CAMBRIDGE MUSICAL TEXTS AND MONOGRAPHS

# RUCKERS

*A harpsichord and virginal building tradition*

CAMBRIDGE MUSICAL TEXTS AND MONOGRAPHS

*General Editors: Howard Mayer Brown, Peter le Huray, John Stevens*

The series Cambridge Musical Texts and Monographs has as its centres of interest the history of performance and the history of instruments. It includes annotated translations of important historical documents, authentic historical texts of music, and monographs on various aspects of historical performance.

PUBLISHED

Ian Woodfield *The Early History of the Viol*

Rebecca Harris-Warrick (trans. and ed.) *Principles of the Harpsichord by Monsieur de Saint Lambert*

Robin Stowell *Violin Technique and Performance Practice in the Late Eighteenth and Early Nineteenth Centuries*

Vincent J. Panetta (trans. and ed.) *Treatise on Harpsichord Tuning by Jean Denis*

John Butt *Bach Interpretation*

*to John and Sheila Barnes*

# Contents

# Illustrations and tables

PLATES

FIGURES

GRAPHS



TABLES

# Conventions and definitions

During the course of this work it became clear that a number of new terms had to be defined, the meaning of terms already in use had to be restricted or altered slightly, and new words and terms introduced. Most of these terms are defined or made clear in the text. A word adopted specially for this work is *clavecimbel*. This word (sometimes spelled beginning with a 'k') was used in sixteenth-, seventeenth-, and eighteenth-century Flanders to mean 'plucked stringed keyboard instrument'. It was a generic term which could mean either virginal or harpsichord. Because, in the translation of documents, it could not be translated directly, and because it avoided the inelegant use of 'plucked stringed keyboard instrument' in the main text, I have used it with its old classical meaning. In modern Flemish *klavecimbel* means harpsichord only.

Two other Flemish words used throughout the text are *voet* (foot) and *duim* (inch – literally, thumb), and their plural forms *voeten* and *duimen*. These are the sixteenth-, seventeenth-, and eighteenth-century Antwerp units of measurement and are discussed in the text and appendices. Lengths are quoted in millimetres (mm) and, where applicable, nominal lengths are also quoted in duimen and voeten. String scalings are measured from centre to centre from one bridge pin to the other. Plucking points are measured from the centre of the nut pin to the centre of the quill plucking the string in question. String scalings and plucking points are always quoted in millimetres even when not stated.

I have used a shorthand notation to refer to particular instruments. This consists simply of the date of the instrument and the initials of the rose in the soundboard (or the initials of the maker if the rose is missing). This is the same system as that used in the 'Ruckers' article in *The New Grove Dictionary of Music and Musicians*, ed. Stanley Sadie (London, 1980). For example, 1639 IR refers to the harpsichord made in 1639 by Ioannes Ruckers. If more than one instrument was made in a single year by a maker, then the date is followed by a lower-case letter of the alphabet, e.g. 1620a AR, 1620b AR, 1620c AR, etc. When the date of an instrument is uncertain it has been placed in parentheses: e.g. (1626) AR is an undated virginal by Andreas Ruckers whose date has been estimated from its Ruckers number.

A concept introduced specially for this work is that of 'reference pitch'. It is not clear that there was any fixed pitch standard during Ruckers' time, nor is it clear that the pitch of any one type of Ruckers instrument was considered as standard. However, in order to refer the pitches of Ruckers instruments to one another, the pitch of the 6-voet virginal, the normal 6-voet harpsichord, or the upper manual of a normal double-manual harpsichord, all with the same string scalings, has been taken as a reference. This pitch survived into the late seventeenth and the eighteenth centuries and is closest to our present modern pitch standard. This pitch is here called 'reference pitch' and is denoted by R (see p. 57). Other pitches are referred to this by counting the number of diatonic notes these are from R. For example, R + 2 is a major second above R, R − 4 is a fourth below R, R + 9 is a ninth above R, etc. Note that R + 1 and R − 1 do not exist.

When referring to keyboard compasses and to notes within the compass, a modified Praetorius/Helmholtz notation similar or identical to that currently adopted by most modern authors has been used:

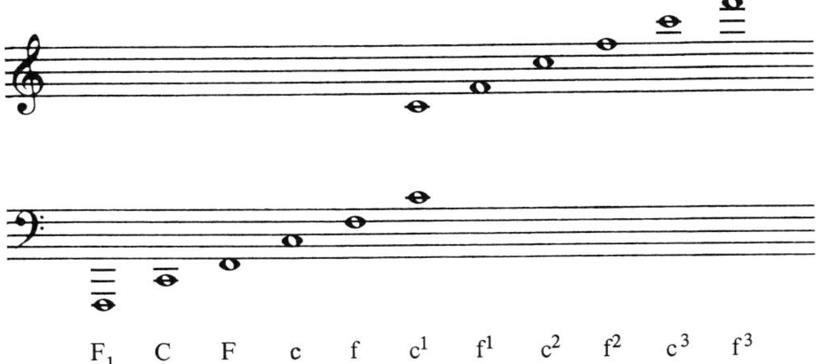

Accidentals are given their meantone names, e.g. e♭ and not d♯, c♯ and not d♭, etc. On instruments at transposed pitch, or when referring to the 4′ stop, the notes are always named according to the played key and not the sounded pitch. If an accidental note is missing at the beginning or end of a compass, then the missing note is replaced by a comma: e.g. C,D means that there is no C♯ between the C and D, and $g^2$,$a^2$ means that there is no $g^{\sharp 2}$ between $g^2$ and $a^2$. 'Pitch c' refers to the pitch of the note $c^2$ at reference pitch, and the scaling of an instrument is the length of the string sounding pitch c. The length of a string for any other note can be referred to pitch c and its equivalent scaling calculated as outlined in Chapter 4.

The convention used here for referring to the order of the registers for describing the disposition is exemplified as follows:

← 4′
→ 8′
← 8′ dogleg
← 8′

Here the 4′ register is furthest from the player and plucks to the left. There are two 8′ registers near the player and they both pluck to the left. The second register is a dogleg register and can be played from either manual. The order of the registers in this convention is the opposite to that used by Hubbard.

Generally, references to the work of other authors or to archival sources are given as footnotes. Exceptional are the three 'standard' works which are referred to in the text without notes. These are the books by Boalch, Russell and Hubbard, which are respectively:

Donald Boalch, *Makers of the Harpsichord and Clavichord, 1440–1840* (London, 1956; revised edn, Oxford, 1974).
Raymond Russell, *The Harpsichord and Clavichord* (London, 1959; reprint, ed. Howard Schott, London, 1973).
Frank Hubbard, *Three Centuries of Harpsichord Making* (Cambridge, Mass., 1965).

Authentic Ruckers/Couchet instruments are always referred to using the shorthand notation already referred to or possibly according to their number in the listing under 'Ruckers' or 'Couchet' in the second revised edition of Boalch's book. Thus, for example, B. 57 refers to the false '1636a Hans Ruckers' harpsichord in the Palace of Holyroodhouse in Edinburgh.

# Acknowledgements

This study was made possible only through the co-operation and help of the many owners and museum personnel in charge of the instruments examined during the course of this study. I would like to thank them and the many others whose help and friendly advice and assistance have enabled me to complete this work.

My thanks and gratitude go out to: Dr Jeanette Abery, Dr Rob van Acht, Dottoressa Clelia Alberici, Dr Horst Appuhn, Lode Bauwens, the late Hubert Bédard, Josianne Bran-Ricci, William Bright, Dr John Catch, Dottoressa Luisa Cervelli, the late Madame de Chambure, Christopher Clarke, the late Richard Clayson, William Dowd, Leonard Elmhirst, Philippe Fritsch, Andrew Garrett, Sheridan Germann, Florence Gétreau, Kenneth Gilbert, Dr Clemens von Gleich, Martha Goodway, Bertil Grahn, Göran Grahn, Friedemann Hellwig, Dr Hubert Henkel, Christianne Jaccottet, Dr Jean-Pierre Jelmini, Dr Dieter Krickeberg, Barbara Lambert, Dr Jeannine Lambrechts-Douillez, Michael Latcham, David Ley, Laurence Libin, Dr Mark Lindley, Tom McGeary, René de Maeyer, Peter Maxwell-Stuart, Dr John van der Meer, Dr Nicolas Meeùs, Claude Mercier-Ythier, François Meyer, Mette Müller, Scott Odell, the late Vere Pilkington, Stewart Pollens, Jerome Prager, Dr Nicholas Renouf, Richard Rephann, Dr Rudolf Reuther, the late J. J. K. Rhodes, Dr J. van Roey, Comte Xavier de Sade, the late Dr Konrad Sasse, Martin-Christian Schmidt, Dr Jim Tait, Fritz Thomas, Michael Thomas, the late W. R. Thomas, Peter Thornton, The Lord Tollemache, Raymond Touyère, Mia van Vaerenbergh, Dr Christian Väterlein, Kurt Wittmayer, and Denzil Wraight.

Eddie Clark and Peggy Loudon have very kindly helped with the typing and retyping of the manuscript for me. I would certainly not have been able to complete this work without their help. I also appreciate the many friends who helped with the photographs and collating in the final stages, and especially James Grant, whose reading greatly improved the style and logic of the final content.

I would particularly like to record my thanks to John Barnes, whose systematic and methodical approach has been the model for carrying out the research involved in this study, and the source of many of the ideas and concepts given here. I would also like to thank Dr Rita McAllister for her many helpful suggestions. I would like to thank Professor Peter Williams, who initially suggested that this study might take the form of a doctoral dissertation, who has read most of the manuscript, and who has offered innumerable suggestions for its improvement. The enthusiasm and support of Penny Souster and all those at Cambridge University Press for this project is much appreciated. I am greatly indebted to Lucy Carolan, my subeditor.

### *Illustration acknowledgements*

The decorated capitals at the beginning of each chapter, and the decorated tail-pieces are printed from blocks held in the Plantin-Moretus Museum in Antwerp. The execution of these blocks took place at a time contemporary with the early members of the Ruckers family. I would like to thank the Mayor and Aldermen of the City of Antwerp for their permission to reproduce these in this work.

The photographic plates come from many sources: the A.C.L., Brussels, Plates 4.1 and 9.2; the Boston Museum of Fine Arts, Plate 3.4; Christopher Clarke, Veron, France, Plate C.4; the Courtauld Institute Galleries (Princes Gate Collection), London, Plate 1.2; Hugh Gough, New York, Plate 11.1; the Haags Gemeentemuseum, The Hague, Plates 5.1 and C.5; the George F. Harding Museum, Chicago, Plate C.3; the Koninklijke Bibliotheek, The Hague, the plate in Appendix 19; Graf Landsberg-Velen and Kurt Wittmayer, Plate 6.3; the Metropolitan Museum of Art, New York, Plates 3.1, 5.8 and 7.3; the Musée Instrumental du Conservatoire National Supérieur de Musique, Paris, Plates 3.13, 7.9 and F.1; the Rockoxhuis Museum and the Kredietbank, Antwerp, Plate A2.1; the owners of the 2½-voet virginal, Plates 3.8 and A3.1; the Plantin-Moretus Museum, Plate 1.1; the Russell Collection, Edinburgh, Plates C.1 and F.3; the Musikinstrumenten-Museum des Staatlichen Institut für Musikforschung Preussischer Kulturbesitz, Berlin, Plate 3.14; the Stiftelsen Musikkulturens främjande, Stockholm, Plate 10.1; the Smithsonian Institution, Washington, D.C., Plate 3.6; the Trustees of the National Gallery, London, Plate 6.4; the Vleeshuis Museum, Antwerp, Plates 5.2 and C.7. My thanks to all of the individuals and institutions for permission to reproduce these plates. All of the rest of the plates are of photographs taken and printed by myself and I would like to thank the owners and museums in charge of the instruments for having given permission to take these.

Finally I would also like to thank Darryl Martin who provided all of the line drawings for the figures and tables.

# Introduction

In approaching a study of the Ruckers family and their instruments, I have always tried to get as much information as possible from the instruments themselves. This approach has involved not only a study of the materials used, and the Ruckers construction methods, but also a close examination of the scalings and pitch of the instruments, the decoration, numbering and the types of instruments made. Of necessity this has also involved a study of the original state of each type of instrument, and of the subsequent states of many of the instruments adapted for later musical use. Although they are no less important than the actual instruments, I have used documents and archives only secondarily to confirm or elucidate features found from a study of the instruments. Thus generally there is little reference made throughout this work either to archival sources or the work of other authors.

The study of the instruments of a given builder is greatly affected by the number of extant examples of his work. The task of someone studying the Kirkman family, with over 150 surviving instruments, is vastly different from that of someone studying the ten or so remaining instruments attributed to Baffo. Boalch lists altogether 190 instruments under the headings 'Couchet' and 'Ruckers'. But if one deletes those which are listed twice, are unauthentic, or have disappeared, one is left with about one hundred instruments which are the genuine products of the Ruckers/Couchet family workshops. About sixty of these are harpsichords, with the distribution of singles and doubles being roughly equal. The rest are all virginals of a number of different sizes and types.

Although the production of the Ruckers family is spread over a period of about a hundred years covering the end of the sixteenth century until the end of the seventeenth century, and although this production is divided among the output of six different individuals, a comparison of all their instruments reveals an extremely stable and conservative building tradition. The differences across this time span and from builder to builder are so few as to make the instruments of any one type almost identical except in the details of the decoration. It is the relatively large number of surviving instruments and the conservative building tradition that make a comparative study of the Ruckers instruments particularly valuable and meaningful.

The Ruckers tradition of clavecimbel building occupies a place in the field of organology which cannot be compared with that of any other. The family's influence on the later style of harpsichord and virginal building spread through and dominated the whole of Northern Europe during the eighteenth century, and elements of the Ruckers design have even been carried on into the design of the modern piano. In fact the Ruckers family is to the clavecimbel as Stradivarius is to the violin. The beauty of sound of the Ruckers instruments resulting from their excellent design and the care exercised in the making of the soundboard and bridges made them famous at the end of the seventeenth century and throughout the eighteenth century. And this reputation for excellence has not declined even down to the present day. Like Stradivarius violins, Ruckers clavecimbels were altered to bring them up to date with later musical fashions and requirements. A major part of this study has been both to analyse the types of alterations that the instruments underwent, and to determine in a methodical way the original state and disposition of the altered instruments. Stradivarius violins were faked and counterfeited in the hopes of deceiving some hapless client. Ruckers harpsichords were also counterfeited, and non-Ruckers instruments were given a Ruckers rose and signature, and then sold at an enormous profit. Clearly, it is necessary to be able to distinguish the authentic (if drastically altered) Ruckers instruments from those which are unauthentic, and this has also been one of the objects of writing this book. The large number of surviving instruments, coupled with the importance of the Ruckers tradition to the later harpsichord building style, makes them the obvious choice for a detailed study.

When writing this book I have imagined my reader already to have had some basic knowledge about the construction and history of keyboard instruments. In order to keep the size of the book in reasonable proportion, it was necessary to start at a reasonably advanced level. The novice in this field must therefore look elsewhere for the definitions of some of the terms, and for a discussion of the fundamentals of some of the concepts used. The books by Russell and Hubbard and a number of the books and articles given in the selected bibliography should be referred to first by those with no previous knowledge of the subject.

I have not given any scale drawings of complete instruments here. A number of museums (such as the Russell Collection in Edinburgh) and private individuals publish plans of Ruckers instruments under their care, and I have assumed that the serious student would have one or more of these available to use in conjunction with this book. Scale diagrams of a whole instrument reduced to the size of a page in this book would be neither accurate enough nor detailed enough to be of any real use. Instead I have included plan-view photographs of both the soundboards and internal structure of some typical instruments, all at the same scale. These show more detail than a scale drawing, and also give a feel of the workmanship and construction of the instruments that is not possible from a line drawing.

Some of the conclusions and results of this work have been published by me previously:

'The numbering system of Ruckers instruments', *The Bulletin of the Brussels Museum of Musical Instruments*, IV (1974), 75–89.

'The determination of the original compass and disposition of Ruckers harpsichords' and 'The stringing and pitches of Ruckers instruments', *Colloquium: Ruckers Klavecimbels en Copieën* (Antwerp, 1977), 36–47 and 48–71.

'Ioannes and Andreas Ruckers – A quatercentenary celebration', *Early Music*, VII, 4 (1979), 453–66.

'Ruckers – The instruments', 'Couchet', co-author of 'Harpsichord', 'Spinet', 'Virginal', *The New Grove Dictionary of Music and Musicians*, ed. Stanley Sadie (London, 1980).

All of this previously published material has been completely reworked and updated before it was included here.

CHAPTER ONE

# Ruckers family history and the Guild of St Luke

nly in the right political, social and economic climate is it possible for trades such as weaving, printing, painting or instrument building to flourish. A market must exist with a clientele sufficiently wealthy to buy the product of the trade, and there must be a prevailing sense of political calm and of prosperity. The Ruckers and Couchet families lived in Antwerp in the Low Countries in a period of political stability and commercial prosperity combined with a cultural and artistic flowering. The Guild of St Luke protected and controlled the artists, among whom were included the instrument builders, in such a way that unwanted competition was largely prevented, and so the members of the Guild, with little competition and an expanding market, were able to thrive.

## ANTWERP AND THE NETHERLANDS AT THE TIME OF THE RUCKERS FAMILY

Towards the end of the fifteenth century, with the silting of the Zwijn, Bruges lost her port and, with shipping greatly restricted, her cultural and economic decline followed. Almost concurrent with the silting of the Zwijn, a series of floods deepened and widened the Scheldt, a large river with its estuary opening out just to the north of Bruges. On the Scheldt's east bank, Antwerp had even before then been an excellent port, and it now became the new home of the shipping, trade guilds and banks formerly centred in Bruges. Europe's first real *bourse* or stock exchange was founded in Antwerp in 1460, and in the early decades of the sixteenth century the diamond industry was established there. This expanded greatly when the Jewish diamond craftsmen, expelled from Portugal, settled in Antwerp. Gradually Antwerp became the chief port and the commercial and cultural centre of the Netherlands, and indeed of western Europe.

Charles I of Spain (1516) succeeded to the throne of the Holy Roman Empire as Charles V in 1519. Born and educated in the Low Countries, he ruled the area with a powerful but benevolent hand. Antwerp's life was stimulated by the Spanish and Portuguese discoveries in the New World and the riches brought back from them to Europe. Trade and culture flourished and a wealthy middle class developed, whose members were eager to adorn their new houses with the best paintings, fine furniture, sculpture, bronzes, rugs and drapery, and whose appetite for silver and gold, books, pottery, medallions and jewellery was insatiable. By 1550 Antwerp had surpassed even Venice in commerce and the arts.

Like the rest of Europe, however, Antwerp was beset by religious strife in the second half of the sixteenth century. Charles V was a champion of the Roman Catholic faith and he vigorously repressed the Protestant heresy. Despite this the number of Calvinists grew. In 1556 Charles' son, Philip II of Spain, succeeded to power. Unlike his father, Philip had little sympathy with or understanding of the attitudes and wishes of the Lowlands' populace. His heavy taxation and fanatical suppression of the Protestants made him very unpopular. In 1567 an open revolt took place in which the united efforts of the Catholics and Protestants were forced against the Spanish. The Duke of Alva was sent in and, under orders from Philip II, a period of bloody and enforced repression took place. In order to estabish Spanish dominance over the local population Alva built a fortified citadel on the southern ramparts of Antwerp's city wall to protect the city from invasion, and to garrison his

Spanish troops and protect them from the citizens of Antwerp.

In 1576 these troops, after enduring a long period of hardship and lack of pay, stormed out of the citadel and ran mad through the streets. In the resultant sacking of Antwerp – the so-called 'Spanish Fury' – hundreds of buildings and homes were burned and plundered, women were raped, works of art were destroyed and an estimated 8,000 lives were lost. Antwerp never really recovered from the disaster.

In the disorder after the 'Fury' the Calvinists seized and held power and destroyed Alva's citadel. But in 1585, after an extended siege, Antwerp again fell to the Spanish under Alessandro Farnese, Duke of Parma. Under Parma the Protestants were sent into exile, and much of the population, capital and enterprise emigrated, mostly to the United Provinces to the north.[1] During the years following 1585, Antwerp's population fell from over 80,000 to only 42,000. Economic, political and religious freedom were sharply curtailed. Gradually, by 1595, the population in Antwerp had increased to 47,000 and a renewed period of peace and prosperity ensued without the crowding and the resultant plague, disease and fires of the earlier years.

Under Albert of Austria and Isabella, daughter of Philip II, who made their state entry into Antwerp in 1599, the city experienced a continued period of peace and splendour. In 1609 the Twelve Years' Truce was signed with the Protestant-held United Provinces, and Antwerp entered into its second Golden Age. By 1612 Antwerp's population was 53,000 and it remained at this level until well into the eighteenth century. Commercial and cultural life again flourished. Rubens, Jacob Jordaens and Jan Brueghel executed major painting commissions and established an international reputation. The printing presses of Plantin were as busy as they had ever been. And the two Ruckers sons, Andreas and Ioannes, entered the Guild of St Luke and established themselves as instrument builders of the highest order.

In 1621, with the expiry of the Twelve Years' Truce, tension increased somewhat between the Protestant Dutch Provinces and the Spanish Netherlands, but outright conflict was avoided, in great part due to the skilful diplomatic efforts of Ruckers' contemporary Peter Paul Rubens. After 1635, when Isabella died without an heir, sporadic fighting took place with the Calvinist Northern Provinces. Nonetheless, the difficulties were not serious enough to affect greatly the artistic and economic life in Antwerp. Then finally in 1648 the Treaty of Münster and the Peace of Westphalia recognized the independence of the United Provinces. It also gave the Dutch full control of the estuary of the Scheldt and therefore of Antwerp's port. The Amsterdam merchants demanded that the river be closed to navigation, and this ensured the final cultural and economic decline of Antwerp. By 1655 the last important members of the Ruckers and Couchet families had died and, like Antwerp's commercial and artistic life, the production of Ruckers instruments ceased. Instruments continued to be built in the Ruckers style by the Couchet sons, who were the heirs to the old tradition. These later instruments exhibit considerable innovation, but the number produced was very small, probably as a result of the lack of a local market and the removal of the commercial focus of north-western Europe from Antwerp to Amsterdam. By 1706 the last of the harpsichord-building Couchets was dead, and the Golden Age of harpsichord building in Antwerp came to an end.

## RUCKERS FAMILY HISTORY

The biographical details of the Ruckers family have been of interest to researchers for over a century now, and in the course of this time a great deal has been learned about its various members. One of the earliest, and still one of the most important contributions to the field was published in 1859 by Génard[2] and further details were added in 1863[3] and 1864.[4] Somewhat more recently a publication of 1942[5] has made further contributions. And the indefatigable energy of Dr Jeannine Lambrechts-Douillez has brought this research together and added much new information to our knowledge of the Ruckers family.[6] Most of the information about the family

[1] It was probably during this time that Marten van der Biest moved from Antwerp to Amsterdam; see J. Lambrechts-Douillez, 'Archief documenten betreffende de Ruckers familie', *Bulletin of the Brussels Museum of Musical Instruments*, IV (1974), 38.

[2] P. Génard, 'Les grandes familles artistiques d'Anvers: Ruckers', *Revue d'histoire et d'archéologie*, I (Brussels, 1859), 458ff.

[3] L. de Burbure, 'Recherches sur les facteurs de clavecins et les luthiers d'Anvers', *Bulletins de l'Académie Royale de Belgique*, Series 2, XV, 2 (Brussels, 1863), 1.

[4] P. Rombouts and T. van Lerius, *De Liggeren en andere Historische Archieven der Antwerpsche Sint Lucasgilde*, 2 Vols. (Antwerp – The Hague, 1872–76; facs., Amsterdam, 1961).

[5] J. A. Stellfeld, 'Bronnen tot de geschiedenis der Antwerpse clavecimbel – en orgelbouwers in de XVI^e^ en XVII^e^ eeuwen', *Vlamsch Jaarboek voor Muziekgeschiedenis* (Antwerp, 1942), 3–110.

[6] J. Lambrechts-Douillez, 'Muziekinstrumenten te Antwerpen', *Tijdschrift van de Stad Antwerpen*, XIII (Antwerp, 1967), 100–1.
'De klavecimbelbouw te Antwerpen: een kunstambacht van wereldformaat (einde zestiende – begin zeventiende eeuw)', *Antiek: Tijdschrift voor Liefhebbers en Kenners van Oude Kunstnijverheid*, III (December 1968), 237–52.
'Biographical notes on the Ruckers–Couchet family', *Galpin Society Journal*, XXII (1969), 98–9.
*Antwerpse Klavecimbels in het Museum Vleeshuis* (Antwerp, 1970).

history that follows has been taken from one of her publications. But despite the large amount of work that has been done, there are still a number of important gaps in our knowledge of the histories of almost all of the members of the Ruckers family. The features and dating of some of the instruments built by the Ruckers and Couchets enable us to make conjectures about some of the missing details. But it now seems doubtful that all of the lacunae in our knowledge of the family history can ever be filled in, as the relevant documents seem to have disappeared in the course of time. Whatever additional new information may be found can only come from a careful and complete study of the Antwerp church and city archives and the other historical sources in Belgium and Holland. The continuation of this work is being carried out by Dr Lambrechts-Douillez and her team.

The name Ruckers comes from the Christian name Ruckaert or Ryckaert (English, Richard). 'Ruckers' is thus a linguistic abbreviation of the patronymic Ryckaertszoon or Ruckaerts (in English, Richardson or Richards). In the archives of the Antwerp cathedral and the Guild of St Luke, the name appears written in the forms Ruyckers, Rueckers, Rieckers, Rueckaers, Rycardt, Rickaert, Ruckeerts, Ryckers, Ricaert and Ruckaert.

As with many of the names associated with instrument building in Antwerp, the family seems to have come to the Lowlands from Germany.[7] Albrecht Dürer, on a trip to the Netherlands and Antwerp in 1520, depicted a Master Arnold of Seligenstadt (near Frankfurt am Main).[8] It has been possible to show that the person sketched by Dürer was one Arnold Rucker or Rücker, who, although he also worked in Mathias Grünewald's workshop in Aschaffenburg as a woodcarver, was best known to his contemporaries as an organ builder. Arnold Rucker built organs in Marburg-an-der-Lahn, Aschaffenburg, Würzburg, Amorbach, and probably in other Franconian towns including his native Seligenstadt, in the period from 1508 to 1536. No direct connection has yet been discovered to link Arnold Rucker of Seligenstadt with the Ruckers family of Antwerp, but the similarity in the name, and the fact that all of the Flemish Ruckers were also involved with the repairs and tuning of the church organs in Antwerp, strongly suggest that there is a family relationship between the two.

### *Hans Ruckers*

The founding member of the Ruckers family was Hans Ruckers. His father was Frans Ruckers and he was born in Mechelen (Malines), but the exact date of his birth is not known. On 25 June 1575 Hans Ruckers married Adriana (Naenken) Knaeps (or Cnaeps) in the cathedral (Onze Lieve Vrouwekerk) in Antwerp, and Marten van der Biest, who was another clavecimbel builder, and Adam Boest were witnesses to the ceremony. It is known that on 5 July 1597 he was still alive, but also that, according to the will of his great-great-granddaughter Rebecca Ruckers, he died 'in the century of 1500 in the years of 90', so that he must have died in 1597, 1598 or 1599.[9] Recent work by Dr Lambrechts-Douillez has shown that he was already dead on 14 September 1599.[10] The cathedral records from Christmas 1597 to Christmas 1599 give:

> Received as the dues for the funeral, 1598, Hans Rycardt. 4 gulden, 1 stuijver, 6 den.[11]

and, although the spelling of the surname is unusual, it seems clear that the entry refers to Hans Ruckers and that the time of his death can be placed during 1598. From this and the date of his marriage it seems likely that Hans Ruckers was born about 1550, since he would then have been about twenty-five at the time of his marriage and roughly fifty years old at the time of his death.

Two factors have contributed to a certain amount of

'Antwerpse klavecimbels, oude muziek herleeft', *Actuele Onderwerpen*, AO 1310 (Goes, 1970).
'The Ruckers–Couchet instruments in the Museum Vleeshuis: restoration or copy?, *Colloquium: Restauratieproblemen van Antwerpse Klavecimbels* (Antwerp, 1971), 44–8.
'Documents dealing with the Ruckers family and Antwerp harpsichord-building', *Keyboard Instruments: Studies in Keyboard Organology*, ed. Edwin M. Ripin (Edinburgh, 1971), 37–42.
'Archief documenten betreffende de Ruckers familie', and 'Catalogus Ruckers: documenten en instrumenten', *Bulletin of the Brussels Museum of Musical Instruments*, IV (Brussels, 1974), 33–54 and 65–70 respectively.
'The Ruckers family and other harpsichord makers', *The Connoisseur*, CXCIV, 782 (1977), 266–73.
'Couchet', *Algemene Muziekencyclopedie*, II (1979), 262.
'Aperçu historique sur la facture de clavecin à Anvers au XVI$^{e}$ et XVII$^{e}$ siècles, *La facture de clavecin du XV$^{e}$ au XVIII$^{e}$ siècle* (Louvain-la-Neuve, 1980), 59–66.
See also the Ruckers family history, with M.-J. Bosschaerts-Eykens, serialized in *Mededelingen van het Ruckers-Genootschap*; I (Antwerp, 1982); II (Antwerp, 1982); III (Antwerp, 1983); IV (Antwerp, 1984); V (Antwerp, 1986).

[7] Edwin M. Ripin, 'Antwerp harpsichord building: the current state of research', *Colloquium: Restauratieproblemen van Antwerpse Klavecimbels* (Antwerp, 1971), 12–23.

[8] Friedrich Ernst, 'Master Arnold Rucker', *Galpin Society Journal*, XXII (1961), 35–9.

[9] Ernest Closson, 'Quelle est l'année de la mort de Hans Ruckers, le vieux?', *Le guide musical*, LVII, 38–9 (1911), 571–2.

[10] Lambrechts-Douillez and Bosschaerts-Eykens, *Mededelingen van het Ruckers-Genootschap*, I, 10 and 15.

[11] 'Onfanck van de rechten van de kerckelycken, a[nn]o 98. Hans Rycardt. 4-, 1-, 6.'

confusion about the death date of Hans Ruckers. In the first place, both Hans and his eldest son Ioannes were referred to by others, and called themselves, by any one of the different forms of the name Ioannes, Joannes, Johannes, Jan and Hans. Thus in the will of Rebecca Ruckers, Hans Ruckers and Ioannes Ruckers, father and son, are both referred to as Ioannes. Also in the cathedral records for 1598 and 1599 we find:

> To Hans Ruckers, for the maintenance of the organ at his salary for two years at the rate of 6 pounds Flemish per year paid for the years 1598, 1599 at St Bavon's. 12 pounds Flemish.[12]

Here it seems certain that since Hans Ruckers had died in 1598, his son Ioannes had succeeded his father in the upkeep of the cathedral organ.

Secondly, Ioannes Ruckers used a rose in the soundboard of his instruments from 1598 until at least 1616 which used the initials 'HR', i.e. Hans Ruckers. This rose (in fact several different castings were used) is, however, slightly different and quite distinguishable from the HR rose used by Hans Ruckers the father from 1579 to 1598 (see pp. 159–61).[13] In order to avoid confusion in this work, I will always refer to the father as Hans, and to his eldest son as Ioannes.

Hans Ruckers joined the Guild of St Luke in 1579. The painters, engravers, printers, glaziers, and other Antwerp artists all belonged to the Guild of St Luke and, in 1557, ten clavecimbel makers banded together to form an autonomous group within the Guild whose profession would be recognized like that of the painters or goldsmiths. Counting the original ten clavecimbel builders, Hans was the nineteenth to be inscribed in the Guild records after 1557 as *Claversinbalmakerre*. Thus in 1579, in a town with a population of only about 80,000, there were probably about fifteen to twenty master clavecimbel makers in Antwerp, probably each having his own workshop, apprentices, workers and servants.

After 1579 Hans Ruckers' name appears regularly in the membership accounts and in the Bussenboek, the register of the contributors to the emergency relief fund for the members of the Guild of St Luke. After 1591 Hans Ruckers was engaged on a yearly basis to tune and maintain the cathedral organ, and his name appears regularly in the cathedral accounts. In 1593 he even installed and tuned fourteen or fifteen ranks of pipes (registers) in the cathedral organ, for which a special payment was made.[14] In 1597, when he was near the end of his career, he is described in the document in which he bought a house on the Jodenstraat (see below) as an *orgelmaker ende clavesingelmaker*, i.e. as an organ builder and harpsichord maker.[15]

In 1594, on the last day of February, he was made a *poorter* or citizen of Antwerp. It is still a mystery why Hans Ruckers' registry as a poorter came so late, as it would normally have been impossible for him to join the Guild of St Luke without already being an Antwerp citizen. It has been suggested that the original documents relating to Hans Ruckers' citizenship may have been lost during the 'Spanish Fury' of 1576 or the Spanish siege and occupation of 1584–85, and that this loss was then later corrected in 1594.

Also in 1594, Hans Ruckers is recorded as having been involved in a civil suit with one of his former employees, Staes van Bueren. In the proceedings of the case we find that Staes van Bueren built a case for a harpsichord which was then finished and sold by Hans Ruckers. It is not clear whether Ruckers paid van Bueren for the building of the case after the completion and sale of the instrument. Also involved was the loan of money by Hans Ruckers' wife to Staes van Bueren's wife after the latter's purse was stolen in the Antwerp fish market. An interesting sidelight of the case is that Staes van Bueren went north for a time around 1587 to work in Amsterdam for Marten van der Biest.

On 5 July 1597 Hans Ruckers bought a house called 'de cleyn clavecingel' ('the little clavecimbel') on the north side of the Vaertstraat, commonly known as the Jodenstraat, or the Street of the Jews. This was probably near the house that they had been renting since 1584. It was a large house located between the house of the late Goosen Karest, whose house was known as the 'groote clavecimbele' ('the big clavecimbel'), on the east side, and the House of God of the Carmelites, which was to the west and also at the back on the north side of the Ruckers house. It is described as being near the beginning of the Jodenstraat, and as having 'a gate, large courtyard, pump, rain cistern, drains, store rooms, kitchen, business premises and all appurtenances thereto situated and located in the . . . Jodenstraat' (see Plate 1.1).

The document dealing with the purchase of the house in the Jodenstraat seems to be the last that exists relating to the life of Hans Ruckers. The house was transferred to Hans Ruckers' widow, Adriana Knaeps, on 14 Sep-

[12] 'aen Hans Ruckers, van de orghelen te onderhouwen voer synn gagie van twee jaren tegen 6lb. t'sjaers bet. pro annis 98, 99 te bamisse 12 lb.'

[13] In particular the 5-voet virginal dated 1604 in the Brussels Instrument Museum, No. 2927, is signed 'IOANNES ET ANDREAS RVCKERS ME FECERVNT' and uses the HR rose otherwise used only by Ioannes from 1598 to 1616.

[14] A further interesting musical connection with the cathedral is that the cathedral organist Servaes van den Muelen was the godfather of Hans Ruckers' third son, who was called Servaes.

[15] Lambrechts-Douillez and Bosschaerts-Eykens, *Mededelingen van het Ruckers-Genootschap*, III, 12.

Plate 1.1 Detail of a map of the City of Antwerp by Virgilius Boloniensis (1565). The darkened area shows the probable site of Hans Ruckers' workshop with 'a gate, large courtyard, pump, cistern, drains, store rooms,' etc. This later became Ioannes Ruckers' workshop, and also probably that of Ioannes Couchet. Copyright Plantin-Moretus Museum, Antwerp.

tember 1599, and became the sole property of their eldest son Ioannes on 31 October 1608 (see below). It seems to have served as Ioannes' workshop and living quarters at least until his death in 1642, and may also have belonged to Ioannes Couchet. It was sold by Hans Ruckers' great-grandson, a cloth merchant, in 1656.

Hans Ruckers and Adriana Knaeps had in all eleven children, of whom five survived into adulthood. All of these children were baptized in the cathedral and this, together with the fact that several of the grandchildren and great-grandchildren became priests or nuns, suggests that the family maintained its Roman Catholic faith throughout the period of religious strife in Antwerp. The three children of Hans Ruckers and Adriana Knaeps of interest to us here are Ioannes Ruckers, Andreas Ruckers, and Catharina Ruckers, who became the wife of Carel Couchet and the mother of Ioannes Couchet. Hans Ruckers' widow, Adriana Knaeps, died on 29 March 1604.

### *Ioannes Ruckers*

Ioannes Ruckers was the eldest of Hans Ruckers' children to survive into adulthood, the heir to the Ruckers' tradition, and probably the greatest of the members of the harpsichord- and virginal-building family. He was baptized on 15 January 1578.[16] In 1598 and 1599, and in practically every year until 1642, his name appears in the Antwerp cathedral accounts for the tuning and maintenance of the organ, initially at the rate of 6 guilders per year, and increasing to 42 guilders by 1625. He also tuned the organ of the St Jacobskerk in Antwerp after 1617, where his yearly salary varied from 28 to 30 guilders, and maintained the organ in the church of the Antwerp Citadel.

In March 1604, Ioannes' mother, Adriana Knaeps, died and, as eldest son, he would have taken over the running of the family home and workshop at the age of twenty-six. Later on in the same year, on 14 November 1604, Ioannes Ruckers married Maria Waelrant, daughter of Raymondus Waelrant, organist at the Cathedral of Our Lady in Antwerp, and granddaughter of Hubert Waelrant, the organist, music publisher, composer, and teacher who helped to formalize the extension of the hexachord and the method of solmization to include the note *si* (i.e. *b*). Ioannes and Maria Waelrant were married in Antwerp cathedral and had three daughters who survived into adulthood: Francisca, Maria and Elizabeth. It seems likely there were some children who did not survive early infancy, as Francisca, the eldest, was born in March 1607, two-and-a-half years after Ioannes and Maria's marriage. Maria Waelrant died in 1613, when Ioannes was only thirty-five years old, and he apparently never married again. Probably because he and Maria had no surviving male children, Ioannes Ruckers took on his nephew Ioannes Couchet as an apprentice to carry on the virginal- and harpsichord-building business.

The virginal dated 1604 and signed 'IOANNES ET ANDREAS RVCKERS FECERVNT', now in the Brussels Museum of Musical Instruments (No. 1917), indicates that the two brothers were working together in partnership in 1604, although neither is known to have been a member of the Guild of St Luke at that time. On 31 October 1608, an agreement was drawn up between Ioannes and his brother Andreas whereby the family home on the Jodenstraat became the sole property of Ioannes, although even before this Andreas was building, numbering and signing his own instruments and must therefore have been working independently of him (see p. 9 and Chapter 3, p. 51).

The date of Ioannes Ruckers' entry into the Guild of St Luke is not certain but the registers of the Guild for 1611 give:

Hans Ruckers, sone, claversigmaker

and this is generally accepted as referring to Ioannes Ruckers. This may be substantiated by the first appearance of an IR rose in a Ioannes Ruckers instrument in 1612 (however, Ioannes Ruckers continued to use the old HR rose at least until 1616, and the dating of the 1612 instrument is not at all certain: see the catalogue entry (1612) IR, p. 245).

From 1614 until his death he was the organ and harpsichord builder to the archducal court in Brussels.[17] It may well have been this court appointment which inspired Ioannes to have the three rather sophisticated IR roses cast for use in his instruments. At any rate after 1616 he ceased using the somewhat primitive HR rose and used only the more elegant IR roses. Also connected with his court appointment is a document dated 1623 in which Jan Ruckaerts, Peter Paul Rubens, Jan Brueghel, Robrecht

[16] *A priori* it is not entirely clear if this date is given in the style of Brabant or in the new style. Until roughly the third quarter of the sixteenth century in Brabant, Flanders, etc. the New Year began not on 1 January but at the movable date of Easter. This date could therefore be either 15 January 1578, or 15 January 1579. However, since Andreas Ruckers was born on 30 August 1579 (which is unambiguous), it seems clear that Ioannes must have been born in January 1578, since the period between January and August 1579 would be too short for the conception, gestation and successful birth of a child at this time.

[17] J. A. Stellfeld, 'Johannes Ruckers de jongere en de koninklijke kapel te Brussel', *Hommage à Charles van den Borren* (Antwerp, 1945), 289ff.

de Nole, and Rombout Rasiers were all, because they were in the service of the court, exempted from carrying out the civic watch duties around Antwerp's town walls (see Plate 1.2). When in 1636 his only surviving daughter, Maria, married Eduard Snaeyers, a painter and later dean of the Guild of St Luke, the wedding dowry was considerable, indicating that Ioannes was by then a very wealthy man. In 1642 Ioannes Ruckers was involved in a court case with the civic aldermen, who challenged not his exemption from personal watch duty but whether he had been freed from making the usual tax contribution to the maintenance of the watch. The outcome of the case is not stated. Ioannes Ruckers died on 29 September 1642, and the burial took place on 1 October 1642. The direction of the workshop and the eventual continuation of the Ruckers tradition was then undertaken by Ioannes Couchet.

### *Andreas I Ruckers*

Andreas Ruckers was the second surviving son of Hans Ruckers and Adriana Knaeps. He was baptized on 30 August 1579, and on 25 January 1605 was married to Catharina de Vries (Catharina was the sister-in-law of the painter Jacob Jordaens). As was mentioned before, Andreas was working with his brother Ioannes in 1604, and the numbering of the Andreas instruments indicates that he was probably signing and numbering his own instruments from 1605 onwards (see Chapter 3, p. 51). Perhaps the two brothers initially shared their father's old workshop until, in 1608, 'de cleyn clavecingel' became the sole property of Ioannes, by which time Andreas and his family must have been living elsewhere. Although there is no record of Andreas' entry into the Guild of St Luke, his extant instruments indicate that from 1608 he signed his instruments himself, and used his own individual A R rose. In 1616 Andreas Ruckers is described as living 'bij kerckhof, bij scoenkramen', that is, near the cathedral churchyard (now the Groenplaats with the impressive bronze of Rubens) and the Shoemarket (Schoenmarkt). This was only about 500 metres from the Jodenstraat and Ioannes Ruckers' workshop, which itself was only about 200 metres from Rubens' house and studio.

Andreas Ruckers and Catharina de Vries had seven children, among whom were Andreas II, who carried on the harpsichord building tradition in the Ruckers family, and Anna, who became the second wife of Johann Davidszoon de Heem, the most famous of all the Antwerp still-life and flower painters. Although the Ruckers soundboard paintings and the oil paintings of de Heem have a kindred aesthetic spirit, the quality of the painting and the excellence of the technique of de Heem far exceeds that exhibited on the Ruckers soundboards, and there is no indication at all that Ruckers soundboards were painted by anyone with the skill and competence of de Heem.

Around 1644 Andreas I Ruckers was living in the Huidevetterstraat (The Tanner's Street) adjoining the Jodenstraat, and therefore probably just a few metres from Ioannes Ruckers' workshop. It is not clear at what stage Andreas II Ruckers began to work in his father's workshop, although other children in the family often started learning their craft at about twelve to fifteen years of age. Andreas II would have been this age in about 1620, and therefore probably started his apprenticeship with his father at about this date. Also unclear is the father–son commercial relationship after Andreas II joined the Guild of St Luke in 1637/38. The 1644 single-manual harpsichord signed 'ANDREAS RVCKERS DEN OVDEN ME FECIT ANTVERPIAE' suggests that the two were building instruments in separate workshops by 1644. And the (1651)a A R single harpsichord signed 'ANDREAS RVCKERS AND.[REAS] F.[ILIVS] ME FECIT ANTVERPIAE]' implies that, despite his seventy-two years, Andreas I was still actively building instruments in 1651.[18] Andreas I died sometime between June 1651 and 24 March 1653.

### *Andreas II Ruckers*

Little is known of the life of Andreas II except that he was baptized on 31 March 1607. On 12 June 1637 he was married to Joanna Haechts (Haeghts or Hex), probably in Mechelen (Malines). The couple had six children, the third of whom was called Ioannes, presumably after Ioannes Ruckers (his great-uncle), who was his godfather at the baptism on 6 February 1642.

During 1637/38 Andreas II also became a member of the Guild of St Luke and a master harpsichord builder. It seems likely that this is connected with his marriage and with his probable establishment as an independent harpsichord builder with his own workshop separate from that of Andreas I. Andreas I was certainly still building instruments in 1644. And since Andreas II took the trouble to sign himself 'Andreas Ruckers Jr.' in 1651, they were probably both working separately at the time the (1651)a A R instrument was built. The two Andreases were therefore working concurrently for at least thirteen,

[18] However, any argument based on this instrument is very flimsy, since it is not entirely clear that the date is not 1641 instead of 1651. The painting of the penultimate figure in the date was touched up in a recent restoration, and the result is a most unconvincing '5' – see Chapter 7, p. 161, and Catalogue, p. 269.

Plate 1.2 A portrait of the family of Jan Brueghel the Elder by Sir Peter Paul Rubens (1577–1640). The Ruckers, Brueghel, and Rubens were all wealthy middle-class Antwerp burghers, and this portrait is a good example of how the Ruckers and Couchets might have looked and dressed. Courtauld Institute Galleries, London (Princes Gate Collection).

and probably fifteen years. They both signed themselves ANDREAS RVCKERS ME FECIT, often without making the distinction of whether it was father or son who made the instrument. It is thus difficult to distinguish the late work of Andreas I from the early instruments built by Andreas II. It may be possible to differentiate them on the basis of the style of the decoration, but such a distinction is both difficult and hypothetical (see p. 157).

Andreas II's wife, Joanna Haechts, died of the plague at the age of forty-four in about July 1653, leaving six small children aged one to fourteen. Andreas II was thus faced with the loss of his father, followed shortly by the loss of his wife, and then the problem of looking after six children all of whom were minors. Andreas II died soon after, between 28 April 1654 and 8 February 1655, leaving his six children without either of their parents. Orphaned, the children had to be put into the care of guardians.

### *Ioannes Couchet*

Catharina Ruckers was a daughter of Hans Ruckers and a sister of Ioannes Ruckers and Andreas I Ruckers. In 1611 she married Carel Couchet, and Ioannes Couchet was their only surviving child, born on 2 February 1615. In 1625 his mother died, and his father, Carel Couchet, then married Catharina Wortelmans less than four months later. There were at least four children from this second marriage, all half-brothers and half-sisters to Ioannes Couchet. According to a letter from Gaspard Duarte to Constantijn Huygens, Couchet went to work for and was apprenticed to his uncle Ioannes Ruckers in about 1626 (see Appendix 17, p. 305). But the date is probably closer to 1625, when he was aged only ten, and probably followed shortly upon the death of his mother Catharina. Couchet worked with his uncle until Ruckers' death in 1642. On 26 December 1643 he married Angela van den Brant, and three of their sons, Ioannes II, Ioseph Ioannes and Abraham, all became members of the Guild of St Luke and carried on the family harpsichord building tradition into the fourth generation.

In 1642/43, the registers of the Guild of St Luke record, along with the death and death dues received for Ioannes Ruckers, the entry of Ioannes Couchet as a master harpsichord builder. In 1646/47 Couchet is recorded in the accounts of the Antwerp cathedral as having carried out special repairs to the organ, and the records of a number of the other major churches in Antwerp indicate that Couchet was also entrusted with their maintenance and repair. Ioannes Couchet died on 4 April 1655, after a sickness during which Couchet and Angela van den Brant made their will. By 6 April, the news of Couchet's death had reached Constantijn Huygens in The Hague, and Huygens noted 2 April as the date of death of Couchet in his *Dagboek* or diary. On 8 April Huygens wrote a short epitaph in the form of a poem to Couchet's memory (see Appendix 19, p. 307) From this it would appear that Couchet might have been a hunchback, or deformed in some way.

After Couchet's death, his widow, Angela van den Brant, continued the direction of the clavecimbel workshops. On 4 July 1656 she entered into a business relationship with Simon Hagaerts, whereby Hagaerts had to teach her son Petrus the art of clavecimbel building for a period of eight years.[19] Hagaerts had to produce instruments at prices which were specified, and share all profits equally. In exchange, Angela van den Brant committed her son for the eight-year period of the apprenticeship which was to begin on Petrus' twelfth birthday on 24 June 1660, and agreed to pay Hagaerts a fee of 200 guilders for Petrus' training. She also agreed to allow Hagaerts to use Couchet's patterns and jigs, measurements, and notes, and also the clavecimbels that she had inherited from her late husband. On 11 April 1657 the contract was updated, giving slightly higher prices for the different types of instrument, and in 1661 the partnership ended when an agreement was drawn up releasing both parties from the previous contracts.

In 1656, a year after Couchet's death, the 'cleyn clavecingel' in the Jodenstraat, the home of the Ruckers and Couchets for almost sixty years, was sold by the family heirs.

### *The Couchet sons*

Of the four sons of Ioannes Couchet and Angela van den Brant very little is known. Ioannes II Couchet joined the Guild aged only eleven in 1655/56, the year in which his father Ioannes I died (this was also the year in which Joris Britsen joined the Guild). Petrus Ioannes, the second son, is not mentioned in the registers of the Guild. Perhaps he did not take to the profession, since, under the terms of the 1661 contract between his mother and Simon Hagaerts, he would have been released from his apprenticeship only a year after beginning to work with Hagaerts. Both Ioseph Ioannes (aged fourteen) and Abraham (aged eleven) joined the Guild in 1666/67 as sons of a master. By 1694 Ioseph Ioannes had become insane and was taken into a rest home. He must have become worse and was later taken into the care of a religious order in the Cloister in Lier. He recovered somewhat in 1703, but was then readmitted a number of times. He died insane in

[19] Lambrechts-Douillez, 'Couchet', *Algemene Muziekencyclopedie*, II (1979), 262.

the Cloister in October 1706. In the saddest of circumstances, the great Ruckers–Couchet clavecimbel building tradition finally came to an end.

### *'CR'*

Two virginals of a type and construction very similar to those built by the Ruckers family survive with a rose bearing the initials CR, but otherwise without any signature.[20] The workmanship in these instruments is very rough and suggests to me that the instruments are the work of an apprentice learning his craft. These instruments have been linked with the sixteenth-century organist Christoffel Ruckers from Dendermonde, between Antwerp and Brussels. However, the C to $d^3$ chromatic compass and details of the decoration found on these instruments point to a date of construction in the second half of the seventeenth century, so that there can be no connection whatever between these virginals and Christoffel Ruckers. Their chief interest thus seems to be that they were *not* built by any of the Ruckers, although built at the end of the period when the Ruckers family were still active.

### RUCKERS AND OTHER ANTWERP ARTISTS

As has already been mentioned, the members of the Ruckers family were related to, or connected with a number of the the well-known figures in Antwerp's cultural history. Marten van der Biest, another clavecimbel builder, was a witness at Hans Ruckers' wedding and took a workman from Ruckers' workshop after moving to Amsterdam. Ioannes Ruckers' grandfather-in-law was Hubert Waelrant, the composer and theorist, and his father-in-law was the organist in the Antwerp cathedral. Andreas I Ruckers was related by marriage to Jacob Jordaens, the painter. And Johann Davidszoon de Heem, one of the greatest still-life painters of all time, was Andreas II Ruckers' brother-in-law. Ioes Karest, whose brother had owned the property adjoining 'de cleyn clavecingel' on the Jodenstraat, may also have been related to the Ruckers by marriage. On 18 March 1542, Karest was married to Christina Rughers, whose relationship with the Ruckers family, although unknown, is at least a possibility. She was Karest's second wife but did not survive long, as Karest was married a third time on 18 November 1545.

Another interesting relationship with the Antwerp harpsichord-building fraternity occurs through Willem Gompaerts, who became a master harpsichord builder in the Guild of St Luke in 1560, nineteen years before Hans Ruckers. In 1593 Gompaerts was godfather to Catharina Ruckers, who was later to marry Carel Couchet and to become the mother of Ioannes Couchet. Also, on 31 October 1610 Gompaerts took part with Elizabeth Waelrant in the baptismal ceremony of a daughter of Ioannes Ruckers and Maria Waelrant. Was Gompaerts Hans Ruckers' teacher and master? These two connections suggest that Gompaerts, if not actually related to the Ruckers, must have been a long-standing friend of the family, and one of the best candidates for the rôle of Hans Ruckers' teacher.

Ioannes and Andreas Ruckers must have been on familiar terms with both Rubens and Brueghel, and Ioannes and the latter two must have been amongst the most respected of Antwerp's citizens, since all three were exempted from the town watch duty and tax in consideration of their services to the court. Ioannes Ruckers' and Rubens' houses were within a minute's walk of one another, and although it is known that Rubens sometimes painted the lids of Ioannes' instruments, unfortunately no harpsichord or virginal lid painted by Rubens is known to have survived (see the Gerbier–Windebank correspondence, Appendix 16, p. 304). Their relationship was probably not just commercial. They would likely have known one another socially, been of comparable class and led comparable and inter-connected lives. For example, Rubens received commissions for the high altar painting and the 'Descent from the Cross' from the cathedral where Ioannes Ruckers maintained and tuned the organ. Jan Brueghel is credited with the lid painting of the 1612 IR harpsichord along with van Balen and Paul Bril. Also, the 1608 AR harpsichord bears a lid painting ascribed to Pieter Codde, a member of the Rubens school.

The Ruckers would obviously have encountered many of the important musicians working in the Low Countries at the time. Sweelinck bought a harpsichord which was probably by one of the Ruckers in 1604. Pieter Cornet, Peter Philips and John Bull were all organists to the Chapel Royal at the court of Albert and Isabella in Brussels at the same time that Ioannes Ruckers held his court appointment there. Philips worked in Antwerp from 1590 to 1597, and Bull was organist at Antwerp cathedral from 1617 to 1628; both would have known Ioannes Ruckers, who tuned and repaired the cathedral organ. (For a further discussion of the contemporary musical life in Antwerp, see Chapter 12, p. 218.)

The Couchets too were very highly placed in the Antwerp economic and social scale. Ioannes Couchet's father, Carolus Couchet, was a surgeon and sometime

[20] One of these is in the Musée de Croix, Namur; the other is in the Metropolitan Museum of Art, New York.

dean of the Guild of barbers and surgeons. Both Carolus Couchet and Ioannes Couchet owned numerous properties in Antwerp and were regularly involved in selling and buying mortgages and collecting rents. Ioannes Couchet's father-in-law by Carolus' second marriage, Adrianus Wortelmans, was a successful painter, and often worked for Ioannes Ruckers. Jacques Champiom, who styled himself 'de Chambonnières', was the harpsichord player to the court of Louis XIV, and owned and played a harpsichord by Couchet. Chambonnières is regarded as the father of the French school of harpsichord composers, and Constantijn Huygens, himself one of the greatest of the seventeenth-century European writers and scholars, was very proud that he also owned a harpsichord by the same builder as the harpsichordist to the French court. Huygens wrote that Couchet's death was a great waste for the lovers of fine harpsichords, and the news of his death was something over which he felt extreme regret (see Appendix 19, p. 307).

The members of the Ruckers and Couchet families took part in and contributed to the second economic and artistic flowering in Antwerp. They were acquainted with many of the distinguished people who moved in cultural and educated circles not only in Antwerp but in the whole of Western Europe.

## THE GUILD OF ST LUKE

The existence of the Guild of St Luke in Antwerp can be traced back as early as 1382. The apostle Luke was the patron saint of the painters, and throughout its entire history in Antwerp, the Guild of St Luke was dominated by the painters of fine art. But other groups of artists and artisans also belonged to the Guild including sculptors, engravers, printers, gold- and silver-smiths, potters, chest makers, craftsmen in glass, etc. By no means all of these were creative artists. Even among the painters, many members of the Guild churned out the same uniform product to the same pattern day in and day out. Others were clearly artisans and craftsmen – the chest makers, bookbinders, cabinet makers – and still others, the booksellers, printsellers, and art dealers, had a solely commercial interest in the products of the other members of the Guild of St Luke. There were also a small number of outsiders whose relationship to the Guild is not certain. Among these are, for example, the drapers, carpet merchants, pedlars, schoolmasters, doctors (St Luke is also the patron saint of the medical fraternity), brushmakers, grocers and even a varnish maker, a 'geographist' and a seller of pens!

The main purpose of the establishment of the Guilds, and membership in them, seems to have been to prevent outside competition. The Guild regulations enabled the number of people engaged in any one trade to be strictly controlled. All people who were members of the Guild also had to be citizens of Antwerp, and this meant that a travelling artist or artisan could not suddenly set up in business in Antwerp in competition with the Guild members unless he planned to settle there permanently and take up citizenship. Prices of the Guild products could be established and regulated so as to be favourable to the Guild members.

But the Guild system also helped to maintain standards. Normally one was not admitted to the Guild without submitting a 'masterpiece' for approval by the other masters. Usually this test piece was the product of a long apprenticeship under one of those who was already a master in the Guild. If the exhibition piece did not meet the standards of the other masters, membership could be refused or withheld until a further period of apprenticeship had been served.

There was, however, a great deal of discrimination and nepotism within the Guilds. The fees charged to the apprentices and journeymen were very high indeed and the registration charges rose much more rapidly than the general rate of inflation in Antwerp. By making the conditions of entry into the Guild more and more difficult, the masters assured themselves of the inexpensive labour of their apprentices for a longer period of time. Ioannes Couchet, for example, worked in his uncle's workshops for at least sixteen years, and did not become a journeyman builder until the eventual death of his master. Also, the sons of the established masters were admitted as '*wijnmeesters*', usually at a fraction of the cost of the regular member, and often without submitting a 'masterpiece'. These practices meant that entry into the Guild was either impossible or at least very difficult for those without influence or money or both.

Also, as in any system where human activity has been regulated by a set of inflexible rules, innovation and inventiveness were stifled, and the products of the Guild workshops tended to become standardized. New ideas took a long time to become accepted and established, since the system fostered the situation in which the product of the student was like that of his master. For example, although the number of instrument models from the Ruckers workshops is quite large, each model is highly uniform from builder to builder, and shows virtually no development or evolution through three generations of building and across a time span of about eighty years.

During the period in which the Ruckers family was active, membership in the Guild for harpsichord and virginal builders was compulsory. This had, however, not always been the case. Before 1557 the building of harpsichords and virginals was carried on freely without corporate restraint. Hence, before 1557, membership in the Guild was 'open' and only a few masters registered as *clavesimbalmakere* are to be found in the ledgers of the Guild. In 1557 ten clavecimbel makers applied to the Guild authorities for regulation and control of harpsichord and virginal building in Antwerp. The application was formally accepted in 1558; after that time the trade was 'closed' and could only be carried on by those who were Guild members and recognized formally as either master or apprentice.

The regulations accepted by the Guild authorities (see Appendix 12, p. 300) exempted the ten applicants from submitting a test piece as a condition for their membership in the Guild, but also laid down the conditions for the submitting and examination of test pieces produced by prospective members from 1558 onwards. The clavecimbel builders were to have the same rights, responsibilities and freedoms (including partial exemption from watch duty) as the other members of the Guild of St Luke, and above all they would be protected from outside competition, since no one would be allowed to make or sell a clavecimbel in Antwerp without being a Guild member. The final stipulation accepted by the Guild was that each instrument should be provided with the maker's distinctive 'mark' or emblem displayed in an obvious place on the instrument.

There seems little doubt that the 'mark' referred to is the decorative rose placed in the soundboard. Although the rose usually displayed the initials of the builder, instruments by van der Biest (a signatory of the 1558 agreement) and Grouwels have geometrical rosettes. In fact instruments by these builders have identical geometrical rosettes, so that not only are the initials of the makers not displayed, but the roses are therefore also not characteristic of the builder.[21] Also, the earliest Hans Ruckers instrument, the 1581 HR double muselar mother-and-child virginal, has three original geometrical parchment and wood rosettes, but lacks the usual lead rose with the HR initials and the angel playing the harp. It is also noteworthy that the early rose used by Ioannes Ruckers is almost indistinguishable from that of his father Hans, and that after 1637 the rose of the two Andreases, father and son, seem to be absolutely identical. Thus the way this final regulation was interpreted and exercised by the clavecimbel makers is not entirely clear.

## CONDITIONS OF WORK IN THE GUILD WORKSHOPS

Unfortunately very little is known about the nature of the Guild workshops during the period when the Ruckers were active. We do not know how big the workshops were, how many people worked in them, and we know very little about the actual conditions of work for apprentices, workers and servants. An analysis of the numbering system used by the Ruckers (see Chapter 3) shows that about thirty-five to forty instruments per year were being produced in the Andreas Ruckers workshop, and there seems little to indicate that the other Ruckers workshops produced fewer instruments than this. Thus, on the average, one new instrument came out of each workshop almost every week. Such a high rate of production seems to imply an industrial enterprise unlike even the largest harpsichord workshops of today.

A workshop of this size would, for example, have had to produce about 5,000 jacks in one year, and this in itself may have been enough to keep one person employed full time (if indeed the jacks were produced on the premises – see, however, p. 126). By way of comparison, the workshops of both Plantin the printer, and Rubens, both of whom were contemporary with the Ruckers family, are still extant in Antwerp. These are both enormous, and it is easy to visualize the Ruckers' harpsichord and virginal workshops as of a comparable size. It is known, for example, that Plantin kept sixteen printing presses busy full time, and employed about eighty people as compositors, printers, collators, proof-readers, binders and shop assistants.

A small insight into the working conditions in the clavecimbel workshops, albeit from a period considerably before the Guild regulations of keyboard instrument production in Antwerp, is provided by a contract between Ioes Karest and his brother Goosen. The Karest family (their father was called Jan (Ioannes)) came from Cologne, probably shortly before 1515. Goosen is recorded in the ledgers of the Guild of St Luke as early as 1519 as an apprentice painter studying under Peeter Mathijs. In 1529 he became a *vrijmeester* or journeyman painter. His brother Ioes was already registered in 1523 as a master *clavichordimaker* and qualified to 'sculpt and paint' his own instruments.

For some reason Goosen decided to become an instrument builder, and in 1537 (1538 new style) a contract (see

[21] The 1580 Marten van der Biest mother-and-child virginal in the Germanisches Nationalmuseum, Nuremberg (MI 85), and the Iohannes Grouwels 6-voet virginal (*c.* 1580) in the Brussels Museum of Musical Instruments (No. 2929).

Appendix 11, p. 299) was drawn up outlining the conditions whereby Goosen would study under his brother Ioes (if Goosen was about sixteen when he began his apprenticeship in 1519, he must have been about thirty-five when he began his apprenticeship with Ioes). First, it is interesting that, although Goosen was already a master in the Guild of St Luke and registered as such, he was required to undergo a further apprenticeship to qualify as a clavecimbel maker. Secondly, considering Goosen's age (Ioes was presumably older than Goosen) and the fact that the two parties to the contract were brothers, the conditions of the apprenticeship seem unduly harsh.

Although Ioes supplied the necessary materials for Goosen to work with, Goosen had to supply his own tools. During the three years of his apprenticeship, Goosen could work only for Ioes and not for himself or a third person, and he had at the same time to provide for his own livelihood. He was expected to work extremely long hours, spending from eleven to fourteen hours per day with only a one-and-a-half-to-two-hour midday break, and by candlelight if necessary. Any lost time had to be made up at the end of the three-year period.

In return Goosen was paid six stuijvers per day by Ioes, who taught him the construction, tuning and playing of virginals and harpsichords. If either party broke his part of the contract a fine amounting to forty times Goosen's daily wage was to be paid. It is difficult to assess the relative value of the wage paid to Goosen – it was probably at least sufficient to support him and perhaps his family. But otherwise the general conditions of the contract seem relatively severe – long working hours with no insurance against lost time through sickness or injury, difficult working conditions, including working by candlelight in the early morning and late evening. Also, considering the blood relationship between Ioes and Goosen, one wonders at the conditions of work in the more usual cases of unrelated master and apprentice.

## THE COUCHETS AND THE RUCKERS TRADITION

As has already been made clear, the Couchets were directly related to the Ruckers family – Ioannes Couchet was Hans Ruckers' grandson. But it is also extremely important to note that the instruments built by the Couchets – especially Ioannes Couchet – belong to the Ruckers tradition as much as those of Andreas II Ruckers, who was also a grandson of Hans. Ioannes Couchet worked in Ioannes Ruckers' workshop for sixteen years and the instruments of Couchet are built so much in the style of Ioannes Ruckers that instruments by the two builders are, aside from the rose and signature, virtually indistinguishable. In fact, many of the late instruments signed by Ioannes Ruckers may indeed be entirely the work of Couchet. Thus the product of the Couchet workshops is as much a part of the Ruckers tradition as those instruments signed by one of the Ruckers. In the subsequent part of this work I will therefore, for the sake of conciseness and readability, not always write 'Ruckers/Couchet tradition', or 'Ruckers/Couchet instruments'. But the contribution of the Couchets is always implied when I speak of the 'Ruckers tradition' and 'Ruckers instruments'.

CHAPTER TWO

# The pre-Ruckers instruments and traditions

Alongside the clavecimbel-making tradition which was developing in the Low Countries in the sixteenth century were other traditions evolving in their own ways in other parts of Europe. Of these the Italian school was particularly distinctive and individual. The early Germanic school at the beginning and middle of the sixteenth century strongly influenced the Flemish tradition, which in turn set the pattern for the Ruckers style around the end of the century. Before discussing the instruments of the Flemish school built by the Ruckers family it is important to understand some of the characteristics of the sixteenth-century Italian school, and also the features of the pre-Ruckers Germanic and Flemish schools as a background to the later Ruckers tradition.

## THE EARLY ITALIAN TRADITION

### *Sixteenth-century Italian construction*

By about 1520, harpsichord and virginal building in Italy seems already to have developed into a mature tradition with its own distinct characteristics. Unlike most harpsichords and virginals made in Northern Europe after about 1580, which have thick cases often of poplar or lime, the early Italian instruments have thin case sides of cypress usually only about 6mm thick. In order to add rigidity to these thin walls the top of the case is stiffened by the addition of slim battens decorated with elegant mouldings. Because of the lack of strength in the case sides, the spine is too weak to support hinges and the weight of a lid. The instruments are therefore placed in a stout outer case, usually plainly decorated, which can be used to protect the entirely separate inner instrument.

From a construction point of view the whole of the case and internal framing in Italian harpsichords is built up from the baseboard. The wrestplank is attached at its ends to two heavy wooden bars which are, in turn, attached to the baseboard. Triangular-shaped bracing blocks called 'knees' are placed at the edge of the baseboard around the inside of the instrument. Often the soundboard liner is let into and attached to the top of the knees. The soundboard is glued to the top edge of this liner and the strings are attached to pins driven into the soundboard and liner along the bentside and tail. The baseboard is usually reinforced with stiffening boards glued on their edge, and the bentside and tail liners, which have to withstand the string tension, are braced with flying buttresses running from the soundboard liners obliquely down to the baseboard. To this extremely rigid structure, which supports the soundboard and sustains the string tension, are attached the case sides. Because of the strength and rigidity of the internal framing these case sides can be made very thin, and indeed the thin walls serve only to enclose the internal bracing and structure and add virtually nothing to the strength and rigidity of the existing framework. The case sides are attached to the knees and liners, and characteristically overlap and are attached to the edges of the baseboard. The sides terminate at the front with scroll-sawn cheeks beside the ends of the keyboard.

The thinness of the wood in Italian case sides greatly facilitated the bending of the bentside, which was probably attached to the instrument directly without first being exposed to a heat or moisture treatment. This is particularly important with Italian harpsichords, some of which also have a much deeper and more constant curve to their bentsides than their contemporary North European instruments. Most sixteenth-century Italian harpsichords were originally disposed 1 × 8′, 1 × 4′ and had long string lengths designed for iron stringing. They went up to a top note of $f^3$, and so, note for note, the treble part of the compass had string lengths similar to many eighteenth-century instruments built in the Flemish tradition. However, the bentside in Italian instruments follows the shape of the bridge much more closely than it does in the instruments built in the North European schools, and so these Italian instruments characterisically have a bentside which is much more strongly curved. A few Italian instruments built in this period were slightly different in being disposed with either 2 × 8′ or 1 × 8′ without the octave, and having a compass going only to $c^3$. These instruments were designed to be strung with shorter strings of brass, and therefore, even though the compass only went to $c^3$, the shorter string lengths resulted in a similar sharp treble curvature in the bentside.[1]

The jack guides in Italian instruments were normally of the box-slide type. That is, each jack was guided in a single long slot morticed in a deep piece of wood. This guide often did not run parallel to the nameboard but rather, with the instrument viewed in plan, was angled so that the bass end of the jack guide(s) was further from the nameboard than the treble end, and the wrestplank was tapered to compensate for this. This gave the required bass plucking points and also tended to reduce the bentside curvature slightly. Often the angle of the registers was sufficient to necessitate the angling of the individual jackslots in the guides.

The key touchplates in Italian instruments are normally of box, except in the more elaborate, highly decorated instruments, when they are of ivory. The sharps are usually of ebony, ebony-topped fruitwood, or some other dark hardwood such as bog chestnut or bog oak. The keys are usually of beech, chestnut or poplar, and are guided at their tails with slips of wood which move in a slotted diapason rack.

The bridges and nuts in Italian instruments are of a basically rectangular cross-section with parallel front and rear surfaces and a delicate moulding along the top surface. These bridges are much smaller in cross-section than the type of bridge found on most North European harpsichords and virginals, but, like their northern counterparts, are tapered slightly to give a larger cross-section in the bass than in the treble. Often the ends of the bridges are carved with delicate scrolls which extend the bridges toward the case sides beyond the top and bottom bridge and nut pins. These scrolls have a purely decorative function and often are detrimental to the tone at the extreme ends of the compass because they stiffen the freely vibrating soundboard area near the ends of the bridges.

The Italian virginals of the sixteenth century are polygonal in shape and closely follow the principles of construction of the harpsichords regarding internal framing, case thickness, bridge shape and cross-sectional area, scalings etc. Naturally the virginals are disposed with only one set of unison strings. The main feature which is characteristic of Italian virginals and which instantly distinguishes them from the early North European virginals also made with thin cases is the position of the keyboard. The keyboard of the Italian virginal projects out from the case of the instrument itself, whereas the keyboard of the northern instruments is recessed into the case. The cases of the Italian virginals are thus narrower front to back and perhaps somewhat more elegant in shape than those of the early North European instruments.

### *Italian string scalings and stringing materials*

#### The concept of string scalings

Basic to the design of any keyboard instrument is the length of the strings used. The early builders of virtually all European traditions designed their instruments so that the strings were, with a small safety factor, very close to the breaking point of the material being used. Instruments designed to sound at pitches different from one another would therefore have string lengths which differed in a regular way. For example, the c string of an instrument designed to sound at a pitch a tone higher than another would have the same length as the corresponding d string of the instrument designed for the lower pitch, if both were designed for strings of the same material. If the stringing materials were not intended to be the same, but the pitch of two instruments was designed to be similar, then the instrument designed for the stronger stringing material would have longer strings, note for note, than the instrument with weaker strings. But the strings in both instruments would be equally near to their respective breaking points. The problem which has caused a considerable amount of confusion in the past is that some Italian instruments of the sixteenth century were designed to use iron treble strings, and some were designed to use treble strings of brass (an alloy of copper and zinc). This is further complicated by the co-existence of pitch standards a tone apart, of various regional pitch standards, and the existence of instruments designed to transpose by intervals of a fourth or a fifth.

[1] W. R. Thomas and J. J. K. Rhodes, 'The string scales of Italian keyboard instruments', *Galpin Society Journal*, XX (1967), 49–62.

In order to be able to compare instruments designed to sound at different pitches, and designed for different treble stringing materials, it is necessary to compare their string lengths. Usually in the treble part of the compass the string lengths halve with each octave rise in pitch, and double with each octave drop in pitch. Therefore specifying the length of one of the treble notes in this part of the compass effectively specifies the length of all of the other strings there. By convention the note whose length is specified so that comparisons between different instruments can be made is that of $c^2$, an octave above middle c. Thus, for example, if $c^2$ has a length of 350mm, $c^1$ would be 700mm long, and $c^3$ would be 175mm long. The notes between the *c*s would then have lengths which are in regular inverse proportion to their pitch, and which can be calculated mathematically. The length of $c^2$ is called the *pitch scaling* of the instrument, and the string lengths of an instrument are collectively called the *scalings*. Thus instruments with short scalings are designed for a high pitch or to use strings of a weak material which cannot stand such a high pitch, or both, and the converse is true for long-scaled instruments.

Because the Greek philosopher Pythagoras observed the relationship between the pitch and length of a vibrating string where the tension was kept constant, we say that an instrument whose scalings halve and double accurately in the treble has *Pythagorean scalings*. In fact, in the treble part of the compass where the scalings are Pythagorean, strings of different diameters are normally used, and therefore the tensions in all of the strings in this part of the compass are not the same. Nonetheless the strings in the part of the compass where the scalings are Pythagorean are all equally near breaking point, a fact which the non-mathematical student of organology will simply have to accept.

### Critically stressed strings

The reason that the strings have scalings which place them under tensions very close to their breaking point is an acoustical one which relates to the musical properties of the string itself. The string in any keyboard instrument vibrates not just in its basic fundamental mode even though it is the fundamental mode of vibration that is recognized by the ear as the musical pitch of the string. As well as the fundamental mode of vibration, the string vibrates in many higher modes which we call partial sounds or simply partials. For a string without any stiffness, these partials are exact integral multiples of the frequency of the fundamental. Thus if, say, the fundamental frequency is 100Hz or 100 vibrations per second, the frequencies of the partials are 200Hz, 300Hz, 400Hz, 500Hz, 600Hz, etc. Because the partials form a perfect harmonic series above the fundamental, they produce a sound which the ear recognizes as musical. The metal strings of a harpsichord or virginal, however, are not completely flexible, and the partials do not form the ideal perfect harmonic series above the fundamental. The frequencies of the partials are always slightly sharp, or slightly higher, than those of the perfect harmonics. The amount by which the partials of the strings are out of tune depends on many factors including the stiffness of the metal of the wire being used for the strings, the diameter of the string, and the length of the string. The lesser the stiffness, or the smaller the diameter of the string, or the longer the string, then the closer are the frequencies of the partials to those of a pure harmonic series. In fact the partials of the strings in most well-designed stringed instruments have a stiffness, diameter and length which produces a sound with partials approximating closely to a pure harmonic series.

Most people have experienced the effect of de-tuning a string on a guitar, violin or keyboard instrument. At the pitch for which the string was intended to sound, the result is a clear, pure sound which is instantly recognized as being musical. If the string is slackened, the sound becomes dull, false and unpleasant, and the effect becomes worse the more the string is slackened. Obviously the greater the tension in the string, the more musical is the effect of the sound that it produces. However, it is not possible to increase the tension in the string indefinitely, as the string will eventually break. The string is therefore tuned as high as possible, leaving a small safety factor below the ultimate breaking point, so that the sound it produces is clear and musical. Such a string is said to be *critically stressed*. It is at a working tension slightly below its ultimate breaking strength.

The early builders of stringed instruments of all kinds seem to have recognized the musical importance of designing instruments with critically stressed strings even though the physical reasons for this had not been formulated. They soon discovered by experiment what the maximum length of a string could be for a given pitch, so that, allowing for a small safety factor, the sound produced by the string was not only musically acceptable, but rich and pleasing.

The obvious problem with using critically stressed strings throughout the entire compass is that the bass strings would be unreasonably long. By using shorter strings in the bass, and changing the stringing material to one which is weaker and less stiff than iron, the quality of the sound is maintained despite the reduction in the string lengths. This reduction, which I shall call 'foreshortening', is not arbitrary but a definite part of the design of the instrument. The implications of the foreshortening of the bass scalings is further discussed in Chapter 4, p. 55.

### Iron and brass as treble stringing materials in Italian instruments

The scalings, compass and disposition of most extant sixteenth-century Italian harpsichords have been altered.[2] Most extant Italian harpsichords now have one keyboard and two sets of unison 8′ strings, with a compass and scalings typical of those harpsichords built in the late seventeenth century. Although the disposition with two sets of unison strings does occur as an original feature of a few sixteenth-century instruments, most originally had either only one set of strings,[3] or, more frequently, they had two sets of strings, one of which was at the octave to the other. An additional feature of sixteenth-century Italian instruments, whether harpsichords or virginals, is that the treble compass went to $f^3$. Later seventeenth-century and early eighteenth-century instruments, or indeed the sixteenth-century instruments which were later altered, were usually given a treble compass which went only to $c^3$.

Comparing these instruments, an interesting correlation becomes apparent. The virginals with a compass to $f^3$ have long scalings; those that go only to $c^3$ have short scalings. The harpsichords that were originally designed to have an octave register also have long scalings; those with only unison strings, or with a top note which only goes to $c^3$, have short scalings.

The reason for the correlation between a long scaling and a top note of $f^3$ in virginals, and the use of an octave register in harpsichords, is simply one of space constraints. For example, a virginal with a short (brass) scaling of, say, 285mm at $c^2$ would have a scaling at $f^3$ of only 106mm. A top string this short leaves no space beside the angled box-slide register for the bridges to sit out over freely vibrating soundboard. On the other hand, a virginal whose $c^2$ string length is 345mm (a typical iron scaling) would have an $f^3$ 129mm long, giving 23mm more space around the treble ends of the bridges. Similarly, a harpsichord with a 4′ register cannot reach to $f^3$ using $c^2$ scalings of 285mm; the 4′ strings in the extreme treble would be only 53mm long – too short to allow space between the nut and bridge for the two registers (for a single row each of 8′ and 4′ jacks) and an area of freely vibrating soundboard. A harpsichord with a 4′ and a $c^3$ scaling of 345mm, however, would allow the 4′ $f^3$ to have a length of 64mm, giving 11mm more space for the 4′ bridge. Thus a virginal which reaches to $f^3$, or a harpsichord with a 4′ register reaching to this note, must have long treble scalings, and this in turn means that they must be strung in iron. A virginal or harpsichord which goes only to $c^3$ in the treble can use short scalings intended for brass stringing and still produce a good sound in the extreme treble, since the string lengths still allow an area of soundboard which can vibrate freely around the ends of the bridges near the registers.

Those instruments which use iron treble stringing, like their North European counterparts, revert to the use of brass strings in the tenor and bass. The reason for this is simply that doubling the length of the long iron strings down into the bass would result in an extremely long instrument. Foreshortening the scalings in the bass to a point where yellow brass (and red brass in the lowest basses) can be used considerably reduces the physical size of the instrument. But using only brass to string the whole instrument has two distinct advantages over using brass bass strings and treble iron strings. First, the tuning stability is increased, since all of the strings are of one material and so they all change equally if the temperature rises or falls. Secondly, there is a noticeable 'break' in the quality of the sound at the transition between the brass and the iron strings. Instruments strung just in brass do not suffer the interruption in the tone quality caused by the transition from brass to iron stringing.[4]

Since most sixteenth-century virginals had a treble compass to $f^3$, and the harpsichords went to $f^3$ and had an octave stop, Italian instruments of this period had long scalings ($c^2$ = about 345mm) and were strung in iron strings. For most of the seventeenth century and part of the eighteenth century the compass regressed to $c^3$ in the treble and the octave was abandoned to the 2 × 8′ disposition, and so both the virginals and harpsichords had short scalings of about 285mm for $c^2$, suitable for stringing in brass.

The iron- and brass-strung instruments with these scalings would have originally sounded at a pitch which was probably slightly below the current modern pitch standard of $a^1$ = 440Hz. However, there is now considerable evidence, too detailed to outline here, that another pitch a tone higher than this was in common current use.[5] These instruments have scalings of about 305mm for iron stringing and of about 255mm for brass stringing. Naturally not all instruments fit rigidly into such a neat

2 John Barnes, 'The specious uniformity of Italian harpsichords', *Keyboard Instruments: Studies in Keyboard Organology*, ed. Edwin M. Ripin (Edinburgh, 1971), 1–10.

3 Friedemann Hellwig, 'The single-strung Italian harpsichord', *Keyboard Instruments*, ed. Ripin (Edinburgh, 1971), 37–41.

4 See Chapter 4 for a discussion of how iron, yellow brass and red brass are used in Ruckers instruments, with typical scalings for each.

5 Work in progress by the author.

scheme. Builders working to variant local pitch standards, and with variant local standards of length measurement, produced instruments whose scalings are outwith this simplified pattern. Nonetheless, a large number of instruments exist which were clearly designed to sound at R either with iron scalings of about 345mm or brass scalings of 285mm, and to sound at R + 2 either with iron scalings of 305mm or brass scalings of 255mm.

Shortridge[6] and Barnes[7] independently noticed the way in which the treble scalings of many Italian keyboard instruments grouped into the two categories, long and short. They proposed that, by analogy with the Ruckers double-manual harpsichords (see p. 41), the scaling difference between the two categories of instrument corresponded to a pitch difference of a perfect fourth between them. Thus they held that the $f^3$ key of the long-scaled instrument would sound the same note and pitch as the $c^3$ key of the short-scaled one. However, both Barnes and Shortridge found that the average difference in the scalings of the two categories of instrument corresponded to less than the expected interval of a fourth and was closer to a major or minor third.

The chief difficulty here is that this is a process of averaging over not just one builder or tradition but a number of different builders working at different times and in different locations. Taking an average in this way also ignores the difference of a tone between the two common pitch standards. In fact the ratio between the lengths of the typical iron and brass scalings, 345mm/285mm = 1.21, is indeed between a just major third (5/4 = 1.25) and a just minor third (6/5 = 1.20). This in itself suggests that the reason for the scaling difference between the two categories is a result not of a pitch difference between them but of a difference in the treble stringing material.

### *Disposition and sound of sixteenth-century Italian harpsichords*

By far the most common original disposition of sixteenth-century Italian harpsichords is 1 × 8′, 1 × 4′, like that of the Ruckers instruments in their original state. But some harpsichords had an original 1 × 8′ or a 2 × 8′ disposition. The strings are to the left of their corresponding jacks in the single-strung 1 × 8′ harpsichords, and analogously, the low-pitched string is on the left, and the octave string is on the right of the jack in those instruments with an octave. This arrangement is characteristically Italian and the opposite of that found on the Flemish instruments disposed with 1 × 8′ and 1 × 4′. Unlike the northern instruments, the Italian instruments with an octave stop often have no separate hitchpin rail glued to the underside of the soundboard for the octave strings. Instead the octave strings are hitched to pins which are simply driven into the plank-sawn cypress soundboard and then reinforced underneath with a large drop of glue placed at the point where the hitchpin penetrates through the soundboard. There are very few Italian harpsichords originally built with two manuals, and none that I know of from the sixteenth century.[8]

The sound of a sixteenth-century Italian instrument, whether brass or iron strung, is pungent, powerful, immediate and engaging. Despite the totally different principles of construction it is remarkably similar to that of the sixteenth- and early seventeenth-century North European instruments. The chief difference is that the sound of the Italian instrument has a somewhat greater attack and slightly less sustaining power, both almost certainly due to the lighter bridge cross-section and the resulting greater flexibility of the bridge and soundboard. That is, because the combined flexibility of the bridge and soundboard is greater than in the North European instruments, the energy of the string after plucking is radiated into the air more quickly during the initial stages of the sounding of the note. The note is therefore louder initially – i.e. it has more attack – but it dies away quickly since the energy of the string is all dissipated in the initial attack of sound.

## THE EARLY GERMANIC TRADITION

### The Hans Müller harpsichord of 1537

The earliest dated North European stringed keyboard instrument is not of Flemish origin, but Germanic. It is a single-manual harpsichord in the Raccolta Statale degli Antichi Strumenti Musicali (formerly the Evan Gorga Collection) in Rome, and is signed 'GOTTES WORT BLEIBT EWICK BEISTAN DEN ARMEN ALS DEN REICHEN DURCH HANS MULLER CV LEIPCiK IM 1537' (The

[6] John Shortridge, 'Italian harpsichord building in the 16th and 17th centuries', *Contributions from the Museum of History and Technology: United States National Museum*, Bulletin 225, Smithsonian Institution, Paper 15 (Washington, D.C., 1960), 93–107.

[7] John Barnes, 'Pitch variations in Italian keyboard instruments', *Galpin Society Journal*, XVIII (1965), 110–16; J. H. van der Meer, 'Harpsichord making and metallurgy: a rejoinder', *Galpin Society Journal*, XXI (1968), 175–8; John Barnes, 'Italian string scales', *Galpin Society Journal*, XXI (1968), 179–81; John Barnes, 'The stringing of Italian harpsichords', *Der klangliche Aspekt beim Restaurierung von Saitenklavieren*, ed. Vera Schwarz (Graz, 1973), 35–40.

[8] The Italians' use of two-manual harpsichords was quite different from that north of the Alps. Most of the surviving two-manual instruments have no manual coupler and 4′ on the upper, and the two unison 8′s on the lower manual. Such a disposition might have been used for an echo or antiphonal treatment of fantasias.

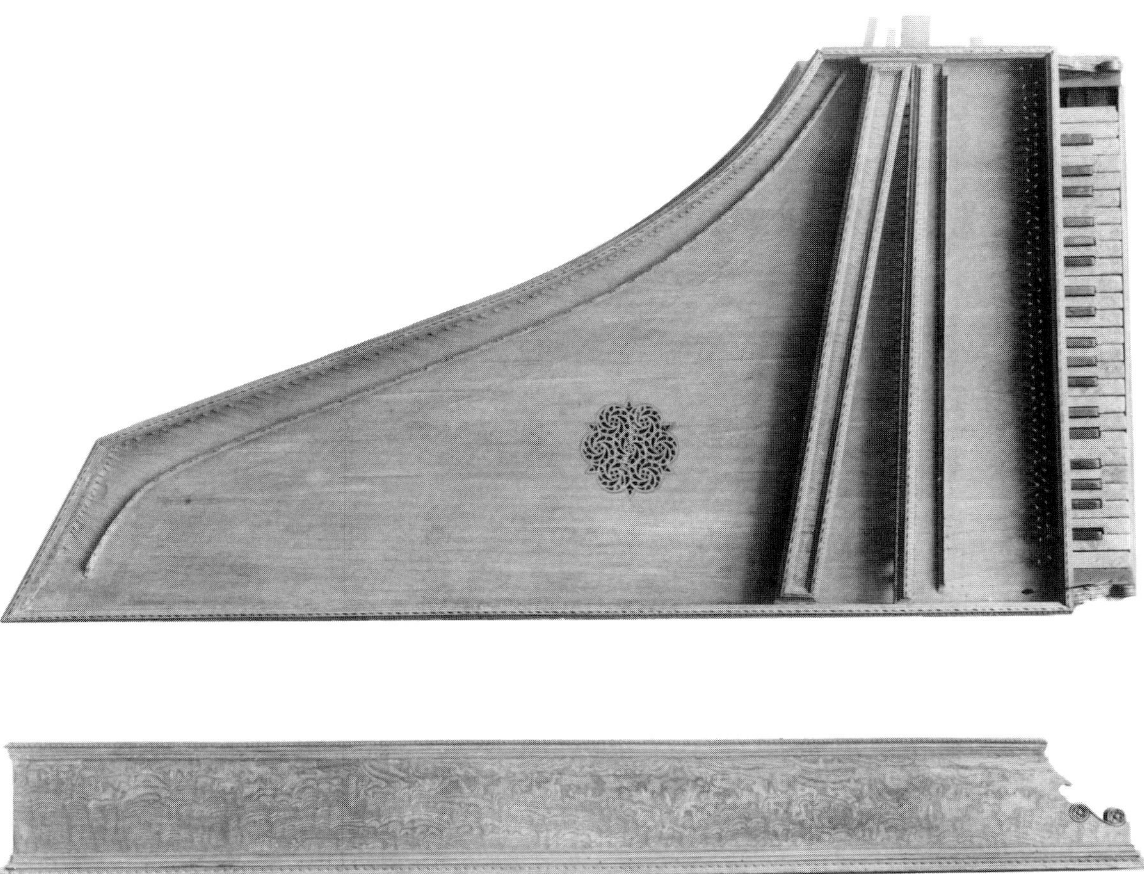

Plate 2.1 Plan view and spine side of the Hans Müller harpsichord of 1537. The original position of the bridges is clearly visible in the plan view. The keyboard is in its low-pitch position. The spine and case are made of figured 'Hungarian' ash, which was later imitated in the printed papers used to decorate the interior of the lid and flap of the Ruckers clavecimbels. Scale 1:10.

word of God remains forever to help the poor [as much] as the rich. [Made] by Hans Müller in Leipzig in 1537).[9] This interesting and extremely rare instrument shows features which are characteristic both of the contemporary Italian school and of the late fully-developed Flemish tradition. It is not clear, however, whether the tradition in which the Müller instrument was built grew out of the Italian tradition, or whether the Italian and Germanic traditions are separate developments of some yet earlier common tradition.

The Müller harpsichord is 1494mm long, 416mm wide at the keyboard and 187mm high. Compared with other single-manual harpsichords it is therefore rather small, and one is immediately led to expect an instrument at a higher pitch than normal. The bentside, unlike that of those instruments built in the Italian tradition, has a shallow curve despite the fact that the bentside follows the original position of the bridge quite closely. The shallowness results mostly from the fact that the treble compass goes only to $a^2$, instead of the $f^3$ common in contemporary Italian instruments.

The original compass was C to $a^2$ without the accidentals C♯ at the bottom and $g\sharp^2$ at the top, i.e. C,D to $g^2$,$a^2$ with forty-four notes. The keyboards are arranged so that the tails of the top and bottom two keys are straight and parallel, with a space between for the 'missing' accidentals. The strings and jackslots also appear to be arranged with a gap at the top and bottom for the missing accidentals, but with altogether forty-six pairs of strings and jackslots, and so two more than the number of notes on the keyboard. However, the arrangement of keys, strings, and jackslots results from the fact that the key-

9 This instrument is described in considerable detail in a booklet by Luisa Cervelli and J. H. van der Meer, 'Conservato a Roma il più antico clavicembalo tedesco', *Palatino: Rivista Romana di Cultura*, X 3–4 (Rome, 1966), 265–8.

board is capable of being shifted laterally by an amount equal to the width of one natural to achieve a transposition of a tone. In either position of the keyboard two sets of strings are not required: one end set and the set third from the same end. The transposition by one tone produces certain problems in tuning which are discussed in relation to a Ruckers instrument in Appendix 7, p. 293.

The Müller harpsichord is disposed with two sets of unison strings but three rows of jacks. Two of these rows are placed in roughly the 'usual' position and one row of jacks is placed near the nut to give a nasal-sounding register similar to the lute stop common on eighteenth-century English harpsichords. Clearly two sets of jacks originally plucked the same string and one set plucked the other, but it is now not possible to say what the original plucking directions of the jacks were.

As it presently stands, the bridge is not in its original position (see Plate 2.1), but is displaced towards the bentside to lengthen the scalings. In this position the bridge is placed asymmetrically between the cutoff bar and bentside, rather than in a more-or-less central position between the two. Also, because of the distortion of the scale produced by moving the bridge, the present treble string lengths do not double with each octave drop in pitch. With the bridge in its present position the scalings are approximately correct for brass stringing at a pitch corresponding to $a^1 = 440$Hz. It would thus appear that the instrument was probably altered in Italy in the eighteenth century to give scalings which would have 'modernized' the instrument to make it useful for playing at the then contemporary pitch.

Traces of the original position of the bridge, running along a roughly medial line between the cutoff bar and bentside, are still visible, and in particular a number of bridge-pin positions are visible where the original pins penetrated through the bridge into the soundboard. From these the original scalings of the harpsichord can be estimated. These yield treble string lengths which double with each octave drop in pitch in a way that is much more accurate than the present scalings. The average scalings for the estimated original position of the bridge are about $c^1 = 374$mm ($c^2 = 187$mm) with the keyboard in the low-pitch position, and $c^1 = 332$mm ($c^2 = 166$mm) in the high-pitch position. These scalings immediately suggest iron treble stringing and pitches respectively an octave and a ninth above normal pitch (that is pitches of R + 8 and R + 9 in the pitch scheme suggested for the Ruckers instruments; see p. 223).[10]

From a construction point of view the Müller harpsichord is framed and built quite differently from the contemporary Italian instruments, although still with some isolated Italianate features. The case sides sit on top of the baseboard, rather than overlapping it as with instruments built in the Italian tradition. The baseboard itself is made like the later Flemish instruments with the grain of the wood running transversely under the keyboard, and lengthwise under the soundboard. The internal 'knees' of the Italian instruments are lacking, and the internal strengthening is achieved by means of upper and lower braces running just below the soundboard and at baseboard level respectively, from the bentside to the spine, in the manner of most later North European harpsichords.

The case sides of the Müller are very thin and are strengthened around the top edge of the instrument with a moulded batten; in this respect the Müller is very Italianate. The scroll-sawn cheek pieces are also very much in the Italian tradition. The rows of jacks are angled across the soundboard in the Italian way, but the jacks are guided by a series of holes pierced in the soundboard itself and in a lower guide, rather than with a box-slide. The tradition of the jacks passing through holes pierced in the soundboard continued in the later Flemish virginal tradition and is also found in at least one early Anglo-Flemish harpsichord, namely that built by Lodowijk Theeuwes (see p. 26).

The soundboard is made not of spruce nor fir, as is normal with North European harpsichords and virginals, but rather of cypress, like many Italian instruments. There is a large rosette carved in the cypress wood of the soundboard itself in a style very reminiscent of lutes of the period. This feature is one not found in either the Italian or the North European traditions, in which the roses are always let into the soundboard. Because the jackslots are pierced through it, the soundboard runs the full length of the instrument. The wrestplank is a narrow bar of wood (beech?) only 32mm wide behind the nameboard, leaving both the bridge and the nut located over freely vibrating soundboard. The bridge and nut have a moulded top edge and scroll-carved ends in the Italian style.

Most of the internal framing and the case of the Müller harpsichord is of a coniferous softwood. But one feature of the Müller which is individual to it is the case veneer. This is of a highly-figured wood called Hungarian ash,

[10] The other possibility is that the pitches involved might have been R + 4 and R + 5, a fourth and a fifth above normal pitch with treble stringing in brass. Using the ratio of the Ruckers brass-to-iron scalings (see p. 61) the scalings for the Müller would then be expected to be about $c^2 = 218$mm and 193mm respectively. Even allowing for a considerable error in estimating the original scalings of the Müller harpsichord, these long scalings seem to exclude this possibility.

which was very popular in German and Swiss furniture and for internal wood panelling during the Northern High Renaissance. Hungarian ash is ordinary European ash (*Fraxinus excelsior*) and is not indigenous exclusively to Hungary. It is, rather, ash which is selected specially for this particular figure (just as fiddle-back maple or sycamore are not from a particular type of tree, but from specially selected or specially grown trees). Ash sometimes grows with wavy, rather than circular, rings usually only on one side of the tree. If this wood is cut through the wavy rings in a roughly tangential direction, then the boards so obtained will have this extremely strong figure. The tradition of using Hungarian ash seems to have been carried to Flanders with the German-speaking craftsmen who migrated there. The wood itself must have been lacking in Flanders, however, and this seems to have been the origin of the Hungarian ash wood-grain papers which were used as an imitation on the Flemish instruments (see p. 131). The use of this wood on the cases of German instruments seems to have lasted for a long time, since it is found as late as 1639 used on the outside of the case of a doll's-house virginal in the Germanisches Nationalmuseum.

There is no evidence on the spine of the instrument that the Müller ever had a lid, and this plus the thin case sides suggests that the instrument had an outer carrying case like its Italian counterpart. The tradition of this separate construction was probably also carried by the Germanic artisans to Flanders, and is to be found, for example, in the two earliest surviving Flemish virginals dated 1548 and 1550 by Ioes Karest, which have separate outer cases for protection and transportation. Traces of abrasion on the lower surface of the Müller baseboard discovered recently by Pietro Pattachiola[11] seem to confirm the original existence of an outer case. This case must have had three longitudinal battens on the inside lower surface which constantly abraded the baseboard of the inner instrument each time it was moved in and out of the outer case.

### Early Germanic virginal-building tradition

No very early Germanic virginals built at about the same time as the Müller harpsichord seem to have existed. However, there are two virginals, both probably dating from the first half of the seventeenth century, which exhibit many of the features of the pre-Ruckers Flemish virginals. These two instruments are the doll's-house virginal (already referred to) in the Germanisches Nationalmuseum, Nuremberg, and a full-sized anonymous virginal of compass C/E to $c^3$ in the Museum Carolino Augusteum, Salzburg.[12] The latter instrument was probably intended to sound at a pitch one tone above normal, or R + 2 (see p. 223).

Both of these instruments are hexagonal in shape, like the 1548 virginal by Ioes Karest. The keyboards are recessed, rather than projecting from the front of the case as is normal with Italian instruments (as mentioned before); this recessing of the keyboards is one of the most characteristic features common to all virginals built in the northern part of Europe. Like the virginals of Karest, but unlike the later Ruckers virginals, the nameboard above the keys is fixed and does not slide out. In order to be able to remove the keys, therefore, a small batten along the lower part of the nameboard is removable, enabling the keyboard first to be lifted up to clear the front keywell moulding, and then to be withdrawn.

A feature found on the Salzburg virginal but not on the later Ruckers virginals is the presence of keyblocks at either end of the keyboard. Normally, even in the early Flemish virginals, there are no keyblocks between the ends of the keys and the keywell cheek pieces. However, the existence of keyblocks on a virginal which was later falsified to appear to be a Ruckers ('1620 HR', see p. 278), but which was almost certainly made in Antwerp, shows that even this feature was carried over from the German tradition into some of the instruments built in Flanders.

## EARLY FLEMISH INSTRUMENTS

### The two virginals by Ioes Karest

The earliest Flemish clavecimbels are the two polygonal virginals by Ioes Karest. The earliest of these, dated 1548, is in the Brussels Instrument Museum and has been described in detail by Ripin[13] and Meeùs.[14] The second Karest virginal, dated 1550, is located in the Raccolta Statale degli Antichi Strumenti Musicali[15] (Inv. No. 812) and is mentioned in one of the catalogues of Franciolini.[16]

[11] Personal communication. My thanks to Sig. Pattachiola for pointing this out to me.

[12] J. H. van der Meer, 'Beiträge zum Cembalobau im deutschen Sprachgebiet bis 1700', *Anzeiger des Germanischen Nationalmuseums* (Nuremberg, 1966), 103–33.

[13] Edwin M. Ripin, 'On Joes Karest's virginal and the origins of the Flemish tradition', *Keyboard Instruments: Studies in Keyboard Organology*, ed. Edwin M. Ripin (Edinburgh, 1971), 65–73.

[14] Nicolas Meeùs, 'La facture de virginals à Anvers au 16$^{e}$ siècle', *Bulletin of the Brussels Museum of Musical Instruments*, IV (1974), 55–64.

[15] Luisa Cervelli, 'Per un catalogo degli strumenti a tastiera del Museo degli Antichi Strumenti Musicali', *Accademie e Biblioteche d'Italia*, XLIV, 4–5 (1976), 305–43.

[16] Edwin M. Ripin, 'The instrument catalogues of Leopoldo Franciolini', *Music Indexes and Bibliographies*, IX (Hackensack, N.J., 1974), 10, 25, 50 and 58.

Both of these instruments are signed 'IOES KAREST DE COLONIA', followed by the date.[17]

Although the two instruments are quite different in size, and therefore probably intended to sound at a different pitch, they have many features in common. Both are polygonal in shape, although the larger Rome instrument has a curved 'bentside' running roughly parallel to the bridge. The case sides of both instruments are thin (about 7mm) and made of sycamore or maple. In order to protect their rather delicate structure, these instruments had to be kept in a heavy outer case which was equipped with a lid and lockable front flap; and indeed the outer cases of both instruments survive. The case sides are flush with the outer edge of the baseboard, a feature concealed beneath a moulded batten which surrounds the instrument along its lower edge. The top edge of each virginal is also reinforced with a moulded batten, and comparison of these mouldings on the two instruments shows that they were made with the same moulding plane. The most prominent rounded feature of this moulding is decorated with stripes of black paint alternating with clear unpainted wood in a sort of 'barber pole' effect. Other parts of the mouldings are decorated with small squiggles and dots of black paint. Both the inside and outside of the case of the Brussels virginal are inscribed with Latin mottoes. The outside of the Rome Karest has a beautiful hand-painted Renaissance grotesque decoration in dark blue and black, with intertwined vines, leaves, fruits and flowers interspersed with, and sometimes connected to, human and griffin heads. Although the dolphin does not feature in this decoration, the general impression is very similar to that of the later painted and block-printed paper dolphin patterns (see Plate 7.4, p. 131). Both virginals probably originally had painted soundboards. But only traces of a soundboard painting are left on the Brussels Karest. The Rome Karest, however, has a soundboard painting in a good state of preservation with flowers and the usual blue borders and arabesques. It is thus the earliest instrument with its soundboard painting still intact.

The two Karest virginals have similar keyboards. The sharps are of bog oak decorated about half-way along the sharp with four scribed lines and a small edge nick between the two middle lines. These decorated sharps are typical of instruments built in Flanders until about 1580. The naturals, like those on the Müller, are of a highly-figured dense wood, which is probably either briar or maple (sycamore?) root. The poplar keylevers are guided at the back by a brass pin moving in a vertical slot in the rack, in a manner typified in later Flemish virginals.

The soundboard in both virginals is a coniferous wood which is probably spruce. The bridges are made with rounded inward- and flat outward-facing surfaces, and a 'step' moulding along the top of the bridge into which the bridge pins are driven. There are two roses in both virginals. The Brussels Karest has one large circular rose and a smaller rose in the shape of a Gothic window. These are filled with a pierced gilded geometrical pattern of interlocking squares cut and embossed in vellum or heavy paper. The Rome Karest has two circular roses both similar in style to the usual Italian pierced Gothic roses.

The jacks are guided by a series of slots cut through the leather-covered soundboard, with the jacks paired together in the same slot. A similar leather-covered board extending between the two keywell braces is used

[17] The signature of the Rome virginal is not original, although it apparently existed at the time that Franciolini compiled his catalogue.

Plate 2.2 Plan view of the virginal by Ioes Karest, 1550. Traces of the original soundboard painting can be seen. The curved 'bentside' is unique to this instrument. Scale 1.10.

Table 2.1 *Comparison of the scalings in two virginals by Ioes Karest*

| | Rome Karest of 1550 | | Brussels Karest of 1548 | | |
|---|---|---|---|---|---|
| Note | Measured scalings | Corrected scalings | Measured scalings | Corrected scalings | Ratio of corrected scalings |
| $f^3$ | 114mm | 111.7mm | – | – | – |
| $c^3$ | 166.5 | 169.8 | 139mm | 136.2mm | 1.247 |
| $f^2$ | 273 | 267.5 | 211.5 | 215.7 | 1.240 |
| $c^2$ | 346.5 | 353.4 | 286 | 280.3 | 1.261 |
| $f^1$ | 488 | 478.2 | 388.5 | 396.3 | 1.207 |
| $c^1$ | 592.5 | 604.4 | 511.5 | 501.3 | 1.206 |
| f | 836 | 819.3 | 679 | 692.6 | – |
| c | 990 | 1009.8 | 885 | 867.3 | – |
| F | 1229 | 1204.4 | 1116 | 1138.3 | – |
| C/(E) | 1347.5 | 1374.5 | 1163 | 1139.7 | 1.206 |

as a lower jack guide. This lower guide, though sometimes called a 'counter soundboard', has no acoustical function whatsoever. It might better be called a 'noise-board', since it tends to amplify the sound of the jacks passing up and down through it, and it was soon replaced in instruments built slightly later by a narrow board stiffened along its edges to minimize the noise made by the jacks.

The chief differences between these two instruments lie in their compass, size and scalings. The compass of the Brussels instrument is C/E to $c^3$, forty-five notes, and that of the Rome Karest is a full C,D to $f^3$, fifty-three notes, chromatic except for the missing bottom C♯. Both of these compasses are unusual for instruments built during this period – the Rome compass has no contemporary counterpart and even the compass of the Brussels Karest might have been expected to be the more limited C/E to $a^2$ usual at this time. In order to assess the difference in pitch between the two virginals I have compared their scalings in the table above.

Here the lengths of the strings for the notes *c* and *f* have been compared, and one immediately recognizes another difference in the two instruments, arising because of their difference in compass. Because the jacks are placed in pairs between the strings, the strings have to be moved apart to provide enough space for the jacks and quills. This means that strings are alternately slightly longer and slightly shorter than that which would give mathematically uniform scalings. On the Brussels Karest ending with $c^3$ at the top the *c* strings are all slightly too long and the *f* strings too short, whereas on the Rome virginal ending with $f^3$ at the top it is the *f* strings which are too long and the *c* strings which are too short. The amount of lengthening or shortening amounts to about two per cent and each of the measured scalings has been corrected by this amount, taking care that the required amount is added or subtracted in each case. It should be noted that, even as corrected, the scalings are not nearly as Pythagorean as those found in Ruckers instruments (p. 58).

Because one instrument has a short-octave bass and the other has an (essentially) chromatic bass compass, I have not compared the scalings below $c^1$ except at bottom C, since the amount and rate of the intermediate foreshortening will be different for the two instruments. The ratio of the scalings is about 1.25 near $c^3$, and close to 1.20 around $c^1$ and for the bottom note C, these corresponding to pitch differences of a major and minor third respectively when using the same stringing material for both virginals. Thus the smaller Brussels virginal should probably be tuned about a major or minor third higher than the larger virginal by Karest in Rome. The Rome Karest has scalings (353.5mm) similar to those of Ruckers (355mm – see p. 61) and should probably be tuned to roughly the same pitch, that is to 'reference pitch' R. The possibility that the smaller Brussels virginal should be strung in brass and tuned to the same pitch as the larger virginal can be rejected on the grounds that the two instruments would then be expected to have a bottom string of the same length, material and tension. Since the bottom string of the Brussels Karest is shorter in roughly the same proportion as the treble strings, it seems that, like the Ruckers instruments analysed in Chapter 4, the smaller instrument has strings which were designed to be shorter by a constant multiplying factor throughout the whole of the compass.[18] Since this multiplying factor is close to 6/5 = 1.20, a just minor third,

[18] Also, there is considerable iconographic evidence showing contemporary small Flemish instruments with iron treble strings (Ripin, 'On Joes Karest's virginal', and in view of the otherwise universal use of iron treble stringing in Flanders one is forced into excluding the possibility of brass treble stringing in one instrument and iron treble stringing in the other.

both for the lowest note and for the notes near the centre of the compass, it seems likely that this is the pitch to which it was designed to be tuned. A pitch a minor third above R does not belong to the scheme found for the Ruckers instruments (p. 223) and I have not been able to find any reference to the musical use of an instrument at this pitch.

### The 'Duke of Cleves' rectangular virginal of 1568

The earliest extant Flemish virginal which is rectangular in shape is the so-called 'Duke of Cleves' virginal in the Victoria and Albert Museum in London.[19] This is a highly-decorated instrument and, although its shape derives partly from a purely decorative motive, it is built in a style which is quite different from the two Karest virginals just described, and more like the virginals which later became the typical product of the Flemish workshops. The case is in sarcophagus form with rounded sides sloping inwards towards the baseboard. The sides are thick and of walnut, richly carved with figures of trophies and musical instruments. The impression is of a heavy chest, quite unlike the light delicate cases of the two Karest virginals just described. The fragile inner instrument has been combined with its heavy outer case in the Cleves virginal without, however, trying to counterfeit the impression of an inner instrument in an outer case as is common in many Italian instruments.

Various parts of the case are decorated with Latin mottoes, among which is included the date 1568, and the coat of arms of William, Duke of Cleves, Berg and Jülich (1516–92). The soundboard is decorated with blue scallops and arabesques and naturalistic painted flowers. Although it has been suggested that these soundboard decorations date from a later period, iconographic evidence (see Ripin, footnote 13) from instruments painted in the 1560s indicates that virginals during this period normally had this form of decoration, and the Rome Karest of some eighteen years earlier also has its original painted soundboard.

The keyboard is recessed into the case, in typical fashion. The keyboard is, however, not original and the present compass of A to $f^3$ (forty-five notes) is highly atypical. The most likely original compass is C/E to $c^3$, also with forty-five notes. The compass and scalings seem to have been altered a number of times and this involved moving and repinning the bridges and adding more jackslots to the soundboard and lower guide. However, the extreme treble and bass ends of the right-hand bridge are near their original positions, and the original position of the middle sections of the bridge can be seen on the soundboard. Thus, assuming a C/E to $c^3$ compass, the scalings can then be estimated:

$$c^3 = 170\text{mm}$$
$$c^2 = 325\text{mm}$$
$$C = 1300\text{mm}$$

Comparing these with the scalings of the slightly later Ruckers virginals (see Chapter 4) suggests that the Cleves virginal was originally intended to sound at a pitch of R + 2.

### The 1579 claviorganum by Lodowijk Theeuwes

One of the clearest links between the early Germanic and the Flemish traditions is provided by the harpsichord part of the claviorganum built by Lodowijk Theeuwes in 1579 and now in the Victoria and Albert Museum, London.[20] Although the instrument was made in London in 1579, it is probably more representative of instruments built in Antwerp ten to fifteen years earlier. Theeuwes was the son of a clavecimbel maker of the same name who worked in Antwerp, and was admitted to the Guild of St Luke in 1561. His style of building was obviously that of the other Flemish builders of this period. But by 1568 Theeuwes was living in London in the parish of St Martin's Le Grand,[21] and was building clavecimbels there.

The Theeuwes harpsichord is built in a style intermediate between the German Müller harpsichord and the later Flemish instruments typified by those made by the Ruckers family. The case sides are about 12mm thick – thicker than the earlier Müller and Karest instruments (7–9mm) but thinner than the 14–16mm typically found in Ruckers instruments. The case of the Theeuwes is of oak instead of the usual poplar found in Flemish instruments, and this seems to be one of the features of this harpsichord which Theeuwes had picked up while living in England. On the other hand the case material seems generally to have been relatively unimportant to the classical builder – he seems to have used what was cheap

[19] Raymond Russell, *Victoria and Albert Museum: Catalogue of Musical Instruments: I: Keyboard Instruments* (London, 1968), No. 11, p. 40, and Howard Schott, *Victoria and Albert Museum: Catalogue of Musical Instruments, Volume 1: Keyboard Instruments* (London, 1985), No. 5, p. 26.

[20] Russell, *Catalogue*, No. 16, p. 48, and Schott, *Catalogue*, No. 9, p. 40; also Thomas McGeary, 'Early English harpsichord building: a reassessment', *The [English] Harpsichord Magazine*, I No. 1 (October 1973), 7–19; John Koster, 'The importance of the early English harpsichord', *Galpin Society Journal*, XXXIII (1980), 45–73; Wilson Barry, personal communication.

[21] Philip James, *Early Keyboard Instruments from their Beginning to the Year 1820* (London, 1930; repr. London, 1960), 29.

and ready to hand. Mouldings are applied inside the main case walls in such a way as to counterfeit the appearance of a light inner instrument inside a protective outer case. This suggests that other Flemish (and perhaps English) builders used this interior construction to imitate instruments like the Müller which were stored in such a case. However, in all later instruments of both the virginal and harpsichord type which are still extant, the cases are thick (i.e. about 16mm) and there is no hint of a counterfeit inner instrument. The case sides are flush with the outer edge of the baseboard in the usual fashion, and the internal framing is typically Flemish, consisting of boards placed on edge on the baseboard, and flat under the liners, both running from the spine to the bentside.

The keys are missing, but the balance rail remains and the balance pins indicate that the original compass was C to $c^3$ chromatic, forty-nine notes. This chromatic compass, although not always required for the music composed during the period in which the Theeuwes was built, is often essential when playing English music of the late sixteenth century, and must be considered typical of instruments built in England at this time, when the C/E short octave seems to have been almost universal in most other parts of Europe (see Chapter 12, p. 220).

Because the 4′ nut and bridge are not original, the 4′ scalings are unreliable. But although the 8′ bridge and nut are both original to the instrument, they are both slightly displaced from their original positions and the bridge pins do not fully relate to the position of the jackslots. However, the displacement of the bridge is greatest only in the extreme treble, and the scalings near $c^2$ are now not appreciably different from the original. At present the long $c^2$ string is about 365mm, which seems to suggest that the harpsichord (and organ) were originally intended to sound at a pitch slightly below R. The value of R arrived at in Chapter 4 (p. 62) is somewhere between 413Hz and 419Hz, corresponding to the Ruckers averaged scalings of 355mm. The Theeuwes $c^2$ scaling of 365mm suggests a pitch of about 402–408Hz. This seems to be confirmed by John Koster's estimation of the pitch from one of the pipes remaining from the claviorganum, which, referred to $a^1$, gives about 392–404Hz.[22]

The jacks are guided by slots cut in the soundboard like the Müller, and by three rows of separately movable lower register slots which may be used to engage or disengage each of the rows of jacks with stop knobs located at the front of the instrument. Unlike the Müller, however, the three rows are all spaced close together and run parallel to the nameboard in a position foreshadowing that of the gap and registers in the later Flemish harpsichords. Like the Müller, the soundboard wood runs continuously for the full length of the instrument from the nameboard to the bentside and tail. The wrestplank is only about 50mm square in cross-section, and therefore both the bridge and the nut sit on freely vibrating soundboard, a feature not found again on a later North European instrument.

There are three rows of tuning pins, which, in conjunction with the three rows of jacks, suggests the disposition 2 × 8′, 1 × 4′. However, in addition to the non-original 4′ nut and bridge there are other features of the 4′ stop which are somewhat dubious. The 4′ hitchpin rail seems rather crudely made and there is no cutoff bar on the spine side of the 4′ bridge, which has caused McGeary[23] to suggest that the 4′ might not be original to the harpsichord. Nevertheless, the upper belly rail, supporting the soundboard immediately behind the far row of jackslots, is cut away in the treble to allow the 4′ hitchpin rail to pass. This could only have been done before the soundboard was glued into the instrument. On the other hand this does not prove that the 4′ stop is original, since the hitchpin rail may originally have served only as a cutoff bar for the 8′ bridge.

However, the hitchpin rail itself is cut away at the soundboard level to allow the 4′ bridge to vibrate freely in the extreme treble. Also underneath the present 4′ nut, there are clear signs of the original nut, which must have been tall and narrow in the style of the present 8′ nut and bridge. The three rows of tuning pins were marked out together, and it is necessary for one set of strings to pass through holes in the 8′ nut. The holes for these strings are very neatly marked out and drilled suggesting that they constitute original work, since normally later alterations are not carried out with such a clean hand. It thus seems that the 4′ is probably original and that the extremely advanced 2 × 8′, 1 × 4′ disposition must also be accepted as original.

The remaining original section of the 8′ bridge of the Theeuwes harpsichord has a series of brass hooks, one for each note, whose function probably explains this apparently advanced disposition. These hooks have a hand-filed thread on one end which is screwed into the top of the 8′ bridge about half-way between the short and long strings. The top part of the hook is flattened and slightly bent so that the flattened section is displaced about 5mm from the axis of the section screwed into the bridge. As the hook is screwed into the bridge the flattened top section moves around from one side to the other. This hook could have been positioned so that it was just

[22] See Koster, 'The importance', p. 54. Koster gets a pitch for $c^3$ of 933–960Hz. Calculating $a^1$ from this (equal temperament) gives $a^1$ = 392–404Hz.

[23] See McGeary, 'Early English harpsichord building'.

touching the long 8′ string, and would produce a buzzing sound similar to the harpichordium found on the later Ruckers muselar virginals or the bray on Renaissance harps. However, unlike the harpichordium stop, it could not have been engaged and disengaged for the whole (or half) of the register at once. It is likely therefore that the long 8′ choir was permanently brayed, with the bray on each string in that choir having to be adjusted individually. The disposition should probably therefore be viewed as 1 × 8′ (quill), 1 × 8′ (brayed), 1 × 4′, and not 2 × 8′, 1 × 4′ in the sense of the later seventeenth- and eighteenth-century instruments.

One complete jack and one jack tongue (lodged in a hole in the 8′ nut) survive. The jack is well made and of a mature and sophisticated design. It has one oval damper hole similar to that found in Ruckers 4′ jacks (see p. 121). It is not clear that this jack belonged to a 4′ register, however; the jackslots in the soundboard are all of the same width, so that all three rows probably had just one damper hole (unlike the Ruckers jacks which have wider 8′ jacks with two damper holes). The use of oval holes for the dampers in this, the earliest extant harpsichord made in England, was not carried on into the later English tradition as it was in Antwerp where it appears often even in some eighteenth-century instruments. Oblong damper holes are found in the jacks of only one isolated example of English keyboard instrument making, namely the John Crang spinet of 1758 in the Victoria and Albert Museum, London.[24] The Theeuwes jack is slightly tapered in width and thickness, and the tongue is retained in its neutral position with the usual hog's bristle. The angled bass of the tongue slot in the jack is covered with soft white (kid?) leather to prevent the tongue from clicking. Both the tongue in the complete jack, and the one lodged in the instrument have, most remarkably, iron quills, which seem to be original. There are no signs that the quills have ever been replaced or tampered with. The quill slots are very small both in width and thickness; this in itself suggests that the quills have always been of metal (which is probably why they have managed to survive). Among other instruments, the clavicytherium dated *c.* 1480 at the Royal College of Music in London was reported by Hipkins[25] as having had traces of brass plectra in 1885. It is therefore possible that more of these early instruments may have been quilled with metal plectra, and that this is not just a feature of the early claviorgana, where the harpsichord had to compete with an organ which was probably fairly loud and rich in harmonics.[26] The effect achieved with the harpichordium operating on metal-plucked strings combined with narrow-scaled pipe organ tone would be surprising to the modern ear!

### Virginals built at a time contemporary with Hans Ruckers

By the time Hans Ruckers had joined the Guild of St Luke in 1579 and had started to build instruments, the style and construction of the virginals built in Antwerp had stabilized and become fairly uniform. These instruments differ little from those built during the next seventy to eighty years by the various members of the Ruckers family and so will not be described in detail here (see Chapter 5). They were the typical heavy-cased, iron-strung, rectangular virginals built almost entirely out of poplar. But although essentially similar to the later standard Ruckers models, they are slightly different in the details, many of which seem to characterize the instruments built during the period from about 1570 to 1590.

By this time the keyboard compass had already become fairly standardized at C/E to $c^3$ (the most common exception is C/E to $a^2$), which remained the usual virginal compass until the Ruckers family ceased building instruments at the beginning of the second half of the seventeenth century. The keys were made with the usual bog-oak sharps and bone natural touchplates. But the sharps on virginals during this period usually retained the extra decoration also found on the very earliest Flemish virginals. Instead of the plain sharps found on later instruments and up to the present day, these were decorated with four scribed lines and a small edge nick filed on either side of the sharp between the two centre lines. This decoration then matched the corresponding scribed lines and nicks found in the bone on the natural touchplates just in front of the sharps. Virginals which have decorated sharps are the following:

Hans Bos, *c.* 1570, Monasterio de Santa Clara, Tordesillas, Spain

Iohannes Grouwels, *c.* 1580 (compass C/E to $g^2$, $a^2$), Brussels Museum of Musical Instruments, No. 2929

Marten van der Biest, 1580 (mother and child), Germanisches Nationalmuseum, Nuremberg, No. MI85

Hans Ruckers, 1581 (mother and child), Metropolitan Museum of Art, New York, No. 29.90

[24] This feature was pointed out to me by John Barnes.

[25] A. J. Hipkins, *The Pianoforte* (London, 1896), 74. There seems to be no evidence at present of metal plectra in the jacks of this instrument.

[26] From a careful examination of the remaining organ parts, and the space formerly occupied by the organ pipes, Wilson Barry (personal communication) has found the following organ disposition:

| | |
|---|---|
| Stopped diapason | 8′ |
| Flute (stopped wood) | 4′ |
| Principal (bass: stopped wood; treble: open wood) | 2′ |
| Cymbel (repeating metal) | ¼′ |
| Regal | 8′ |

Hans Ruckers, 1583, Instrument Museum of the Conservatoire NSM, Paris

The Artus Gheerdinck virginal built in 1605 and now in the Germanisches Nationalmuseum, Nuremberg, No. MINe 95, also has decorated sharps but, having been built in Amsterdam[27] out of the mainstream tradition, is atypical of instruments built at this late date.

Most of the instruments just mentioned also have slightly ornate bridges. The later Ruckers virginals have plain simply-made bridges of an irregular cross-section, with all of the surfaces planed flat (see p. 76). The earlier virginals, however, usually have either or both of the front or rear surfaces planed to a rounded shape. The cross-section and strength of these bridges is roughly the same as that of the flat-surfaced bridges, so that rounding the sides of the bridges probably serves no acoustical purpose, and was done strictly from an ornamental point of view.

Another feature of the virginals built from about 1570 to 1590 concerns their roses. The later Ruckers virginals had a single lead rose with the figure of an angel playing a harp between the maker's initials. It is usually assumed that this is the distinctive mark which the Guild regulations required each member to place in or on his instrument. However, many of the instruments built after the acceptance of the Guild regulations in 1557 do not have such a lead rose. Also, there is often more than one single rose decorating the soundboard. For example, the Hans Bos virginal does indeed have a lead rose with a representation of a small pipe organ and the initials 'HB', but it also has a parchment geometrical rose, and a third empty rose hole which presumably also contained a geometrical rose.[28] Furthermore, the Marten van der Biest mother-and-child virginal has two geometrical parchment roses in the 'mother' and one in the 'child', but no lead rose. The Iohannes Grouwels virginal in Brussels has but a single geometrical parchment rose. There seems no reason to doubt the originality of the roses in any of these instruments.

All three of the van der Biest mother-and-child roses are completely different, but the slightly smaller left-hand rose in the mother virginal is identical in size and design with the Grouwels rose. It thus would seem that these parchment roses had a common origin and that different virginal makers used one and the same type of soundboard rose, perhaps purchased from a common supplier. Since these parchment roses are therefore not at all distinctive it seems unlikely that they qualify as the characteristic mark required by the Guild. Was the signature, usually on the jackrail, the required distinctive mark? Or was the Guild regulation simply ignored by the instrument builders? Or was the Guild itself perhaps ineffective in enforcing the regulations?

## EARLY FLEMISH DOUBLE-MANUAL HARPSICHORDS

### The Brussels three-register double harpsichord *c.* 1580

The Brussels Instrument Museum has the good fortune to possess not only the earliest Flemish virginal by Ioes Karest, but also what is probably the earliest Flemish double-manual harpsichord.[29] The instrument bears the museum number 2934, and unfortunately is neither signed nor dated. It is in an extremely dilapidated state, and appears at first sight to be a very uninteresting and unattractive instrument. It has undergone a number of alterations including a case ravalement to give the rather conservative $G_1/B_1$ to $c^3$ compass.[30] However, the original keyframes and most of the original keys remain, and from the pinning and repinning of the balance rail, and from the renumbering of the keys it is possible to establish not only the original compass, but also that of three subsequent states.

There seems no doubt that the instrument is of Flemish origin. It is of poplar construction with thick case sides sitting on the baseboard, which is planed flush with the case walls around the bottom edge. The internal framing is in the general Flemish style, having baseboard braces placed on their edge and upper-level braces placed flat underneath the soundboard liners, with both types of bracing running from the spine to the bentside. The bridges are heavy, have flat surfaces with the usual irregular cross-section like Ruckers bridges, and the registers and buff stop originally projected through the cheek in the usual way.

However, although it seems certain that the harpsichord is Flemish in origin it seems equally certain that it is not by one of the Ruckers family.[31] The usual Ruckers

[27] Alan Curtis, 'Dutch harpsichord makers', *Tijdschrift van de Vereniging voor Nederlandse Musiekgeschiedenis*, XIX, 1/2 (Amsterdam, 1960/61), 44–46.

[28] See the illustrations 25 and 30 in Donald Boalch, *Makers of the Harpsichord and Clavichord, 1440–1840* (Oxford, 1974), 2nd edn only.

[29] The possible importance of this harpsichord was first noticed by Edwin M. Ripin, and pointed out to me by Nicolas Meeùs. See Boalch, Ruckers No. 26.

[30] This was later crudely altered to C to $f^3$ chromatic. A complete description of the intermediate states of this harpsichord will be the subject of a future paper by the author.

[31] The instrument is, however, ascribed to Ruckers by both Boalch (number 26) and the 5th edn of *Grove's Dictionary* (Hans Ruckers number 21).

Plate 2.3 Anonymous early Flemish double-manual harpsichord (Brussels Museum of Musical Instruments, No. 2934).
Scale 1:10.

construction marks on the soundboard above the 4′ hitchpin rail are lacking and there are no positioning holes on either side of the bridges and nuts as invariably found on Ruckers instruments (see Chapter 6, p. 106). There are also no nails underneath the bridges securing them to the soundboard. Furthermore, although the internal framing is in the style of Ruckers, the rear tool-box brace is lacking, and the edges of the upper level braces and the soundboard liners are not broken with a chamfer as in Ruckers instruments. Nor are the dimensions, such as the case height and the length of the tail, typical of a Ruckers harpsichord. And although part of the plan of the registers and string band is marked out on the original portion of the baseboard, this is done in a way quite different from the 1594 HR harpsichord (which, aside from being the only known harpsichord by Hans Ruckers, is also one of the few Ruckers instruments in which the string band is marked out on the baseboard). All of these features point to a builder who had, in some aspects, a considerably different construction procedure from that of any of the members of the Ruckers family.

On the other hand, the bentside case joins are like those on Ruckers instruments (see p. 188), the original keyboard three-octave span is 500mm, the (now empty) rose-hole diameter is 65mm, the bass section of the 8′ bridge was originally back-pinned from C/E to c, and the original 8′ $c^2$ bridge pin is 49cm from the back of the nameboard (see p. 175). All of these are among the characteristic features of a Ruckers instrument (see Chapter 9). But the important deviations from the Ruckers' usual practice suggests to me not only that the harpsichord is Flemish, but that it was made by one of Hans Ruckers' contemporaries in Antwerp where the relationship between the various builders would be very strong, yet with slight but noticeable differences from workshop to workshop.

Hence, keeping this all in mind, an attempt can be made to determine the original state of the harpsichord. The pinning of the balance rail on both manuals makes the original compass clear. The first three naturals in the bass of the upper manual are missing and in their place traces remain not of a solid block, as is usual with Ruckers harpsichords, but of a small framed box, possibly with a lid originally. The upper manual then begins with a C/E short octave and reaches to a top note of $a^2$ (including $g^{\#2}$). The lower manual also begins with a C/E short octave and continues on to $d^3$ (with $c^{\#3}$). The upper manual sounded at reference pitch R and the lower manual was pitched a fourth lower at R − 4, like the later Ruckers double-manual harpsichords. Identification of the pitch of the $c^2$ string using the 49cm rule, and the original bridge-pin positions found using the 500mm three-octave span (see Chapter 8), confirms the compass of both the upper and lower manuals and their pitch assignment. The important difference between the compass of this harpsichord and the Ruckers standard-model double-manual harpsichord is that the Ruckers doubles reached a minor third higher. The shorter compass of the Brussels harpsichord is one of the features which points to an early dating, since the C/E to $a^2$ compass was common on keyboard instruments built in the period between 1550 and 1580 or 1590.

However, although the compass of the keyboards of this harpsichord can be determined unequivocally, the original disposition is not as easy to reconstruct. A series of scribed lines is drawn on the original portion of the baseboard under the gap. Four lines running the full width of the instrument are traversed by a series of short lines which seem to indicate the positions of the *c* and *f*# strings on both upper and lower manuals. The four lines underneath and parallel to the gap almost certainly indicate that the instrument was originally designed for three registers (Ruckers single-manual harpsichords have two registers and three similar lines, and Ruckers double-manual harpsichords have four registers and five lines drawn equispaced underneath the gap). The wrestplank was replaced in the course of the case ravalement, but there seems no indication that the gap width was altered in the process. This gives a present gap width of only 64mm, whereas the gap width in a normal four-register Ruckers double is 73mm. This and the narrow jackrail mortice (the jackrail is missing) all seem to confirm that the harpsichord was originally intended to have only three registers. Ripin has found iconographic evidence for a three-register double-manual Flemish harpsichord, and he attributes the harpsichord depicted by Brueghel to Ruckers.[32] But if one accepts the accuracy of the painter in depicting the three registers correctly, then I feel that one must accept that a number of other features of the instrument in the painting are not in the style of Ruckers. This means that the instrument painted can at best be attributed only generally to the Antwerp school and not to one of the members of the Ruckers family, and that it does not follow from this evidence that any of the Ruckers made three-register harpsichords.

However, acceptance of the fact that the Brussels harpsichord originally had only three registers then leads immediately to the problem of the original distribution of three registers among two manuals. Because of the alterations to the instrument and because the original jacks have been lost, the original arrangement must of

[32] Edwin M. Ripin, 'The two-manual harpsichord in Flanders before 1650', *Galpin Society Journal*, XXI (1968), 33–9

necessity remain conjectural. And yet I believe the instrument retains sufficient features that the original arrangement can be postulated with some certainty.

It is clear from the repinning of the bridges that the harpsichord originally had only one set of 8′ strings and one set of 4′ strings, 1 × 8′, and 1 × 4′. Furthermore, there is no evidence either on the 8′ or 4′ bridge or along the 4′ hitchpin rail that there were doubled strings for the e♭/g♯ notes. Thus when the player went from one manual to the other he had to retune these strings to avoid the meantone 'wolf'. Both the upper- and lower-manual keytails were marked out by using a punch through the upper and lower registers to leave an oblong indentation on the tail of the key at the future location of each jack similar to that used by the Ruckers (see p. 118). It is clear from these marks that the upper-manual keys have been shortened, since only half of the oblong indentation is visible at the extreme end of each key. Since the mark occurs at a position in the middle of the near row of jacks, the upper-manual keylevers were shortened to operate a dogleg register for the rear row of jacks in the most recent state of the instrument. This alteration would give the usual eighteenth-century disposition with 1 × 8′ on the upper manual and 2 × 8′, 1 × 4′ on the lower. From the position of the indentations on the lower manual it seems clear that the upper-manual keys have been shortened by an amount equal to one full register width. This would mean that the *middle* row of jacks was originally a dogleg register which could be operated from either manual.

The most likely disposition is then:

← 4′
→ 8′ dogleg
← 4′

This would then mean that the 8′ strings could be played from either manual without altering the register. Probably the 8′ register would be left on most of the time, except when using the 4′ as a solo stop. With the 8′ register on, the appropriate 4′ register (depending on the manual being used) could be added for added volume and brilliance. Because there is only one row of 8′ jacks the notes e♭ and g♯ *must* be retuned when moving from one manual to the other, since the same jack plucks the corresponding 8′ string on both manuals. However, at this early period the range of modulation of the music was relatively small and the key signature of the pieces seldom involved more than one or two accidentals. So there would seldom have been the need to retune when changing manuals. The Ruckers doubled-string arrangement for the e♭ and g♯ notes is surely a development arising out of a later musical need for pieces both to modulate further from their home key, and to involve a key signature with more accidentals. The Ruckers doubled-string system could have been used on this harpsichord for the 4′ stop, although there was probably little need for such a system when this instrument was built.

The Ruckers system is a distinct advance over this system, since one can switch from one manual to the other immediately without retuning the troublesome e♭/g♯ strings. Whether this advance can be attributed to Ruckers or not can never be confirmed because of the lack of instruments from this period and relevant documentary evidence.

### The Brussels 16′ double-manual harpsichord

A second interesting double-manual harpsichord is also to be found in the Brussels Museum of Musical Instruments (No. 2510).[33] It has an 'HR' rose[34] in the soundboard which is similar to the roses in a number of other fake Ruckers instruments: a '1636 Ioannes Ruckers' double-manual harpsichord in the Palace of Holyrood House, Edinburgh (p. 281), a '1637 Hans Ruckers' also in the Brussels Museum of Musical Instruments (No. 4276, p. 280), and a '1658 Hans Ruckers' in the Germanisches Nationalmuseum, Nuremberg (No. MINe 84, p. 280). Apparently all of these instruments must have passed through the same faker's hand, and he placed a recast Hans Moermans rose, modified by changing the 'M' to an 'H', in the soundboard of each instrument to deceive potential buyers into thinking that the instruments were by a member of the Ruckers family. Although the Brussels instrument appears to be of Flemish origin, it has many features which are quite unlike any other Ruckers instrument, and it is quite certain that it is not by any of the Ruckers.

It is an extremely long instrument (over 2800mm) and has three bridges for 4′, 8′ and 16′ choirs of strings. However, it has been very extensively altered, and its present disposition dates from a later alteration. Nonetheless there is a separate soundboard and bridge for the 16′ strings raised above the level of the soundboard for the 8′ and 4′ bridges, suggesting that the 16′ stop might be original. A careful analysis of the original state of the instrument has been made by John Koster,[35] who has shown that the harpsichord did indeed originally have a register at 16′ pitch!

[33] Boalch, Ruckers No. 25. See John Koster, 'A remarkable early Flemish transposing harpsichord' *Galpin Society Journal*, XXXV (1982), 45–53.

[34] See Boalch, *Makers of the Harpsichord and Clavichord*, Plate 27, which is a photograph of the rose in the Brussels 16′ double-manual harpsichord fake 'Ruckers'.

[35] See Koster, 'A remarkable early Flemish transposing harpsichord'.

One of the registers in the instrument has an irregularly spaced arrangement of jack mortices and blank spaces similar in principle, although not in detail, to the upper-manual register in a normal Ruckers double-manual harpsichord. Also, there are three sets of metal plates on the 8′ nut similar to those on Ruckers double-manual instruments for the doubled $e^{\flat}/g^{\sharp}$ strings, and both of these features strongly suggest that this was originally a transposing double-manual harpsichord.

Koster shows that one manual of this instrument was originally at reference pitch R and had a compass of $C_1/E_1$ to $a^2$ (with $g^{\sharp 2}$), and that the other keyboard was pitched at R − 4, and had a compass of C/E to $d^3$, like the lower manual of the early double-manual transposer described above. It is now impossible to tell which manual was the upper, and which the lower, but it did indeed have a keyboard sounding $C_1$, an octave below C.

### The earliest Ruckers double-manual harpsichord of 1599

The earliest Ruckers double-manual harpsichord is dated 1599 (1599 HR), a year after Hans Ruckers had died, and must therefore have been made by one or both of Hans Ruckers' sons, Ioannes and Andreas. This harpsichord has been carefully examined and is discussed in more detail on pages 177ff. In its original state it had doubled strings for the notes $e^{\flat}$ and $g^{\sharp}$, and therefore must originally have had four registers like the usual later models of Ruckers double. However this harpsichord is of particular interest, since it originally had the same compass as the keyboards pitched at R − 4 on the two early anonymous Brussels instruments described above, namely C/E to $d^3$.

CHAPTER THREE

# The types of instrument built by the Ruckers, and the Ruckers numbering system

ever since the seventeenth century have as many different models of keyboard instrument come from a single family or school of clavecimbel building as from the Ruckers/Couchet workshops. Unlike most of the eighteenth-century keyboard-instrument builders, who built very few different models of instrument, the members of the Ruckers family built at least twenty clearly distinguishable models of harpsichord and virginal. Such a large number of different instrument types present a selection of different pitches, tone qualities, combinations of instrument types and keyboard compasses. Before going on to a discussion of the numbering and of the construction of Ruckers instruments it is necessary to have a clear idea of the different models which were built. Although many of these models will be described here briefly, the complete identification and determination of all of the instrument types will be left to Chapters 4 and 8.

## THE MODELS OF RUCKERS VIRGINAL

Ruckers virginals exist in a number of different lengths. Careful comparison indicates that these measurements were not random and arbitrary, and that the different sizes of virginal were not designed to be tuned to arbitrary pitches. Rather, only specific lengths of virginal were made, and each size was tuned to its own pitch which was related musically to the pitch of the other lengths of virginal.

As they were being built the cases and action parts of the virginals were marked by the makers with two numbers, one above the other. The upper number appears to be simply the overall length of the instrument in *voeten* or Flemish feet. Confirmation of this is provided in Table 3.1. The Flemish foot has been calculated here on the assumption that it contained eleven *duimen*, and that each *duim* – the equivalent of the modern inch – contained 25.88mm (see Chapter 5, p. 69).[1]

The practice of referring to the instruments according to their length must have been common in the late seventeenth century. Klaas Douwes in 1699 referred to the length of the virginals in the following way:

> some clavecimbels are six feet long, some five feet, some four feet, some three feet, and some even smaller.[2]

Because of the way the virginals were numbered, the Ruckers must also have referred to their instruments in

[1] Edwin M. Ripin, 'The "three foot" Flemish harpsichord', *Galpin Society Journal*, XXIII (1970), 35–9, and W. R. Thomas and J. J. K. Rhodes, 'Harpsichord strings, organ pipes, and the Dutch foot', *The Organ Yearbook*, III (1973), 112–21, both suggest that the Flemish voet contained 11 duimen. Ripin suggests that the duim was 25.7mm or 26.6mm in length, and Thomas and Rhodes give 25.8mm. Jeannine Lambrechts-Douillez, 'Aperçu historique sur la facture de clavecin du XVe au XVIIIe siècles', *La facture de clavecin du XVe au XVIIe siècle* (Louvain-la-Neuve, 1980), 59–66, gives the Antwerp voet as 0.2868m, so that one duim would be 26.07mm. In 'Bronnen in verband met lengtematen te Antwerpen in gebruik tijdens de 17de eeuw', *Mededelingen van het Ruckers-Genootschap*, IV (Antwerp, 1984), 7, Dr Lambrechts-Douillez notes that the voet was almost always divided into 8 parts, each called a line, and not 11 as stated by Thomas and Rhodes above, although the division into 11 was found in rare instances.

However, none of these values gives consistent results when applied to the existing instruments. The value of the duim used here is the 'large duim', one of two different measures both of which seem to have been used simultaneously in the Rucker workshops, and has been calculated on the basis of the lengths of the extant unaltered virginals (see Appendix 1 and the beginning of Chapter 5).

[2] Klaas Douwes, *Gronnnndig Ondersoek van de Toonen der Musijk* (Franeker, 1699; facs., Amsterdam, 1970), 105; see Appendix 8.

Table 3.1 *Lengths of different Ruckers virginal types*

| | length | | | | | |
|---|---|---|---|---|---|---|
| | modern | | | Flemish | | |
| instrument | mm | inches | feet | duimen | voeten | Ruckers upper number |
| (*c*. 1600) HR, Castello Sforzesco, Milan | 1709 | 67.3 | 5.61 | 66.0 | 6.00 | 6 |
| 1604 HR, Brussels Museum, No. 2927 | 1424 | 56.1 | 4.67 | 55.0 | 5.00 | 5 |
| 1629 IR, Brussels Museum, No. 2511 | 1282 | 50.5 | 4.21 | 49.5 | 4.50 | 4½ |
| 1613b AR, Brussels Museum, No. 2928 | 1138 | 44.8 | 3.73 | 44.0 | 4.00 | 4 |
| (*c*. 1600) HR, Castello Sforzesco, Milan | 820 | 32.3 | 2.69 | 31.7 | 2.88 | k |
| (*c*. 1610)a AR, private, Australia | 711 | 28.0 | 2.33 | 27.5 | 2.50 | ? |

this way, and other Antwerp builders must also have used this convention. Georgius Britsen, for example, used an upper '3' when numbering the little 1676 3-voet virginal (length = 883mm = 3.10 voeten) in the Brussels Museum of Musical Instruments (No. 2923).

Some Ruckers virginals are large composite instruments consisting of a unison and octave instrument together. The unison instrument has strings that are the same length as the normal 6-voet virginals and the pitch is therefore the same, but the case is usually made slightly larger so that the small octave instrument can be stored inside it. These double virginals are obviously *de moeder met het kind* – the mother with the child – referred to by Reynvaan[3] in his dictionary of music. When marking these virginals, the Ruckers placed an *m* on the large mother instrument and a *k* on the *kind* or child, as the upper part of the composite number.

As well as being specified according to their lengths, the virginals are also differentiated according to their tone quality. Douwes was the first to define the instrument types according to the sound they produced:[4]

> Clavecimbels are musical instruments which are very agreeable in the sound, and are therefore used mostly for pleasure and entertainment. They are best suited for playing all types of melodies and musical pieces. There are different types. In some the jacks are placed in the middle between the bridges, and these are the most common type. They are called *Muselars*. In some the jacks are placed close to the left hand bridge, and these are called *Spinetten*. The little ones are called *Scherpen* because they have a high and sharp sound.

Plates 3.1 and 3.2 show the soundboards of two 6-voet Ruckers virginals, and distinguish clearly the muselar from the spinett virginal. These two instruments have the same scalings, and are therefore at the same pitch, but clearly the jacks attack the strings at different points and the resulting tone quality of the two types of virginal will be very different. The muselar virginal (Plate 3.1) has its keyboard placed towards the right-hand side of the instrument, and the jacks pluck the strings, not near their middle as Douwes suggests, but about one-third of the way along their length.[5] In muselar virginals both bridges are on an area of freely vibrating soundboard, and the sound produced is bold, round and flutey – quite unique among the sound of plucked keyboard instruments. Also unique to the muselar virginal is the harpichordium stop. This consists of a series of soft metal hooks placed in a wooden bar underneath the right-hand ends of the strings. The bar with its hooks can be slid back and forth alongside the straight bass section of the bridge to engage and disengage the stop. When the stop is engaged the tops of the hooks just barely touch the ends of the strings and produce a rattling, buzzing sound similar to that produced by the bray on the Renaissance harp. The harpichordium operates only on the bass strings and provides an accompaniment of striking contrast to the flutey treble sound.

The spinett virginal (Plate 3.2) plucks the strings at a point along the string which is roughly the same proportion of the string's length as in a harpsichord, and therefore has a tone that is more similar to the harpsichord than to the muselar virginal. The keyboard is placed near the left-hand side of the instrument and the left-hand bridge nearest the jacks rests on a solid piece of wood so

[3] Joos Verschuere Reynvaan, *Muzijkaal Kunst-Woordenboek* (Amsterdam, 1795), 115; see Appendix 9.

[4] Douwes, *Grondig Ondersoek*, 104–5.

[5] A string plucked exactly in the middle, at the nodes of the even-numbered partials, produces a sound which lacks these partials. Tuning an instrument with strings plucked at their centres is very difficult because the even-numbered partials necessary for tuning fifths (ratio of frequencies of the two notes = 3/2) and major thirds (ratio = 5/4), the most common intervals used by the tuner, are missing.

Plate 3.1 1581 HR 6-voet (mother) muselar virginal. Scale 1:10. Copyright, Metropolitan Museum of Art, New York. Gift of B. H. Homan 1929 (29.90).

that only the right-hand bridge can vibrate.[6] Presumably because the geometry of the larger spinett virginals imposes a smoothly-curving shape on the right-hand bridge, these instruments do not have a harpichordium stop, which would need a straight section of bridge along which it could operate. But even on the muselar virginals the harpichordium stop is notoriously difficult to adjust and regulate despite the fact that the amplitude of vibration of the more centre-plucked strings is relatively great. The harpichordium would be even more difficult to regulate in the end-plucked spinett virginals, where the amplitude of vibration of the string is relatively small – doubtless another reason why the harpichordium is found only on the muselar type of virginal.

No 5-voet spinett virginal exists which is made by one of the Ruckers. However, there is no particular reason to suppose that the Ruckers did not in fact make such virginals, and it is presumably only a quirk of fate and the law of probability that none now survives. 5-voet spinett virginals were probably produced in only small numbers: Douwes, above, says that the muselar type was the most common. Among the twenty extant 6-voet Ruckers virginals only four are of the spinett type: i.e. about one in five is a spinett virginal. Assuming that 5-voet spinett virginals were produced in about the same proportion, it is therefore not surprising that none of the four surviving 5-voet virginals is of the spinett type. However, 5-voet spinett virginals were made in Antwerp. One example is the 1636 Cornelius Hagaerts virginal in the Rockox House in Antwerp (see Appendix 2, p. 286).

Douwes mentions clavecimbels 6 voeten, 5 voeten, 4 voeten, 3 voeten and 2 voet 4 duimen long. But two Ruckers virginals exist which are 4½ voeten in length and are marked as such (see Plates 3.4, 3.5 and 3.18). One of these is a spinett virginal (1629 IR) and the other is of

[6] See Nicolas Meeùs, 'Épinettes et "muselars": une analyse théorique', *La facture de clavecin du XV^e au XVIII^e siècle* (Louvain-la-Neuve, 1980), 67–78. Note that the 5-voet spinett virginal of 1636 by Cornelius Hagaerts in the Rockox House, Antwerp (see Appendix 2) does not have a solid support underneath the left-hand bridge, so that both bridges contribute to the sound produced.

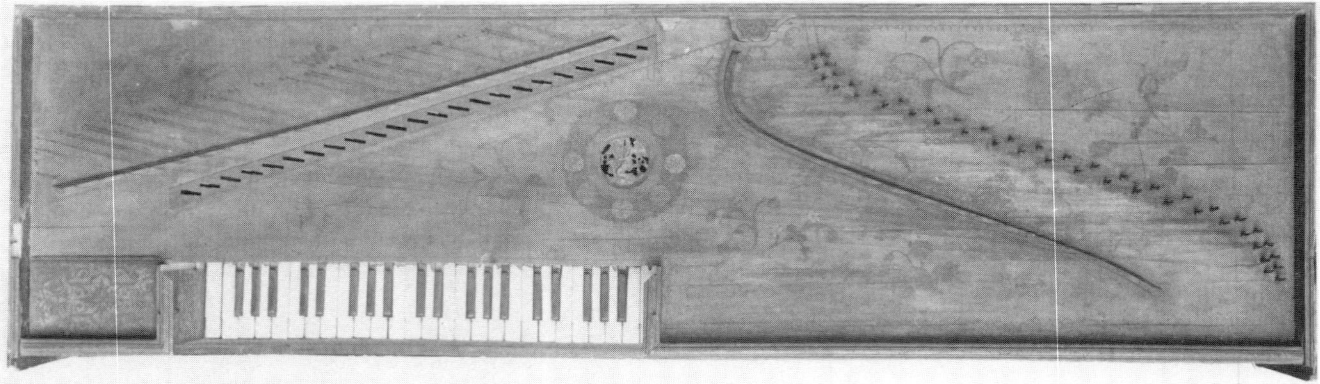

Plate 3.2 (*c.* 1600) HR 6-voet (mother) spinett virginal. Scale 1:10.

Plate 3.3 1604 HR 5-voet muselar virginal. Scale 1:10.

Plate 3.4 1610b AR 4½-voet muselar virginal. Scale 1:10. Copyright, Boston Museum of Fine Arts, Boston.

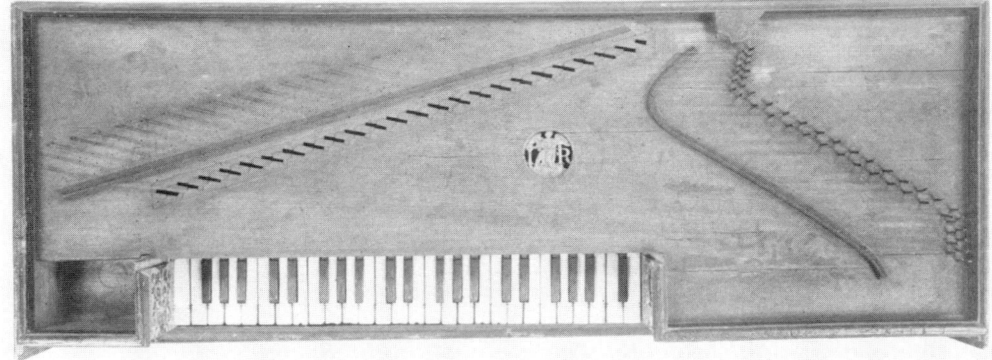

Plate 3.5 1629 IR 4½-voet spinett virginal. Scale 1:10.

Plate 3.6 1620a AR 4-voet spinett virginal. Scale 1:10. Copyright, Smithsonian Institution, Washington, DC.

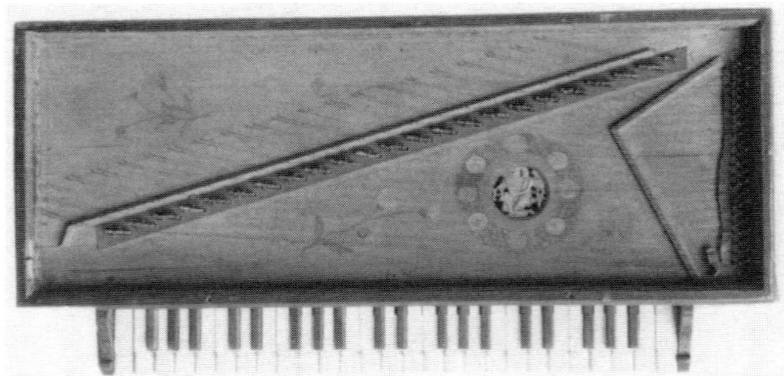

Plate 3.7 (*c*. 1600) HR child spinett virginal. Scale 1:10.

Plate 3.8 (*c*. 1610)a AR 2½-voet spinett virginal. Scale 1:10. By courtesy of the owners.

Plate 3.9 (*c.* 1600) HR mother and child spinett virginal. The child is in its coupled playing position with the jackrail of the mother removed.

the muselar type (1610b AR). There are no muselar virginals shorter than 4½-voet in length. The reason for this is one of geometry. The bass strings of the 4-voet virginals, for example, are only about 920mm long. To design a 4-voet muselar virginal the bass jacks would have to be placed about one-third to half of the way along the length of the bass string. The keyboard, which is about 650mm wide for a C/E to $c^3$ compass, would then position the bass jacks at one-third to half of 920mm, with the treble jacks 650mm to the right of this. This would then mean that the treble jacks would have to be placed to the right of the right-hand bridge. In other words, a muselar virginal 4 voeten or smaller in length is a geometrical impossibility.

All extant 3-voet virginals originally occurred in conjunction with 6-voet instruments as a mother-and-child combination. Unlike other builders such as Britsen, the Ruckers never seem to have built any 3-voet virginals as separate instruments on their own. Also, probably because of space limitations in the mother instrument, the child instruments are not quite 3 voeten in length, but are 2 or 3 duimen less.

The child instruments fit into a space in the body of the mother virginal beside the keyboard. If the mother is a spinett virginal the child fits to the right of the mother's keyboard; if the mother is a muselar virginal, the child fits to the left. But there is a slot in the baseboard of the child instrument under the tails of the keylevers enabling the child to be played while placed on top of its mother. The jackrail of the mother is removed, the child is positioned above the keyboard of the mother, and the jacks of the mother then operate the keys and jacks of the child through the slot in the baseboard. Because the child sounds an octave higher than the mother, this allows an octave and unison sound from the virginals similar to that of the harpsichord with a $1 \times 8'$, $1 \times 4'$ disposition. But clearly the possibility also exists of two separate players playing the two instruments together side by side, either with the child slightly withdrawn from the mother to make its keyboard accessible, or with the two instruments completely separated.

There is only one extant example made by the Ruckers (*c.* 1610a AR) of the little virginal which Douwes describes as being 2 voet 4 duimen long (see Appendix 3). It is at a pitch an octave above the 5-voet instruments, at R + 9 (see p. 57) and is in fact not 2 voet 4 duimen in length, but exactly half the length of the 5-voet instrument, i.e. 2 voet 5½ duimen or 2½ voet long. This particular instrument does not have a slot in its baseboard, and this, along with its very high and sloping sides, strikingly suggests that it was not meant to be the child part of a 5-voet mother-and-child combination. At first glance it seems strange that no 5-voet mother-and-child combinations exist. Just as the 6-voet mothers are sometimes a few duimen longer than the nominal 6 voeten to accommodate the child instrument, so a 5-voet instrument could easily be made to hold a 2½-voet virginal. But such a combination has not been found.

The reason for this seems clear, and is related to the geometry of the instrument and the width of the keyboard (see Appendix 3, p. 289). The keys of a 2½-voet virginal are cranked in towards the centre of the string band and the jacks are squeezed together into a space much narrower than usual in such a way that the jacks and keytails would not match the normal spacing in a 5-voet 'mother'. The two could therefore not be used together as in the 6-voet mother and child.

Since the 4-voet, 3-voet (child) and 2½-voet virginals all occur only as end-plucking spinett virginals, they would all have a similar tone quality. They would also all have a very high tessitura relative to, say, one of the large 6-voet instruments. All three types were built in Antwerp as independent instruments, even though the 3-voet instruments are most familiar as the child part of a double virginal. It seems very likely therefore that these small virginals are the *Scherpen* which Douwes says 'have a high and sharp sound'.

The virginal models may be summarized as follows:

| | |
|---|---|
| 6-voet spinett mother and child | 6-voet muselar mother and child |
| 6-voet spinett virginal | 6-voet muselar virginal |
| 5-voet spinett virginal* | 5-voet muselar virginal |
| 4½-voet spinett virginal | 4½-voet muselar virginal |
| 4-voet spinett virginal | |
| child spinett virginal | |
| 2½-voet spinett virginal | |

* None now extant, but it would have been like the 1636 Cornelius Hagaerts virginal in the Rockox House, Antwerp.

The keyboard compass of Ruckers virginals is almost universally C/E to $c^3$. Some of the earlier sixteenth-century Hans Ruckers instruments have the more restricted C/E to $a^2$ compass. Also, the only 4½-voet spinett virginal (1629 I R) has the unusual compass C/E to $d^3$. The reason for so large a compass is not clear, but may have been to allow the *pitch* of the top note to match the top $c^3$ note of the smaller 4-voet instrument pitched a tone higher (see Chapter 4).

Only one Ruckers virginal is polygonal; all the others are rectangular. Like the earlier Karest virginals (see pp. 23ff), the 1591a H R is a six-sided spinett virginal. However, the layout of this instrument is exactly the same as the other Ruckers 6-voet spinett virginals in scalings, plucking points, keyboard compasss, etc. The difference is simply that the inactive parts of the soundboard of the more usual rectangular instruments have been eliminated and a polygon fitted around the musical part of the instrument. Therefore, because the 1591a H R spinett virginal is neither acoustically nor musically different from the normal rectangular spinett type, I do not feel that it qualifies as a separate model of its own.

The different models of Ruckers virginal are at six clearly defined and different pitches (see Chapter 4). The pitch differences between the models are not arbitrary, but correspond to the simple musical intervals of a tone, a fourth, a fifth and an octave. Nowhere else in the history of keyboard instrument building do we find such an array of virginal models and pitches. The existence of these instruments at well-defined intervals from one another must be considered amongst the most important contributions of the Ruckers to our knowledge of musical practice and instrument building in the sixteenth and seventeenth centuries.

## THE STANDARD TYPES OF HARPSICHORD

There are also a number of different models of Ruckers harpsichord. However, these types are at relatively few pitches, and their variety is more an indication that harpsichords were made with different compasses, and in a few isolated cases with different dispositions.

Also like the virginals, the harpsichords were marked with a composite sign consisting of a cipher above a number. The cipher is the same for single- and for double-manual harpsichords; some examples of these marks are shown in Plates 3.21, 3.22 and 3.25.

### *Single-manual harpsichords*

The most common type of single-manual harpsichord has the same scalings (and therefore sounds at the same pitch) as the 6-voet virginals, but is slightly longer than 6 voeten in length – usually about 6 voet 4 duimen (1810mm). These harpsichords have only two rows of jacks and two sets of strings and are disposed 1 × 8′, 1 × 4′:

← 4′
→ 8′

Their original compass is universally C/E to $c^3$.

Plate 3.10 1645 IC standard single-manual harpsichord. Scale 1:10.

### *Double-manual harpsichords*

The standard model of double is considerably longer than the single, at 8 voeten or slightly less (average about 2240mm). The two keyboards are completely independent and not capable of being coupled, each operating only two rows of jacks, as in the single-manual harpsichords. There are only two sets of strings, one an octave above the other, so that the four registers are disposed:

← 4′
→ 8′
← 4′
→ 8′

Since the jacks of both manuals operate on the same two sets of strings, only one manual can be used at a time, otherwise damper interference would occur (it is assumed that the dampers of all registers were cut so that when the register was withdrawn, the dampers moved away from the strings to allow them to vibrate freely when plucked by the row of jacks on the other keyboard: see Chapter 6, p. 123).

The upper-manual keyboard consists of a block of wood three naturals in width followed by keys with a compass of C/E to $c^3$. The keyboard and jacks of the upper manual pluck strings whose scalings are the same as in the standard single-manual harpsichord and the 6-voet virginal, and so the upper manual is at the same pitch as these instruments. The lower manual has a compass of C/E to $f^3$, with the keys arranged so that they are displaced to the left of the upper-manual keys by an interval of a fourth. Thus the c key on the lower manual plays the same string as the G key on the upper manual: the $c^3$ key on the upper manual plays the same strings as the $f^3$ key on the lower manual, etc. (see Plate 6.12, p. 117).

Because the lower manual effects a transposition downwards of a fourth, the Ruckers double-manual harpsichords have become known as transposing harpsichords.[7]

## SPECIAL MODELS OF RUCKERS HARPSICHORD

Single-manual Ruckers harpsichords were made at pitches higher than the standard '6-voet' harpsichord described above. One harpsichord exists (1627 AR) which is 1232mm long (about 4 voet 4 duimen) and is

[7] Sibyl Marcuse, 'Transposing harpsichords in extant Flemish harpsichords', *Musical Quarterly*, XXXVIII (1952), 414. Richard Shann makes some very unsound arguments about the use of transposing harpsichords in 'Flemish transposing harpsichords: an explanation', *Galpin Society Journal*, XXXVII (1984), 62–71.

Plate 3.11 1638b IR standard double-manual harpsichord. Scale 1:10.

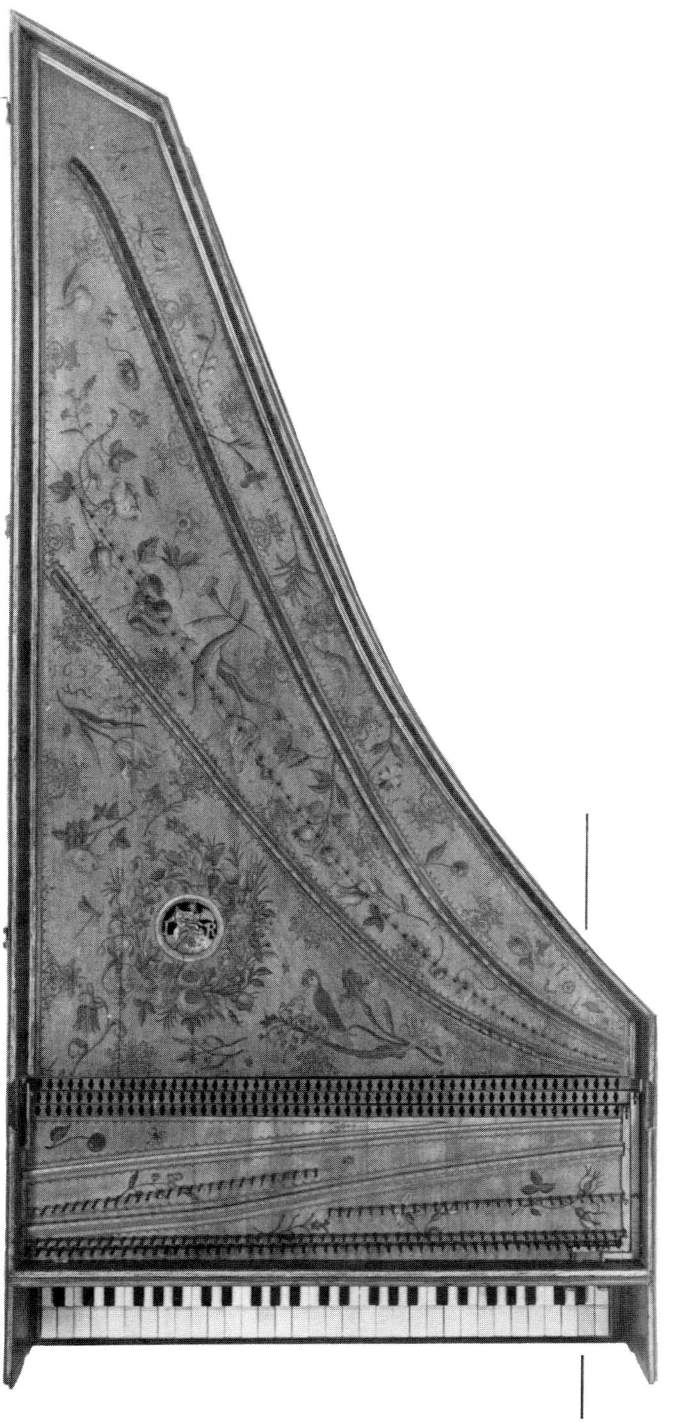

Plate 3.12 1637a IR wide single-manual harpsichord. The original width of the inside of the case is marked by the line. Scale 1:10.

thus a nominal '4-voet' harpsichord.[8] This harpsichord has the same scalings and is at the same pitch as the 4-voet virginals. It has the usual C/E to $c^3$ compass and also the usual two-register unison and octave disposition (see Plate C.5, p. 262). No smaller Ruckers harpsichord is known than the 1627 AR '4-voet' harpsichord.[9]

As well as the standard short-octave singles, the Ruckers also made 6-voet single-manual harpsichords with a chromatic bass octave to C. These have the same scalings and are at the same pitch as the standard 6-voet harpsichords and virginals. One of these harpsichords (1639 IR) originally had an extended treble compass to $d^3$, rather than the usual treble compass finishing at $c^3$. These instruments are the same length as the standard 6-voet singles but are wider by the amount occupied by the 'extra' naturals in the compass. Most of these chromatic-bass-octave singles have been in England at least since the eighteenth century, and this along with the fact that sixteenth- and seventeenth-century English music often requires a chromatic bass octave suggests that they were made as special export models for the English market. Sixteenth- and seventeenth-century English composers and players, used to the native chromatic-bass-octave instruments, would have wanted their new harpsichords to have all of the chromatic and diatonic notes below B♭ (see Chapter 8, p. 176, and Chapter 12, p. 229), and the Ruckers appear to have catered specially for this market. Even in Antwerp, in the Couchet workshops these chromatic-bass-octave single-manual harpsichords were referred to as having 'de bassen recht vuyt [*sic*] op sijn engels' ('the basses straight on in the English way').[10]

Although they are each unique examples of their type and are really all late instruments out of the mainstream Ruckers tradition, some interesting harpsichords were built by the Couchets which indicate the way that musical taste was moving in the second half of the seventeenth century. The 1652 IC harpsichord was unusual in originally having a disposition of $2 \times 8'$ with no $4'$, and an original compass which was C to $d^3$ chromatic. The (*c.* 1650)b IC harpsichord was originally a long single with the usual $1 \times 8'$, $1 \times 4'$ disposition, but with an extended bass compass of $F_1$, $G_1$, $A_1$ to $c^3$. A single by Ioseph Ioannes Couchet (1679 IC) has a chromatic C to $c^3$

[8] See J. H. van der Meer, 'A Flemish "quint" harpsichord', *Galpin Society Journal*, XVIII (1965), 117.

[9] Ripin, 'A "three foot" Flemish harpsichord', 35–9. The instrument described is anonymous, is dated 1724, and although its scalings match those of the 3-voet child Ruckers virginals, it has many non-Flemish features. Its Flemish provenance has not been established and to me it looks more like an Italian than a Flemish instrument.

[10] J. Lambrechts-Douillez and M. J. Bosschaerts-Eykens, '1. Dokumenten betreffende de familie Couchet', *Mededelingen van het Ruckers-Genootschap*, V (Antwerp, 1986), 25 and 28.

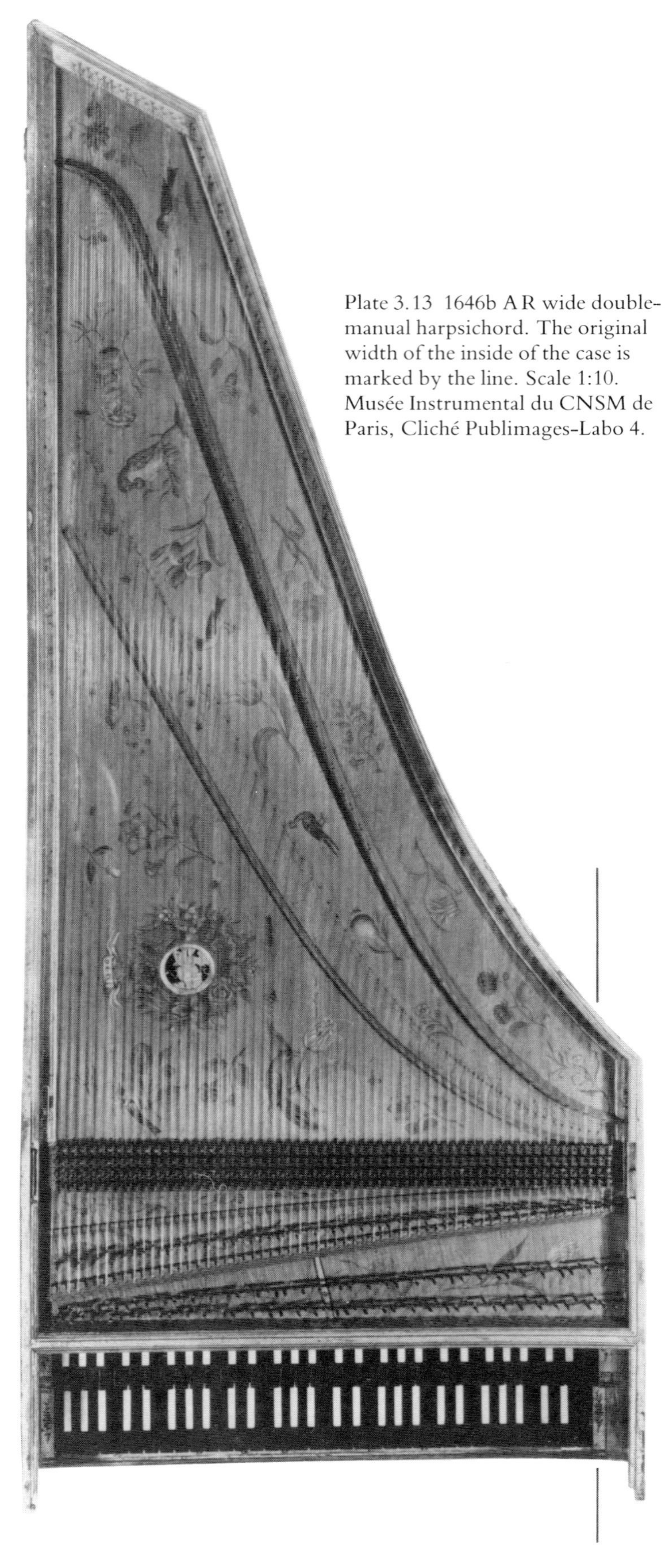

Plate 3.13 1646b AR wide double-manual harpsichord. The original width of the inside of the case is marked by the line. Scale 1:10. Musée Instrumental du CNSM de Paris, Cliché Publimages-Labo 4.

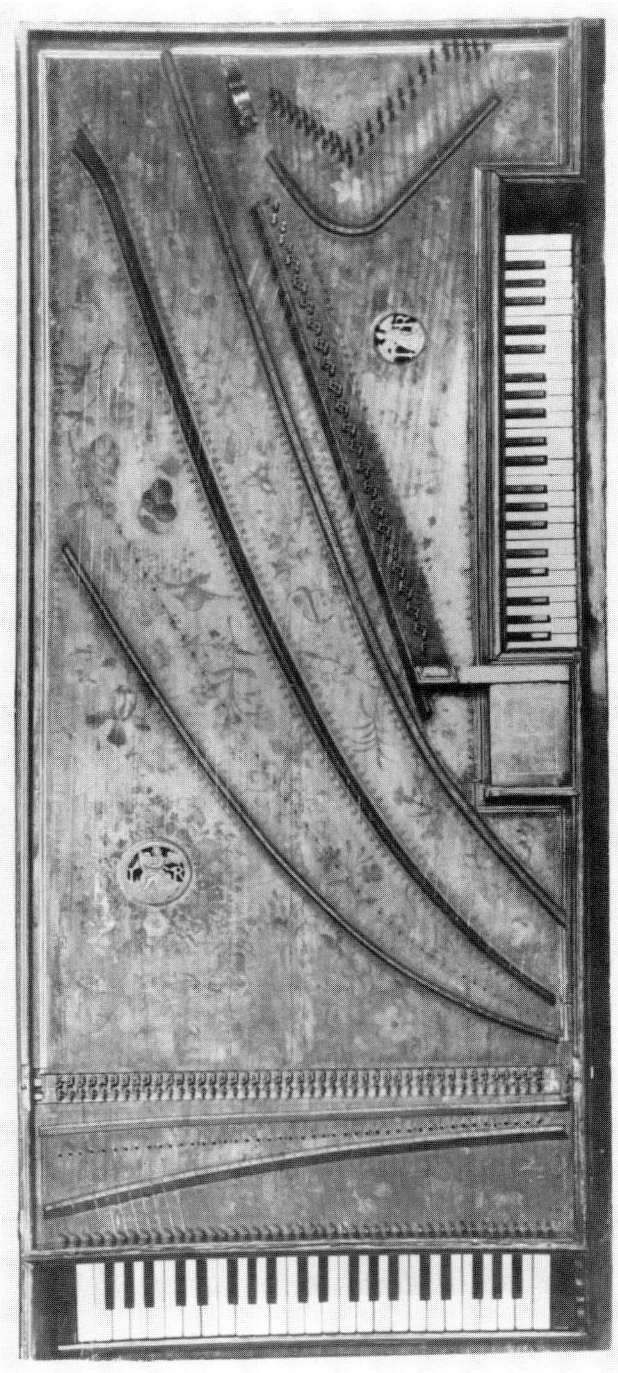

Plate 3.14 n.d. IR single-manual harpsichord/virginal combination. Scale 1:10. Copyright, Musikinstrumenten-Museum des Staatlichen Institut für Musikforschung Preussischer Kulturbesitz, Berlin.

compass, a disposition of 1 × 8′, 1 × 4′, but three rows of jacks with two rows of 8′ jacks separated by the 4′ row and both plucking the same string. And the 1680 IC in its original state as a single-manual harpsichord, possibly also by Ioseph Ioannes, probably had a compass of $F_1$, $G_1$, $A_1$ to $d^3$ with an unknown disposition. The most unusual Couchet single is the n.d. IC harpsichord, which was originally about 2630mm long, and had a compass of almost five octaves from $F_1$ to $d^3$, $e^3$.

As with the singles, the Ruckers also made chromatic-bass-octave double-manual harpsichords. In these instruments the disposition is the same as with the standard-model double and the two keyboards differ in pitch by a fourth, but the pitch rôle of the keyboards is reversed (see Chapter 8, p. 180). The lower manual, at the same pitch as the 6-voet virginals and harpsichords, has a chromatic compass of $G_1$ to $c^3$. At the bass end of the keyboard, the upper manual has a block three naturals wide followed by keys with a compass of F to $f^3$ chromatic. This keyboard operates jacks plucking strings a fourth lower in pitch than the corresponding keys and jacks of the lower manual. These chromatic-bass-octave doubles are the same length as the standard model short-octave doubles, but they are two natural notes wider.

Only one other non-standard type of double is known (1612a HR). Neither the disposition nor the compass of the second manual of this harpsichord can be determined with certainty, but one of the manuals must have had a compass of C/E to $d^3$ at a pitch a *fifth* lower than the pitch of the 6-voet harpsichord and virginals (see Chapter 8, p. 178).

## RUCKERS COMBINED HARPSICHORD AND VIRGINAL

One of the most unusual models of Ruckers instrument is the harpsichord/virginal combination. These are large rectangular instruments in which the virginal fills up the space beside the harpsichord bentside, with the virginal keyboard at the rear of the right-hand longside of the instrument. The harpsichord part may have either one or two manuals. In the single-manual version the virginal is at the octave to the harpsichord part. One double-manual harpsichord/virginal combination exists; in this the harpsichord is the standard model described above and the virginal is an octave above the lower-manual keyboard (i.e. it is at the same pitch as the 4-voet virginals).

The extant Ruckers instruments of all types are classified in Appendix 6 according to their original states.

## THE NUMBERS FOUND ON THE DIFFERENT MODELS OF RUCKERS INSTRUMENTS

Related to the different models of clavecimbel built by the Ruckers are the marks and numbers written on many of them.[11] Unfortunately a great many Ruckers instruments have been so drastically modified in order to conform to later musical taste, that no part of them remains which bears this original marking. There are, however, several extant instruments which still retain at least one original marked part.

These marks and numbers are most commonly found on the action parts of the instruments: the upper and lower keylevers, the upper and lower jacks in each register, the registers themselves, and on the keyframe. In virginals, they are almost always found on the tail of the board at the bass end of the keyframe. The number is sometimes also written on the baseboard below the keyframe, underneath the jackrail, in the case mortice for the jackrail, on the back of the nameboard in virginals, and on the rear of the namebatten and lower-manual batten in double-manual harpsichords. There are also isolated cases where the number is scratched with a sharp tool on one of the frames of the instrument, or, more rarely, is written in rather large red numerals.[12]

Plates 3.15–3.26 show typical examples of these marks on various Ruckers and Couchet instruments. These are written with quill or brush in ink, and are apparently in a hand characteristic of each of the Ruckers workshops. On Ioannes Ruckers instruments, they are in one type of handwriting which is different from that found on Andreas Ruckers instruments, etc.

## THE INTERPRETATION OF THE RUCKERS NUMBERING SYSTEM

As has been seen earlier, the upper part of the Ruckers number clearly represents the length of the instrument in Flemish feet in the case of the single virginals, and *m*oeder and *k*ind in the case of the double mother-and-child virginals. The cipher which appears as the upper part of the number on the harpsichords, whether double or single, is the ligature *ſt*: the letters St run together in this way in ordinary Flemish handwriting of the sixteenth and seventeenth centuries.[13] This cipher clearly stands for *staartstuk* or *staertstuk* (harpsichord, literally 'tail-piece').

The explanation of the lower number is not at first obvious, since if all the numbers appearing on Ruckers instruments are arranged in chronological order a seemingly arbitrary arrangement results. However, if arranged according to the type of instrument, and to the member of the family who built the instrument, the numbers do increase uniformly and chronologically (see Table 3.2, p. 54). For example, if one considers the 6-voet virginals of Andreas Ruckers,

1617 A R $\frac{6}{23}$

1620b A R $\frac{6}{27}$

1633a A R $\frac{6}{70}$

it can be seen that the lower number gradually increases with time. Because of this uniform increase, one is led to the conclusion that we are dealing here with serial numbers applied separately to each member of the Ruckers family and to each model.

It is very enlightening to plot these lower numbers from various instruments in graph form as a function of the date, for each model of instrument and for each of the various members of the Ruckers family. Graph 3.1 shows the numbers plotted against the date for Hans and Ioannes Ruckers and for Ioannes Couchet. Similarly, Graph 3.2 shows a plot of the numbers of the two Andreas Ruckers, father and son. Making sense of these curves is not easy. Only fifty Ruckers instruments are numbered, and of these fifty only thirty-four are instruments in which the date and authorship are completely unambiguous. In some cases the serial number increases more or less uniformly over a long period of time, such as in the example above and that of the 6-voet virginals of Ioannes Ruckers. But in many cases it is clear that, after the serial number has reached a value of 50 or 100, the numbering started again from 1. With some instrument types this restarting of the serial number occurs very frequently. This I have taken to mean a high rate of production for these types of instruments.

In drawing the lines and curves through the points of Graphs 3.1 and 3.2, I have tried to relate the production of instruments to the history of each of the members of the Ruckers family as far as we know it. But because of the paucity of reliable numbers, and the inadequacy of our knowledge of the family history, many of the conclusions drawn are at best only tentative. In some cases so

[11] These marks have been discussed by me in 'The numbering system of Ruckers instruments', *The Brussels Museum of Musical Instruments Bulletin*, IV (1974), 75–89. Since writing this article many more Ruckers numbers have been discovered which alter some of the conclusions arrived at in this article.

[12] For example, the number *2* is written on the lower surface of the lower jack guide of the 1640b A R, and the number *59* is also written in sanguine on the lower guide of the 1639a A R child virginal.

[13] This was kindly pointed out to me by Dr J. Lambrechts-Douillez of the Vleeshuis Museum, Antwerp.

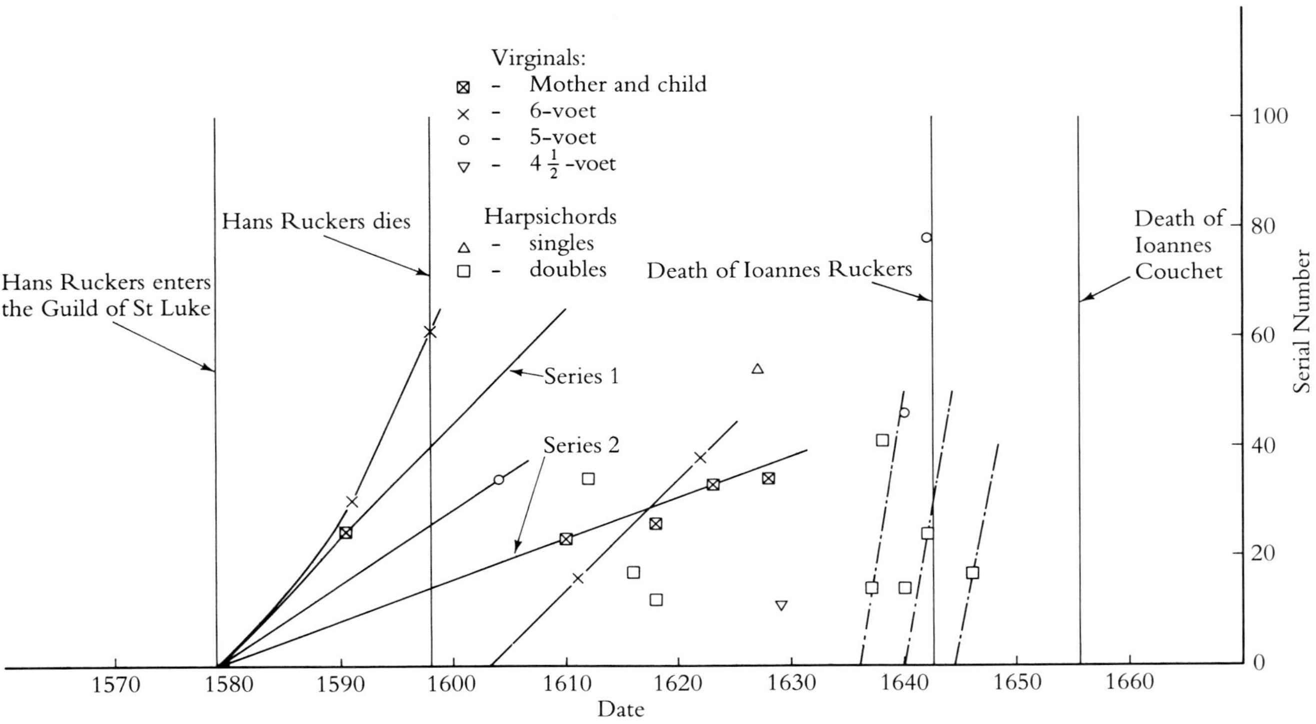


Graph 3.1 Serial numbering of the clavecimbels of Hans Ruckers, Ioannes Ruckers, and Ioannes Couchet.

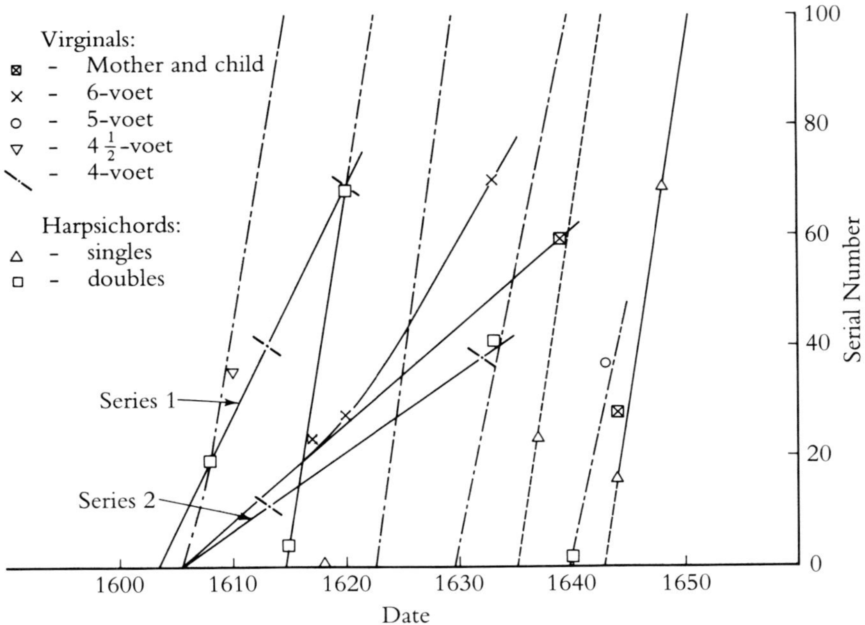


Graph 3.2 Serial numbering of the clavecimbels of Andreas Ruckers I and Andreas Ruckers II.

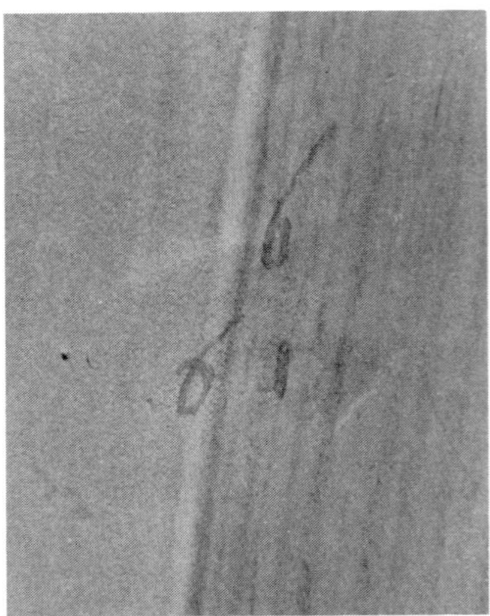

Plate 3.15 The Ruckers mark on the 1598 HR 6-voet spinett virginal.

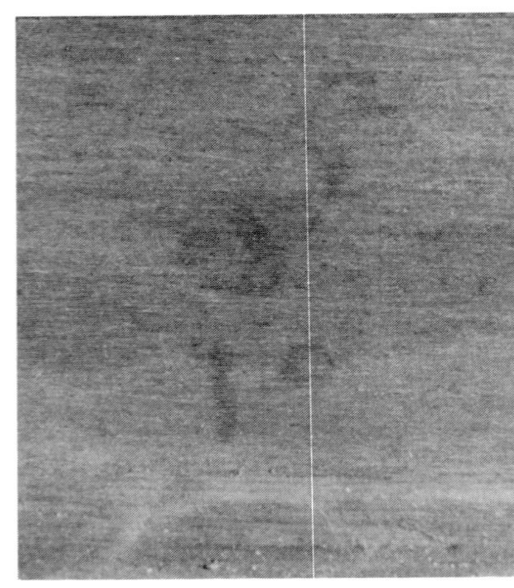

Plate 3.16 The Ruckers mark on the 1591a HR polygonal spinett virginal, with (below) a clearer view of the mark and number.

Plate 3.17 The Ruckers mark on the 1643a AR 5-voet virginal.

Plate 3.18 The Ruckers mark on the 1629 IR 4½-voet virginal.

Plate 3.19 The Ruckers mark on the 1613a AR 4-voet virginal.

Plate 3.20 The Ruckers mark on the 1610 HR mother and child virginals.

Plate 3.21 The Ruckers mark on the 1640b AR double-manual harpsichord.

Plate 3.22 The Ruckers mark on the 1608 AR double-manual harpsichord.

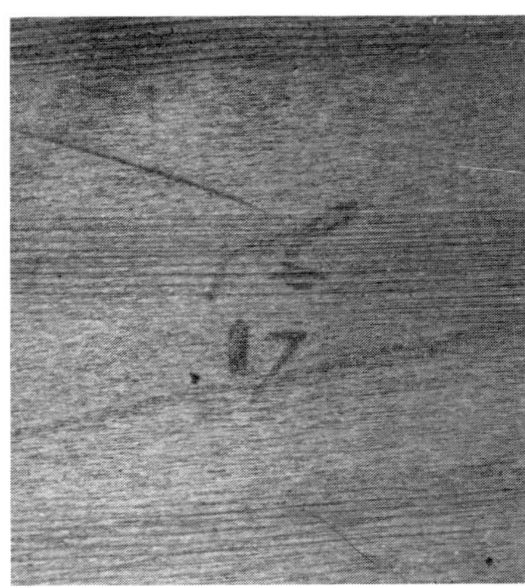

Plate 3.23 The Ruckers mark on the 1616 HR 'French' double-manual harpsichord.

Plate 3.24 The Ruckers mark on the 1619 IR double-manual harpsichord/virginal combination.

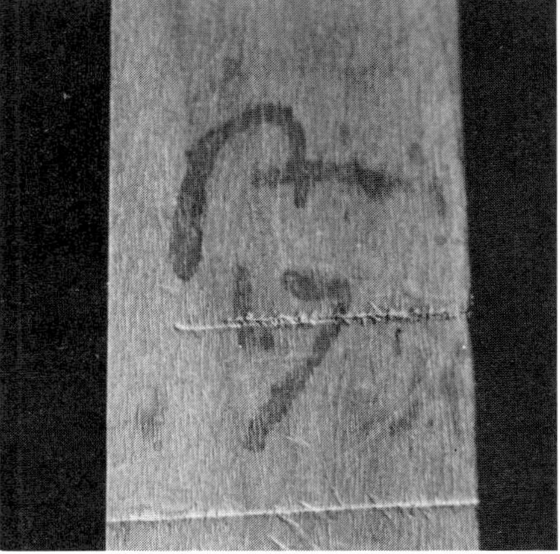

Plate 3.25 The Ruckers mark on the 1646 IC double-manual harpsichord.

Plate 3.26 The Ruckers mark on the 1627 AR 4-voet harpsichord.

little data exists that lines could not be drawn through the points at all.

Looking first at the Hans and Ioannes Ruckers and Ioannes Couchet production in Graph 3.1, vertical lines have been drawn corresponding to the death of Hans Ruckers in 1598, of Ioannes Ruckers in 1642, and of Couchet in 1655. The 1591a HR polygonal and the 1598 HR rectangular spinett virginals both appear to belong to the same number serial, even though the upper part of the number on the 1591a HR is not a 6 (see Plate 3.16) and the 1598 virginal was probably made by Ioannes Ruckers in the year of his father's death. The other numbers for 6-voet virginals are all from the output of Ioannes Ruckers, and appear to indicate that the numbering restarted in about 1598. The dates for the 6-voet virginals of 1636 and 1638 are both suspect, as neither now appears on an original part of the instruments. If both are correct then the position of these points on the graph indicates that the numbering was not always strictly chronological. This may have arisen if the instruments were made and numbered in batches, and then pulled one by one more or less at random from the batch for decorating, finishing and dating.

The same situation occurs for the mother-and-child virginals of 1623 and 1628 – the serial numbers are only one apart, although the instruments differ in date by five years. Also, although there seems to be a more-or-less regular increase in the numbering of the mother-and-child instruments beginning in 1579, the number 26 in 1618 is somewhat lower than what one might expect. The (1591)b HR mother-and-child virginal is dated only on the lid painting. On the basis of the other mother-and-child numbers one would expect that it should be dated shortly before 1615. However, the style of the roses and the soundboard decoration all indicate that the instrument was made by Hans Ruckers, so that the date must be sometime before his death in 1598. It thus seems that there were two series of numbers for the mother-and-child virginals, both probably originating in 1579, when Hans Ruckers joined the Guild (see Graph 3.1). The Milan mother-and-child virginal has the number 15, and its date has been estimated to be about 1600 using the Series 2 numbers. Its soundboard decoration is in the style of the 1598 HR 6-voet virginal, the 1610 HR mother-and-child virginal and the 1612a HR double harpsichord, seeming to corroborate this estimation of the date. The other possibility – that the 15 belongs to the earlier Hans Ruckers serial numbering – can be eliminated on a number of grounds, despite the lavish lid painting and the red-painted curved lower surface on the nameboard/faceboard double moulding, both of which are typical of Hans Ruckers instruments. Under Series 1, the number 15 would put the date of this instrument at about 1586, and this is totally at odds with the soundboard decoration, the painting of the wreath and the signature which uses IOHANNES and not HANS.

The production of double-manual harpsichords, where many serial numbers exist, poses some interesting problems. The serial numbers 14 and 41 for the 1637 and 1638 doubles seem to indicate a very large production of double-manual instruments. These are followed by the numbers 14 for 1640 and 24 for 1642, suggesting that production had slowed down greatly. A more sensible explanation might be that the 1637 double was made at the beginning of the year and the 1638 double at the end, so that the average rate of production was about $(41 - 14)/2 = 27/2 = 13.5$ instruments a year. If then the 1640 had been numbered at the end of the year and the 1642 at the beginning (so that in fact only one year separated them), this would indicate a comparable production of $(24 - 14)/1 = 10$ instruments per year. Probably, like the virginals, the double-manual harpsichords were also made in batches and the lack of precise chronology in the numbering, or the existence of an apparently variable rate of production, could be explained if the instruments were not pulled from the batches for finishing in strict order.

The above analysis suggests that after reaching about 50, the serial number started again from 1 in 1639. If the serial again went to 50 and started from 1 in 1644 and the production was maintained at the same level, then the production curve coincides with the serial 17 for the 1646 Couchet double harpsichord. This is not surprising, since Couchet had been in Ioannes Ruckers' workshop since 1627, and having probably worked on the instruments whose serial numbers are given above as belonging to the production of Ioannes Ruckers, he would no doubt have continued the same serial system after Ruckers' death in 1642.

Too few numbers exist to attempt to draw curves through the double-manual serial numbers 34 and 12 for 1612 and 1618 respectively. The 1616 double has the anomalous number 17, probably because it is one of the large chromatic-bass-octave 'French' doubles, which may have been numbered with a different serial from the standard-model bass short-octave doubles.

One of the surprising features of the production of Ioannes Ruckers is that only one of his single-manual harpsichords is numbered, despite the fact that several of those singles that survive have their original baseboards, on which one would expect to find a number. The reason for numbering the case and action parts of instruments must have been to avoid mixing up the various pieces of otherwise identical instruments in a busy workshop with several instruments of the same type under construction simultaneously. The lack of a serial number on most of the Ioannes singles suggests that, during a large part of his career, he made very few instruments of this type, possibly only on a one-off basis so that there was no possibility of interchanging the action parts. This seems to be confirmed by the fact that of the extant Ruckers standard singles only two out of sixteen are by Ioannes Ruckers.

The situation seems to have changed markedly for Ioannes Ruckers' successor, Ioannes Couchet, at least as far as the special long single-manual harpsichords with a compass of $F_1$, $G_1$, $A_1$ to $c^3$ are concerned. The only extant example of this type of harpsichord, the (*c.* 1650)b IC in the Metropolitan Museum, New York, has the serial number 34 but is undated. The very fact that it was numbered indicates that this model was being produced in such large numbers that several were under construction in the workshop at the same time. Couchet refers to this model of harpsichord in a letter (see Appendix 18) which can be dated to the latter part of 1648,[14] saying that he had only just begun to make this type of instrument. Such long singles were thus in production from 1648 until 1655, when Couchet died. Even if the Metropolitan Museum instrument was made in 1655, the serial number 34 would indicate an average production of about seven of these long chromatic-bass-octave singles every year. Couchet had found himself a best-selling model which appealed to a clientele with musical tastes different from those of the first half of the seventeenth century. It is also likely that the date of this instrument is closer to 1650 than to 1655; it must at any rate be later than 1648.

Graph 3.2, showing the serial numbers for Andreas Ruckers, reveals several interesting features. There appear to be two series of numbers for the 4-voet virginals. Series 1 rises very sharply, indicating a high rate of production at about 4 instruments per year, and the other, Series 2, represents a much slower rate of production averaging about 1.5 instruments per year. Why there are two lines can only be guessed: does one of them represent the production of Andreas himself, and the other that of one of his apprentices? Or were there perhaps two workmen building cases and parts, each numbering his own instruments, which were then later decorated and finished by someone else? The fact that they both seem to originate in the period around 1605 certainly suggests that they are indeed two genuinely separate serials which mark the beginning of Andreas' active production.

The date of Andreas' entry into the Guild is not known. But he was married in 1605 and worked with Ioannes in the same workshop until 1608. The 1604 HR 5-voet virginal is signed IOANNES ET ANDREAS RVCKERS FECERVNT, indicating that the two brothers were signing instruments together in 1604. However, the fact that his 6-voet and 4-voet virginal numbering serials both appear to start around 1604–05 indicates that Andreas, although still working together with Ioannes in the family workshop, began then to number (and probably to sign) his own instruments. Unfortunately no dated instruments by Andreas Ruckers from before 1608 exist to confirm whether or not Andreas and Ioannes were numbering and signing instruments independently during the subsequent period when they were sharing the same workshop. However, a combined harpsichord and virginal of 1606 by Andreas Ruckers alone is listed among the instruments for sale in Paris in the eighteenth century,[15] and another harpsichord dated 1606 by Hans Ruckers alone (Ioannes used an HR rose at this date) appears in an inventory of instruments confiscated from the French aristocracy.[16] Thus at about the time of Andreas' marriage in 1605, the two brothers began to work on an independent basis: Ioannes continued his

[14] Edwin M. Ripin, 'Antwerp harpsichord-building: the current state of research', *Colloquium: Restauratieproblemen van Antwerpse Klavecimbels* (Antwerp, 1971), 12–22.

[15] Eugène de Bricqueville, *Les ventes d'instruments de musique au XVIII^e^ siècle* (Paris, 1908), 15 (see Appendix 15, pp. 302ff). The authenticity of this instrument, of a type unlikely to have been faked in the eighteenth century, seems undoubted. Another harpsichord by Andreas dated 1601 (pp. 11–12) is listed as being 7 pieds 3 pouces long (2355mm). But this is about 10cm longer than a normal Ruckers double-manual harpsichord and is therefore probably unauthentic.

[16] See No. 78 in Albert G. Hess, 'The transition from harpsichord to piano', *Galpin Society Journal*, VI (1953), 84, and Raymond Russell, *The Harpsichord and Clavichord* (London, 1959; reprint, London, 1973), p. 152, No. 13.

father's serial numbering and continued the serials he had restarted after Hans' death in 1598, and Andreas began his own serial numbering for all instrument types.

Several single-manual harpsichords by Andreas have numbers, from which his production rate can be estimated. The 1644b AR (serial number 16) and 1648 AR (serial number 69) indicate an approximate production of between eleven and eighteen singles a year, depending on when in these years the instruments were numbered and dated. Assuming a production of about thirteen singles per year by drawing a line through the 1644 and 1648 points, with the serial going up to 100 (instead of 50 as for Ioannes), puts the serial numbers for the 1637 AR and (1651)a AR singles on the same production curves, with the serials begining in about 1635, 1643 and 1650. The number 1 on the 1618 AR single indicates that a serial started in this year, and suggests that another single-manual serial started in about 1627 or so, or roughly midway between 1618 and 1635 – i.e. a new single-manual harpsichord serial began about every eight-and-a-half years. This would mean that, at a slightly slower initial rate of production, the first single-manual serial numbering could also have begun in about 1605.

Andreas' production of double-manual harpsichords can be estimated only from the numbers of the 1615 AR (serial number 4) and the 1620c AR (serial number 68). Again depending upon whether these instruments were numbered at the beginning or end of these years, the production rate could have been between eleven and sixteen instruments per year. The serial number 19 on the 1608 AR double indicates that by 1608 Andreas' production was already well established, and had in fact begun well before 1608. If we assume a somewhat slower initial rate of production than in the 1615–20 period, the 1608 serial also suggests that Andreas' production of double-manual harpsichords began about 1605. The serial number 41 of the 1633b AR indicates that there was probably a set of intermediate serial numbers (starting perhaps in about 1623?), but there are no other intermediate numbered double-manual Andreas harpsichords to confirm this.

Considering the present scarcity of 4½-voet virginals, the serial number 35 for the 1610b AR virginal is very surprising. In view of the small number of surviving 4½-voet instruments, I feel that this serial cannot be interpreted to indicate that Andreas had a high rate of production after 1605 of 4½-voet virginals. The most likely explanation is that the number is a continuation of Hans Ruckers' production and serialization which was maintained by Andreas (rather than Ioannes) after Hans' death in 1598.

As only the 1643 5-voet instrument by Andreas Ruckers has a serial number, nothing can be said about Andreas' rate of production of 5-voet virginals.

It would appear from the previous analysis, at least of the single-manual harpsichord, that the serial numbers of Andreas II were a continuation of those of Andreas I. The 1644a AR single is signed ANDREAS RVCKERS DEN OVDEN ME FECIT, whereas the 1651a AR single is signed ANDREAS RVCKERS AND[REAS] F[ILIVS] ME FECIT, so that these can definitely be ascribed to Andreas I and Andreas II respectively. However, just as the Couchet double harpsichord numbering seems to continue the Ioannes Ruckers serials, so the Andreas II single serials seem to continue those of Andreas I. Probably, therefore, the serial numbers cannot be used to distinguish the production either of Ioannes Couchet from Ioannes Ruckers, or of Andreas I from Andreas II Ruckers.

As has already been seen, one of the practical advantages of understanding the method by which the Ruckers numbered their instruments is that it enables one to estimate a date for an instrument which retains its number, but which has otherwise lost any trace of its date of manufacture. This has been done for the (1605) AR single-manual harpsichord and the (1626) AR 'motherless' child, in a manner similar to that described for the Ioannes Ruckers instruments.

One of the most interesting instruments which retains its mark given it by Ruckers, but which does not fit into any of the categories previously described, is the 1627 AR 'quint' harpsichord in the Gemeentemuseum, The Hague. This is a small instrument with the normal width of a Ruckers single-manual harpsichord, but only 1231mm long instead of the usual 1839mm or so for a harpsichord at normal pitch. It is thus 4 voet 3.6 duimen long. The inscription which appears on it is shown in Plate 3.26. This is clearly '4 *ſt*', a 4-voet *Staartstuk*, corresponding exactly to the 4-voet virginal which has the same scalings as this harpsichord. The lack of a serial number suggests that this was an unusual, perhaps unique, instrument made to special order, which did not need to be distinguished from other instruments of a similar type in the workshop.

Also of interest is the sign on the combined double-manual harpsichord with a virginal in the bentside, dated 1619, by Ioannes Ruckers, located in the Brussels Museum (No. 2935). A great deal of this instrument is not original, but it does retain its original keyboards and keys. The top $c^3$ key of the harpsichord upper manual bears a cipher which is probably the usual '*ſt*', but no serial number (see Plate 3.24). This would also seem to indicate an instrument made to special order, or the absence in the workshop of other instruments of the same type with which it could be confused.

The polygonal virginal of 1591 in the Gruuthuuse, Bruges, by Hans Ruckers, has a cipher written in a very flowing hand above the serial number 30 (Plate 3.16). The exact meaning of this cipher is not understood, but it may refer to the unusual polygonal shape of the instrument. The serial number, however, seems to fit in with those for the more usual rectangular 6-voet virginals and it has therefore been included with these in Graph 3.1. Among the 6-voet virginals it should be noted that the two Hans Ruckers instruments and the 1617 Andreas Ruckers are all left-plucking spinett virginals. So far as their serial numbering is concerned at least, the Ruckers did not seem to distinguish between these and the more usual centre-plucking muselar virginals.

Since the numbers of both the mother and of the child are the same, the numbers of the missing instrument for the 'childless mothers' and the 'motherless children' can quite naturally be inferred. Also, an instrument like the 1628a IR virginal in the Brussels Museum (No. 2926), which at first sight appears to be a normal 6-voet virginal, is revealed originally to have been a double mother and child. The exterior of this instrument has been entirely veneered over and the keyboard compass has been extended into the space formerly occupied by the child, so that its original appearance has been completely disguised. However, the presence of an *m* on the keyframe instead of the *6* characteristic of a single virginal proves that it was originally a double mother-and-child instrument.

Only the first digit of the number on the 1620 IR 6-voet virginal in Boston remains. A *3* is clearly visible on the original C/E keylever, but a second digit has been cut away during the process of a compass alteration. From the curve for the 6-voet virginals in Graph 3.1, the number must originally have been about 33–35.

Another advantage of understanding the Ruckers numbering system is that by assuming a more-or-less uniform production and extrapolating the curves obtained, one can obtain an estimate of the number of instruments that the various members of the Ruckers family built. Because of the scarcity of numbers for Hans Ruckers, Andreas Ruckers the Younger and Ioannes Couchet, and since there are no serial numbers with which to estimate the number of 4-voet virginals or single-manual harpsichords for Ioannes Ruckers, I have had to base my calculations only on the number available for Andreas the Elder. This results in an estimate of about thirty-five to forty instruments of all types per year during the latter part of his active production.

At this rate Andreas was producing one new instrument in a little more than a week, including one single- and one double-manual harpsichord every month. This is much greater than my original estimate of the Ruckers production rate,[17] and seems to indicate that the Ruckers' workshops were quite large, employing a number of assistants and apprentices. It is likely that the Ioannes workshop produced as many if not more instruments than Andreas. And this represents the production of only two workshops in a town with a population of only 50,000. Antwerp's position as a port was clearly very important to the Ruckers, since such a high rate of production, supplemented by the output of the workshops of the other clavecimbel builders, would soon have saturated a local market.

Unfortunately we have no idea of the exact number of people working in the Ruckers workshops. From the Karest contract (see Appendix 11) we see that the workshop employees and apprentices worked long and hard hours. The instruments themselves indicate that the sharps and jacks were not made in the workshops, but were bought from a common source of supply (see pp. 120 and 126), and so would not require workshop staff for their production. The decoration of the soundboard and case indicates that each workshop employed its own decorator, and personal experience suggests that a production rate of one instrument every eight to nine days or so is about the rate at which one person fluent in the style and technique could decorate a Ruckers instrument.

To the best of my knowledge, the only other makers who have both numbered and dated their instruments were all working in the eighteenth century. Baker Harris, Johannes Hitchcock, Johann Gottlob Horn, Johann Paul Krämer, Longman and Broderip and Shudi–Broadwood are among those whose production can be calculated. By way of comparison, J. P. Krämer made about twenty-three clavichords per year; Shudi made only about eight harpsichords per year at the beginning of his career, and this increased to a fairly steady rate of twenty-six during the latter part of the Shudi–Broadwood partnership. The Ruckers were also producing about twenty-six harpsichords per year, but in addition made all of the different types of virginals as well. It is figures such as these which bring their workshops into focus more readily than any other. They imply a large workshop and workshop staff, a vast number of tools and jigs, and a large reserve stock of well-seasoned wood for the cases and soundboards.

[17] See footnote 1.

Table 3.2 *Ruckers instrument serial numbers*

*Hans Ruckers*

6-voet virginals

| | |
|---|---|
| 30 | 1591a HR |

mother-and-child virginals

| | |
|---|---|
| 24 | (1591)b HR |

*Ioannes Ruckers*

mother-and-child virginals:

| | |
|---|---|
| 15 | (*c.* 1600) HR |
| 23 | 1610 HR |
| 26 | 1618a IR |
| 33 | 1623 IR |
| 34 | 1628a IR |

4½-voet virginals

| | |
|---|---|
| 11 | 1629 IR |

5-voet virginals

| | |
|---|---|
| 46 | 1640a IR |
| 78 | 1642a IR |

6-voet virginals

| | |
|---|---|
| 61 | 1598 HR |
| 16 | 1611 HR |
| 20 | (1614) HR |
| 3? | 1620 IR |
| 38 | 1622 IR |
| 68 | (1638)a IR |
| 70 | (1636) IR |

single-manual harpsichords

| | |
|---|---|
| 54 | 1627a IR |

double-manual harpsichords

| | |
|---|---|
| 34 | 1612b HR |
| 17 | 1616 HR |
| 12 | 1618b IR |
| 14 | 1637b IR |
| 41 | 1638b IR |
| 14 | 1640b IR |
| 24 | 1642b IR |

*Ioannes Couchet*

double-manual harpsichords

| | |
|---|---|
| 17 | 1646 IC |

large single-manual harpsichords

| | |
|---|---|
| 34 | (*c.* 1650)b IC |

*Ioannes and Andreas Ruckers*

5-voet virginals

| | |
|---|---|
| 34 | 1604 HR |

*Andreas Ruckers*

mother-and-child virginals

| | |
|---|---|
| 36 | (1626) AR |
| 59 | 1639a AR |
| 28 | 1644b AR |

4-voet virginals

| | |
|---|---|
| 11 | 1613a AR |
| 38 | 1632 AR |
| 40 | 1613b AR |
| 69 | 1620a AR |

4½-voet virginals

| | |
|---|---|
| 35 | 1610b AR |

5-voet virginals

| | |
|---|---|
| 37 | 1643a AR |

6-voet virginals

| | |
|---|---|
| 23 | 1617 AR |
| 27 | 1620b AR |
| 70 | 1633a AR |

single-manual harpsichords

| | |
|---|---|
| 2 | (1605) AR |
| 1 | 1618 AR |
| 23/24 | 1637 AR |
| 16 | 1644a AR |
| 69 | 1648 AR |
| 2 | (1651)a AR |

double-manual harpsichords

| | |
|---|---|
| 19 | 1608 AR |
| 4 | 1615 AR |
| 68 | 1620c AR |
| 41 | 1633b AR |
| 2 | 1640b AR |

*Ioseph Ioannes Couchet*

large single-manual harpsichords

| | |
|---|---|
| 1 | 1679 IC |

CHAPTER FOUR

# The stringing and pitches of Ruckers instruments

Numerous factors must be considered by a builder to help him decide upon the stringing to be used for a clavecimbel. Because of the importance of the gauges and string materials used in determining the final sound, the rôle of both the diameter and the material of the string must be clearly understood. The string must provide a fundamental tone with a set of partials above it that are as close as possible to integral multiples of the fundamental frequency, and at the same time it must provide enough energy to cause the soundboard to radiate the resulting sound into the air surrounding the instrument.

## SOME ACOUSTICS OF CLAVECIMBEL SOUNDBOARDS AND STRINGS

To provide a set of partials as pure as possible, the string should be as flexible as possible, and under the maximum possible tension. The flexibility of the wire can be increased by making the string as thin and long as possible and by using an inherently flexible material. For any given pitch, the length of the string is increased until its tension is such that it is just on the point of breaking. Since this breaking point is unaffected by the diameter of the string for wire of uniform properties, the ideal string will have a large ultimate breaking stress and a small Young's Modulus (i.e. little stiffness). Unfortunately, of the materials commonly available, those of high breaking stress are also quite stiff, so that the desirability of one material over another is not very great.

In order to impart enough energy to the soundboard to cause the string to radiate its sound into the surrounding air, the lighter and extremely flexible string materials such as gut and silk must be rejected as lacking the inertia necessary to cause sufficient motion in the soundboard, in favour of heavier metal strings. The most suitable and readily available are iron and copper-alloy (yellow and red brass) strings. Iron is slightly less stiff in relation to its breaking point than the copper-alloy materials, and is therefore marginally the preferable material. As the ultimate breaking stress of iron is somewhat higher than that of the strongest brass material, iron scalings are longer than brass scalings in order that iron be close to its breaking point. However, the use of critically-stressed iron throughout the entire compass of keyboard instruments would result in unreasonably long strings in the bass. For example, an instrument at the same pitch as a 6-voet virginal would require strings about 2.84 metres long for low C if it were strung in iron right to the bottom note. The problem is avoided by shortening the bass strings and using the softer, more flexible copper-alloy strings up to a point permitted by their breaking strength. Moreover, copper alloy gives a better sound than the stiffer iron in this part of the compass.

Given that the strings must be of metal, one must arrive at a compromise diameter where the energy of the radiated sound is as great as possible by using a string which is on the one hand large in diameter, but on the other hand small enough to ensure that the stiffness of the wire does not seriously affect the purity and musical acceptability of the partials produced. Choosing the gauge of the wire had to be done by experiment; the final choice, being subjective, varied from individual to individual, and from time to time according to aesthetic judgement. Nonetheless certain physical constraints would affect the choice by the person carrying out the experiment.

Physical theory shows that in order for an acoustical radiator to be efficient, the size of the radiator should be approximately equal to or greater than that of the wavelength of the propagated radiation. In the treble part of a harpsichord or virginal this is indeed the case, so that the fundamental note in the string as well as all of the shorter wavelength partials are radiated by the soundboard there. But in the bass of the instrument the dimension of the radiating soundboard is only about one-tenth of the wavelength of the fundamental tone being sounded. A simple experiment shows that in the bass, the fundamental tone is not radiated at all. If one removes from a harpsichord the jack of the lowest note, its string can then be plucked in the middle with the soft part of the fingers of one hand. In this way the fundamental will be excited very strongly in the string. Any weak odd partials also excited can be damped out by touching the string near the bridge or nut momentarily with the soft part of a finger of the other hand, leaving only the fundamental note excited in the string. The string will then be seen to be vibrating with a large amplitude, but the soundboard will radiate absolutely no sound.

How then do we sense the fundamental tone when the string is plucked and sounded normally? The answer seems to lie in the way the sound is perceived by the ear and brain. When a string is plucked sharply near one end, its partials are excited, and the ear and brain create the impression of a fundamental from the structure of these partials. If the partials are all exact multiples of the fundamental, then the fundamental is just the difference tone between successive partials contained in the harmonic series of the string. If the partials are not exact multiples of the fundamental, then the ear will perceive a band of difference tones rather than a single unique fundamental. Such a note will have a totally unmusical character, and the impression of the fundamental will be lacking. It is thus very important that the partials be as close as possible to pure harmonics by ensuring a long, thin string sounding as near its breaking point as possible, and with as little inherent stiffness as possible.[1]

In the bass of the instrument, however, there are reasons for preferring heavier strings. First, they compensate for the inefficiency of the soundboard in the bass. Secondly, they are more stable in pitch: a long thin bass string voiced loud enough to match the treble notes is displaced by the quill to such an extent that the pitch of the string is initially slightly sharpened due to the increased tension, and then becomes flatter as time progresses after it is released from the quill. Calculation shows that even though the bass strings are much heavier and thicker than those in the treble, the inharmonicity caused by their stiffness and thickness is more than compensated for by their length. In fact, for any normal stringing plan, the inharmonicity of the treble strings is greater than it is for the bass strings. The amount of inharmonicity in the bass strings is critical because the fundamental tone is not radiated by the soundboard, and the impression of the fundamental is determined by the tuning accuracy of the partials. Inharmonicity in the treble strings does not matter so much, because the soundboard radiates the fundamental tone there, and the inharmonic upper partials are so high in frequency as to be outwith the range of normal hearing.

As will shortly become clear, the historical instrument builders and designers, and writers on the subject had a remarkable insight into these factors, even though this was perhaps much more intuitive than the explanation given above. Klaas Douwes,[2] although he lived some fifty years after the Ruckers family had ceased production, throws much light on the instruments already under study. Douwes mentions three different types of stringing material, and lists the actual gauge numbers of the strings for different sizes of instrument, although unfortunately he does not give the diameter equivalents for these gauge numbers. In order to understand better the scalings and string gauges that Douwes gives it is necessary first to understand the pitch scheme of Ruckers instruments. It will then become clear, I think, that Douwes' lists apply perfectly to Ruckers clavecimbels, and close analysis of the strings and gauge numbers on some extant instruments may give some indication of the actual sizes of Douwes string gauges.

## THE PITCHES OF RUCKERS INSTRUMENTS

Whereas the absolute pitch of a wind instrument can be determined within very narrow limits, this is not the case with a stringed instrument, because any given string can be tuned up or down over a limited range and still remain musically acceptable. However, a comparison of the ratio of string lengths is a good indicator of the relative pitch of two instruments. Such a comparison shows that the Ruckers/Couchet family built instruments at pitches differing by fixed amounts, corresponding to common musical intervals. Furthermore, the study of these pitch relationships should throw light not only on musical practice during the period contemporary with the Ruckers, but also on some of the design principles utilized, if not invented, by the Ruckers family.

The discussion in Chapter 3 introduced the different models of clavecimbel made by the Ruckers and Cou-

[1] A more complete discussion of the acoustics of soundboards and stringing including the important effect of the string's internal damping is in preparation by the author.

[2] Klaas Douwes, *Grondig Ondersoek van de Toonen der Musijk* (Franeker, 1699; facs., Amsterdam, 1971), 104–24. See Appendix 8.

Table 4.1 *Lengths and proposed pitches of Ruckers virginals*

| Instrument | Length mm | Length duimen | Length voeten | Ruckers upper number | Proposed pitch |
|---|---|---|---|---|---|
| (*c.* 1600) HR | 1709 | 66.0 | 6.00 | 6 | R |
| 1604 HR | 1424 | 55.0 | 5.00 | 5 | R + 2 |
| 1629 IR | 1282 | 49.5 | 4.50 | 4½ | R + 4 |
| 1613b AR | 1138 | 44.0 | 4.00 | 4 | R + 5 |
| (*c.* 1600) HR | 820 | 31.7 | 2.88 | k | R + 8 |
| (*c.* 1610)a AR | 711 | 27.5 | 2.50 | ? | R + 9 |

chets.[3] Above middle c ($c^1$) each of these models exhibits Pythagorean scalings which halve in length for every octave rise in pitch. Thus in this region the relative pitch of two notes bears a strict mathematical relationship to the string length: for example, the string sounding the note $g^2$ is two-thirds the length of the $c^2$ string a fifth lower. If another smaller instrument whose $c^2$ key activates a string which is the same length as the $g^2$ string on the larger instrument, then we can be fairly certain that the two instruments are meant to sound a fifth apart. Obviously if the historical builder was not using both critically-stressed strings as described above and Pythagorean scalings, it would not be so easy to establish these relative pitch relationships.

Douwes mentions 6-voet, 5-voet, 4-voet, 3-voet and 2-voet 4-duimen instruments. Edwin M. Ripin[4] has suggested pitch assignments for the first four of these instruments, based on the scalings given for them by Douwes, but without reference to extant instruments. It therefore remains to compare the scalings in order to determine the relative pitches of some surviving instruments.

Table 4.1 shows the length and proposed pitches of a number of Ruckers virginals. The instruments chosen for study here are of necessity those whose scalings and dimensions have remained unaltered up to the present day. Because of the small number of surviving unmodified instruments, this has meant that examples built at various periods had to be chosen from the workshops of both Ioannes and Andreas Ruckers. Despite this, the degree of accuracy and standardization of the Ruckers workshop practice results in a wholly convincing comparison, which strongly suggests that the lists in Douwes are indeed applicable to Ruckers instruments.

In making the calculations in Table 4.1, as in Chapter 3, p. 34, the Flemish voet is taken to have eleven duimen each of length 25.88mm.[5] The resulting lengths in Flemish voeten are then clearly equal to the upper half of the Ruckers number-symbol normally found on various parts of the action and elsewhere on the instrument (see Chapter 3).

Here the pitch of the 6-voet virginal has been defined as 'reference pitch' or 'R'.[6] The pitches R + 2, R + 4, R + 5, R + 8 and R + 9 are a major second, a fourth, a fifth, an octave, and a ninth above reference pitch.

The virginals at a pitch of R + 4, the 4½-voet virginals, are absent from Douwes' lists. He mentions them in terms neither of their scalings nor of their stringing. Using the Ruckers number to estimate the number of instruments of this type which were produced, it seems likely that few 4½-voet virginals were made. For example, by 1629 Ioannes Ruckers had built only eleven 4½-voet virginals, whereas he had produced thirty or more of each of the other types of virginal at this same date. Because of their scarcity it is quite possible that they were unfamiliar to Douwes and hence omitted from his work.

The last entry in Table 4.1 at a pitch of R + 9 is mentioned by Douwes in terms of its length, and its stringing list is given, but without a mention of its scalings and therefore without any implication of its relative pitch. However, using the scalings of the one extant example of this type of instrument by Ruckers, this pitch assignment is confirmed just as with the larger instruments.[7]

3 The instrument models to be discussed here are only loosely related to those surveyed by Frank Hubbard in *Three Centuries of Harpsichord Making* (Cambridge, Mass., 1965), 57–8. I have also not attempted to follow the system for harpsichords of William Dowd, 'A classification system for Ruckers and Couchet double harpsichords', *Journal of the American Musical Instrument Society*, IV (1978), 10666–13.

4 Edwin M. Ripin, 'The "three foot" Flemish harpsichord', *Galpin Society Journal*, XXIII (1970), 35ff.

5 See footnote 1, Chapter 3, and Apendix 1.

6 Calling this pitch standard 'R' gives it an apparent importance which is completely anachronistic, since it makes it seem as though R was a desired standard or norm, which it was not. This disadvantage is, I think, offset by the graphic clarity and ease with which one can then refer the other pitches to this. Note that R + 1 and R − 1 do not exist.

7 A second confirmation of this pitch assignment has been made by a careful analysis of Douwes stringing lists. See G. Grant O'Brien, 'The stringing and pitches of Ruckers instruments', *Colloquium: Ruckers Klavecimbels en Copieën* (Antwerp, 1977), 48–71.

### *Ruckers virginal scalings*

Comparison of the scalings of the various Ruckers virginals is made in Table 4.2. Here it can be seen that, for example, the $c^1$ string of the child virginal has about the same length as the $c^2$ string of the 6-voet (mother) virginals, confirming the proposed octave difference in pitch between them. Similarly, the $g^1$ string in the 4½-voet virginal measures 356mm, about the same length as the $f^1$ string in the 4-voet virginal; this confirms the R + 4 and R + 5 pitch assignments in relation to the length of $c^2$ for the instrument at R. These pitch comparisons may be made for the other instruments for the lengths given in the table. But the relative string lengths can also be used to determine the relative pitches of these virginals by comparing the lengths of the strings for the same note. Dividing the string length of the 5-voet virginal by that of the 6-voet virginal for the note $f^1$, for example, gives a ratio of 0.88, and confirms that the pitch relationship between the two is R + 2 (ratio for a just major second = 8/9). The other ratios are: R + 4, a just fourth = 3/4; R + 5, a just fifth = 2/3; R + 8, an octave = 1/2; and R + 9, a major ninth = 4/9.

The scalings in Table 4.2 are plotted in Graph 4.1 in such a way that the actual sounding pitch of each type of virginal has been taken into account. Thus the scalings of the 5-voet virginal are plotted two semitones higher in pitch than the 6-voet one, the 4½-voet virginal a fourth higher, the 4-voet virginal a fifth higher, the child virginal an octave higher and the 2½-voet virginal a ninth higher than reference pitch. In each of these plots the curve becomes linear above the played note $c^1$. The best straight line was fitted to the points above played $c^1$ using the method of least squares, subject to the restriction that the line gave points whose scalings decreased by half with each octave increase in pitch. This gives an average scaling converted to reference pitch for these six virginals of $c^2 = 354.8 \pm 4.2$mm.

It is important to note that the scalings of the various sizes of virginal are in proportion to the instrument's pitch, not only in the treble part of the compass, where it is normally strung with iron, but also in the tenor and bass where copper-alloy strings are used. For example, the child's C string is half the length of the 6-voet C string; the 4-voet C string is two-thirds the length of the 6-voet C string, etc. and the ratios for the other intervals given above will all confirm the proposed pitch assignments for the notes in the bass as well as in the treble. The full significance of this will be pointed out in the discussion of the stringing materials used.

### *Ruckers harpsichord scalings*

The scalings of three harpsichords are treated in an analogous way in Table 4.3. The instruments under consideration are the following:

(1) The lower manual of the 1638b IR double-manual harpsichord at sub-quart pitch and its octave at quint pitch;

(2) The 1644a AR single-manual harpsichord at reference pitch and its octave;

(3) The 1627 AR 4-voet single-manual harpsichord at quint pitch and its octave a twelfth above reference pitch.

The three rows of figures at the bottom of the table do not really belong to the pitch scheme for Ruckers instruments, as they are not the basic scalings of the instruments but merely the octave scalings to the unison register. The basic scalings are of course to be found in the unison string lengths comprising the first three rows of figures, and confirmation of the proposed pitches can be seen at a glance by comparing the $f^1$ scaling of the 1627 AR, the $c^2$ scaling of the 1644a AR, and the $f^2$ scaling of the 1638b IR harpsichord unison scalings. Other equivalent comparisons lead to the same pitch assignments, and, as outlined for the virginals above, these are confirmed by comparing the ratios of relative string lengths to the ratios for the corresponding intervals between the proposed pitches.

The values of the bass scalings of the larger harpsichords are roughly the same as those of the virginals. But

Table 4.2 *Ruckers virginal scalings in millimetres*

| Instrument | Length | Scalings C | F | c | f | $c^1$ | $f^1$ | $c^2$ | $f^2$ | $c^3$ | Proposed pitch |
|---|---|---|---|---|---|---|---|---|---|---|---|
| (*c.* 1600) HR | 6-voet | 1397 | 1366 | 1131 | 936 | 708 | 527 | 367 | 269 | 183 | R |
| 1604 HR | 5-voet | 1204 | 1156 | 969 | 803 | 621 | 464 | 330 | 243 | 163 | R + 2 |
| 1629 IR | 4½-voet | 1055 | 1017 | 858 | 716 | 549 | 402 | 274 | 198 | 139 | R + 4 |
| 1613b AR | 4-voet | 916 | 881 | 742 | 608 | 473 | 348 | 243 | 175 | 122 | R + 5 |
| (*c.* 1600) HR | child | 689 | 673 | 562 | 465 | 354 | 261 | 178 | 136 | 89 | R + 8 |
| (*c.* 1610)a AR | 2½-voet | 606 | 599 | 507 | 418 | 320 | 226 | 147 | 114 | 75 | R + 9 |

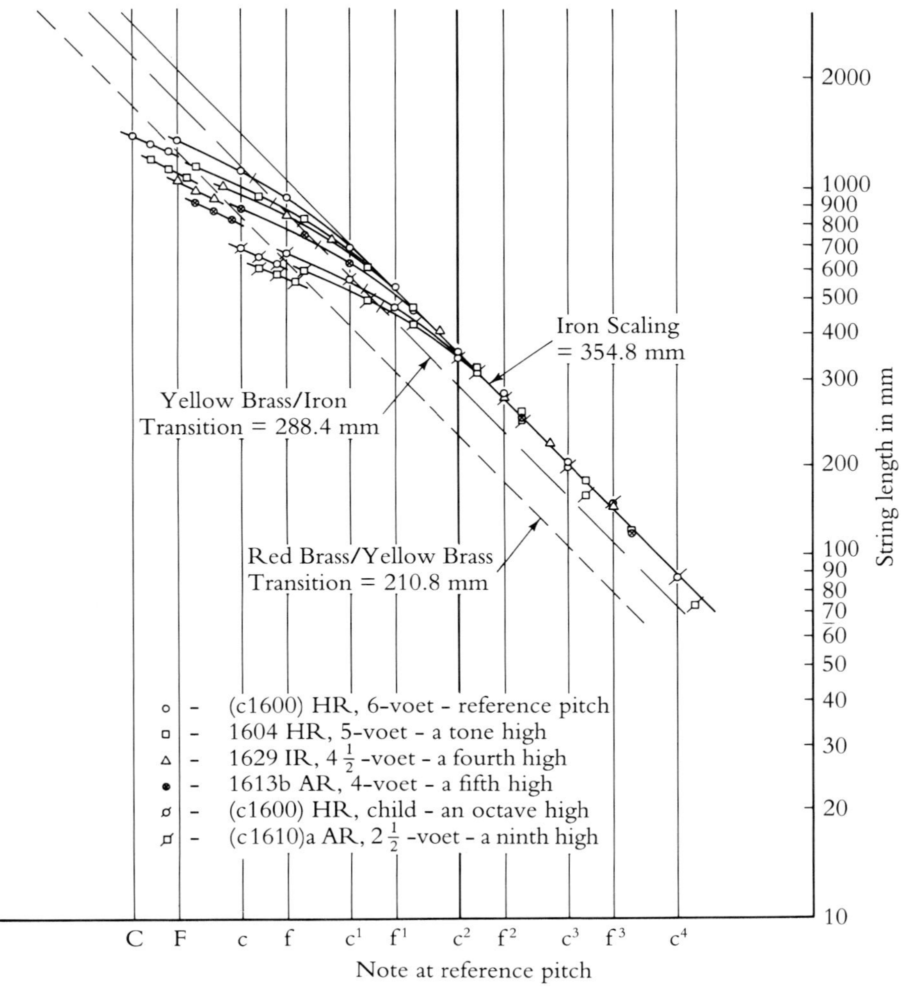


Graph 4.1 Ruckers virginal scalings.

the bass scalings of the harpsichord octave stops are all notably longer in comparison with the unisons, especially in the case of the quint harpsichord. This seems to arise because space constraints are less serious for the octave stop of a harpsichord, requiring less foreshortening in the bass. Surprisingly, for comparable instruments, the bass scalings of the virginals are slightly *longer* than those of the corresponding unison strings of the harpsichords.

The scalings of Table 4.3 are plotted in Graph 4.2 in a manner similar to that carried out for the virginals. As before, the curves are linear above the played note $c^1$, and

Table 4.3 *Ruckers harpsichord scalings in millimetres*

| Instrument | C | F | c | f | Scalings $c^1$ | $f^1$ | $c^2$ | $f^2$ | $c^3$ | Proposed pitch |
|---|---|---|---|---|---|---|---|---|---|---|
| 1638b IR | 1693 | 1644 | 1413 | 1196 | 891 | 704 | 477 | 354 | 235 | R − 4 |
| 1644a AR | 1365 | 1346 | 1125 | 940 | 683 | 528 | 358 | 270 | 177 | R |
| 1627 AR | 886 | 876 | 749 | 628 | 461 | 356 | 238 | 178 | 121 | R + 5 |
| 1638b IR | 958 | 931 | 754 | 621 | 452 | 348 | 235 | 175 | 113 | R + 5 |
| 1644a AR | 745 | 720 | 575 | 475 | 343 | 278 | 179 | 135 | 88 | R + 8 |
| 1627 AR | 543 | 529 | 419 | 339 | 237 | 175 | 117 | 89 | 60 | R + 12 |

again the points were fitted to a line with a slope of − ½ by the usual linear regression analysis. The resulting average scaling at reference pitch is $c^2$ = 355.2 ± 0.8mm.

Weighting the harpsichord and virginal results equally gives an average scaling at reference pitch of $c^2$ = 355.0 ± 2.5mm. This scaling could be thought of as the basic scaling used by the Ruckers, from which they calculated the scalings of the treble strings of all of their instruments, both virginals and harpsichords. Obviously because of workshop techniques and simple problems of geometry – for example, the curved bridges which one would expect on the small virginals at R + 8 and R + 9 are approximated by bridges consisting of two straight-line mitred segments – individual cases must be treated separately and exceptions will be found which lie outwith these error limits. Nonetheless, there is a clear pitch relationship between the various sizes of instruments which is closely tied to their scalings. This relationship is much more accurately confirmed for the extant Ruckers instruments than for the string scalings given by Douwes. This is probably because Douwes was rounding off the lengths he measured to the nearest whole or half duim, whereas I have treated the scalings measured to the nearest millimetre (see Appendix 5).

## RUCKERS STRINGING MATERIALS

Before considering the gauge numbers which Douwes gives, it is important to note that, regardless of the size of the instrument, the three notes of the short octave are always strung in red brass ('Roode'), the notes from F to c♯ are always strung with yellow brass ('Geele'), and the notes from d to $c^3$ with iron ('Witte') strings (see pp. 294 and 295). This results simply because of the fact that the

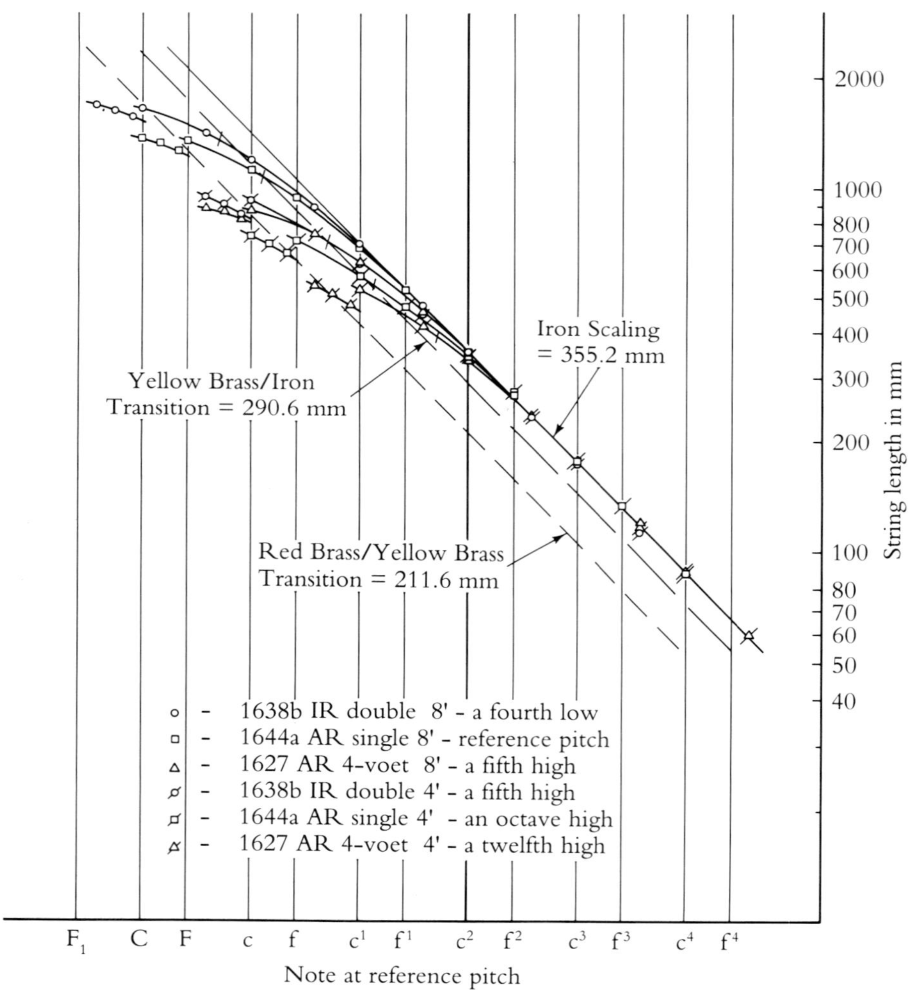


Graph 4.2 Ruckers harpsichord scalings.

same compromise foreshortening occurs in all models of instrument. The scalings at the transitions between stringing materials, corrected for the pitch of the instrument, are thus the same in all cases. On Graph 4.1, plotting the scalings of Ruckers virginals corrected for their pitch, the transitions from yellow brass to iron between the notes $c^{\sharp}$ and d have been marked with a short diagonal, and these points have also been fitted to a line with a slope of − ½ which, like the line for the iron scalings, halves with each octave rise in pitch. The resulting long-dashed line passes through pitch $c^2$ at a scaling of 288.4mm so that each point on this line can be thought of as having a scaling, referred to pitch $c^2$, of 288.4mm. Similarly the transitions between red and yellow brass all occur at approximately the same scaling given by the short-dashed line, which, referred to pitch $c^2$, has a value of 210.2mm. Thus for Ruckers virginals critically-stressed yellow brass has a scaling equivalent of 288.4mm, and red brass of 210.2mm.

Carrying out a similar procedure, assuming the same transition notes for the harpsichords (Graph 4.2), gives results which are less consistent than those for the virginal scalings. This is mainly because of the scalings with the longest and shortest values: the bass scalings of the double-manual harpsichord are slightly too much foreshortened, and the octave scalings of the quint harpsichord are longer than expected. Nonetheless, it would appear that the transition from one string material to another should occur at the same *played* notes for the harpsichords as for the virginals, and this further confirms the common scaling and bass-foreshortening compromise for all Ruckers instruments.

The question then arises as to whether Douwes' lists are specifically for virginals, or whether they apply equally well to harpsichords.

There are a number of factors which point to the lists being intended for virginals. Harpsichords were built approximately 6 voeten, 4 voeten, and 3 voeten in length, but the inclusion of the 5-voet and the 2-voet 4-duimen instruments points to virginals being intended here. Also, Douwes refers elsewhere[8] to the 6-voet instruments:

> But I should also say that such clavecimbels as are called six-voet are not fully 6 voeten long, but are approximately ⅓ of a voet shorter. Then in a similar way the 5, 4, and 3-voet also have not the full length, but are normally a bit shorter . . .

It seems clear that the confusion here arises because Douwes is using the Dutch voet with 12 duimen instead of the Flemish voet used by Ruckers with only 11.[9] Thus an instrument labelled by the Ruckers as being 6 voeten long would be somewhat shorter than 6 Dutch voeten. If Douwes were talking about harpsichords this confusion would not have arisen, and in fact the harpsichords, being somewhat longer than the equivalent virginals, are almost exactly 6 and 4 Dutch voeten in length.

Nonetheless, despite the fact that Douwes seems to be referring specifically to virginals, there seems no reason to suppose that the stringing lists he gives cannot be applied to harpsichords as well. Douwes does not mention any difference in the stringing of the centre-plucking muselar and the left-plucking spinett virginals, and indeed even the Ruckers themselves did not seem to distinguish between the two when numbering their instruments (see p. 53). Since the plucking ratios of the harpsichords are roughly the same as those of the spinett virginals, it would seem that the gauge lists are equally applicable to the harpsichords. Thus these stringing lists should apply equally well to the 6- and 4-voet harpsichords and (corrected for their pitch) their octaves, and to the corresponding virginals, if only the gauge equivalents were known.

Each of the three materials used by the Ruckers family to string their instruments was at a pitch and tension just below the point of breaking, while allowing a small margin of safety. Even if one knew the ultimate breaking strength of such materials, one would still be unable to calculate the pitch to which the instruments were intended to be tuned, as it is impossible to estimate what this safety margin was. However, the scalings of a number of late eighteenth-century French instruments by Pascal Taskin are known:[10]

Table 4.4 *Comparison of Taskin's and Ruckers' scalings*

| Material | Taskin's scalings | Ruckers' scalings | | |
|---|---|---|---|---|
| | | Virginals | Harpsichords | Average |
| iron | 364.0mm | 354.8mm | 355.2mm | 355.0mm |
| yellow brass | 292.6mm | 288.4mm | 290.6mm | 289.5mm |
| red brass | 231.4mm | 210.8mm | 211.6mm | 211.2mm |

These results indicate in all cases that Taskin's scalings were longer than Ruckers', implying a lower pitch in France. The difference may of course be due to the manufacture in eighteenth-century France of stronger

8 Douwes, *Grondig Ondersoek*, 107.

9 The duim units used by Douwes and by the Ruckers are only slightly different, but this difference is not sufficient to alter the argument here. See W. R. Thomas and J. J. K. Rhodes, 'Harpsichord strings, organ pipes and the Dutch foot', *Organ Yearbook*, III (1973), 112–21.

10 See G. Grant O'Brien, 'Some principles of 18th-century harpsichord stringing and their application', *Organ Yearbook*, XII (1981), 160–76. See also footnote 1.

wire. If the breaking strengths of some of these wires were known, physical theory, using the scalings and material density, could be used to determine the highest pitch that the strings could stand. However, until these breaking strengths are determined, nothing definite can be said about the absolute value of Ruckers' pitch standard, although Taskin's pitch standard is known to have been about 409Hz.[11] If one assumes for the moment that both Ruckers and Taskin used wire of the same breaking strength, and that they both chose scalings which gave the same safety factor between the working stress and the ultimate breaking stress of the strings, then the scalings would reflect a true difference in pitch standard. Leaving aside the value of the Ruckers red brass scaling because of the inaccurate way in which it is determined, as well as the apparent variable quality of the material itself, then compared with Taskin's pitch and scalings, Ruckers' iron and brass scalings correspond to pitches of 419Hz and 413Hz respectively. This is a pitch roughly one semitone flat to modern pitch at 440Hz.

The ratio of Ruckers iron to brass scalings is 355.0/289.5 = 1.226. Considered in terms of the corresponding musical interval, the ratio of these two scalings is somewhere between a major third (5/4 = 1.25) and a minor third (6/5 = 1.20). Considering van Blankenburg's suggestion[12] that copper (alloy) strings were sometimes used in the treble, a Ruckers 6-voet instrument strung throughout in brass would then sound between a major and a minor third lower than reference pitch. Similarly, a 5-voet instrument would sound between a tone and a semitone lower than reference pitch, and this seems to contradict van Blankenburg's claim that the 5-voet virginals were suitable for copper (alloy) stringing.[13] (On a strictly practical level, however, it should be noted that copies of the little 4½-voet virginal, tuned to modern pitch approximately a semitone higher than the pitch which Ruckers seems to have used, are ideally suited for brass stringing in the treble, although the bass strings are then much too short to sound well at the new pitch about a major third lower than that originally intended.)

## RUCKERS STRING GAUGES

Having carefully examined most of the Ruckers instruments in Europe and America, I have come to suspect that three of the instruments that I have seen, although all have been slightly altered, reflect seventeenth-century stringing practice and may be of some help in determining an approximate value for each of the gauge sizes given by Douwes (see Appendix 8). Two of the instruments have old, but not original, strings. The 1612b HR double in Amiens has eighteenth-century string-gauge numbers marked on it, and these markings are in good agreement with the string sizes found on the other two instruments. In all three cases it would appear that the person who carried out the alignment tried to copy the Ruckers stringing with the equivalent eighteenth-century gauges.

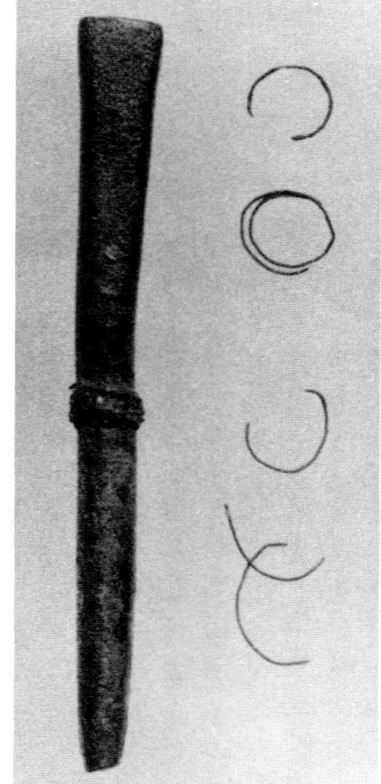

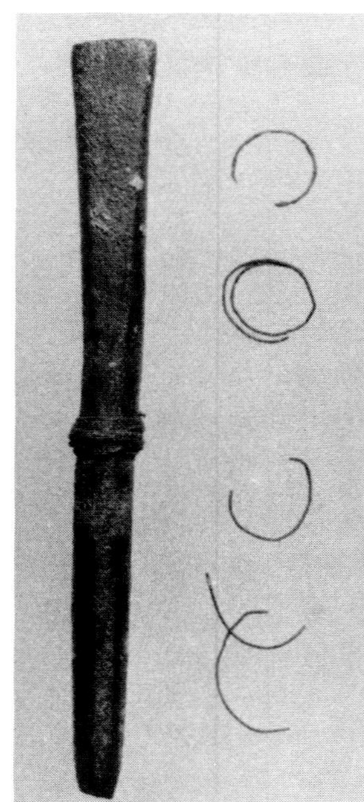

Plate 4.1 Tuning pin and wire from 1644a AR single-manual harpsichord. The wire in loose fragments and the wire rusted to the pin is of 0.31mm in diameter.
Copyright, A.C.L., Brussels.

The first instrument found which seems to represent seventeenth-century stringing practice is the 1644a AR single-manual harpsichord in the Vleeshuis Museum, Antwerp. This harpsichord was extended by two notes in both the treble and bass to widen its compass to C to $c^3$ chromatic, and the 4′ register was replaced by an 8′ one. But other than this very little has been done to it and it retains many original features. However, all that remains of the strings are a few loops of wire on the tuning pins. Most, but not all, are relatively recent and either 0.25mm or 0.33mm in diameter, and used without discretion throughout the entire compass. But the present short-string $f^2$ tuning pin, or the original $g^2$ tuning pin, has about ten coils of very old wire rusted to it – see Plate 4.1.

11 Hermann Helmholtz, *On the Sensations of Tone* (London, 1855; facs., New York, 1954), 495, gives the frequency measured by Lissajous of a 1783 tuning fork of Pascal Taskin as 409Hz.

12 Quirinus van Blankenburg, *Elementa Musica* (The Hague, 1739; facs., Amsterdam, 1972), 175; see Appendix 10.

13 The results given here also contradict the pitch assignments of Thomas and Rhodes, 'Harpsichord strings'.

The approximate diameter of this wire can be measured and it was found to be 0.31mm. Wrapped over the coils rusted to the tuning pin is more recent wire of diameter 0.305mm, apparently copying the string-gauge size of the earlier wire with the closest available equivalent. As will be shown, it seems likely that the wire rusted to the tuning pin is the original seventeenth-century wire, and probably the only bit of original wire left on any Ruckers instrument.

Moreover, the lowest note was strung with brass wire of diameter 0.63mm, and the tongue axles in some of the broken jacks were also of brass wire of diameter 0.64mm. It seems probable then that the 0.305mm wire wound over the rusted wire on the tuning pin, and the 0.63mm wire in the bass were an attempt to copy the original sizes of 0.31 and 0.64mm respectively. If these correspond to gauge 10 and to gauge 1, the smallest and largest gauges Douwes calls for on 6-voet clavecimbels, then the intermediate sizes can be calculated by assuming a logarithmic relationship between successive gauge numbers.[14] The ratio between the successive diameters is then

$$r_g = \left(\frac{0.64}{0.31}\right)^{\frac{1}{9}} = 1.084$$

and the gauges larger than gauge 1 can be obtained by successively multiplying 0.64mm by this factor. The results of this can be seen in Table 4.6, which gives the sizes of the intermediate gauges. Wires of some of these intermediate sizes were found to exist on the instrument, and some gauge transitions occurred at the same notes as those given in Douwes' lists for 6-voet clavecimbels. But there were two few old strings on the instrument to give much confidence in the string gauges calculated in this way.

The 1618b IR double-manual harpsichord in Schloss Cappenberg, Westphalia, also shows evidence of having been restrung at the time of a petit ravalement with the nearest available string gauges to those of the original stringing. This harpsichord originally had the usual unaligned keyboards, similar to those on the 1638b IR. The keyboards have now been aligned and the treble compass extended to $d^3$, giving a compass of $G_1/B_1$ to $d^3$. Other than this the instrument has been very little altered and it also retains many of its original jacks, dampers, keyboard and balance-rail cloths, etc. Many more of the strings have survived than on the 1644a AR instrument. Hence the hitchpin loops as well as the tuning-pin coils could be examined, and the workmanship of these compared, so that some obviously recent strings could be identified.

The problem associated with this instrument is that, being a double-manual harpsichord, it is not included in the gauge lists given by Douwes. However, because the upper part of the compass of the upper manual has the same compass, pitch and scalings, it seems most probable that the gauges used in the treble were the same as those used in the 6-voet virginal and harpsichord. In the bass one might then expect the use of gauges perhaps one or two heavier than in the 6-voet instrument, the additional length of the double-manual instrument compensating for the lower pitch. With this in mind, gauge numbers were assigned to the measured values of the string diameters, and averages were calculated for each gauge.[15] Assuming that these average diameters bear a logarithmic relationship to the gauge number as before, the logarithm of each of the above diameters was taken and the results fitted by the usual regression analysis to a linear equation (a first-order polynomial), weighting each diameter according to the number of strings from which the average diameter was calculated. The result of this calculation gives the gauge sizes listed in Table 4.5,

Table 4.5 *Ruckers string gauges based on the extant strings on the 1618b IR double-manual harpsichord, and the 1644a AR single-manual harpsichord*

| | 1618b IR | 1644a AR |
|---|---|---|
| gauge 00 | 0.75mm | – |
| gauge 0 | 0.69mm | – |
| gauge 1 | 0.63mm | 0.640mm |
| gauge 2 | 0.59mm | 0.590mm |
| gauge 3 | 0.54mm | 0.545mm |
| gauge 4 | 0.50mm | 0.503mm |
| gauge 5 | 0.46mm | 0.464mm |
| gauge 6 | 0.42mm | 0.428mm |
| gauge 7 | 0.39mm | 0.395mm |
| gauge 8 | 0.36mm | 0.364mm |
| gauge 9 | 0.33mm | 0.336mm |
| gauge 10 | 0.31mm | 0.310mm |
| gauge 11 | 0.28mm | – |
| gauge 12 | 0.26mm | – |
| gauge ratio $r_g$ | 1.084 | 1.084 |
| drawing ratio $r_d = r_g^2$ | 1.175 | 1.175 |

[14] The reason for the logarithmic nature of these results has been pointed out by W. R. Thomas and J. J. K. Rhodes, 'Harpsichords and the art of wire-drawing', *Organ Yearbook*, X (1979), 126–39. At each stage of drawing the ratio of the length of the wire before and after drawing was kept constant. Thus the ratio of the cross-sectional area before and after drawing, the drawing ratio $r_d$, is also a constant. The gauge ratio $r_g$, the ratio of successive gauges, is thus related to $r_d$ by the simple equation:

$$r_d = r_g^2$$

[15] Details of these calculations are found in O'Brien, 'The stringing and pitches'.

which have been extrapolated to both heavier and lighter diameters than those given by the measurements themselves.

These are probably the only two instruments with extant strings on which any evidence of Ruckers stringing practice is likely to be found, since there are no other Ruckers instruments known to me which have strings of any great age.[16] But the gauge markings on the 1612b HR double in Amiens tend to confirm the string sizes found on these two instruments.[17] This double was given a very conservative alignment and petit ravalement in France in 1730. The keyboards were aligned and the compass extended from fifty to fifty-three notes by adding a split $B_1/E^\flat$ key and the top two notes $c^{\sharp 3}$ and $d^3$. The disposition was left with only $1 \times 8'$, $1 \times 4'$ on each manual and no manual coupler. The gauge numbers were marked on the bridges and these are shown in Table 4.6 along with their eighteenth-century French equivalents.[18]

Comparing the string diameters on the 1618b IR and the 1612b HR doubles and the 1644a AR single in Table 4.6 gives fairly close agreement. It would indeed appear that all three instruments were strung at some later period using strings which came from different gauge systems, but which attempted to copy the original Flemish stringing found on the instruments before they were altered.

The gauge ratio of the strings found on both the 1618b

[16] The 1581 HR virginal may have come to the Metropolitan Museum, New York with at least some sixteenth- or seventeenth-century strings, but all traces of these were lost in a recent restoration. Plates of the soundboard of the instrument taken before the restoration are tantalizing and show that the three notes of the short octave were strung quite heavily with two strings twisted around one another. The use, say, of twisted yellow brass strings instead of the softer red brass would give strings which were both flexible enough to produce accurately-tuned partials, and massive enough to radiate sufficient sound energy for these lowest bass notes. The use of twisted strings for the lowest basses therefore makes good acoustical sense, and is a valid alternative method of stringing a clavecimbel's lowest notes. My thanks are due to Stewart Pollens, of the Metropolitan Museum, for his patient help in pursuing this matter.

[17] Hubert Bédard, 'Harpsichord of 1644 by Andreas Ruckers: on putting it in playing condition', *Colloquium: Ruckers Klavecimbels en Copieën* (Antwerp, 1977), 109–18.

[18] See O'Brien, 'Some principles'.

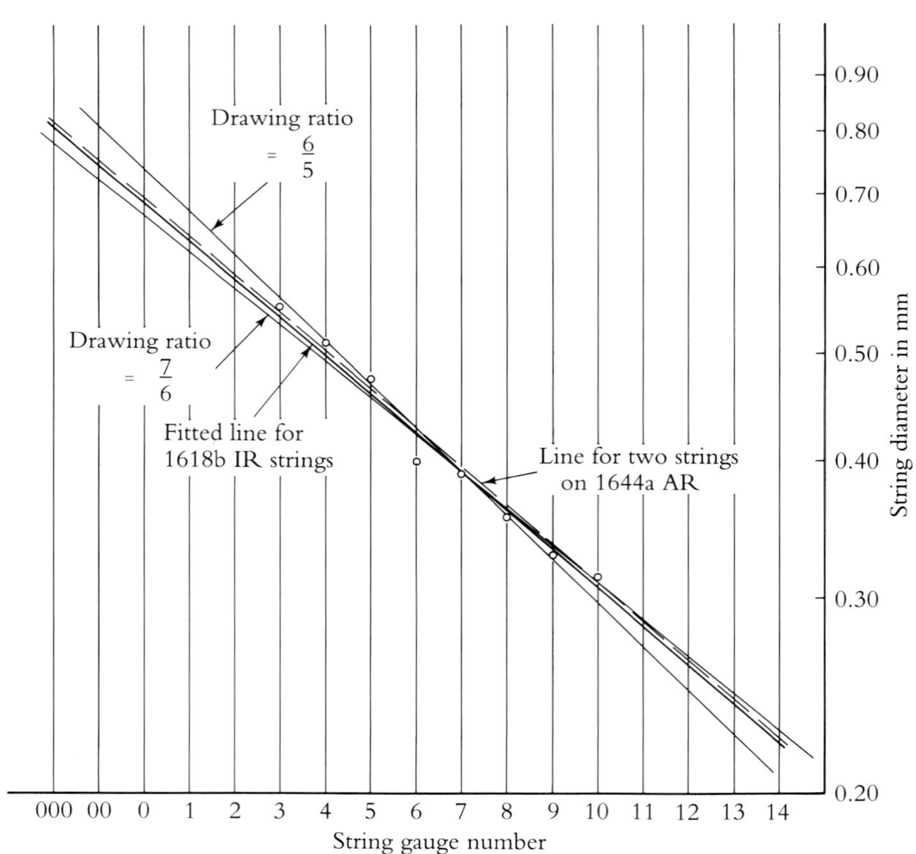


Graph 4.3 Ruckers string-gauge diameters.

Table 4.6 *Evidence for original stringing on three Ruckers harpsichords*

| Note | Douwes gauge | Material | 1618b IR old strings: Proposed gauge | 1618b IR old strings: Fitted diameter | 1612b HR French gauges: Gauge number | 1612b HR French gauges: Gauge diameter | 1644a AR old strings: Proposed gauge | 1644a AR old strings: Fitted diameter | Note |
|---|---|---|---|---|---|---|---|---|---|
| $G_1$ | --- | | 0 | 0.69 | | | | | $G_1$ |
| $A_1$ | --- | | 1 | 0.63 | *0* | 0.61 | | | $A_1$ |
| $B_1$ | --- | | | | | | | | $B_1$ |
| C | 1 | | | | | | 1 | 0.64 | C |
| D | 2 | | 2 | 0.59 | | | 2 | 0.59 | D |
| E | 2 | brass | | | *1?* | 0.54 | | | E |
| F | 3 | | | | | | | | F |
| $F^\sharp$ | --- | | | | | | 3 | 0.55 | $F^\sharp$ |
| G | 3 | | 3 | 0.54 | *2?* | 0.48 | | | G |
| $G^\sharp$ | --- | | | | | | | | $G^\sharp$ |
| A | 4 | | | | | | 4 | 0.50 | A |
| $B^\flat$ | 4 | | | | | | | | $B^\flat$ |
| B | | | | | | | | | B |
| c | 5 | | 4 | 0.50 | *2?* | 0.48 | 5 | 0.46 | c |
| $c^\sharp$ | | | | | | | | | $c^\sharp$ |
| d | | | | | | | | | d |
| $e^\flat$ | | | | | | | | | $e^\flat$ |
| e | 6 | | 5 | 0.46 | | | 6 | 0.43 | e |
| f | | | | | | | | | f |
| $f^\sharp$ | | | | | | | | | $f^\sharp$ |
| g | | | | | *3?* | 0.43 | | | g |
| $g^\sharp$ | | | 6 | 0.42 | | | | | $g^\sharp$ |
| a | | | | | | | | | a |
| $b^\flat$ | | | | | | | | | $b^\flat$ |
| b | 7 | | | | | | 7 | 0.40 | b |
| $c^1$ | | | | | | | | | $c^1$ |
| $c^{\sharp 1}$ | | | 7 | 0.39 | | | | | $c^{\sharp 1}$ |
| $d^1$ | | | | | *4* | 0.38 | | | $d^1$ |
| $e^{\flat 1}$ | | | | | | | | | $e^{\flat 1}$ |
| $e^1$ | | | | | | | | | $e^1$ |
| $f^1$ | | | | | | | | | $f^1$ |
| $f^{\sharp 1}$ | 8 | | | | | | 8 | 0.36 | $f^{\sharp 1}$ |
| $g^1$ | | iron | 8 | 0.36 | | | | | $g^1$ |
| $g^{\sharp 1}$ | | | | | | | | | $g^{\sharp 1}$ |
| $a^1$ | | | | | *5* | 0.34 | | | $a^1$ |
| $b^{\flat 1}$ | | | | | | | | | $b^{\flat 1}$ |
| $b^1$ | | | | | | | | | $b^1$ |
| $c^2$ | | | | | | | | | $c^2$ |
| $c^{\sharp 2}$ | 9 | | 9 | 0.33 | | | 9 | 0.34 | $c^{\sharp 2}$ |
| $d^2$ | | | | | | | | | $d^2$ |
| $e^{\flat 2}$ | | | | | | | | | $e^{\flat 2}$ |
| $e^2$ | | | | | *6* | 0.30 | | | $e^2$ |
| $f^2$ | | | | | | | | | $f^2$ |
| $f^{\sharp 2}$ | | | | | | | | | $f^{\sharp 2}$ |
| $g^2$ | | | | | | | | | $g^2$ |
| $g^{\sharp 2}$ | | | | | | | | | $g^{\sharp 2}$ |
| $a^2$ | 10 | | | | | | | | $a^2$ |
| $b^{\flat 2}$ | | | 10 | 0.31 | | | 10 | 0.31 | $b^{\flat 2}$ |
| $b^2$ | | | | | 7 | 0.27 | | | $b^2$ |
| $c^3$ | | | | | | | | | $c^3$ |
| $c^{\sharp 3}$ | --- | | | | | | | | $c^{\sharp 3}$ |
| $d^3$ | --- | | | | | | | | $d^3$ |

IR Cappenberg and the 1644a AR Vleeshuis harpsichords is $r_g = 1.084$. This gives the drawing ratio $r_d = r_g^2 = 1.175$. This is very close to the ratio 7/6 = 1.167, and suggests that the proportion of the length of the wire after drawing to the length before drawing was given by this simple ratio. It is clear that this is the drawing ratio of the gauge system which replaced the Ruckers system and not of the original Ruckers wire. However, to the extent that the gauge transitions occur at roughly the points for the Douwes lists, this is probably also near the gauge ratio for the Ruckers wire.

It is extremely important to point out that the string diameters given by the list above are much heavier than any eighteenth-century gauge system. For an eighteenth-century English or French harpsichord, strings for the note $c^3$ would typically be 0.21mm in diameter, whereas for a Ruckers 6-voet clavecimbel they would be about 0.31mm. Assuming they sounded at the same pitch for the sake of argument, this implies a tension approximately 2.3 times higher in the seventeenth-century instrument. This increased tension would result in a large increase in the volume of sound produced, which may explain why many paintings of the time show harpsichords played with their lids closed.

The increased tension puts a greater strain on the case of the instrument, which is partly offset by the fact that the seventeenth-century harpsichords had only one set of 8′ strings whereas the later ones had two sets. However, I feel it necessary to stress that the data on which the calculated diameters are based is open to considerable question. Before using these diameters to string an historical instrument, it must be completely clear that the instrument is able to stand the strain imposed upon it, and in no case would I recommend that any Ruckers or Flemish instrument be strung with these gauges if it has been altered to the disposition with two 8′ sets of strings from its original disposition of 1 × 8′ and 1 × 4′, as this could result in an excessive overall tension which might well lead to permanent damage to the instrument.

The proverb below is one of many, ten of them dealing with musical instruments, inscribed on the walls and ceilings of the New Lodge at the Percy estate in Leckingfield, and in the British Museum (MS Royal 18 D ii). See Francis M. C. Cooper, 'The Leckingfield proverbs', *Musical Times*, CXII (1972), 547–50.

A slack strynge in a virgynall soundeth not aright
It dothe abyde no wrastynge it is so louse and light
The sounde borde crasede forsith the instrumente
Throw mysgovernannce to make notis which was
not his intent.

Leckingfield Proverb, *c.* 1518–23

CHAPTER FIVE

# The construction of virginals

Except for the wrestplank, the structural part of all Ruckers instruments is of poplar (*Populus*, probably *Populus canescens* or *Populus nigra*). This wood is used for the baseboard, case sides and internal framing as well as for the lid, lid flap, front flap, keys, keyblocks and jackrail. Although technically a hardwood, poplar is in fact a soft open-textured wood, very susceptible to indentation and scratching. It is very light and extremely tough. The wood used in Ruckers instruments has sometimes mistakenly been identified as lime (*Tilia vulgaris*), which is, however, much heavier and denser and more close-grained than poplar, although similar in that both lack any strong distinction between the spring- and summer-growth woods. The timber used in Ruckers instruments often has streaks of grey and a reddish or reddish-brown tinge suggesting that the species involved is *Populus canescens*, which has a characteristic reddish-brown heartwood.

All joins in the case, lid, baseboard and action are secured with hot glue. Hot glue consists mostly of gelatin, and is made from animal bones, skins and intestines. The glue is dissolved in water and usually kept hot in a water bath. When hot the glue is watery and runny, but at room temperature it becomes rubbery and jelly-like. Any join made with hot glue must be made before the glue cools down to its jelly consistency, otherwise a great deal of the strength of the glue-joint is lost. This means that the surfaces to be glued should be pre-heated in order that, after application to the wood, the glue remain liquid while the joint is quickly clamped or secured. The short working time before the initial 'set' of the glue is strongly reflected in the methods used by the Ruckers in the construction of their instruments. In particular, much use is made of wooden pegs in securing the joint between two parts. The thin film of glue between the sides of the peg and the hole it is driven into cools and sets within a few seconds, after which the peg can be neither driven further into its hole nor extracted from it. The pegged joint becomes completely solid and without any further need of clamping. Normally, once the joint is pegged, any initial clamping used can be removed and the next joint clamped and pegged. Clearly, gluing two surfaces or joins using pegs is not always necessary or possible, and other methods of gluing surfaces together will be discussed as they arise.

All parts of the Ruckers instruments were made by hand and this is reflected in their construction, dimensions and finish. The wood was hand sawn, joints and surfaces were planed by hand and the individual parts were assembled, glued and finished by hand. This results in a variability in case dimensions and wood thicknesses, especially in such non-acoustical parts of the instrument as the case, internal framing, and lid. It also means that many of the internal invisible surfaces are left with saw marks not planed away, large knots, wavy grain with chip marks, corners not square, etc. Although Ruckers workmanship has been decried by many, it must in deference also be pointed out that the actual joinery is tight and sound, and the skill and craftsmanship exhibited in the making of the soundboard, bridges and registers is unsurpassed. The disparity in the attention paid to different parts of the instrument can only be explained by the Ruckers' intuitive or learned knowledge of which parts of the instruments were important to the sound and action and which not, and therefore of where careful attention and precision were necessary. It is clearly a question of the attitude of the builders and not of their inherent skill. They were primarily interested in the

Plate 5.1 The 1640a IR 5-voet muselar virginal gives a good idea of the original appearance of a Ruckers virginal. Copyright, Haags Gemeentemuseum, The Hague.

sound and action of their instruments and not in their static non-resonant parts.

In studying the Ruckers instruments it must be remembered that they were built without the aid of drawings or stable templates. This, coupled with the dimensional variability resulting from the handwork itself, is also reflected in the construction and marking out of the instruments. Generally this means that, as construction progressed, each new part was marked out from those already made. Any variability and lack of standardization was compensated for by matching parts to be made to those already existing. One needs then only to get the order of construction right.

Therefore in studying what follows on the construction of Ruckers virginals and harpsichords one must try as much as possible to adopt a seventeenth-century frame of mind. One must remember that these instruments were made entirely by hand, without a technical drawing as a standard reference, and using hot glue. Within this framework, which almost certainly did not seem limiting to them, the Ruckers worked quickly and efficiently and turned out a surprisingly large number of some of the most beautiful-sounding instruments in the history of keyboard-instrument making.

## VIRGINAL BASEBOARDS

One of the important characteristics of the Flemish school of harpsichord and virginal building is that the edge of the baseboard extends right to the edge of the instrument with the case sides resting on it, rather than overlapping it as is usual with instruments built in the Italian tradition. Naturally, this reflects a difference between the two traditions in the order and way in which the parts of the instrument were assembled.

Like the rest of the case, the baseboard is made of poplar. The grain of the wood runs lengthwise so that the maximum strength is achieved in the direction of the string tension. At the same time the baseboard has good dimensional stability parallel to the strings, since the humidity coefficient of expansion is small in the direction of the grain of the wood.

The thickness of the baseboard varies considerably from about 11mm to 14mm in different instruments, but is usually near the nominal half a small duim (12.7mm). After planing, the inside surface of the baseboard was probably left completely untreated. It is possible, however, that the outer lower surface was sized with glue or shellac, as is shown by the characteristic brown discoloration normally found on the lower baseboard surface. The upper interior surface of the baseboard is marked out with double scribed lines to indicate the positions of the case sides, the keywell and keywell braces, the nameboard liner and the lower keywell moulding.

The positions of these lines on the baseboard were punched with a sharp awl at several places along the lines. Once the lines were scribed, the baseboard could be used as a plan and base onto which the instrument could be built. Holes were drilled between the lines, and, as the case sides and braces were fitted to the scribed plan, wooden pegs inserted into these and matching holes along the lower edge of the case side-pieces held the framework temporarily in position as it was being assembled on the baseboard. After the case was assembled and the soundboard glued in position, the baseboard was fixed permanently in position and its edges planed flush with the case sides.

The baseboard was fixed to the case of the instrument by means of wooden pegs and was only lightly glued in place. The pegs used for fixing the case sides to the baseboard have pointed ends, are about 2 duimen (52mm) in length and 5mm across, and seem originally to have been made either square and tapered or rather irregular in section. But in either case, being of soft poplar, they assume the rounded shape of the hole after they are driven into position. The pegs were usually, but not always, glued in place and sometimes the glue near the peg holes has spread, attaching the baseboard even more strongly to the case sides and framing.

Except in the child virginals which fit inside the case of the larger mother virginals, the keywell flap was attached to the front edge of the baseboard by means of wire hinges. The number, position and nature of these hinges will be discussed later. Also attached to the baseboard at the position of the front edge of the keyframe are two blocks of wood with chamfered edges – the keyboard hold-down blocks. Turnbuttons fixed to these blocks are used to hold the keyframe firmly in position. The top surface of the baseboard in the keywell including these blocks was painted black to render this area unobtrusive under the keys.

## VIRGINAL OUTER CASE AND FRAMING

An analysis of the length of the poplar case of the various sizes of Ruckers virginal, coupled with a knowledge that the foot unit used in Antwerp at the time of the Ruckers contained eleven units and not twelve, leads almost immediately to a solution of the way in which the members of the Ruckers family specified their instruments (see Chapter 3). But knowing the number of subdivisions in the voet, and knowing that the virginals were labelled according to their length in voeten also enables one to calculate the length of the duim and voet in use in the Ruckers workshop. In Appendix 1, I have taken the length in millimetres of each extant unaltered virginal and divided this by the nominal length in duimen. For the 6-voet virginals, for example, this means that the length in millimetres is divided by 66 duimen. A few of the 6-voet instruments have lengths which are not exactly 6 voeten: the 1598 HR and 1617 AR spinett virginals are 2 duimen shorter, and the mother virginals are one to three duimen longer than 6 voeten. However, averaging over all of these instruments including those shorter than 6 voeten, and correcting the length where it is obviously greater or less than the nominal value as above, one gets a value for the subdivision of the Antwerp voet of 25.880mm (see Appendix 1, p. 284). This I have called the large duim.

Dividing the width of the various sizes of virginal by this value gives measurements which are integral or half-integral multiples of this large duim (see Table 5.1).

It would seem equally reasonable to expect that the case heights, the frame dimensions and the spacings of the various parts of the instruments should also be integral or half-integral multiples of the same duim unit. However, all these small distances turn out to be slightly less than this.

The slight discrepancy might be explained by assuming that the case planks came to the workshops in dimensions which were exact multiples of the 25.88mm duim, and were then reduced in width by planing in the process of finishing. However, against this is the observation that many of the scribed lines on the baseboards of Ruckers instruments are also separated by distances which are slightly less than integral multiples of this dimension. Since it is unlikely that awkward units of length would be used for what are otherwise highly arbitrary distances, I concluded that there were two standards of length in use in the Ruckers workshop at the same time.

The large duim equal to 25.88mm was used to measure large distances greater than one voet such as case lengths and widths; the other, the short duim equal to 25.48mm, I have calculated from small measurements of less than one voet. In all some seventy-five measurements of case heights, the width of the wrestplank, framing dimensions, soundbar spacings, spacings of scribed lines on baseboards and other dimensions of about or less than 1 voet were averaged to arrive at the value of the small duim. Although it might seem inconvenient and confus-

Table 5.1 – *Lengths and widths of Ruckers virginals expressed in duimen*

| | | Length | | Width | |
|---|---|---|---|---|---|
| Instrument | Type | mm | duimen | mm | duimen |
| 1620d AR | 6-voet | 1708 | 66.00 = 66 | 492 | 19.01 = 19 |
| 1604 HR | 5-voet | 1424 | 55.02 = 55 | 479 | 18.51 = 18½ |
| 1629 IR | 4½-voet | 1282 | 49.54 = 49½ | 478[a] | 18.47 = 18½ |
| 1613b AR | 4-voet | 1138 | 43.97 = 44 | 441 | 17.04 = 17 |
| (1626) AR | child | 801 | 30.95 = 31 | 300 | 11.59 = 11½ |

[a] Only one other 4½-voet virginal exists (1610b AR). It is 452mm or about 17½ duimen wide. The difference in the dimensions of these two virginals almost certainly arises because the 1629 IR is a spinett virginal, whereas the 1610b AR is a muselar virginal.

ing to use two different standards of length in the same workshop, I see no other way of resolving the discrepancy in the measurement of long and short distances. It was obviously not a problem to the Ruckers: the same situation obtained in all of their workshops over a time span of more than a hundred years. They must have had both short and long measuring sticks, the two not being calibrated to quite the same standard.

In units of the 25.48mm small duim the height of the case sides (not including the thickness of the baseboard) are close to:

| | | |
|---|---|---|
| mother virginals | 10 duimen | 255mm |
| 6-voet virginals | 9 duimen | 229mm |
| 5-voet virginals | 8 duimen | 204mm |
| 4½-voet virginals | 7½ duimen | 191mm |
| 4-voet virginals | 7 duimen | 178mm |
| child virginals | 5 duimen | 127mm |

Other measurements which are integral multiples of the small duim will be discussed as they arise.

It is important to notice that the nameboard and faceboard of the mother, the 6-voet, and the 5-voet virginals are always about ½ duim (about 13mm) lower than the outer case sides. But they are the full height in the smaller 4½-voet, 4-voet, and child virginals. Also, being hand finished, the thickness of the case sides, the front flap, and lid varies from about 15mm to 13mm, or sometimes even less for the small sizes of virginal. The nameboard and faceboard are always somewhat thinner than the case sides – about 11–12.5mm.

The top edge of the case sides is decorated with a characteristic moulding profile. The depth of this moulding varies for each member of the Ruckers family, and according to the date of the instrument. But the basic profile is always the same; it was one of the features of Ruckers instruments copied by builders in other countries in the late seventeenth and eighteenth centuries. The smaller virginals with their thinner case sides usually have the profile standing on edge, otherwise it would leave only an extremely narrow ledge of wood along the top of the side. The virginal nameboard and faceboard have a double profile with the two mouldings placed back to back (see Fig. 5.1). The lower angled surface of the added moulding is sometimes rounded in the early instruments of Hans Ruckers.

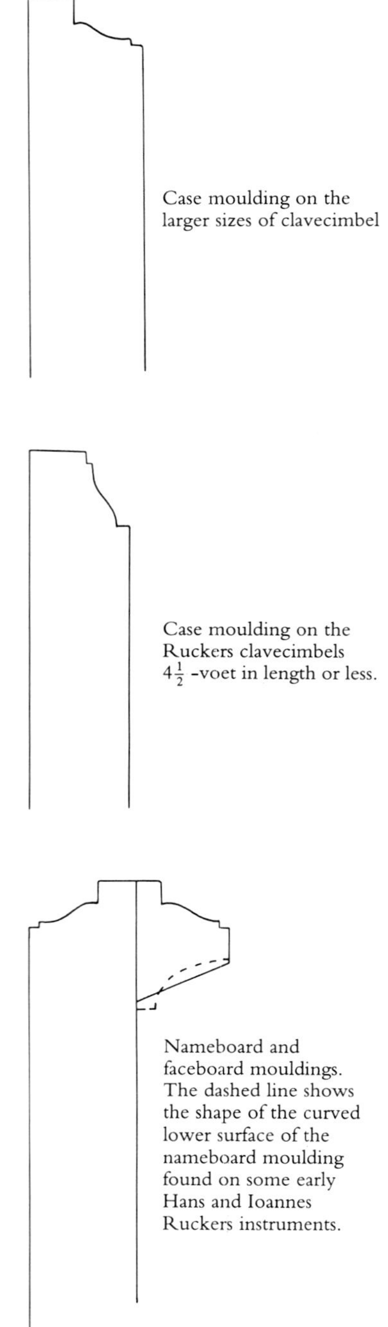


Fig. 5.1 Case mouldings and nameboard/faceboard mouldings on Ruckers clavecimbels. Scale 1:1.

The basic strength and rigidity of a virginal are almost entirely provided by the baseboard, case sides and soundboard liners. In addition, the sides of the keywell, reduced in height inside the virginal, extend to and are let into the spine of the instrument. The nameboard liner extends to the left-hand side of the instrument and is let into the left-hand soundboard liner, which also helps to provide some rigidity. Otherwise the case sides and liners support the string tension unaided by any other interior bracing.

The corner joints in the case and the keywell/faceboard joints of the Ruckers virginals are simple 45° mitred joints without dovetails or complicated joins. The faceboard is let into the sides of the ends of the case with simple mortices. In the smaller sizes of virginal where the case sides and faceboard are the same height, the top part of the faceboard is mitred into the case ends so that the moulding at the top of the case matches the moulding of the faceboard and runs continuously around the inside of the instrument with a 45° mitre at each corner. All case, faceboard/case and faceboard/keywell joins are pegged with small (about 3mm in diameter) wooden pegs for stability during gluing and to increase the ultimate strength of the joint.

Except for the nameboard liner, the soundboard liners onto which the soundboard is glued are usually about 2 small duimen (about 51mm) high and about 15–20mm in width. In all sizes of virginal (and harpsichord) the upper surface of the liners is placed 2 small duimen (about 51mm) below the top of the case, and the lower outer edge of the liner is characteristically chamfered off. The nameboard liner behind the nameboard is about 5 small duimen (127mm) narrower than the total case height: there is a space about 3 duimen below it to allow access for the keyboard plus the 2 duimen above it to the top of the case sides. The left extension of the nameboard liner is usually about the same height as the other liners in the instrument. This extension supports or provides part of the framing of a little toolbox in the left-hand corner of the instrument. Also, in muselar virginals, a block glued to the side of the nameboard liner extension braces the soundboard under the left-hand jackrail support.

The liners are glued and secured to the case sides and to one another with wooden pegs. The ends of the keywell braces are let into the spine and also secured with wooden pegs. The rear vertical edges of the higher front part of the keywell braces are let into the nameboard liner, and nails are driven into the back of the latter to fix it in position.

The nameboard itself is not a structural part of a Ruckers virginal but is removable. It slides in and out of two slots in the keywell braces just in front of the nameboard liner. The added moulding at the top of the keywell braces is mitred to match that of the nameboard. In the larger sizes of Ruckers virginals the nameboard must be taken out before the keyboard can be removed. Some non-Ruckers Flemish virginals, however, have a fixed nameboard which does not extend down to the level of the top of the keys, but which has instead a removable moulded batten just over the keys, allowing them to be extracted. The child and 2½-voet Ruckers virginals are exceptional as regards the construction of the nameboard. In the child virginals the nameboard does not exist as such, since the keys project from the case, and the front of the case is one continuous straight board. So all Ruckers child virginals have a paper-decorated removable batten above the keys which is held in place with two small wooden pegs. Also the keyframe is not removable in child virginals, since the balance rail is fixed to the baseboard. Therefore the keys may be removed only one at a time after removing the papered batten from above the keys. In the 2½-voet virginals (see Appendix 3) a removable keyframe, held in position with turnbuckles on the keyboard hold-down blocks, is provided. The keyframe and keyboard are removed only after lifting out a batten (like the namebatten in harpsichords) which fits into appropriate slots in the keyblocks.

## VIRGINAL WRESTPLANKS AND HITCHPIN RAILS

The wrestplank is made of oak (*Quercus, spp.*) rather than the softer and weaker poplar of the rest of the instrument. In the larger virginals of the spinett type the wrestplank consists simply of a long piece of oak about 2½ by 1¼ small duimen (about 64mm by 32mm) running diagonally across the rear left of the instrument roughly parallel to the direction of the bridge. This is lap-jointed to a short extension for the bass tuning pins running parallel to the right side of the case, and ending at the back of the faceboard. With the smaller 4-voet and 4½-voet spinett virginals and all sizes of muselar virginals (not including the 4-voet, child, and 2½-voet virginals, which are only of the spinett type) the wrestplank is composed of three sections jointed together in such a way that its shape closely follows that of the bridge. This produces a lap joint in the wrestplank which is well away from the side of the case and about half-way from the front to the spine of the instrument. The joint is supported by a poplar post nailed at its top end to the lap joint itself and with its other end standing on the baseboard. The support post is used to withstand any downward thrust on the tuning pins when they are placed in position and during tuning. The wrestplank in the child and 2½-voet virginals consists solely of a single piece of oak parallel to and attached to the right-hand side of the case.

In all models the wrestplank is let into the liners in such a way that its sections extend right out to the case sides. The sections are glued and pegged to both case sides and liners, thus anchoring the plank firmly to withstand the tension of the strings. The soundboard is then glued to the top surface of the wrestplank as well as to the liners. In most sizes of muselar virginal, because the bass end of the right-hand bridge would extend over the upper surface of the bass section of wrestplank, the wrestplank is cut away at the soundboard level to allow the bridge to vibrate freely there. For the same reason, the wrestplank is cut away near the treble end of the bridge in the spinett virginals.

The tuning pins are placed alternately in two rows along the length of the wrestplank. The tuning-pin diameter is chosen in proportion to the length of the string – smaller pins being used for the shorter, higher-pitched strings to provide greater ease and accuracy of tuning. Thus, normally, different-sized tuning pins are used in the treble and bass of any one instrument and the smaller, higher-pitched virginals have smaller tuning pins than the larger instruments. Typically the bass tuning pins in a 6-voet virginal are about 4.1mm in diameter and the treble pins about 3.4mm, with the change in diameter occurring somewhere between $c^1$ and $a^1$. By comparison, the treble tuning pins in the smallest child virginals are about 3.0mm or slightly less.

The tuning pins themselves are round pieces of wire rod flattened slightly (probably cold) for the tuning hammer at one end, and slightly tapered over a length of about 10–15mm at the other. Unlike the tapered tuning pins and holes in a viol, lute or violin, the holes drilled in the wrestplank have parallel sides and are somewhat smaller than the untapered shank of the tuning pin. By bruising and slightly compressing the wrestplank wood, the tuning pin itself forms its own tapered hole. Because the pin gradually moves down into its tapered hole with wear, and because it is initially placed only about 12mm deep in the hole, it never works loose even after centuries of repeated tunings.

The tuning-pin locations in a number of virginals are lettered in ink with the note name of each pin. Although evidence of this has disappeared through wear or abrasion in most virginals, it was probably an original feature of all Ruckers instruments.

The spinett virginals have a wide piece of poplar about 1 small duim (about 25.5mm) thick and several duimen wide running diagonally across the rear left-hand corner of the instrument parallel to the register. This is let into the liners and used both as a hitchpin rail for the strings and to support the non-sounding bridge on this side.

In the muselar virginals, where the left-hand bridge is the main sounding bridge, the spine and left-hand soundboard liners act as the hitchpin rail. The lowest bass strings in the muselar virginals are raised slightly at the hitchpin end on a block of wood glued to the soundboard and left-hand case side. Thus the downward pressure exerted by the heavy bass strings, which are under approximately twice the tension of the treble strings, is greatly reduced. Despite this the downward string pressure has caused the soundboard and bridge in a number of Ruckers muselar virginals to sink to such an extent that the sounding portion of some of the strings touches the soundboard or the register leather.

### VIRGINAL LID AND KEYWELL FLAP

Except for the child, all models of Ruckers virginal have a lid and a keywell flap. The lid is hinged along the spine, and the keywell flap is hinged to the front edge of the baseboard. Although axle hinges were sometimes used for harpsichord lids, both the lid and keywell flaps on virginals seem invariably to have had only wire hinges. The keywell flap is thus not removable, and gets in the way of the player's knees unless a standing or high sitting position is adopted.

The wire hinges used for the lid and keywell flap consist simply of two short sections of wire bent in half across one another. Angled holes are drilled at the edges of the pieces being hinged and the paired wire ends of the hinge inserted into them. The wire ends left projecting out of the hole are then bent over and hammered into the grain of the wood flush with the surface, thus preventing the hinge from pulling out. These wire hinges were apparently positioned after the instrument was decorated, since the splayed ends of the spine hinges are visible on top of the block-printed papers around the soundwell of the instrument, and above the inside painted surface of the lid and keywell flap.

Four wire hinges were normally used on both the lid and keywell flap of the 5- and 6-voet virginals, and only three hinges on the 4- and 4½-voet instruments.

The keywell flap is recessed into the left- and right-hand case sides so that when closed it is flush with the front edge of the sides. It is held in the closed position by a brass or wire retaining hook fastened to the side of the keywell brace nearest the middle of the virginal. The hook engages a wire eye made and secured like the wire hinges, and this is placed on the inside of the keywell flap. Unlike the rest of the case sides, the keywell flap has no moulding.

The lid usually overhangs the case by about 10–12mm on the sides, 6–8mm along the front, and is flush along the spine. The lid was normally held closed with two hooks on the keywell flap entering into two wire eyes in the front lid overhang. But at least one virginal (1643a AR) had a lock and hasp similar to that normally found on double-manual harpsichords.

The lid was retained in the open position with a cord running from the lid to the case side. The holes for this cord are about 1 duim (about 25mm) below the top and near the middle of the side of the case, and in a matching position in the lid. The holes for the lid cord are about 3mm in diameter. No direct evidence of the size or the material of this cord in virginals has been found in my investigations.

## VIRGINAL TOOLBOX

The 6-, 5-, 4½-, and 4-voet Ruckers virginals of both the muselar and spinett types are provided with a small toolbox. This is placed to the left of the keywell behind the faceboard and is usually against the left-hand case side. The lid on the toolbox is pivoted along one of its long edges and is tapered in thickness from about 12–13mm at the pivoted edge to 8–9mm at the free edge.

On muselar virginals the soundboard provides the bottom of the toolbox. Two walls of the toolbox are built onto the soundboard and the other two are provided by the left case side and faceboard. One of the walls built onto the soundboard is perpendicular to and let into the faceboard, and moulded on top like the rest of the case walls and faceboard. The other wall is lower and acts as a stop under the thinned free edge of the toolbox lid.

The toolbox in spinett virginals is a ready-made part of the construction of the virginal and consists of the well immediately to the left of the key touchplates. Here, the tapered lid is positioned to pivot at soundboard level. In some spinett virginals the toolbox is provided with a floor above the level of the baseboard, but in others the toolbox extends right down to baseboard level.

## VIRGINAL SOUNDBOARDS

The soundboard in all Ruckers instruments is made of European spruce (*Picea abies*, or more properly *Picea excelsa*). Nothing seems to be known of the country of origin of this wood except that it was not the Low Countries themselves. The annual rings, marked by the contrast between the light springwood and the darker summerwood, are both highly prominent and closely spaced, indicating that the country of origin was colder and drier than Flanders and had an extreme variation between the summer and winter average temperatures. It seems likely therefore that the wood came from central or northern Europe. The Alps or Carpathian Mountains are possible sources but have obvious problems of transportation to Antwerp. The Antwerp city records indicate, however, that there was an enormous timber-shipping trade in Flanders in both softwoods and hardwoods such as oak with the Baltic countries, and this seems to be the most likely source of the wood used by Ruckers and the other Flemish builders.[1]

The soundboard wood is usually accurately quartered, although there are instances when the grain is as much as 20° off the quarter. Individual boards often consist of both widely and closely spaced rings, and there seems to be no consistent pattern in the way in which these are used when making soundboards. Often it is clear that adjacent planks are successive slices from the same tree, there being no tendency to use, say, close-grained wood for the treble part of the compass, reserving the wide-grained wood for the bass. It was simply used as it came. This had the considerable advantage that the direction of the grain was the same in adjacent planks, thus eliminating problems when planing the soundboard down to final thickness.

However, although the Ruckers family seem to have placed little importance on the spacing of annual rings and accuracy of quartering, they took great care with thinning. The soundboards of any one maker over his entire lifetime were thinned across their entire area consistently to an accuracy of a few tenths of a millimetre.

In both the 1611 HR and 1643a AR muselar virginals (see Fig. 5.2) the soundboards were about 3.5mm thick under the tenor part of the left-hand bridge. From here the soundboard was thinned in all directions to about 2.8mm along the outer edge of all of the sounding part of the left-hand bridge, to about 2.6mm under most of the bridge itself, and tapering to about 1.8mm at the rear right corner. The soundboard is thickest and stiffest near the tenor and bass, and most flexible in the treble parts.

The upper touch bar on the keyboard rack, and the lower register guides are often of poor-quality soundboard wood 4.5–5.0mm thick. It is quite probable that this wood was rejected, unworked wood of the original thickness which was found convenient for use as lower guides.

The initial reduction in thickness was probably carried out using a plane. The final thinning and finishing of the soundboard was, however, done with a furniture scraper. A scraper works more slowly than a plane, removing only a small amount of wood with each stroke, and is very useful in an accurate finishing of the soundboard. Furthermore, the scraper is virtually insensitive to the direction of the grain of the wood, so that the soundboard cannot be damaged in the final thinning, as might happen when accidentally planing against the direction of the wood.

[1] D. Eckstein, T. Wazny, J. Bauch, and P. Klein, 'New evidence for the dendrochronological dating of Netherlandish paintings', *Nature*, CCCXX (3 April 1986), 465–6, show that the oak used in Netherlandish panel paintings came from North Poland around Gdansk. It is therefore very likely that the oak, and possibly the beech, poplar and soundboard spruce, came from this area as well. Even if the Ruckers construction material did not come from exactly this area, the Baltic generally is a likely source.

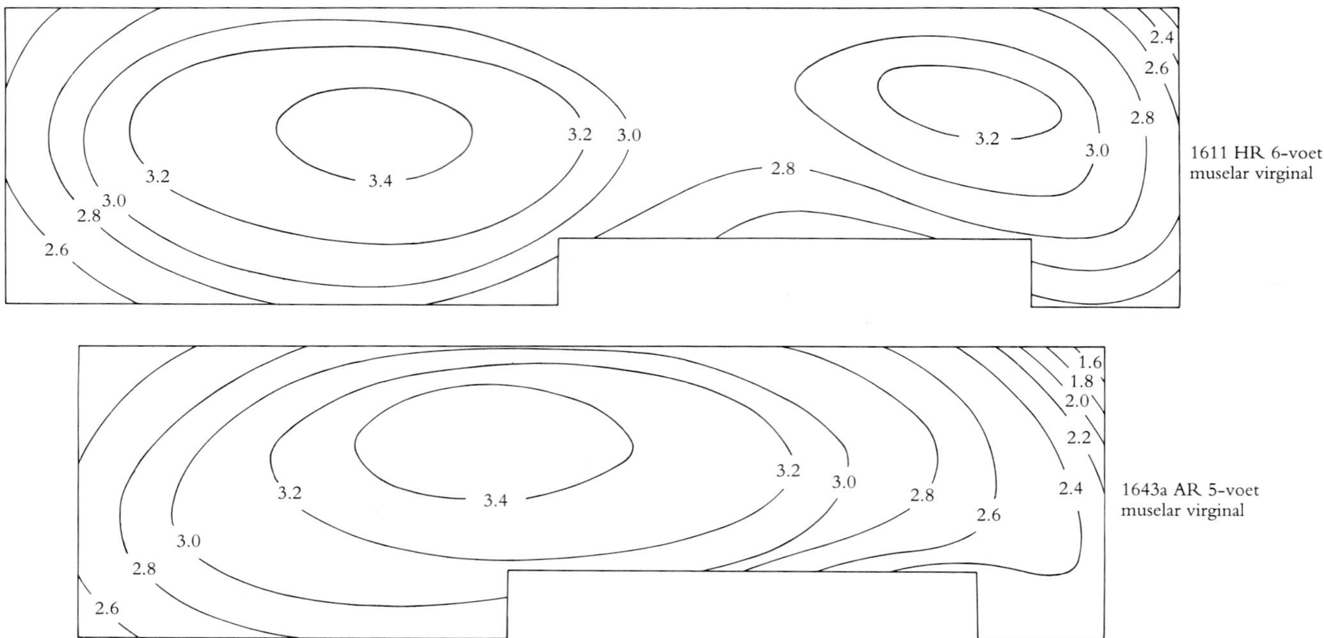


Fig. 5.2 Comparison of the soundboard thickness contours in two typical muselar virginals. Scale 1:10.

Used on a softwood such as spruce, a scraper produces an immediately recognizable effect. Although removed to the same extent as the harder summerwood in planing and sanding operations, the springwood, because of its soft spongy nature, is slightly compressed in the scraping operation. Left to 'relax' for a day or so, or if dampened slightly, this compressed wood rises up above the summerwood, and stands proud in ridges along the soundboard. This slightly ribbed texture is one of the most distinctive features of a genuine Ruckers soundboard.

Before the soundboard was painted, it was sized to fill the porous wood and to prevent the paint from running away along the grain of the wood. The material used as a size is not known, but was probably something simple and readily available in the workshop such as diluted glue or shellac. The subsequent chemical breakdown of the organic material in the size, together with the discoloration of the wood itself, has contributed to the present mellow amber-brown colour of the surface of the Ruckers soundboards.

## VIRGINAL SOUNDBOARD BARRING

The effect of the barring in all Ruckers instruments is to render the freely-vibrating treble soundboard area smaller than the bass. This accords with the law stating that in order for an acoustical radiator to be efficient, the physical dimensions of the radiator must be roughly the same as the wavelength of the propagated radiation. In this case the size of the radiating soundboard should be of the same order as the wavelength in air of the note being played. In the treble part of the compass this is roughly true, and the wavelength of the notes being radiated (about 30 cm) is of the same order of magnitude as the soundboard dimension.

In the bass region, the radiating area of soundboard is much less than the wavelength of, say, 'cello C in air (about 5m). In order to set as much soundboard area in motion as possible, the soundboard is made stiffer by making it thicker and the bridge cross-section is made heavier in the bass. Coupled with heavier bass stringing, this ensures that as large an area as feasible is caused to radiate in this part of the compass. Despite this, for the very lowest notes, the *fundamental* tone is not radiated enough to be audible by itself. For the low notes the impression of a sounding fundamental is created in the ear and brain of the listener from their analysis of the upper short-wavelength harmonic partials which are radiated by the soundboard (see p. 56). The centre-plucking muselar is very weak in upper partials in comparison with the end-plucking spinett virginal, and it is thus necessary for the muselar to radiate the few low partials it produces with a greater efficiency than for the spinetts. This is done by giving the muselar virginals a much larger soundboard area in the bass.

The barring of a typical muselar virginal is shown in

Plate 5.2 The soundboard barring and internal construction of a typical 6-voet muselar virginal (1650a IC). Scale 1:1. Copyright, Vleeshuis Museum, Antwerp.

Plate 5.2. The soundboard area immediately behind the keyboard is deadened by soundbars running perpendicularly from the nameboard liner to the lower-guide brace. In order to avoid the soundboard radiating the noise made by the jacks moving up and down in the register, it is covered with leather and the wood underneath is cut away so that the jacks touch only the leather. Also, the soundboard is stiffened by the cutoff bar running behind it and the lower-guide brace in front of it. The right end of the lower-guide brace is cut away so that it does not touch the soundboard near the right-hand end of the bridge. The radiating soundboard area around the right-hand bridge is contained between the right-hand soundbar and the lapped wrestplank, whose shape roughly matches that of the bridge. Since the bass end of the right-hand bridge would otherwise sit solidly on it, part of the wrestplank is cut away at soundboard level, as has been mentioned before.

The left-hand bridge radiating area is controlled by the cutoff bar and a shaped block of wood normally about 25mm thick attached to the spine soundboard liner near the bass keywell brace. Only the two earliest muselar virginals, the 1581 HR and the (1591)b HR virginals, have a much lighter piece of wood about 6mm thick restricting the tenor soundboard area in a way similar to that found in the *c.* 1580 Iohannes Grouwels virginal (Brussels Museum of Musical Instruments No. 2929). In the treble the cutoff bar extends all the way to the spine in the earliest Hans Ruckers instruments, but stops short of the spine and rapidly expands in height in the later instruments of his sons. The left-hand end of the cutoff bar extends to (and is often let into) the left side soundboard liner. Typically the poplar cutoff bar is about 45mm high and 20mm wide at the base with sides angled at close to 10°; the poplar soundbars are usually about 15mm high and 10–15mm wide at the base, with their sides angled either at 10° or 15° (see pp. 102ff).

Plate 5.3 shows the barring of a typical 6-voet spinett

Plate 5.3 The soundboard barring and internal construction of a typical 6-voet spinett virginal (modern copy by the author of the (*c.* 1600) HR virginal). Scale 1:10.

virginal. Here also, the area immediately behind the nameboard liner is deadened by soundbars running to a cutoff bar placed immediately beside the jack register. The rear right soundboard area is deadened with soundbars running from the wrestplank to the spine soundboard liner. The noise of the jacks moving in the registers is eliminated by the use of leather on the top surfaces of both the upper and lower guides and also by the position of the cutoff bar and hitchrail immediately on either side of the register. The left-hand bridge does not sound on a Ruckers spinett virginal, since it is placed above the massive hitchpin block.

The radiating soundboard area of the right-hand bridge is contained between the wrestplank, the right-hand extension of the nameboard liner, and the two soundbars to the left of the treble part of the bridge. Since the treble end of this bridge runs directly over the wrestplank, a part of the wrestplank near the soundboard level is cut away at the bridge position to free the soundboard and bridge and allow them to vibrate freely there. Normally the soundbars in a 6-voet spinett virginal are about 15mm high and 10–11mm wide at the base; as usual, the sides are angled at close to either 10° or 15°. In the spinett virginals the cutoff bar beside the register slots is usually only marginally bigger than the soundbars.

In both the spinett and muselar virginals the larger soundboard bars such as the cutoff bars and the large register bars have rounded scallops about 2 duimen (51mm) cut in their ends, and the smaller soundbars such as those behind the nameboard liner have shorter scallops only 1 duim (25mm) long. These scallops render the extreme ends of the soundboard bars almost flush in height with the soundboard, and often linen tapes were glued over the scalloped ends of the bars to prevent the bars from breaking loose from the soundboard. In addition to restricting and controlling the vibrating soundboard area, the sound- and cutoff bars help to hold the soundboard flat and level, and prevent the distortions which would be produced as a result of the down- and side-draught of the strings.

## VIRGINAL BRIDGES

The left-hand bridge is, in both muselar and spinett virginals, practically always of beech (*Fagus sylvatica*). The right-hand bridge is usually also of beech, although sometimes of cherry (*Prunus avium*), especially in the large spinett virginals, where the bridge is a continuous curve sawn from the plank. In some rare cases cherry is used for both bridges. In muselar virginals the right-hand bridge consists of two separate sections. The treble section for $f^{\sharp 1}$ to $c^3$ is slightly curved, and is mitred to a straight section in the tenor and bass for the notes from C/E to $f^1$. It is along this straight section that the harpichordium stop slides.

Virginal bridges have the same cross-sectional shape as harpsichord bridges (see Fig. 6.9, p. 104) and were almost certainly made in the same way, since the angles of the faces to the horizontal and vertical are the same as those of harpsichord bridges (see p. 104). Both right-hand and left-hand bridges have a larger cross-sectional area in the bass than in the treble and, along with the soundboard tapering and barring, this helps to ensure that a sufficiently greater area of soundboard is set in vibration in the bass than in the treble, as is necessary for efficient acoustical radiation.

The bridges were positioned on the soundboard during gluing by means of pairs of pins driven into the soundboard and placed on either side of the bridge. These pins not only located the bridges in their correct position, but also ensured that the bridges did not slide around on the soundboard while they were being glued in place. The positioning pins were later removed and the pairs of empty holes in the soundboard beside the bridges are left as evidence of their use. After the bridges were glued to the soundboard they were further fixed in position with small iron nails[3] placed from below the soundboard between the paired positioning-pin holes.

The bridge pins are made of brass wire sharpened at one end, and are slightly heavier in the large virginals than in the small ones. The 5- and 6-voet instruments usually have bridge pins 1.1–1.2mm in diameter, and the 4½- and 4-voet child virginals have pins 0.9–1.0mm in diameter.

There is a slight difference between spinett and muselar virginals in the bridge pinning and the hitchpin arrangement. The muselar virginals alone are equipped with a harpichordium on the right-hand bridge. Because of the large space occupied by each of the hooks on the harpichordium, they have to be almost evenly spaced, and the strings and bridge pins on the bass section of the right-hand bridge must therefore also have a corresponding uniform spacing. In order to allow space between the strings for the jacks, alternate strings diverge, with a consequent close spacing of successive pairs of strings on the left-hand bridge.

[2] The left-hand bridge of the 1581 HR muselar mother virginal follows the tradition of many mid-sixteenth-century instruments in having slightly curved faces. The right-hand bridge of the mother and both bridges of the child have the usual flat sides.

[3] The virginal part of the 1594 HR instrument used sharpened pieces of brass wire bent over against the soundboard instead of the usual iron nails. I am indebted to Martin-Christian Schmidt for pointing this out to me.

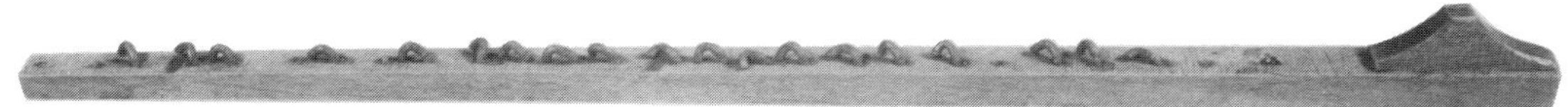

Plate 5.4 A typical harpichordium batten and hooks (1604 HR 5-voet muselar virginal). Scale 1:2.

The harpichordium is never found in spinett virginals and the strings in this type of instrument can run almost completely parallel to one another, spaced in pairs along both bridges so as to allow clearance for the jacks between them. Running diagonally under the left-hand bridge in Ruckers spinett virginals is a solid plank of wood, which serves both to deaden this bridge and as a hitchpin rail.

In muselar virginals the bass end of the left-hand bridge sits on a very large and flexible soundboard area. In order to relieve the downward string pressure on the soundboard in this region, the bottom octave of strings, that is, the nine notes C/E to c inclusive, are back-pinned. These strings run, without any side-draught, back to hitchpins on a raised block, roughly the same height as the bass end of the bridge. This reduces both the downward and sideways pressure on the bridge produced by the heavy bass octave of strings. Since there is no problem of the left-hand bridge sinking in a spinett virginal, it is not back-pinned, and there is no hitchpin block to raise the strings in the bass.

In both spinett and muselar virginals, side-draught is provided by angling the strings towards the spine at both bridges. This side-draught is usually of the order of 7–11°. Except for the bass octave in the muselar virginals, there is also a slight down-draught in the strings, since the hitchpins are driven directly into the soundboard, forcing the ends of the strings down from bridge height to soundboard level.

## THE HARPICHORDIUM STOP

As has been mentioned, only muselar virginals have a harpichordium stop.[4] Why it is not found on spinett virginals is not absolutely certain. Practical experience shows, however, that the harpichordium operates reliably only when the amplitude of vibration of the strings is large, that is, it works especially well in the bass. Since end-plucking spinett virginals do not produce such a large amplitude of vibration in the strings, even in the bass, as muselar virginals, the operation of a harpichordium in a spinett virginal may have been found to be too uneven because of the critically small tolerances required. This may also explain why, after its early appearance on the treble bridge section of the early 1581 HR virginal and the difficulties experienced adjusting it, the harpichordium was not used there on later surviving muselar virginals.

The stop operates by sliding beside the straight bass portion of the mitred bridge on the notes from C/E to $f^1$.[5] It consists of a bar of poplar beech into which hooks of lead[6] have been fixed (see Plate 5.4). The bar is tapered so that its upper surface runs parallel to the top of the bridge about 6–7mm below the strings, and the bar extends beyond the strings in the bass to allow a fingerstop to be fixed to it, by means of which it is operated. The bar is held in position against the bridge, and its range of motion is constrained at either end by small chamfered blocks of wood. It is also held down against the soundboard by three iron pins placed horizontally into the side of the bridge; these pins extend out of the bridge to press against the upper surface of the bar containing the hooks, and are usually located above or near the chamfered blocks.

The hooks themselves are 1.8–1.9mm in diameter and, being of lead, are easily regulated by bending them slightly so that they just touch the strings. The point of contact of the hooks with the strings is about 12mm from the bridge pin at $f^1$, and 15mm at C/E. When engaged, the top horizontal surfaces of the hooks are directly underneath and lightly touching their respective strings. The vibration of the string against the hook produces a snarling sound which is probably more novel to the modern ear than it was in Ruckers' time.

Praetorius[7] refers to this stop as an *Arpichordium*, to be found in virginals, and consisting of brass (*sic*) hooks

[4] Here the word harpichordium is used to mean a stop and not an instrument. See, however, A. Neven, 'L'Arpicordo', *Acta Musicologica*, XLII (1970), 230–5, and Luisa Cervelli, 'Italienische Musikinstrumente in der Praxis des Generalbass-Spiels: Das Arpichord', *Bericht über den siebenten internationalen Kongress, Köln, 1958* (Kassel, 1959), 76–8.

[5] As mentioned, the 1581 HR mother virginal in the Metropolitan Museum, New York is an exception. It has a split harpichordium covering the entire range of the instrument. The bass section covers C/E to $e^1$; the treble part covers $f^1$ to $c^3$.

[6] N. Meeùs of the Brussels Museum of Musical Instruments has had the metal of the 1604 HR harpichordium analysed by the Koninklijk Instituut voor het Kunstpatrimonium; the analysis showed that the harpichordium hooks were more than 99% lead with only small traces of tin.

[7] Michael Praetorius, *Syntagma Musicum II: De Organographia* (Wolfenbüttel, 1619; facs., Kassel, 1958), 67.

below the strings. He says that the sound produced in a virginal was similar to that produced on a harp: here he was clearly referring to the 'bray' commonly found on the Renaissance harp, which also produced a buzzing, snarling sound.

## VIRGINAL REGISTERS

The register for the jacks in a virginal consists simply of a series of holes pierced in the soundboard. Both the lower guide and the soundboard registers are covered with sheepskin leather about 30–33mm wide, and the soundboard wood and the wood of the lower guide is cut away so that the jacks touch only the leather. This, in conjunction with the barring and framing under the soundboard, results in an extremely quiet action.

Unlike most of the contemporary virginals made in Italy, and the slightly later virginals and spinets made in England, the jacks in Ruckers virginals are placed two to a slot, rather than each having its own slot. This means that the jacks rub against one another slightly as the keys are depressed. In the usual forty-five-note C/E to $c^3$ compass there are therefore twenty-two double slots taking the jacks from C/E to $b^2$ plus one narrow single slot at the top for the $c^3$ jack.

Since the space occupied by one octave of keys at their tails is the same as that of the touchplates, the space occupied by one octave of jacks in a direction parallel to the spine (or parallel to the keyboard) must be the same as that of the keys. Thus the three-octave spacing of the jackslots, like the key touchplates, is 500mm when measured parallel to the long direction of the instrument. Therefore the eighteen paired slots in three octaves must be spaced at an interval of 500/18 = 27.78mm. The total spacing of the forty-five notes in the C/E to $c^3$ compass is then 22.5 × 27.78 = 625mm. Twenty-seven naturals at the front of the keyboard occupy 27 × 500/21 = 643mm, to which must be added about 3–4mm clearance at both sides. The width of the keywell is then about 650mm wide – the actual width varies from 645mm to 652mm.[8] The keywell is therefore about 25mm or 1 duim wider than the total space occupied by the jacks and jackslots.

Near the ends of the register leathers, lines are scribed on the soundboard surface at positions corresponding to the insides of the keywell braces. On each side is another scribed line about 12–13mm (½ duim) in towards the centre of the keywell; these coincide with the outside edges of the C/E and $c^3$ jackslots, and are 625mm from one another in a direction parallel to the spine. These construction lines often run underneath the register leather and the bridges, indicating that the marking out, and probably the cutting of the jackslots, was done before the soundboard was encumbered with bridges or cutoff bars and soundbars.

In the two construction lines at the outside edge of the C/E and $c^3$ jackslots and just behind the front edge of the register leather there are invariably two nail holes. These were made by the nails used to fix the lower guide in position under the soundboard so that the slots in both could be cut simultaneously. The corresponding nail holes in the lower guide are sometimes covered by its leather, indicating that the leather of the lower guide was not always cut at the same time as the wood. Thus in some cases the leather was glued to the lower guide after the slots were cut in the wood, and was then cut from the underside using the holes in the wood as a guide. Either way, there are no construction marks on the lower guide to aid in the cutting out of the jackslots.

The jackslots in the soundboard are marked out with scribed lines uniformly 27.8mm apart for the notes from C/E to $b^2$, and half this amount for the top $c^3$. In addition to this two long lines 17.0–17.5mm apart and running parallel to its length are scribed onto the leather strip. These two long lines, intersected by those 27.8mm apart, then determine the extremes of the ends of the jackslots. The sides of the slots are cut at a constant angle about 5° steeper than the angle of the strings. This ensures a longer plectrum length than if the jackslots ran parallel to the string direction.

The sides of the jackslots in the soundboard and lower guide, like the slots in the wooden part of the lower guide in harpsichords, were probably cut with a chisel sharpened to a very small angle (see pp. 113ff). However, a chisel will not cut soft leather satisfactorily without tearing, and the leather shows clear signs of having been first cut out with a knife held vertically. After the holes in the wood have then been punched the wood is cleared away underneath, so that the jackslot opens out, ensuring that the jack touches only the leather without coming into contact with the wood.

Usually the lower guide was of poplar or spruce and reinforced underneath with a layer of parchment glued to it before the slots in the wood were opened out. This seems to have been done to prevent the splitting of the short-grained wood between the guide slots. The soundboard slots were not so reinforced, since the grain of the soundboard, running diagonally past the slots, is always much longer than the short grain of the longitudinal wood of the lower guide.

In muselar virginals the lower guide is attached both to

[8] The Hans and Ioannes Ruckers instruments have a keywell about 645–648mm wide; Andreas Ruckers instruments are 650–652mm wide.

the lower guide brace behind the register slots in the soundboard and to the top of the keywell braces – often a shallow slot is made in the keywell braces specifically for the lower guide. The guide is nailed to the upper surface of the keywell braces and to the lower edge of the lower-guide brace which extends up to support and deaden the soundboard near the soundboard registers. The free edge of the lower guide is stiffened with a small bar about 14mm by 18mm in cross-section, leaving a space about 30–35mm wide for the leather between the guide brace and the stiffening bar.

The lower guide in the spinett virginals has two small stiffening bars on either side of the leather strip and jackslots, and is nailed to the upper surface of the keywell braces.

### BRIDGE-PINNING IN VIRGINALS

The bridge pins on a virginal must position the strings under the constraints of two factors. First, the pins must locate the strings on the bridges so that the string lengths correspond to the usual scalings at the pitch of the instrument concerned. Secondly, the strings must be the correct distance from the jacks to ensure the proper mechanical functioning of the instrument; the plectra must be neither too short nor too long, and the strings must not come into contact with the neighbouring jacks or strings.

The method by which the Ruckers decided the correct scalings of the strings is not entirely clear. The marking of the pin positions on the bridge was probably done before the top edge of the bridge was chamfered away, so that any evidence of their existence has now disappeared.[9] The paired holes beside the bridges in the soundboard used to locate the bridge during gluing do not seem to bear any fixed relationship to any note or pitch, nor do their positions usually correspond to the same notes on the left- and right-hand bridges. This is in marked contrast to the rôle of the positioning holes beside the bridges in the laying out, positioning and pinning of the harpsichord bridges. The position of the right-hand bridge seems to have been determined previous to gluing the bridge by means of scribed lines indicating the position of its right edge. The location of this scribed line must have been made in relation either to the case sides or, more likely, to the left-hand bridge.

The position of the string relative to the jacks is usually marked on the soundboard register leather. A small pinprick in the leather indicates the position of the string in relation to the *back* surface of each jack. This locates the strings about 2.0mm from the rear of the jacks and ensures that the strings will not touch them. It also, in conjunction with the angle of the jackslots relative to the strings, determines the plectrum length. In most virginals this is found to be about 3.6mm, measured from the jack surface to the outside edge of the string. The total plectrum length depends upon the amount the jack tongue is recessed behind the front of the jacks, as well as the amount the plectrum projects beyond the string.

Once the jackslots had been cut through the soundboard and leather register, and the string positions were marked on the register, the bridges could be positioned and glued to the soundboard. Since the strings run parallel to one another (the deviation even in muselar virginals is not great) a jig fixing the angle of the strings to the spine could be used to mark the string and bridge-pin position on the two bridges. Such a jig might consist simply of a board or light framework with one edge at the same angle as the angle of the strings to the spine edge of the soundboard. The edge corresponding to the string position must be long enough to reach from the left- to the right-hand bridge at C/E. If this edge is placed over the string-position marks on the leather registers, then the two bridges will intersect the edge of the jig, and the bridge-pin positions can be marked, one note at a time, on the two bridges.

Clearly a slight error in positioning either bridge, but especially the left bridge, will result in a deviation from the desired value of the string scale. Comparing virginal scalings one finds variations within one instrument type of up to fifteen per cent (more than two semitones, or plus or minus one semitone). The average variation is much less than this, but the fact that such deviations do occur reflects the method of marking out the bridge-pin positions. Also, these scaling variations provide information which sheds light on two other aspects of the building of these instruments.

First, it was of prime importance to the Ruckers that the instrument operated well. That the strings were neither too close nor too far away from the jacks was more important than consistently accurate scalings. Secondly, the magnitude of the scaling variation is an approximate measure of the safety factor represented by the difference between the working stress and the ultimate breaking stress of the wire material used for the strings. The large variations quoted above occur in the foreshortened bass part of the scale. In the treble these variations amount to at least seven per cent, this representing slightly more than a semitone in pitch variation. Therefore the spread between the working and ultimate breaking stress must have amounted to at least seven per

9 The virginal part of the 1594 HR instrument in Schloss Köpenick, East Berlin has the intended position of the $c^1$ bridge pin marked on the rear surface of the right-hand bridge.

cent, and obviously a somewhat larger safety factor would have to have been used to avoid string breakages due to humidity variations, etc.

## GLUING THE VIRGINAL SOUNDBOARD INTO THE CASE

After the jackslots had been cut in the soundboard, the cutoff bar and soundbars glued in position, and the bridges glued down and marked and drilled for pinning, the soundboard had to be glued into the case. Muselar and spinett virginals must have differed slightly in the procedure used immediately preceding the actual gluing of the soundboard to the liners.

For muselar virginals the lower-guide support with the attached lower guide had to be glued to the soundboard and fixed to the keywell braces at more or less the same time as the soundboard was glued into the instrument. It is not clear whether the lower guide and support were fixed to the keywell braces and the soundboard glued to the top of the lower-guide support at the same time as the soundboard was glued to the liners, or whether the lower-guide support with the lower guide attached was first glued to the soundboard and then, after the soundboard was glued into position, the lower guide was nailed to the keywell braces. The first possibility is easier and would involve a method similar to that used to glue the soundboard to the wrestplank. Also, in muselar virginals the bass end of the large cutoff bar for the left-hand bridge is usually let into the left cheek liner, and the recess for this would have to be made before the soundboard could be glued into position.

In the spinett virginals the lower guide is not attached to the soundboard and would therefore almost certainly have been fixed to the keywell braces before the soundboard was glued down. But the feature which most distinguished the Ruckers end-plucking spinett virginals from the centre-plucking muselar virginals is the heavy hitchpin plank across the near left-hand corner of the instrument. This plank can only have been let in, glued, and pegged to the liners before the soundboard was glued in place.

Apart from the differences in the details just mentioned, it seems likely that the basic method of gluing the soundboard into the case was the same for both muselar and spinett virginals. The soundboard in both types of virginal is pegged to the liners along its outer edge except for the nameboard liner in the keywell. Here it is possible to hold the soundboard down against the liner with ordinary clamps, thus making pegging unnecessary. Along the rest of the edge of the soundboard it seems most likely that the soundboard was held in place during gluing with stiff battens nailed over the edge of the soundboard into the liners. A similar system seems to have been used for gluing the soundboard to the wrest-plank and hitchplank in the spinett virginals and to the lower-guide brace in muselar virginals. In both, the spacing between the pegs in the soundboard is too great (4–5 duimen = 105–130mm) and the soundboard too thin to ensure proper gluing of the soundboard by means of the pegs alone. These pegs, then, are probably just filling the nail holes left after removing the battens used to hold the soundboard against the liners and other structures below it during the process of gluing.

## VIRGINAL KEYFRAMES AND KEYBOARDS

The keylevers, keyframe, balance rail and rack in all Ruckers virginals are made of poplar. The keyframe consists of four pieces of wood which form an irregular polygonal shape and are joined together with pegged half-lap joints. The sides of the keyframe are parallel to one another and leave a few millimetres clearance inside the keywell of the instrument into which the keyframe will fit. The front of the keyframe runs approximately parallel with the angled balance rail, and the rear of the keyframe is roughly parallel with the rack and thus with the angled lower guide and jackslots. The rack and key-frame touch the spine of the instrument on the treble side, and the board forming the bass side of the keyframe extends beyond the rear of the rack to the case spine. The boards of the keyframe are 12–14mm thick.

The balance rail consists of a piece of poplar about 34mm wide and tapered in height from about 12.5mm at the edge near the player to 9 or 10mm at the rear. The top surface of the balance rail is then approximately parallel to the bottom surface of the keys. Because the bass keys are much shorter than the treble keys, the balance rail is placed at an angle on the keyframe so that the lever ratio of the bass and treble keys is roughly the same. This produces the same mechanical advantage in the keylevers throughout the compass, so that the player experiences a uniform touch from bass to treble. Considering only the natural keylevers and taking the ratio between the distance from the end of the natural touchplate to the natural balance point, and the distance from the natural balance point to the end of the keylever, one gets an average balance ratio or mechanical advantage of about 0.53–0.56. Exceptional are the 4-voet and child instruments, which have keys with a greater mechanical advantage (about 0.63) than the larger instrument. In all models the balance point of the sharps is about half a duim (12.7mm) behind that of the naturals. The balance pins are made of iron wire about 1.8–2.1mm in diameter and are just long

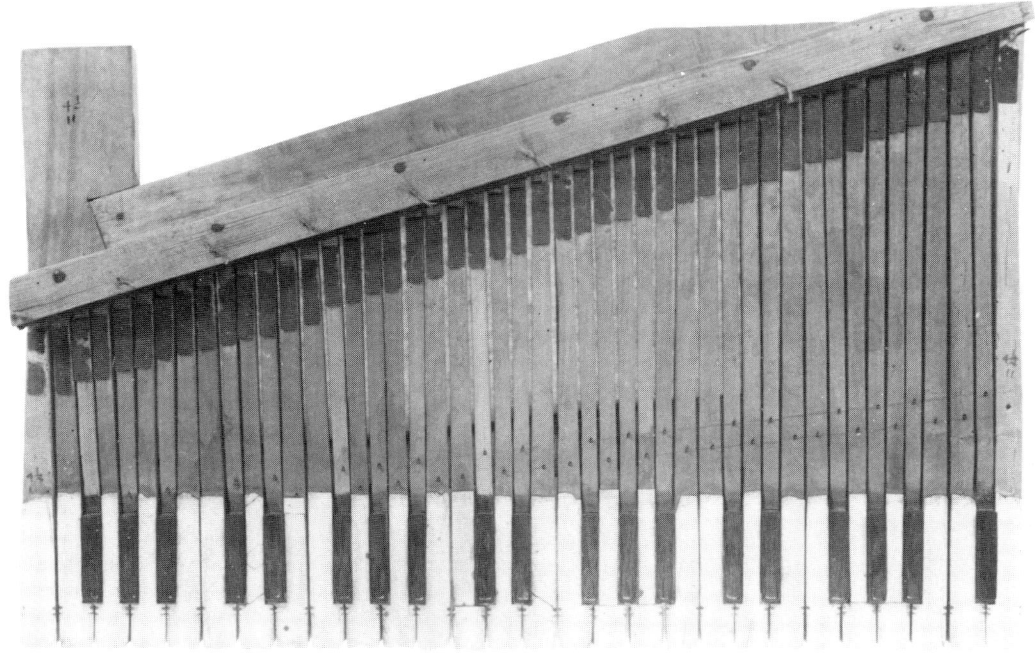

Plate 5.5 Keyframe and keyboards from the 1629 IR 4½-voet spinett virginal. Scale 1:5.

enough to protrude above the tops of the keylevers. In fact, in the bass, the balance point is so far towards the player that the balance pins are underneath the natural keyplates, in which case the pins are driven further into the balance rail so that they just clear the lower keyplate surface.

The poplar board or keyplank from which the keylevers were cut is about half a duim (12.7mm) in thickness, and 6–8mm narrower than the instrument keywell to allow clearance for the end keylevers. Both the front and rear edges of the keyplank were angled at about 10° to the perpendicular so that the lower surface of the keylever is shorter than the upper one. Before the keys were cut apart the keyplank was fixed in both the treble and bass to the balance rail – sometimes the holes for the nails used to fix the keyplank in position are visible both in the top and bottom keys and in the ends of the balance rail. But usually the keyplank was fixed by nailing it at the exact position of the balance pin for the top and bottom keys, thus removing evidence of this procedure. The keyframe with the keyplank fixed to it was then inserted into the instrument and held in its final position. A punch having the basic dimensions of a jack, but with a small oval or rectangular end, was inserted into each jackslot and jack position in turn to make a punch mark on the keyplank. These punch marks accurately located the future position of the jack centre on the end of the key and could be used to mark the position of the rack pin in the end of the key, as well as the saw line between the ends of the keylevers.

It is probable that, after removing the keyframe with the attached keyplank from the instrument, a series of marks to locate the position of the rack guide pins[10] were made along the rear edge of the keyplank at points corresponding to the centre of each jack punch mark. Naturally, there is no evidence left of the lines scribed between the punch marks to guide the sawing out of the keylevers. Likewise all evidence of the scribed lines to guide the sawing of the keyfronts has disappeared, except for the line delineating the back edge of the touchplate fronts and front end of the sharps. This line can be seen when a natural plate has been removed or has come loose and is reproduced underneath the natural keylevers at a point which is the same distance (about 33mm in virginals) from the angled keyfront below the key as above it.

However the keyfronts were marked out, it was done such that the three-octave span averages about 500mm (one octave = 166.7mm). The origin of this octave span is obscure, but it may well have arisen by giving the twenty-four natural notes of the earlier F to $a^2$ compass a width of 2 Flemish feet (2 voeten have a length of 569mm, which is close to the 571mm width of twenty-four naturals with a three-octave span of 500mm). The space between the natural tails and the sharps is divided up to give wide tails to the *c*s, *e*s, *f*s and *b*s. The tails of the *d*s, *g*s and *a*s are some 3–4mm narrower, making it very difficult for a player to get his fingers between the sharps to depress these keys.

It seems clear that the holes for the balance pins were marked out and drilled through the keyplank into the balance rail after the keylevers were marked out, but before the nails holding the keyplank temporarily in position were removed. The slots in the rack were also marked out at this stage, by offering the block to be used for the rack up to the rear edge of the keyplank and marking the rackslot positions from the marks already made to locate the guide pins. In this way any irregularities in marking out the positions of the guide pins are copied onto the rack so that the two eventually match one another.

The rack consists of a block of poplar about 1 duim (25.5mm) thick into which the rackslots are cut. Each rackslot is about 8mm deep and opens out into the rack block so that the rackslots as seen from above have a triangular cross-section. The top of the rack block is tapered downwards from front to back and is capped with a thin (5mm) piece of poplar or soundboard wood projecting out in front of the rackslots about 16mm. Called the upper touch-limit bar, this strip of wood, in conjunction with the cloth strips tied underneath it, limits the upward motion of the key and jack. Usually the top ends of the key levers (for about ½ duim= 13mm) have been carved to match the upward slope of the rack upper touch-limit bar. This means that the

[10] This procedure must have been slightly different for the child virginals, which do not have a keyframe, but in which the balance rail and rack were fixed permanently to the baseboard. In this situation, the baseboard must have been fixed temporarily in position so that it and the keyboard could be detached from the rest of the case during the various stages of the marking out of the keyboard and rack.

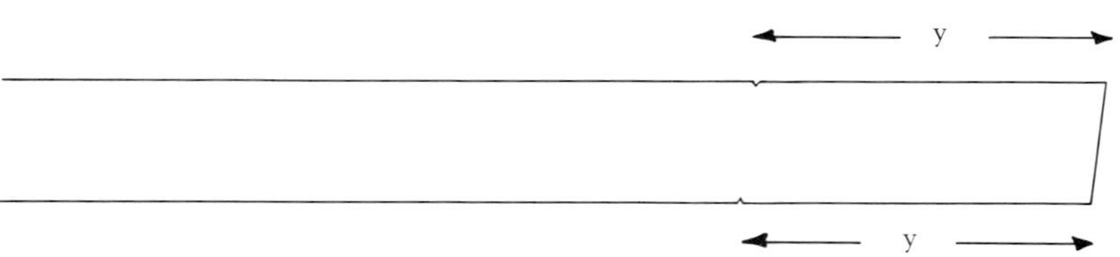

marks made to position the rack guide pins have been chiselled away, except where the occasional key has been missed and remains flat at the end. The overall height of the rack block is not tapered from bass to treble, unlike the harpsichord keyboard rack (see p. 115). The rack is glued to the keyframe and held in place at either end with wooden pegs driven in from underneath.

Once the keyplank was removed from the balance rail for sawing out, the keyframe was placed back in the instrument and the positions of the top and bottom jacks (usually C/E and $c^3$) were punched on the top surface of the keyframe. These two keyframe punch marks were probably used to position the finished rack, by lining the marks up with the top and bottom rackslots.

The natural touchplates are made of bone – probably from beef cattle. Since the bone plate overhangs the wood of the keylever slightly at the recesses for the sharps, it is clear that the bone was glued to the keylevers after the keys were cut apart. The plates are about 2–2.5mm thick at the near end, tapering to about 1mm at the far end. Each keyplate is decorated with four lines scribed across the plate just in front of the sharps. On each side of the key between the two middle scribed lines there is an elliptical nick made with a small round file. Flattish bevels are made along the sides of the touchplate in front of the nearest scribed line, and the front of the touchplate is slightly rounded. The top of the bone plate was incompletely smoothed (apparently with a furniture scraper) and then buffed to polish it. The buffing compound remains as dark deposits in the blood pores of the bone, giving the keyboard a rich and variable texture. Most instruments with original keyboards and keys which have not received too much use show that the tails of the naturals were lettered with their note name in red (possibly sanguine).

Although they have disappeared even on most Ruckers and Couchet instruments where the original keyboards survive, decorative embossed arcades covered the near ends of the keylevers. The bone plates overhang the keylever at the front by 2–3mm so as to protect the arcade below it. The arcade consists of a pierced design incorporating Gothic arches and trefoils embossed on heavy paper glued to a red-stained or dyed parchment. The red pigment used to colour the parchment is highly light-sensitive and has often faded completely. Hebrew script is clearly visible through the pierced embossed paper on the parchment used on the two earliest Ruckers virginals (1581 HR, 1583 HR).

Two types of arcades must be distinguished. In the first type, apparently used exclusively by Hans Ruckers, Ioannes Ruckers and Ioannes Couchet, the embossing is rounded and smooth in texture. The second type, used only by the two Andreas Ruckers, is more angular and the foliate parts of the design are indented (see Plate 5.6).[11]

The sharps on Ruckers keyboards are of bog oak or bog chestnut. This wood is obtained from a peat bog or moor, from trees (sometimes partly petrified) which have lain for centuries saturated with the dark alkaline water of the moor. The wood is usually cut so that the rings run parallel to the top of the keylever. This gives a smooth upper surface, with the pores of the wood on the vertical sides of the sharps. The early Hans Ruckers virginals, like most of the other sixteenth-century Flemish virginals, had sharps decorated with scribed lines and nicks similar to the naturals. But the instruments of later Ruckers had sharps without decoration.

The usual type of sharp had a slightly sloping front surface and parallel vertical sides. The width of the sharps and the narrowness of the natural tails make it virtually impossible for a player to get his fingers between the sharps, which perhaps says something about the type of fingering used by the contemporary instrumentalists. Somewhat narrower sharps with sloping sides are sometimes found, especially on the instruments by Andreas Ruckers the Elder, which just allow the players' fingers enough room to play the natural tails. Usually the top and bottom surfaces of the sharps run parallel, but the later instruments of Ioannes Couchet have sharps which taper in height, being lower at the back than at the front.

In all Ruckers instruments the sharps were made initially slightly overlength. After the sharps had been glued in place, the keys and keyframe were placed in the instrument in their final position. When the nameboard was slid into place it would be stopped from dropping into its normal position by the over-long sharp. Then a line scribed or cut along the top of the sharps at the position of the front surface of the nameboard could be used to indicate the correct length of each sharp. The sharps were then sawn to length in position on the keylever, and the excess length chipped away. The slight sawcut in the keylever at the rear of the sharp, and the clearing of the upper surface of the keylever, and the short chamfered edges just behind the sharp, are among

11 A third arcade design, found only on the 1643a AR 5-voet virginal, consists of a head surrounded by two wings embossed on thin paper without any piercing whatsoever. This is, in fact, the same arcade as is found on the 1605 Artus Gheerdinck virginal made in Amsterdam (MINe 95, Neupert Collection) in the Germanisches Nationalmuseum, Nuremberg. This winged head design is not found on any other Ruckers virginal or harpsichord. Although there is no proof one way or the other, this design seems spurious to the Ruckers tradition; probably the arcades were removed from another Amsterdam instrument and reused on the 1643a AR virginal.

Plate 5.6 Key arcades on Ruckers clavecimbels.
Top: Arcade type found only on instruments by Hans Ruckers, Ioannes Ruckers and Ioannes Couchet.
Bottom: Arcades found only on instruments signed by Andreas Ruckers. Scale 1:1.

Plate 5.7 Keys of the 1581 HR virginal showing the decorated sharps found on many early Flemish instruments by Hans Ruckers and his contemporaries.

the distinguishing characteristics of the genuine Ruckers keyboard.

The sharp keylevers were recessed underneath in front of the balance pin so that the key would rock at the balance pin and not foul with the near edge of the sloping balance rail. Also, because of the width of the jacks and keylevers and the closeness of the jacks to one another, both the keytails and the lower part of the jacks were narrowed, so that each key would operate only its own jack and not interfere with the adjacent ones. The keylevers are, furthermore, tapered in cross-section, being narrower underneath than on top, apparently in an effort to lighten them. Usually the top edges of the tails of the keylevers are slightly chamfered.

The keyframe is held in position at the rear by two chamfered blocks glued to the case spine. The rear edges of the keyframe slide underneath these and fit snugly between them and the baseboard. Two chamfered blocks glued to the baseboard at the near edge of the keyframe are each equipped with a turnbutton to hold the keyframe down, and the blocks themselves hold the keyframe tightly in position against the spine. The baseboard and turnbutton blocks are painted black underneath the touchplates and sharps. The tops of the keylevers behind the sharps are also painted black.

As with all keyboard instruments, cloth or felt in the keyboard keeps action noise to a minimum. Ruckers instruments use a felted wool cloth, tightly woven, combed to draw the fibres out of the material, matted and pressed. The result is a firm durable material of great resilience which, used as an action cloth in the keyframes, gives a firm, crisp touch, quite unlike the spongy effect of modern piano-action felt. The same material appears to have been used as damper cloth in the jacks; being strongly matted together, the individual fibres and threads of the material do not pull apart with repeated contact with the strings.

The warp and weft of this cloth are of the same thickness of yarn and it is woven in a simple, tight 'over one, under one' tabby weave, with about 22–26 warp threads per 2.5cm and a weft beaten to 10–15 threads per 2.5cm. There are two distinct types of cloth in Ruckers actions, which can be distinguished by their appearance and thickness.

The thicker type of cloth, for example, is used as a single layer on the balance rail. Compressed tightly between the jaws of a vernier caliper, its thickness is about 1.8mm. Characteristic of this type of cloth are loose surface fibres more than 15mm in length and all lying in one direction after having been pulled out of the woven fabric in the combing process. The cloth is cut to the full width of the balance rail and held in place only by the balance pins. Additional square bits of leather or folded card about 0.9–1.1mm thick are used on top of the cloth underneath the sharps to raise the sharp keylevers to the level of the naturals. This is necessary because of the slope of the balance rail, which puts the sharp balance point lower than that of the naturals.

The same heavy cloth is used on the keylever top surface underneath the jacks. Pads of this cloth are positioned over the punch marks used in the marking out of the tails of the keylevers, only the ends of the pads being glued so that there is actually no glue under the pad where the foot of the jack makes contact. The pairwise positioning of the jacks, two to a jackslot, produces a corresponding pairwise pattern in the jack pads.

The thinner type of cloth is about 0.9mm thick when tightly compressed, and the fibres on the surface are relatively short and not combed to lie only in one direction (i.e. it has no nap). This cloth is used in the jackrail and as dampers in the jacks, and both above and below the keylever tails in the rack. In the rack it is usually in three or four layers tied at regular intervals with coarse linen thread to the upper touch-limit bar of the rack. Underneath the keylever tails two layers of cloth about 1 duim (25mm) wide are used, tacked with small tacks at the ends, and usually at positions about one-third and two-thirds along the length of the cloth strips as well. The thickness and number of cloth strips in the rack, in conjunction with the keylever thickness and the height of the rack itself, determines the depth of touch of the keylevers. In Ruckers virginals which retain their original keyboard cloths the depth of touch is found to be about 9mm in the base and 8mm in the treble, measured at the end of the natural keylevers. This is slightly more than in harpsichord keyboards.

In the few instruments which retain them, original action cloths are usually dyed black. Two Ruckers harpsichords (1618b I R, 1640b A R) have apparently original cloth dyed red in the rack, but only black cloth seems to have been used in virginal keyboards. On the other hand only red cloth seems to have been used for the jack dampers.[12] The outside layer of the cloth in the rack and jackrail has often lost its outer matted felting through wear or insect damage, and the threads of the weft and warp are clearly visible. The interior surfaces of such cloth should be carefully examined for the features described above before disregarding it as being non-original.

[12] The damper cloths in the child part of the Marten van der Biest double virginal of 1580 in the Germanisches Nationalmuseum, Nuremberg (M1 85) appear to be original and are dyed green.

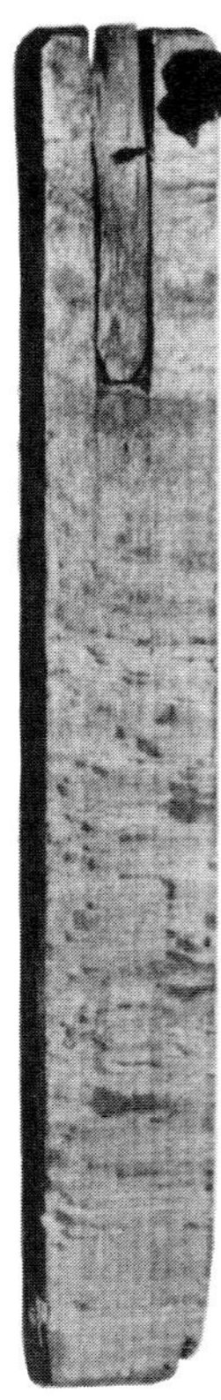

Plate 5.8 A typical Ruckers virginal jack and tongue made of quartered beech (from the child portion of the 1581 HR virginal). The (slightly damaged) damper is probably original. Scale 1:1. Copyright, Metropolitan Museum of Art, New York. Gift of B. H. Homan, 1929 (29.90).

## VIRGINAL JACKS AND JACKRAIL

Ruckers virginal jacks, like the jacks used in the harpsichords, are made of quartered beech and have oval damper holes instead of the morticed slots common in eighteenth-century instruments (for a detailed description of Ruckers jacks see pp. 121ff).

Both the virginal and harpsichord jacks have the same rounded 'mouse ear' type of damper cloths. This type of damper is particularly effective in the larger muselar virginals. If a damper with a flat lower edge (found only rarely even in eighteenth-century instruments, but commonly used by modern builders) is used in the bass section of the larger centre-plucking muselars, the amplitude and inertia of the string is great enough to throw the jack up again and again until the energy of the string is dissipated. If the lower edge of the damper is angled or rounded, however, the string is gradually, but rapidly, damped as the angled edge of the damper approaches the string and the jack returns to its rest position.

The ability to absorb the energy of the string is enhanced by using two dampers instead of just one. The problem of the rapid absorption of such energy is clearly not as great in spinett virginals and harpsichords, but even here doubled dampers with rounded or sloping lower edges are normally used. Nevertheless, the small 2½-voet, child and 4-voet virginals, which occur only as spinett types (and the 4′ stop in harpsichords), have jacks with only one damper.

Since the upper touch-limit bar on the rack controls the depth of touch of the keys, the jackrail in a Ruckers instrument serves only to prevent the jacks from jumping out of their slots and to reflect them as quietly and quickly as possible back into their playing position. It does not control the depth of touch. The jackrail is made of a solid piece of poplar with moulded upper edges, and sides which overhang the recess into which the jacks enter. To my knowledge only one Ruckers virginal survives with its original jackrail cloths, the 1622 IR 6-voet muselar virginal in the Metropolitan Museum, New York. This virginal jackrail has two layers of the thinner action cloth already described (compressed thickness of each layer = 0.9mm) tacked with pairs of tacks at both ends and along one-third and two-thirds of its length.

A tongue in the treble end of the jackrail fits into a blind groove in a decorated and carved block glued to the spine side of the instrument (except for the little 2½-voet and child virginals, where the blind groove is located just below the moulding on the right-hand side of the case and is cut directly in the case itself). With the spinett virginals the bass end of the jackrail fits into a recess in the left-hand case side. A small mortice in the end of the jackrail fits around a wire loop fixed into the case recess, and a wire or brass hook nailed to the top of the jackrail engages in the wire loop to hold the jackrail in position.

In the muselar virginals a heavy block is glued to the left extension of the nameboard liner at soundboard level. A decorative carved block which serves as the bass jackrail support is glued to the soundboard at this point.[13] A tongue in the bass end of the jackrail fits into a recess in this jackrail support, and a turnbutton turns to cover the tongue in the recess, and to hold the jackrail in position.

The jackrails of the muselar virginals are usually slightly tapered, being somewhat wider in the bass than in the treble. Spinett virginals, on the other hand, usually

[13] In the 1610b AR virginal, the only muselar 4½-voet virginal, the bass end of the jackrail fits into an extension of the left-hand keywell brace out over the soundboard and is secured with a turnbutton.

Plate 5.9 A typical signature on a virginal jackrail (1638a IR).

have parallel-sided jackrails. In all instrument types, the overhanging sides of the jackrail are carved with gently curved arches at both ends, gradually cutting the overhang away to the level of the top of the padded recess.

Since there is no name-batten on a virginal, the Ruckers signature is found on the jackrail, instead of the decorative block-printed papers found on harpsicord jackrails. The signature – IOANNES RVCKERS ME FECIT ANTVERPIAE – without the date is typical.

Plate 5.10 The double-arcaded stand from below the 1611 HR 6-voet muselar virginal.

CHAPTER SIX

# Construction of Ruckers harpsichords

Since many parts of Ruckers harpsichords are identical with or similar to those of the virginals, and since it appears that the same workmen, using the same methods and procedures, were involved in the making of harpsichords as virginals, there are many points of similarity in the construction of the two types of instrument. Most of the woods and other materials are the same, much of the decoration is similar, and the attention paid to the structural parts and to the musical and acoustical parts is the same. The construction of harpsichords reflects the lack of stable templates or technical drawings, the use of hot glue to join the various parts together, and the pragmatic approach already seen from the previous chapter.

## HARPSICHORD BASEBOARDS

As with Ruckers virginals, harpsichord baseboards are made of poplar and are usually near ½ small duim (12.7mm) in thickness. The grain of the wood runs parallel to the long direction of the instrument except at the front under the keyboards. Here a plank about 10 duimen (250–260mm) in width whose grain runs at right angles to the spine is joined to the planks running lengthwise by means of an oblique scarf joint. This achieves dimensional stability and strength where it is needed most – parallel to the direction of the strings under the body of the instrument, and to the long axis of the action under the keyboards. The lower outside surface of the baseboard seems to have been sized with glue or shellac, although the interior surface is completely untreated. As with the other instruments of the Flemish school, the baseboard is flush with the outside case sides, and the instrument is built up on the baseboard. The layout of the instrument is punched on the baseboard and the punch marks joined up with scribed lines.

The baseboards extend right out to the edges of the case, and the case sides and nameboard, baseboard braces (including the toolbox braces), keyblocks, and keywell moulding are all marked on the baseboard. In addition, single-manual harpsichords have three scribed lines under the gap marking its two registers, and doubles have five lines indicating the four registers in the gap in a similar way. These lines do not give the exact position of the registers above them, however. The near line under the gap coincides with the far edge of the wrestplank. This line is 8 duimen (206–207mm) from the inside face of the nameboard in both single- and double-manual harpsichords, the only exception being the little quint harpsichord (1627 AR). The rear register line scribed under the gap is further back than the rear edge of the gap itself. The upper belly rail in Ruckers harpsichords is, however, not perpendicular to the baseboard, but sloped (see pp. 94 and 114–15), and the rear line coincides with a line projecting down from the front surface of the belly rail to the baseboard. This line, in conjunction with the position of the rear edge of the top of the gap, thus determines the slope of the upper belly rail. The central scribed line under the gap in double-manual harpsichords indicates the position of the rear ends of the upper-manual keys. As well as the extra lines under the gap, double-manual harpsichords have two additional lines across the keywell portion of the baseboard to position the papered batten in front of the upper-manual keyboard.

The spacing of the scribed lines on the baseboard for the internal bracing, the gap lines, and the cheek, spine, and nameboard is remarkably consistent from one instrument to another for each member of the Ruckers

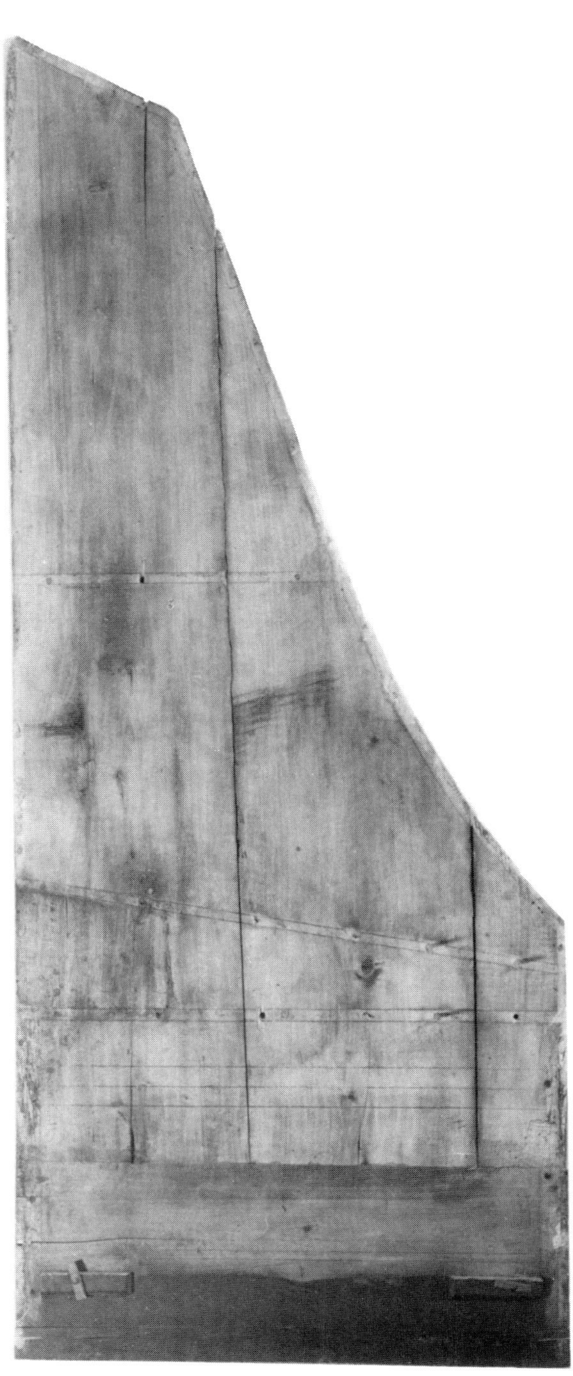

Plate 6.1 The interior surface of a single-manual harpsichord baseboard. The scribed lines for the baseboard braces and case-sides, and the 3 scribed lines marking the gap can be seen clearly (1644a AR). Scale 1:10.

family. One may assume from this that the position of these lines was scribed using a marking-out rod of some type, which was individual to each member of the family. The shaping of the bentside, on the other hand, is somewhat erratic and it appears that no two Ruckers instruments had exactly the same curvature of bentside, no doubt because it was impossible to expose each bentside to exactly the same heat treatment and because of the variable nature of the bentside wood. However, the scribed lines on the baseboard for the bentside do follow the bentside, of whatever shape, quite closely. Hence it would appear that the bentside was itself used as a template.

Harpsichord baseboards, like those of virginals, are fixed by means of wooden pegs on to the case sides. (Indeed, the scribed lines on the baseboard, as well as providing a plan from which the instrument could be built, also served to locate the holes for the pegs centrally in the case sides and baseboard braces.) Again like those of virginals, they are only lightly glued to the case sides and braces, although the glue used on the wooden pegs sometimes spreads, causing localized secure gluing of the baseboard to the case. The keyblocks are glued to the inside of the case and are also pegged to the baseboard from below. Keyframe hold-down blocks with turnbuttons are glued to the baseboard at the sides of the keywell to fasten the keyframe in position, and these and the baseboard under the keys are painted black. The keywell flap, hinged at the bottom to the near edge of the baseboard, seems to have been a universal feature of double-manual and single-manual harpsichords. The front edge of the baseboard originally carried three wire hinges for this flap. In addition, the little toolbox flap on the spine is also fixed with two wire hinges to the spine edge of the baseboard.

## HARPSICHORD CASE SIDES AND INTERNAL FRAMING

With few exceptions the lengths of virginals are relatively standard, and this standardization is reflected in the identification of the instrument type in the numbering system used by the Ruckers. No such standardization seems to occur in the length of single- and double-manual harpsichords. The single-manual harpsichords vary in length from about 70 to 72 duimen (1,813 to 1,864mm) and doubles from about 85½ to 88 duimen (2,210 to 2,274mm). Although the latter dimension is almost exactly equal to 8 Flemish voeten,[1] there is only

[1] Klaas Douwes (see Appendix 8) refers to harpsichords which are 8 voeten long. He is clearly referring to harpsichords and not to virginals since he calls them *Steert-stukken*. These are also referred to by Duarte in his letters to Huygens (see Appendix 17). He says, 'The extreme length of the large clavecimbels is 8 voeten more or less . . .'. Clearly these instruments were not exactly 8 voeten long.

one harpsichord of this length (1628b IR), so no particular significance can be attached to this. Most doubles in fact measure close to 87 duimen or about 2,250mm. Indeed, even the little 1627 AR quint harpsichord, identified by Ruckers as '4 St' (that is, 4-voet *Staertstuk*) is about 48 duimen (1,232mm) long or about 4 duimen longer than 4 voeten.

The widths of the harpsichords, being determined basically by the compass of the instrument, are much more standardized than the lengths, because the number of different compasses used by the Ruckers in their instruments was small. The usual C/E to $c^3$ single-manual harpsichord had an inside case width of about 690mm, and the standard double with a lower-manual compass of C/E to $f^3$ an inside case width of about 760mm. The larger, less common singles and doubles with chromatic basses had inside case widths in proportion to their compasses (see p. 173).

The height of Ruckers harpsichord cases was also highly standardized. Single-manual harpsichords are either 9 or 9½ small duimen (229 or 242mm) high (measured excluding the baseboard thickness).[2] Double-manual instruments seem universally to have been built with case sides, not including the thickness of the baseboard, 10 small duimen high (255mm). To determine the original number of manuals of an instrument which has been greatly altered one therefore simply measures the case height, providing of course that this has not also been altered. Although there is a statistically small sample from which to make general conclusions, there are two 9½-duimen-high single-manual harpsichords with a strapwork outer decoration, and six 9-duimen-high singles with a marbled outer case. Thus one may also be able to use the case-height measurement to say something about the type of original decoration of single-manual harpsichords.

Why instruments with a strapwork outer decoration have higher case sides is not clear, but it is probably because the strapwork pattern would appear unduly cramped with a case height of only 9 duimen. That they changed the case height simply to suit the type of decoration implies to me that the Ruckers attached little acoustical or musical significance to the case height or the internal cavity volume. The choice of the case height was at any rate more or less arbitrary, since only integral or half-integral units of the duim were used. There seems to have been no attempt to control the volume of the internal cavity of their instruments by using smaller fractions of the duim unit. However, the volume of the instrument is not a function of the case height alone, since it also depends upon the length and width of the harpsichord. The standard short-octave and the large 'French' double-manual harpsichords have a range of notes covering exactly the same pitch, but the volume of the two types of instrument is much different. No attempt was made to equalize the volume of the two types of instrument by changing the case height or the length in order to compensate for the larger width of the 'French' double.[3]

The thickness of the poplar case sides varies from instrument to instrument, from 12.5mm to 16mm. Though double-manual instruments sometimes have slightly thicker case sides than singles, the average thickness in both is about 14–15mm. The bentside, unlike the other case sides in Ruckers harpsichords, is variable in thickness along its length. Usually it is about 15.5mm thick near the tail, thinning to about 12.5mm at the point of strongest curvature, and then thickening again to the original 15.5mm at the cheek. This variation seems to reflect the way in which the bentsides were constructed and bent.

The three combined virginal-and-harpsichord instruments (1594 HR, 1619 IR and n.d. IR) provide the best clues as to the way the Ruckers made their bentsides. These instruments have an internal bentside forming a partition between the harpsichord and virginal parts of the instrument and used as a hitchrail for the strings of both parts of the instrument. (This partition reaches in height only to the soundboard level and the soundboard runs over its top edge for the full length of the instrument.) Because the bentside is completely hidden and requires no finishing or decoration, it was left untreated after the bending had been carried out. All three instruments show that the concave surface of the internal bentside was strongly heated over an open fire. Indeed, in the region of strongest curvature, the surface of the wood is slightly charred. The ends of the bentside show streaks of black soot indicating that the fire may have been of pitch, oil, or wax, although a rapid fire of wood shavings would produce a similar effect.

After heating the bentside over the fire it was bent, perhaps over a former, perhaps simply by compressing the two ends of the bentside together between two walls, or perhaps by drawing the ends together with a twisted rope. No traces of the procedure remain on any of the surviving instruments, however. The variety in the

[2] The one exception is the 1636 AR which was originally a single with a case depth of 10 duimen.

[3] Edward L. Kottick, 'The acoustics of the harpsichord: response curves and modes of vibration', *Galpin Society Journal*, XXXVIII (1985), footnote 20, finds that the internal cavity of a harpsichord case in no way acts like a Helmholtz resonator. Therefore the internal volume can have no effect on the vibrations of the strings or soundboard and is in no way coupled with them. It is therefore not surprising that changing the case height by arbitrary amounts was not found to affect the sound of the Ruckers instruments.

amount of heat produced by the fire, and in the position on the bentside which received maximum heating and was most readily bent, would produce strongly variable results. This variation could also be produced if the ends of the bentside were drawn together by compression or rope tension to produce the curvature, rather than by using a former. Interestingly, from a comparison of the scribed lines on the baseboard with the present position of the bentside on the 1644a AR single-manual harpsichord, it is clear that the bentside had slightly straightened out between the time when the baseboard lines were scribed and the time when the bentside was fitted to the rest of the case sides and secured to the baseboard in its final position. This 'relaxing' or straightening is characteristic of wood which has been bent using heat. The amount the bentside straightens will depend at least in part on the time interval between when it was used as a template to scribe the lines on the baseboard, and when it was fitted and secured into the instrument.

The interior bentsides in harpsichord/virginal combinations have a uniform thickness along their length. However, in the more usual harpsichords where the bentside was an external case side and had to be prepared to take the paint for the outer decoration, the soot and charred wood had to be planed away from the surface with a round-bottomed compass plane. Most material had to be removed in the region of strongest heating (and therefore where the greatest curvature occurred). The bentside is thinnest at the point of greatest curvature not because it was made thinner there to facilitate bending, but because this is where the bentside needed the greatest amount of cleaning up after the bending had taken place.

The original exterior decoration of the 1618b IR double-manual harpsichord has been completely removed, and replaced with a plain varnished finish. The discoloration produced by the heating of the bentside previous to bending is clearly visible under the varnish, showing that some discoloured, heat-affected wood still remained before the case was painted.

The bentside is fitted to the tail and cheek with a characteristic join (see Fig. 9.2), which differs from the usual eighteenth-century mitred and dovetailed case joins. In the Ruckers bentside joins, only the moulded part of the case side forms a mitred join. In all Ruckers and most sixteenth- and seventeenth-century Flemish harpsichords, the tailpiece overlaps the bentside and the bentside overlaps the cheek. This characteristic construction is one of the distinguishing features of a genuine Ruckers instrument which may be of help in identifying a counterfeit instrument.

The tail/spine join is a simple mitre joint and it and all other joins are pegged together during gluing with 3mm pegs. The pegs are placed in the overlapping side at the bentside joins – i.e. in the tail at the tail/bentside join, and in the bentside at the bentside/cheek join (see Figs. 9.1 and 9.2).

The ends of the wrestplank are let about 6mm into the cheek and spine, and secured with large oak pegs about 5–6mm in diameter driven through the case side into the wrestplank. In addition the wrestplank is pegged along the near edge to the nameboard with small 3mm pegs.

The entire top edge of the case is decorated with an ogee moulding identical with that used in the virginals. The nameboard is somewhat thinner than the other case sides (11–12mm) and, like the faceboard and nameboard in virginals, is capped with two opposing ogee mould-

Plate 6.2 The treble section of the bentside on the 1618b IR double-manual harpsichord, which has had its outer decoration removed. As well as the scorching of the bentside wood, the dowels used to fix the internal baseboard braces, the internal case-joins, and the bentside liner are also visible.

ings (see Fig. 5.1). The nameboard is let into the spine and cheek on either side, and the opposing ogee mouldings are mitred into the mouldings on the spine and cheek. The nameboard is secured with 3mm pegs from the outside of the case into the ends of the nameboard.

All Ruckers harpsichords, whether doubles or singles, seem originally to have had upper registers which projected out through the cheek. The projecting ends of each register could be grasped by the player and moved back and forth to engage or disengage the jacks of that register. The hole for the register in the cheek is the width of the gap and the height of the register plus the thickness of the bone plates glued to the top surface of the ends of the registers. The cheek usually, but not always (e.g. 1637 A R), also contained a hole through which the end of the buff stop projected and was operated.

The lid was hinged to the top of the spine side of the instrument. Most single-manual instruments used wire hinges for the main lid. Like the hinges used on the lid and keywell flap of the virginals, these consisted simply of two pieces of wire bent in half across each other. The paired wire ends were then inserted into angled holes in the lid and case side, splayed apart and hammered into the grain of the wood to prevent them from pulling out. The same type of hinge was used for the front keywell flap and the spine toolbox lid, and, in single-manual harpsichords, for the lid flap hinged to the main lid. A few singles (e.g. 1637 A R and 1651b A R) and all double-manual harpsichords used an axle strap hinge of a characteristic pattern (see Plate 7.41) to hinge the main lid to the spine. In doubles, strap hinges seem to have been necessary simply because of the weight of the large heavy lids – wire hinges would have been too flimsy. These hinges were nailed to the lid and case side with short, stubby, round-headed brass nails. Double-manual harpsichords also had small decorative axle hinges to hinge the lid flap to the main lid instead of the wire hinges used on singles. The strap hinges (see Plate 7.41) were also held in place with small brass nails.

Wire hooks, which fitted into wire loops in the overhanging edge of the lid, were nailed to the bentside and served to keep the lid firmly closed. To hold the keywell flap closed, wire hooks, which were nailed to the spine and cheek in the keywell, mated into wire loops on the keywell flap itself. Normally a lock on the outside of the keywell flap mated to a hasp attached to a strap hinge on the lid flap. Otherwise, two wire hooks on the keywell flap mated into wire loops in the overhanging edge of the lid flap.

Ruckers virginals have no specific internal framing or bracing, but rely on the case sides and structure of the instrument itself for the stability and the strength necessary to resist the tension of the strings. Ruckers harpsichords, on the other hand, have a clearly-worked-out method of internal framing and bracing which adds to the strength and stability provided by the case sides and joints. Since the 8′ strings are hitched to the bentside and tail liners, the tendency is naturally for the bentside and tail to collapse inwards, and any framing system must provide bracing which prevents this from happening.

The internal framing in Ruckers harpsichords occurs at two levels: the lower-level baseboard braces at and above the baseboard, and the upper buttresses just below the liners. The lower braces consist of poplar boards placed vertically on the baseboard at right angles to the spine. These are about 3 small duimen (77mm) high and are let about 6–7mm into the spine at one end, and the bentside or cheek at the other. The ends of these are pegged to the case side and their lower edge is pegged to the baseboard with 5mm pegs.

The baseboard brace nearest the player forms the lower belly rail. The keyframe (the lower-manual keyframe in double-manual harpsichords) butts against this brace, and two chamfered blocks glued to the side of the brace hold the rear edge of the keyframe firmly against the baseboard. Immediately behind the lower belly rail, another baseboard brace makes a small angle with the belly rail. This angled brace is usually about ½ voet to 7½ duimen (140–191mm) from the belly rail at the spine end, and one duim (26mm) at the cheek end. These two braces are called the toolbox braces.

A rectangular opening in the spine allows access to the space between the two braces, probably for storage of tools, the tuning key, spare quills, strings, etc. Usually this toolbox space did not extend right along to the cheek, but stopped at a wall glued between the two toolbox braces about half-way along the width of the instrument. A chamfered board nailed to the top edge of the toolbox braces provided a top over the toolbox, and a small flap hinged to the baseboard provided access to the toolbox opening. The flap was held closed with a wooden turnbutton nailed to the spine, and opened with a loop of leather passing through a hole near the centre of the flap and glued or nailed to its inside. A stop glued to the spine on the inside of the case of the instrument prevents the toolbox flap from hinging past its normal closed position and becoming wedged between the two toolbox braces. This stop hangs about 6mm below the top edge of the toolbox opening so that when the flap is closed it is flush with the rest of the spine.

Behind the toolbox braces, and running from the spine to the bentside, are two more baseboard braces in double-manual harpsichords and one in single-manual harpsichords. These braces keep the baseboard flat, and hold

Plate 6.3 The internal framing and soundboard barring of a typical Ruckers double-manual harpsichord (1640b IR). The method of fixing the soundboard rose, and the veneer on the lower surface of the wrestplank are not original. Scale 1:10. Photograph: Kurt Wittmayer. By permission of Graf Landsberg-Velen.

the bentside, cheek and spine at a constant distance from one another, and the case sides at a right angle to the baseboard.

The upper-level braces consist of boards running from the bentside to the spine placed flat underneath the lower edge of the soundboard liners. Each brace is about 2 duimen (50mm) wide and is nailed at each end with two nails into the liners. The lower edge of each of these braces is chamfered in a way which seems characteristic of the Ruckers family, and which also seems completely aesthetic and non-functional (see Fig. 9.3). In some instruments the upper-level braces are perpendicular to the spine; in others they run obliquely across the instrument, not quite perpendicular either to the bentside or the spine. These upper-level braces – two in single-manual harpsichords, and three in doubles – maintain the integrity of the upper section of the bentside. Buttressing the bentside against the spine at a level which is close to that in which the string tension acts prevents any tendency of the bentside to collapse inwards.

Besides supporting the soundboard, the liners also add to the overall strength and rigidity of the instrument. They vary in dimensions – usually about 45–52mm wide and 15–20mm thick. The tail liner, which has to withstand the tension of the heavy bass strings, is usually both wider and thicker than the other liners. Like the bentside, the bentside liner is thinner near the region of maximum curvature. It seems likely therefore that it too was bent by heating over an open fire, and later thinned to remove the charred wood where the bending was the most pronounced.

The top surface of the wrestplank, excluding the veneer, and the liners along the spine, tail, bentside and cheek, are all placed 2 small duimen (51mm) below the top edge of the case. The liners are glued to the case sides, and the bentside liner is, in addition, pegged to the bentside with 5mm pegs placed at intervals of about 5–6 duimen (125–155mm). The joins in the liners at the case-side corners are all simple mitred joints. The liners in the harpsichords of the Ruckers and most of the other Flemish builders of the sixteenth and seventeenth centuries extend past the upper belly rail into the gap and under the wrestplank at both the spine and cheek sides. In some examples, the liners even extend under the wrestplank right to the nameboard, although they usually stop slightly short of it. Beyond the gap, the liners are cut to fit around the (sometimes rather irregular) shape of the wrestplank.

The belly rail is usually 15–16mm thick, and positioned at an angle to the vertical with its lower edge further to the rear of the instrument than the top edge. This is to accommodate the jacks, which are splayed apart at their feet as a result of the way that the lower guides are made (see pp. 114–15). As mentioned earlier, a line projecting down from the front surface of the belly rail coincides with the rear transverse line scribed on the baseboard under the gap and this line must have been used to determine the angle of the upper belly rail in conjunction with the position of the rear edge of the gap. It is, however, not entirely clear how the gap width was determined, since there is no construction mark either on the baseboard or liner to indicate this.

The upper belly rail does not extend to the spine and cheek case sides, but is let into the liners about 6–8mm at either end, and is therefore left with an air gap at either end below the liners. The upper edge of the belly rail is planed flush with and parallel to the top of the liners, providing a surface to which the front edge of the soundboard is glued and pegged. Two pairs of wires straddle the gap between the wrestplank and the top of the belly

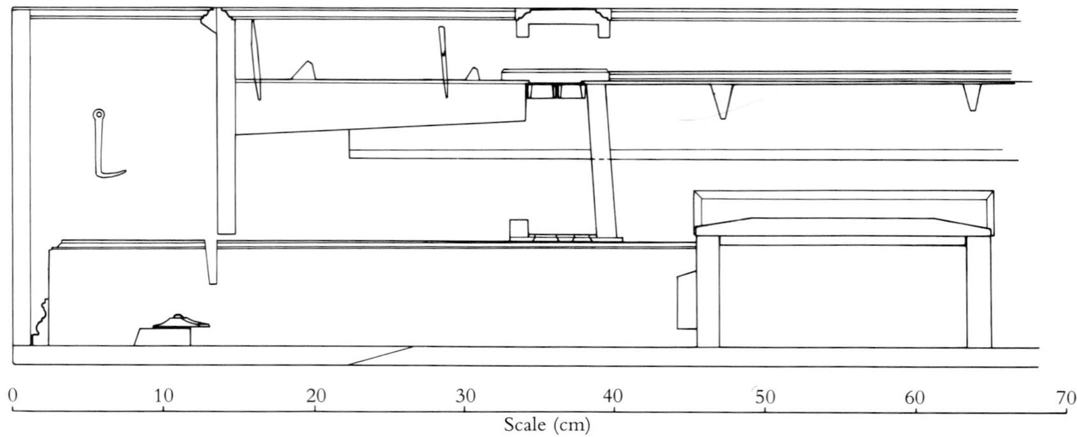


Fig. 6.1 Section through the bass keywell of a typical Ruckers single-manual harpsichord (based on the 1645 I C). Scale 1:5.

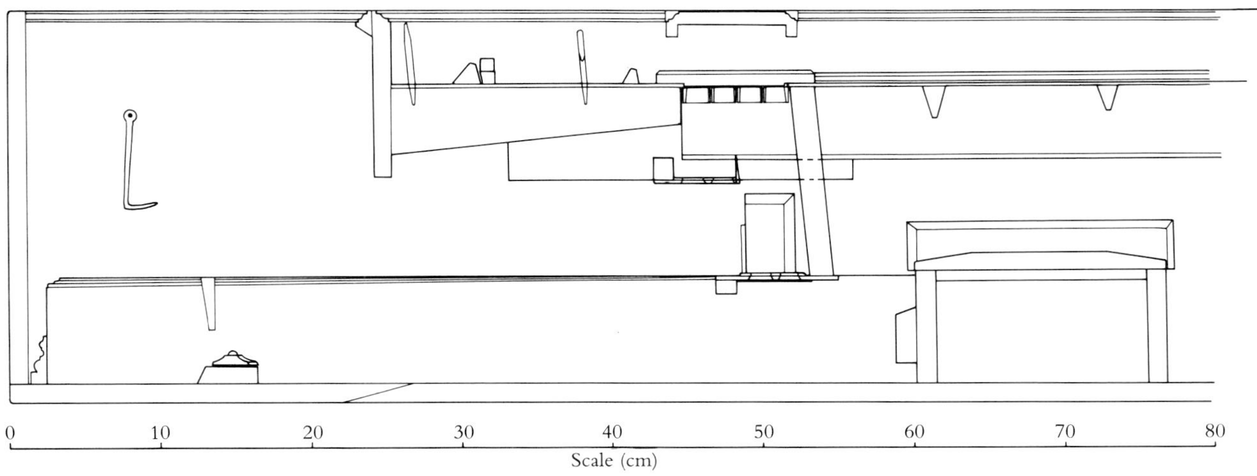


Fig. 6.2 Section through the bass keywell of a typical Ruckers double-manual harpsichord (based on the 1638b IR). Scale 1:5.

rail, and support the registers with one wire underneath and one above them in each pair.

The lower guide is nailed along its length to the lower edge of the upper belly rail. It is then attached to the rear top surface of the bass and treble keyblocks and may, in double-manual instruments, be let into the keyblocks so that its top is flush with the top surfaces of the keyblocks. This allows the upper-manual keyframe to slide as far over the top of the lower guide as is necessary to line up the upper-manual keys under the upper-manual guide and jacks.

The upper belly rail thus extends from the top of the keyblocks to the soundboard, and serves as a means of support and attachment for both the soundboard and the lower guide.

In double-manual instruments, the extra lower jack guide for the upper manual is attached underneath the liners on the cheek and spine sides. In order to increase the distance between the upper registers and the lower guide, an additional strip of wood 10–15mm deep is sometimes glued to the lower surface of the liners, and the lower guide is attached to this strip instead of the liner. The strip usually extends under the wrestplank in one direction, and beyond the belly rail in the other such that the belly rail is let into the strip as well as into the liner. If, as in some doubles, the cheek liner is made specially wide, the additional strip is not then necessary on this side.

The keyblocks at the bass and treble ends of the keyboards are glued to the case sides and pegged to the baseboard. A characteristic moulding, which I have called the keywell moulding (see Fig. 6.3), runs along the baseboard between spine and cheek just in front of the keys, and from which the keyblocks extend backwards to the lower belly rail or first toolbox brace.

Besides the direct function of supporting the lower jack guide and the upper manual in double-manual harpsichords, the keyblocks also have an indirect function which strongly affects the acoustical performance of a harpsichord. Since the octave spacing of the strings and the keys in a Ruckers harpsichord is the same, the keyboard width and the width of the string band are the same (neglecting the extra width of the two outside natural keys). If there were no keyblocks, the case sides would be adjacent to the top and bottom keys, and in consequence, also very close to the top and bottom strings. Because of the width of the liners, the bridges at both their treble and bass ends would sit on top of the liners, and this would seriously impair the quality of the lowest and uppermost

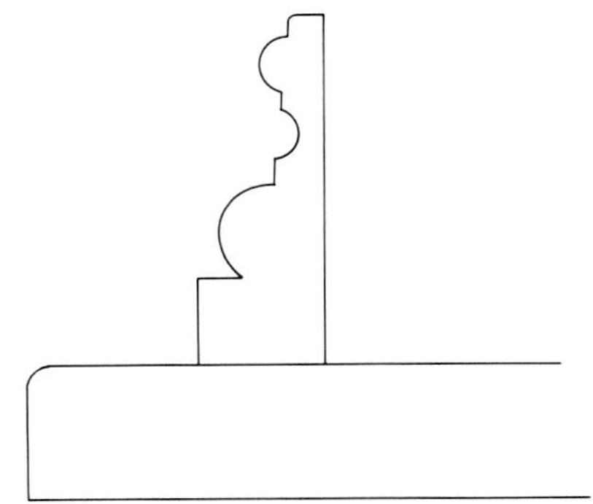

Fig. 6.3 Profile of the keywell moulding used on the baseboard in front of the keys in both harpsichords and virginals. Scale 1:1.

notes. Widening the case by inserting keyblocks whose width is greater than the width of the soundboard liners moves the case sides and liners away from the ends of the bridges, thus maintaining the quality of the notes into the extreme treble and bass by allowing the bridges and soundboard to vibrate freely there.

## THE MAIN LID, LID FLAP AND KEYWELL FLAP IN HARPSICHORDS

The main lid, lid flap and the keywell flap, like the rest of the case of the instrument, are all of poplar wood, and are usually 12–14mm thick. The main lid on both single- and double-manual harpsichords overhangs the tail and bent-side by 10–15mm, but is flush along the spine. The break between the lid and lid flap is just behind the gap, and the edge of the main lid is stiffened by two transverse bars with ovolo mouldings, one on the outer and one on the inner surface of the lid (see Fig. 6.4). These bars have functions, however, in addition to stiffening the lid.

The bar on the outer surface of the main lid has an ovolo moulding along one edge, the other being flush with the edge of the lid. Three hinges placed along the edge of this bar attach it to the lid flap. The bar on the inner surface of the main lid has ovolo mouldings along both edges, and one edge of the bar projects beyond the edge of the lid to overlap the break between the main lid and lid flap. This overlapping seems to be to prevent dust and dirt from falling through the small gap at the lid break onto the soundboard, but especially into the jacks and registers. I have therefore called this lower batten the dustcatcher moulding.

The lid-flap design varies slightly between single- and double-manual harpsichords. On singles the lid flap is simply a jointed board stiffened along the edge hinged to the main lid with another bar like that on the lid. The double-manual lid flap, in addition to being larger, is stiffened differently from the lid flap used on singles. Here the jointed board used for the flap is both stiffened on the outside at the spine and cheek edges with ovolo moulded bars, and also framed on the inside surface with mitred bars bearing an elaborate moulding (see Fig. 6.4). The effect of the inner mouldings, especially if the inside of the lid is painted rather than decorated with block-printed papers, is that of a framed painting. Because of the way the flap is hinged (see Fig. 6.4), the surface of the frame and the inside of the lid are flush when the lid is closed. Thus the inside surface of the lid flap and the main lid are in the same plane in single-manual harpsichords but are offset in doubles. Also, because of the additional

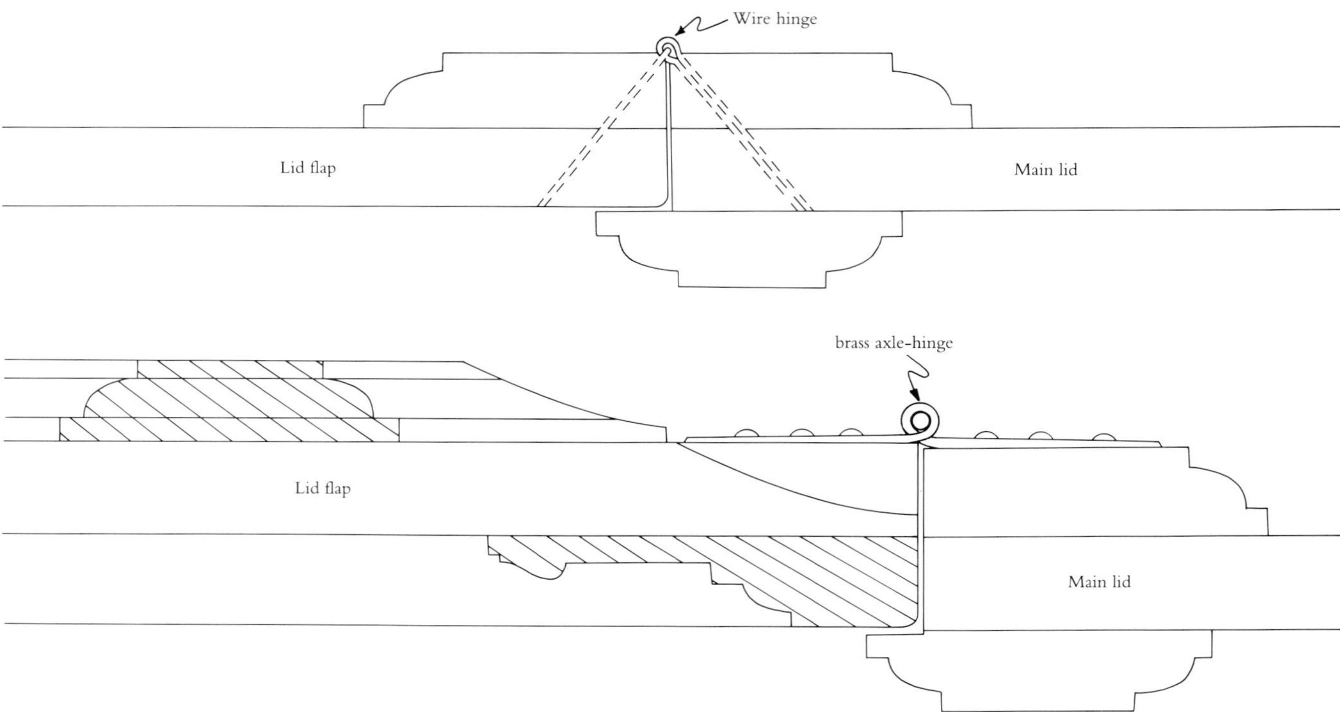


Fig. 6.4 The mouldings on the main lid and lid flap on Ruckers harpsichords (sections at the main lid/lid flap join). Above, for a single-manual harpsichord, and below for a double-manual harpsichord. Scale 1:1.

size of the double-manual main lid, an extra transverse stiffening bar with ovolo mouldings along both edges was added to the top of the main lid at about the mid-point along the length of the instrument.

The lid flap, unlike the main lid, overhangs the case sides along the spine as well as along its other two outside edges. The Ruckers never seemed to have used a single large lid without the break between the main lid and the lid flap, though the Couchet sons did not always follow this tradition (see the catalogue entry for n.d. IC). Although a number of seventeenth-century paintings show instruments built very much in the style of Ruckers harpsichords with a single-piece lid, there are usually other features which are also uncharacteristic of Ruckers instruments, leading to the conclusion that the instruments depicted were not made by one of the Ruckers family.

The harpsichord lids were held open, not with a lid stick, but with string cords. With the main lid closed, the lid flap could be hinged back, and held in position by a cord running from a 3mm hole in the spine above the wrestplank and just behind the nameboard, to one about half-way along the spine side of the lid flap. The lid flap could then be held back at an angle to the vertical by gravity and could be used in this position as a music support by resting the music on the jackrail. The main lid could also be hinged back past the vertical and was held open in this position by a cord running from another 3mm hole in the bentside above the soundboard to a hole in the bentside portion of the lid. The stability of the main lid in the open position is increased by the weight of the lid flap. Hinged freely on the main lid and falling back under its own weight, it increases the tendency of the lid to overbalance. The lid cords can be seen in a number of contemporary paintings, as for example, in 'A young woman playing a harpsichord' by Jan Steen (see Plate 6.4).

This lid arrangement prevents the harpsichord from being placed close to a wall. In turn, this leaves the toolbox accessible and means that the spine side is normally visible, and therefore decorated. Eighteenth-century harpsichords, using a lid stick to hold the lid open, could be placed close up to a wall so that the spine was not visible; it was therefore usually left undecorated.

The keywell flap is a simple unmoulded board hinged to the baseboard with three wire hinges. It fits into a recess in the front edge of the spine and cheek and is held closed by one or two hooks in the inside of the keywell on the cheek and spine. These hook into wire eye loops on the inside of the keywell flap. Some harpsichords have a pin (often a tuning pin) projecting out of the case side in one or both of the case recesses for the keywell flap. This pin fits into a small slot in the keywell flap when it is in the closed position and prevents the keywell flap from being pulled up if an inadvertent attempt is made to open the lid flap without first unlocking it or unhooking it from the lid flap.

Plate 6.4 'A young woman playing a harpsichord' by Jan Steen (1626–79). The main lid of the harpsichord is held open with a lid cord (not visible). The cord for the lid flap, which can be used to hold the lid flap open with the main lid closed, can be seen hanging below and to the left of the music. Reproduced by courtesy of the Trustees, The National Gallery, London.

## THE HARPSICHORD WRESTPLANK

Unlike the rest of the structural part of the Ruckers harpsichord, which is made of poplar, the wrestplank is of oak (*Quercus, spp.*). It is let about 6mm into the spine and cheek and pegged and glued to the nameboard, spine and cheek, as well as to the shaped extensions of the spine and cheek liners. In both double- and single-manual harpsichords it is about 45mm thick near the player, and about 26mm (1 duim) thick near the gap. It is cut very close to the quarter, which gives the lower surface a very strong figure with characteristically wide rays. This tapering in thickness and cutting almost exactly on the quarter strongly suggest that the wood was obtained from an oak butt split radially, with the thin central wedges then discarded. Indeed, the 1608 AR double-manual harpsichord wrestplank, where it has not been planed smooth, shows clear signs of splintering and splitting. Later Ruckers wrestplanks often show marks indicating sawing from the log rather than splitting. However, as in the earlier instruments, the wood is still tapered and accurately quartered, and so must have been sawn as a radial section of the tree.

The shape and grain direction of the wrestplank have a number of important consequences. The thickest, strongest part of the wrestplank is located near the 8′ nut and tuning pins where the stress on the wrestplank from the 8′ strings is greatest, leaving the thinner part to support the lesser forces of the lighter 4′ strings. The tuning-pin holes are drilled tangentially to the annual rings, taking advantage of the greater resistance to splitting of the wood in this direction. For the same reason, the wrestplank as a whole is less likely to split under the tension of the strings. The other advantage of using quartered wood is that the humidity coefficient of expansion is greater in the tangential than in the radial direction. Thus the movement of the wood under conditions of changing humidity is minimized in the direction of the strings. This obviously contributes to the overall tuning stability.

The wrestplanks have the same width of 193–196mm (about 7½ duimen) in both double-manual and single-manual instruments and, since they also have the same thickness, are indistinguishable except in their length. The wrestplank is covered on its upper surface with a veneer of soundboard wood about 3–3½mm in thickness. The veneer overhangs the gap edge of the wrestplank by about 2mm and partly covers the edge of the near register. The direction of the grain of the veneer wood matches that of the soundboard wood, and the use of this veneer on the wrestplank seems to carry on the very early tradition of Müller and Theeuwes. In this tradition the jackslots were cut through the soundboard wood as in the virginals, and the soundboard wood carried on beyond the jacks, under the freely-vibrating nuts to the wrestplank at the back of the nameboard.

In Ruckers harpsichords the veneer is pegged to the wrestplank with very small (2mm) wooden pegs. These pegs are spaced regularly across the surface of the wrestplank at an interval of about 4 duimen (102mm), which is unrelated to the width of the soundboard planks used to make up the veneer. This suggests that the sections of the veneer were first jointed together, cut to length, and the whole veneer was then glued to the wrestplank. This was probably done by nailing several boards or strips of wood over the veneer to press it to the wrestplank while the glue cooled and dried. The boards and nails were then removed and pegs were used to fill the holes left by the nails.

After the veneer was glued to the wrestplank, lines were scribed on its surface marking the position of the tuning pins and nuts. The nuts run obliquely across the wrestplank, being further from the gap in the bass than in the treble. The 4′ nut is completely straight but the 8′ nut is curved such that the concave edge is nearest the player. The 8′ tuning pins run in a line parallel to the nameboard about 14mm from it. The 4′ tuning pins run obliquely in a straight line about half-way between the 8′ and 4′ nuts. The name of the key to which each string belongs is written near its tuning pin. In normal double-manual harpsichords the note name written is that of the lower-manual set of keys.

The 4′ tuning pins in Ruckers harpsichords are smaller than the 8′ pins (the exception is the 1627 AR quint harpsichord, where both 8′ and 4′ pins have a diameter of 3.7mm). The smaller pins make the 4′ easier to tune accurately. Unlike virginals, where the size of the tuning pins is graded within one register, harpsichord tuning pins in each register all have the same diameter: about 4.2mm for the 8′ pins and about 3.7mm for the 4′ pins, although variations of 3.8–4.6mm for the 8′, and 3.2–3.7mm for the 4′ tuning pins do occur. The 8′ pins are about 55mm long and about 5mm longer than the 4′ pins. The tuning pins are of iron wire rod, and their outer surface is usually striated with marks left by the drawing plate used to pull the rod down to the required diameter. The sharp edges on these striations help prevent slippage when the strings are coiled on the tuning pins.

The top of the tuning pin has been hammered lightly to provide a flat bearing surface for the tuning hammer. The lower section of the tuning pins used by Ruckers, and by all of the historical builders, was tapered. As this section was driven into the undersized parallel-sided hole in the wrestplank, it bruised and compressed the wood into a shape exactly right for the tapered shape of the pin. Usually the bottom 13mm (½ duim) of the pin is tapered and the pin is put in the wood to a depth of about 19mm, thus ensuring that the pin is aligned in its hole. The hardened compressed wood around the tapered shank of the pin ensures a tight-fitting, long-wearing bearing surface which will not loosen even if the pin slowly wears its way deeper into the hole.

The holes drilled in the wrestplank for the tuning pins are placed at a slight angle to the vertical – about 5° to 6° – such that the top of the tuning pin leans away from its corresponding nut. Drilling the 4′ tuning-pin holes at an angle presents no problems, but drilling the 8′ pin holes would require an exceptionally long drill bit. To avoid this the tuning-pin holes were presumably drilled in the wrestplank before it was positioned and glued into the case sides. Further weight is given to this hypothesis by the fact that the lower surface of the tapered wrestplank is at an angle of about 5½° to the upper surface. With the wrestplank placed on a horizontal surface, drilling vertically would automatically incline the holes at the correct angle. If this theory is correct, then the wrestplank veneer must have been glued to the wrestplank, the nuts glued in position, and the nut pins marked out so that the tuning-pin positions relative to the nut pins could also be determined and marked out. Having the wrestplank out of the instrument would also facilitate the gluing and clamping of the nuts in position.

Like the soundboard bridges and the bridges in virginals, the harpsichord nuts characteristically have a cross-section with angled faces. Also, like the bridges, the nuts are tapered in height and cross-section from bass to treble (see pp. 104–6 for a complete description of the angles of the faces and the probable method of making the bridges and nuts). Table 6.1 (p. 105) gives typical values of the dimensions of the nuts in a single- and a double-manual harpsichord. Also like the bridges, the nuts are positioned prior to gluing with pairs of pins on either side of the nut. These positioning pins are usually placed at or near the notes *c* and *f*♯, and the holes remaining may be of some help in determining the original pitch and compass of the instrument. They are a characteristic feature of Ruckers and some of the other Flemish builders. Normally, the holes left by the positioning pins in the wrestplank were filled with small wooden plugs cut off flush with the top of the wrestplank veneer.

All Ruckers harpsichords seem originally to have had a buff stop, with soft buff-leather pads touching the strings near their ends and producing a sound which is rapidly damped away like that of a harp or lute (it is sometimes called the harp stop or the lute stop). This stop consists of pads, probably of soft oil-tanned ox or moose leather about 5.5mm thick, glued to the top surface of a bar of beech or poplar placed against the 8′ nut. The pads are usually about 10mm high in the bass and 8mm high in the treble. They are also tapered in width from about 4mm at the top to 6mm at their base. The doubled e♭/g♯ strings on double-manual harpsichords (see p. 108) require special pads which are higher than normal and specially shaped so that the edge of the buff pad comes in contact with both strings simultaneously. The buff stop is split near the middle. Like the registers, the treble section projects through the cheek and can be operated by reaching around to the side of the instrument. The bass section was operated by a finger stop like that on the virginal harpichordium, or by a pin in a block glued to the top of the buff bar near the spine.[4] Both sections of the stop are turned on by pushing the buff bar towards the centre of the instrument, so that the treble pads are on the right, the bass pads are on the left of the strings. This means that the special pads for the e♭/g♯ strings have to be shaped differently on the bass buff bar from those on the treble bar. Also, contrary to the suggestion by Hubbard (p.63), it means that the two sections of the buff bar cannot be joined together to operate as one. Furthermore the original split-buff system is not readily adaptable to the instruments which have later had a second 8′ set of strings added.

The buff stop is held in place like the harpichordium stop in virginals. Small chamfered blocks of wood hold the bar against the 8′ nut, and horizontal wires placed in the nut hold the bar down against the wrestplank veneer. The friction between the bar and the blocks and wires, which is necessary to hold the stop in position, is increased by the bend introduced in the buff bar by the curvature of the nut. When engaged, the bar is stopped partly by the resistance of the pads against the sides of the strings and partly by a small carved block of wood placed at the position of the split in the buff stop (see Plate 6.5). One of the 4′ tuning pins passes through the low tapered end of this small block and the other end is let into a V-shaped nick in the nut. The presence of the V-shaped nick in the 8′ nut proves the former existence of a split buff in those instruments which have subsequently lost it, and also reveals where the split occurred. Also the scalloped border decoration painted around the buff bar, retaining block, and centre stop block provides further proof of the original existence of a buff stop and whether or not it was split. If the nut is original, the holes for the wires used to hold down the buff stop will also indicate whether or not the instrument originally had a buff.[5]

The split between the two sections of the buff stop occurs between the notes f¹ and f♯¹ in single-manual harpsichords. In a Ruckers double, where the two

[4] Both the treble and bass sections of the buff stop are operated by finger stops on the 1637 AR single, rather than by projecting the right-hand section through the cheek. Later instruments by Andreas Ruckers revert to the usual system.

[5] The two harpsichords signed by Ioannes Couchet (1645 IC and 1646 IC) which retain their original wrestplanks and nuts show clearly that the buff stop was not split, but was a continuous batten covering the entire register from treble to bass. These instruments both show traces of the chamfered blocks used to hold the buff batten against the nut, and both have holes in the side of the 8′ nut for the iron pins which held the batten against the wrestplank veneer. But there is no trace of the block or the 'V' notch in the 8′ bridges which are necessary for a split buff.

manuals are at different pitches, the split in the buff occurs at a different note (but the same pitch) on each manual – at $f^1/f^{\#1}$ on the 'f' keyboard and at $c^1/c^{\#1}$ on the 'c' keyboard.

## HARPSICHORD SOUNDBOARDS

The soundboard is the major acoustical element in any Ruckers instrument. The importance of the soundboard seems to have been clearly understood by all of the members of the Ruckers family, for it and the bridges, keys, registers and jacks are made and finished with a delicacy, accuracy and care that is atypical of the rest of the instrument. This indicates that the case was prepared by an entirely different person from the maker or makers of the soundboard, bridges, and action.

The soundboard is made of softwood which has been identified microscopically as *picea*, or spruce (probably *Picea abies*, or more properly *Picea excelsa*).[6] The wood is cut on the quarter so that one sees the edges of the annual rings and the silvery shimmer of the sides of the rays on the surface of the wood. Why it was quartered is not clear. Preliminary research on the vibrations of harpsichord soundboards[7] shows clearly that the soundboard is acting as an acoustical radiator, and not an acoustical resonator. This means that the soundboard is acting as a whole like a large piston driving the air above it up and down. In this way the soundboard converts the energy of vibration of the string into sound energy around the instrument. The extent to which the soundboard area breaks up into small sections with nodes and antinodes is insignificant. Therefore since the soundboard is not a resonating system, the velocity of travel of the waves in the soundboard is not an important acoustical factor, and hence the difference in the velocity of a sound wave in the radial and tangential directions in the soundboard wood is not important. So the wood is not quarter-sawn for acoustical reasons (many Italian soundboards use plank-sawn cypress to no acoustical or musical disadvantage). One clear non-acoustical advantage of using quartered soundboard wood is that the humidity coefficient of expansion is lower for quartered than for plank-sawn spruce, so that a quartered soundboard is dimensionally more stable under conditions of changing humidity. The soundboard is also therefore less subject to splitting when cut on the quarter, since the internal forces of tension (or compression) due to change in humidity are also reduced.

Plate 6.5 Detail of the wrestplank of the 1638b IR showing the position of the split in the buff stop and the carved block between the bass and treble sections of the buff battens.

The width of the individual planks of wood in a soundboard are usually integral multiples of the small duim, although one does, rarely, encounter half-integral widths as well. Usually adjacent planks show the same pattern of rings, indicating that they are successive slices cut from the tree. Such an arrangement would ensure that the grain of the wood in every plank was lying in the same direction. This is important when planing the soundboard to thickness: the wood can be planed in the same direction over the whole of the soundboard area, thus avoiding damage to the soundboard caused by lifting the grain of the wood with the plane. No attempt was made to use, say, wide-grained wood in the bass, and narrow-grained wood in the treble. Although the soundboard wood is usually close- and straight-grained, there are many cases where it is open-grained (1646 IC) or rather variable in texture. The soundboard often shows a fine shimmering silvery figure characteristic of well-quartered wood, but this is sometimes lacking, and the wood may be up to 20° off the quarter. Also, as is characteristic of spruce, the soundboard wood often contains pitch pockets whose existence has usually been disguised underneath the soundboard painting.

The Ruckers apparently paid a great deal of attention to the thickness of their soundboards. After the individual planks were glued together, the soundboard was carefully and accurately planed to thickness to give it the correct flexibility and weight in each section of its area. Fig. 6.5 shows the thickness of the soundboard of the 1640b AR double-manual harpsichord. The soundboards of Ioannes Ruckers harpsichords are even more strongly tapered, being about 4.3mm thick under the

[6] My grateful thanks to Mrs A. Miles of the Forest Products Research Laboratory, Princes Risborough, who carried out the identification of the soundboard and 8′ bridge woods (see below) for me.

[7] Further work on the acoustics of the soundboard and strings is in progress by the author.

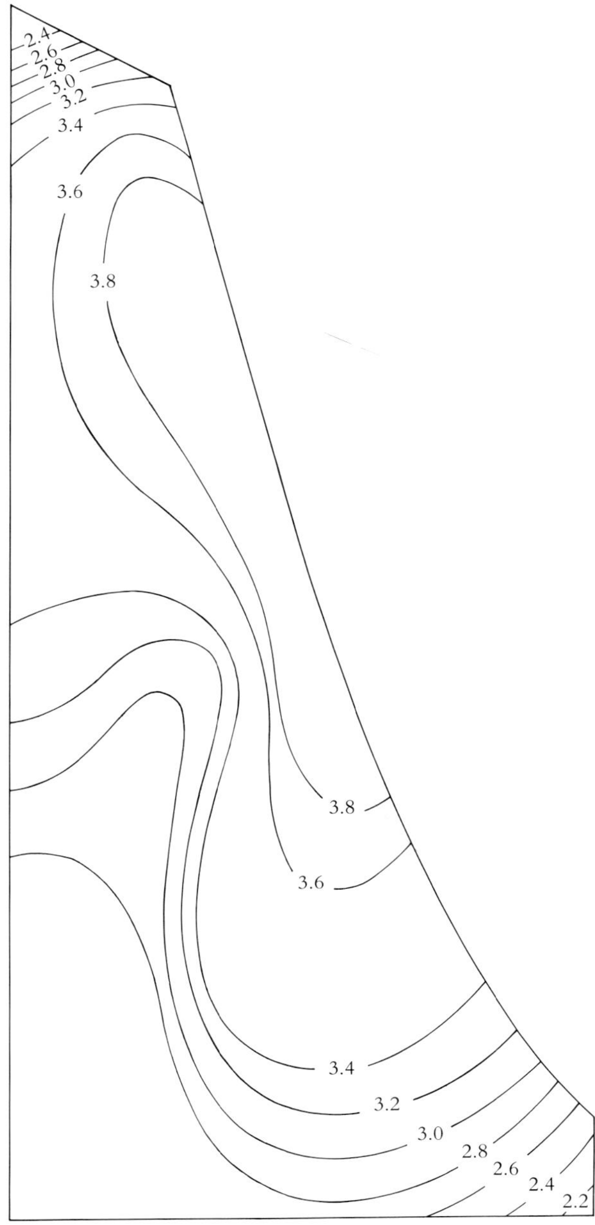


Fig. 6.5 The soundboard thickness contours for the 1640b AR double-manual harpsichord. Scale 1:10.

tenor part of the bridge and less than 2mm in the treble.[8] Thus the soundboards are much thicker under the tenor and bass part of the bridge than elsewhere, tapering away to become thinnest near the tail/spine corner and in the extreme treble part of the compass. The Couchet and later Ioannes Ruckers instruments seem also to vary the thickness of the tenor and bass regions of the 4′ bridge separately from those of the 8′ bridge.

The effect of the tapering is quite definite. In the treble the bridges lie almost at right angles to the grain of the soundboard, and this, coupled with the small distance of the bridges from the 4′ hitchpin rail and the belly rail in the treble, tends to make the soundboard and bridges very stiff there. This is offset by making the soundboard very thin in the treble. Clearly the opposite is true in the tenor and bass, where both the angle between the bridge and the soundboard grain is small, and the distance of the bridges to the case sides and hitchpin rail is large, producing a much more flexible system. To overcome this the soundboard is made thicker in the bass to avoid the 'banjo effect', where the sound energy of the string is radiated very quickly and dies away almost immediately. Also, being stiffer, a larger part of the soundboard is set in motion, increasing the effective area of the soundboard and, in turn, increasing the strength of the fundamental and lower partials of the radiated sound. It also helps to support the heavier bass strings.

As with the virginals, the soundboard wood was probably initially reduced in thickness using a plane and then the final adjustments were made with a scraper. The final finishing using a scraper gives the characteristic ribbed texture of the soundboard surface in Ruckers instruments, and in those of a number of other sixteenth- and seventeenth-century Flemish makers (see pp. 73–4).

After the final tapering to thickness, the upper surface of the soundboard was sized as a preparation for the soundboard painting. The material or materials used to size the soundboard have become a rich golden-brown colour and have produced a fairly shiny surface. The coloration is probably the result of the degradation of the organic matter in the size preparation. It seems likely that the material used was a simple, easily accessible material commonly found in the workshop, and not a complex special preparation. Gum arabic, egg white (glair), or varnish might have been used, but the most likely and readily available materials were thinned shellac, or a glue size made by thinning down the glue used for gluing the instrument together. Since the surface of the soundboard is not sticky when touched by the moistened finger, it seems likely that the final size was not glue or gum arabic, although the ribbed texture of the surface seems to indicate that a water-based size was applied initially. Perhaps the board was first glue-sized and then, when this had dried, it was given a final coat of thinned shellac.

[8] The difference in the thickness of the soundboards in Ioannes and Andreas harpsichords may be the reason that Andreas often used a stiffening bar glued to the bentside liner to increase the rigidity of the soundboard there, since, being too thin, it was otherwise too flexible in the area near the stiffening bar.

## SOUNDBOARD BARRING AND HITCHPIN RAILS IN HARPSICHORDS

There are two separate hitchpin rails in harpsichords, one for the 4′ strings and one for the 8′ strings. The 8′ strings are hitched to the bentside and tail soundboard mouldings. These are made of a thin moulded strip about ¼ duim (6.5mm) high sitting on the soundboard adjacent to the case walls. The 8′ hitchpins are driven into this moulding, through the soundboard and into the liners. Since the soundboard moulding is the same low height above all of the soundboard, there is a large down-draught for the heavy bass 8′ strings, where the bridge is very high and the distance from the bridge to the hitchrail is relatively short.

The 4′ hitchpin rail consists of a curved poplar bar between the 4′ and 8′ bridges under the soundboard, and is always in one piece sawn from the plank. At the treble end it was either let into the cheek liner in a manner similar to the bass end, or it was supported by and usually let into a block glued to the cheek liner or belly rail. It tapers very little in thickness from bass to treble and is usually about 20–25mm thick along most of its length. It is, however, much wider in the bass than in the treble, tapering from 50–60mm in the bass to 13–18mm in the treble.

The position of the 4′ hitchpins on the soundboard was probably determined according to the following procedure, deduced from construction marks on the soundboard itself. Before being glued together, the 4′ hitchpin rail and soundboard were positioned temporarily in the instrument. With the baseboard removed and the instrument on its side, a line was scribed on the lower surface of the soundboard along the whole length of the near edge of the 4′ hitchpin rail.[9] The soundboard was then removed and placed upside down so that a fine pointed object (a fine nail or pin?) could be driven through from the lower to the upper surface of the soundboard. Four or five of these holes were spaced all along the scribed line. The soundboard was turned over and the 4′ hitchpin rail laid on top of it so that the hitchrail lined up with the pierced holes. Short lines passing through the holes pierced from below were scribed on the soundboard along the edge of the 4′ hitchpin rail. At this stage the hitchpin rail was in the same position above the soundboard that it would eventually occupy below. The hitchpin rail was then drawn back towards the tail and bentside edge of the soundboard by an arbitrary amount always less than half the width of the hitchpin rail at each point along its length. Another line was scribed along the entire length of the player side of the hitchpin rail, into which the 4′ hitchpins were later driven. This method ensured that all of the 4′ hitchpins would find their way firmly into the wood of the hitchrail, and not miss it on one side or the other. The line scribed underneath the soundboard could also be used to locate the 4′ hitchpin rail when gluing it to the lower surface of the soundboard.

As well as carrying the 4′ hitchpins and helping to support the tension of the 4′ strings, the 4′ hitchpin rail forms a natural soundbar and barrier between the 4′ and 8′ bridges. The vibration of the soundboard around the 8′ bridge is limited on one side by the tail and bentside, and on the other by the spine and 4′ hitchpin rail. Similarly the vibration of the 4′ soundboard area is confined between the 4′ hitchpin rail on one side and the spine and cutoff bar on the other side. Since the area of soundboard allotted to each part of the compass is very important to the final tone of the instrument, the positioning of the 4′ hitchpin rail and the cutoff bar has an important acoustical effect.

The cutoff bar runs diagonally under the soundboard so that the 4′ bridge is more or less half-way between the 4′ hitchpin rail and the cutoff bar. Behind the cutoff bar a number of smaller soundbars run perpendicular to the spine and stiffen and deaden the area of soundboard between the cutoff bar and spine. Of course the soundbars, cutoff bar and 4′ hitchpin rail, in addition to acting as acoustical barriers, also perform the important structural duty of helping to hold the soundboard flat. Glued to the soundboard, they help counteract distortions in the soundboard caused by the down- and side-draught in the strings. Nevertheless, the unsupported parts under the bridges are often considerably distorted by sizeable undulations in the soundboard surface. Also, despite the heavy case structure and the strength of the barring and bridges on the soundboard, there seems not to be a single harpsichord without the characteristic split at the treble end of the bridges. These must be accepted as part of the consequences of classical harpsichord design and construction.

The cutoff bar and soundbars are of poplar and have the same basic cross-section in all Ruckers instruments (see Fig. 6.6). They are wider at the base than at the top and the angle of the sloping sides ($\alpha$) is close either to 10° or to 15°. The constancy in the angles of the sides of the cutoff and soundbars suggests that they were made in a

[9] In Ioannes Ruckers instruments only the player side of the 4′ hitchpin rail is scribed under the soundboard. In some of the late Andreas Ruckers instruments both sides are scribed, although no use seems to have been made of the line along the far side of the rail except perhaps to help in gluing the hitchpin rail to the lower surface of the soundboard.

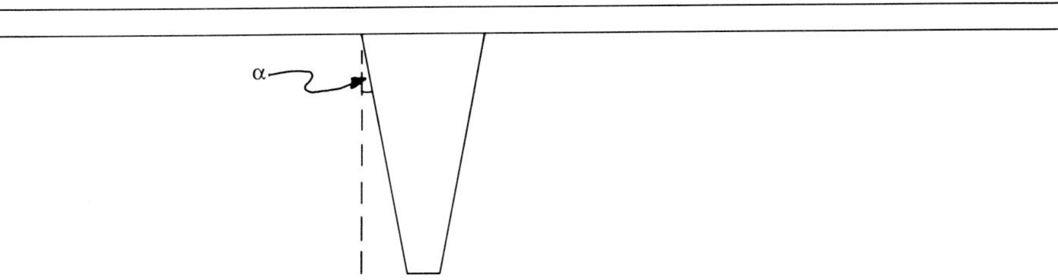


Fig. 6.6 Cross-section of typical soundbars and cutoff bars in Ruckers clavecimbels.

jig which always produced the same angles regardless of the size of the bar.

One such jig is easily made by gouging out two angled channels in a plank of wood, as in Fig. 6.7. A rectangular bar of wood, which is the same height and the same width as the base of the soundbar required, is placed first in the left angled channel. The shaded area is planed away from the bar by holding the plane parallel to the top of the jig and workbench. The bar is then turned end-for-end and placed in the right-hand channel and the shaded area again planed away. The Ruckers must have used two such jigs, one with $\alpha = 10°$ and another with $\alpha = 15°$, which produced bars which were close, but not necessarily exactly equal, to these angles. The method used to make soundbars and cutoff bars follows closely the probable procedure used also in the making of bridges (see pp. 104–6).

Arched scallops were removed from the ends of the soundbars and cutoff bars leaving the extreme ends of the bars only 1–2mm high (see Fig. 6.8). The scallops in the larger cutoff bars are about 2 duimen (51mm) long and about 1 duim (25mm) long in the smaller soundbars. The reason for the scalloped cutouts at the ends of the soundbars is probably structural rather than acoustical. If the soundbars were left full thickness at the ends they would be totally rigid throughout their entire length, and any tendency of the soundboard to distort near the end of the soundbar would result either in the soundboard splitting nearby or in the glue joint at the end of the soundbar giving way. The flexibility of the ends of the soundbars prevents concentrated areas of stress there.

Before gluing on the soundbars, their position was marked in red underneath the soundboard with a sanguine pencil. The soundbars are usually separated from one another at regular intervals measuring an integral or half-integral number of duimen. The ends of the soundbars are angled to butt tightly against the cutoff bar at one end, but at the other there are several millimetres of clearance between the soundbars and the spine liner. Similarly, several millimetres of clearance are left between the ends of the cutoff bar and the spine liner and the belly rail. This clearance was probably left to ensure that the ends of the bars did not get trapped between the soundboard and liners when the soundboard was glued in place. The spine ends of the soundbars and both ends of the large cutoff bar are secured with linen tape glued over their scalloped ends to the soundboard.

The joins in the planks of the soundboard in much of its freely-vibrating area are covered on the lower surface with strips of parchment about 1 duim (25mm) wide. These strips shrink slightly when the moisture of the glue used to fix them evaporates, which not only strengthens the joint but actually tightens it. They do not run under the bridges, 4′ hitchpin rail or the cutoff and soundbars; their position and length is marked in red with sanguine previous to gluing.

## HARPSICHORD BRIDGES

The 8′ bridge in Ruckers harpsichords is almost always made of cherry (*Prunus avium* – commonly called wild

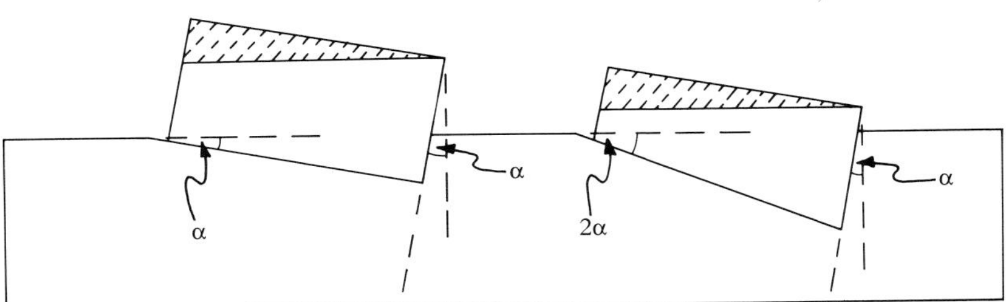


Fig. 6.7 Cross-section of a jig for making Ruckers soundbars and cutoff bars.

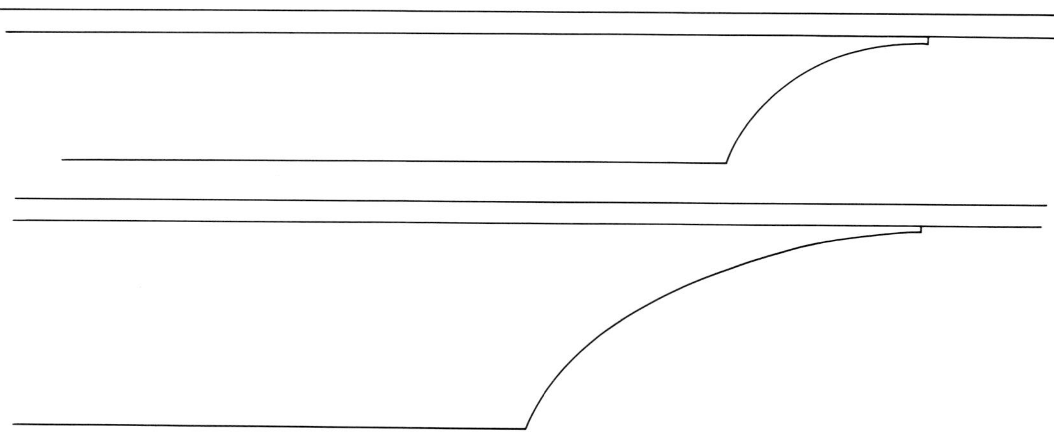

Fig. 6.8 Scalloped ends of Ruckers soundbars (above) and cutoff bars (below). Scale 1:1.

cherry, European cherry or gean).[10] The heartwood of wild cherry characteristically turns dark brown on long exposure to air and light, and thus Ruckers 8′ soundboard bridges, because of their age, are always deep brown rather than the pale pink usually associated with freshly-sawn or planed wild cherry. There are four Ruckers harpsichords, however, with original 8′ bridges not of cherry. The 1636 A R, 1637 A R, (1651)a A R and 1645 I C single-manual harpsichords all have 8′ bridges of beech. The 4′ bridge, however, is always of beech. This bridge has a much smaller section and no regions of sharp radius of curvature, and can be made from a straight piece of wood which is then bent and held in shape solely by the glue and by the nails driven into it from underneath the soundboard. However, the thicker 8′ bridge, with its sharp curvature at the bass end, is sawn from the plank and not bent.

Like the nuts, the bridges are tapered in height and width from bass to treble, both being heavier in the 8′ than the 4′ (see Table 6.1). Both also have a characteristic shape with angled flat surfaces (unlike some early Ruckers virginals, no Ruckers harpsichord has bridges and nuts with curved faces). The dimensions and the angles of the faces of most original nuts and bridges on both harpsichords and virginals can be seen in Table 6.1; they show two distinct configurations (see Fig. 6.9). The angles of the faces of the nuts and bridge are not always exactly 45°, 55° and 80°, but there is a remarkably consistent set of data giving angles very close to these for the two configurations. (In a few rare cases the front face is at right angles to the soundboard or wrestplank instead of being angled at 80°.) The 4′ bridge almost always has configuration (b), the 8′ bridge and usually the 4′ nut have configuration (a), and the 8′ nut may be either (a) or (b).

Such consistency suggests that a jig of the type used to make the soundbars was used to make the nuts and bridges. Also, the obvious relationship between the angles 45°, 55° and the 10° angle from the vertical suggest that the two configurations may somehow be interrelated. In fact, if the chamfered top edge of the nut or bridge is ignored, the relationship between the two configurations becomes obvious (see Fig. 6.10). They were almost certainly made using the same jig, by choosing a different surface as the eventual base of the bridge or nut.

Those nuts and bridges which were made from straight pieces of wood and later bent could be made by

[10] Rather confusingly, 'bird cherry' is *Prunus padus*.

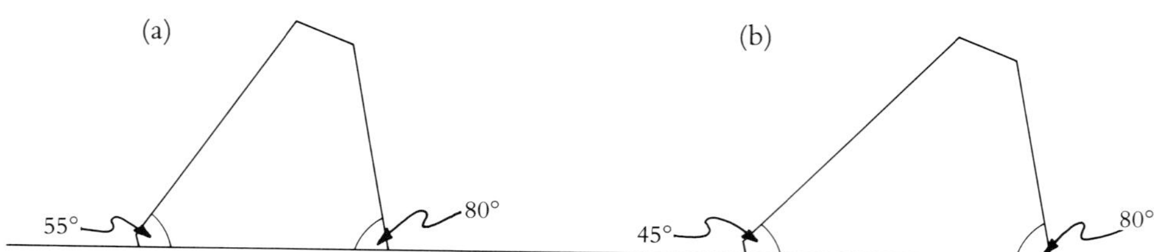


Fig. 6.9 The two configurations of Ruckers nuts and bridges.

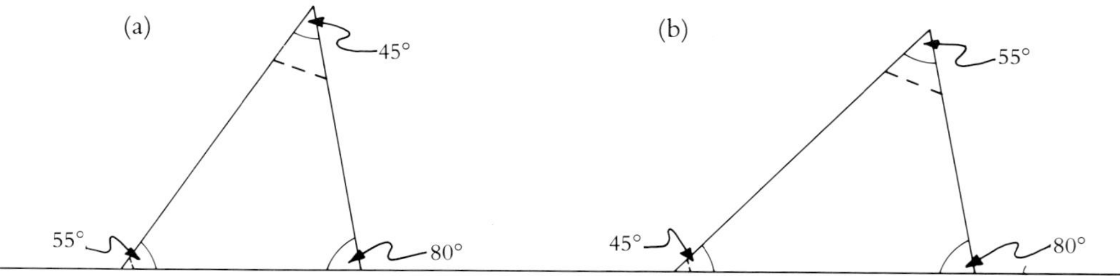


Fig. 6.10 The shape of Ruckers nuts and bridges before removing the chamfered edges.

Table 6.1 *Dimensions of the nuts and bridges in typical single-manual (1645 IC) and double-manual harpsichords (1638b IR). All measurements are in mm.*

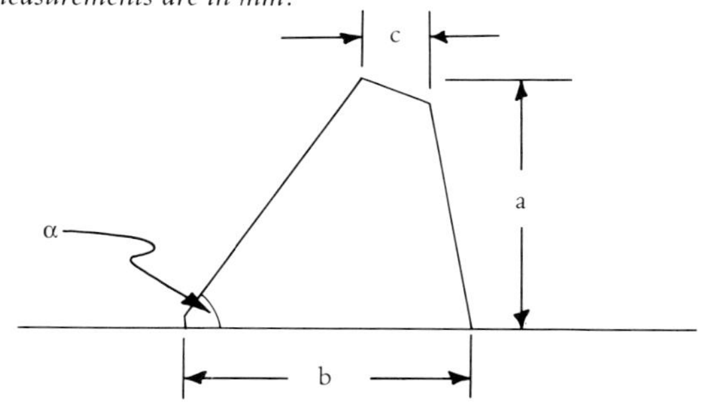


1645 IC single-manual harpsichord:

| | | C/E | c | $c^1$ | $c^2$ | $c^3$ | |
|---|---|---|---|---|---|---|---|
| 8′ bridge | a | 17.0 | 14.7 | 13.9 | 12.4 | 11.2 | |
| | b | 16.9 | 15.6 | 15.4 | 14.5 | 12.2 | $\alpha = 55°$ |
| | c | 4.5 | 4.9 | 5.3 | 4.8 | 4.1 | |
| 4′ bridge | a | 6.3 | 6.2 | 6.4 | 6.5 | 5.9 | |
| | b | 9.7 | 9.4 | 9.0 | 8.5 | 7.8 | $\alpha = 45°$ |
| | c | 4.5 | 4.2 | 4.0 | 3.6 | 3.3 | |
| 8′ nut | a | 14.5 | 13.1 | | 12.5 | 11.9 | |
| | b | 17.4 | 16.7 | | 15.0 | 15.0 | $\alpha = 55°$ |
| | c | 5.2 | 5.3 | | 4.4 | 4.4 | |
| 4′ nut | a | 9.8 | 9.4 | | 8.4 | 7.4 | |
| | b | 11.6 | 11.1 | | 9.8 | 9.2 | $\alpha = 55°$ |
| | c | 4.4 | 4.1 | | 3.7 | 3.7 | |

1638b IR double-manual harpsichord:

| | | $G_1/B_1$ | C | c | $c^1$ | $c^2$ | $c^3$ | |
|---|---|---|---|---|---|---|---|---|
| 8′ bridge | a | 16.8 | 16.7 | 15.0 | 13.7 | 12.7 | 11.1 | |
| | b | 18.0 | 18.6 | 17.7 | 14.8 | 12.3 | 11.5 | $\alpha = 55°$ |
| | c | 4.5 | 4.8 | 5.0 | 4.6 | 4.7 | 4.6 | |
| 4′ bridge | a | 7.3 | 7.3 | 6.8 | 6.5 | 6.7 | 6.8 | |
| | b | 11.0 | 10.8 | 10.0 | 9.3 | 8.9 | 8.8 | $\alpha = 45°$ |
| | c | 4.4 | 4.2 | 3.9 | 3.6 | 2.8 | 3.0 | |
| 8′ nut | a | 12.7 | | 11.8 | | 11.4 | 10.9 | |
| | b | 17.6 | | 16.5 | | 15.1 | 14.5 | $\alpha = 45°$ |
| | c | 5.0 | | 4.5 | | 4.1 | 3.9 | |
| 4′ nut | a | 9.2 | | 8.8 | | 8.1 | 8.3 | |
| | b | 10.5 | | 10.4 | | 9.7 | 10.0 | $\alpha = 55°$ |
| | c | 4.2 | | 3.7 | | 3.4 | 3.3 | |

starting with a square piece of beech as long as required, which was cut diagonally to give two pieces with a cross-section in the shape of a right-angled isosceles triangle. This could then be planed to the desired shape and configuration as follows. With a very simple jig, consisting of a plank of wood slotted like the soundbar jig, but with the cross-section shown in Fig. 6.11, the piece to be made into a bridge or nut is first placed in the left-hand slot and against a bench stop. With the plane kept parallel to the top of the jig and workbench, the sawn surface is planed smooth. It is then placed in the right-hand slot and planed at the 80° angle. At this stage the decision is made about which configuration to use and the piece tapered by planing away more wood at one end than the other. Either the left or right sloping surface is given the correct dimensions for the base of the bridge or nut being made, and the dimensions of the other sides are then fixed by geometry.

The height of the piece is established by placing the bridge or nut on its base and planing away the apex of the triangular cross-section until the required height is reached. The chamfer could be given to the piece at this stage, or the top surface could be left flat and parallel to the base. The latter possibility would leave a bearing surface for clamping to the soundboard or wrestplank and also facilitate drilling the nut or bridge-pin holes. There is in fact a lack of any construction or marking-out lines on the top of the bridge, which suggests that the marking out and drilling of the pin holes was done when the top surface of the bridge or nut was flat, and that the top was later chamfered away removing any construction marks in the process.

The use of the type of jig just described is not as convenient with a curved sawn bridge as with a straight one, even though the surfaces have the same angles. Nonetheless, since the only configuration for the 8′ sawn bridges in harpsichords and virginals appears to be type (a), adding one more slot to the jig, as in Fig. 6.12, enables even the curved bridge to be placed in the jig and a spoke shave or compass plane to be used to smooth and taper the sides of the bridge after the 55° surface has been sawn out.

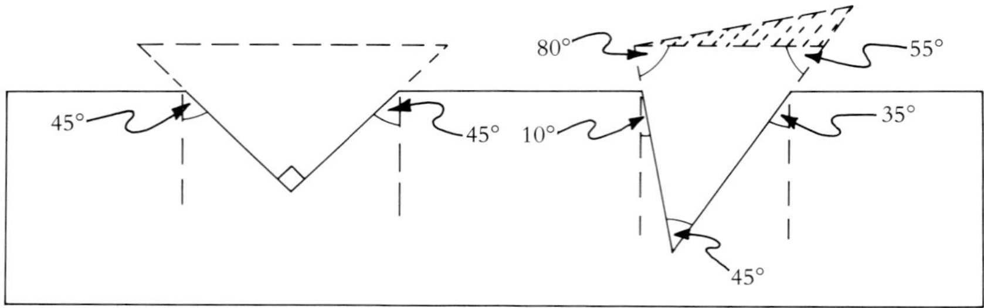


Fig. 6.11 Cross-section of a jig for making Ruckers bridges and nuts.

The sharp lower edge of the rear sloping surface of the bridge or nut was removed to provide a small bearing surface for the positioning pins used to hold the bridge in place during gluing to the soundboard. Pairs of positioning pins, one on either side of the bridge or nut, were placed at or near the notes *c* and *f*♯ at regular intervals every six notes throughout the compass. Even in the case of the sawn bridges, the shape of the bridge was altered slightly by bending to give the desired scalings, and then holding it in its final position by the positioning pins.

A number of clues exist to suggest how the Ruckers positioned the bridges to give their instruments the desired scalings, although some details remain hypothetical. As with the virginals, there is considerable variation in the string scalings from instrument to instrument and from one maker to another. This again suggests that, like the virginal bridges, harpsichord bridges were positioned as accurately as possible to give the correct scalings, but that the primary concern was with spacing the strings accurately relative to the jacks and quills to ensure the correct mechanical operation of the instrument.

The important clues to the procedure used to locate the bridges are the construction marks on the soundboard, some of which were scribed before the bridges were glued in position. These marks consist of a heavy pin-prick indentation in the soundboard wood, with a short scribed line running away from it. These marks can always be found corresponding to the played note $c^1$ (the lower manual $c^1$ in the normal double-manual harpsichord) for both the 8′ and 4′ bridges. In many instruments all of the played notes *c* and *f*♯ are also marked. In all cases the positions of the pin-prick marks on the soundboard correspond precisely with the pin-pricks on the register(s) for the notes *c* and *f*♯ when the register end is held against the spine (see pp. 110ff for a discussion of the making of the registers). It thus appears that, whatever their number, these marks were positioned relative to the spine and have no direct bearing on the separation of the nuts and bridges and therefore on the scalings. This is further borne out by the fact that the marks are not always covered by the bridges as they would be if they had been used to determine the scalings.

After the position of the *c* and *f*♯ strings relative to the spine had been marked, the position of the nut and bridge pins was presumably determined by measuring out from the nameboard, upper belly rail, or one of the rows of jacks. I have found that the bridge pin of the pitch c note ($c^2$ at 8′ pitch) is always within a few millimetres of 49cm (19 duimen) from the back of the nameboard, whether the instrument is a double- or single-manual harpsichord. However, even though the pitch c bridge pin may have been determined by measuring its position from the back of the nameboard, none of the other notes seems to be as accurately or consistently located relative to the nameboard, and this is especially true of the *c* and *f*♯ played notes in the bass. To add further to the confusion it must be noted that it is the position of the played note *c* on the lower manual of the normal double-manual harp-

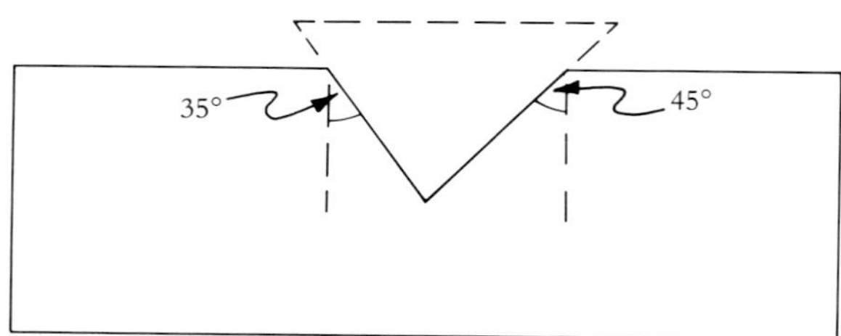


Fig. 6.12 Cross-section of a jig for shaping the sawn 8′ bridges.

sichords which is located by the positioning holes, and not pitch c.

Nonetheless, I feel the best available hypothesis to be that the bridge-pin positions of the *c* and *f*♯ played notes were marked out on the soundboard relative to a reference line – probably the back of the nameboard – and that these marks are now covered over by the bridges. Alas, I have never had the opportunity of seeing a bridge removed from a Ruckers soundboard, nor do I know of anyone who has. The positioning holes beside the bridge would then be located as closely as possible over the marks measured from the back of the nameboard. But because handmade bridges are slightly non-uniform, the line of bridge pins was not always located at the same position relative to the side of the bridge and relative to the positioning holes. Once the bridges were glued to the soundboard, the final pin positions were marked out on the bridges (using a bar – the same one used to mark out the register – with regularly-spaced notches in it?) from the spine edge of the soundboard. Thus, each pin may have been slightly ahead of or behind its intended position, especially in the tenor and bass, where the bridges run at a very oblique angle and where a slight sideways shift in the string position would greatly alter the position of the pin along the bridge.

This would then explain two interrelated characteristic features. First, the large angle between the treble bridges and the strings would result in a consistently accurate positioning of the treble bridge pins (including that of the pitch c bridge pin) relative to the nameboard, and therefore to accurate and consistent treble scalings. Secondly, the small angle between the strings and the bridges in the tenor and bass results in rather non-uniform scalings and positioning of the bridge pins relative to the nameboard in the bass. Also, for the same reason, the final position of the bridge pin may be considerably different from that actually marked on the soundboard and may not be exactly beside the pairs of bridge positioning holes. It also means that although found very close to the *c* and *f*♯ bridge pins in the treble, the positioning holes may be a semitone or more away from those notes in the tenor and bass.

The method of clamping the bridges and nuts to the soundboard and wrestplank during gluing remains a complete puzzle. Personal experience has shown that using the positioning pins as clamps as well as a means of positioning is not efficient. It works well for the nuts on the wrestplank where the pairs of pins are close together, but in the tenor and bass of the bridges the distance between successive sets of pins is too great to ensure adequate clamping between them. Perhaps weights were placed on the bridges during gluing, or deep-throated clamps may have been used. Or the necessary pressure may have been provided by 'go-bars' similar to those used in French eighteenth-century workshops.[11]

After gluing, the bridges were nailed from below to the soundboard as insurance against the glue softening or breaking loose and releasing the bridges. In early Ruckers harpsichords (1594 HR, 1608 AR) the nails were simply bits of heavy brass wire driven through the soundboard into the bridge and then bent over and hammered into the grain of the soundboard wood. In later harpsichords small iron tacks were used. Whatever their type, they were always driven into the bridges between the pairs of positioning holes, ensuring that the nail would always be located centrally in the bridge.[12] The holes left by the pairs of positioning pins beside the nuts were usually plugged with small wooden nails, although those in the soundboard were left open and unplugged. This is probably because the nuts are much closer to the player and the holes in the wrestplank are therefore more likely to be noticed than those in the soundboard.

The bridge-pin positions in harpsichords may have been marked out with the soundboard removed from the instrument to avoid interference between the end of the marking-out stick and the bentside. This could easily have been done by holding the spine side of the soundboard against a wall or vertical surface (in lieu of the spine) and measuring out, perhaps with a notched bar, the position of the bridge pins from this surface. The nuts could have been marked out in the instrument, but could also have been marked out in a similar way before the wrestplank was glued in place. After marking out, the holes for the bridge and nut pins could be drilled. The pins themselves may also have been driven into position at this stage, although it was probably not done until after the soundboard was glued into the instrument and the soundboard was painted. (Painting the soundboard with the pins in the bridges is most uncomfortable!)

Throughout most of the compass the strings are parallel with the spine. In the lowest octave the strings run

11 Reference to go-bars are quite frequent in eighteenth-century inventories – see P. J. Hardouin, 'Harpsichord making in Paris: Part I, eighteenth century', *Galpin Society Journal* X (1957), 13. Hubbard, who translated this article, seems to be responsible for translating 'goberge' into American English 'go-bars'. André Jacob Roubo, in *L'Art du Menuisier* (Paris, 1769–75) in Part IV, 'Vocabulaire Raisonné', p. 1285, gives 'Goberge – tringle de bois qu'on place entre le plafond de la boutique & l'ouvrage, pour fixer ce dernier sur l'etabli.' ('Go-bar – bar of wood which one places between the ceiling of the workshop and the piece being worked, to fix the latter to the workbench.') In Scotland they are known as 'dwangs'.

12 Because of the large spacing between the pairs of positioning holes in the tenor and bass, it is unlikely that these nails were the actual means of clamping the bridge to the soundboard during gluing.

obliquely, being further from the spine at the ends of the bridges than at the nuts. Increasing the distance of the bridges from the spine in this way increases the flexibility of the bass ends of the bridges and enables them to vibrate as freely as possible. In some instruments the treble strings are also angled slightly away from the cheek, probably for a similar reason. Not surprisingly, instruments built during the same period by the same maker have bridge and nut pins at the same relative position to the spine, indicating a standard method of spacing the strings. Such instruments do not, on the other hand, have equally consistent scalings. This seems to be a consequence of the method just described to locate and pin the bridges.

As mentioned before, in double-manual harpsichords the same string is used to play the notes of the two manuals sounding a fourth apart (for a detailed description of the double harpsichords with manuals which were probably a tone apart, see Chapter 8, p. 179). If the instrument is tuned in meantone, eleven of the strings in each octave will be properly tuned to the correct pitches for both manuals. However, the note tuned to g♯ on the 'f' keyboard is pitched about $^4/_{10}$ of a semitone (41 cents) below the required e♭ on the 'c' keyboard. Consequently, in each octave the two keyboards require eleven shared strings plus two separate strings, one for each keyboard. If the twelfth string were also shared then it would have to be tuned correctly either to g♯ or to e♭, depending on the manual being used and the requirements of the music.

The essential components which enabled two strings to be used for these notes and avoided the necessity of retuning when changing manuals were small brass plates driven into shallow notches let into the 8′ and 4′ nuts at each e♭/g♯ string position. The brass plate is notched to position its strings with a slight horizontal and vertical displacement relative to one another (see Plate 6.6). This displacement is greatest at the nut, and gradually decreases along the length of the strings until they have only a slight horizontal displacement at the bridge.

Since the pitch of the e♭ (a♭) string is slightly higher than the g♯ string (see Appendix 7), it was always the shorter string and placed to the right of each doubled set (see Fig. 6.13). The jacks plucking the higher strings had long quills which could not drop low enough to pluck the low strings. Similarly, the short jacks had short quills which were not long enough to pluck the higher strings during the upward travel of the jack. The dampers of the shorter jacks had to be adjusted so that they did not interfere with the higher strings. In this way the jacks of each manual pluck only their respective strings, and the retuning of the e♭/g♯ notes is avoided.

Plate 6.6 The 4′ (above), and the 8′ (below) transposing plates for the e♭/g♯ strings on the 1615 AR double-manual harpsichord.

After the bridges were glued to the soundboard and the bridge-pin positions marked out, the soundboard was glued into the case. The drips of excess glue running down the insides of the case show how this was done. These indicate that the case was the right way up when the liners were glued, and when the soundboard was glued to the liners and belly rail. But the excess glue beside the edges of the 4′ hitchpin rail does not run down its sides. Thus the 4′ hitchpin rail was glued onto the soundboard before the soundboard was glued into the instrument. Gluing the hitchrail to the soundboard was done using one or more wooden positioning pegs placed in the line of the 4′ hitchpins. The holes for these pegs were probably drilled after the soundboard and hitchrail had again been placed temporarily in their final position in the instrument. With the soundboard then placed upside-down and with a short peg in the positioning hole, the hitchpin rail could be glued in position using the positioning peg(s) and the line scribed previously along the side of the 4′ hitchpin rail to locate it correctly. The excess glue squeezed out from between the surface of the soundboard and hitchrail would then collect and lie beside the 4′ hitchpin rail without moving any further.

Before the soundboard was glued into its final position, the top of the cheek liner and belly rail were chiselled away near the treble ends of the bridges to increase both the effective area of radiating soundboard for the top notes and the flexibility of the soundboard, so as to improve the tone at the top of the compass. In some

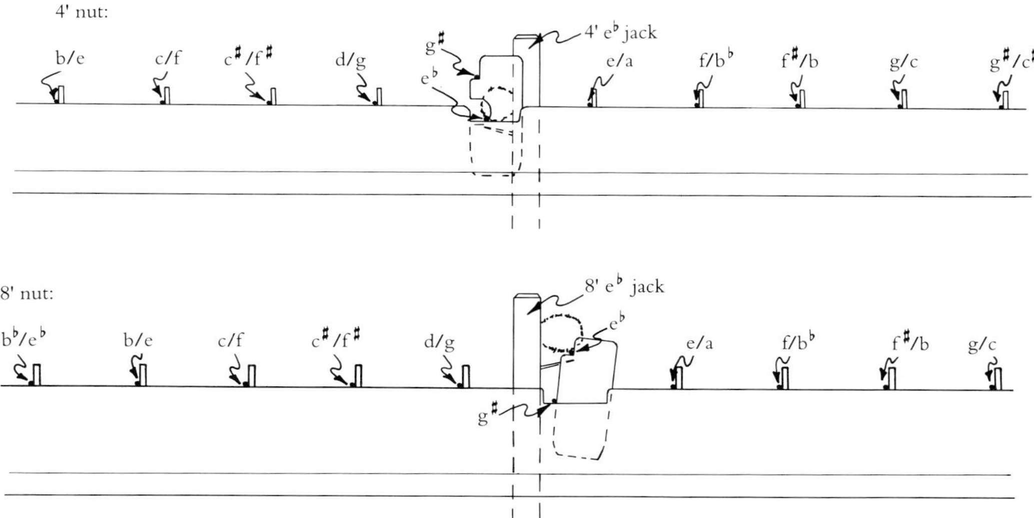


Fig. 6.13 The arrangement of the strings on the e♭/g♯ transposing plates in the normal double-manual harpsichord. The figure shows the 4′ nut and the 8′ nut perpendicular to the plane of the strings. The jacks shown plucking the *e*♭ strings belong to the upper-manual 'c' keyboard; the lower-manual *g*♯ jacks for the 'f' keyboard would be behind the jacks shown and would pluck the other string on the transposing plate. Scale 1:1.

instruments the spine liner is also cut away near the ends of the 8′ and 4′ bridges; this improves the response of the lowest notes of the harpsichord.

The only traces of how the soundboard was glued into the instrument are the wooden pegs through the soundboard into the upper belly rail. These are small (3mm) pegs located at intervals of 5–6 duimen (125–156mm) near the gap. Because of the flexibility of the thin soundboard along this edge, these pegs could not have been the only means of holding the soundboard to the belly rail during gluing. As with the virginals, a batten must have been nailed temporarily over the edge of the soundboard to provide the necessary rigidity to hold it flat. After the glue had dried, the batten and nails were removed and the nail holes plugged with the small wooden pegs. The other edges of the soundboard are covered by the soundboard mouldings, which hide any evidence of how the soundboard was held in place there. These mouldings are also pegged every 5–6 duimen to the soundboard and liners, but it seems unlikely that the mouldings were glued to the soundboard at the same time that the soundboard was glued to the liners. Such a double gluing operation would be so complicated that the glue on the liners would have partially set before the soundboard mouldings could be positioned, glued, and pegged. The edges of the soundboard must have been glued to the liners using battens nailed over the soundboard edges, and the soundboard mouldings later glued and pegged to the soundboard in a separate gluing operation.[13]

The 4′ hitchpins must have been driven into the soundboard after it had been decorated, since the soundboard painting often passes underneath these pins as if they did not exist. The 8′ hitchpins and the 8′ and 4′ bridge pins were probably put in at the same time as the 4′ hitchpins. They are all of brass, and the size of the pin used is graded according to the function it has to serve. The 4′ bridge and nut pins are about 0.9–1.0mm in diameter, slightly smaller than the 8′ bridge and nut pins, which are 1.1–1.2mm in diameter. The 4′ hitchpins are about 1.3–1.4mm and the 8′ hitchpins 1.5–1.8mm in diameter. The hitchpins are bent over slightly towards the tail to prevent the strings from slipping off. In double-manual instruments there are two bridge pins and two hitchpins placed side by side for the e♭/g♯ paired strings. Even in altered instruments, pairs of plugged holes are visible in the line of 4′ hitchpins. The existence of the paired pins or their plugged holes on all Ruckers harpsichords (except the 1612a HR) originally with two manuals is proof that the keyboards were not aligned.

There is a slight down-draught in all strings, since the 4′ strings are hitched at the soundboard level, and the 8′ strings are hitched to the soundboard moulding/hitchrail

[13] In the course of the restoration of the 1764/83 Goermans/Taskin in the Russell Collection, Edinburgh, carried out by the writer, it was found necessary to remove the spine soundboard moulding. It was clear that Goermans in 1764 had glued the soundboard and the soundboard moulding in separate gluing operations using a method similar to that described here.

about 6½mm high throughout its length. Unlike that of many eighteenth-century harpsichords, the 8′ hitchpin moulding is not made higher in the bass to reduce the large downward pressure on the bridge from the heavy bass strings. In addition to the down-draught, the strings also have a side-draught of about 5°, except for the bass octave of 8′ strings. The notes C/E to c (nine notes) in short-octave instruments, or the chromatic notes C to c in single- or $G_1$ to G in double-manual harpsichords (thirteen notes) are back-pinned on the 8′ bridge. The back-pinned strings run straight back to the hitchpins without any side-draught, although occasionally the very lowest notes are pinned so that there is a slight side-draught pulling the bridges towards the spine, instead of away from it as happens higher up in the compass. None of the 4′ strings is back-pinned.

## HARPSICHORD REGISTERS

The upper registers guide the jacks and position them relative to the strings. Each register consists of two parts: a 'comb' between whose teeth the jacks move up and down, and a capping piece which covers the openings at the end of the teeth in the comb. The wood used is beech (*Fagus sylvatica*), cut on the quarter so that the quartered figure is visible on both the top and bottom surface of the registers, and on the side formed by the capping piece. Because of their obvious importance to the correct mechanical operation of the instrument the registers were made with a care, skill and accuracy equal to that exhibited in the construction and preparation of the soundboard, nuts and bridges.

The entire row of jacks is engaged or disengaged by moving the register (and with it the jacks) towards or away from the strings. In the engaged position the quills are positioned under the strings and pluck the string when the corresponding key is depressed; when disengaged, the quills no longer make contact with the strings. The only original disposition indicated by a study of the extant Ruckers harpsichords is 1 × 8, 1 × 4′.[14] Thus the single-manual instruments have only two registers, while the doubles have four with one 8′ and one 4′ on each manual.[15]

All the registers from one instrument were marked out together before the individual sections were cut apart. Longitudinal scribed lines on both the top and bottom surface of the registers mark the ends of the jackslots. Pin-pricks, probably made using the same notched bar postulated for the pinning of the bridges and nuts, are visible along the near edge of the near register (register 1). These pin-pricks occur in pairs and could have been made by first pricking the positions of one side of the jackslot, then moving the notched bar along by an amount equal to the width of the jackslot and pricking the position of the other side of the jackslot; or the two pricks were made simultaneously with a double-pointed marking tool. Knife cuts about 1mm deep pass through the pin-pricks; these were presumably made by holding a set square along the ledge of the register plank to ensure that the cuts were parallel to one another and perpendicular to the long direction of the registers. Since the 4′ and 8′ registers were marked out simultaneously, the 4′ and 8′ jackslots (and jacks) are therefore all of the same thickness.

At this stage of the marking out, the board must have been cut apart into the individual register strips, and the sawn surfaces planed flat and smooth. The sides of the jackslots were sawn so that they opened outwards towards the bottom of the register at an angle to the perpendicular of about 13°. The sawcuts were made slightly inside the knife cut marking the two sides of the jackslot so that the knife cuts were not quite touched by the saw. The accuracy of the width of the jackslot opening is therefore determined by the accuracy of the marking out with the knife and not the accuracy of the sawing. The width of the jackslot openings is thus very constant along the register, and this width even from instrument to instrument and maker to maker varies between the relatively narrow limits of 3.6mm and 3.8mm. The block remaining between the two sawcuts in the middle of the jackslot was cleared away and the side of the slot cleaned out.

Because of the way in which the lower guides are constructed (see pp. 113ff) the space between the rows of jacks at the level of the lower guide is greater than that at the level of the registers. Thus the rows of jacks converge into the jackrail and are splayed apart at the level of the keys. Because each row of jacks rises at a different angle through the registers, the ends of the jackslots in each register are angled to suit the angle of the jacks passing through them. In a double-manual harpsichord, for example, the outer ends of the jackslots of the first and fourth registers are more steeply angled than those of the two inner registers.

[14] The 1652 IC by Ioannes Couchet and the 1671 IC, probably by Ioseph Ioannes Couchet, were both originally singles with a 2 × 8′ disposition. The use of the 2 × 8′ disposition by Couchet is also mentioned in the correspondence between Couchet and Huygens (see Appendix 18).

[15] Two late instruments by the Couchets are exceptions. The 1652 IC and 1679 IC both originally had only two sets of strings but had three registers. In this case one set of 8′ strings was plucked by one or other of two different sets of jacks separated by the third row. The difference in the plucking points of these two widely separated jacks would cause a distinct difference in the timbre of the sound produced from the same string.

Plate 6.7 Typical Ruckers harpsichord upper registers (1638b IR). From top to bottom the plate shows: the top view of a 4′ register; the bottom view of an 8′ register; the capping piece on the side of a 4′ register; and the top view of the near 8′ register showing the pin-pricks and knife marks used in the marking out of the registers. Scale 1:1.

The wrestplank veneer overhangs the far edge of the wrestplank and the soundboard overhangs the near edge of the upper belly rail by about 2mm. The registers in the gap between the wrestplank and the upper belly rail are partly covered by this overhang on each side. In order to prevent the jacks from binding against the wood overhanging the gap, the near and far sides are made wider than the other sides of the registers.

Thus, because of the asymmetrical way in which the registers are constructed, it is possible to determine the original order in which the registers were placed in the instrument. Also, the registers were 'numbered' by a series of punch marks near the left-hand end of the registers. The near register has one punch indentation, the second has two, and in doubles the third has three and the fourth – the farthest from the player – has four indentations. Each jackslot is recessed on one side with an almost vertical slot opposite the jack tongue, which ensures that the tongue does not bind on the side of the jackslot when the jack returns to its rest position. These tongue recesses are placed in the middle of the jackslot for the 8′ jacks with two dampers and near to one end for the asymmetrical 4′ jacks with only one damper. The difference in the positioning of the tongue recess as well as the narrower width of the 4′ registers enables one to distinguish the 4′ from the 8′ registers.

Plate 6.8 The arrangement of the bass jackslots in the registers of a normal double-manual harpsichord (1638b IR).

In all cases in which the original registers remain it is clear, both from the punch indentations on the ends of the registers and the angling and width of the end wall of the jackslot, that the 4′ register was placed nearest the soundboard and the 8′ register nearest the player. Also, the tongue recesses (as well as the original pinning of the bridges and nuts) indicate that the 4′ jacks plucked to the left and the 8′ jacks plucked to the right. This then establishes the original disposition of Ruckers harpsichords, which is, in single-manual instruments:

← 4′
→ 8′

and in doubles:

← 4′
→ 8′
← 4′
→ 8′

Except perhaps for the 1612a HR double (see p. 179), no original Ruckers instrument is known to me which indicates an original disposition other than these, although some of the late Couchet instruments are exceptional.

Because of the cranking down of the keys in the upper manual of the normal double-manual harpsichord (see pp. 116–17), caused by the interweaving of the short octave on the two manuals, the upper-manual registers have to be made specially to suit the arrangement of the notes. The upper-manual and lower-manual pitches are compared in the diagram below:

Lower-manual register:
C F D G E A B♭ B c c♯ d e♭ e f f♯ g g♯ a b♭ b c c♯ d e♭ e f f♯ g g♯ a
Upper-manual register:
C D E F G A B♭ B c c♯ d e♭ e f f♯ g g♯ a b b♭ c c♯ d e♭ e

Thus the slots of the upper-manual registers are interspersed with blank spaces (see Plate 6.8). This arrangement is necessary only on the normal short-octave instruments and would not have been necessary on the extended-compass instruments (1616 HR, 1627c IR, 1628b IR and 1646b AR) with a chromatic bass octave. A possible arrangement of the keys in the instrument postulated to have its keyboards a tone apart in pitch (1612a HR) is given on p. 179.

A detail found on most, but not all, sets of original registers is a number of pin-pricks on the top of the register near the tongue recess for selected notes throughout the compass. The 1638b IR and the 1640b AR doubles have pin-pricks on the lower manual 8′ register for the played notes c, $f^{\sharp}$, $c^1$, $f^{\sharp 1}$, $c^2$, $f^{\sharp 2}$, $c^3$ and $f^3$; the 1637 AR single has pricks on both the 4′ and 8′ registers for the notes C/E, c, $f^{\sharp}$, $c^1$, $f^{\sharp 1}$, $c^2$, $f^{\sharp 2}$, and $c^3$. In the latter case the pin-pricks are each on the same side of the jackslot as the corresponding tongue recess.

These pricks are all very close to 3.6mm from the position of the side of the jack on the 1638b IR double-manual lower 8′ register. Like those on the virginal registers, these pin-pricks seem to indicate the intended position of the string relative to the jack, and thus the length of the quill. Assuming that the same distance applies to the 4′ register, then the total space between successive 4′ and 8′ strings is just equal to the space occupied by the quills and jacks with the 4′ and 8′ registers in exact alignment. One can check this as follows: the space between successive 8′ strings is determined by the three-octave span and is equal to 500mm/36 = 13.88mm. The space between the 4′ and 8′ strings for adjacent notes varies between 2.8mm and 3.0mm and averages about 2.9mm. Therefore if the 4′ and 8′ registers are accurately aligned, the space occupied by the quills, jacks and strings is:

| | |
|---|---|
| 3.6mm | space occupied by the quills |
| 3.6mm | |
| 3.8mm | width of the jacks |
| 2.9mm | separation of the 8′ and 4′ strings |
| 13.9mm | total |

Therefore with the 4′ and 8′ registers in their correct operational alignment the jacks in a Ruckers harpsichord should be centred in the space between the 8′ and 4′ strings of the same note. This practice of aligning the registers is probably a continuation of the old tradition found in the early Germanic and Flemish harpsichords. In these instruments (e.g. the 1537 Müller and the 1579 Theeuwes harpsichords) the jackslots are pierced through the soundboard in straight rows centred between the string for each note.

As with the virginals, the total plectrum length depends upon the amount the tongue is recessed behind the side of the jack and the amount the quill projects beyond the string. The existence of the register pin-pricks does, however, give at least some idea of the quill length used. Also, the jack-to-string distance has been shown to be 3.6mm in both virginals and harpsichords.

The ends of the register project through a hole pierced in the cheek, and the registers are engaged and disengaged by reaching around to the side of the instrument and pulling or pushing on this register extension. The extension of the register, consisting of the part inside the cheek and the part which projects about 10mm beyond the cheek, is covered on its top surface with a bone plate similar to the bone used for the key touchplates. Near the very end of the register the bone and wood are pierced with two round holes 4–4.5mm in diameter. Cords or ribbons of cloth or leather passed through these holes to assist the grasp of the player turning the register on or off.

The lateral motion of the register involved in engaging and disengaging it is controlled at the treble end of the register. Tuning pins, usually the same size or slightly smaller than the 4′ tuning pins, are positioned near the middle of each register just inside the cheek surface. These pins are fixed in the cheek liner, which spans the gap and extends under the wrestplank. Slightly oval or rectangular slots in the registers around the tuning pins allow the register a small lateral motion, and the position of their ends determines the engaged and disengaged positions.

In order to hold the registers in the positions required by the player, a beech or poplar block or register yoke covered on its lower surface with soft sheep's leather is placed over the registers next to the cheek (see Plate 6.9). Notches are cut in the side of the block so that it does not interfere with the pins driven into the registers and cheek liners. The ends of the block are slightly recessed underneath so that the lower leather-covered surface extends down to the top of the registers at a level slightly below the soundboard and wrestplank veneer. Two hand-made screws through the ends of the block into the wrestplank and cheek liner (these are the only screws that would be found in an original Ruckers harpsichord) provide a variable amount of friction between the leather and the top of the registers. Turning the screws in or out regulates the friction until it is sufficient to hold the register in position during playing, but not enough to prevent it being engaged or disengaged as desired by the player.

The bass ends of the registers are covered with a smaller poplar block positioned against the spine over the gap. This block is fixed permanently in position with a small brass nail at either end. This bass register yoke does not touch the registers, but serves to prevent dust and foreign objects from entering and fouling the space between the ends of the registers and the spine. The punched indentations numbering the register are normally hidden underneath this bass register block.

As well as being supported at the cheek and spine, the registers are held between two pairs of wires which span the gap. The upper wire is in the shape of an inverted 'U' staple, which is driven into the top surface of the wrestplank at one end and the top of the belly rail at the other before the wrestplank veneer or soundboard are glued into position. The lower wire is driven through a hole in the side of the belly rail into the far edge of the wrestplank at a distance below the top surface corresponding to the depth of the registers. Clearly these wires are located at positions between the jacks so as to avoid interference with the mechanical operation of the instrument.

The lower guides in Ruckers harpsichords are very similar to those already described for the virginals. They consist of a thin board of poplar or spruce soundboard wood between 2.5mm and 4.5mm in thickness, covered on its upper surface with sheep's leather 1.5–2.0mm thick and on its lower surface with parchment. The jackslots are pierced through this combination of materials. The parchment helps to reinforce the weak short-grained wood between the individual jackslots. The wood provides the basic structural rigidity of the

Plate 6.9 The treble arrangement of the registers in a Ruckers harpsichord (1637 AR). The bone plates normally covering the register projections are missing; otherwise the arrangement is original.

lower guide and supports the upper layer of leather. The wood is cut away under the leather jackslot so that the leather alone bears on the sides of the jacks, guiding them noiselessly as they move up and down.

The lower guides are marked out in a manner very similar to the upper registers. Longitudinal lines along the length of the leather mark out the position of the ends of the 4′ and 8′ jackslots. A series of paired pin-pricks along the player side of the lower guide marks the position of the sides of the jackslots, and must have been made in the same way as the pin-pricks on the near upper register. As with the sides of the jackslots in the upper registers, the jackslot sides in the lower guide seem to have been marked out with a knife guided by a set square held against one of the long sides of the lower guide. In the case of the lower guides, however, the knife cuts do not extend across the whole width of the guide. The knife cuts are made only along the side of the jackslot itself and do not extend between the 8′ and 4′ rows of jackslots or from the pin-pricks to the 8′ jackslots. Frequently, however, one sees a small nick in the surface of the leather through the pin-prick where the knife was lined up with the prick before being moved down to cut the side of each 4′ and 8′ jackslot. Often the knife cut slightly overshoots the far end of the jackslots, indicating that this side of the lower guide was nearest to the person cutting the slots.

After the leather, and perhaps the top surface of the wood, was cut with a knife, the jackslot holes were punched through the wood and lower layer of parchment with a chisel. The upper belly rail of the 1627 AR quint harpsichord was used as a backing piece during the cutting of the lower guides, and it shows shallow chisel marks made when the jackslot holes were punched through: a fortunate accident, since it gives detailed information about the cutting process. These marks show that the sides of both the 4′ and 8′ jackslots were cut with the same chisel; two cuts were made on the sides of the wider 8′ jackslots in order to cut the full length of the jackslots. As seen on the backing piece, most of the cuts for the sides of the jackslot are parallel, but a number of the jackslots appear as cuts which are not parallel and either diverge or converge in the jackslot opening. This indicates that both sides of the jackslots were not cut simultaneously with a double set of parallel chisels. Instead, each side of the jackslot was cut separately with a single chisel, and sometimes a slight rotation of either the backing piece or the lower guide itself between cutting one side of the jackslot and the other caused the observed irregularity in the backing-piece marks. Clearly the knife cuts made previously in the upper leather surface would serve to guide the chisel in piercing the sides of the

Plate 6.10 The bottom surface of the upper-manual and the top of the lower-manual (below) lower guides from the 1618b IR double-manual harpsichord.

jackslots. The ends of the jackslots were cut separately with a narrow chisel. The pattern of chisel cuts on the backing piece suggests that the ends of the jackslots were cut in one operation and the sides in another, since there is a marked misalignment of the end and side cuts at one end of the register. In both cases the cuts were made vertically, however, as the width and length of the jackslot cut marks on the belly rail are the same as the width and length of the jackslots in the lower guide itself. Experience has shown that the chisel used to cut these slots must be sharpened with a cutting and supporting edge with an angle much less than the usual 20° or so, in order to avoid causing cracks in the short-grain between the jackslots.

After the vertical cuts were made and the wood and leather plugs were removed from the jackslot holes, the lower guide was turned over and the holes were opened out by angling all four sides of the jackslot, apparently with a knife. This was done so that all of the wood and the lowest portion of the leather was angled, leaving only the leather part of the jackslot with vertical sides. Thus the jack touched nothing but the leather part of the jackslot.

Because the ends of the lower guide jackslots open out underneath, a certain minimum distance must be left between the rows of jacks in the lower guides in order to ensure sufficient structural strength in the wood between the jackslot rows. Usually at least 6mm is left between the 4′ and the 8′ row of jackslots. This is considerably more than the distance between the ends of the successive jackslot rows in the upper registers; for this reason, the rows of jacks are further apart at their feet, which, in turn, is the reason that the belly rail must be angled.

The lower guide in single-manual harpsichords is glued and nailed to the lower edge of the belly rail; it sits on top of and is nailed to the keyblocks at its ends. A rectangular bar is glued to the top of the lower guide along the near edge to add rigidity.

In double-manual harpsichords also, the lower-manual lower guide is nailed and glued to the lower edge of the belly rail. But in doubles the guide is let into and nailed to the top surface of the keyblocks and the stiffening bar is attached to its lower surface, both of these changes being necessary to allow the upper manual to slide along the top of the keyblocks and overlap the edge of the lower guide without interfering with it at the rear. Wooden pegs angled through the ends of the stiffening bar into the sides of the keyblocks under the lower guide further secure and support the lower-manual guide. The upper-manual guide is nailed to the lower surface of the deep cheek liner and to a block glued underneath the spine liner. Both edges of the upper-manual guide are stiffened with reinforcing bars. The near bar is roughly 14mm square in cross-section and similar to the one used on the lower-manual guide. But the bar on the far edge of the guide, which must be squeezed between the 4′ row of jacks of the upper manual and the 8′ row of jacks of the lower manual, must be very narrow to avoid interference with the jacks. It is usually only about 2.5mm thick and often tapered to half this at its top edge.

## KEYBOARDS AND KEYFRAMES IN HARPSICHORDS

The single-manual keyboard and lower-manual keyboard in double-manual Ruckers harpsichords are constructed in a manner very similar to the virginal keyboards. The poplar keys, guided at the rear in a rack, are placed on a rectangular half-lapped poplar frame. This is usually 12½–13mm thick, and each half-lap joint is glued and pegged together with two or three small pegs.

The rack is placed near the rear edge of the frame, and is also glued and pegged in place. The slots in the rack which guide the keylever endpins widen into the wood and are triangular in shape when viewed from above. The top of the rack is sloped upwards from back to front, and is capped with a thin (4½–5mm) piece of poplar or poor-quality soundboard wood. This capping piece is nailed to the rear portion of the top of the rack and overhangs the front by about 12mm. It serves, with several layers of woollen cloth attached to its lower surface, to limit the upward motion of the tails of the keys, and is called the upper touch bar. The height of the touch bar above the keyframe is usually somewhat greater in the bass than in the treble. Because of the greater overall flexibility of the strings in the bass, which is a result of their length, the jacks must raise the bass strings further before they pluck. Thus the jacks and keylever tails must move further in the bass than in the treble, and this can only happen if the rack is also slightly higher in the bass than in the treble.

The balance rail is placed on the near board of the keyframe. A line is usually scribed on the frame to locate the position of one edge of the balance rail. The 1615 A R lower-manual keyframe still has two metal pins beside the balance rail, driven into the scribed line, and presumably used to locate the balance rail during gluing; they are similar to the positioning pins which must have been used to locate the nuts and bridges during gluing.

The single-manual and double-manual lower keyframes are held in place at the rear by two chamfered blocks glued to the front surface of the lower belly rail (or the near toolbox brace), under which the keyframe slides when the keys and keyframe are put in position in the instrument. The front of the keyframe is held by two keyframe hold-down blocks which are the same thickness as the keyframe. These are located beside the keyblocks on the baseboard and along the near edge of the keyframe, and prevent it from sliding towards the player. A turnbutton with chamfered edges is fixed with a nail to the top of the hold-down blocks, and a wing of the turnbutton can be rotated over the top surface of the keyframe to hold it firmly against the baseboard.

The upper-manual keyframe in doubles is quite different from that just described. The upper manual sits on top of the lower-manual keyblocks and slides in and out of the instrument like a drawer. The upper-manual keyblocks are an integral part of the keyframe and are carved with a characteristic scroll pattern at the near ends. These

Plate 6.11 The keyframe hold-down block and turnbutton for the bass end of the lower keyboard in the 1618b IR double-manual harpsichord.

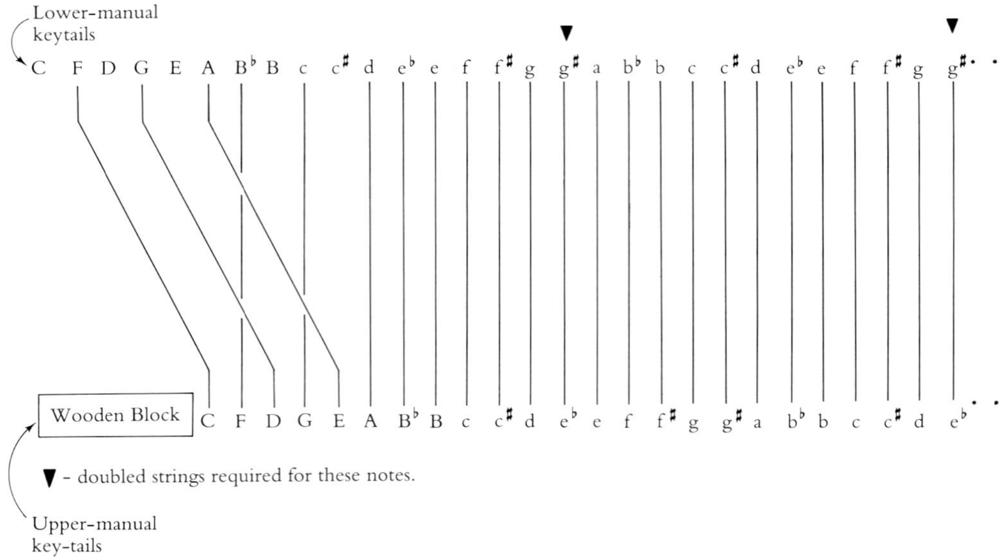


Fig. 6.14 Schematic arrangement of the upper-manual bass keys in the normal Ruckers double-manual harpsichord.

keyblocks are approximately the same thickness as the keyblocks beside the lower manual and are pegged and glued to the keyframe, which consists simply of a single plank of wood about ½ duim (12½mm) thick. The plank of wood is long enough to fit with a small clearance between the spine and cheek sides of the keywell, and extends in width from the front to the rear of the keylevers. Because of the close spacing of the rows of jacks in the registers, and because the keylevers have to reach all the way under the first two rows of jacks, there is no space at the ends of the keylevers for a rack. The upper-manual keys are therefore guided by iron pins located between the keylevers near their tails. These pins are iron wire rod about 2.0mm in diameter driven into the keyframe plank, and the sides of the keys are planed away to allow the keylever tails just to pass between the successive pins with a small clearance.

The limit of the upward motion of the tails of the upper-manual keys is controlled, in the absence of the usual rack, by a rectangular bar let into the top of the upper-manual keyblocks and spanning the full width of the keyframe between the keyblocks. This upper touch bar is placed over the tails of the keys, usually immediately behind the row of 2.0mm guide pins between the keys. In order to prevent the middle of the rather flexible bar from bending upwards when a large number of keys is depressed simultaneously, an additional piece of wire rod located between a pair of keys near the middle of the compass ties the upper touch bar to the keyframe plank. This wire rod is bent over at its ends into the grain of the bottom of the keyframe plank and the touch bar, thus preventing the touch bar from bending upwards.

In the normal type of Ruckers double-manual harpsichord, the upper manual is pitched a fourth higher than the lower manual. Both manuals begin in the bass with the usual short octave, and have the compasses C/E to $c^3$ on the upper manual and C/E to $f^3$ on the lower. Because of its smaller compass, there are three naturals less in the bass of the upper manual than in the lower manual, and the space for these naturals is occupied by a block of wood, moulded with an ovolo moulding and decorated with one of the larger block-printed paper patterns on its upper surface.

The irregular sequence of the notes of the short octave on the two manuals produces a special problem in obtaining the required notes for the jacks of the upper manual from the pitches of the strings tuned to suit the lower manual. Schematically the situation at the tails of the keys of the two manuals is represented in Fig. 6.14. The notes of the lower manual with its short-octave bass fill out the whole width of the keyboard. After the wooden block three naturals in width, the short octave of the upper manual begins. But whereas the correct pitches for the upper manual (except for the e♭/g♯s) are available on the lower manual for the notes F, G, A and higher, the pitches for the upper-manual short-octave notes C, D and E are found much lower down in the bass of the lower-manual keys and strings. In order that the upper-manual keys operate jacks which pluck strings at the correct pitch, they must crank down to the position of

Plate 6.12 The original arrangement of the upper- and lower-manual keys in the 1638b IR double-manual harpsichord.

the lower-manual keys by an amount equal to the width of four keytails. The original arrangement used to achieve this remains only in the 1638b IR double and is shown in Plate 6.12.

The extended-compass doubles with a chromatic bass octave in both manuals (1616 HR, 1627c IR, 1628b IR and 1646 AR – the 'French' doubles) would not have required the cranked keys found in the normal double-manual harpsichords, since the notes of both manuals follow in the usual sequence. A possible arrangement of the keys for the tone transposition scheme postulated for the 1612a HR double is shown on p. 179.

As mentioned previously, the upper manual slides in and out of the instrument on the top surface of the lower-manual keyblocks. In order to prevent it from sliding too far back into the instrument a chamfered bumper block is glued to each case side under the gap and just above the

Plate 6.13 Keywell of the 1638b IR, showing the namebatten, papered lower-manual batten, the upper-manual bass block and the carved upper-manual keyblocks.

lower-manual lower guide. Sometimes, a piece of the same buff leather used for the buff-stop pads is glued to the edge of the bumper blocks to act as a buffer between the keyframe and the bumper block. The upper manual is prevented from sliding out of the instrument towards the player by the lower-manual batten. This tapered batten, decorated with a block-printed paper pattern and a moulding, runs between the two keyblocks immediately behind and above the lower-manual keys. This batten slides into tapered slots in the keyblocks and is held in place by gravity so that it is readily removable. The back surface of the batten is located immediately in front of the upper-manual keyframe. Hence only when the batten is removed can the upper manual be slid forward and out of the instrument.

The upper-manual batten or namebatten is similarly fitted into two tapered slots in the upper-manual keyblocks, and runs immediately above and behind the upper-manual keys. Although it is also easily lifted out of its slot, it only needs to be removed if the upper-manual keys have to be removed from the balance pins after the upper manual is slid out of the keywell.

The balance rails in double- and single-manual harpsichords can vary in width from 35mm to 50mm. They taper in height from the front down to the rear, at an angle which is slightly greater than the angle of the keys to the keyframe.

The single-manual and double-manual upper keylevers are made from a jointed plank of poplar about ½ duim (12.5–13mm) thick, and the lower manual of a double, with much longer keys, is about 14.5–15mm thick to give added stiffness to the longer keylevers. Except for the tails of the upper-manual keys, both the front and rear ends of the keylevers are angled at 7°–10° so as to make the top surface of the key longer than the bottom surface.

Before marking out the actual keys a number of longitudinal lines were scribed on the keyplank to mark out a number of features. Lines near the front of the keyplank were used to mark, on the top and bottom surface, the cut for making the recesses in the naturals for the sharps (see the diagram on p. 82). In single-manual harpsichords this distance $y$ is about 33mm; in doubles $y$ is about 27.5mm for the upper manual and 29.0mm for the lower manual, although individual harpsichords have values differing slightly from these. Another line on the top surface, approximately 105–115mm from the front of the keyplank, marks the end of the natural keyplates.

Near the middle of the keyplank, two scribed lines mark the keylever balance points. The balance line for the sharps is about 13.5mm behind the natural's balance line in singles and in double lower manuals, and about 16–

17.5mm in the upper manuals of double harpsichords. The balance pins are usually about 2.1mm in diameter. The holes in the keys for the balance pins had to be enlarged to allow the balance pin to pass through readily, and to allow the keylever to rock about the balance pin. No evidence has been found to suggest how the balance hole was enlarged, although the holes have been found to open out towards the top and the bottom, placing the pivot point half-way up the thickness of the keylever.

The location of the balance line along the length of the key is one of the most important factors affecting the feel or touch of the instrument under the fingers of the player. In order to compare the relative position of the balance point of different instruments by different makers, one can compare the balance ratio of the keylevers. This can be defined as the ratio of the length of the front of the keylever, from the end of the natural's touchplate to the natural's balance point, to the length of the rear of the keylever from the natural's balance point to the tail of the keylever. Defined in this way, the balance ratio is just equal to the mechanical advantage of the keylever.[16] The larger the numerical value of the balance ratio, the greater the mechanical advantage of the keylever, and the lighter the touch experienced by the finger of the player.

For virginals the balance ratio has been found to be between 0.53 and 0.56. For Ruckers harpsichords with two rows of jacks instead of the virginals' one, the balance ratio must be somewhat greater to give the keys the same 'feel'. Single-manual and lower-manual harpsichord keyboards usually have a balance ratio of about 0.59–0.61 and the upper-manual keyboards a ratio of 0.53–0.58 or virtually the same as that for virginals. These balance ratios have all been measured for the treble keys, but usually the balance rail and line of balance pins is slightly angled so as to make the mechanical advantage of the bass keys less than that of the treble keys. The amount by which the balance rail is angled varies in different instruments, but the intention to angle the balance rail seems always to be present.

The reason for angling the balance rail in this way is unclear. In fact it seems the opposite of what one would logically do to achieve a uniform touch weight across the compass. The bass notes need a stronger plectrum requiring more force to cause it to pluck the string. Thus the mechanical advantage or balance ratio should be greater, not less, for the bass keys than for those in the treble in order to obtain an even touch weight. One possible explanation of the angling of the balance rail is that it was an attempt to even out the depth rather than the weight of the touch across the compass of the instruments. Since the height of the rack is greater in the bass than in the treble, the motion of the tails, and therefore the fronts, of the keylevers would also be greater in the bass than in the treble if the balance rail were not angled. Angling the balance rail has the effect of reducing the motion of the fronts of the keylevers in the bass, and therefore of producing the same depth of touch throughout. If this is indeed the reason for angling the balance rail, then the Flemish builders gave a greater importance to the uniformity in the depth of touch than to the uniformity in the force required to cause the jacks to pluck.

Behind the scribed lines for the balance pins there is usually a pair of lines running from the tails of the keys in the bass to the balance-pin lines in the treble. These lines serve to order the keys, since, if one of the keys is misplaced on the keyboard when reassembling them, its pair of oblique lines will be seen to be out of alignment with the lines on the neighbouring keys. Keyboards which do not have these lines have keys which are numbered in ink behind the balance-pin line for the sharps.

The upper manual in the double-manual harpsichords also has a scribed line near the tails of the keylevers which marks the position of the guide pins between the keys. Usually the cloth glued to the top of the tails of the keys under the feet of the jacks begins at this line.

The keys were marked out at the front with a three-octave span close to 500mm. Thus each of the seven naturals in each octave occupies, on average, $500/(3 \times 7) = 23.81$mm. The sharps are located so that the *d*, *g*, and *a* natural tails are about 11.5mm wide after cutting out, and the *c*, *e*, *f* and *b* naturals are 15.5–16mm wide.

The tails of harpsichord keys were marked out in a manner very similar to the virginals. The keyplank was temporarily fixed to the keyframe, probably using the outer balance-pin holes after these had been drilled through the keyplank into the balance rail. The keyplank and keyframe were placed temporarily in the instrument in their final position and a punch, inserted in both the 8′ and 4′ jackslots, made a double set of oblong marks along the rear of the keyplank. The reason why both the 4′ and 8′ jack positions were punched is unclear. It would be necessary to punch both only if there were considerable misalignment of the two. Both registers were aligned at the level of the lower guide, and, as has already been pointed out (p. 112 of this section), the upper registers also seem to have been designed to be used in the aligned position. Therefore, the jacks of both registers are also aligned and the second punch mark seems to be redun-

[16] To be fully accurate one should measure from the point of application of the force exerted by the finger on the natural's touchplate, and from the line of action of the centre of gravity of the jacks on the tails. The above definition is, however, accurate and practical enough to allow a meaningful comparison to be made.

dant. However, the cloth jackpads under the feet of the jacks were glued over these marks after the keylevers were cut out. In most but not all instruments, the cloth strips are glued only at their ends and not in the middle of the strip where jack feet were actually resting. Perhaps both jack positions were punched simply as a guide for gluing these cloth strips in place (see Plate 6.14).

The position of the rack pin on the end of the keylever was located along the centre line of the two punch marks on the keyplank, and the position of the slots in the rack were in turn marked out from the rack-pin positions. This seems the most likely way to explain the fact that, although the rack slots are not uniformly spaced, they follow exactly any irregularity in the spacing of the back pins. Presumably the lines for cutting the tails of the keylevers were marked out by spacing them mid-way between the punch marks made through the jackslots, although any sign of this marking out has been lost in the process of cutting out and trimming the keys.

On the single-manual and lower-manual keyboards there is also a punch mark on the keyframe for the position of the 4′ jacks for each of the top and bottom notes. The top and bottom rackslots line up with these marks on the keyframe and it seems likely that their purpose was to position the rack and rackslots. The position of the guide pins at the tails of the upper-manual keys must have been marked out and drilled after the keytails had been marked out, but before removing the keyplank to saw out the keylevers.

The sides of the keylevers were trimmed, probably with a spokeshave, after the keylevers were sawn out of the keyplank. A considerable amount of wood was shaved off the sides of the keylevers near their tails leaving relatively large gaps between the ends of the keys. More wood was removed from the lower part of the side of the key, both at the front and at the tail, giving the keylever a slightly trapezoidal cross-section. Characteristically a tiny sliver of wood was chamfered off the top edge of the tail section of the keylevers.

Plate 6.14 The keylever tails, natural touchplates and sharps from the lower manual of the 1638b IR double-manual harpsichord. The black paint on the keylever sides below the sharps is not original – only the top of the keylever behind the sharp was originally painted black.

When the keys were being sawn apart and the sharp keylevers sawn out of the recesses in the natural keys, a large amount of wood was removed from the near end of the recess. The absence of this wood means that the natural keyplates overhang the wood at the recess, and the sharps considerably overhang the front ends of their keylevers.

Like the virginal keys, the Ruckers harpsichord natural keyplates are of bone and the sharps are of bog oak. The bone keyplates are 2–2½mm thick at the front and usually taper in thickness to half this or less at the rear, and consist of one single piece of bone without a join between the head and tail sections. The front of the keyplate overhangs the wood of the keylever by about 2mm and the embossed arcade (see Chapter 5, Plate 5.4) was glued to the sloping keyfront under the keyplate overhang. Four decorative lines are scribed in the naturals' keyheads just in front of the sharps, and a small elliptical nick made with a round needle file between the middle two lines on each side of the touchplate. In double-manual harpsichords the length of the front of the touchplate, from the rear scribed line to the near edge, is about 2mm greater for the lower-manual keys than for those of the upper. The top edges of the touchplates were bevelled along the front and up the side to the first decorative line, and the bevel and the front corners of the keyhead were rounded slightly before or during the buffing and polishing of the keyplates. The tails of the keyplates were lettered with the note name of each natural key in a red material which may have been sanguine or perhaps a red dye or ink. The red pigment used to letter the keyplates was fugitive and evidence of the lettering of the keyplates is often difficult to find again, although traces usually exist on the little-used bass and treble keyplates.

The bog oak used for the sharps varies in colour from a dark brown-umber to an almost black charcoal-grey, and this apparently reflects a difference in the organic composition of the moor or bog in which the wood was found. The sharps are normally about 63–67mm long, with very little difference between those found in single- and double-manual harpsichords except that the upper-manual sharps are a few millimetres shorter than those on the lower manual. Like the naturals the sharps are buffed to polish them and any sharp edges and corners are rounded off.

The most usual type of sharp found on Ruckers harpsichords with their original keyboards is rectangular in cross-section. These sharps are about 12mm high and 10.5–11.3mm wide, and have a front sloping at about 15° to the vertical. But a number of instruments by both Ioannes and Andreas Ruckers have sharps which are only about 9mm high, and tapered in width from 7.5mm at the top of the sharp to 10.5mm at the base. Instruments which have sharps with these sloping sides are usually dated in the period 1618 to 1627, and the standardization in the size and shape of the sharps suggest to me that they were supplied from a common source to both the Andreas and Ioannes Ruckers workshops. The sharps on the 1646 IC double are unique among the instruments of the Ruckers family. They are also made of bog oak, and the sides are very slightly sloping – between 1° and 2° to the vertical. Their most distinguishing feature, however, is that they slope in height from about 11½mm at the front to 7½mm at the rear of the sharp. To my knowledge, this is the earliest known instrument with its original sharps which slope in height from front to back.

The sharp glued onto the keylevers was slightly overlong (this may also argue for a common supplier, who produced sharps of only one 'standard' length, which was used for virginals and both single- and double-manual harpsichords). Because of this, the keyboard battens (lower-manual batten and namebatten) would not come to rest in their final positions in their slots because they would sit on the ends of the sharps. Thus after the sharps were glued to them, the keylevers were placed on the keyframe in the instrument and a scribed line made along the tops of the sharps just in front of the keyboard battens. The sharps were then cut off to length and the excess wood at the tail was chiselled off the keylever. The wood of the keylevers was usually penetrated slightly by the saw cutting through the end of the sharp, and the wood just behind the sharps was often slightly splintered in the process of chiselling away the excess portion of the sharp. Characteristically, in cleaning up the keylever wood behind the sharps, two scalloped chamfers were made on the top edges of the keylever. The top of the keylever just behind the sharp including the scalloped chamfers was painted black, although the sides of the keylever under the bog oak sharp were left unpainted. The lower surface of the sharp keylevers is cut away in front of the balance point so that the keylever does not interfere with the balance rail or the balance-rail cloth when a sharp is depressed.

The wood of the bog oak sharps was practically always cut so that the rings were horizontal. Thus the sides of the sharps contained the quartered ray figure of the oak and the yearly lines of open pores of the soft early wood. The tops of the sharps are therefore relatively free of pores. Although the earliest Ruckers virginals had sharps which were decorated with nicks and transverse scribed lines, I know of no Ruckers harpsichord keyboards with decorated sharps.

The cloths used in the keyboards of harpsichords are of the same types as those used for virginals (see p. 85). A heavy black cloth with long surface fibres pulled out in the matting process is used on the balance rail and on the ends of the keylevers under the feet of the jacks. The compressed thickness of this cloth is about 1.8mm. Because the slope of the balance rail is steeper than the angle of the keys, the sharp keylevers, which balance near the lower rear edge of the balance rail, would all be slightly below the level of the natural keylevers. To avoid this a piece of white leather or folded card was placed on the sharps' balance points to bring the keylevers all to the same level (see Plate 6.15).

The lighter cloth used for the rack, jackrail and jacks has a compressed thickness of 0.9–1.1mm. Usually that in the rack is dyed black, but two double-manual instruments (1618b IR and 1640b AR) have rack cloths dyed red, like that found in the jacks. I know of only two harpsichords which have their original jackrail cloths (1624 AR and n.d IR (Berlin)); these cloths are dyed black in both cases.

Plate 6.15 The keys and balance rail of the upper manual of the 1618b IR double-manual harpsichord. The white patches of folded playing card on the sharp balance pins are original.

The number of layers of cloth used in the rack of harpsichords varies slightly, since the height of the rack also varies. Double upper-manual keyboards usually use three layers of cloth under the upper touch bar and two layers on the keyframe under the tails of the keys. The cloths are tied to the upper touch bar with loops of linen thread which pass through the cloth into small holes in the touch bar and are then tied at the top surface. The double layer under the tails of the keylevers is tacked to the keyframe with pairs of tacks at the ends and at one-third and two-thirds of the length of the cloth strips.

Single-manual and double-manual lower keyboards usually have four layers of cloth attached to the upper touch bar on the rack. These strips are rather narrow (about 12–15mm) and are tied through holes in the touchbar with linen thread in a manner similar to that used for the upper-manual upper touch cloths. The double layer of cloth under the tails of the keylevers is also attached like that of the upper manual with pairs of tacks at the ends, and one-third and two-thirds along the length of the strip.

In as many as possible of the harpsichords with original rack cloths, the depth of touch has been ascertained by measuring the total motion of the near ends of the bone natural keyplates. The upper-manual depth of touch has been found to lie between 6.5mm and 7.0mm, and the lower-manual and single-manual depth of touch is about 7.5–8.0mm. This is somewhat less than the 8–9mm found in Ruckers virginals, and about the same as that found for eighteenth-century English and French makers.

Besides the decorative lines and nicks on the bone plates, the naturals are also decorated with arcades on the keyfronts under the slight overhang of the bone touch-plates. These arcades are composed of two layers: a front design embossed on heavy paper pierced through to leave only the raised embossed pattern, glued to a rear layer of red parchment. Apparently the embossing and piercing were carried out simultaneously, since on one instrument (1637 AR) a defect in the piercing of the design in one corner is reproduced on each arcade. Two slightly different embossed patterns are to be distinguished. Hans and Ioannes Ruckers and Ioannes Couchet used a rounded type of embossing; the two Andreas Ruckers used an indented type of embossing (see Plate 5.4). The red-dyed parchment backing is glued to the front of the keylever. The dye used for the parchment backing is fugitive and is usually completely faded. The original red colour can therefore be seen only where the embossed pattern has protected the parchment from light and air and subsequently become detached.

## RUCKERS JACKS

The material and methods of construction used in Ruckers virginal and harpsichord jacks are identical and so the two will be described here together. The length of the jacks and the number of dampers used are appropriate to the size and pitch of the instrument concerned.

Ruckers jacks are made of beech (*Fagus sylvatica*) cut on the quarter with the quartered figure visible on the widest face of the jack. It is not clear whether the quartering was an attempt to achieve the maximum stability in shape and dimension in the jacks, or whether it shows that the jacks may have been cut apart by splitting, to avoid the laborious task of sawing them apart. Beech splits cleanly and easily in a radial direction, and indeed most jacks are very accurately quartered, as would be the case with jacks which were split apart. Some instruments do have jacks which are slightly off the quarter, although not enough to exclude completely the possibility of their having been split from the jack blank. The way they are cut does, at any rate, provide the maximum strength and dimensional stability possible with wood. A disadvantage of using beech which is accurately quartered is that the extremely hard rays in beech tend, even when using a very sharp plane, to splinter slightly and provide a slightly uneven, textured surface which is quite unlike the silky-smooth finish possible with plank-sawn beech (see Plate 6.16).

The jacks are made to fit the jackslides so that a fairly large amount of slack is tolerated in the long direction of the jackslot, but with a very close fit to the width. This ensures that the tip of the quill is always in the same position relative to the string before plucking. The play between the sides of the jack and the jackslot is only about 0.1–0.2mm, whereas in the long direction it may be between 0.5 and 1.0mm.

Ruckers jacks, like the jacks of most harpsichord builders of the classical era (except for the Italians), are tapered in width and thickness along the length of the jack. This means that, as it rises out of the register when a key is depressed, the jack becomes gradually looser and free in its slot. Normally a jack is actually thicker at its top than the width of the jackslot. Even without its dampers it would thus not fall through the jackslot if the keys were removed, but would bind in the jackslot near the top of the jack. A typical 8′ jack tapers in thickness from about 3.9mm to 3.0mm and in width from 13.7 to 13.1mm, and fits in a jackslot which is 3.8mm by 14.4mm. Similarly a 4′ jack of the same thickness tapers in width from about 12.1mm to 11.7mm and fits a jackslot 3.8mm by 12.6mm.

The dampers in Ruckers jacks fit in oval holes. These

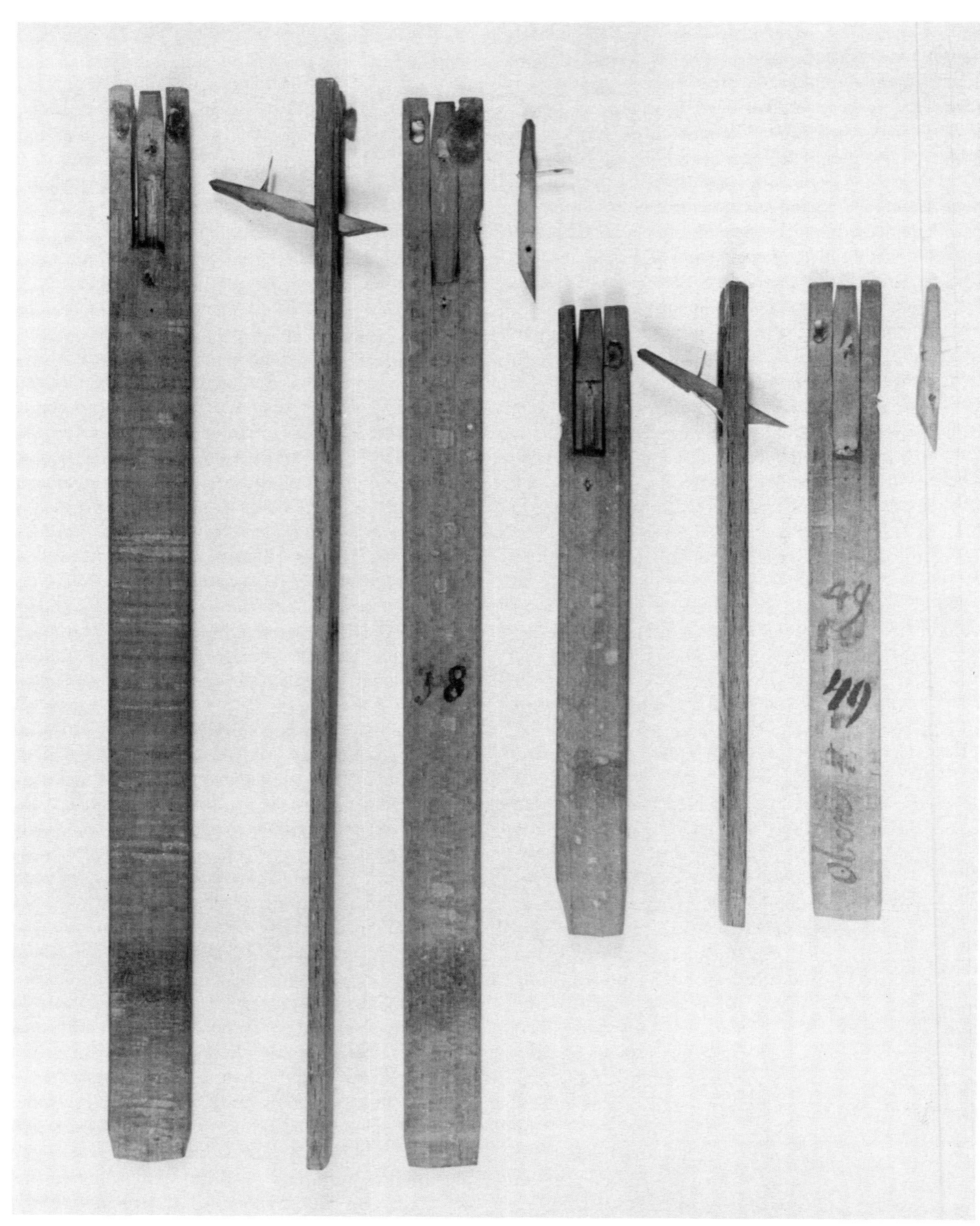


Plate 6.16 Original Ruckers jacks from a double-manual harpsichord (1618b IR). Scale 1:1.

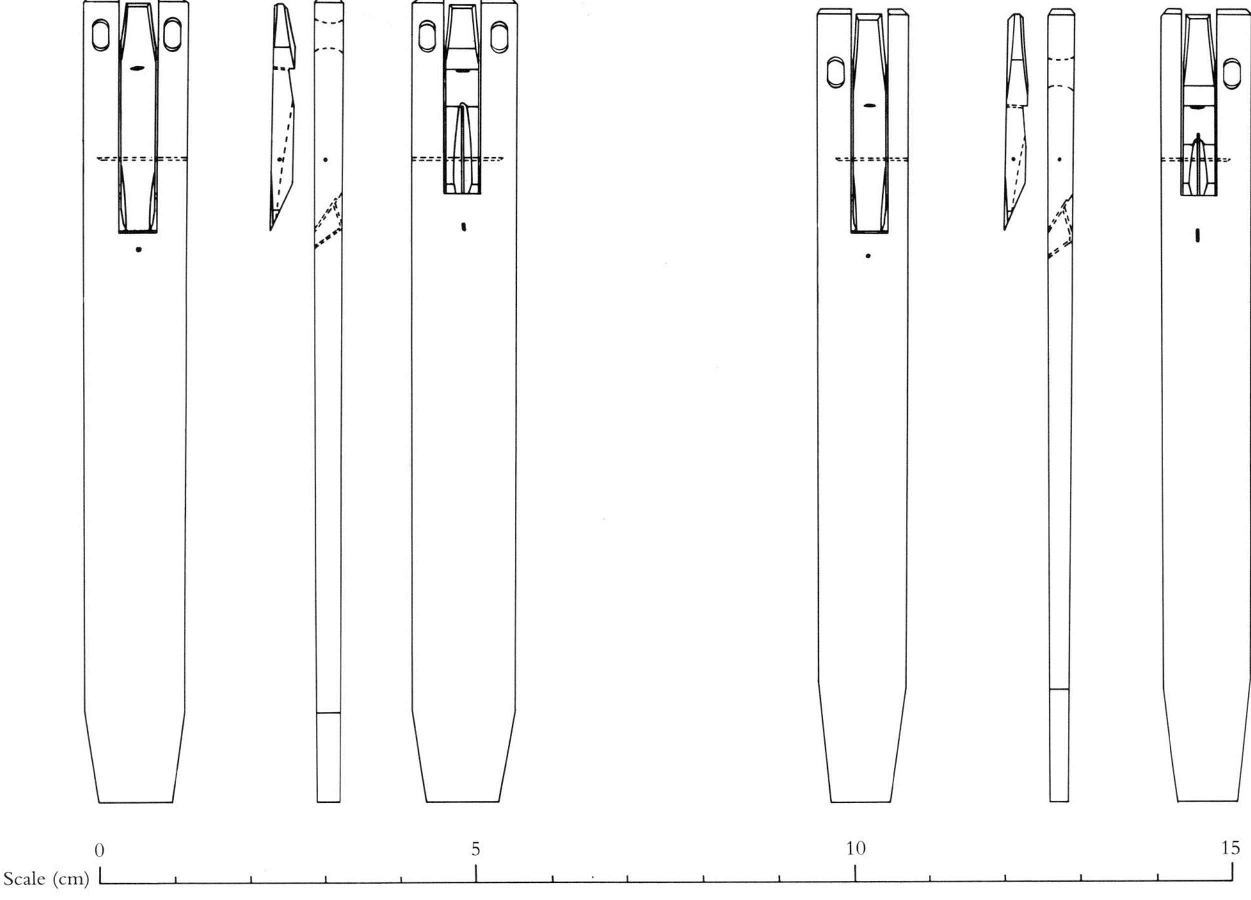


Fig. 6.15 Typical jacks from a Ruckers harpsichord (measured from the 1618b IR upper-manual jacks). Scale 1:1.

holes do not seem to have been made by drilling two holes close together and then clearing away the excess wood between them, but by means of a sharp semi-circular tool (a gouge?) which cut out the top and bottom of the hole working from both the front and back surfaces towards the middle of the jack. The hole produced in this way is longer, but not wider, at the front and rear surfaces of the jack than it is in the middle of the jack, and this pinches the damper cloth tightest near the middle of the hole (see Fig. 6.15). At the front and rear of the jack the damper holes are about 4.2mm long and about 3.6mm long near the middle; they are about 2.0–2.3mm wide. They are often placed very close to the mortice in the jack for the tongue: sometimes the wall between the damper hole and the tongue mortice is little more than paper thin. Because the wood in the hole must have been chiselled or gouged out, the damper holes must have been made in the jacks before the tongue mortices were cut, otherwise the wood between the damper hole and the tongue mortice would have ruptured through.

The dampers and damper holes used in Ruckers jacks seem unusual to one accustomed to the more common type of flag damper in a straight damper slot. Yet the use of this type of damper and damper hole spanned the period from 1579 to 1770 (in instruments by Theeuwes and Delin respectively). A number of Ruckers instruments survive with their original jacks with this type of damper hole, and several instruments (among them the 1618b IR, 1640b AR and 1644a AR harpsichords) retain at least traces of their original dampers. In addition, the child part of the Marten van der Biest double virginal has some original dampers; the 1651b AR harpsichord has jacks dating from its petit ravalement which have oval damper holes and some old dampers which clearly copy the earlier Ruckers style.

These dampers have a characteristic rounded shape (somewhat like a large mouse's ear). They were apparently made with a piece of wedge-shaped cloth rounded along the short side of the wedge opposite the apex. If the two sides of the apex are folded together and the apex inserted into the damper hole, the apex may be grasped and the damper pulled up snugly into the hole. The damper itself then assumes the characteristic 'mouse ear' shape automatically, and the apex end of the damper can be cut off flush with the back of the jack.

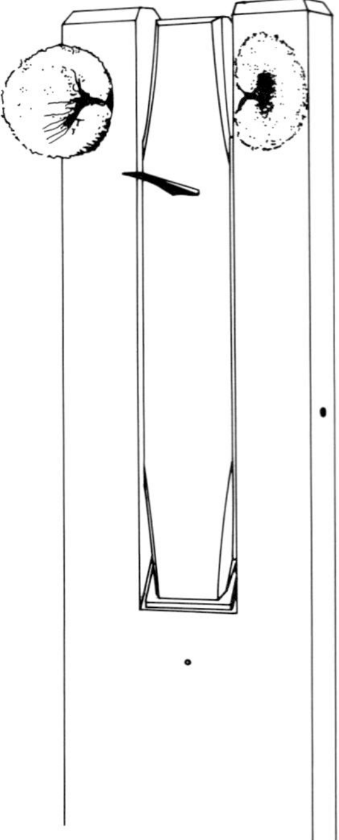

The edge of the resulting damper comes into contact with the string at an angle to the horizontal. The string is brought gradually to rest as the damper descends onto the string, rather than being damped suddenly by a flat horizontal lower surface. This effect is extremely important in damping the muselar virginal strings, as has been explained previously, but it is also a very efficient method for damping the strings of a harpsichord.

The fact that the lower edge of the damper makes contact with the string at an angle also has another important consequence especially relevant to the operation of the double-manual harpsichords. Since the damper does not rest on top of the string, it completely loses contact with the string as the register is drawn away when disengaged. This is an essential feature of a double-manual harpsichord, since both upper-manual and lower-manual jacks operate on the same string. When one set of jacks is engaged and the other disengaged, the dampers of the jacks in the register turned off must not make contact with the strings, otherwise they would permanently damp the strings and the desired register would not sound. Thus both the dampers and the quills must be drawn away from the strings when the double-manual register is disengaged.

The 'mouse ear' type of damper produces an interesting effect in an instrument with two 8′ strings for each note. If one 8′ register is turned off, its strings are left undamped and free to vibrate in sympathy with the other 8′ register. When the jack of the note being played returns to rest it will damp its own string, but the undamped 8′ string vibrating in sympathy will continue to sound after the key is released. Although no Ruckers harpsichord appears to have survived which was originally disposed with two 8′ registers, Ioannes Couchet and Ioseph Ioannes Couchet made harpsichords with this disposition (1652 IC and 1671 IC; see Chapter 12, pp. 222–3).

The sides of the tongue mortice were scribed on the front and rear of the jack with a mortice gauge. The scribed lines are usually about 4.1mm apart, but the actual tongue mortice may be up to a millimetre wider than this. The bottom of the mortice is angled at about 40° to the front surface of the jack. This angled surface acts as a stop for the bottom of the tongue and a small piece of white (kid?) leather is glued to its surface to prevent the click which would otherwise result when the tongue comes to rest the instant after the string is plucked, and again when the quill passes over the string on its return.

The bristle which holds the tongue in position is held in the body of the jack by the friction produced between the scaly surface of the bristle and the hole for it below the tongue mortice. The amount of friction is increased by bending the bristle sharply inside the jack body to increase the force exerted on the sides of the hole by the bristle. The bristle hole angles up from below the middle of the front of the tongue mortice to emerge from the rear of the jack, only to re-enter the jack body again at a shallow angle and emerge from below the top of the angled surface at the bottom of the tongue mortice (see Fig. 6.15). These two angled holes are carefully drilled so that the bristle does not actually project from the rear surface of the jaacck.

The tongue, usually of beech but sometimes of cherry, pivots on an axle placed through the side of the jack and across the tongue mortice. In the 4′ jacks, the axle pin always passes through the thin side of the tongue mortice, and lodges in the thicker side which has the damper hole in it. Usually the axle is a piece of brass wire 0.63mm in diameter (probably gauge number 1 in the gauge system used by the Ruckers; see p. 63) which is sharpened at one end. The axle hole in the tongues, in the only two instruments where measurement of this is possible (1618b IR and 1644a AR), were both 0.75mm in diameter. The axle hole is placed quite low on the tongue, so that the point at which the bristle touches the tongue is well away from the axis of rotation of the tongue and so that the moment of the force of the bristle returning the tongue to its rest position is as great as possible.

The sides of the tongue are chamfered near the top and bottom to avoid interference between the tongue and the sides of the mortice. The top and rear edges of the tongue are also often shaped with delicate, fine chamfers which serve only a decorative purpose. Except for these chamfers the front of the tongue is flat. The back of the tongue angles steeply at the bottom so that only the very bottom edge of the tongue touches the angled bottom of the tongue mortice. The top of the tongue is thinned at the back to reduce the amount of wood above the quill. An asymmetrical notch is also made in the back of the tongue with one edge of the notch at the edge of the quill slot. Just below this notch is the longitudinal groove for the bristle. A total of about 0.2–0.5mm clearance was left between the tongue and the sides of the tongue mortice.

The quill slot in the tongue is a simple rectangular or lenticular-shaped hole passing through the middle of the tongue. This slot is angled upwards at an angle of 10–12°, and this angling of the quill has a number of significant consequences. Probably the most important is that after plucking the strings, the quill will always slide past the string on its return. The weight of the jack suspended from the angled quill has a strong component which pushes the quill and tongue back allowing the quill to 'escape' over the string. This ensures that the quills and jacks do not hang on the strings, as may sometimes happen with quills which are perfectly horizontal, and is consistent with the general importance which seems to have been placed by the Ruckers on reliability in the action of their instruments.

Angling the quill upwards also affects the reliability of the action in another more subtle way. When a key is depressed and the jack begins to rise, the angled quill draws the jack towards the string. Thus, regardless of the amount of play between the jack and the sides of the jackslot, the jack always comes into the same position relative to the string and the amount of 'bite' of the quill is constant. This is, of course, not the case with horizontal quills, which will project under the string by a different amount each time the key is depressed depending on the amount of play between the jack and the sides of the jackslot. The resulting uneven plucking is especially noticeable in the playing of trills or ornaments.

The reliability produced by angling the quill can also affect the voicing of the instrument. Since the quill automatically adjusts the position of the jack relative to the string, one may safely have only a small amount of quill projecting beyond the string and still be certain that the string will be plucked. This amount, adjusted during voicing, is one of the factors which most affects the final sound of the instrument. If a large amount of quill projects past the string, the quill displaces the string sideways as well as vertically and the string is released vibrating in a plane angled to the vertical. This effect is generally recognized as being detrimental to the sound produced (clearly only the vertical component of the string's vibration can be radiated by the bridges and soundboard), and thus the smaller the sideways displacement of the string the closer its plane of vibration will be to the vertical. The angling of the quill aids this effect, since only by angling the quill can one increase the vertical displacement in the plucking process without increasing the sideways movement of the string. Although there is no indication of how the Ruckers may have actually voiced their quills, they were certainly both long and angled; these are features which are recognized today as contributing to good voicing and a reliable action.

There are a number of essential differences between the 4′ and 8′ jacks. The 4′ jacks have only one damper, as opposed to the two used in the 8′ jacks. This means that one of the forks forming the sides of the tongue mortice on the jack body can be narrower than the one pierced with a damper hole. Thus the 4′ jacks are narrower than the 8′ jacks, with their tongues located asymmetrically. The positions of the tongue mortices in the 4′ jackslots in the upper registers are correspondingly asymmetrical. Also, because the 4′ strings are located in a plane below the 8′ strings, the quills and dampers on the 4′ jacks are lower down the jacks than on the 8′ jacks. However, the difference in the distance from the top of the jack to the quills on the 8′ and 4′ jacks is less than the distance between the planes of the 8′ and 4′ strings. For example, on the 1618b IR double, the dampers and quills are about 3.7mm lower on the 4′ jacks than those on the 8′ jacks, but the average distance between the levels of the 8′ and 4′ strings is 5.5mm. Therefore, if the 8′ and 4′ jacks are cut so that the 4′ speaks first, then the length of the 4′ and 8′ jacks will automatically be almost identical, and the two jacks will reach and rebound from the jackrail cloth together. This has been checked and corroborated on the 1640b AR double, where the length of jacks has not been altered, and which still retains a number of 4′ and 8′ jacks from the same note and manual whose lengths can be compared. Thus the plucking order must have been adjusted to make the 4′ jacks speak first for each note, and the position of the quills and dampers on the jacks was chosen to give a similar mechanical motion of both types of jacks in order to achieve this. That the 4′ jacks should speak first on Ruckers instruments is consistent with the later eighteenth-century practice in England, France and

Plate 6.17 A typical signature on a harpsichord namebatten (1638b IR). Scale 1:5.

Flanders, where the 4′ was, as far as I know, always chosen to speak first with the usual 2 × 8, 1 × 4 disposition.

In double-manual harpsichords the jacks for the $e^{\flat}/g^{\sharp}$ notes must have been respectively longer and shorter than their neighbours. Although I have kept a careful watch for original jacks which belonged to these notes (the upper-manual jacks would be numbered 12, 24, and 36, the lower-manual ones 17, 29 and 41), I have unfortunately never found any. It is possible that special jacks and tongues had to be made for the unusual geometry of these notes.

The narrow sides of the jacks are usually cut away at the feet, reducing the area of the jack touching the end of the keylevers. All four edges of the top of the jack are trimmed away with fine chamfering. The chamfered edges, the quartering of the beech wood for the body of the jacks and the oval damper holes are some of the most immediately recognizable characteristics of original Ruckers jacks.

As the number of instruments which retain their original jacks is relatively large, it has been possible to compare the style and workmanship of the jacks in different instruments. As might be expected, the jacks vary in the shape and chamfering of the tongues in particular, and in the chamfering of the jack body and the piercing of the damper holes as well. In view of this it is particularly surprising to find that the two instruments 1618b IR and 1618 AR have jacks which are identical in dimension and in the detail of the decorative chamfers on the tongue and jack body. This suggests that, like the sharps, the Ruckers may have obtained their jacks from a common supplier rather than making them themselves. Unfortunately, there are no other instances of instruments built at nearly the same time by different builders which retain their jacks for comparison. However, the fact that the style of the jacks varies during the course of the career of any given builder seems to suggest that the supplier or workman making the jacks changed from time to time, since the building style tended otherwise to remain very constant.

## HARPSICHORD JACKRAILS

Except that they are wider, the harpsichord jackrails are very similar in shape and function to the virginal jackrails. They have an inverted 'U' cross-section with a moulding profile similar to the case moulding along the top edges. The overhanging edges are carved away at the ends of the jackrail so that only the flat 'backbone' of the jackrail is let into the spine and cheek case sides. Each end of the jackrail is slotted for an iron loop which is driven into the jackrail mortice in the case sides (see Plate 6.9). A flat brass hook, or an iron wire hook, nailed to the top of the jackrail engages in the iron loop in the jackrail case mortice and holds the jackrail in position at each end. The case mortice is not mitred to match the jackrail moulding in any original Ruckers harpsichord. It is instead a simple parallel-sided mortice which has the same width and a slightly greater depth than the end of the jackrail.

Two layers of the thinner (0.9mm compressed thickness) black woollen cloth used by Ruckers is tacked to the inside lower surface of the jackrail. The tacks holding the cloth in place are located in pairs at the ends of the jackrail and roughly one-third and two-thirds along its length. This cloth damps the sound of the jacks rebounding off the jackrail so that they return quickly and quietly to their neutral position.

Whereas the Ruckers signature is always found on the jackrail of the virginals, the harpsichord signature is found on the namebatten above the keys. The jackrail is therefore decorated with a block-printed paper pattern. I have found that in all instruments in which the signature is found on the jackrail, it can be shown to have been painted on the jackrail at a later period.

## HARPSICHORD STANDS

The number of harpsichords which still retain their original stands is very small. Those stands that do seem to be original are similar in style to the seventeenth-century Flemish furniture and interior decoration seen in the Plantin-Moretus Museum, the Rubens House, the Rockox House, or the Vleeshuis Museum in Antwerp. They are made of oak stained a very dark brown and varnished or shellacked.

Most of the original stands are in three essential parts. The front and rear parts which go under the keywell and tail of the instrument are a pierced fretwork structure decorated with turned buttons, split appliqués and hanging 'acorns'. Between the two endpieces is a stretcher of turned columns and fretwork arcades with more turned 'acorns' hanging in the arcades – see Plate 6.18. The stands vary in height from 680mm to 770mm – the former being comfortable for a player seated on a chair of normal height, the latter feeling comfortable only when one is seated on a high chair such as those common in seventeenth-century Flanders. Instruments which retain stands of this type are the 1620c AR, 1616 HR and the 1627 AR harpsichords. The 1624 AR and the '1629 IR' fake in Antwerp (p. 281) have parts of this type of stand under them; the 1624 AR is a cut-down version of a virginal stand.

Plate 6.18 A Ruckers carved, turned and arcaded harpsichord stand (a copy by the author of the stand under the 1620c AR double-manual harpsichord).

The 1640a AR single-manual harpsichord has a stand (which is not original to it but is reputed to have once belonged to the 1648 AR single) with bulbous legs and plain moulded stretchers in the style of many Flemish dining tables. This stand is about 580mm high. The 1608 AR double-manual harpsichord has a stand which is probably almost as old as the instrument, with an upper and lower frame matching the shape of the instrument, separated by carved square legs. Originally about 720mm high, this stand is in the style of English seventeenth-century furniture and therefore likely to have been built for the instrument after it arrived in England. Underneath the later eighteenth-century paint the stand is painted brick red, probably to match the original red marbling of the rest of the instrument.

CHAPTER SEVEN

# The decoration of Ruckers instruments

Ruckers instruments are decorated to produce a visual effect that is as rich as the aural. The case and lid exterior were painted either with a rather simple imitation marble, or with an imitation iron strapwork, brass studs and large semi-precious stones against a marbled background. Most of the interior surfaces such as the soundwell and keywell were decorated with block-printed papers, and the interior of the lid, if not also ornamented with paper patterns and Latin mottoes, was painted in oils, often by one of the great Flemish artists of the day. The soundboard and wrestplank were decorated with paintings of flowers, birds, insects, scampi and occasionally with a small scene depicting human or animal figures. The focus of the soundboard is the gilded rose surrounded by a floral wreath. This rose, along with the date painted on the soundboard or wrestplank, identified the maker and the year in which the instrument was built. The case sides, the tops of the keyblocks, the jackrail, and the keyboard and lid battens were decorated with varnished ogee, ovolo or composite mouldings which were sometimes partly painted over with red or black lines, and the keyfronts were decorated with Gothic-pattern embossed arcades in paper and parchment.

## FLEMISH PRINTED-PAPER DECORATIONS

The two earliest Ruckers instruments, the 1581 HR double virginal and the 1583 HR 4-voet virginal, have original painted decorations in the soundwell and keywell. All subsequent instruments are (or show signs of originally having been) decorated with block-printed paper patterns. In the two early Hans Ruckers instruments the painted decorations are very similar in style to the more common paper patterns. In the soundwell the designs are in only two colours – the background colour plus the white design. In the keywell more colours are used and produce a striking effect. Also a feature of these

Plate 7.1 A modern spinett virginal copied by the author from the (*c.* 1600) HR, showing the style of Ruckers decoration. The stand is copied from that of the 1650 IC muselar virginal.

Plate 7.2 A modern copy of a 'French' double-manual harpsichord made by the author, showing the style of Ruckers decoration. The stand is copied from that of the 1620c AR double-manual harpsichord.

first two virginals are the pairs of medallions on the nameboard with effigies of the Spanish royalty and aristocracy. The cost of these painted instruments must have been high, and, clearly in an effort to reduce their cost, the later instruments were decorated with the inexpensive paper patterns.

The decorative paper patterns used by the Ruckers family, and probably by most of the instrument makers in the Guild of St Luke, are printed from wood-blocks and are usually in the shape of long strips. These strips were joined end to end to form a continuous pattern which covered most of the interior surfaces except for the soundboard.

The paper onto which the patterns were printed was made by hand one sheet at a time. The raw material consists of linen and cotton rags beaten and mixed with water. The pulp mixture was brought into a vat where it was kept in a state of agitation to ensure even mixing by a kind of paddle or hog. The paper-maker or vat man picked up a layer of the pulp on a mould consisting of a mesh of fine parallel wires tightly stretched or 'laid' between the sides of a wooden frame. The wires of the mould are close enough together to retain the fibres on the supper surface, and far enough apart to allow the water to drain away. It is these wires with the occasional transverse chain wires, on which the pulp collects more or less unevenly, that produce the characteristic ribbed texture of hand-made paper.

The layer of pulp was removed from the mould onto a felt cloth. The resulting sheet of paper was covered by another sheet of felt, until a pile consisting of alternate layers of paper and felt was formed. This was then pressed in a screw press in a series of operations, first of all with the felts and later with them removed, to squeeze out all excess water and to give the surface of the sheets the required finish. The paper was then sized with one of various sorts of fillers according to the purpose to which it was going to be put, and hung and allowed to dry.

The paper produced by this method and used by the Flemish builders is of an extremely fine quality without any coarse fibres and with little surface texture. It is quite strongly sized so that the ink does not bleed into the paper. The thickness of the paper which they used is about 0.085–0.12mm, with a weight of about 60–70 grams per square metre.

The exact type of ink used to print these papers is not known. However, the standard ink used during this period consisted of lampblack or powdered charcoal ground in a linseed varnish. The fact that boiled linseed

Plate 7.3 The 1581 HR muselar mother and child double virginals. The decorations are all hand-painted on this instrument, and no use is made of the block-printed paper patterns. Copyright, Metropolitan Museum of Art, New York. Gift of B. H. Homan, 1929 (29.90).

oil made a varnish of good binding and drying properties was already known to Flemish painters in the fifteenth century, and paints based on it were used during this period for inking wooden printing blocks. It seems almost certain that the papers were printed in a press, as press printing had superseded manual rubbing of the blocks or type as early as 1440, and since the linseed varnish inks were used for letter-press, it is likely they were also used to print the blocks.

The patterns were cut into the surface of a plank-sawn piece of hard, even-textured wood. Blocks dating from the period in which the Ruckers were active in the Plantin-Moretus Museum Collection in Antwerp are made of pear, apple, cherry and box. Because the wood is cut plankwise, the cutter has to pull the knife towards himself. The technique of wood engraving was a later development and is done on end-grain boxwood using a graver pushed away from the cutter. During printing the part of the block cut away is not inked, and the pattern printed results from ink transferred from the uncut flat sections of the block onto the paper. Obviously the patterns consisting of a black background with the pattern in white were quicker to cut than the corresponding negative pattern, since less wood had to be cut away, and this may explain the rather large numbers of this type of 'black' pattern.

### *The wood-block pattern books*

Many of the patterns used by the Ruckers family were taken from Renaissance pattern books which were printed expressly for the use of decorators, gold and silversmiths, embroiderers, lace-makers, etc. The patterns are wonderfully inventive and exhibit a great beauty of form and design. Based on Arabic art, they make use of stylized vines, leaves, ribbons, and bands interlaced together, sometimes in the form of knots or geometrical patterns, and sometimes as exotic arabesques.

*La fleur de la science de pourtraicture* by the Renaissance artist Francesco Pellegrino[1] (signed Francisque Pellegrin, Paris, 1530) is one of the two identifiable source books of the Ruckers paper patterns.[2] In it I have discovered the origins of four of the Ruckers papers. This book, along with two similar books by Peter Quentel and Giovanni Tagliente both printed in 1527, was among the first to be printed which introduced the elements of Arabic design into Western art in a way grammatically correct and yet thoroughly confident and inventive.

The second pattern book is by Balthasar Sylvius.[3] In 1939 Scheuleer[4] discovered three Ruckers patterns in this book, but in fact it is the source of at least twelve complete patterns, and the border patterns of four others. It was published in Antwerp in 1554 under the title *Variarum protractionum quas vulgo Maurusias vocant* ... This was the time of the 'Golden Age' in Antwerp, when there was a flourishing trade in the new port in all sorts of articles, such as decorated cups, plates, vases, goblets, boxes, knife sheaths, as well as lace, embroidery, trimmings, braids, etc. Obviously a book such as this would find a ready market.

The patterns in these books are remarkable for their freedom and rhythm. None of the designs is completely symmetrical: the basic outlines of most of the patterns give the appearance of symmetry, but slight, unobtrusive asymmetries avoid mechanical solidity and stiffness.

Such asymmetries show that some of the designs have suffered a mirror reversal in being copied from the pattern books, and some have not. The mirror reversal was a natural consequence of the process of copying and cutting the blocks. The original design from one of the pattern books was glued face uppermost onto the wood-block and the pattern cut through the paper into the wood. After cutting, the original paper was removed using warm water to dissolve the glue. The prints produced from the resulting block were then all mirror images of the original. Prints without the mirror reversal are produced by gluing the original pattern with its printed face towards the surface of the block. If the paper on the block is dampened slightly, it can then be carefully rubbed off, leaving only the inked pattern and the surface fibres of the paper glued to the block, so that the pattern is clearly visible for cutting. The glue is again dissolved after the cutting is completed and the printed pattern produced from the resulting block is an almost exact

[1] Pellegrino was a Florentine and, along with Benvenuto Cellini and Rosso Fiorentino, came to work on the Château de Fontainebleau from 1534 to 1536 for François I. The great King's Gallery at Fontainebleau is one of their finest achievements and a major contribution to the rapidly-developing Renaissance style. Rosso Fiorentino originated the heavy strapwork borders surrounding the painting in the King's Gallery; these contrast markedly with the light airy arabesques of Pellegrino (see pp. 139 and 140). Pellegrino died about 1552.

[2] A (perhaps unique) original copy is in the Bibliothèque de l'Arsenal in Paris. There is a modern edition limited to 300 copies printed by Jean Schmidt in Paris in 1908.

[3] Balthasar Sylvius was born in 1518 in 's-Hertogenbosch, in what is now Southern Holland. He was already living in Antwerp in 1543. In the ledgers of the Guild of St Luke he is inscribed under the name 'Balten Bos' as a journeyman *copersnyder* in 1551, the same year that Pieter Brueghel (the Peasant Brueghel) became a master.

[4] Daniel F. Lunsingh Scheurleer, 'Over het ornament en de autenticiteit van bedrukte papierstrooken in twee clavierinstrumenten', *Mededelingen van de Dienst Voor Kunsten en Wetenschappen der Gemeente's-Gravenhage* (The Hague, 1939), 45. See also: Ernest Closson, 'L'ornementation en papier imprimé des clavecins anversois', *Revue Belge d'archéologie et d'histoire de l'arte*, II/2 (1932), 105.

duplicate of the original. Most of the patterns used by the Ruckers have been copied in this way, without the mirror reversal.

### *The Ruckers wood-block paper patterns*

The Pellegrino and Sylvius pattern books are the source of most of the patterns used by the Ruckers. Although I have made an exhaustive search of the large European libraries, no other pattern books have been found with any of the Ruckers patterns in them. The stylistic similarity of many of the remaining patterns does seem to indicate that a third pattern book was the source of these designs, but that this book has now disappeared. A few of the designs are quite unlike any of the others and may have come from yet other pattern books, or may have been made up by the wood-block cutter without reference to already published patterns.

The origin of the dolphin pattern, Types 3 and 4 below, is particularly intriguing. Although I have found the dolphin motif as a constant feature of Renaissance ornament and of many of the pattern books that I examined, none was identical with or even very similar to those found on Flemish instruments. With such a traditional design, it seems highly improbable that the exact origin of this version of it can be located. The dolphin pattern is painted in the keywell of the Iohannes Grouwels virginal (c. 1570), No. 2929, in the Brussels Museum of Musical Instruments, and this, along with the other painted decorations on the instrument, seems to be original. A number of paintings and engravings[5] as early as 1548 show this traditional dolphin motif. And the Ioes Karest virginal of 1550, in Rome,[6] is painted with a mannerist grotesque design very similar to the dolphin pattern (see Plate 7.4). The paper pattern used by the Flemish instrument makers was a cheaper version of this traditional design.

It seems that the pattern Type 2 below was also one of the traditional patterns of the St Luke builders. A similar pattern is painted on the faceboard and keywell of the Lodewijck Grouwels virginal dated 1600 (made in Middleburg shortly after Grouwels had moved there from Antwerp) in the Crosby Brown Collection of the Metropolitan Museum, New York, as well as appearing on the papers of several Flemish instruments.

Plate 7.4 The case decoration of the 1550 Karest virginal in Rome, painted in blue-black monochrome.

The Hans Bos virginal in the monastery of Santa Clara in Tordesillas, Spain, has not only the two patterns mentioned above, Types 2 and 3, but also another pattern, Type 16, which provides an interesting clue to the origin of these papers. This pattern appears on only one Ruckers harpsichord (1640b IR), and that an instrument probably sixty years later than the Bos virginal. The fact that the patterns used by two quite independent builders at different times have a common pattern book as origin suggests that probably all of the Guild members bought their papers from a common source. Further, the fact that the paper Type 15/30 uses patterns taken from both the Pellegrino and the Sylvius books points to there being but one person making the blocks and utilizing both sources. Doubtless also a member of the Guild of St Luke, this person cut and printed a number of patterns, some traditional and some taken from pattern books, and he and his successors supplied them to all the instrument builders working in Antwerp.

Another interesting pattern used by the Ruckers family is the imitation wood-grain pattern Type 1, which is clearly not the type of pattern that would be found in a pattern book. I have discovered a version of this pattern in the so-called 'Winkelriedhaus' from Stans in Switzerland. The coffered ceiling of the banqueting hall from the second floor of this house is now in the Schweizerisches Landesmuseum, Zurich; it is dated about 1563. Similar, but not identical, papers have been found by Dr Horst Appuhn of Schloss Cappenberg in the rooms in Kloster Isenhagen and Kloster Weinhausen, and in a number of sixteenth-century German letter-safes.[7] In all of these, the paper pattern is meant to imitate the wood grain of plank-sawn figured ash (usually called Hungarian ash). Panelling on walls and ceilings, cupboards and wardrobes was often of figured plank-sawn ash, sometimes with the larger flat surfaces inlaid with intarsia arab-

[5] Plates 54 and 57 in Edwin M. Ripin's 'On Joes Karest's virginal and the origin of the Flemish tradition', *Keyboard Instruments: Studies in Keyboard Organology*, ed. Edwin M. Ripin (Edinburgh, 1971).

[6] No. 812 of the Museo degli Strumenti Musicali. See Luisa Cervelli, 'Per un catalogo degli strumenti a tastiera del Museo degli Antichi Strumenti Musicali', *Accademie e Biblioteche d'Italia*, XLIV, 4–5 (1976), 305–43.

[7] Horst Appuhn, *Kloster Isenhagen: Kunst und Kultur im Mittelalter* (Lüneburg, 1966), 82; *Riesenholzschnitte und Papiertapeten der Renaissance* (Unterschneidheim, 1976), 87–92.

esques, and was very fashionable during the High Renaissance. In the Winkelried ceiling the coffered areas with the imitation wood-grain papers are boldly set against genuine figured-ash panels in the framing!

The Winkelried ceiling contains two very similar wood-grain papers. The first of these (see Plate 7.5) closely resembles the earliest example of the wood-grain paper to be found on a Ruckers instrument, the 1591a HR virginals. Unfortunately the figured wood pattern is barely visible on this instrument, but the same pattern is also found on the 1598 HR virginal (see Plate 7.6). A careful comparison reveals that the earlier Winkelried pattern and that on the 1598 HR are mirror images of one another; the 1598 pattern contains much more detail than the earlier one. Both patterns have a cleverly-designed edge symmetry with an axis along the centre of the long direction of the paper. If the papers are glued in place by rotating each successive paper through 180° relative to

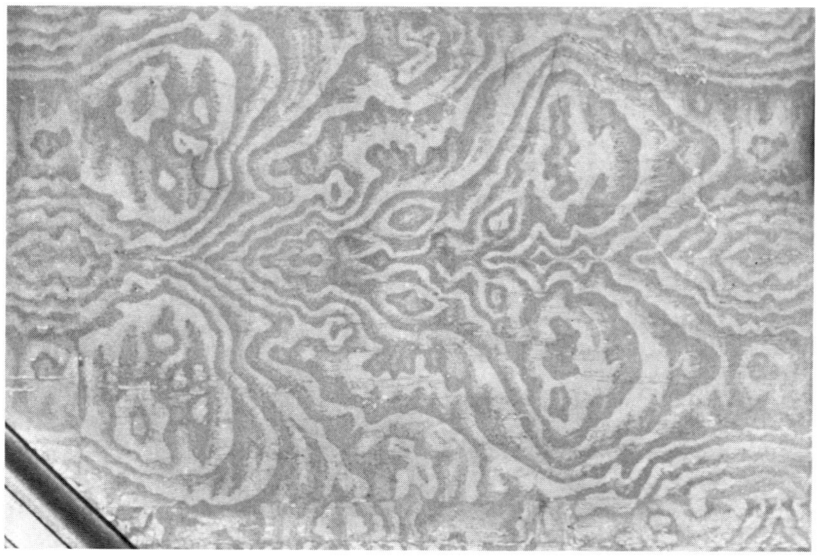

Plate 7.5 The wood-grain paper (*c.* 1560) from the Winkelriedhaus, Stans, Switzerland (now in the Landesmuseum, Zurich). Scale 1:4.

Plate 7.6 The wood-grain paper from the 1598 HR spinett virginal. Scale 1:4.

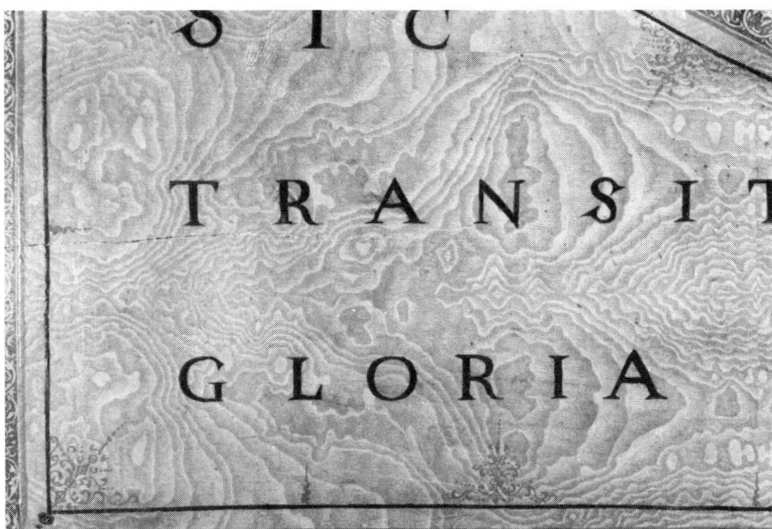


Plate 7.7 The wood-grain paper from the 1627 A R harpsichord. This pattern, unlike the two above which are brown, was printed with green ink and used after 1623. Scale 1:4.

the preceding one, the wood-graining matches at the join in the two papers. The upper and lower surfaces of the papers are also ingeniously designed so that, if the papers are placed directly one above the other, the wood-grain pattern of one paper matches the next, flowing without an apparent break from paper to paper. The repetition cycle of the papers is thus so large that the eye is easily deceived into believing that, as with natural wood, the wood-grain pattern does not repeat at all.

It seems fairly certain that the 1598 H R pattern was cut from the earlier Winkelried pattern simply by taking a sheet of the Winkelried paper, gluing it to a block, and enhancing the detail somewhat in the process of cutting it. Similarly, the 1598 wood-grain pattern and all of the subsequent wood-grain patterns (see Plate 7.7) differ by the same mirror reversal, produced by a second similar recutting of the pattern. These three wood-grain patterns thus represent three generations of woodcuts spanning the period from the Winkelried ceiling, in 1563, to 1651 when the last Ruckers instrument which still has this pattern was built.[8]

The first two patterns (Plates 7.5 and 7.6) are used in a way which clearly imitates wood. The pigment used to print the pattern, although now greatly darkened, seems to have been natural Italian sienna, and the original effect, against a background of off-white paper, must have been very similar to the appearance of the grained figure in the natural ash wood. All blocks of this pattern printed after 1598, however, are printed using a light olive-green pigment. This green pattern can no longer have been meant to imitate wood grain. Either the Ruckers simply liked the shimmering effect, or, more likely, it was meant to imitate watered silk or camlet. These artificially patterned materials were popular as early as the beginning of the sixteenth century, and became very fashionable in the first half of the seventeenth century. However, despite the more common later use of this green-printed paper to imitate silk, I have chosen to call this the wood-grain paper because of its original purpose.

The block-printed papers, in addition to being used inside the main lid, lid flap and keywell flap, were put to a number of other uses. As already mentioned, the keywell was decorated with one of the wide paper patterns. In the large virginals and single-manual harpsichords this is often one of the dolphin patterns. On double-manual harpsichords, however, the most common keywell patterns are Type 12 in the Andreas instruments, and 21 or 22 in Ioannes doubles. These patterns fit quite well on the narrow nameboard; on the spine and cheek part of the keywell the papers are placed side by side with the rope or chain edging removed so that only the central portion of

[8] The history of this wood-grain pattern may be even longer, with yet an additional generation of papers. Also in the Schweizerisches Landesmuseum in Zurich is a papered door from the Techtermann-haus, the 'Haus zu Salmen', which came from Fribourg in Switzerland. The door is believed to have been papered in about 1540, and the papers used are very similar, although not identical, to the wood-grain papers on the 1598 H R virginal. They are, however, related, and may well be the parent of the Winkelried papers. They are in such poor condition that a photograph does not show enough of the detail for an accurate comparison to be made. The occurrence of both of these papers in Switzerland definitely points to this country as the origin of the wood-grain paper.

Plate 7.8 Original engraved pattern from the book by Balthasar Sylvius (1554) (above), and the block-printed pattern found on the 1610 HR child virginal (below). Scale 1:2.

the paper is used. The smaller virginals, which have narrower case sides, use one of the narrower patterns such as Type 12 in the keywell and on the faceboard.

In the child virginals the whole of the outer case is covered in a paper pattern: Types 5 or 12 are often used. An interesting variant is the child part of the 1610 HR double virginal in Brussels, which has two strip patterns still joined together. Paper Types 24 and 28 are both taken from Sylvius, where they occur together on the same page one above the other. This is the way they appear on the virginal (see Plate 7.8): clearly, when the pattern was taken from the Sylvius book, the page was left as it was and glued face down to the block. The extra leafy arabesque designs were added on either side, probably by cutting them from a second copy of the Sylvius pattern book, since the added arabesques are slightly different from one another (although each is identical to one of the internal arabesques of the pattern).

The narrow strip patterns are used to decorate the soundwell on the interior case sides above the soundboard. One of the most commonly occurring soundwell patterns is the Pellegrino pattern Type 13. In the large 6- and 5-voet virginals the faceboard and keywell are lower than the case sides. The strip pattern used on this part of the soundwell has to be narrower than that on the spine and sides of the instrument: thus for these instruments two different papers are used in the soundwell.

The harpsichord jackrails are also decorated with paper patterns (the virginal jackrails bear the maker's signature and are therefore not papered). The double-manual jackrails are wider than those on singles, and strip patterns of the appropriate width are chosen to suit. The lower-manual batten on doubles is papered, and often the top of the lid on the virginal toolbox and the top of the block at the bass end of the upper-manual keyboard in doubles are covered with a section of one of the paper patterns. Although the keyblocks (only the lower-manual keyblock in doubles) usually have a design painted on them in Ioannes Ruckers harpsichords, they are often decorated with one of the narrow strip patterns in harpsichords signed by Andreas Ruckers.

The wood-blocks from which the Ruckers patterns were printed are competently cut, but without any particular skill or refinement. In comparison with the superb contemporary woodcuts used for botanical illustrations, book decorations, etc. which are preserved in the Plantin-Moretus Museum in Antwerp, the wood-blocks used for the Flemish instruments are second-rate. The exact source of these papers is a mystery – it was not a block cutter of the first order, and it does not seem to have been the instrument makers themselves, unless one of them made the papers as a sideline and sold them to his colleagues.

The papers which appear on the instruments show that the blocks gradually became chipped and damaged, resulting in a number of defects in the finished prints. The later prints generally show more of these defects, indicating that the blocks were reused regularly to make fresh copies and that they were probably both very badly stored and cut in a relatively fragile wood. This would explain why a number of the patterns were recut giving new versions of the same pattern. This gradual change in the wood-block patterns is very important as a useful tool in estimating the date of some instruments. Clearly if an undated instrument retains one or more of the paper patterns found also on a number of other dated instruments, it would be possible to give an estimate of its date by comparing the defects in the prints.

Rather surprisingly, nothing seems to have been done to protect the papers from damage after they were applied. Many of the papers have since been covered with a protective coat of varnish, but the large number of instruments which survives untreated indicates that the papers were applied and then left to fend off the ravages of time without any additional protection.

## CATALOGUE OF BLOCK-PRINTED PATTERNS FOUND ON RUCKERS CLAVECIMBELS

Each of the paper patterns and each of the original designs as printed in the books by Sylvius or Pellegrino are here reduced in size by a factor of 2:5. It will be noticed for those patterns which have been taken from one of these source books that the pattern found on the instrument is slightly larger than the original. The probable reason for this is that when the original pattern was cut it was first glued to the wood-block with a water-soluble glue (such as hide glue). The water in the glue would expand the paper slightly as it was glued in place so that the wood-block design was slightly larger than the original. The same enlargement would again occur when the printed pattern was glued to the instrument. Thus the paper patterns as found on the instruments are larger than the originals as a result of *two* expansions caused by the use of water-based glue.

### TYPE 1

*Early type* Found on: 1591a HR, 1598 HR

TYPE 1 (*cont*)

*Late type* Found on: 1623 IR, 1628a IR, 1629 IR, 1637b IR, 1638a IR, 1640a IR, 1642a IR, 1615 AR, 1618 AR, 1620a AR, 1624 AR, 1627 AR, 1632 AR, 1633a AR, 1635 AR, 1637 AR, 1640a AR, 1644a AR, 1648 AR, (1651)a AR, 1654 AR

TYPE 2

Found on: (*c.* 1600) HR, 1642a IR, 1620a AR, 1643a AR.
This pattern is usually used on the front flap or, using only half of the pattern, is sometimes used to decorate the lid of virginal toolboxes. It is also used on the 'C.R.' virginal in Namur, and the Iohannes Bos virginal in Tordesillas, Spain.

TYPE 3

*Early type* Found on: 1591a HR, 1594 HR, 1598 HR, 1611 IR, 1640a AR, 1640b AR

*Late type* Found on: 1640a IR, 1637 AR, 1648 AR, (1651)a AR

These two patterns are used only in the keywell and on the faceboard. The late type is a mirror reversal of the early type. The early type also occurs on the 'C.R.' virginal in Namur, and on the Iohannes Bos virginal in Tordesillas, Spain.

TYPE 4

Found on: (*c.* 1600) HR, 1623 IR, 1644a AR, 1645 IC.

This pattern is a negative of the early Type 3 paper, and was probably cut from the same original design as there is no mirror reversal between it and this paper. It is also used only on the keywell and faceboard.

TYPE 5

Found on: (*c.* 1600) HR, 1639 IR.
This pattern is painted on the keywell of the 1639 IR instrument, but it was almost certainly used originally as a paper, and then later painted in when the paper became damaged and was removed.

TYPE 6

Found on: 1642a IR, 1608 AR, 1643a AR, 1644a AR, 1648 AR, 1654 AR

TYPE 7

Found on: 1633a AR

TYPE 8

Found on: 1591a HR, 1598 HR, 1629 IR, 1642a IR, 1618 AR, 1620a AR, 1637 AR, 1640a AR.
There are practically no two versions of this pattern which are exactly the same. It seems to have been printed from a number of different blocks.

TYPE 9

Found on: 1618a IR, 1638a IR, 1613c AR, 1620d AR, (1626) AR, (1651)a AR.
Without the two narrow border strips, this pattern is often used in the soundwell of the child virginals. As a border pattern to Type 1 it is used both with and without its own border strips.

TYPE 10

Found on: 1623 IR, 1640a IR, 1620d AR, 1624 AR, 1632 AR, 1635 AR, 1637 AR, 1654 AR.
A similar pattern, cut from an entirely different block, is to be found on the 1605 Gheerdinck virginal, in the Germanisches Nationalmuseum, Nuremberg.

TYPE 11

Found on: 1598 HR

TYPE 12

Found on: 1599 HR, 1611 HR, 1618a IR, 1623 IR, 1640a IR, 1642a IR, 1610b AR, 1613b AR, 1613c AR, 1615 AR, 1620a AR, (1626) AR, 1627 AR, 1643a AR, 1644b AR

TYPE 13

Found on: 1599 HR, (*c.* 1600) HR, 1609 AR, 1610b AR, 1615 AR, 1633b AR, 1635 AR, 1636 AR, 1637 AR, 1640b AR, 1644a AR, (1651)a AR.
Source: Francesco Pellegrino, 1530. This is by far the most commonly-used soundwell paper.

TYPE 14

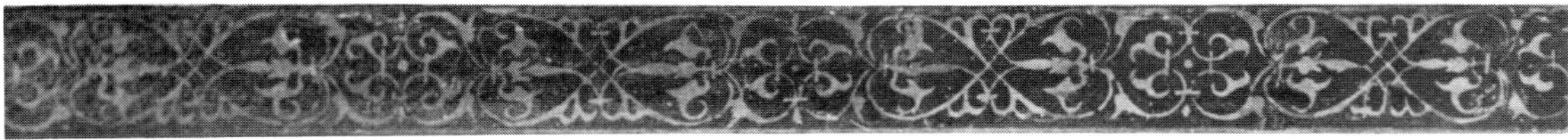

Found on: 1624 IR.
Source: Francesco Pellegrino, 1530. This is clearly the negative of the Type 13 above.

TYPE 15

Found on: 1598 HR.
Source: Francesco Pellegrino, 1530, the central pattern only. The top and bottom border patterns are Type 30 (see below).

TYPE 16

Found on: 1640b IR.
Source: Francesco Pellegrino, 1530. This paper is also found in the soundwell of the Iohannes Bos virginal in Tordesillas, Spain.

TYPE 17

Found on: 1598 HR, 1617 IR, 1640a IR, 1642a IR, 1620a AR, 1620d AR, 1624 AR, 1648 AR.
Source: Balthasar Sylvius, 1554. This pattern was obviously enlarged and redrawn before being cut as a woodblock.

TYPE 18

Found on: (*c.* 1600) HR, 1618b IR, 1640a AR.
Source: Balthasar Sylvius, 1554.

TYPE 19

Found on: 1611 HR, 1634 AR.
Source: Balthasar Sylvius, 1554.

TYPE 20

Found on: 1628b IR, 1637b IR.
Source: Balthasar Sylvius, 1554.

TYPE 21

Found on: 1618b IR, 1624 IR, 1627b IR, 1628b IR, 1637b IR, 1638b IR.
Source: Balthasar Sylvius, 1554. This pattern seems to have been used only by Ioannes Ruckers in the keywell of his double-manual harpsichords.

TYPE 22

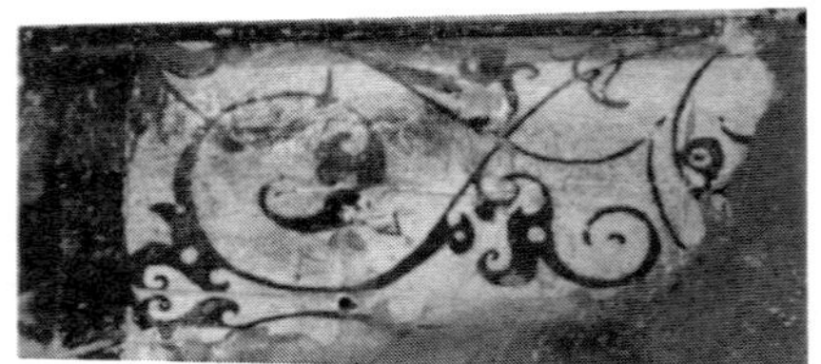

Found on: 1640b IR, 1635 AR.
Source: Balthasar Sylvius, 1554. No complete version of this paper is known to exist, but it is clearly the negative of Type 21.

TYPE 23

Found on: (*c.* 1600) HR, 1611 HR, 1638b IR.
Source: Balthasar Sylvius, 1554.

TYPE 24

Found on: 1610 HR, 1628b IR, 1637b IR, 1638b IR.
Source: Balthasar Sylvius, 1554. (See Type 28.)

TYPE 25

Found on: '1634 IR'
Source: Balthasar Sylvius, 1554. Strangely, this pattern, although it exists on no genuine Ruckers instrument, is found on the '1634 Ioannes Ruckers' fake harpsichord of *c.* 1720 in Ham House, London. Since the pattern is one of those in the book by Sylvius, it seems likely that the person who made the fake harpsichord copied the pattern from a genuine Ruckers instrument in the eighteenth century.

TYPE 26

Found on: 1610 HR, 1623 IR.
Source: Balthasar Sylvius, 1554.

TYPE 27

Found on: 1627 AR, 1645 IC.
Source: Balthasar Sylvius, 1554.

TYPE 28

Found on: 1610 HR, 1623 IR, 1627 AR.
Source: Balthasar Sylvius, 1554. Type 24 and Type 28 appear engraved in the Sylvius book one above the other, and appear together this way on the outside of the 1610 HR child virginal. (See Plate 7.8.)

TYPE 29

Found on: 1612a HR, 1628 AR.
Source: Balthasar Sylvius, 1554.

TYPE 30

Found on: 1598 HR.
Source: Balthasar Sylvius, 1554. This is the border of Type 15.

## RUCKERS PAINTED SOUNDBOARDS

The origin of the painted soundboards on Flemish instruments is not at all clear. What does seem certain, though, is that the tradition of painting the soundboard certainly did not come from Italy. It may have come to Flanders from Germany, along with the other traditions in keyboard-instrument building. The earliest paintings depicting Flemish virginals and harpsichords show that the soundboard decoration often consisted only of a scalloped edging which outlined the inside of the case, the bridges, rose and jack mortices, with arabesques joined to the edging and placed at any corners and also at intervals along the edging.[9]

Traces of pigments have been found on the soundboard of the Ioes Karest virginal of 1548 in Brussels, and the 1550 Karest virginal in Rome has a fully developed soundboard painting with blue scalloped borders, blue arabesques, and fruit and flower paintings. It is thus the earliest extant instrument with a painted soundboard. This, along with its beautiful grotesque outer decoration, its elegantly curved 'bentside' and the unusually large compass of C,D to $f^3$, makes it one of the most interesting and precious of early Flemish instruments.

But although the origin of painting flowers, fruit, etc. on clavecimbel soundboards is not certain, the tradition of this type of decoration has considerable precedent. The stylized flower and figure painting found in illuminated books, peasant furniture, and on pottery, armour, and 'Dutch' tiles is very similar in concept and execution. When there was at the time a passion for gardening, exotic plants and birds, and when, at the height of the 'Tulpomania' aberration, a single exotic tulip plant could be sold for a fortune, it is not surprising to see this type of decoration on harpsichord and virginal soundboards.

### *Pattern books for Ruckers soundboard paintings*

It is clear from an examination of Ruckers soundboard paintings that each builder had his own painter and that each painter worked in a consistent style over a period of several decades. In addition to using his own style of arabesque, each soundboard painter used the same motifs and groupings of flowers, fruits and animals again and again, and each had his own characteristic technique of applying the paint. The similarity in the individual decorative elements from soundboard to soundboard are so consistent for each painter over such a long period of time, that it seems almost certain that the decorators were each working from pattern books from which they copied their designs onto the soundboards, rather than painting each flower or bird from memory. The position, orientation, spacing and size of individual elements varies on different soundboards by the same decorator, but details such as the proportions, outlines, colours and shading of the individual elements remain the same.

Just as there were traditional patterns used for the block-printed papers, there were also doubtless workshop patterns used by the Ruckers which were not taken from published pattern books. Clearly the garland or wreath around the rose was one such workshop design which would not have come from a pattern book. But the popularity and large numbers of printed herbals and *florilegia* that existed at this time suggest that the Ruckers soundboard designs, if not copied directly, were at least inspired by these pattern books.

It is very difficult to associate a particular pattern book with a Ruckers soundboard painter or design. Each soundboard painter would interpret the engraved designs in the manner of his usual painting style. It is possible to imagine two different soundboard decorators using the same engraved pattern book to produce painted motifs which are so dissimilar as to disguise their common origin.

The other problem of associating one of the published *florilegia* with a given Ruckers soundboard painter is that, in the days before copyright, such flower books were copied and republished again and again by new 'authors'. This usually meant that a previous flower or animal design was copied onto the engraving plate and re-engraved. Each time this was done the image suffered a mirror reversal. Some of the designs copied onto Ruckers soundboards have this mirror reversal either because the decorator was working from a second-generation copy of the pattern book, or because the reversed image would fit better into the space he needed to fill or would better synchronize with the rhythm of the adjacent designs. I have been able to associate only one set of printed pattern books with Ruckers soundboard-painting designs, some with and some without the mirror reversal. The pattern books were the *Florilegium* and *Avium Vivae Icones* (*Living Images of Birds*) by Adrian Collaert[10], and were used by the soundboard painter

[9] See Ripin, 'On Joes Karest's virginal', Plates 54, 55, 56, 57 and 58.

[10] Adrian Collaert, born about 1550–60, a citizen of Antwerp, died 29 July 1618. He became a master in the Guild of St Luke as a *figuersnyder* or engraver; his father was a master of the Guild and presumably also an engraver. His wife was Justa Galle, the daughter of Philip Galle, another famous engraver. Collaert was co-dean of the Guild of St Luke in 1596/97 and corporate dean in 1597/98, and would therefore have been aware of Hans Ruckers' death in 1598. He is recorded regularly in the Registers of the Guild as having taken in apprentice engravers, and in his later years is recorded as a contribu-

working on the late instruments signed by Andreas Ruckers. The date of publication of the *Florilegium* is unknown but thought to be about 1590.[11] The *Avium Vivae Icones* was published in Antwerp in 1610, and posthumously in Amsterdam in 1625. Collaert also published two other pattern books of interest: *Piscium Vivae Icones* (Antwerp, 1611 and Amsterdam, 1634) and *Animalium Quadrupedium* (Antwerp, ?1612). Unfortunately I have not found any specific examples of the use of these other pattern books by any of the Ruckers soundboard painters.

Collaert's *Avium Vivae Icones* is a collection of engravings of domesticated, wild, European, and exotic birds, and designs from it are easily recognizable on late Andreas Ruckers soundboards. Most of the birds illustrated depict the common European species: the sparrow, raven, eagle, partridge, starling, goldfinch, etc., and a few exotic birds like the turkey and the parrot. The latter are easy to identify on the soundboards, but the European species are less easy to recognize because they are so stylized. Plate 7.9 shows the Collaert turkey engraving and the turkey depicted on the soundboard of the (1651)a A R single-manual harpsichord. Here there is no mirror reversal. The same turkey is seen in a similar position, but sitting on the stem of a tulip(!) on the 1640b A R double, and with a mirror reversal sitting on a strawberry on the 1633b A R double. Plate 7.10 compares the parrot holding a cherry on the 1640b A R double soundboard with the Collaert engraving. Here there is clearly a mirror reversal. Plate 7.11 shows a comparison of the Collaert hoopoe and that found on the 1623 A R double harpsichord. Here the soundboard painter, who may be different from that of the previous two examples, is less confident and more naive, but the source of his design seems still to have been Collaert. Naturally there are numerous other concurrences between the engravings in the *Avium Vivae Icones* and the late soundboard paintings of Andreas Ruckers which cannot all be itemized here.

Collaert's bird engravings exhibit a clear attempt at a naturalistic representation of the animals involved, even if they are not completely anatomically correct. The illustrations below show that the painter of the late instruments of Andreas Ruckers treats these engravings with considerable freedom, resulting in a highly stylized representation of the birds concerned. This is also true of the flower patterns which the late Andreas painter took from Collaert's *Florilegium*. Plates 7.12–7.14 show comparisons of numerous flowers engraved by Collaert and those found on the later instruments of Andreas Ruckers. These illustrate beautifully the meaning of artistic licence, but also show that the decorator of the late Andreas Ruckers instruments was definitely using Collaert's *Florilegium* as a source book for his soundboard paintings.

In the work of other painters who decorated Ruckers soundboards I have not been able to trace the use of any particular printed pattern book. The decorator who worked on the early Ioannes Ruckers instruments is notable for a style almost like that of a tinted engraving. The leaves are painted in flat green paint and then the outlines and veining are added with quill and ink, as though the painter were copying the black engraved lines onto his soundboard. Even the flower heads are sometimes outlined and shaded in ink, and the birds and insects are also treated in this way. His flower groups most resemble those engraved by Crispin van der Passe, but it is not possible to identify unequivocally any of these with the early Ioannes paintings.

The soundboard paintings on the early Andreas instruments are like those on the early clavecimbels by Ioannes Ruckers, being outlined with quill and ink; they must also be derived from an engraved (or woodcut) pattern book. These are not so much paintings as drawings in paint; there is no use of the methodical building up of paint, or of the brush-stroke. The effect is flat and linear, and results in a very stylized representation. But although the paintings of the late Andreas soundboards, on which we see the designs taken from the Collaert books, are also very stylized, they are painted and not drawn in paint. The painter who used the most sophisticated technique and who produced the most naturalistic paintings was the late Ioannes Ruckers/Ioannes Couchet soundboard decorator. Here the paint is applied methodically in layers, and glazes are used to create shadows and highlights. Use is made of the brush-stroke both to give colour and to create form. The effect gives shape and depth in a manner not achieved by the other decorators and in a style which begins to approach the flower paintings of Bosschaert, van Kessell and de Heem.

However, none of the Ruckers painters is to be compared with the fine art painters. They were simply highly efficient decorative artists. The results they produced are stylized and naive, colourful, and thoroughly charming.

tor to various Guild benevolent funds. See P. Rombouts and T. van Lerius, *De Liggeren en andere Historische Archieven der Antwerpsche Sint Lucasgilde* (The Hague, 1872–6; facs. Amsterdam, 1961), 1 (1872), 273.

11 A copy of Collaert's *Florilegium* in the British Library has a facing page (which may be unrelated to the rest of the book) dated 1586.

Plate 7.9 Comparison of the turkey in Collaert's *Avium Vivae Icones*, and that on the soundboard of the (1651)a A R single-manual harpsichord.

Plate 7.10 Comparison of the parrot in Collaert's *Avium Vivae Icones*, and that on the soundboard of the 1646b A R double-manual harpsichord.
Musée Instrumental du CNSM de Paris, Cliché Publimages-Labo 4.

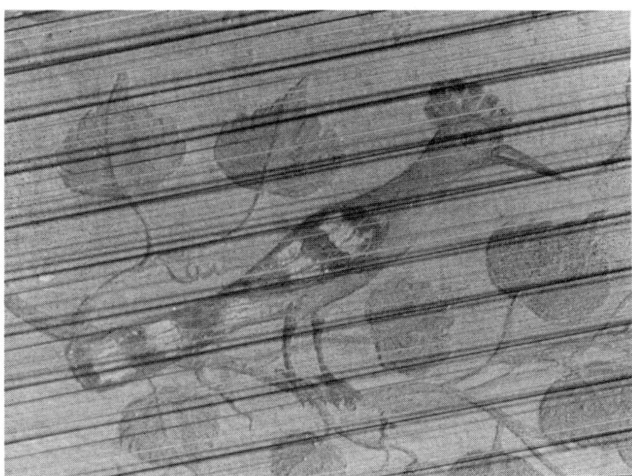

Plate 7.11 Comparison of the hoopoe in Collaert's *Avium Vivae Icones*, and that on the soundboard of the 1623 A R double-manual harpsichord.

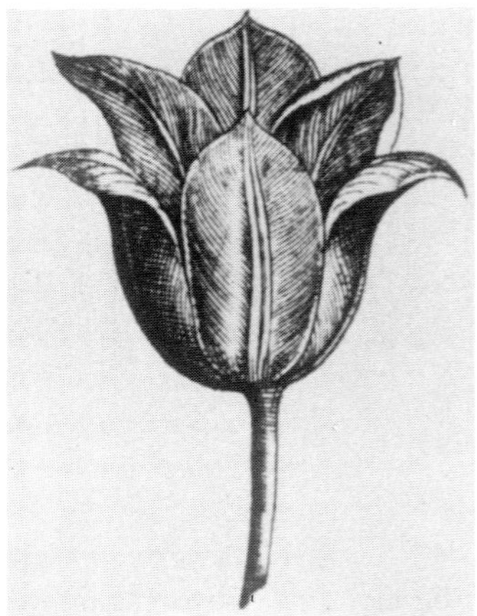

Plate 7.12 Comparison of the tulip from Collaert's *Florilegium*, and that on the soundboard of the 1640a A R single-manual harpsichord.

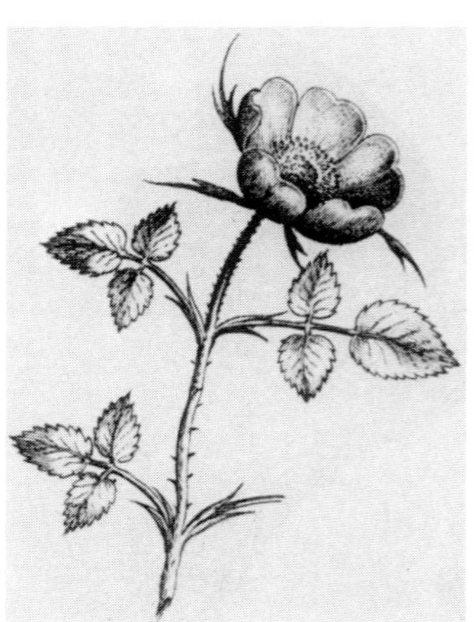

Plate 7.13 Comparison of a rose from Collaert's *Florilegium*, and that on the soundboard of the 1640a A R single-manual harpsichord.

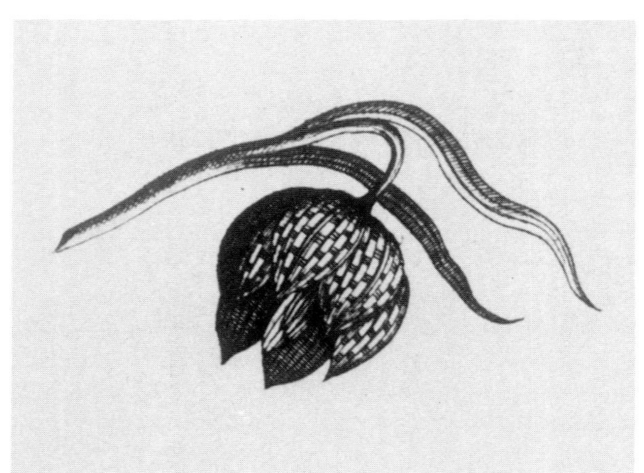

Plate 7.14 Comparison of a fritillary from Collaert's *Florilegium* with that on the soundboard of the 1633b A R double-manual harpsichord.

## STYLES AND PERIODS OF RUCKERS SOUNDBOARD DECORATION

Because the soundboard-painting style of each Ruckers decorator is relatively constant over a period of several decades, the soundboard painting can be a useful guide to the authentication of a Ruckers instrument, and to the dating and the identification of the member of the family who built the instrument. It is therefore worthwhile to examine each soundboard-painting style in detail in order to identify the salient characteristics of the decorators. There are five, or perhaps six, different styles, each with its characteristic blue borders and arabesques, and each with a different painting technique and choice of designs and motifs.[12]

### *Early Hans Ruckers style*

It is very difficult to distinguish the later instruments of Hans Ruckers from the early ones of his eldest son Ioannes. Ioannes would have been nineteen years old when Hans died in 1598, and therefore old enough to have been making his own instruments even though not yet registered with the Guild of St Luke as a master builder. The last clavecimbel with an extant soundboard painting in the style of earlier Hans Ruckers instruments is the 1591a HR polygonal virginal in Bruges. The 1594 HR harpsichord/virginal combination in East Berlin has lost virtually all traces of its soundboard painting, and the next instrument, a 6-voet virginal dated 1598, has an HR rose like that of the earlier Hans instruments, but is signed IOHANNES RVCKERS FECIT ANTVERPIAE and has a soundboard painting in the style of the other early instruments by Ioannes Ruckers. It therefore seems likely that the 1598 HR virginal is by Ioannes and not Hans, although there is no reason why the soundboard painter should not have worked for Hans and then later, after Hans Ruckers' death in 1598, for his son Ioannes. As we shall see below, a later soundboard painter worked for Ioannes Ruckers and then for Ioannes Couchet when he had taken over the workshop after Ruckers died.

The same decorator worked for both Hans Ruckers and Marten van der Biest (and perhaps Iohannes Grouwels). The style of this decorator is particularly easy to identify from the lacy blue wreath surrounding the rose (he does not use a floral or foliate wreath). The soundwell and keywell painted decorations are also in the same style in instruments by these builders, and were obviously done by the same decorator. Usually this person paints a red band inside the wreath and around the rose, with black and white 'pearls' spaced regularly along the band. The flowers usually have either four or five petals and these are painted in a very characteristic way with a prominent green sepal between each petal regardless of the type of flower. The flower heads are done in a somewhat more painterly style than on the early Ioannes and Andreas instruments, but the stems and leaves are thin, straight and pointed, making them look very stiff and rigid. The effect is much like that of dried straw flowers

[12] Sheridan Germann, 'Regional schools of harpsichord decoration', *Journal of the American Musical Instrument Society*, IV (1978), 64–74.

Plate 7.15 The soundboard of the 1581 HR child virginal showing the typical Hans Ruckers 'straw-flower' soundboard painting style. Scale 1:5.

scattered about the soundboard, and I usually call this the 'straw-flower' style. Cherries and other small individual fruits, leaves and olives are scattered among the flowers and blue arabesques. This decorator does not seem to have painted birds, scampi, animals or human figures.

### *The early Ioannes style*

The same decorator worked in the Ioannes Ruckers workshop from at least 1598 until 1624, and his soundboard-painting style is remarkably consistent over this period. The early soundboards are slightly stiff, and somewhat sparsely painted in comparison with the later ones, but the painting technique and the motifs chosen remain consistent over the entire period.

One of the most characteristic features of this soundboard painter is the way the wreath is painted around the rose. Instead of the red ring surrounding the rose bevel, as on Hans Ruckers instruments, the Ioannes decorator used two thin concentric red rings with a wide white band between them. A red rope pattern is painted onto the central white band. On some double-manual soundboards each loop in the rope has a grey dot at its centre. Surrounding the ring with its rope pattern is a wreath of intertwining myrtle leaves with small red, white, and blue flowers dotted among them. Two crossed stems originate at the bottom and oscillate from one side of the wreath to the other, with leaves curling out to intermingle on either side. As with the Hans and early Andreas wreath paintings, concentric circles are scribed with a sharp object into the soundboard wood to use as guidelines while painting the decorations around the rose.

Another striking feature of the early Ioannes painter is the way the leaves and some of the flower heads are outlined in black ink. The leaves are painted without shadows or highlights in a solid flat green (or sometimes each half of the leaf is painted in a different shade of green). This is outlined in black ink, and the veining is inked in over the paint normally on only half of each leaf. Some flower heads are also painted in solid flat colours which are then outlined in ink. The effect is strikingly similar to the designs in a tinted engraved pattern book. But the flower heads which are painted by mixing colours and by applying successive layers of paint to give highlight, shade and form are not outlined and shaded in ink. Overall, the flower groups consist of a pleasant mixture of large flowers – tulips, irises, peonies, roses and lilies, with smaller marigolds, cornflowers, lilies-of-the valley, fritillary, borage, columbines, heart's-ease, forget-me-nots, etc. filling up the space of the soundboard.

Sometimes a bird is perched on one of the flower stems. The black and white magpie, and the red-breasted, black-backed stone-chat are particularly common, but the goldfinch and parrot also occur. There are never any large fruits but small empty spaces are filled up with single leaves, small fruits, bees, butterflies, moths, or flower buds. And a spindly strawberry plant with long stems to its leaves, fruit and blossoms is also quite characteristic. Because of the general flatness of the paint, and the use of ink outlines and shading in most of the motifs, the result is very stylized. But despite this stylization the effect is always naturalistic enough to make the decorator's intent clearly recognizable.

The blue arabesques are usually quite tall and tapering with a pronounced central axis, like those of the early Andreas painter. But the Ioannes arabesques are lighter and more lacy than those of Andreas, which tend to be rather solid and heavy. A considerable part of the lightness of the arabesques is achieved by individual dots of paint placed near, but not touching, the arabesque. These early Ioannes arabesques are much more symmetrical than those of the Couchet or late Andreas painter, although mechanical symmetry is avoided by balancing the left and right halves of the arabesque in such a way that the eye is deceived into thinking that both halves are identical even though small asymmetries exist. The variety and inventiveness displayed in the arabesques is extraordinary when one examines the small number of basic elements used in their construction. Although they are usually quite large, the arabesques may also be no more than a few curls and dots of paint added to the scalloped border, with all possible variations in between. Arabesques in the same style are painted in red on the wood-grain paper on those instruments with papered lids and flaps, but these are never as large and intricate as the blue arabesques found on the soundboard.

In addition to the blue arabesques and scalloped borders, the early Ioannes soundboards usually have a few 'bubbles' consisting of six or eight dots surrounding a larger central dot, and 'stars' which are just 'bubbles' with lines drawn out from the dots of the 'bubbles'. These 'stars' and 'bubbles' float freely among the arabesques and flower decorations, but are used only very sparingly.

On the virginals the date is placed on the soundboard. But on the harpsichords the date is written on the wrestplank rather than the soundboard (except for the last extant harpsichord decorated by this painter, the 1624 IR double in Colmar, which is dated on the soundboard between the rose and the spine). A number of Ioannes harpsichords from this period which have undergone a ravalement and lost their original wrestplank or wrest-

Plate 7.16 Wreath painting on the 1618b IR double-manual harpsichord.

Plate 7.17 (above) and Plate 7.18 Examples of early Ioannes soundboard paintings. At the beginning (1612a HR) the composition was rather sparse (above), compared to that at the end (1624 IR) of this painter's career (below). Scale 1:4).

plank veneer are dated either on the non-original name-batten or jackrail, but it seems almost certain that the date was originally painted on the wrestplank.

### *The late Ioannes Ruckers/Ioannes Couchet style*

Ioannes Couchet came to work as an apprentice in Ioannes Ruckers' workshop around 1625–27. Couchet would then have been only ten or eleven. This period also marks the appearance of a new soundboard decoration style on Ioannes Ruckers instruments. The two events seem coincidental, however, and it is highly unlikely that the young and inexperienced Couchet began to decorate the soundboards signed by Ruckers. The output of the workshop was such that an apprentice would not have had time to do all the decoration and learn the art of harpsichord building at the same time. Most importantly, we know from the decoration on a recently discovered instrument that the same decorator was working for Gommarus van Eversbroeck in 1659, four years after Couchet died.

This decorator worked for Ioannes Ruckers from about 1627 (there are no dated instruments from the period between 1624 and 1627) until Ruckers' death in 1642, and then for Couchet, until Couchet's death in 1655. This decorator is probably the most painterly and naturalistic of all the Ruckers decorators. He uses his paint in layers, building it up gradually to create form and depth. There is no use of ink for outlines or veining. The use of the rope pattern and wreath of myrtle leaves was abandoned for an extremely rich and finely-painted floral wreath, which is separated from the rose by a black circle painted around the gilded soundboard bevel.

The late Ioannes Ruckers/Couchet decorator used a much lower, somewhat rectangular arabesque, usually consisting of two double 'S' curves with spirals at the ends. The 'S' curves are decorated and elaborated with dots and squiggles in such a way that, although balanced, the arabesque is rather asymmetrical. The 'star' and 'bubble' motifs are not used at all by this decorator.

Besides the characteristic arabesques and the painterly way in which the paintings are executed, the late Ioannes Ruckers/Couchet decorator is characterized by a number of other features. He often paints the flowers in groups with the stems and leaves of different species crossing, whereas all of the other Ruckers soundboard decorators paint each flower separately. Large fruits such as pears, peaches, plums, lemons, etc. are common motifs; also characteristic are single or paired scampi painted between the 8′ bridge and the bentside. The harpsichords usually have one or more large colourful and naturalistic parrots (but no other species of bird). The position and colouring of these parrots, the floral wreath paintings, as well as a number of the individual flower motifs, are identical on different late Ioannes Ruckers/Couchet soundboards, indicating that the decorator was closely following his workshop pattern books. The arrangement of the motifs on the soundboard varies, however, each soundboard painting being composed individually by selecting from the painter's repertoire of motifs. The date is always painted on the soundboard – on the harpsichords it appears between the spine and bass end of the 4′ bridge.

The single-manual harpsichord by Gommarus van Eversbroeck of 1659 in the Instrument Museum of the Conservatoire NSM, Paris, has a soundboard and lid decorated by the late Ioannes Ruckers/Couchet painter. Although some new motifs appear, many are the same as those found on earlier Couchet instruments – the style of the arabesques and the manner of actually applying the paint are also the same. The existence of this isolated example of a non-Ruckers instrument painted by one of the Ruckers decorators proves conclusively that the Ruckers/Couchet instruments were not decorated by the builders, but rather by a workshop employee, or at least by someone who contracted to do the decoration for them.

### *The early Andreas style*

Andreas Ruckers I set up his own workshop separately from his brother Ioannes around 1605. The only instrument which survives from the period in which Ioannes and Andreas worked together, the 5-voet virginal of 1604 in Brussels, is decorated by the early Ioannes decorator. But from 1608 until at least 1624 it is clear that a different decorator was working exclusively for Andreas Ruckers.

This decorator seems to have changed his style during his career more than any of the other soundboard painters. The soundboard paintings from 1608 to about 1618 are done in expanses of flat colour, with shading in the flowers and veining in the leaves done in ink. The ones done from about 1620 to 1624 have more shading in paint in both the leaves and the flowers, with less use of ink. Like the early Ioannes painter, the contemporary Andreas decorator uses a red and white rope pattern immediately surrounding the rose. The wreath paintings of the 1608 and 1609 harpsichords have small flowers scattered among the intertwined leaves. But from 1614 the flowers are large and occupy almost the whole of the width of the band of leaves in the wreath. (The exception to this occurs in the small child virginals, which lack the wreath and have instead only the red and white rope patterns and a few blue arabesques.) Moreover, only the instruments after 1614 have bird and animal motifs.

Plate 7.19 The wreath painting of the 1637a IR harpsichord. The usual black ring around the edge of the rose bevel has been gilded over during a retouching of the soundboard painting. Scale 1:2.

Plate 7.20 A typical example of the soundboard painting by the early Andreas soundboard painter (1620c AR). Scale 1:2.

One of the early Andreas painter's most characteristic features is the sinewy shape he gives to his flowers: the stems and leaves snake their way across the soundboard in a style unlike that of any other decorator. Also, the paint, especially on the leaves, is built up in thick impasto.

Like the early Ioannes arabesques, the Andreas arabesques of this period are tall and tapering with a strong central axis; they are strongly and heavily painted and make use of double 'S' bends and rounded arcs of circles. Also characteristic is the large number of 'stars' and 'bubbles' scattered among the flowers and arabesques. These are more intricate and inventive than those of the early Ioannes painter, and are very numerous.

A feature of both the early and late Andreas decorators, not found with any of the other Ruckers painters, is the decoration of the inside of the harpsichord lid and lid flap with motifs similar to those found on the soundboards.

Plate 7.21 The wreath painting of the 1640a A R single-manual harpsichord. Scale 1:2.

The early Andreas painter seems to have been especially fond of using birds and animals around the Latin mottoes on the wood-grain papers.

The date is always painted on the soundboard by the early Andreas painter. Usually there is also an elaborate red arabesque on either side of the date. On the harpsichords the date is painted between the rose and the spine, or on the lid. The date is recorded only on a non-original namebatten or jackrail on a number of Andreas instruments from this period, probably because the original dated lid is now missing.

### *The late Andreas style*

As with the Ioannes instruments, a new soundboard painter began working in the Andreas workshop in the period between 1624 and 1627. It is not known if the occurrence of a change in decorator in both workshops at about the same time is related.

The style of this soundboard decorator is more painterly than that of the early Ioannes and Andreas decorators, but is not any more naturalistic, making identification of some of the species portrayed very difficult. The shapes of many of the flowers and birds are distorted and exaggerated, giving them a very unnatural appearance. The painting technique is characterized by long, narrow brush strokes. The long thin highlights in particular give the painting a striped appearance which is easily recognized. The rose is surrounded by a floral wreath and not the stylized foliate wreath of the earlier soundboards. A characteristic feature of this decorator's harpsichord (and some virginal) soundboard paintings is the way the wreath is held by two angels, one on either side. The leaves of the flowers are rather narrow and pointed, and the stems straight, giving the painting a rather stiff appearance somewhat similar to the 'straw-flower' style of Hans Ruckers.

As mentioned earlier, many of the numerous flower

Plate 7.22 Soundboard painting on the 1633b A R double-manual harpsichord. The ribbon containing the date (not legible here) can be seen between the wreath and the spine. Scale 1:4.

and bird species used by the late Andreas decorator are taken from Collaert's *Avium Vivae Icones* and *Florilegium*. Also very characteristic of this painter are the scenes with animal and human figures. Among these we find a courting couple being served with wine, a gentleman taking off his hat to a musician playing his fiddle to a dancing dog, a knight on his mount, and even a group of monkeys playing instruments and singing. There are usually a number of insects, flies, butterflies, moths and, not found on any other style of soundboard painting, dragonflies. On the single-manual harpsichords the date is painted simply in red, but on double-manual harpsichords the date is painted in red across a white ribbon scroll between the rose and spine: a style unique to the doubles decorated by this painter.

The arabesques of this decorator's style are low, but slightly more tapered than those of the late Ioannes Ruckers/Couchet painter. They are exceptionally beautifully painted, making use of the natural flow of the paint from the brush in a way not characteristic of the other decorators. The arabesques are balanced but in fact highly asymmetrical, and this produces a vitality and rhythm lacking in the arabesques of the other Ruckers soundboard painters.

Although Johann Davidszoon de Heem was Andreas I's son-in-law and Andreas II's brother-in-law, there is no indication that he painted any of the Ruckers soundboards. De Heem's skill and competence are far greater than that exhibited on any of the Andreas soundboard paintings.

### *Distinguishing instruments by Andreas I and Andreas II on the basis of their soundboard paintings*

Andreas II became a member of thhe Guild of St Luke at the age of thirty in 1637 (Andreas I was then fifty-eight). It seems probable that Andreas II, who was also married in 1637, set up his own workshop then independently of his father. He might have engaged his own soundboard painter to work for him, but in fact the single-manual harpsichords of 1637 in Nuremberg and of 1648 in Copenhagen, and some details of the 1644 6-voet double virginal in Leipzig, are all painted with a somewhat different style of arabesque, and the leaves are shaded differently, although the motifs and flower heads are painted in a very similar style. Are two decorators involved here? The differences in the painting styles are probably marked enough to justify a division into two separate decorators. But the single harpsichord in Antwerp of 1644 signed ANDREAS RVCKERS DEN OVDEN ME FECIT ANTVERPIAE (i.e. by Andreas I) and the single in Traquair House, Innerleithen signed ANDREAS RVCKERS AND [REAS] F[ILIVS] ME FECIT ANTVERPIAE (by Andreas II) seem definitely to have been decorated by the same person. It thus does not seem possible to make a distinction between the instruments of Andreas I and Andreas II on the basis of the decoration. Even though the soundboard decoration style seems slightly different on some instruments, I have decided not to subdivide the late Andreas instruments into two separate styles, since this does not lead to a distinction between the instruments of the two Andreases, and because the 1637 and 1648 harpsichord paintings still bear a strong resemblance to the other late Andreas instruments.

## SOUNDBOARD PREPARATION, PAINTING MEDIA AND PIGMENTS

A number of Ruckers soundboards are varnished over the wood and paint of the soundboard paintings. But most of the Ruckers soundboard paintings are unvarnished and the paint has a light, fresh appearance rather than the thick oily impression of paint under varnish. It is clear that the varnish is a later addition and that it was not Ruckers normal procedure to varnish their soundboards after painting.

On the other hand it is equally clear that the soundboards were prepared in some way before painting and that the paint was not applied directly to the bare wood. All genuine Ruckers soundboards are shiny and reflective underneath the matt appearance of the painted groups, and the pores of the wood are filled. The material used to size the soundboard is unknown, but was probably a simple thin glue, or more likely a shellac preparation (see p. 101). Both of these could fill the wood grain to prevent the paint from running along the pores away from the intended edge of the painted surface.

No rigorous investigation has, to my knowledge, been carried out to determine the painting medium or pigment materials used by the Ruckers soundboard painters. Whatever the painting medium is, it is highly water soluble. This means that it is not oil, egg tempera, or any oil emulsion. The most likely possibility is gum arabic, which was used on soundboards in eighteenth-century France and gives similar effects to those found on Ruckers soundboards. Also possible are cherry gum, which produces similar effects to gum arabic and which would have been available locally. A glue size made either from animal or fish bones is also a possibility, although less likely in view of the well-established use of gum media in other branches of decorative art.

The pigments available to the Ruckers soundboard painters are quite restricted in number. It is unlikely that a scientific analysis of the pigments will lead to a palette much different from that which is suggested here. The list which follows has been compiled on the basis of several contemporary manuals on painting which give the preparation and use of painting grounds, media, and pigments,[13] and also a modern knowledge of sixteenth- and seventeenth-century pigments.[14]

*White*: Lead white (flake white)
*Black*: Ivory black or bone black; lampblack; charcoal black or vine black
*Brown*: Italian umber and burnt umber; brown ochres; asphaltum
*Red-brown*: Iron oxide reds – Venetian red, English red, Indian red, Pozzuoli red, etc.
*Red*: Red ochres and red earth; burnt sienna; carmine and cochineal (unstable in water colours); vermilion (cinnabar); red lead (minium – heated flake white); Indian lakes
*Orange*: Realgar (heated orpiment); orange lead (minium)
*Yellow*: Yellow ochre (sienna); massicot (heated flake white); orpiment; Naples yellow
*Green*: Malachite (mountain green or green verditer); terre verte; verdigris (Spanish green)
*Blue*: Ultramarine; azurite (blue verditer); smalt; indigo

It seems almost certain that some colours such as orange, green, and purple would have been made by mixing pigments of the primary colours. It is thus possible that the actual number of pigments used by the Ruckers decorators was very small.

## RUCKERS ROSES

The rose is the focal point of a Ruckers soundboard. Surrounded by a wreath painted on the soundboard, the rose and soundboard bevel are gilded with gold leaf, probably using varnish as a size. The Ruckers roses portray an angel playing a harp with the initials of the builder on either side. The rose is cast with four tabs around its outer edge, over which cloth strips were glued to the lower surface of the soundboard when the rose was glued in position in the rose hole.

It has often been supposed that the rose was made from a lead-tin alloy similar to that used for organ pipes. However, analysis of the material of two Ruckers roses shows that the material of the rose is almost entirely lead. The composition has been found to vary from about 98%

[13] T. T. de Mayerne manuscript in the British Library (Sloane, No. 2052). This has been carefully analysed by J. A. van de Graaf, 'Het de Mayerne manuscript als bron voor de schildertechniek van de barok', diss., University of Utrecht, 1958; Zahira Véliz, 'Francisco Pacheco's comments on painting in oil', *Studies in Conservation*, XXVII, 2 (1982), 49–57.

[14] R. S. Gettens and G. L. Stout, *Painting Materials – A Short Encyclopaedia*, (New York, 1942; reprint, New York, 1966); Rosamond Harley, *Artists' Pigments c.1600–1835* (London, 1982).

Plate 7.23 Hans Ruckers rose (1594 HR single-manual harpsichord/virginal combination). Scale 1:1.

lead with 1.7% tin impurity for the 1594 HR single-manual harpsichord[15] to 99.9% lead with about 0.1% copper impurity for the 1608 AR double.[16] This variation in composition is well within the limits of what one would expect from the impurities present in naturally occurring lead ores, and indicates that there was no attempt to introduce tin to produce an alloy similar to organ-pipe metal. A few of the early roses of Ioannes Ruckers in instruments datable from the period 1598 to 1616 are of the usual castings for this period, but are made of papier mâché.

The very earliest Hans Ruckers instrument, the double muselar virginal of 1581 in New York, is exceptional in that it does not have a rose with the maker's initials. Instead it has three parchment-and-wood soundboard roses cut in geometrical patterns. All of the other Hans Ruckers instruments have the rose shown in Plate 7.23. The 1594 HR harpsichord/virginal combination in Köpenick, East Berlin, has this rose in the virginal part and a parchment-and-wood rose in the harpsichord part. The (1591)b HR double muselar virginal in Cambridge, Mass. and the (*c.* 1600) HR double spinett virginal have the metal HR rose in both the mother and the child parts. But here the rose in the mother has the usual diameter of 65mm, although the child part has an appropriately smaller rose of diameter 58mm. In all subsequent Ioannes and Andreas double virginals, the rose is of the same diameter in both mother and child.

All instruments with the rose shown in Plate 7.23 are signed HANS RVCKERS ME FECIT ANTVERPIAE. But during the period between 1595 and 1598 (unfortunately

[15] Martin-Christian Schmidt, 'Ein Beitrag zum Cembalobau von Hans Ruckers aus instrumentenkundlicher und handwerklicher Sicht', *Neue Museumskunde*, XXI, 1 (1978), 63.

[16] I would like to express my thanks to Dr Jim Tait of the Research Laboratory of the National Museums of Scotland, who carried out the X-ray fluorescence analysis of the 1608 A R rose material for me.

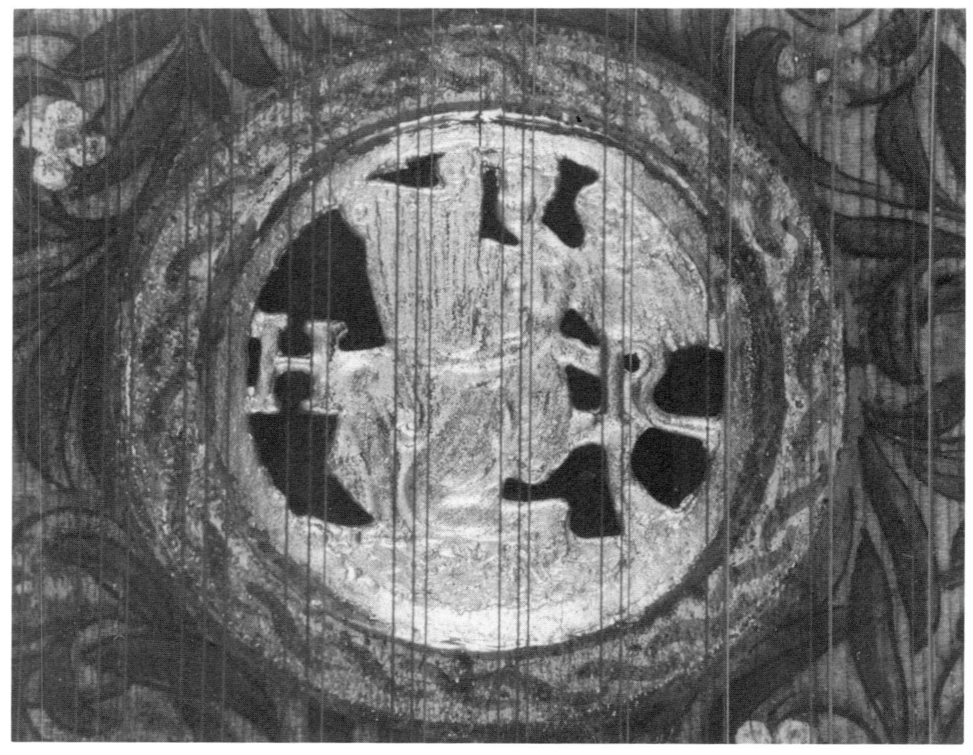

Plate 7.24 and Plate 7.25 Two castings of the HR rose used by Ioannes Ruckers before 1616. The top rose (1612a HR) is sometimes cast in papier maché. The bottom rose is from the 1610 HR mother virginal. Scale 1:1.

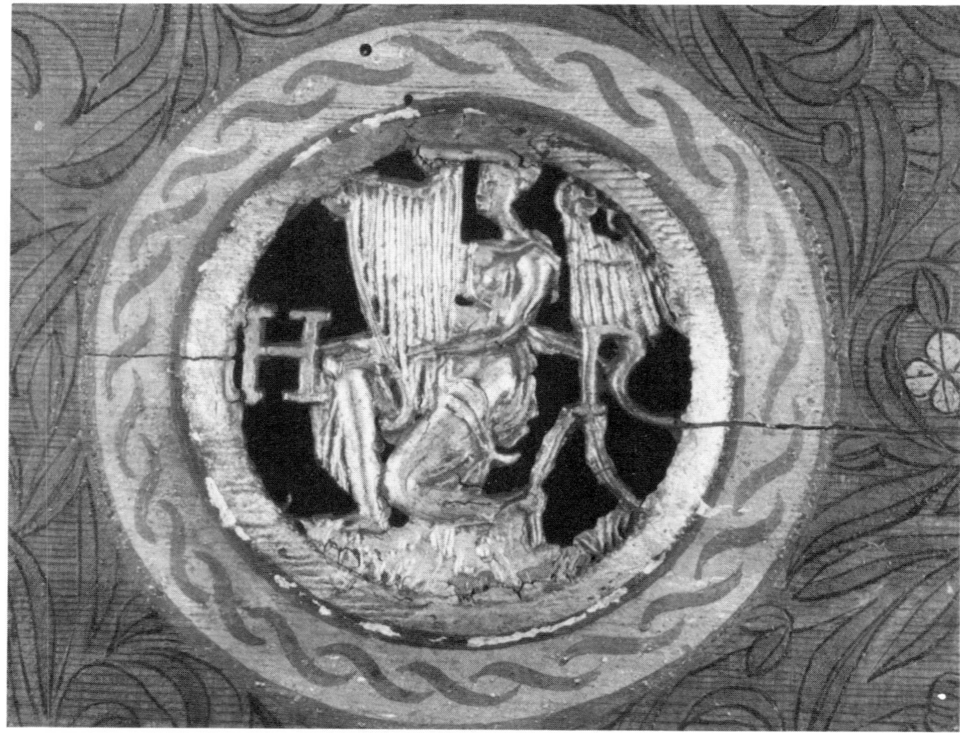

none of the instruments from this period has an original date), instruments begin to appear with the signature IOHANNES RVQVERS ME FECIT ANTVERPIAE and a rose which still has the initials HR, but which differs from the earlier rose in several details, notably in the absence of the angel's right wing (Plate 7.24). The combination of the change in both the signature and the rose seems to suggest that the later instruments are by Hans Ruckers' son Ioannes. Two instruments which can be dated 1598 and 1599, of which one was certainly built after Hans Ruckers' death in 1598, had the later rose and signature and can be ascribed to Ioannes Ruckers. This then leaves only four virginals and one single-manual harpsichord/virginal combination which can be ascribed to Hans. There is no surviving double-manual harpsichord by Hans Ruckers.

Up until 1615, and his court appointment, Ioannes Ruckers used a rose similar to that shown in Plates 7.24 and 7.25. A number of different castings were made and, as mentioned above, sometimes the rose was made of papier mâché instead of the usual lead alloy. But the figure of the angel is always lacking its right wing. Also, after 1599 the instruments are signed using the form IOANNES RVCKERS rather than IOANNES RVQVERS. One instrument from this period, however, has the signature IOANNES ET ANDREAS RVCKERS FECERVNT and the date 1604, and is clearly from the period in which the two brothers were sharing their father's old workshop. This period ended in about 1605 when Andreas I set up a workshop independently of his brother and began using the AR rose shown in Plate 7.34.

In 1615 Ioannes Ruckers was appointed clavichord and clavecimbel builder and tuner to the archducal court of Albert and Isabella in Brussels. Perhaps as a sign of his new status, he decided to alter his roses in a way which is not only elegant, but which does not seem to have been done before or since. Instead of having just one rose recast, he used three different models, one for virginals, another for single-manual harpsichords, and a third for doubles. These roses have the initial IR instead of the earlier HR also used by his father.[17]

The rose used in the virginals built by Ioannes Ruckers after 1615 is shown in Plate 7.26, and has, like the earlier HR rose and the AR rose used in all instrument types, a diameter of about 65mm. It has a characteristic star-shaped pattern on the rear surface, consisting of four equally-spaced intersecting lines. This pattern seems to have been produced by a backing plate used to squeeze out excess lead during casting, and is lacking on the Andreas Ruckers and Ioannes Couchet roses. In his single-manual harpsichords Ioannes used a 73mm-diameter rose (Plate 7.28) and in doubles the larger 85mm-diameter rose shown in Plate 7.29. When authentic, both of these harpsichord roses are hollowed out on the rear surface; this was done by tipping out the excess lead from the mould before it had completely cooled and solidified. Because they have a much greater relief than the other Ruckers roses, this hollowing considerably lightens them (see Plate 7.33).

Sometime between 1638 and 1642 (the 1640a IR 5-voet virginal has lost its original rose) it appears that the old mould for the virginal roses was broken or lost, and a new virginal rose had to be cast. This new rose is very similar to the old one but is larger and of a slightly different design (see Plate 7.27). It is found only in the 1642a IR Stockholm virginal, made in the year of Ioannes' death. The use of a different rose for each type of instrument was carried on by Ioannes Couchet, who simply used the same Ioannes Ruckers designs, but changed the second initial from an R to a C in the new castings. Naturally, Couchet copied the newer Ioannes Ruckers virginal rose. Plates 7.30 to 7.33 show the three types of Ioannes Couchet soundboard roses. Like the Ioannes Ruckers harpsichord roses, the authentic Couchet harpsichord roses are also hollowed out on the rear surface. The only virginal IC rose (1650a IC) has a flat rear surface.

The two Andreases, father and son, were less inventive and used only one type of rose in all instrument models. Several designs occur, however. The rose shown in Plate 7.34 was used from 1608 to 1636. Around 1637, perhaps for the occasion of Andreas II's entry into the Guild of St Luke, a new but only slightly different AR rose was cast (Plate 7.35). This later rose seems, however, to have been used by both the elder and the younger Andreases after 1637. It should be noted that the (1651)a AR single has a different rose (see Plate 7.36) from the post-1636 one shown in Plate 7.35. This harpsichord is signed ANDREAS RVCKERS AND[REAS] F[ILIVS] ME FECIT and is therefore definitely by Andreas II. Does this mean that this is the only surviving late instrument actually made by Andreas II, and that all of the others with the rose shown in Plate 7.35 are by Andreas I? The problem is complicated by the uncertainty of the date of the (1651)a AR harpsichord, which has been given as 1651 in the literature, but which appears to have read 1641 before it was retouched during a restoration by J. J. K. Rhodes (see Plate 7.37). Another harpsichord of 1651, in the Victoria and Albert Museum, London, has the usual post-1636

[17] The name Hans is a variation of Hannes or Johannes, the Germanic form of Ioannes (in English, John). Both the Germanic Hans and the Flemish Jan were used as familiar forms in sixteenth- and seventeenth-century Flanders.

Plate 7.26 The Ioannes Ruckers virginal rose (1629 IR) used from 1617 to 1640. Scale 3:4.

Plate 7.27 The Ioannes Ruckers virginal rose (1642a IR) used in 1642. Scale 3:4.

Plate 7.28 The Ioannes Ruckers single-manual harpsichord rose (1637a IR) used after 1617. Scale 3:4.

Plate 7.29 The Ioannes Ruckers double-manual harpsichord rose (1618b IR) used after 1617. Scale 3:4.

Plate 7.30 The Ioannes Couchet virginal rose (1650a IC). Scale 3:4.

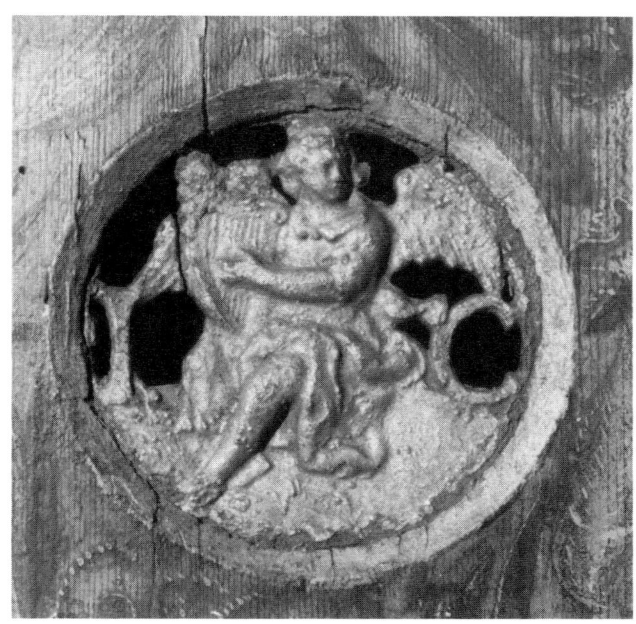

Plate 7.31 The Ioannes Couchet single-manual harpsichord rose (1645 IC). Scale 3:4.

Plate 7.32 The Ioannes Couchet double-manual harpsichord rose. Scale 3:4.

Plate 7.33 Rear view of the Ioannes Couchet double-manual harpsichord rose. Scale 3:4.

Plate 7.34 The Andreas Ruckers rose used in all types of instruments from 1608 to 1635 (1613b A R). Scale 3:4.

Plate 7.35 The Andreas Ruckers rose used in all types of instruments from 1636 to 1654 (1644a A R). Scale 3:4.

Plate 7.36 The Andreas (II?) Ruckers rose in the (1651)a A R single-manual harpsichord. Scale 3:4.

Plate 7.37 The retouched painting of the date on the (1651)a A R single-manual harpsichord. Was this 1641 before being retouched?

type of rose, as does the 1654 AR harpsichord in Nuremberg. Andreas I was dead by 24 March 1653, so the 1654 AR harpsichord must have been made by Andreas II. Why then the spurious appearance in 1641 or 1651 of the Plate 7.36 rose? Clearly the rose type cannot be used to distinguish the work of Andreas I from Andreas II, just as the soundboard painting style cannot (see p. 157).

## LID AND KEYWELL-FLAP DECORATION

In addition to having painted keywell and soundwell decoration, the earliest Ruckers instruments also have painted lids and keywell flaps. The only surviving examples of contemporary lid paintings are found exclusively on virginals (for example, see Plates 3.9 and 7.3). They are colourfully if somewhat stiffly executed in oils. Like the soundboard paintings, they are stylized, naive decorative art; they do not belong to the fine art of Marten de Vos (1532–1603) or Vredeman de Vries (1527–1606), although they are not far removed from the canvases of, say, Marten van Valckenborch (1535–1612) or Joris Hoefnagel (1542–1600), all of whom were active around 1580 to 1600.

These early lid decorations are genre paintings portraying elegantly-dressed figures, some dancing, lounging, courting, eating, making music, boating etc. The scenes usually include a bower or a fountain, a mediaeval castle, a canal or river with a boating party, and sometimes a hunting scene. They seem designed to show the wealthy middle class in elegant surroundings, quietly enjoying their leisure.

The Marten van der Biest double virginal in Nuremberg and the Iohannes Bos virginal in Tordesillas seem to be painted by the same artist as the early Ruckers instruments, and the Iohannes Grouwels virginal in Brussels is painted in a very similar style. The Bos virginal and the (*c.* 1600) HR double virginal are interesting hybrids combining a painted lid decoration with a papered keywell, soundwell and front flap.

A number of later Ruckers instruments have painted lid decorations; some of these are also genre paintings. Most of them, however, belong to the sphere of fine art and are by well-known Flemish painters: Pieter Codde II (1608 AR), Jan Brueghel I, Hendrik van Balen and Paul Bril (1612 IR) and Artus Wolfort (1640b IR and 1646b AR). Many instruments have extremely fine lid and lid-flap paintings by anonymous artists (1628b IR, 1632 IR, 1638b IR, 1642b IR, 1614 AR, 1628 AR, 1636 AR, n.d. IC). These and others are dealt with individually as they arise in the catalogue. The correspondence between Balthazar Gerbier and Sir Francis Windebank (Appendix 16) indicates that even Rubens was commissioned to paint a Ruckers harpsichord lid, although unfortunately no such painting has survived.

But most Ruckers clavecimbels probably originally had papered lid and keywell-flap decorations. The interior lid decoration consisted of the wood-grain papers with Latin mottoes written across them; these were surrounded by a patterned paper strip, a strip of clear varnished wood, and finally a border next to the edge of the lid painted in black. The joins between the interior wood-grain paper and the strip border, and the strip border and the varnished wood are each covered by a thin (3–4mm wide) red line painted in a water-soluble vermilion paint. About 12–15mm inside the edge of the paper strip pattern there is another 3–4mm-wide line painted in black around the edge of the wood-grain papers. (Occasionally this line is painted in vermilion, in which case the printed strip edges are covered with black paint instead of the usual red.) The corners of these thin edgings, whether black or red, are elaborated with a trefoil, a tear-drop, or some other ornament, depending on the decorator and period in which he was working.

In single-manual harpsichords the lid flap is a flat surface like the main portion of the lid and is decorated in a way similar to the main lid. In double-manual harpsichords, the lid flap is framed with a heavy moulding (see Fig. 6.4). Here the printed strip pattern touches the inside of the moulding and the wood-grain pattern fills up the whole of the area inside this. The edge of the strip pattern next to the moulding is not painted over with a thin line, but the rest of the papered surface is decorated like that of the main lid.

The keywell flap is decorated either with one of the wider paper patterns alone (the dolphin pattern Type 3 or 4 was not used, however), or with the wood-grain paper with a Latin motto surrounded by a narrow strip pattern. Of the wide strip patterns Type 2 is by far the most common keywell-flap paper, although Types 12 and 15 also sometimes occur. Because the keywell flap is very narrow, the clear varnished border is often lacking. If present, it is, like the black edging, narrower than on the main lid or lid flap.

The Latin mottoes are painted in black Roman capitals on the wood-grain papers. The mottoes seem to have been chosen to suit the space they were intended to fill: SIC/TRANSIT/GLORIA MVNDI, for example, is particularly well suited to the main lid of a harpsichord, which is narrow at the top and wide at the bottom. Virginal lids, on the other hand, usually have four-word mottoes with words each of roughly the same number of letters. Short three-word mottoes such as ACTA VIRVM PROBANT are used for harpsichord keywell flaps, and longer four- and five-word mottoes are used on virginal keywell flaps.

Plate 7.38 Interior lid decoration of the 1633a AR 6-voet virginal. Scale 1:10.

When the mottoes did not quite match the space they were required to fill, extra 'bubbles', 'stars', arabesques or other ornaments were used to fill up any left-over space. In many Andreas Ruckers lids and lid flaps the spaces around the mottoes were often filled with motifs similar to those on the soundboard.

The line mottoes used on authentic Ruckers instruments are the following. These do not, of course, include unusual mottoes which have been added to genuine Ruckers instruments by later restorers. Those words in parentheses are variants and only sometimes present.

GLORIA DEO
OMNIS SPIRITVS LAVDET DOMINVM
MVSICA DVLCE LABORVM LEVAMEN (or MVSICA LABORVM DVLCE LEVAMEN)
SCIENTIA NON HABET INIMICVM NISI INGNORANTEM [*sic*]
ARS NON HABET INIMICVM NISI IGNORANTEM
DVLCISONVM REFICIT TRISTIA CORDA MELOS
MVSICA MAGNORVM (EST) SOLAMEN DVLCE LABORVM
AVDI VIDE ET TACE SI VIS VIVERE IN PACE
ACTA VIRVM PROBANT
CONCORDIA RES PARVAE CRESCVNT DISCORDIA MAXIMAE DILABVNTUR
SOLI DEO GLORIA (ET SANCTVM NOMEN EIVS)
SIC TRANSIT GLORIA MVNDI
MVSICA LAETITIAE COMES MEDICINA DOLORVM
CONCORDIA MVSIS AMICA

Plate 7.39 Interior lid decoration on the 1648 AR single-manual harpsichord. Scale 1:10.

MVSICA DONVM DEI
NON NISI MOTA CANO

The sources and significance of some of these mottoes are discussed in an interesting article by Thomas McGeary.[18]

## OUTER-CASE DECORATION

The virginal outer-case decoration seems always to have been done in imitation green porphyry marble. This consists of a dark olive-green background colour onto which off-white paint tinted with the base colour has been splattered while the base colour was still wet. The splattered paint gives the surface a rough texture which is often visible under subsequent layers of more recent paint. This technique was used from the first Hans Ruckers virginal of 1581 until the 1640s. The entire case sides were painted from top to bottom in imitation porphyry without any upper and lower grey (imitation iron) bands, although some of the early Hans Ruckers virginals have a thin white line painted around each side of the lid about 35mm from the edge of each face. I have not found any other type of virginal outer-case decorations which I can definitely identify as being original.

The harpsichords have a slightly more elaborate outer-case decoration. They were painted to imitate either a red marble with grey iron straps above and below, or a complicated strapwork pattern with large round or faceted stones held in place by grey iron straps studded with brass buttons against a red marbled background.[19] The marbling is done with a brown/red (iron oxide?) background which was allowed to dry before the scumble was added. The scumbling was done with semi-transparent layers of paint in several shades of grey, a pinkish-yellow ochre and black and white, or sometimes just using darker and lighter shades of the background colour. This seems to have been done with the fingers without the use of a mop or solvent to soften the scumble. The result is not very realistic. The stones of the strapwork pattern are 'marbled' in a manner similar to the background marbling, and highlights and shadows are added to the stones, brass studs, and iron strapping to give the appearance of depth.

The lid and keywell flap are also marbled to match the case sides. Usually the outer reinforcing mouldings on the harpsichord lids and the lid hinges, which are decorative in their own right, are marbled over as though they

[18] Thomas McGeary, 'Harpsichord mottoes', *Journal of the American Musical Instrument Society*, VII (1981), 5–35.

[19] See p. 90 for a discussion of the case heights of instruments with the strapwork decoration.

Plate 7.40 Typical plain outer case marbling on a harpsichord (1637b IR). Scale 1:3.

Plate 7.41 Outer case strap-work decoration on a harpsichord (1637 A R). Scale 1:3.

did not exist. Again, all the Ruckers harpsichords I have seen seem originally to have been marbled either plainly or with the strapwork design. But I think that even the most ardent admirer of the Ruckers would have to agree that the marbling technique of the Ruckers decorators is at best primitive, and it is little wonder that the original marbling was later removed or over-painted.

## MOULDINGS

The top of the case sides of Ruckers clavecimbels were decorated on the inside edge with an ogee moulding which was left as clear varnished wood, without paint or gilding. On the larger harpsichords and virginals this is positioned normally, but on the smaller virginals (the 4½-voet, 4-voet, child and 2½-voet) with thinner case sides, the moulding is placed sideways at 90° to the usual position, in order to leave more wood on the top edge of the case side. This top edge is painted black and borders with the iron straps of the outer-case marbling. The top of the nameboard in harpsichords and the entire face-board and nameboard in virginals is capped with a double moulding consisting of two of the case ogee mouldings placed back to back. A characteristic of the earliest Ruckers instruments (and early Flemish instruments generally) is that the lower surface of this added part of the moulding is rounded instead of being flat (see Fig. 5.1, p. 70). The keyblocks in harpsichords (only the lower-manual keyblocks in double-manual harpsichords) also have this same case ogee moulding left in clear varnished wood with the top of the keyblock painted black. Slight differences in the ogee mouldings on the same instrument, and the way in which the mouldings on the keyblocks are cut, indicate that a left- and a right-handed moulding plane were used. Use of these two planes is essential to eliminate any problems of planing against the grain direction, and enables the two mouldings on either edge of the jackrail, for example, to be made by planing both in the same direction. The lid, lid flap and keywell flap are left unmoulded.

The composite keywell moulding at the bottom of the keywell along the front of the baseboard is also left in varnished wood except for a red stripe in the central concave part of the moulding (see Fig. 6.3). The flat unmoulded bottom part of this batten, the edge of the baseboard and the front-flap recesses in the case sides are all painted black. On the smaller 4½-voet and 4-voet sizes of virginal only the bottom part of this moulding is used, thus decreasing its total height. This probably means that the moulding plane used to cut it had two blades, one of which was withdrawn to cut the lower moulding for the small virginals. This same half-moulding also appears on the lower-manual batten of double-manual harpsichords.

The soundboard moulding and the moulding on the 8′ hitchpin rail on harpsichords, and the small raised block for the hitchpins of the bass strings in muselar virginals, are left entirely in clear varnished wood. The ovolo mouldings on the interior dustcatcher batten are also varnished, with the central flat portion of the batten painted black. The moulded parts of the wide interior lid flap on double-manual harpsichords are left in clear varnished wood and the flat sections are painted black. The harpsichord namebatten and its moulding is also left clear, and the signature, bordered by two thin (about 2mm) black lines, is painted in Roman capitals onto the varnished wood. In double harpsichords the lower-manual batten is decorated with a paper strip pattern with a thin border of vermilion paint around the paper. The rest of the batten is left clear. The moulded part of the top of this batten is the same shape as the bottom part of the lower keywell moulding below the ends of the keys, as already explained (see Fig. 6.3).

Both edges of Ruckers jackrails have ogee mouldings with the same profile as those on the case sides. On harpsichords, the top surface of the jackrail is painted black and covered with one of the paper strip patterns surrounded by a red vermilion line, and the mouldings are left as usual in varnished wood. On virginals the jackrail always bears the signature of the builder, and this is painted in a manner similar to that of the harpsichord namebatten with black Roman capitals between two narrow black lines on clear varnished wood. Because the virginal jackrail is tapered in width the letters of the signature get smaller and, in proportion, slightly closer together towards the right-hand end of the jackrail. The virginal jackrail supports are also left clear and are decorated on the sides with arabesques of a style similar to those on the soundboard, with dots and 'I's on their edges.

On Ioannes Ruckers double-manual harpsichords the sides of the lower-manual keyblocks are decorated with a rope pattern with dots at the centre of each loop in the rope. The keyblocks on Andreas doubles and some singles are covered with one of the strip patterns. The curved ends of the upper-manual keyblocks of both Andreas and Ioannes Ruckers doubles were left undecorated and entirely in clear varnished wood.

## KEY ARCADES

Although these are now missing on most Ruckers clavecimbels, the keyboards probably all originally had arcades on the keyfronts of the natural keys under the bone plates. The bone plates project about 3mm beyond the angled front end of the wood of the natural key, and this helps somewhat to protect the arcades. But owing to their extremely fragile nature and their exposed position, they have been damaged and lost on most instruments with original keyboards.

Each arcade consists of two parts: the front of the arcade is of a heavy paper embossed with a Gothic design of arches and florets (see Plate 5.6, p. 84). The edges of the design are incised to leave the embossed pattern pierced with holes through which the background, the second part of the arcade, can be seen. This background is of parchment or paper dyed red. The dye used to colour the background was highly fugitive (and therefore probably one of the lakes). It has now usually discoloured to a dark brown except where a bit of the pierced Gothic design has broken away to expose the unaltered original background colour. On the two earliest Ruckers instruments, the background is a piece of reused parchment with Hebrew characters written on it. It has been suggested that this might reflect the fact that Hans Ruckers lived on the Jodenstraat, the Jewish Street. But Ruckers did not buy 'de cleyn clavecingel' on the Jodenstraat until 1597, or until at least fourteen years after these instruments were made. Nonetheless there were many Jews living in Antwerp at this time and it is not surprising to find a disused parchment written in Hebrew on these instruments.

It appears that the front paper part of the arcade was embossed and incised in one operation. The cutting of each arcade is exactly the same as every other, and often a slight error in the cutting is repeated again and again on each arcade.

Two slightly different arcades appear to have been used (see Plate 5.6). The most common type is found on instruments by Ioannes Ruckers and Ioannes Couchet. A second type has a sort of indented embossing and was used on instruments by Andreas Ruckers.

## LOCKS AND STRAP HINGES

The strap hinges and the locks often found on Ruckers instruments are at once both functional and decorative. Strap hinges seem always to have been used on the lid of double harpsichords, probably because wire hinges were too weak to support the weight of the large lid. But the decorative lock and hasp also found on doubles seem to be a part of the luxury of a large instrument. On single harpsichords and on virginals the lid and flap usually have simple wire hinges and simple wire hook-and-eye closures. But some single harpsichords and some virginals have brass strap hinges and a decorative lock, presum-

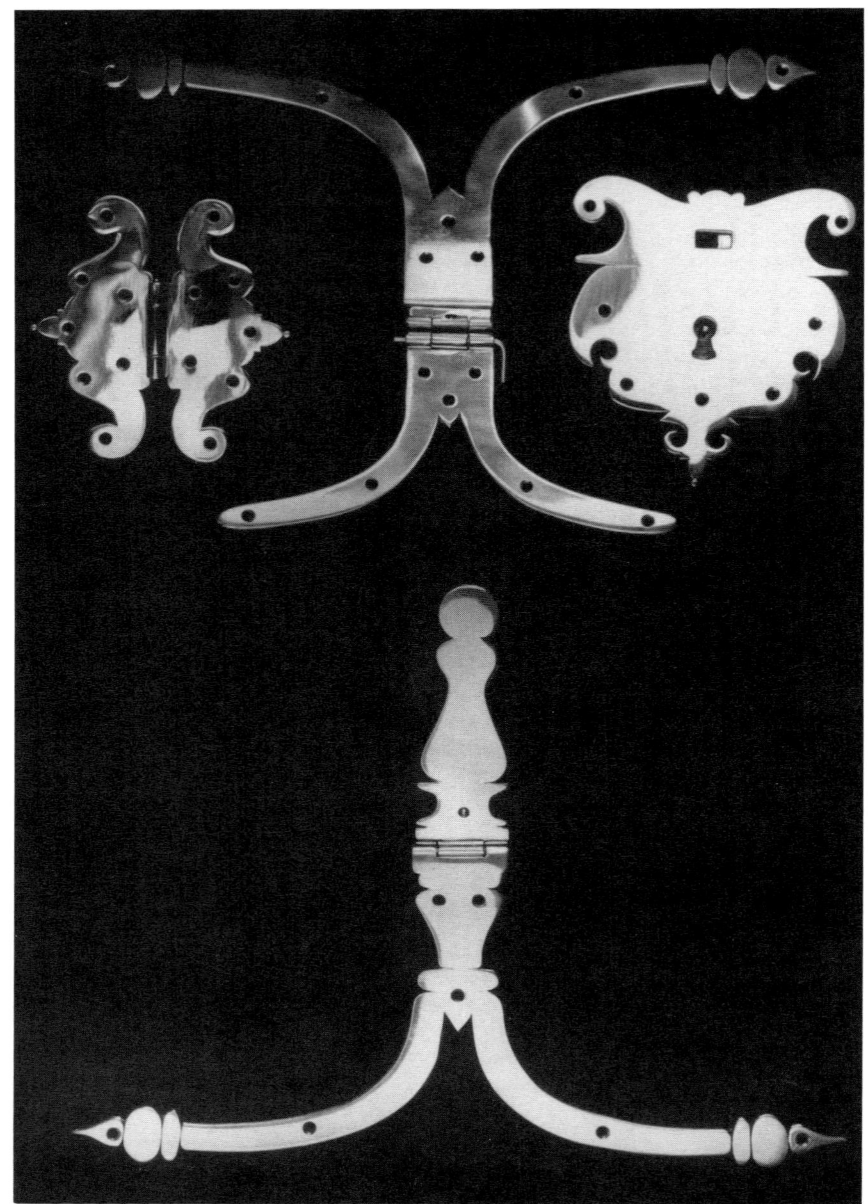

Plate 7.42 Typical Ruckers hardware. Above (from left to right) are a lid-flap hinge, a spine main-lid strap hinge and a lock escutcheon. Below is the lock hasp and strap hinge. (These are modern copies by the author.) Scale 1: 2.

ably because the clients who bought these instruments could afford the extra luxury. Plate 7.42 shows a typical main lid-strap hinge, a lid-flap hinge and a lock.

## IN CONCLUSION

The purpose of the paper patterns used by the Ruckers family on their instruments seems to have been to imitate the painted vine- or scroll-work, or perhaps the niello or intarsia that was popular in this period. One of the important principles of High Renaissance decoration was that the imitation of exotic woods, marble, ivory or any natural material was in bad taste. The fact that most of the decoration on Ruckers instruments is imitative should probably be ascribed not so much to bad taste as to the changing fashion at the beginning of the Baroque, when natural materials were freely imitated, often to the point where it would have been easier to use the genuine substance. This changing taste seems to be indicated clearly in the Ruckers instruments. The two earliest dated instruments, the 1581 HR and the 1583 HR virginals, both have a beautiful and intricate hand-painted decoration. The next two dated instruments, 1591a HR and 1594 HR, were both originally papered. But although the 1581 HR double virginal had painted interior decoration, and not the cheaper papered patterns, the original exterior decoration of the mother virginal was the usual *faux* porphyry marble which was used to decorate all of the succeeding virginals. Thus even at this early date the use of imitation marble in an instrument intended for the Spanish aristocracy was not considered in bad taste. It was a minor step in terms of the changing taste, from the painted interior decoration, to the paper patterns on the keywell, soundwell and lid, and a major step in reducing the cost of the instruments. Clearly there was fierce competition among the Guild of St Luke instrument builders for the custom of the increasingly wealthy middle-class Antwerp population. The changing taste fitted nicely into the desire to reduce the cost of the instruments in order to make them more competitive and within reach of the pocketbook of the typical Antwerp burgher.

CHAPTER EIGHT

# The determination of the original compass, disposition and pitch of Ruckers harpsichords

Very few of the extant Ruckers instruments have survived without having undergone some sort of modification. The harpsichords' keyboards, disposition, scalings, cases and decoration were altered to suit the music and taste of later periods. Virginals were not only less favoured in the period after the Ruckers were active, but were also not as readily adaptable as harpsichords. It is possible to change the compass of a virginal, but its disposition cannot be altered. The determination of its original state thus amounts to the determination of its original compass.

The original disposition and compass of a harpsichord is obvious when the original keyboards remain intact. Because of the widespread adaptation of the Ruckers harpsichords in the late seventeenth and the eighteenth centuries, only two double- and three single-manual instruments remain with their original keyboards and disposition.

The altered harpsichords vary in the degree to which they have been changed, and usually the difficulty of determining the original compass and disposition increases in proportion to the degree of alteration. Instruments which retain their original keys and keybed, but whose compass has been extended either by removing the keyblocks or widening the case to provide room for the additional keys, usually provide clear indications of the original compass. The difference between the original and the subsequent workmanship of the keys, the repinning of the balance rail, and the alterations to the registers and lower guides give evidence about the original state of the instrument. Examples of this type of alteration are the 1627a IR and the 1644a AR single-manual harpsichords, and the 1618b IR and the 1615 AR doubles.

But more than half of the extant Ruckers harpsichords have been so drastically altered that the simple analysis afforded by the keys or the original balance rail is of no help whatsoever. Typically the case has been widened, the keys, keybed, jacks and registers have been replaced, and the bridges and nuts have been extended and repinned. In some examples the nuts have been moved or the entire wrestplank replaced in the process. In such a situation one must resort to more detailed and careful analysis in order to ascertain the original state of the instrument.

## DETERMINATION OF THE NUMBER OF NATURAL NOTES

The starting point in this analysis is the determination of the number of natural keys which were originally contained between the keyblocks. Friedrich Ernst[1] was the first to point out that the *Stichmass* or three-octave span in Ruckers instruments is near 500mm. Since three octaves contain twenty-one natural keys, the average space occupied by one natural keyplate is 500mm/21 = 23.81mm. For example, the twenty-seven naturals in the common C/E to $c^3$ compass would occupy a space of 27 × 23.81mm = 643mm. The additional space for the bass and treble keyblocks and the clearance at either end of the keys is usually of the order of 47mm for both double- and single-manual harpsichords. Thus in the example chosen the total width of the inside of the case should be about

[1] Friedrich Ernst, 'Four Ruckers harpsichords in Berlin', *Galpin Society Journal*, XX (1967), 63–75.

643mm + 47mm = 690mm. The actual inside case width of a typical single with an original C/E to $c^3$ compass agrees with this to within a few millimetres. Any disparity is certainly less than one key width, so that an instrument with an original inside case width near 690mm must originally have had a compass with twenty-seven naturals, which was almost certain to have been C/E to $c^3$.

The original inside case width can usually be estimated closely from the bentside and nameboard ravalement joins, or the join forming the extensions to the nuts, bridges or soundboard. This in turn can be used to determine the original number of natural keys to within less than half one natural key. Table 8.1 can be used as a guide.

Although not found in Ruckers instruments, some of the compasses in parentheses in Table 8.1 are musically probable and were sometimes used by other contemporary or near-contemporary builders. It is clear that a knowledge of the number of natural keys is not enough to determine uniquely the original compass. For example, an instrument with thirty natural keys could have any one of the C/E to $f^3$, $G_1/B_1$ to $c^3$ or C to $d^3$ compasses, all of which are found on genuine Ruckers harpsichords. The first two of these would have had fifty notes, the last fifty-one. A count of the number of plugged 4′ hitchpin holes, or of the plugged tuning-pin holes, might be enough to determine whether the original compass had fifty or fifty-one notes. But even if it is found to be a fifty-note compass, one has still to decide between C/E to $f^3$ or $G_1/B_1$ to $c^3$. It could be argued that the $G_1/B_1$ to $c^3$ compass is historically less likely, and yet Nicolas Meeùs[2] has shown that this compass is original to the 1646 IC double in the Brussels Instrument Museum. Clearly a more general method for the determination of the original compass and disposition is required.

## MAKING A STRING-BAND STRIP

Because of the special sonority attributed to the Ruckers soundboards, any process of ravalement carried out on

[2] Nicolas Meeùs, 'Le clavecin de Johannes Couchet, Anvers 1646', *Bulletin of the Brussels Museum of Instruments*, I (1971), 15.

Table 8.1 *Inside case width used to suggest possible keyboard compasses*

Based on the Ruckers three-octave span of 500mm, where one natural width = 500mm/21 = 23.81mm.

| Number of natural keys | Width of naturals | Keyblocks plus clearance | Approximate width of inside of case | Possible compass | Number of notes |
|---|---|---|---|---|---|
| 24 | 571.4mm | 47mm | 618mm | (F to $g^2$, $a^2$) | 40 |
| | | | | (F to $a^2$) | 41 |
| 25 | 595.2mm | 47mm | 642mm | C/E to $g^2$, $a^2$ | 41 |
| | | | | C/E to $a^2$ | 42 |
| 26 | 619.0mm | 47mm | 666mm | (F to $c^3$) | 44 |
| 27 | 642.9mm | 47mm | 690mm | C/E to $c^3$ | 45 |
| | | | | (C to $a^2$) | 46 |
| 28 | 666.7mm | 47mm | 714mm | C/E to $d^3$ | 47 |
| | | | | ($G_1/B_1$ to $a^2$) | 47 |
| 29 | 690.5mm | 47mm | 738mm | C to $c^3$ | 49 |
| | | | | F to $f^3$ | 49 |
| 30 | 714.3mm | 47mm | 761mm | C/E to $f^3$ | 50 |
| | | | | $G_1/B_1$ to $c^3$ | 50 |
| | | | | C to $d^3$ | 51 |
| 31 | 738.1mm | 47mm | 785mm | ($G_1/B_1$ to $d^3$) | 52 |
| 32 | 761.9mm | 47mm | 809mm | $G_1$ to $c^3$ | 54 |
| 33 | 785.7mm | 47mm | 833mm | $F_1$, $G_1$, $A_1$ to $c^3$ | 54 |
| | | | | ($G_1/B_1$ to $f^3$) | 55 |
| | | | | ($G_1$ to $d^3$) | 56 |
| 34 | 809.5mm | 47mm | 857mm | $F_1$, $G_1$, $A_1$ to $d^3$ | 56 |
| | | | | ($G_1$ to $e^3$) | 58 |
| 35 | 833.3mm | 47mm | 880mm | $F_1$ to $d^3$, $e^3$ | 59 |

Compasses listed in parentheses were not, to my knowledge, used by the Ruckers/Couchet family.

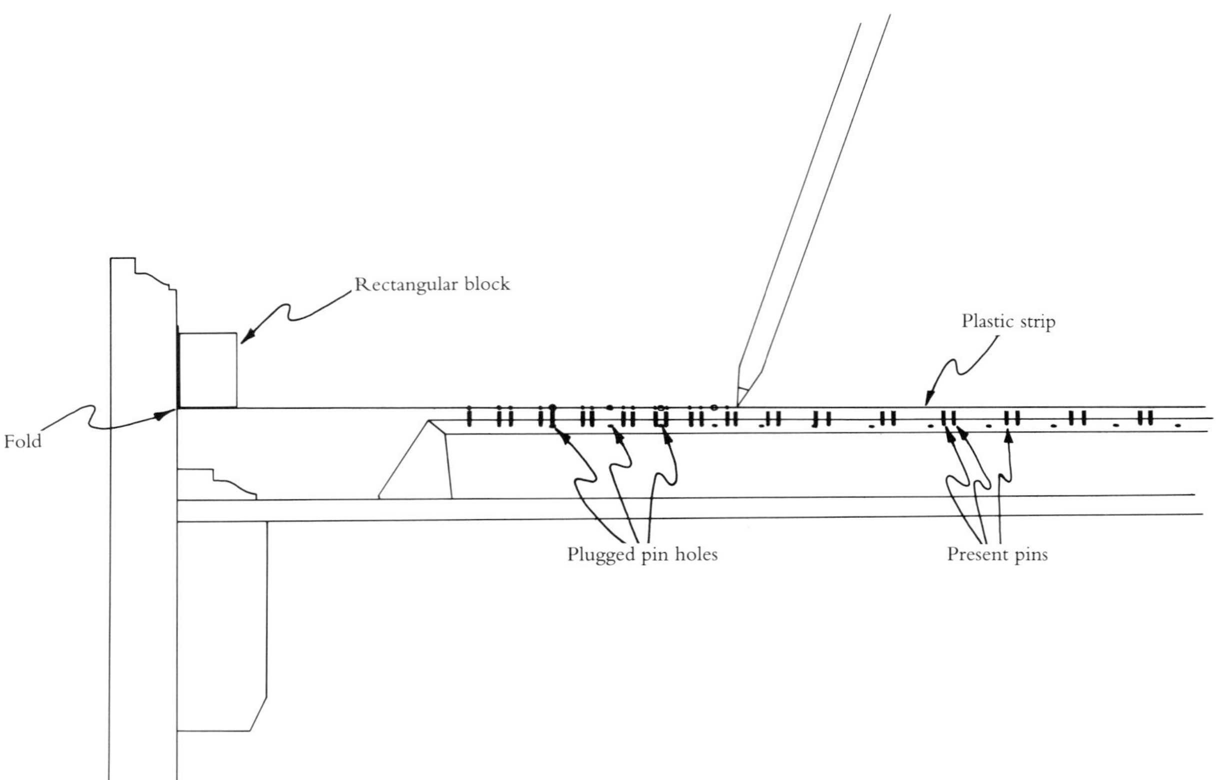


Fig. 8.1 Making the string-band strip.

an instrument tended to treat the soundboard and soundboard bridges as inviolate. Whereas the casework was drastically altered, and the action and wrestplank completely renewed, the most that was normally done to the soundboard was to extend it in the treble and to repin and extend the bridges. Although the 4′ hitchpin rail and bridges may have been repinned a number of times, the plugged holes remaining contain the evidence of the original string-band layout. The problem is only to identify which of the plugged holes correspond to the original Ruckers pinning, and then to determine the relative pitch and the note played by each string which passed over these pins. When working directly from the original instrument itself, or even from an accurate full-scale drawing showing all of the plugged bridge and hitchpin holes, it is difficult to keep track of which are the possible original pin holes and which the subsequent ones, quite aside from the pitch of the associated strings. A more schematic and abstract representation of the string-band is required.

A convenient and permanent record of the pinning of the bridges and 4′ hitchpin rail containing all the information relevant to the original compass and disposition of a harpsichord can be made as follows. A strip of stable transparent plastic drafting film is cut about 2cm wide and slightly longer than the inside width of the instrument being studied. A fold is made in the film about 1cm from one end and perpendicular to the long edge of the strip. The strip is then attached to a small rectangular block of wood so that the fold coincides with one of the 90° edges of the block (see Fig. 8.1). The block is then held against and moved along the spine of the instrument with the fold at the lower spine-side edge of the block. The position of the pins relative to the spine is then marked on the strip by slowly moving the block along, maintaining the strip at right angles to the spine. Different marks are used for the plugged holes and for the actual pinning; the 8′ bridge-pin positions are marked along the back edge, the 4′ bridge-pin positions along the near edge and the 4′ hitchpin positions along the middle of the strip. The plugged holes for the 8′ back-pinning should be marked adjacent to the rest of the bass 8′ pinning. The ends of the original bridges as well as bridge additions, the ravalement join in the soundboard, and the joins in the bentside nameboard and belly rail should also all be marked and identified on the strip.

I have decided to call the strip obtained, after marking the positions of all of the present pinning and plugged holes by moving across the entire soundboard area, the string-band strip. From the resulting mass of marks on this strip one has to identify those corresponding to the original Ruckers pinning. It has already been noted that the keyboard three-octave span is 500mm, and this is also the space occupied by three octaves of strings. With twelve strings in each octave the spacing between successive strings is 500mm/36 = 13.89mm. Using this spacing, a 'standard' strip can be made from a length of the same transparent plastic film, and this standard compared with the instrument string-band strip. Because of the single pinning of the 4′ bridge, it is usually simpler to make the first comparison here. If the two strips are laid down parallel to one another and the standard moved slowly past the strip under study, a position is quickly reached where each of the marks on the standard coincides with one of the marks on the string-band strip. Often the standard positions coincide in places with the plugged holes and in others with the positions of the later pinning. The marks which coincide with the standard are those of the original Ruckers pinning of the 4′ bridge. Since the 4′ strings were always placed to the left and the 8′ strings to the right of the jacks, sliding the standard up and to the right will identify the original 8′ bridge pinning. The marks for the original Ruckers pinning should be clearly identified on the string-band strip.

Ruckers practice was to angle the strings away from the spine in the bass, so that the string positions are compressed together at the bass ends of the bridges. Clearly the standard strip will get out of step with the pin positions for these lowest bass strings. If the bridges have been repinned a number of times it can then be difficult to identify the original pin positions because of their variable spacing. However, the single back-pinning positions on the 8′ bridge will quickly identify the original bass pins, since the back pins were placed directly behind and in line with the bridge pins. Ruckers practice, again highly standardized, was to back-pin the bottom octave of 8′ strings – instruments with a short octave have nine back-pinned 8′ strings from C/E to c inclusive, and instruments with a chromatic bass octave have thirteen back-pinned 8′ strings.

Having identified the marks on the study strip with the original pinning of the instrument, one has then to ascertain the pitch of the string associated with each of these pins. In the case of double-manual instruments this is relatively easy because of the double pinning of the e♭/g♯ strings. At each pair of double plugged holes (most readily identifiable on the 4′ hitchpin rail and the 4′ bridge) one is sure to be dealing with the e♭/g♯ keys. Having identified the original pin positions, one can then work upwards and downwards to identify the bottom and top notes for each manual.

## FINDING PITCH c USING THE 49cm RULE

Identification of the associated pitch of the pins on a single-manual harpsichord is not as straightforward as that of a double. However, I have discovered that the pitch c unison bridge pin (i.e. $c^2$ at 8′ pitch) is 49cm or 19 duimen from the rear surface of the nameboard for both double- and single-manual harpsichords. Thus, except for the little 1627 A R harpsichord in The Hague at quint pitch, it is possible, even when the wrestplank and the nut have been replaced, to identify the pitch c plugged hole in the unison bridge simply by measuring out 49cm behind the nameboard. Identifying this plugged hole on the string-band strip then identifies the pitch of all of the strings above and below 8′-pitched $c^2$.

## USING THE BRIDGE-POSITIONING HOLES TO DETERMINE THE PLAYED NOTES *c* AND *f*♯

Determining the pitch of the strings does not necessarily determine the compass if the pitch of the instrument is other than the normal 'reference' pitch R. The original width of the case determines the number of naturals, and this in turn greatly restricts the number of possible compasses which make musical and historical sense. Other factors such as the back-pinning of the 8′ bridge will help in determining the original compass. But the *played* note for each string, and hence the *relative* pitch, can be determined unambiguously in the following way.

In laying out the position of the bridges and bridge pins, Ruckers practice was to place pairs of positioning pins into the soundboard on either side of the bridges close to the played notes *c* and *f*♯ (see p. 106). The holes for these positioning pins remain beside the bridges and are one of the characteristics of the genuine Ruckers harpsichord. It is always clear whether any pair of positioning holes corresponds to a *c* or to an *f*♯, since a misinterpretation of these possibilities normally means that the instrument would then have the unlikely note *f*♯ as a lowest or highest key. Comparing the played $c^2$ string position determined from the bridge-positioning holes with the position of the pitch $c^2$ string will then determine both the original compass and the pitch of the instrument.

## SOME EXAMPLES OF THE APPLICATION OF THE METHOD

Most of the harpsichords subjected to the string-band analysis were originally the familiar models made by the

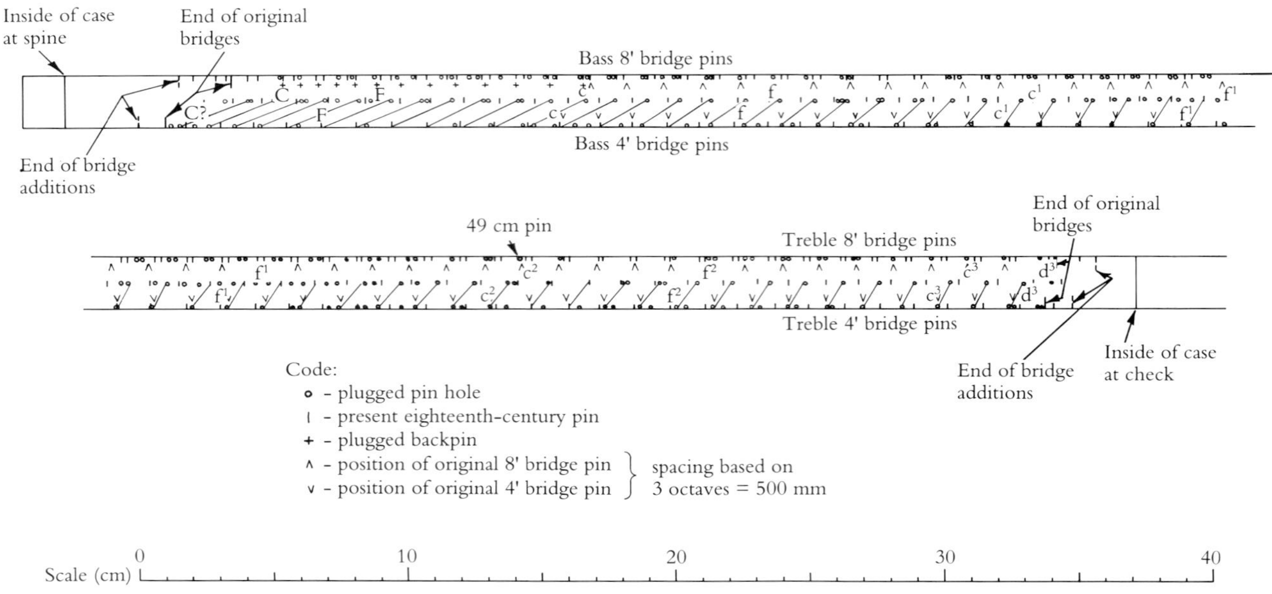


Fig. 8.2 The 1639 IR string-band strip.

Ruckers family. The single-manual harpsichords usually had an original compass of C/E to $c^3$ at 8′ pitch, and the doubles had two manuals, the upper with a C/E to $c^3$ compass at 8′ pitch, and the lower with C/E to $f^3$ at 10⅔′ pitch. However, a number of harpsichords have been found which do not fall into the above categories.

### *The English singles with a chromatic bass*

Two of these exceptional instruments are very similar, not least in that they were both originally, as now, single-manual harpsichords. The first is the 1637a IR in the Russell Collection, Edinburgh. The case of this harpsichord has been widened in the eighteenth century to give its present compass of $A_1$ to $f^3$. The original inside width measured from joins in the bentside and nameboard was about 735mm, implying a twenty-nine natural-note compass. Application of the 49cm rule confirms the C to $c^3$ chromatic compass reported by John Barnes in 1970.[3] An important feature not pointed out by Barnes is that instead of the usual nine strings which are back-pinned on singles having a C/E short octave, there were originally thirteen back-pinned notes on this harpsichord. This also confirms the long octave, since it meant that, as usual, the back-pinning covers the full bottom octave.

Almost identical to this is the 1639 IR single in the Victoria and Albert Museum, London. The case of the instrument has never been widened, but the original keyblocks have been narrowed to allow space for a wider keyboard, the gap has been widened to make room for the third register, and the bridges extended and repinned to back the extra notes and two unison sets of 8′ strings (see Fig. 8.2). The eighteenth-century keyboard of this harpsichord was lost in a fire in Kirkman's workshops in 1835, but the tuning pins, nuts and bridge pins and the registers all indicate that the eighteenth-century compass had fifty-five notes and was probably $G_1$, $A_1$, to $d^3$, with a scaling of 339mm and a three-octave span of only 465mm. The scribed lines on the original baseboard indicate the positions of the original keyblocks and the space between these was originally 722mm. This implies a compass with thirty natural notes (the total inside case width is 758mm, the same as the 1638b IR double in Edinburgh, also with a compass of thirty natural keys). The string-band strip shows that the original compass had fifty-one notes, and applying the 49cm rule to locate the $c^2$ string gives an original compass of C to $d^3$. Like the 1637a IR single in Edinburgh and the 1679 IC in Washington, the chromatic bass octave is confirmed by the presence of thirteen original single back-pins on the bass end of the 8′ bridge. These instruments with a chromatic bass octave to C seem to have been special export models probably made for the English market. In fact two of the four harpsichords with chromatic bass octaves to C (the 1637a IR and the 1639 IR) seem to have been in England from earliest times, and were therefore probably among

[3] John Barnes, 'The Flemish instruments in the Russell Collection, Edinburgh', *Colloquium: Restauratieproblemen van Antwerpse Klavecimbels* (Antwerp, 1971), 35–9.

these special export models. Also, Dr Lambrechts-Douillez has found that in Antwerp itself, in the archival documents dealing with Ioannes Couchet's wife and the Hagaerts, harpsichords with a full chromatic bass octave to C are referred to as *op sijn engels*, or 'in the English style'.[4]

### *The large extended-bass Couchet singles*

During the second half of the seventeenth century the Couchets continued building instruments in the Ruckers style, but with compasses and dispositions not found in the Ruckers instruments built before about 1650. These instruments had the same keyboard and string spacing as Ruckers instruments and so the string-band strip method can be applied to them to determine their original compass and disposition. Except for the 1646 IC, all of the extant Couchet harpsichords were originally singles.

The (*c.* 1650)b IC in the Metropolitan Museum, New York has not been widened and the inside width of the case is 831mm, suggesting that the original compass had thirty-three naturals. The note names, written beside the original row of tuning pins, read (transcribed from the old Flemish script): $F_1$, $G_1$, $A_1$, $B^\flat{}_1$, c . . . $c^3$, confirming the thirty-three-natural-note compass. On this harpsichord, eleven of the bass notes were originally back-pinned, which conforms to the usual practice of back-pinning the lowest octave of strings – in this case from $F_1$ to F without $F^{\sharp 1}$ and $G^{\sharp 1}$. The original unison pitch c bridgepin located using the 49cm rule gave a normal scaling of 353mm, but its string was played by the $b^{\flat 1}$ key. This, together with the $c^2$ string length of 314mm, proves that this harpsichord was one of those which Couchet built to sound a tone above R (see Appendix 18).

The 1680 IC in Boston (ravalé by Blanchet in 1758 and by Taskin in 1781) was altered at least twice in the eighteenth century and apparently also in more recent times. The cheek shows evidence of a lap joint which extended the length of the keywell to convert it from a single to a double. The original inside case width can be estimated and is found to be about 863mm. From Table 8.1 this suggests that the original compass had thirty-four naturals. Using the 49cm rule to give the original position of pitch c locates the plugged original tuning-pin hole for this note in the wrestplank. Counting upwards gives $d^3$ as the pitch of the original top note. This suggests that the original pitch was R and that the original compass was $F_1$ to $d^3$ (or perhaps $F_1$, $G_1$, $A_1$ to $d^3$). Unfortunately the bridges and hitchrail have been pinned and replugged so many times that it is now impossible to distinguish the position of the original from the later pin holes. This, plus the curious lack of any of the usual construction marks on the soundboard, such as the positioning holes beside the original *c* and $f^\sharp$ notes, has made it impossible to confirm definitely either the pitch or the compass of this instrument.

The n.d. IC harpsichord in Stockholm, which may be the last instrument built in the Ruckers/Couchet tradition, can also be analysed in the usual way. It is now a beautifully-decorated double ravalé by Taskin. The case has never been widened, but both the spine and cheek have been lengthened to enlarge the keywell and convert it from a single- to a double-manual harpsichord. The instrument is 887mm wide inside, wide enough for thirty-five naturals plus about 54mm for the keyblocks and clearance at the ends of the keys. Locating the pitch $c^2$ string using the 49cm rule gives $F_1$ as the bottom note, and a chromatic bass octave is confirmed by the presence of thirteen single back-pinned strings on the 8′ bridge. The treble ends of both the 8′ and 4′ bridges are replacements, so that the top note cannot be confirmed directly. A thirty-five-natural-note compass from $F_1$ would give $e^3$ as the top note and a completely chromatic compass would have sixty notes. However, the presence of only fifty-nine original holes (plus later added holes) in the original registers, which were later used as lower guides, suggests that the original compass was $F_1$ to $d^3$, $e^3$. This seems to be confirmed by extrapolating the position of the treble strings on the string-band strip. If the $e^{\flat 3}$ were present, then the top string would be placed very close to the cheek and cheek moulding, giving virtually no free soundboard in the treble. This compass is thus only two notes smaller than the standard $F_1$ to $f^3$ compass which was used in instruments throughout Northern Europe for the next hundred years.

Because the 49cm rule locates the original 8′ $c^2$ note, it might be expected that, as usual, this is also the pitch c note in the n.d. IC harpsichord. However, the original position of the nut shows that the scalings of $c^2$ here were about 315mm, so that the pitch of this harpsichord must have been R + 2, like the (*c.* 1650)b IC in New York.

### *Some unusual double-manual harpsichords*

The 1599 HR harpsichord has an HR rose of the type used by Ioannes Ruckers before 1618 and is therefore the earliest harpsichord by him. It is now an aligned double with a compass of $F_1$ to $f^3$ chromatic and a short scaling suitable for brass stringing throughout (see p. 216). The original width of the inside of the case measured from the joins in the bentside and lower belly rail is about 715mm,

[4] J. Lambrechts-Douillez and M. J. Bosschaerts-Eykens, '1. Dokumenten betreffende de familie Couchet', *Mededelingen van het Ruckers-Genootschap*, V (Antwerp, 1986), 25 and 28.

indicating an original compass with twenty-eight naturals. Examination of the string-band strip shows clearly that there were originally three pairs of doubled e♭/g♯ strings. Considering the lower manual where the pitch $c^2$ string is played by the $f^2$ key, and counting downwards, the lowest note is found to be the E of the usual C/E short octave. Counting upwards, the last original pin hole on the remaining original parts of the bridges corresponds to $g^2$ at 8′ pitch, and $c^3$ at 10⅔′ pitch. However, the original bridges have been considerably shortened during the ravalement and there would have been ample room inside the case for a compass with at least two additional treble notes. The original compass must thus have been C/E to $a^2$ on the upper manual, and C/E to $d^3$ on the lower manual, the latter having the requisite twenty-eight naturals predicted from the inside case width. (It seems impossible to determine whether or not there was originally a top $g^{\sharp 2}/c^{\sharp 3}$ accidental.) The C/E to $a^2$ compass is also found on the 1583 HR virginal at R + 5 in the Instrument Museum of the Conservatoire NSM, Paris, and on the virginal part of the 1594 HR combined harpsichord and virginal in Schloss Köpenick. It is thus a familiar compass in early Ruckers instruments, and represents, along with another non-Ruckers double of the same compass in the Brussels Instrument Museum (see Chapter 2, pp. 29ff), an early form of the Flemish non-aligned double-manual harpsichord.

Another interesting Ruckers instrument is the 1612a HR harpsichord. This is now a brilliantly-lacquered double with a compass of $G_1$, $A_1$ to $f^3$. The depth of both the keywell and the case has been altered, but indicates that the instrument was originally also a double-manual harpsichord, since the original keywell depth would have been too great for a single-manual instrument. The alteration to the case height was made at the top of the case, but the soundboard-to-baseboard distance is still the original 8 small duimen (203mm), also a characteristic of Ruckers double-manual harpsichords (see pp. 90 and 94). The inside width of the instrument measured from the ravalement join in the bentside is 700mm, but the extreme end of the original 8′ bridge extends to a point 685mm from the spine. This indicates that the original cheek must have been at about 710–715mm from the spine (otherwise the treble ends of the bridges would have been sitting on the cheek liner), and thus that the original compass had twenty-eight naturals. A string-band strip has been made for this instrument; the pitch $c^2$ pin on the 8′ bridge and the original Ruckers pinning on the bridges and 4′ hitchpin rail have been identified (the 4′ bridge is not original above the present $g^{\sharp 1}$ pin). Counting downwards from the pitch $c^2$ pin, the bottom note is found to be pitch $A_1$; the top note would be pitch $g^2$. The fact that this is a completely unknown compass historically suggests that the harpsichord was at a transposed pitch. Assuming 10⅔′ pitch, like the lower manual of a normal double, renders the bottom note a D and the top note a $c^3$. This is an equally unlikely compass. However, assuming that the harpsichord originally sounded at 12′ pitch (i.e. at R − 5, where the pitch $c^2$ note was played by a $g^2$ key) gives an E as the lowest, and $d^3$ as the top key.

The positioning holes beside the bridges for the played notes *c* and *f*♯ confirm the assumption that the original compass was C/E to $d^3$, and hence also confirm the R − 5 pitch.[5] But what was the pitch of the second manual? The string-band strip and careful examination of the instrument itself indicates that there were originally no doubled hitchpins for the notes e♭/g♯, nor for any other notes. Excluding those instruments with non-original soundboards, and those which were originally singles, this is therefore the only Ruckers double-manual harpsichord without the doubled strings necessary when using meantone tuning and keyboards a fourth apart in pitch. This suggests that the instrument was originally tuned in some well-tempered system; on the other hand, such tuning systems were virtually unknown in 1612, and meantone tuning was thoroughly ingrained in the musical culture of the Low Countries during this period. Most important of all, the instrument originally had a C/E short octave, so that tonalities with root chords not available in the short-octave bass could not be used, thus negating many advantages of a well-tempered system.

Therefore, keeping in mind the C/E to $d^3$ compass, the lower-manual pitch of R − 5, and the use of meantone tuning, three possibilities suggest themselves. The first possibility is that the two manuals were aligned and at the same pitch. There is no historical precedent for such a disposition. The earliest extant undoubted aligned doubles date from at least forty years later, although documentary and iconographical evidence seems to point to the existence of aligned instruments about ten to fifteen years later.[6] Also, it seems unlikely that an instrument with both manuals at the uncommon R − 5 pitch should survive, whereas there is not a single example of an aligned double at the usual 8′ pitch, or at R − 4. At any rate it would not have been an 'expressive' double, since analysis of the string-band strip shows that the original

[5] The C/E to $d^3$ compass is not unique to this instrument, but is also found on the 1629 IR 4½-voet virginal.

[6] Marin Mersenne, *Harmonie universelle* (Paris, 1636; English translation by R. E. Chapman, The Hague, 1957), 155; Edwin M. Ripin, 'The two-manual harpsichord in Flanders before 1650', *The Galpin Society Journal*, XXI (1968), 33ff.

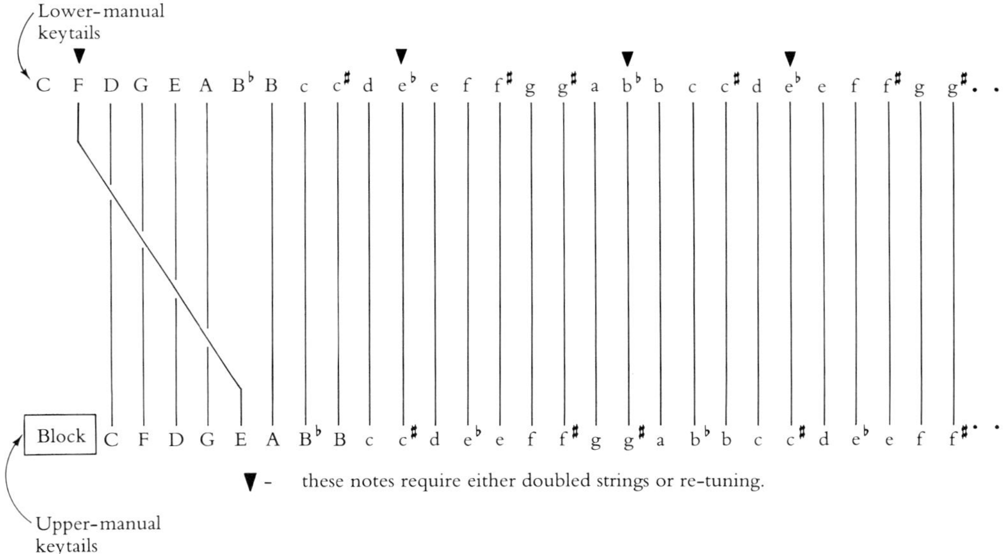


Fig. 8.3 Schematic diagram of a possible arrangement of the upper-manual bass keys in a double-manual harpsichord transposing by a tone.

disposition had only two choirs of strings, one an octave above the other, so that exactly the same disposition would have been available on both manuals. Such an arrangement therefore seems pointless.

A second possibility is that the two manuals were a fourth apart, with compasses of C/E to d$^3$ and C/E to a$^2$, like the 1599 HR harpsichord just discussed, but overall a tone lower in pitch. But such an instrument would still be expected to have the usual four rows of jacks and e♭/g♯ plates on the nuts in the same way as the normal double. These plates had been in regular use since 1599 (e.g. 1599 HR, 1608 AR, 1612b HR, and (1612) IR), so one should expect to find them here. Their absence and the C/E to a$^2$ upper-manual compass, completely anachronistic for 1612, make this possibility very unlikely.

The third possibility is that the instrument was originally a non-aligned double with it's two manuals a tone apart. Such a harpsichord would have keyboards with compasses of C/E to d$^3$ and C/E to c$^3$, and would require only one cranked key in the bass for the short octave (see Fig. 8.3).

With the two manuals a tone apart a conflict in the tuning occurs for *two* sets of notes in every octave, namely c♯/e♭ and g♯/b♭; moreover, the lower-manual F would have to be tuned up a small semitone to F♯ when using the upper-manual E (see Appendix 7).[7] With the tradition of using the e♭/g♯ plates well established, it seems odd that similar plates, two to an octave, would not have been used for the notes requiring retuning on this harpsichord. However, it is not clear that this instrument was like other doubles in having four registers. Traces of the original jackrail mortice remain on the spine, and although its original size is indistinct, it is clear that the jackrail (and hence the register gap) was not originally as wide as in the normal double-manual harpsichord.[8] This seems to indicate another three-slide instrument. The most likely disposition for a three-slide harpsichord (see also p. 32) is:

← 4′
→ 8′ dogleg
← 4′

Here, because the 8′ jacks are common to both manuals, the strings with conflicting tunings *must* be retuned when moving from one manual to another and the plates for the double strings have no purpose, hence their absence.

Assuming that the two manuals were a tone apart would also explain why the lower-manual compass extends to the unusual d$^3$: the upper manual must reach

[7] A player moving from the lower to the upper manual would have to tune the lower-manual F up by 76 cents to give the upper-manual E; the lower-manual *e♭*s and *b♭*s would each have to be tuned down 41 cents to give *c♯*s and *g♯*s respectively on the upper manual.

[8] R. Clayson and A. Garrett, 'Harpsichord by Hans Ruckers the Younger dated 1612: Workshop report on the restoration completed in 1981' unpublished restoration report (Lyminge, Kent, ?1981).

to $c^3$ in order that the contemporary repertoire be playable, and this in turn means that the lower manual, a tone lower, must end at $d^3$.

Although no other Ruckers double-manual harpsichord seems either to have had its manuals other than a fourth apart, or to have had other than four registers, the assumption that the manuals of the 1612a HR double were a tone apart solves the unusual problems associated with this instrument, given that it originally had three registers and one manual at R − 5. The pitch of the second manual at R − 4 is the same as the lower manual of the normal Ruckers double, and the tone difference between the two manuals is just that between Praetorius' *Kammerton* and *Chorton*.[9] That harpsichords were made with a difference of a tone between them is also mentioned by Couchet himself in his letter to Constantijn Huygens (see Appendix 18). This tone difference is also known in organs[10] and most important of all, in the Hans Müller harpsichord (see Chapter 2, pp. 20ff).

An example of another non-standard type of harpsichord build by the Ruckers family is the 1616 HR double. This harpsichord, although it is now an aligned double, still has a disposition with 1 × 8′, 1 × 4′ on each manual. The instrument has never been widened and so retains its original inside case width of 806mm. The one-time $F_1$ to $a^2$, $b^2$ compass, which had thirty-two naturals – two naturals more than the normal Ruckers double-manual harpsichords – could be original. However, the lower manual keys and keybed and the upper-manual keys are all replacements. The upper-manual balance rail is, on the other hand, original and shows traces of the original wooden block in the bass, which was wide enough to replace three natural keys. The first note after the block was originally an F, not the expected E of a C/E short octave, and the top note was $f^3$ four chromatic octaves higher. This four-octave compass, with the bass wooden block three naturals wide, confirms the thirty-two-natural-note inside case width.

The bridge and nuts have not been repinned, the wrestplank retains its original doubled tuning pins and the nuts retain their plates for the doubled $e^\flat/g^\sharp$ strings. There are in fact four sets of doubled tuning pins and nut plates instead of the three sets of the normal Ruckers double. The doubled strings occur at the position of the $g^\sharp$ keys of the original upper manual, fixing the $e^\flat$ key positions of the lower manual and implying a top note of $c^3$, a bottom bass $G_1$, and a chromatic fifty-four-note compass between. Thus not only do both manuals have a chromatic bass compass but the pitch rôle of the two keyboards is interchanged compared with the normal double (see Fig. 8.4). This must be the large instrument referred to by Douwes:[11]

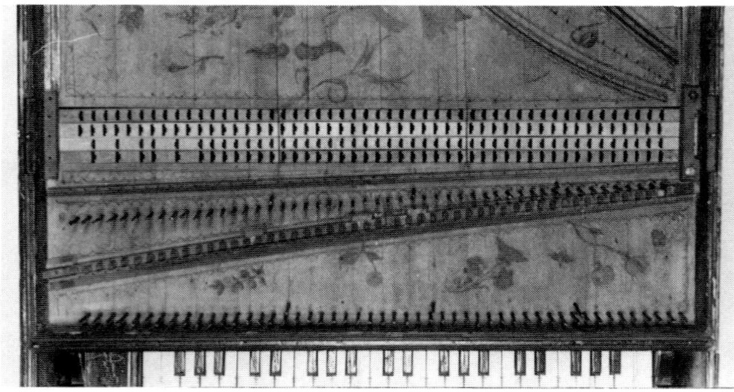

Plate 8.1 Comparison of the wrestplank of the normal (above: 1638b IR) and the 'French' (below: 1616 HR) double-manual harpsichords. Besides being wider, the 'French' double has one extra set of doubled $e^\flat/g^\sharp$ tuning pins and strings for each of the 4′ and 8′ choirs.

> The notes or keyboards of clavecimbels compare with those of most organs, namely from C to C four octaves [C(/E) to $c^3$]. But a few large harpsichords go down lower to G or F [$G_1$ or $F_1$] similar to some large organs and encompass four octaves and a fifth.

The 1616 HR harpsichord is the earliest extant clavecimbel known to me which originally had a chromatic bass compass beginning as low as $G_1$.

All four examples of this type of harpsichord (1616 HR, 1627c IR, 1628b IR, 1646b AR) are found in France and appear to have been there for a very long time. This seems to suggest that this model of double-manual instrument with an extended chromatic bass was specially made for export to France. I have therefore called this model the 'French' double to distinguish it from the normal double with short-octave bass compasses.

[9] Michael Praetorius, *Syntagma Musicum II: De Organographia* (Wolfenbüttel, 1619; facs., Kassel, 1958), 14ff.

[10] H. J. Moser, *Paul Hofhaimer* (Stuttgart–Berlin, 1929), 22 and 177.

[11] See Appendix 8, p. 293.

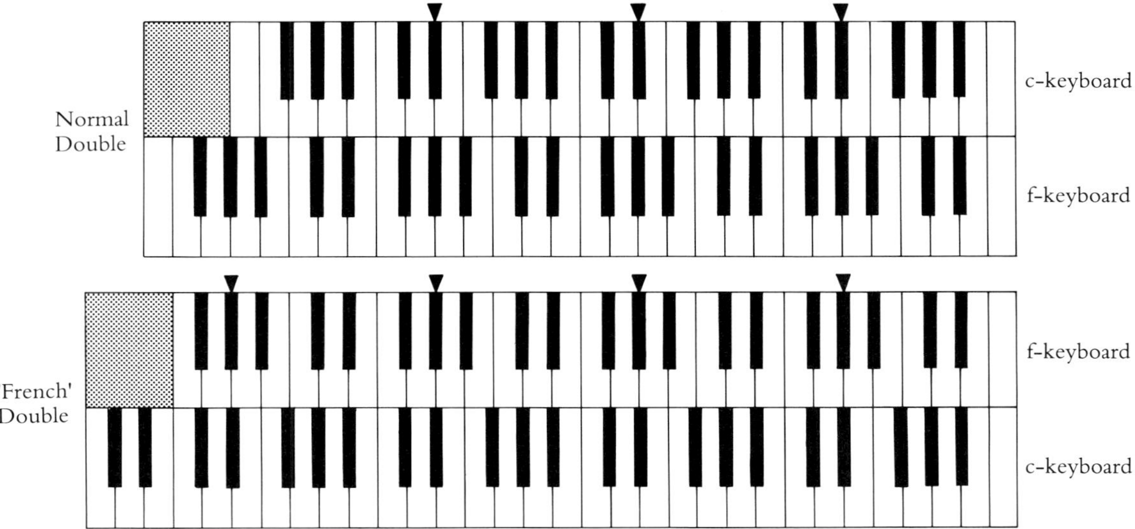


Fig. 8.4 Comparison of the keyboards on the normal (above) and the chromatic bass compass 'French' (below) double-manual Ruckers harpsichord.

*Aligned double-manual harpsichords and the Ruckers tradition*

It should be noted at this point that all the extant Ruckers harpsichords which originally had two manuals were of the non-aligned type[12] with the manuals a fourth apart in pitch (or, in the case of the 1612a HR, a tone apart). Not including the 1612a HR, only five Ruckers harpsichords which are now doubles and which have their original soundboards do not show evidence of the original double pinning of the e♭/g♯ notes. All of these, the 1632 IR, the 1636 AR, 1621AR, 1651b AR and the 1654 AR, were undoubtedly originally four-octave singles (the first two actually still retain their original baseboards, onto which the plan of the instrument has been scribed). In addition, the Couchets made several instruments which are now doubles but which were all originally singles; these have already been discussed. Therefore, since none of the surviving two-manual harpsichords was originally of the aligned type, it seems likely that no aligned doubles were ever made by any of the Ruckers family.

*The 2 × 8′ disposition*

Previously, in identifying the 8′ string positions from those of the 4′ strings, it was assumed that the original disposition was 1 × 8′, 1 × 4′. However, many Ruckers harpsichords were altered, probably early on in their history, to a 2 × 8′ disposition. Might there exist some Ruckers instruments with an original disposition of 2 × 8′, but with later alterations which disguise their original state?

The 1627a IR single in the Berlin Instrument Museum now has this disposition and Alfred Berner[13] suggests that it is original. However, neither the present soundboard nor soundboard bridge is original, and the lack of a 4′ bridge is therefore no indication of the original disposition. Since the original jacks which were reused include both 4′ and 8′ jacks, with one and two damper holes respectively, it seems clear that the original soundboard had both a 4′ and a 8′ bridge, and I can see no evidence that the original disposition was other than 1 × 8′, 1 × 4′.

A careful search has been made for a harpsichord by a member of the Ruckers family which originally had a disposition other than 1 × 8′, 1 × 4′. No instrument signed with the name Ruckers has been found to have had a 2 × 8′ disposition, although two such instruments by the Couchets have been discovered.

[12] The aligned double referred to by J. H. van der Meer, 'More about Flemish two-manual harpsichords', *Keyboard Instruments: Studies in Keyboard Organology*, ed. Edwin M. Ripin (Edinburgh, 1971), 50ff. is undoubtably not a product of the Ruckers' workshops.

[13] Alfred Berner, 'Der Ruckers Bestand des Berliner-Musikinstrumentenmuseums', *Colloquium: Restauratieproblemen van Antwerpse Klavecimbels* (Antwerp, 1971), 53–62.

The first of these is the 1652 IC harpsichord in private hands in France, now a double with the normal 2 × 8′, 1 × 4′ disposition.[14] The 8′ bridge has not been repinned, but a 4′ bridge has been added which runs across the soundboard covering parts of the original soundboard painting. The 4′ bridge also runs over the original barring under the soundboard, which was clearly laid out for just a single 8′ bridge. There was never any provision for a 4′ hitchpin rail, so instead an added strip of wood was glued to the top of the soundboard and the 4′ strings were hitched to this. The present original inside case width is 763mm, implying an original compass with thirty naturals. The present compass is $G_1/B_1$ to $c^3$ with a split E♭, and the 49cm rule locates the present long $c^2$ string, which has the usual Ruckers/Couchet scaling of 353mm. This suggests that the present compass is original except for the bottom split E♭, for which an extra set of strings was added in the extreme bass. This is confirmed by the pinning and position of the lower strings. Although the 1646 IC double also originally had the $G_1/B_1$ to $c^3$ compass, it had this more by default than design, since it is just the transposed compass of the lower manual. The 1652 IC, as well as being the oldest 2 × 8′ Ruckers-family harpsichord, is thus probably the earliest extant harpsichord of any type *designed* to have the $G_1/B_1$ short-octave compass (see p. 230).

The second instrument which originally had a 2 × 8′ disposition is the 1671/73 IC harpsichord (belonging to Kenneth Gilbert) by one of the Couchet sons, probably Ioseph Ioannes. This has also been converted from a single- to a double-manual harpsichord. In so doing, the soundboard has been elaborately respliced to make use of the old wood in the sounding parts of the new soundboard (see Chapter 11, p. 211); as a result all evidence of the original bridges (and their pinning) and the soundboard barring has been lost. However, traces of the original soundboard painting show the original position of the 8′ bridge and rose hole. It is clear from these that there was never a 4′ bridge, nor is there any trace of 4′ hitchpin holes in the soundboard. Therefore this harpsichord also originally had a 2 × 8′ disposition – the only other possibility being the anachronistic 1 × 8′.

Besides the evidence of the 2 × 8′ disposition in existing Ioannes Couchet harpsichords, there is also documentary evidence. Letters between Constantijn Huygens and Gaspard F. Duarte and also between Huygens and Couchet himself (see Appendices 17 and 18) indicate that Couchet made a harpsichord with the extended compass of $F_1$ to $d^3$ and a 2 × 8′ disposition in the summer of 1648. It appears from Couchet's letter that this was the first 2 × 8′ harpsichord he had made. So it was not surprising that such a disposition is not found among those instruments signed by the Ruckers, since only three Ruckers instruments survive dated later than 1648.

## CONCLUSIONS

The use of the string-band strip method to determine the original compass and disposition of a Ruckers harpsichord has a number of advantages quite aside from the relative ease of use and the positive nature of its results. As a record of the major part of the musical alterations to an instrument the strip is permanent and stable, since the humidity and temperature coefficients of expansion for the plastic film are both small. The rolled strip can be stored in a space a fraction of that of a full-scale drawing. The analysis of the original pin spacing can be done later, away from the instrument and at one's convenience. Furthermore, the method is readily applicable to other types of instruments which have undergone alterations. Most seventeenth-century instruments of the Flemish school also used a 500mm three-octave span, and the 49cm rule works on at least two Flemish non-Ruckers harpsichords that I know. Many Italian instruments also used a three-octave span close to 500mm, and this can be used at least to determine the original number of natural keys if not to identify the pitches of the strings.

[14] I would like to express my thanks to William Dowd, Sheridan Germann and David Ley, who supplied me with information about this instrument.

CHAPTER NINE

# Trademarks of Ruckers instruments

Clearly it is important to be able to establish the authenticity of a Ruckers instrument. But genuine Ruckers instruments vary greatly in condition and appearance: some are virtually unaltered, others have been enlarged and redecorated and now bear little visual resemblance to their original state. Counterfeit instruments have been made which imitate the genuine article in almost every stage of alteration found in authentic instruments. When confronted by a new instrument, how is one to decide definitely whether or not it is a genuine product of the Ruckers tradition?

In part, the ability to establish the authenticity of a Ruckers instrument becomes easier as experience is gained. As more and more instruments are examined, recurrent features become apparent which can be used to decide if a new instrument is genuine. After one has seen a number of undoubted examples, all of which have similar features, it is possible to compare these with new instruments which have been altered both musically and decoratively or which may have lost certain of their identifying features such as their rose and namebatten.

In theory a genuine Ruckers instrument must exhibit all of the features outlined in Chapters 5 and 6 on the construction of Ruckers harpsichords and virginals. But in practice it is usually necessary to look for only a few features of the construction and marking out. Fortunately it is only rarely really difficult to decide about the authenticity of an instrument; usually if even a few of the characteristic features are missing or are atypical or wrong, one soon finds that there is nothing that, in detail, is typical of Ruckers' practice. On the other hand, if only some of the characteristics of Ruckers' usual practice are present, more and more features are discovered as the examination continues which are typical of Ruckers' practice, until the evidence that the instrument is genuine becomes overwhelming.

## UNAUTHENTIC RUCKERS INSTRUMENTS

Most unauthentic instruments are the products of eighteenth-century workshops outside of Flanders, and usually they are harpsichords and not virginals. I think it is useful to distinguish three different kinds of unauthentic instruments:

(1) *Counterfeit instruments* are conceived from the start by their builders as instruments designed to deceive their purchasers. They are new instruments built and decorated to resemble Ruckers or Couchet instruments, and probably artificially antiqued to give the appearance of age.

(2) *Redecorated instruments* are later instruments which have come into the hands of a faker, who then gives them the appearance of a Ruckers instrument, for example by adding printed papers or by staining the soundboard to make it appear older than it really is.

(3) *Reattributed instruments* are instruments given a Ruckers signature and rose but otherwise not altered.

Most unauthentic instruments are fairly easily recognized, since the methods involved in their manufacture are usually only superficially like those used in the seventeenth century in the Ruckers/Couchet workshops. Counterfeit instruments are particularly easy to identify, because they usually belong to the counterfeiter's normal local tradition of materials, framing, musical potential, etc. The counterfeiter simply gives his usual type of instrument the decorative appearance of a normal Ruckers harpsichord or virginal. Similarly, redecorated instruments are usually not difficult to recognize, since they also date from a later period, and most reattributed instruments are just eighteenth-century harpsichords with a false signature and a fake rose in the soundboard, with no other attempt to give the appearance of a Ruckers.

Difficulties occur with genuine seventeenth-century Flemish instruments which have later been redecorated or reattributed. In this case the woods used, the framing methods, the case joints, soundboard preparation, and even the construction marks and methods are very similar to those used by the Ruckers themselves. But I have found that even with seventeenth-century Flemish instruments faked by giving them a Ruckers signature and rose there are usually a few of the construction methods which differ significantly from the Ruckers' usual practice and which establish that the instrument is unauthentic.

The problem of a counterfeiter working in Antwerp at a time contemporary with the Ruckers poses serious difficulties, since a good builder working in the same tradition and milieu could probably produce an instrument which is now indistinguishable from the genuine article. However, although the Ruckers were recognized in their lifetimes as fine builders, their instruments do not seem to have achieved their almost mythical reputation until well after the demise of the family. Probably the reputation of the Ruckers in their own time was not sufficiently great to warrant the risks involved in counterfeiting instruments. Also, the Guild of St Luke was set up specifically to guard against such activity. Since there is no record of any action having been taken by the Guild or Courts on behalf of any of the members of the Ruckers family, it seems highly unlikely that any instrument now accepted as genuine might be the product of a seventeenth-century Flemish counterfeiting workshop.

## RUCKERS INSTRUMENT AUTHENTICATION

What then are the characteristics which identify a Ruckers instrument as genuine? It is clear that it must possess all or some of the features of size, construction, original disposition, and decoration already described in the previous chapters. The purpose of the following guide to the identification of a genuine Ruckers instrument is to point out the characteristics which are most often significant in deciding if an instrument under investigation is genuine or unauthentic.

### *Soundboard-construction features*

In even the most drastically altered Ruckers instruments, the soundboard and bridges usually retain their basic integrity, with all of the original construction marks, pinning, finish and materials. It has generally (although unfortunately not always) been realized that the soundboard is the soul of the instrument, and that to tamper with the thickness of the soundboard or bridges, or to alter the basic scalings and plucking points, is to detract from the great beauty and purity of the sound produced by the instrument. So usually the soundboard and bridges remain, and usually it is possible from the soundboard alone to identify a genuine instrument.

The genuine Ruckers soundboard will always have the characteristic ribbed surface texture which was produced by the scraper used in the final thinning of the soundboard. This ribbed texture results when the spongy spring or early wood relaxes into a position above the harder summer or late wood when the wood is sized or sealed after scraping. Although this is a feature of most seventeenth-century North European instruments, it is one lacking in almost all eighteenth-century instruments. In the eighteenth century soundboards were planed and the surface of the wood was left completely flat. Also, Ruckers soundboards were sized or varnished, or both, whereas many eighteenth-century soundboards (especially in France) were unsized, at least in the open areas which were not painted. Because of the degradation of the size or shellac varnish, a genuine Ruckers soundboard has a shiny rich golden brown appearance, easily distinguishable from the flat matt greyish surface of many later soundboards.

The positioning holes on either side of the bridges and nuts are also a characteristic feature of Ruckers soundboards. In harpsichords and in many virginals these paired holes are located near the bridge pins for the notes played by the original *c* and *f*♯ keys, and can therefore also help in the determination of the original pitch and compass of the instrument. Underneath the soundboard one will find small nails or bent-over brass pins driven into the bridges and located between each of the pairs of positioning holes. Later instruments usually have neither the positioning holes nor the nails securing the bridge to the soundboard. Or if one of these features is present, the other is normally not.

The position of the 4′ hitchpins on most eighteenth- and late seventeenth-century North European harpsichord soundboards was not marked out. The hitchpins were simply driven into the soundboard and there is now no apparent indication of how the position of the pins was determined. On Ruckers harpsichord soundboards, in contrast, both the edge of the 4′ hitchpin rail and the line of the hitchpins were marked out on the soundboard. The way in which these lines were used is discussed in Chapter 6; they are shown in Plate 9.1. The presence of

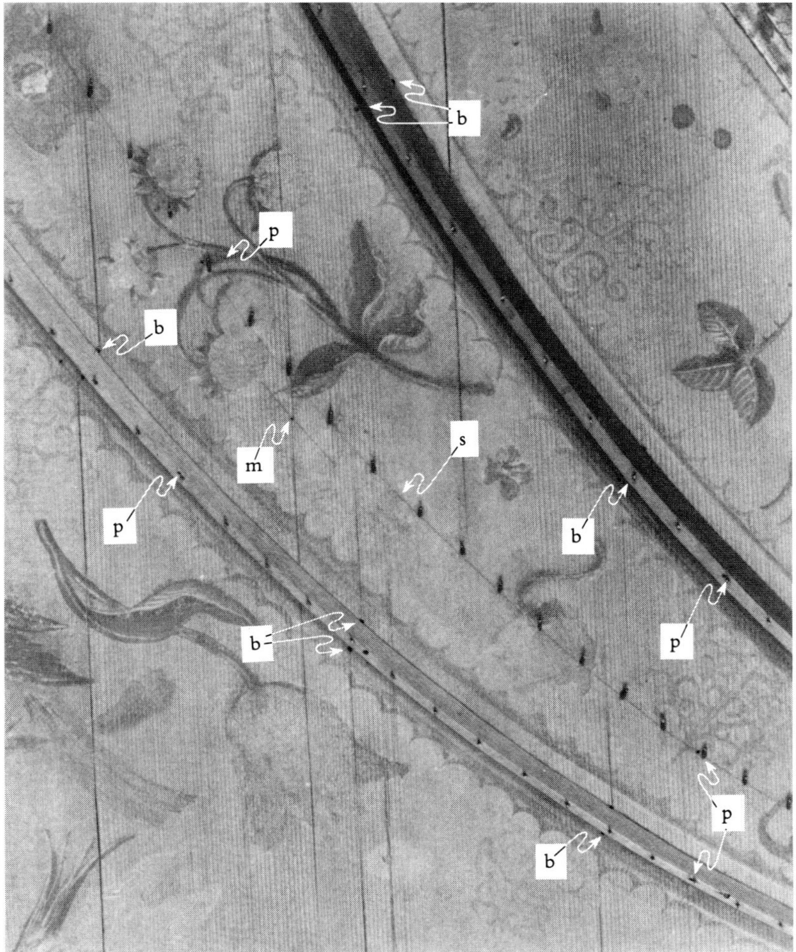


Plate 9.1 Construction marks and features characteristic of a Ruckers soundboard (1638b IR).

b double holes for bridge-positioning pins
p pins, originally double, for the $e^{\flat}/g^{\sharp}$ strings
s scribed line for the 4′ hitchpins
m mark above the edge of the 4′ hitchpin rail

the holes with their associated scribed lines along the near edge of the 4′ hitchpin rail and the scribed line marking the original position of the 4′ hitchpins are among the most characteristic features of a Ruckers or Couchet harpsichord soundboard, and are not often found in instruments built outside Antwerp or even in Antwerp in a later period.

Finally, Ruckers soundboards seem always to have been made of spruce (*Picea*). The distinction between spruce and fir (*Abies*) can be made reliably only by microscopic examination of a thin section of the wood, although the pitch pockets characteristic of spruce are often found disguised under parts of the soundboard painting. As spruce was also used by other North European builders during all periods, the fact that a soundboard is of spruce may not in itself authenticate an instrument. But an instrument with a fir soundboard is almost certainly a product of an eighteenth-century French faker's workshop, since many French builders used fir instead of spruce as a soundboard material.

### *Soundboard decoration*

All Ruckers soundboards seem originally to have been painted. As part of his deception, a forger would therefore paint the soundboard with flowers and birds and include the usual scalloped borders and arabesques. Some eighteenth-century counterfeit instruments have very convincing painted soundboards. But most redecorated, reattributed, and even some counterfeit instruments have soundboards which are clearly not decorated in the style of the Ruckers painters. Even the most clever counterfeiter or faker usually made some mistakes of style, of material, or of dating in executing the soundboard decoration.

Clearly the date, signature and style of the painting must all correlate with the facts known about the Ruckers family. Unaware of the family history, the counterfeiter often made mistakes which were not detected at the time, but which are now plainly obvious. For example, the instruments of Hans Ruckers seem to have been most highly regarded in the past. Partly this must have been because Hans was the founding member of the family workshop, partly it must have been because of the sheer number of instruments with HR roses. But we now know that many instruments with HR roses were made by Ioannes Ruckers after Hans' death in 1598, and before Ioannes' court appointment in 1615 when he began using the IR roses. Not knowing this, the counterfeiter often mistakenly signed an instrument with the name of Hans Ruckers or gave it an HR rose, and then dated it long after Hans Ruckers' death and after Ioannes Ruckers ceased using the HR rose.

In theory, a counterfeiter could have made the very obvious mistake of signing an instrument with the name of one member of the Ruckers family and then imitating the soundboard-style of another. Few seem to have fallen into this trap. But there are a number of instruments where the dating, signature and painting style do not match. The '1590b HR' (see p. 278) double-manual harpsichord in the Instrument Museum of the Conservatoire N.S.M., Paris, now known to be by Goujon, is dated within the lifetime of Hans Ruckers, but has a soundboard painting imitative of the style of the late instruments by Andreas Ruckers. The '1644a HR' (see p. 280) double in private ownership in Switzerland is dated forty-six years after Hans Ruckers' death in 1598 and has a soundboard decorated roughly in the style of the early instruments of Ioannes Ruckers.

### *The use and type of the Ruckers roses*

One of the most characteristic features of a Ruckers instrument is the rose. In any authentic instrument the type of rose used (or if the rose is missing, the rose-hole diameter) must correspond to that of its maker and to the period in which the maker was working. This means that the two types of HR rose, one used by Hans, the other by Ioannes until about 1616, must be in instruments with the correct signature and dating. An instrument with an HR rose dated after 1616 is immediately suspect (e.g. '1644a HR' and '1644b HR'; see p. 280). Similarly, the casting of the AR rose changed around 1636 (see p. 161). An AR rose of the later casting in a putative Andreas Ruckers instrument dated before 1636 is also liable to suspicion (e.g. 1622 AR; B, 89, see p. 282). Ioannes Ruckers used three different types of roses after 1616, and each type had a different diameter. One type was used in virginals, another in single-manual harpsichords, and the third in double-manual harpsichords. Because virginals were less valuable in the eighteenth century, it seems that Ioannes (and Andreas) virginals were cannibalized and their roses used in counterfeit and fake instruments. Thus a harpsichord with an IR virginal rose taken from one of the cannibalized instruments is almost certainly not an authentic product of the Ioannes Ruckers workshop (e.g. '1636b IR'; see p. 281). Conversely, few other builders use the large harpsichord roses adopted by Ioannes. If an instrument without a rose appears from its construction and decoration to be by Ioannes Ruckers *and* it has a large rose hole of the correct diameter, it is almost certainly genuine (e.g. 1624 IR, 1637b IR and 1638b IR).

As has already been mentioned, it was a favourite practice among counterfeiters and fakers to attribute instruments to Hans Ruckers. A fake 'Hans Ruckers' harpsichord had to have an HR soundboard rose, and several methods seem to have been used to satisfy this requirement. Sometimes castings of other makers' roses were used in which the initials were changed. The Hans Moermans rose was used in four known fakes ('1658 HR', 'n.d.a HR', '1637 HR', and '1636a IR', see pp. 277, 280, 281 and 280), with the M changed to an R. Another possibility was to alter either the casting, or in some cases even an original AR rose (possibly from a virginal). The two sides of the A were easily cut at the top, spread apart and made parallel, thus converting the A to an H (e.g. '1573 HR'; see p. 277). Similarly, IR rose castings have been made using the pattern of an AR rose and retaining the left-hand part of the initial A but cutting away the top and bottom of the right-hand part of the letter to make it into an I (e.g. '1634 IR'; see p. 281). When looking at a rose to determine whether or not it is genuine, it must be examined in detail. The two HR roses are very similar, and an AR rose altered into an HR rose can at first glance appear quite genuine.

The rose must also fit the hole it is in. If the rose is either too small or too large for the soundboard hole then it is likely that the rose has been fraudulently placed in the instrument (e.g. '1629 IR'; see p. 281). An examination of the back of the rose may also help to decide its authenticity. Every genuine Ruckers rose has four tabs for gluing it onto the soundboard. Some of the early Ioannes

Ruckers HR roses were made from papier mâché instead of lead, but since the mould was the same, this is only discernible from the back surface of the rose. The three types of rose used by Ioannes after 1616 all have a distinctive appearance from the back: the virginal rose is flat except for four ridged lines forming a star-shaped pattern on the back, and the large harpsichord roses are hollowed out at the back instead of being flat (the large Couchet harpsichord roses also exhibit this feature). The HR roses of Hans, the early HR roses of Ioannes, the Andreas roses and the Couchet virginal roses all have a flat rear surface.

A number of authentic instruments are missing roses or have a crude casting of a rose, and a number of unauthentic instruments have genuine Ruckers roses. Whether or not an instrument is genuine can only be established by considering the type and initials of the rose in the context of all the other features of the instrument.

### *The style of the signature*

Closely related to the type and diameter of the rose in the instrument is the signature on the instrument. Typically, a Ruckers instrument is signed simply: 'X . . . S RVCKERS ME FECIT ANTVERPIAE'. I know of no genuine signature which includes the date. The date is always found on the soundboard or wrestplank. Also the word 'Anno' or 'A°' was never used in the signature.

### *Features of case construction and materials*

Most authentic Ruckers instruments, regardless of the extent to which they have been altered, retain most of the case-side material and some of the internal bracing. To be authentic a Ruckers instrument must be constructed of poplar. Needlewoods (fir, pine and spruce) and lime, which is a much denser and more finely grained wood than poplar, were never used for the case sides or internal framing by any of the Ruckers family. Usually the poplar used is a dull creamy colour with reddish-brown or sometimes greyish streaks (*Populus canescens*?).

The length and height of the case sides are also distinguishing features in Ruckers instruments. The virginals are always close to their nominal lengths in Flemish voeten, although a certain amount of variation occurs between spinetts and muselars, and in that of the large mother instruments. Some idea of the limits of the variation in the length of Ruckers virginals is given in the Table 9.1. (The heights given do not include the thickness of the baseboard. When only one value of the height and length is given it means that there is only one known instrument of that type.)

Table 9.1 *Length and height variation of Ruckers virginals in millimetres*

| Type of instrument | Nominal length | Length | Height |
|---|---|---|---|
| 6-voet mother muselar | 1708 | 1706–1786 | 252–254 |
| 6-voet mother spinett | 1708 | 1708 | 254 |
| 6-voet muselar | 1708 | 1668–1712 | 239–243 |
| 5-voet muselar | 1423 | 1424–1500 | 202–205 |
| 4½-voet muselar | 1281 | 1304 | 191 |
| 4½-voet spinett | 1281 | 1282 | 190 |
| 4-voet spinett | 1139 | 1136–1143 | 177–178 |
| child spinett | – | 795–819 | 122–127 |
| 2½-voet spinett | 711 | 711 | –[a] |

[a] This instrument has sloping case sides

Unlike the virginals, the harpsichords do not seem to have been made in lengths which were measured in whole or half units of the Flemish voet. However, most singles are about 6 voet 4 duimen long, and most doubles are about 7 voet 10 duimen in length. The variation is given in Table 9.2 (parenthetical values are unique, but genuine, examples outwith the normal range).

Table 9.2 *Length and height variation of Ruckers harpsichords in millimetres*

| Type of instrument | Length | Height |
|---|---|---|
| Double-manual harpsichord | 2210–2254 (2274) | 252–254 |
| Single-manual harpsichord | 1813–1829 (1864) | 228–232[a] |
| 4-voet single-manual harpsichord | 1232 | 190 |

[a] The single-manual harpsichords painted with the strapwork decoration instead of the more common marbling are 241–242mm high. Also, I have not included the very late single-manual harpsichords of Ioseph Ioannes Couchet, which are much longer and higher than the dimensions given above.

Although there are some exceptions, few virginals deviate more than a few millimetres from the nominal length in voeten, and the variation in the length of the harpsichords is seldom greater than one per cent from the average. Hence, an instrument which has a length or height deviating markedly from the limits given above must be liable to suspicion.

Virginals were seldom faked or falsified, and I know of only two counterfeit virginals. A few typical features follow which can be checked quickly before a detailed examination of the virginal is made. The case corner-joints must be simple mitred joints pegged together, and

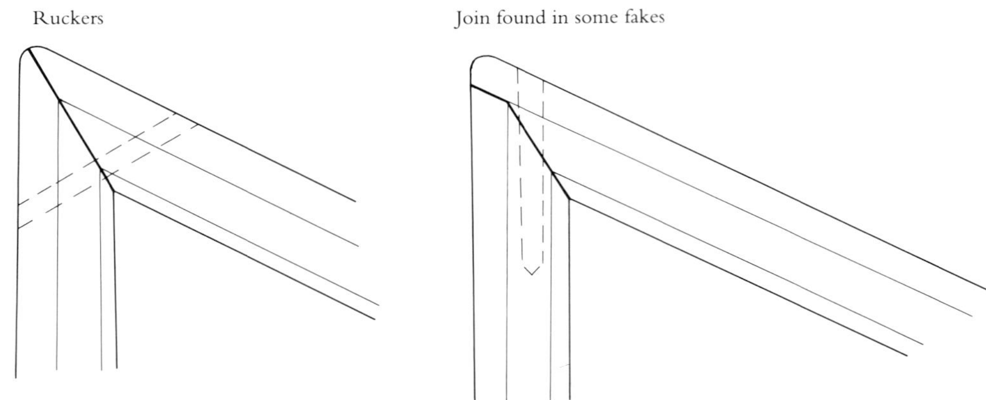


Fig. 9.1 The spine/tail case join. Scale 1:1.

not dovetailed joints. Except for the child virginals, the nameboard is removable to allow access to and removal of the keyboard, rather than having a fixed nameboard and a removable namebatten. There are also no key-blocks beside the keys in a genuine Ruckers virginal – instead, the outside keys are immediately adjacent to the sides of the keywell formed by the two keywell braces. Also, Ruckers virginals have no moulded batten running around the inside of the case above the soundboard (which would be used as a hitchpin rail along the spine and left-hand side of the instrument). The bass strings in the muselar virginals are raised up on a small rectangular block of wood, but other than this there is nothing covering the soundboard near the edge of the case.

In Ruckers harpsichords the case joins are also not dovetailed. The type of join is, however, very characteristic, and will often help to distinguish a genuine instrument from a fake. The spine/tail joint is a simple mitre which is pegged together (see Fig. 9.1).

The tail/bentside and bentside/cheek joins are made as shown in Fig. 9.2. If these joins are simple mitre joints, or if the lapped part of the join is on the wrong case side, then the instrument is almost certainly unauthentic.

Another feature often easily recognized is the way the

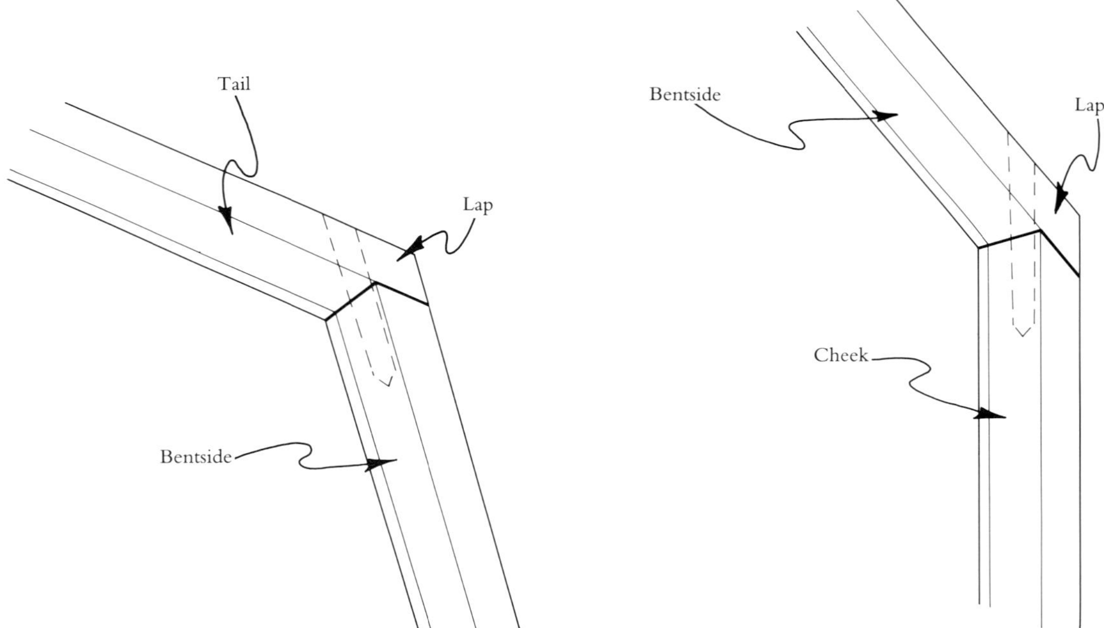


Fig. 9.2 The tail/bentside and the bentside/cheek case joins in authentic Ruckers/Couchet harpsichords. Scale 1:1.

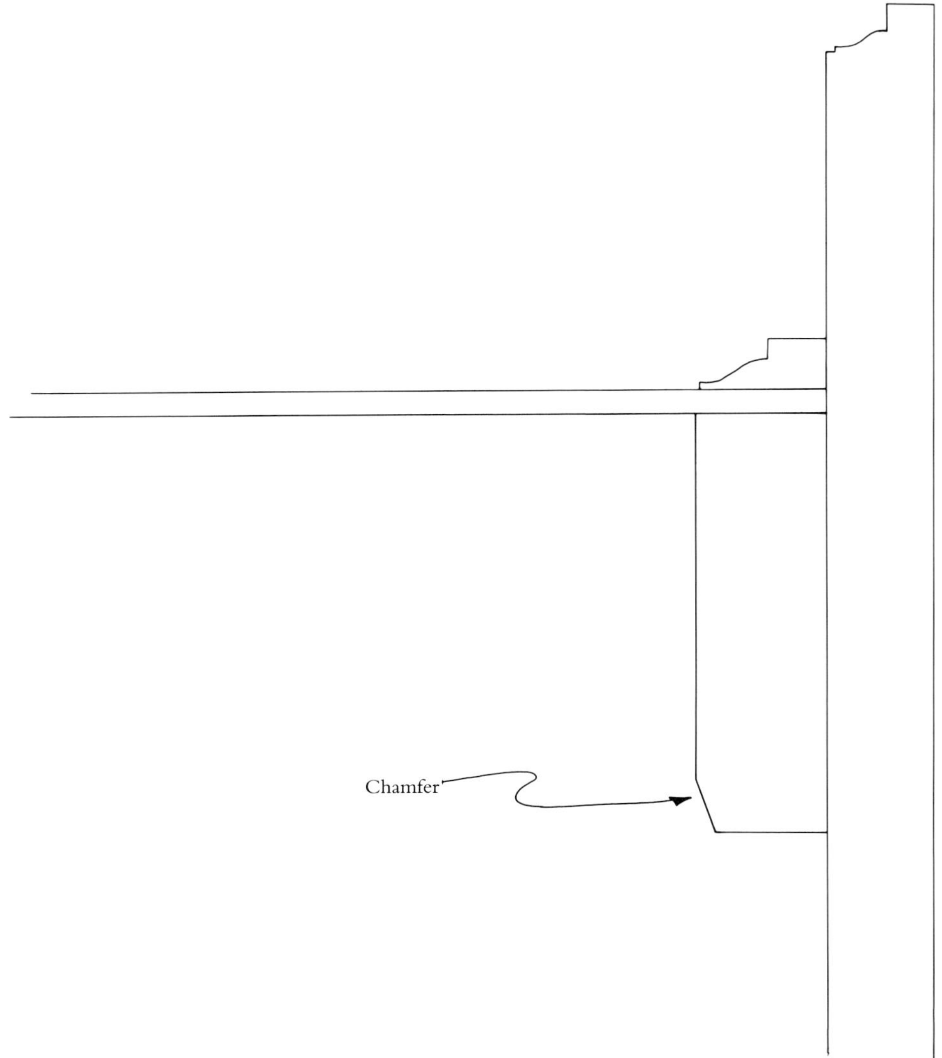


Fig. 9.3 The chamfered soundboard liner in an authentic Ruckers clavecimbel. Scale 1:1.

recesses cut into the spine and cheek for the jackrail are made. In Ruckers instruments the jackrail recess is a simple rectangular slot. In many eighteenth-century instruments the jackrail is mitred into the recess so that the moulding on the case side and jackrail meet at 45°. An instrument with a mitred jackrail recess is therefore liable to suspicion unless the gap and jackrail have been later widened in the process of adding an extra register.

Whether or not the internal framing has disappeared, most instruments will retain the soundboard liners. The dimensions of these liners are not very constant, but they are about 15–20mm thick and 45–65mm high. Usually the tail liner is thicker and higher than the spine or bentside liner. The characteristic feature in Ruckers instruments is that the lower corner of the liner is chamfered, instead of being left as a sharp edge (see Fig. 9.3). This detail is one that even the most fastidious counterfeiter or faker is sure to have overlooked and is very often lacking even on contemporary Flemish instruments falsely attributed to one of the Ruckers (e.g. '1639 A R'; see p. 282).

Besides the chamfering of the soundboard liners, the Ruckers apparently constructed the toolbox in the harpsichords differently from most of the other contemporary Antwerp builders. Ruckers harpsichords have a toolbox on the spine side of the instrument. The lid of the toolbox is cut out of the spine itself and is hinged with wire hinges to the baseboard. The sides of the toolbox are formed by the two baseboard braces which are let into the spine and cheek on either side. The near baseboard brace is just the lower belly rail, against which the keyboard butts and to which are fixed the keyboard hold-down blocks. The rear toolbox brace is the same height as the lower belly rail and runs at a slight angle to it, being further from it at the spine (about 200mm) than at the cheek (about 25mm). If the two toolbox braces were parallel, then the rear one would meet and be let into the bentside, and only the near one (the lower belly rail) would be let into the cheek; angling them ensures that both are let into the cheek-piece. Other seventeenth-century Flemish makers, if they include a toolbox in the construction, usually have toolbox braces that are parallel so that one brace is let into the cheek and one into the bentside at the right. But some Flemish makers simply did not build a toolbox, even though the two 'toolbox' braces, either angled or parallel, may exist. If there is no sign of the former existence of a toolbox flap on the spine, or if the toolbox braces are parallel instead of being slightly angled, the instrument displaying these features is almost certainly not by one of the Ruckers or Couchets.

## DIFFERENCES IN THE CONSTRUCTION METHODS AMONG THE VARIOUS MEMBERS OF THE RUCKERS FAMILY

Considering the long period in which the Ruckers worked – from 1579 for Hans Ruckers, until before 1706 for Ioseph Ioannes Couchet – and considering the fact that at least six different makers were involved, the standardization of the product of their workshops is remarkable. The earliest virginals and the latest harpsichords are slightly different in detail from the rest of the instruments built in this period, but otherwise the instruments are so similar in construction that it would be very difficult to tell which member of the family built a given instrument were it not for the signature, rose and decoration.

The differences in the construction of the virginals between the various members of the family seem to be almost non-existent. I have in fact found only one difference which might help to distinguish which maker built a given virginal, although even this is not universal. The width of the keywell varies slightly in Hans and Ioannes virginals from that in Andreas I and II virginals. In Hans and Ioannes Ruckers virginals the original width of the keywell varies from 645mm to 648mm, and in Andreas Ruckers instruments from 650mm to 652mm. Early and late virginals can be distinguished even if the signature, rose and soundboard decoration have disappeared. Before about 1627 the soundboards would have scribed circles used as a guide in painting the wreath and the red and white rope pattern around the rose. In virginals built after about 1627 these circles were not scribed on the soundboard. Unfortunately the presence or absence of these scribed circles around the rose cannot be used to distinguish Andreas from Ioannes Ruckers virginals, since the decorators working in the two workshops changed the style of painting the wreath at almost the same time (in fact it seems likely that entirely new decorators started working in both workshops at about this time).

Fortunately there are a few more differences between the harpsichords built by Andreas and those of Ioannes Ruckers. Most of these are minor differences and have no bearing on the musical qualities of the instruments. However, although I have not had the opportunity of checking this for a large number of instruments, there does seem to be a major difference in the way the two Ruckers decided upon the thickness of their harpsichord soundboards. Ioannes Ruckers seems to have tapered his soundboards from 4.3mm or more under the tenor part of the 8′ bridge to less than 2mm in the extreme treble. Andreas Ruckers harpsichords on the other hand have soundboards tapered from about 3.8mm in the tenor to about 2.2mm in the treble. This may mean that, being stiffer in the treble, the Andreas Ruckers harpsichords sustain longer and have slightly less attack there. In the bass the extra stiffness of the Ioannes Ruckers soundboards would sustain better and in addition would tend to reinforce the higher harmonics of the strings, increasing slightly the clarity and brilliance in this region of the compass.

The cross-sectional shape of the 4′ hitchpin rail is also slightly different in Ioannes and Andreas Ruckers harpsichords, and this is especially noticeable in the treble. The hitchpin rails in Ioannes Ruckers harpsichords have a distinctly rectangular cross-section in the treble, with one of the shorter faces of the rectangle glued to the soundboard; in Andreas harpsichords the treble section of the 4′ hitchpin rail is almost square (see Fig. 9.4).

In addition there are two minor features which distinguish the late (i.e. post-*c.* 1625) harpsichords of Ioannes and Andreas Ruckers and which are readily visible and measurable from the outside of the instrument. First, the moulding on the soundboard liner/8′ hitchpin rail is different for the two builders, as indicated in Fig. 9.5. Secondly, the harpsichords made after about 1616 have different-sized soundboard rose holes. In Andreas Ruckers harpsichords these are about 65mm in diameter; in Ioannes Ruckers harpsichords the rose hole has a diameter of about 73mm in single- and about 85mm

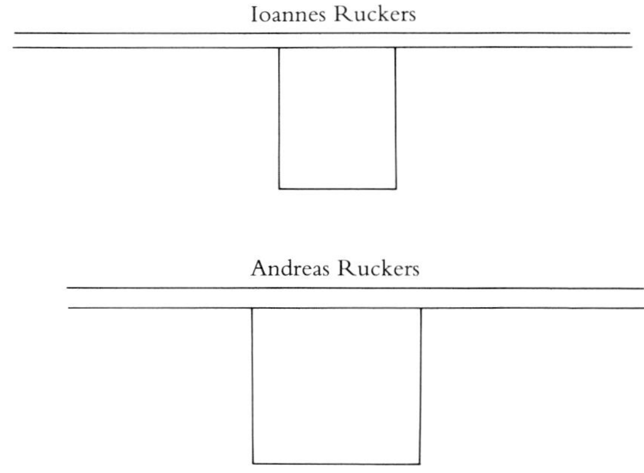


Fig. 9.4 Comparison of the treble section of the 4′ hitchpin rail in Ioannes and Andreas Ruckers harpsichords. Scale 1:1.

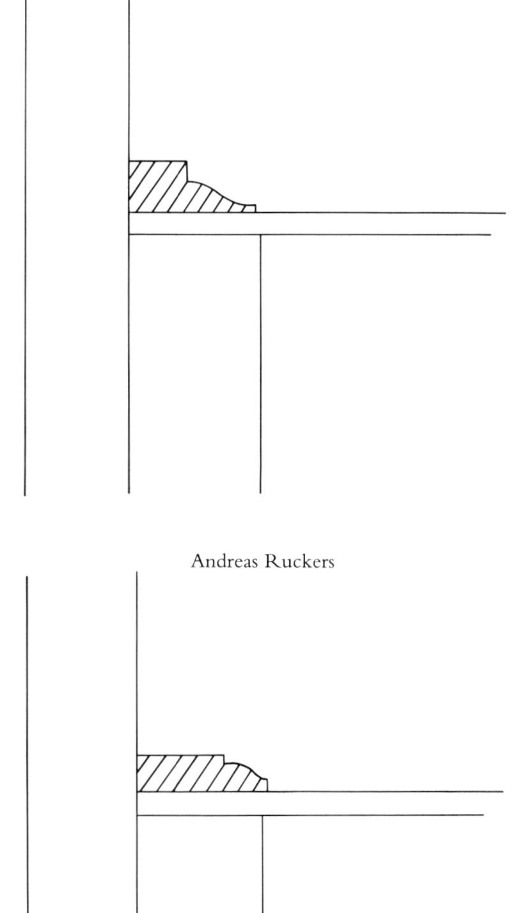


Fig. 9.5 Comparison of the soundboard-liner moulding profile in the post-*c.* 1625 harpsichords of Ioannes and Andreas Ruckers. Scale 1:1.

in double-manual harpsichords. Unfortunately, the two builders used the same soundboard-liner mouldings and rose-hole diameters in their earlier instruments.

## RUCKERS INSTRUMENTS IN PAINTINGS

Harpsichords and virginals are often depicted in Flemish paintings of the late sixteenth and seventeenth centuries. Like the fine interiors of the houses and the elegant furniture they contained, the paintings, rugs, magnificent costumes and musical instruments were all symbols of the increasing wealth of their middle-class owners, who naturally enjoyed being painted with their finery surrounding them. Brueghel, Steen, Terborch, Cornelius de Vos, Catharina de Hemessen, Metsu, Teniers, Frans Floris, Gonzales Cocques, Vermeer, van Kessel, de Zeeuw, and David Ryckaert all painted genre scenes which include either a Flemish harpsichord or virginal. The question is: are the instruments depicted by one of the Ruckers family?

The answer to this cannot, of course, be definitive, since usually neither the signature nor the rose is depicted in the painting. But usually there are a few details of construction and decoration on which to base a decision. However, one is relying on the artist involved to have been accurate in his depiction of the instrument and not to have exercised artistic licence to improve its appearance or to alter its proportions to give a more pleasing balance to the canvas. Most often it is clear that the instrument is *not* by one of the Ruckers.

One of the most obvious construction features of a harpsichord visible on a painting is the lid. If the lid is only in one long section, without the usual break between the lid flap and main lid, then the instrument portrayed is probably not a Ruckers (although Ioseph Ioannes Couchet made the lids for his harpsichords in one piece). All extant Ruckers harpsichords with their original lids are made with the lid hinged near the position of the far edge of the jackrail into two separate sections. If the instrument depicted is a double-manual harpsichord, then the inside of the lid flap should have a wide picture frame of black and yellow varnished wood, since all genuine Ruckers doubles with original lids seem to have this type of lid-flap construction. Also, the lid-stick was not used on seventeenth-century Flemish harpsichords. Either the lid was held open with a cord, or the instrument was placed near a wall against which the lid was leaned.

Other than the hinging of the lid in two sections, few other construction details are normally visible in a painting. Sometimes the keyblocks (and their decoration), key arcades, jackrail, protruding registers, and the nuts and tuning pins are visible in the painting, and details of these will have to be compared with Ruckers' normal practice before it can be suggested that the instrument might have come from the workshop of one of the Ruckers family.

Details of the decoration may also give a clue as to whether the instrument is a Ruckers or not. The marbling of the exterior of the case on the harpsichords should be continuous across the case joins around the instrument. If the marbling is done in panels with vertical borders running up and down the case sides at the joints, then the harpsichord should probably not be attributed to any of the Ruckers. Sometimes the strapwork decoration, with the large semi-precious stones held against a marbled background by iron straps, is depicted instead of the more simple marbled decoration. Details of this decoration must be compared with that usually found on Ruckers instruments (see Chapter 7, pp. 167–8) before attributing the harpsichord to the Ruckers. Since all Ruckers virginals seem to have originally had the speckled off-white-on-green porphyry *faux-marbre*, the depiction of a Ruckers virginal should also have this sort of decoration. On the other hand, I know of no seventeenth-century Flemish (or other) genre paintings of virginals which actually show a green porphyry outer decoration.

Usually the printed papers (which are sometimes identifiable as one of the patterns used by the Ruckers), the case mouldings, the hinged keywell flap, etc. are visible in the painting. These must of course all be in the usual style of the Ruckers. If the lid is papered, then there should be the usual border of varnished wood with a black band surrounding the outer printed strip pattern.

Plate 9.2 shows an instrument in a painting by Jan Brueghel which is probably by one of the Ruckers. The lid is hinged along a line just behind the jackrail, and the lid flap is framed by a wide moulding with the usual black ink and varnished wood decoration. The marbling on the outside of the case is continuous around it and not in panels. The instrument is obviously a transposing harpsichord: the block of wood in the bass of the upper manual next to the C/E short octave is clearly visible. The upper-manual keyblock has roughly the same curved shape as in the usual Ruckers double, and it is also plainly decorated with varnish only. The lower manual has key fronts decorated with white and red Gothic arcades; the artist seems to have forgotten to paint these in on the upper manual. The papers on the batten above the lower manual and the keywell paper are clearly identifiable as Type 17 and Type 12 respectively, and the soundwell paper and the border paper of the keywell flap may be Type 6. The motto on the keywell flap must be [ACTA VIRVM PROB] ANT, which is a motto often found in this location on Ruckers instruments. The mouldings on the case sides and jackrail are of varnished wood, and the arcaded stand (more of which is visible in the whole painting) is typical of those found under some Ruckers instruments. The line of the 4′ tuning pins is visible and even the soft leather buff pads of the buff register can be seen behind the 8′ bridge! So many of the details are correct that it seems very likely that a Ruckers instrument was used as a model by Brueghel – the style of the marbling (like the 1615 A R) and the choice of the papers make it most likely to be by Andreas Ruckers.

## THE VALUE AND IMPORTANCE OF FAKE AND COUNTERFEIT RUCKERS INSTRUMENTS

Although a large proportion of those instruments bearing the name Ruckers is not genuine, virtually none of these unauthentic instruments is without its interest or historical value. Despite the hiatus in musical interest in the harpsichord, which lasted most of the nineteenth century, Ruckers seems to have been known among the collectors and musical historians as one of the great names in the harpsichord world. This had the fortunate result that far more instruments signed with the name Ruckers survived than would otherwise have been the case. But until recently both the genuine and unauthentic instruments were accepted, usually without question, as having originated in the Ruckers workshops. This group of instruments, seen as a whole, exhibited such a variety of types and sizes, with many different compasses, dispositions, types of decoration, etc. that no one questioned their authenticity or found the odd deviant instrument suspect. Had it not been for their Ruckers signature and the inability of the owner to distinguish the genuine from the fake, the non-Ruckers instruments would have been destroyed or lost along with the other instruments of their type. Because of this they are often extremely rare or even unique examples.

Unfortunately, however, there is a popular misconception that because an instrument is a fake or counterfeit Ruckers it is worthless and to be ignored. It is true that a counterfeit banknote does not have the same attraction that a genuine note does, and that a violin labelled Stradi-

Plate 9.2 Detail of a painting 'The Allegory of Hearing' by Jan Brueghel, showing the keyboard of a non-aligned double-manual harpsichord. Both keyboards begin with a C/E short octave, so this instrument is clearly the normal model of double, and not the 'French' model. Many details indicate that the instrument depicted is by one of the Ruckers, perhaps Andreas the Elder. Copyright A.C.L., Brussels.

varius is open to immediate suspicion and is probably not even an Amati or a Klotz which has been falsified by adding a Stradivarius inscription. The same is not true of an unauthentic 'Ruckers' instrument. Even if it is down-graded into being simply anonymous, and in the style of a particular builder or school, its historical and musical value is often greater than it would be if genuine. And its monetary value should therefore be at least as great as if by one of the Ruckers family.

For example, few Flemish virginals exist by any of the Ruckers' contemporaries; only instruments by van der Biest, Bos, Grouwels and Bader survive. But two fake Ruckers virginals, the '1610 HR' in Halle (see p. 278) and the '1620 HR' in Lisbon (see p. 278) are certainly both Flemish, but not by Ruckers. As one of the few instruments which was originally a double virginal, the '1620 HR' in Lisbon is of particular interest and is an especially fine example of its type. Few Flemish harpsichords exist which are contemporary with, but not actually by, one of the Ruckers. But two unauthentic singles, the '1629 IR' in Antwerp (see p. 281), originally with the very wide compass of $G_1$ to $e^3$, and the '1639 AR' in Brussels (see p. 282), give a good idea of the original construction practice of two non-Ruckers singles. Also, three Flemish doubles, the three-slide transposing harpsichord in Brussels (see p. 29), the 16′ transposing harpsichord ('n.d.a HR') also in Brussels (see p. 277 and Chapter 2, p. 32) and the aligned double '1658 HR' (see p. 280) in Nuremberg, are examples of unusual Flemish construction which would almost certainly not have survived had they not all been falsified Ruckers. They are all unique examples of types of instruments which were probably once relatively common and about which we would otherwise be totally ignorant.

Two counterfeit instruments, the '1634 IR' double in Ham House, London (see p. 281) and the '1646 AR' single (see p. 283) (and possibly the anonymous '1623' double owned by Michael Thomas), are by the same builder and were probably constructed about 1700–20 in England. English harpsichords of any sort from this period are very rare, and doubles are particularly unusual. These instruments are therefore especially interesting examples of their type, which do not otherwise exist.

Another benefit we receive as a result of the high survival rate of unauthentic Ruckers instruments is that

Plate 9.3 Plan view of the '1634 IR' (B. 54) English double-manual harpsichord. The shape of the case and the layout of the bridges and 4′ hitchpin rail is notably different from that of Ruckers. Scale 1:10.

the work of some builders is now more common through their fake and counterfeit instruments than through their own signed instruments. For example, only two instruments (both spinets) signed by Jean Claude Goujon exist. However, at least three harpsichords, all attributed to Ruckers, are by Goujon: the 1732 '1615 HR' (p. 278), the 1749 '1590b HR' (p. 278), and the 1757 '1632a IR' (p. 281). These instruments, plus the two genuine Ruckers ravalé by Goujon, the 1632 IR ravalé in 1745, and the 1627c IR ravalé in 1753, all greatly increase our knowledge of Goujon's work and establish him as one of the great French eighteenth-century harpsichord builders.

But probably the greatest benefit we receive from the survival of forged Ruckers instruments is a heritage of outstanding musical instruments. The '1590 HR' Goujon double mentioned above is now recognized as one of the finest eighteenth-century French harpsichords. Another French instrument, the '1636b IR' (see p. 281), is an excellent harpsichord of 1766 by Guillaume Hemsch, brother to the better-known Henri. The '1634 IR' (see p. 281) double by an anonymous English builder is not only interesting as an example of early eighteenth-century English counterfeiting practice, but is also, more importantly, a very fine musical instrument. The '1644a HR' (see p. 280) anonymous French double-manual harpsichord has one of the best sounds I have ever heard. Such instruments are not to be disregarded as mere forgeries; they are extremely interesting and valuable instruments in their own right.

CHAPTER TEN

# The influence of the Ruckers/Couchet tradition on later harpsichord building practice

Keyboard-instrument making in Antwerp seems to have evolved very little during the period of the Ruckers family, with virtually no development or innovation from 1579 to the middle of the seventeenth century. With extremely few exceptions, the virginals and single-manual harpsichords had the compass C/E to $c^3$. Almost all double-manual harpsichords had a C/E to $c^3$ upper-manual and a C/E to $f^3$ lower-manual compass. Any exceptions to these were either the early virginals, with a C/E to $a^2$ compass, or the models with larger compasses apparently made for export: the chromatic C to $c^3$ singles for England, and the chromatic $G_1$ to $c^3$/F to $f^3$ doubles for France.

Not only did the compasses remain the same throughout these seventy-odd years, but also the disposition of the instruments never altered. Most of the virginals built were single virginals, which perforce had only one set of strings. Among these the smaller virginals, which to the modern musician seem especially restricting because of their high pitch and tessitura, were produced in considerably larger numbers than the big 6-voet virginals at a pitch R. Even the mother-and-child virginals, which might be thought more versatile and expressive, seem to have been produced at a rate which remained constant during this entire period. Thus the greater potential of the two manuals of the coupled mother and child does not seem to have been exploited, or at least there was apparently no increase in the musical demand for this variety and contrast.

Similarly, the harpsichord disposition did not change during this period. All harpsichords signed by the Ruckers appear originally to have had the disposition 1 × 8′, 1 × 4′ and not a single contrasting double-manual harpsichord with aligned keyboards seems to have been built by the Ruckers (see p. 181).

The conservatism, both of the building practices of the Ruckers and of the contemporary music, which is implied by these conclusions is rather surprising, since at least some change would be expected during a period of seventy years. Ripin[1] has suggested from iconographical evidence that three-register and aligned doubles were built in Flanders. But if the illustrations he cites can be relied upon for details of compass and number of registers, they must be assumed to be accurate in other details as well. If so, then none of the illustrations is of a Ruckers instrument, since all depict features uncharacteristic of Ruckers' usual practice of construction and decoration (see Chapter 9, p. 191). Although other Flemish builders may have experimented with ways to alter or increase the musical potential of their instruments, this does not seem to be true for the surviving instruments of Hans, Ioannes and Andreas Ruckers.

## IOANNES COUCHET AND THE BEGINNING OF CHANGE

The Couchets, either because they possessed a natural flair for innovation or because they were under pressure from changing musical requirements and taste, broke away from the conservative tradition followed by the Ruckers. That is not to say that the materials or methods of construction used in their instruments were different; in this respect the tradition is continuous and unbroken. Although Couchet instruments clearly belong to the Ruckers school from their outward physical appearance

[1] Edwin M. Ripin, 'The two-manual harpsichord in Flanders before 1650', *The Galpin Society Journal*, XXI (1968), 33–9.

and the methods used in their construction, they practically all exhibit a greater musical potential than the earlier Ruckers instruments.

The last two double-manual harpsichords built in the Ruckers tradition were both built in 1646, a date which marks the end of the epoch in which harpsichords with unaligned keyboards were made. One of these doubles was made by Andreas Ruckers (1646b AR), originally with keyboards having chromatic compasses from F and $G_1$ (see p. 180). Although few examples of this type of large double were made, the construction of this harpsichord cannot be considered a new development, since a similar type of harpsichord existed as early as 1616 (1616 HR). However, the second double, made by Ioannes Couchet (1646 IC), is unusual in having two fifty-note keyboards, the upper manual with a compass of $G_1/B_1$ to $c^3$, the bottom manual a fourth lower with the normal C/E to $f^3$ compass. Couchet is therefore the first person known to have used the $G_1/B_1$ short octave. The 1646 Couchet instrument is also unusual in being a semitone above R, a pitch not found originally in any other Ruckers/Couchet instrument (see p. 271).

The last two Ioannes Couchet harpsichords also introduce new musical possibilities not found in earlier Flemish instruments. Both of these instruments, although originally singles, have since been converted into double-manual harpsichords. One, built about 1650 ((*c.* 1650)b IC), originally had a compass of $F_1$, $G_1$, $A_1$ to $c^3$ and was at a pitch R + 2. Although it had the conventional 1 × 8′, 1 × 4′ disposition, the compass extending down to $F_1$ was very advanced for this period and remained the standard bass compass in most of Europe for the next 150 years.

The second and latest surviving Ioannes Couchet instrument shows even more innovation. This harpsichord (1652 IC) was built originally *without* a 4′ and had a 2 × 8′ disposition. More surprisingly, it had three registers probably arranged as follows:

→ 8′
← 8′
→ 8′

Furthermore, these three registers seem to have been operated by some sort of trapwork connected to pedals or perhaps a genouillère. This is also the first single-manual harpsichord known to have been designed with a bass $G_1/B_1$ short octave.

Documentary evidence relating to these two instruments throws an interesting light on the activity of Couchet (see Appendix 17 and Appendix 18). These are letters written in the spring and summer of 1648 between G. F. Duarte and Constantijn Huygens and between Couchet himself and Huygens. The earlier letters are those from Duarte. From these we learn that Huygens has asked for a 'large harpsichord with one full keyboard down to the octave of G sol re ut [$G_1$]'. Duarte informs Huygens that Couchet could build a harpsichord with three registers disposed 2 × 8′, 1 × 4′ and at a pitch he calls 'Corista' (i.e. at a pitch R). The idea of having two sets of 8′ strings was clearly novel at this time, and the potential for combining the different registers, or using them alone, was realized. The instrument finally built for Huygens had 'a full keyboard down to the octave of ef fa ut [$F_1$] and up to the cadence of the la sol re [$d^3$]'; 'full keyboard' presumably means from $F_1$ chromatic, so that the notes $F^\sharp_1$ and $G^\sharp_1$ may not have been missing as in the (*c.* 1650)b IC harpsichord.

From Couchet's letter it is apparent that the harpsichord was disposed 2 × 8′, notwithstanding Couchet's personal preference for the old 1 × 8′, 1 × 4′ disposition. Although the instrument built for Huygens was at a pitch R (Corista), Couchet also mentions building harpsichords a tone higher (i.e. at R + 2), and nothing further is said of the 2 × 8′, 1 × 4′ disposition mentioned by Duarte. Thus the pitch of the (*c.* 1650)b IC harpsichord at R + 2 is not surprising and might be expected in this and other harpsichords built by Couchet and his sons. Couchet also wisely provided some sort of pitch pipe tuned to a *g*.

## THE COUCHET SONS AND THE DEVELOPING TRADITION

Four of Ioannes Couchet's sons, Ioannes II, Petrus Ioannes, Ioseph Ioannes and Abraham, worked as harpsichord builders. Although Petrus Ioannes began an apprenticeship with Hagaerts, he was released after only a year (see Chapter 1, p. 11) and no harpsichord by him is known to exist[2]. Neither are there surviving instruments

[2] A harpsichord with the signature Petrus Ioannes Couchet and dated 1669 exists in the Gemeentemuseum, The Hague ('1669 IC'; see p. 283). It has an IC virginal rose in the soundboard, and the signature is on a namebatten which, because it fits the later altered width of the instrument, is not original. The authorship of this harpsichord is therefore in doubt. Although the tradition of using a different type of rose in virginals, single-manual and double-manual harpsichords seems to have ended with Ioannes Couchet, it is possible that both the rose and signature were added to this instrument in a later period. In any case, the instrument is built in a style that is quite atypical of the usual Ruckers/Couchet practice. The decoration, soundboard-construction marks, three-octave span of the keyboards and strings, the materials, and the mouldings are all different from those used by the Ruckers and the rest of the Couchet family. I have therefore not included it among those which clearly belong to that tradition. This instrument is, however, similar in many respects to those of Joris

signed by Abraham Couchet, but several harpsichords either signed by or attributable to Ioannes II or Ioseph Ioannes Couchet exist. These exhibit features which clearly show the desire on the part of builders in the second half of the seventeenth century to satisfy the changing musical tastes. The 1671/73 I C harpsichord has been so drastically altered that its original compass cannot easily be determined, but there is no doubt that it originally was disposed 2 × 8′. It was almost certainly at a pitch of either R or R + 2, but this cannot now be determined. Nevertheless, this harpsichord gives evidence of a new preference for a disposition with two sets of 8′ strings rather than the traditional 1 × 8′, 1 × 4′.

The 1679 I C harpsichord in the Smithsonian Museum, Washington, signed by Ioseph Ioannes is preserved in its original musical state. Its compass of C to $c^3$ chromatic must be considered conservative for this date, considering the large compass of some of the instruments built by Ioseph's father some thirty years earlier. Like the 1652 I C, it has three registers, but it has the disposition 1 × 8′, 1 × 4′. There are two 8′ registers of jacks both plucking the same set of strings, and separated by the 4′ register to give the maximum possible tonal difference between them:

→ 8′
← 4′
→ 8′

The 1652 I C harpsichord did not have registers projecting through the cheek, and this along with other evidence (see Catalogue, p. 273) suggests that the registration was originally changed with some sort of a machine. Although the 1679 I C has three registers, they do project through the cheek and there is no evidence that it had a machine stop. However, the two rows of 8′ jacks placed on either side of the 4′ row give clear evidence of the new desire for tonal contrast and variety, just as the machine stop does in the earlier 1652 instrument.

Two further instruments, probably also by Ioseph Ioannes Couchet, show a desire more for an increased range than for tonal diversity. The 1680 I C harpsichord had an original compass with thirty-four naturals from $F_1$ to $d^3$, probably like that described by Ioannes Couchet and Duarte (see Appendix 17 and Appendix 18) with 'a full keyboard' down to $F_1$. The pitch of the instrument, also like that made for Huygens, was at R or Corista pitch.

The large undated Couchet harpsichord in Stockholm (n.d. I C) is probably the last surviving instrument built in the Ruckers/Couchet tradition. Besides being extremely long (as a single it was originally about 2630mm, and so considerably longer than a double-manual Dulcken!), it originally had the very large compass $F_1$ to $d^3$, $e^3$. This compass (with $e^{\flat 3}$) is greater than that found on English instruments of the 1720s and was still being used by Blanchet in the 1730s. The reason for designing such a long instrument is not clear. The (*c.* 1650)b I C and the 1680 I C harpsichords, which also originally went down to $F_1$, are slightly longer than those which went down to $G_1$, but there is no precedent for the length of this unusual harpsichord. At a pitch of R + 2, the bass strings are so long that only the 8′ note $F_1$ could be strung in red brass. If red brass strings were used any higher they would break. Was the instrument therefore designed specifically to have scalings suitable for stringing only in yellow brass right down to the lowest note? Such a possibility suggests that the Couchets were involved in

Plate 10.1 Three-quarter view of the n.d. I C harpsichord. The width of the instrument has never been changed, but the keywell has been lengthened in 1768 by Pascal Taskin to make room for a second keyboard. By permission of Stiftelsen Musikkulturens främjande, Stockholm.

Britsen. The relationship between the Couchet sons and Britsen suggested by Dr Lambrechts-Douillez ('Aperçu historique sur la facture de clavecin à Anvers aux XVI^e^ et XVII^e^ siècles', *La facture de clavecin du XV^e^ au XVIII^e^ siècle* (Louvain-la-Neuve, 1980), 65–6) might be proven if the instrument *were* by Petrus Ioannes Couchet, and a definite link in the building practices of the two could be found.

experiments not only with registration and compass but also with stringing and scalings.

It seems unlikely that only one instrument of this type was built. It also seems clear that the Stockholm Couchet is the prototype for the later eighteenth-century instruments made by Dulcken (although in fact it is even longer and uses longer bass scalings than Dulcken). Thus, the length of Dulcken's harpsichords, which exceeds that of contemporary instruments in France, Germany and England, is not so much an innovation as the continuation of Couchet's practice some sixty to seventy years earlier.

## THE RUCKERS TRADITION IN ENGLAND IN THE EIGHTEENTH CENTURY

It is known that Ioseph Ioannes Couchet died in 1706. But although none of the other members of the Ruckers/Couchet family carried on building clavecimbels into the eighteenth century, the tradition was carried on after their demise.

James Shudi Broadwood, writing in 1838, says that Hermann Tabel brought the Ruckers/Couchet tradition with him from Antwerp to England. Tabel was born in the Low Countries and, according to several sources,[3] worked with the successors of the Ruckers in Antwerp, i.e. with the Couchets. After working for and learning harpsichord building with them, Tabel moved to London in the early years of the eighteenth century (before 1716). There he set up his own workshop and began building and selling harpsichords for the English market.

Unfortunately only one instrument by Tabel survives (for a complete description see Mould, footnote 3), This is a double-manual harpsichord dated 1721 in the County Museum, Warwick. Although it resembles later harpsichords by Shudi, Kirkman and other English eighteenth-century builders, the influence of the Ruckers/Couchet tradition is strong. Unlike the short-scaled, thin-cased instruments by such contemporary builders as Barton and Hancock, who seem to have been influenced by the earlier English virginal-building tradition, the Tabel has thick case sides and long treble scalings suitable for iron stringing. The bridges, although not tapered in thickness as much as in Ruckers instruments, have the usual Ruckers cross-section. Unfortunately the interior is inaccessible and cannot be examined, so the internal framing and soundboard barring cannot be compared with Ruckers normal practice. However, from the fact that Tabel's pupils Shudi and Kirkman used the same style of soundboard barring as Ruckers, it seems likely the Tabel soundboard is also similarly barred. The disposition with $2 \times 8'$, $1 \times 4'$, a dogleg coupler and a lute stop is typical of both earlier and contemporary English harpsichords. However, although the English influence is also apparent in such details as the veneered case, the turned stand and the brass hinges, the influence of the Flemish tradition on scalings, bridge shape and dimensions and soundboard layout is very strong indeed.

In 1718 Burkat Shudi came from the canton of Glarus in Switzerland to London, to work there with Tabel and to learn harpsichord construction from him. Shudi became Tabel's foreman and then, sometime before 1729, began making his own instruments independently of Tabel. In turn, John Broadwood of Cockburnspath in Scotland came to work in Shudi's shop in 1761, and after marrying Shudi's daughter Barbara in 1769, he was taken into partnership with Shudi's son Burkat the Younger. In 1782 Broadwood took over direction of the firm and in 1795 took his son into partnership with him. And thus began the firm of John Broadwood and Sons. This firm, still in business making pianos, can thus trace its origins back to the Couchets and Ruckers, and to the roots of the Flemish clavecimbel tradition.

Shortly after Shudi left Tabel's workshop, Jacob Kirkman, an immigrant from the Alsace, came to work with Tabel, and also eventually became his foreman. After Tabel's death in 1738, Kirkman married Tabel's widow and took over the workshop under his own name. Kirkman carried on building harpsichords and, like the Shudi/Broadwood firm, began building pianos at the end of the eighteenth century. As a piano-building firm they only ceased production in the 1960s.

Kirkman was a prolific builder of harpsichords. Today three times as many Kirkmans as Shudis survive. Assuming the survival rate of instruments by Kirkman and Shudi is the same (about forty per cent), Kirkman must have built about 4,000 instruments, averaging about eighty instruments per year in the 1780s. This rate of production, consisting almost entirely of harpsichords, is twice the annual rate of each of the Ruckers workshops, whose output consisted of both harpsichords and the smaller, less time-consuming virginals. Thus a vast number of harpsichord were built in eighteenth-century England in the Ruckers style, even if one considers only the Shudi and Kirkman workshops. But Hitchcock, Mahoon, Coston, Wilbrook, Crang, Longman and Broderip, etc. were also all building instruments in the Ruckers tradition in the same period.

[3] James S. Broadwood, *Some Notes Made by J. S. Broadwood in 1838, with Observations by H. P. Broadwood, 1862* (London, 1862); W. Dale, *Tschudi: The Harpsichord Maker* (London, 1913; reprint, Boston, Mass., 1978), 21; C. M. Mould, 'The Tabel harpsichord', *Keyboard Instruments: Studies in Keyboard Organology*, ed. Edwin M. Ripin (Edinburgh, 1971), 57.

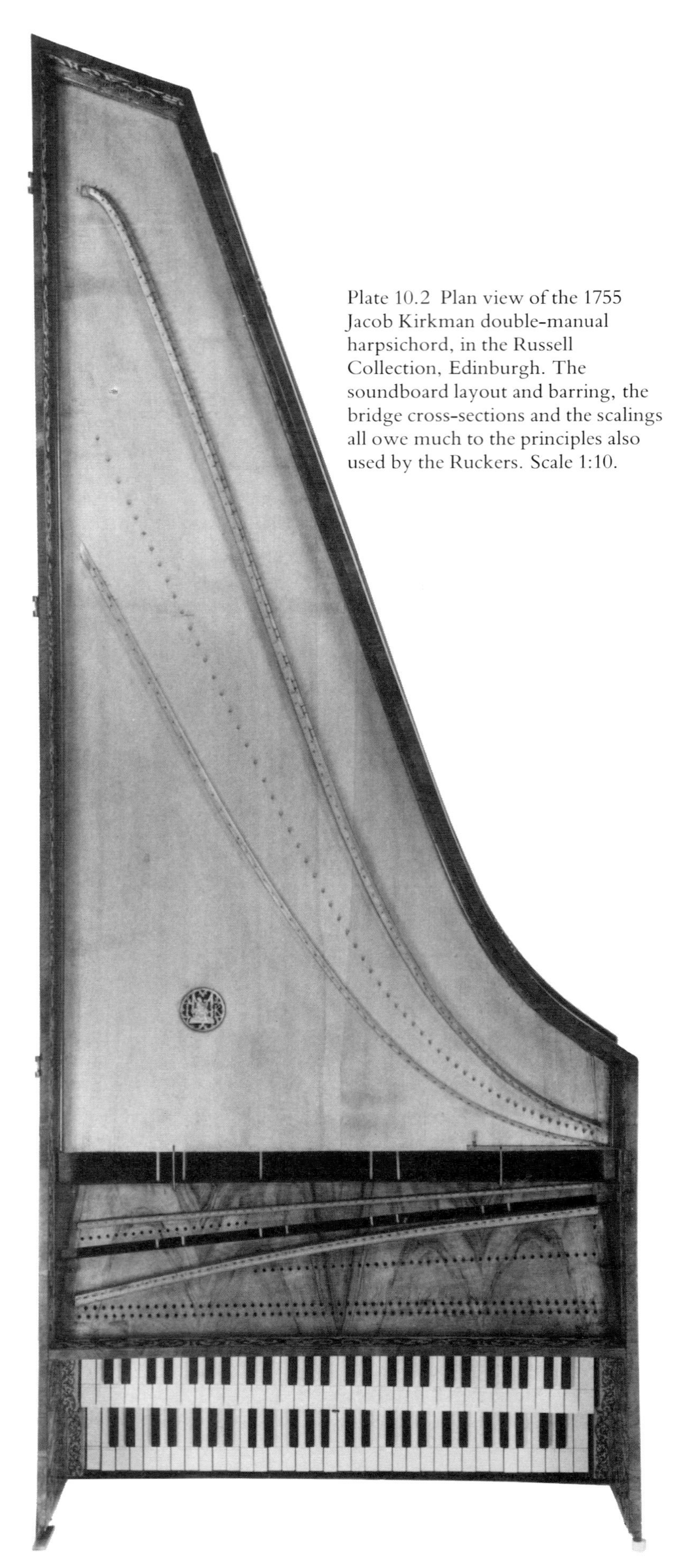

Plate 10.2 Plan view of the 1755 Jacob Kirkman double-manual harpsichord, in the Russell Collection, Edinburgh. The soundboard layout and barring, the bridge cross-sections and the scalings all owe much to the principles also used by the Ruckers. Scale 1:10.

The Ruckers style of construction influenced harpsichord building in England in two ways. A large number of instruments actually built by the Ruckers survived into the eighteenth century; among their owners were Handel, Queen Charlotte and numerous other artists and members of the aristocracy. Because of the beauty of their sound, Ruckers instruments were used as models for the native instruments by the English builders. But also, as explained above, there was a direct master–apprentice succession involving the two most important English builders, Shudi and Kirkman, which went back to the origins of the Flemish tradition.

### THE RUCKERS TRADITION IN EIGHTEENTH-CENTURY FRANCE

The appreciation of the Ruckers style of instrument building seems to have developed rather differently in France. There was no known master–apprentice relationship between any of the French eighteenth-century builders and the Ruckers family. The French harpsichord makers seemed to have absorbed the Ruckers style of building directly from the Flemish instruments imported into France. Much of the activity of the eighteenth-century French makers went into the rebuilding or ravalement of old Flemish instruments, and also into the faking or counterfeiting of instruments. Such activity could not have taken place without understanding the Ruckers style of building before incorporating it into the local tradition. This style is the dominant influence in the construction practice of virtually all of the eighteenth-century French builders.

Because of the lack of extant instruments to study, not a great deal is known about seventeenth-century French harpsichord building, and of course even less is known about that of the previous centuries. However, the few seventeenth-century French harpsichords that survive by Desruisseaux, Tibaut, Vaudry, etc. have a number of features in common. The cases are often made partly of walnut, or walnut is used inside the instrument to line the keywell and ornament the soundwell. The case sides, bridge sections and framing are usually lighter than those found in Flemish (and later French) harpsichords, and the general impression is one of lightness and delicacy compared with the Flemish counterparts. The roses were usually of pierced and layered parchment instead of cast and gilt lead. The scalings are usually shorter – 300–330mm instead of about 355mm – than those found in contemporary Flemish instruments. But probably more important even than the use of shorter scalings, these French harpsichords had soundboards with barring which passed underneath the bridges. Instead of leaving the soundboard area near the bridges completely free and using the barring to control the areas of vibrating soundboard, as in the Flemish tradition, these early French instruments have soundboards made generally stiff by the barring, with no accurate control over the vibrating area near the bridges. Virtually all the surviving French seventeenth-century harpsichords are doubles and date from the second half of the century. They had aligned keyboards, a disposition with $2 \times 8'$ and $1 \times 4'$ and a compass usually of $G_1/B_1$ to $c^3$. The keyboards had black ebony naturals and (usually solid) white ivory or bone sharps, with the ends of the natural keylevers cut away underneath to give an arcade of three connected arches. The stands usually have six to eight spiral-turned legs connected together with a stretcher just above floor level.

However, although French instruments from the first half of the seventeenth century are very scarce, it should be remembered that the Ruckers seem to have built instruments during this period specially for the French market. All the large double-manual Ruckers harpsichords (see p. 180) originally with chromatic basses down to F and $G_1$ are now in France and seem to have been there since earliest times. This almost certainly means that these instruments were made especially for export to France, where the larger compass down to $G_1$ must have been needed. The period in which these instruments (the 1616 HR, 1627c IR, 1628b IR and 1646b AR) were built covers most of the first half of the century. As in other parts of Northern Europe, the use of harpsichords with keyboards at different pitches was known in France and, as in England, the use of a chromatic bass octave was therefore a requirement of the music. (The musical reasons for a chromatic bass octave during this period are not known, since no original French keyboard music now extant requires this.) Also, importation of these instruments over such a long period suggests that they were continuously appreciated in France and that, at least in the first half of the seventeenth century, the limited $1 \times 8'$, $1 \times 4'$ disposition of the Flemish instruments was sufficient for the music being played.

The four extant 'French' doubles are doubtless only a small fraction of the total number of such instruments imported into France in the first half of the seventeenth century. But judging from the number of instruments now extant there, the smaller normal doubles were also imported into France, along with singles and virginals. Because of the number of their instruments in France and especially in Paris, the Ruckers gained a reputation there for having built some of the finest-sounding harpsichords. Apparently these instruments were appreciated even more than the native products, since, by the close of the seventeenth century, such builders as Richard, Nicolas Blanchet and Dumont were building in a style very close to that of the Ruckers. The French instruments had heavier moulded cases of lime (a wood very similar to the poplar used by the Ruckers), and the roses (often copying Ruckers roses but with the initials changed) were of cast and gilt lead. The scalings were similar to those used by Ruckers and the soundboard barring system copied the Flemish model very closely.

By the beginning of the eighteenth century the Flemish style of building seems to have become predominant, and I know of no harpsichords in the style of the Tibaut/Desruisseaux/Vaudry instruments built after 1700. And for the rest of the eighteenth century, builders such as François Étienne Blanchet, Goujon, Goermans, Stehlin, Hemsch, Taskin, Vater, Dedeban, etc. made instruments very much in the Ruckers tradition. They were of course longer instruments with a wider compass, aligned keyboards, and a more versatile disposition. But the structure, framing, scalings, and soundboard construction, layout and barring were all clearly modelled on that found in the Ruckers instruments.

The effect of the Ruckers tradition was felt also through the influence of the Ruckers instruments that were being heard 'in the flesh': many builders were reworking and enlarging them, aligning the keyboards, adding extra strings and generally bringing them up to date. The 1778 Geneva edition of the *Encyclopédie* (see Appendix 13) says:

> The best harpsichords that have been made up to now for the beauty of their tone are those of the three Ruckers (Hans, Ioannes and Andreas) as well as those of Ioannes Couchet, who, all working in Antwerp in the previous century, made an immense quantity of harpsichords, of which a very large number of originals are found in Paris, and recognized as such by the true connoisseurs.

Much of the activity of the French (especially Parisian) builders seems to have been directed towards the ravalement of old Flemish instruments. Of the extant *œuvres* of such builders as Blanchet, Goujon and Taskin, by far the largest number are reworked instruments and not instruments begun and built entirely by the makers themselves. As one would expect, this high proportion of reworked instruments among a builder's output must also have existed in the eighteenth century. In a 1780 inventory of the instruments of Louis XVI at Versailles[4], twenty-three harpsichords are listed. Of these, two are by Blanchet, but a total of eight are listed as having 'claviers de Blanchet'. And of these ravalé harpsichords seven are Ruckers instruments.

The many inventories of eighteenth-century Parisian harpsichord builders[5] all list Ruckers and Flemish instruments among the other effects found in the Paris workshops. Among these we find 'Deux petits clavecins Ruckers pour prendre la table', 'Trois clavecins vieux pour mettre en pièce', '1 clavecin de Ruckers avec ses claviers', etc. Flemish instruments 'à grand ravalement' (i.e. with five octaves, $F_1$ to $f^3$) are common among the other instruments listed. But it is among the inventories where the prices of the instruments are listed that one gets a true idea of how the Ruckers were valued by the French. As an example, the inventory dated 2 March 1737 of the effects of the deceased harpsichord builder Jacques (I) Bourdet (see footnote 5, Samoyault-Verlet, p. 135) lists a number of harpsichords by French builders, mostly of the seventeenth century, valued at up to 80 livres, but averaging about 60. Then we find 'un clavecin . . . à ravalement de Jean Ruckers' with a price of 450 livres, or roughly eight times the average price of the locally made French instruments.

By the eighteenth century, the original decoration of the Ruckers instruments was completely out of date. Even for the seventeenth century, the marbled exterior and papered interiors seem rather provincial and old-fashioned. When the cases of the old Flemish harpsichords were widened, the original decoration was destroyed. So the instruments were redecorated in the current style. In the simplest form the new decoration would consist of a lacquered lid and case, ornamented with bands of gold leaf, and a stand either with cabriole legs in the style of Louis XV, or later with turned and fluted legs in the style of Louis XVI. But the more lavish instruments had paintings inside the lids by one of the fashionable contemporary artists and had more elaborately-carved inlaid or gilt stands and outer-case decoration. Unfortunately most of these sumptuously decorated instruments were lost at the time of the French Revolution. But we can get some idea of what they would have been like from their descriptions in the contemporary sale notices (see Appendix 15). Unfortunately, no extant Ruckers harpsichords have paintings attributable to Watteau or Oudry, or stands with Boule decoration. However, the 1646b AR double-manual harpsichord has a beautiful outer-case decoration in *vernis*

[4] Sybil Marcuse, 'The instruments of the King's Library at Versailles', *The Galpin Society Journal*, XIV (1961), 34–6.

[5] C. Samoyault-Verlet, *Les facteurs de clavecins parisiens: Notes biographiques et documents (1550–1793)* (Paris, 1966). F. Hubbard, *Three Centuries of Harpsichord Making* (Cambridge, Mass., 1965), Appendix C, p. 256; Pierre-J. Hardouin, 'Harpsichord making in Paris: eighteenth century', *The Galpin Society Journal*, X (1957), 10; XII (1959), 73; XIII (1960), 52.

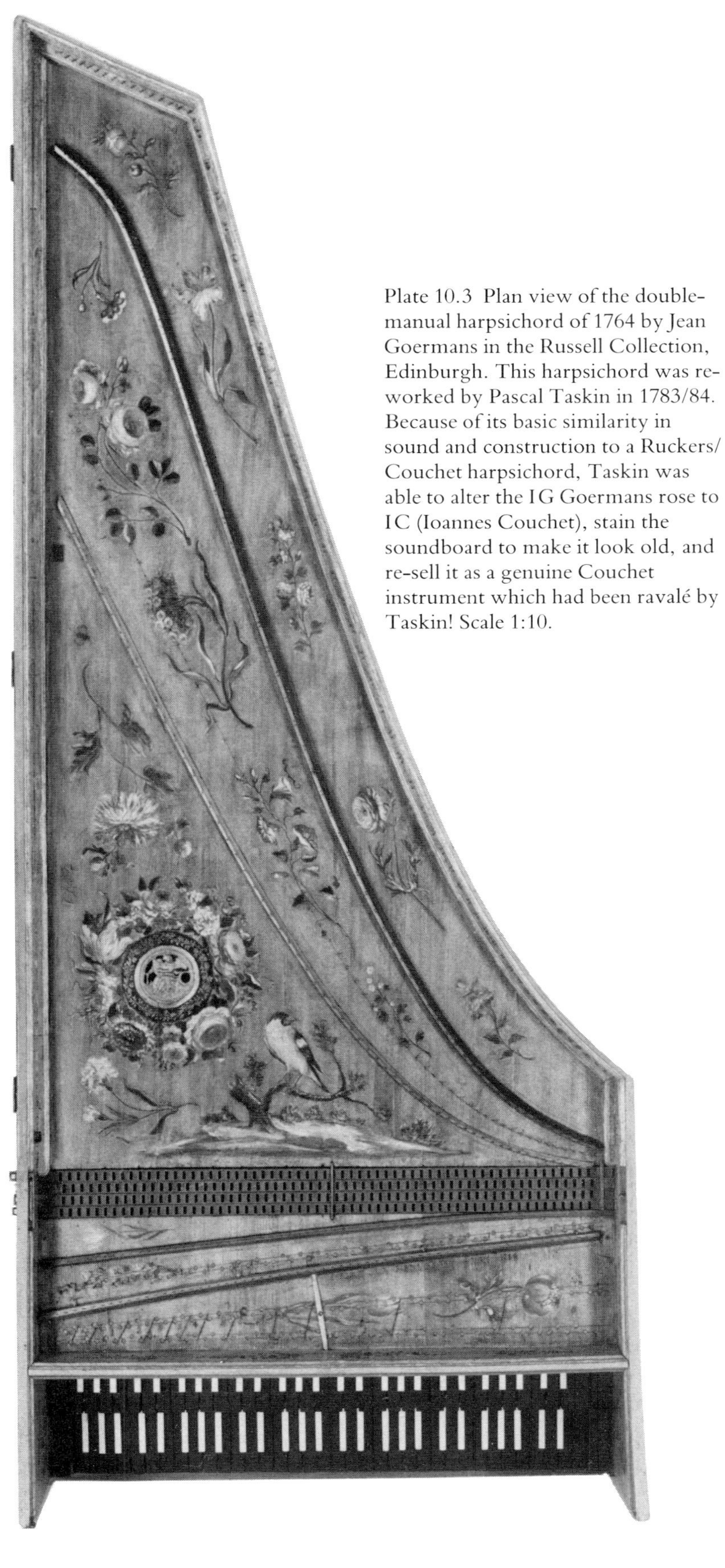

Plate 10.3 Plan view of the double-manual harpsichord of 1764 by Jean Goermans in the Russell Collection, Edinburgh. This harpsichord was re-worked by Pascal Taskin in 1783/84. Because of its basic similarity in sound and construction to a Ruckers/Couchet harpsichord, Taskin was able to alter the IG Goermans rose to IC (Ioannes Couchet), stain the soundboard to make it look old, and re-sell it as a genuine Couchet instrument which had been ravalé by Taskin! Scale 1:10.

*martin* with delicately-painted motifs on a background of gold leaf.

The lists of instruments for sale in Paris (see Appendix 15) usually give asking prices. In the period between about 1750 and 1780 the average price for a double-manual harpsichord made by a Parisian builder was about 300 to 400 livres. A Ruckers or Couchet double, on the other hand, was usually listed for either 600 or 1,000 livres. But sometimes prices as high as 2,000–5,000 livres were asked, and in 1778 a harpsichord listed without details simply as a 'Clavecin d'André Rukers' was on sale for 1,000 louis, or 20,000 livres! Naturally when a harpsichord with a Ruckers nameboard and rose could fetch thirty times or more the price of a new instrument, many builders were unable to resist the temptation to counterfeit Ruckers instruments by faking old Flemish or French harpsichords.

To what extent this practice was an accepted part of the activity of these French builders, and to what extent their clients realized that the instruments they were buying were not genuine, is not known. Perhaps some clients were knowingly deceived, others not. Although some instruments such as the 1788 Taskin harpsichord in Milan signed 'ANDREAS RVCKERS' and the '1590b HR' (see p. 278) by Jean Goujon (made sometime before 1749), are particularly clever imitations of Ruckers instruments, and seem to have been made purposely to deceive, the practice of counterfeiting instruments seems to have been widely accepted. Inventories of the property of many builders made during their active career – as opposed to after their death, when exposing any disreputable activity could not have damaged their future prospects – include entries such as:

A harpsichord by Goujon claiming to be Hans Ruckers
1 harpsichord carrying the name Ruckers, built by the late Paschal Taskin. . .

However, the fact remains that most of these *contrefait* instruments were accepted until recently as genuine. Probably the eighteenth-century buying public was deceived to the same extent as many modern collectors and museums have been. The fact that such a deception was possible shows that the Ruckers style was so well absorbed by eighteenth-century builders that their *contrefait* instruments were indistinguishable from a genuine Ruckers harpsichord *mis à grand ravalement*.

## THE EFFECT OF THE RUCKERS TRADITION IN THE REST OF NORTHERN EUROPE

The Ruckers style of building seems to have made no impact at all on the Italian harpsichord builders of the eighteenth century, and I know of no Italian instruments made in the Flemish style. In northern Europe the influence of the Ruckers tradition was very strong in France and England. But although the Ruckers style did touch upon the harpsichord-making traditions outside these countries, it is useless to try to find a comparable effect on harpsichord building elsewhere in Europe.

In central Europe, because of the lack of harpsichords from the seventeenth century, it is impossible to trace the influence of the Ruckers tradition there, if indeed it existed. In the eighteenth century, harpsichord building in the German-speaking part of Europe was centred mainly around Hamburg in the North and Dresden in Saxony in the East. The instruments of the Hamburg school, typified by builders like Hass, Fleischer and Zell, are in some ways not unlike those of the Ruckers, but have their own particular characteristics. The harpsichord tails, instead of being mitred, are rounded so that the bentside has an elongated 'S' shape. The bridges are usually tall and narrow and have an almost rectangular cross-section. The scalings of the Hamburg instruments are very similar to those used in France and England during this period and, from what little evidence exists, the use of brass and iron, and the actual gauges of the strings, were also similar to those of the English and French eighteenth-century builders. But most important of all, the soundboard barring with the 4′ hitchpin rail separating the 8′ and 4′ bridges, and a cutoff bar running almost parallel to the 4′ bridge, are very similar in concept to that used in the Ruckers tradition. Also, although the cross-section of the bridges has a different shape, their stiffness is roughly the same as that of the Ruckers. Thus, even with the characteristics that differentiate the Hamburg school from the other Ruckers-derived traditions, the instruments of the two disciplines have more features in common than differences.

In Saxony the influence of the Ruckers style was much stronger. The eighteenth-century instruments built in and around Dresden were clearly based on the Ruckers tradition. The cases were heavily constructed with the sides sitting on the baseboard. The tails were mitred and not rounded as in the Hamburg instruments, so that the general appearance of these instruments is also similar to their contemporary Ruckers-derived French and English counterparts. Their scalings are similar and the soundboards are similarly barred and ribbed. Only the shape of the bridges is distinctly different from that of the Ruckers tradition. The instruments of Gräbner and Horn have bridges which, except for a recess cut for the bridge pins and a sloping top behind this, are almost square in cross-section. The bridges in instruments by Hartmann and Johann Heinrich Silbermann (the latter, although work-

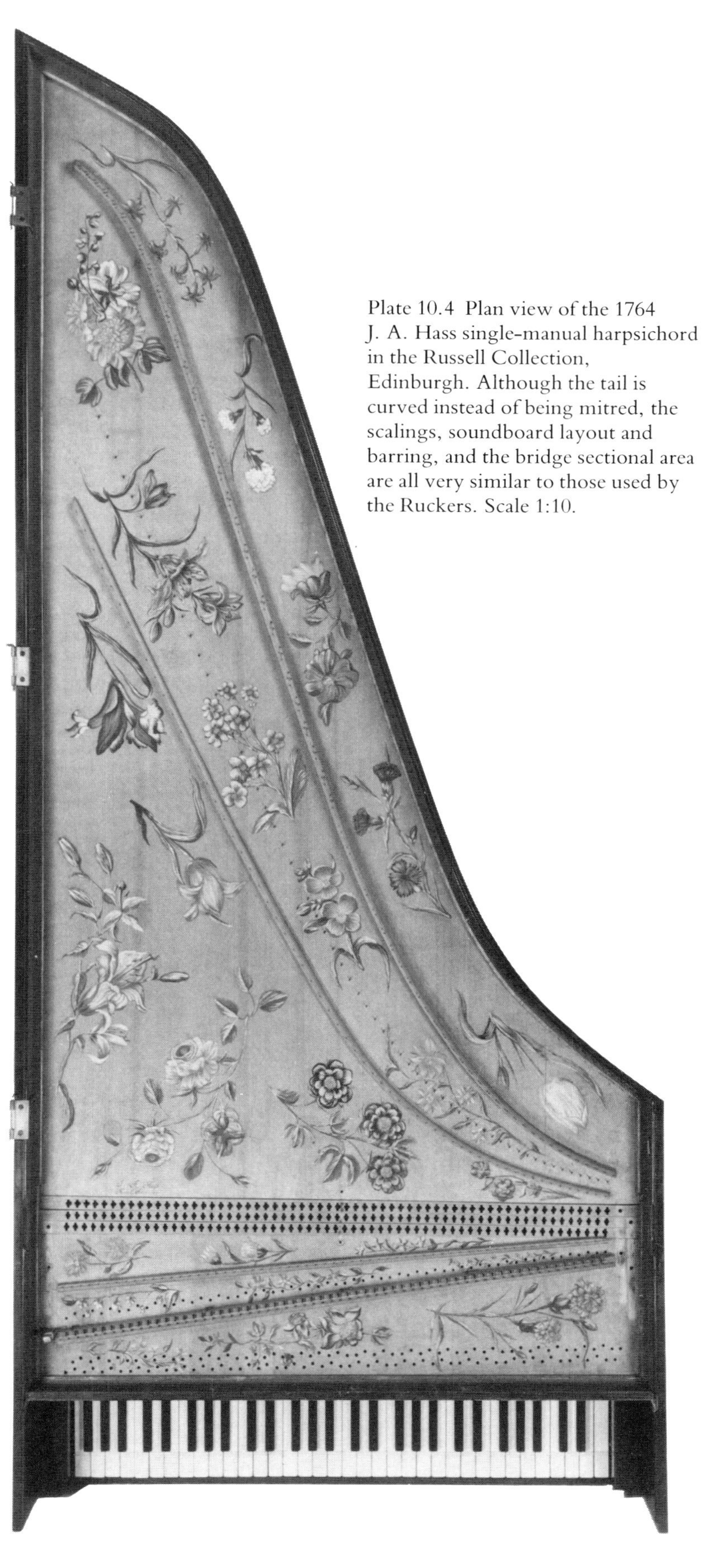

Plate 10.4 Plan view of the 1764 J. A. Hass single-manual harpsichord in the Russell Collection, Edinburgh. Although the tail is curved instead of being mitred, the scalings, soundboard layout and barring, and the bridge sectional area are all very similar to those used by the Ruckers. Scale 1:10.

Plate 10.5 Plan view of the 1668 Stephen Keene spinett virginal in the Russell Collection, Edinburgh. Because virginals were never as popular after 1650 as they had been during Ruckers time, the influence of the Ruckers virginal building tradition is difficult to establish. Nonetheless, the similarity of this instrument to the typical Ruckers spinett virginal (see Plate 3.2) is very strong. Scale 1:10.

ing in Strasbourg, learned his craft from his uncle Gottfried in Freiburg in Saxony) are similar to Gräbner and Horn except that they are slightly wider at the base than at the top of the bridge.

Not surprisingly, the Ruckers tradition was strongly felt in Flanders itself in the eighteenth century. But unlike France and England, and even Germany, eighteenth-century harpsichord building was carried on on a very modest scale in Flanders. We have only a few surviving Flemish instruments from this period by Bull, van den Elsche, and Heinemann. However, Dulcken, working first in Antwerp and then in Brussels, and Delin, working in Tournai, seem to have been more prolific (or at least their instruments tended to survive more). As with their contemporary English and French colleagues, the eighteenth-century Flemish builders made harpsichords in the style of the Ruckers and Couchets, but with a wider compass and a greater musical potential as a result of the addition of an extra set of 8′ strings and sometimes extra registers such as the close-plucking lute stop, the soft leather-quilled peau de buffle stop, etc.

The instruments of Delin particularly resemble those of Ruckers. The soundboard layout and barring, the bridge cross-sections, the scalings – in fact all of the important features of his instruments – are similar to the Ruckers. Delin even used an Andreas Ruckers rose, modifying the initials from AR to AD. Delin also used jacks with blind damper holes – clearly modelled on the jacks found in the earlier Ruckers and Couchet instruments.

The instruments of Dulcken, although they have more individual characteristic features than those of Delin, are also built closely in the style of Ruckers and Couchet. Although the soundboard barring and layout and the bridge cross-section are in the seventeenth-century Flemish style, the scalings are very long (370–385mm, and therefore longer even than the contemporary low-pitched French instruments). The cases of Dulcken's instruments are also longer than those of his contemporary English and French colleagues, who seemed to base their instruments on the two-manual harpsichords of the Ruckers. It seems clear, as mentioned earlier, that Dulcken's instruments are based on the long single-manual harpsichords built by Ioseph Ioannes Couchet.

CHAPTER ELEVEN

# The ravalement of Ruckers and Couchet clavecimbels

Eighteenth-century music made requirements of clavecimbels that the instruments built in the seventeenth century could not fulfil. In order to adapt the Ruckers and Couchet instruments to play the music of the later period it was necessary to modernize them. In eighteenth-century France a harpsichord with a compass greater than four octaves, C to $c^3$, was said to be 'en ravalement', so that any Ruckers or Couchet instrument which had been widened beyond this compass had been 'mis en ravalement'. Modern authors (e.g. Russell, Hubbard, Boalch, Ripin, Chambure) have called the process of alteration ravalement, and have distinguished two types of alteration or reworking of earlier instruments. When only the keyboard compass was widened by using narrower keyblocks or a narrower three-octave span, or both, the process is called 'petit ravalement'. If the case sides were moved out to widen the whole instrument, the process was called 'grand ravalement'.[1] The methods used to achieve these ravalements are almost as numerous as the extant instruments and not all can be dealt with here individually. But the general process, the problems raised during the process and some of the solutions are important and are discussed below.

## RAVALEMENT OF RUCKERS VIRGINALS

Usually when one speaks of ravalement it is in connection with harpsichords. But virginals were also altered to make them more fashionable and suitable for the later musical literature. Virginals are inherently single-register instruments, so only their compass can be widened. The use of the short octave declined when composers began to write in tonalities which required the use of the missing chromatic bass notes as roots for the chords above. Therefore, the most obvious alteration to a virginal was to extend the compass down to C chromatically by adding four notes in the bass (or down to C without C♯, adding three notes). There was no need to lengthen the instrument itself, since the bottom note was still the same, so lengthening the strings was also unnecessary. Usually the bass enlargement was accompanied by an extension of the treble compass up to $e^3$ or $f^3$.

The extension of the virginal compass could be carried out in one of three ways. In the first and most common method the extra keys and notes were added at the ends of the keyboards, registers and bridges, leaving the original spacing of keys, jackslots and strings in the middle. This meant moving the keywell braces out to accommodate the extra width of the added keys, and piercing extra jackslots at the ends of the registers. These tasks were relatively easy to accomplish but posed problems for the strings and bridges of the notes at the extremes of the compass. In the bass, the strings added to extra sections of the bridges were positioned closer to the player and touched the back of the removable nameboard at its right-hand end. A channel was therefore cut in it and the

[1] In eighteenth-century France an instrument 'à grand ravalement' meant that it was an instrument with a five-octave compass from $F_1$ to $f^3$. Anton Bemetzrieder, *Leçons de clavecin, et principes d'harmonie* (Paris, 1771), 13, writes of a pedagogical discourse between a teacher and his pupil. The teacher says: 'In the past harpsichords contained only four octaves from C, to which were successively added, to the left, the seven keys, $B_1$, $B^{\flat}{}_1$, $A_1$, $A^{\flat}{}_1$, $G_1$, $G^{\flat}{}_1$ and $F_1$, and to the right, the five keys $c^{\sharp 3}$, $d^3$, $d^{\sharp 3}$. $e^3$, $f^3$. Today the widest harpsichords have five octaves from $F_1$, or four octaves from C preceded by seven keys, and followed on the right by five. They are called harpsichords "à grand ravalement".'

treble keywell brace so that the bass strings could vibrate freely. In the treble, the added pieces of bridge were so long that they ran onto the area of soundboard above the spine liner. Since the ends of the bridges were therefore not free to vibrate, the added treble notes produced a very bad tone.

The next option, which was much more time-consuming, avoided these problems but created a new problem of its own. Here, the three-octave span of the keyboard was reduced so that a new keyboard and new registers had to be made. Usually this was done by removing the leather of the upper guide from the soundboard and slicing out the portion of the soundboard with the jackslots cut into it. A new piece of soundboard wood was inserted into the hole and covered with a new piece of leather; a completely new lower guide was also made. The new jackslots were cut into these in such a way that the spacing of the slots matched the new narrower keyboard span. Because of the respacing of the jacks, the bridges had to be repinned. But because the geometry of the bridges was based on the original three-octave span of 500mm, the scalings were altered. Quite aside from any pitch changes, the treble scalings were no longer Pythagorean. In those instruments modified by this method but having only a bass extension to the compass, both keywell braces were usually moved outwards to accommodate the wider keyboard. The keyboard was thus effectively moved towards the treble, resulting in shorter scalings and a higher pitch. Comparing the new and old scalings does not give a consistent pitch change throughout the compass, since the new scalings are no longer Pythagorean: at some points they correspond to at least a tone rise in pitch, at others even more.

The final method of widening a virginal compass attempts to avoid both the pitch alteration and the non-Pythagorean scalings. Here the keyboard and registers are remade as above; in addition new bridges are made and positioned to give Pythagorean scalings roughly the same as the original ones leaving the pitch unaltered. But since the original soundboard barring and the placement of structural members under the soundboard was designed for the original location of the bridges, relocating the bridges inevitably comprises the tone of the instrument in its altered form.

Numerous variations of these three methods of ravalement are to be found. Bass-compass extension to $B_1$ ($G_1$/$B_1$?) and treble extensions to $d^3$, $e^3$, $f^3$ or $g^3$ are possible variants. Sometimes the keyboard is moved a semitone or a tone in either direction to centralize it in the new space in the widened keywell. A few mother-and-child instruments have also been ravalé. If the bass keywell brace of a muselar mother virginal is moved to the left, the original space for the child will become too small. This means that, during the ravalement of a double virginal, either the mother's keywell must not be widened or the child must be left permanently in its playing position above the mother (e.g. 1610 HR). The fact that the child no longer fitted inside the mother after the ravalement doubtless explains the separation of many mother-and-child instruments.

## RAVALEMENT OF RUCKERS HARPSICHORDS

Because of the enormous reputation that Ruckers harpsichords later acquired, few escaped without alterations to their compass or disposition. A Ruckers harpsichord in its original state, with a bass short octave and a disposition of only 1 × 8′, 1 × 4′, was very restricting to an eighteenth-century musician. So there was a strong temptation and a very real reason for both musicians and harpsichord builders alike to modernize these instruments. Only two single- (1637 AR and 1679 IC) and one double-manual harpsichord (1638b IR) have survived with their original unmodified disposition and compass (the 1618 AR and 1627 AR singles and the 1637b IR double have now been returned to their original state, but only after the removal of intermediate modifications). Because of their rarity the unmodified instruments are uniquely valuable in our search for an understanding of Ruckers building practices and of the original musical potential of the instruments; they must be the focus of attention for conservation without further alterations or deterioration.

A builder modernizing a single-manual harpsichord could change the compass, disposition and number of manuals. No single-manual harpsichord now exists in which only the disposition was changed without altering the compass. But analysis of the string-band strips made for a number of single-manual harpsichords shows that the first alteration was often to replace the 4′ stop with an 8′ stop, without affecting the compass. This was done by placing the new 8′ string directly above the position of the original 4′ string. Either a new set of jacks was made to pluck the added string or, more likely, the original 4′ jacks were lengthened so that the plectra reached up to the height of the new 8′ strings. Because the added 8′ string was positioned to the left of the pair of jacks for any particular note, the new string was longer than the original by an amount corresponding to an increase in the scalings of almost a semitone. This is a problem that will be encountered throughout this discussion of the ravalement of harpsichords.

### The van Blankenburg problem

Van Blankenburg (1739) recognized this problem (see Appendix 10) and its consequences. He says that because the Ruckers made their scalings as long as possible to give strings with tensions just below the breaking point, increasing the scalings by an amount equivalent to just less than a semitone would inevitably result in string breakages. Because of the fundamental nature of this problem to the ravalement of all harpsichords, I have decided to call it *the van Blankenburg problem* (see Fig. 11.3, p. 213).

Van Blankenburg himself suggests moving the keyboard up towards the treble by one semitone. This has the effect of decentralizing the keyboard in the keywell. Another possibility is to move the 8′ nut in the treble so that the 8′ scalings are decreased by the required amount. This avoids the problem of string breakages, but changes the plucking points and therefore the treble tone colour. No matter how the alteration to give the 2 × 8′ disposition was carried out, it was very common (see Chapter 12, p. 232).

No single-manual harpsichord survives with an altered disposition but without an altered compass, and only one instrument, the harpsichord part of the n.d. IR combined harpsichord and virginal, has its original 1 × 8′, 1 × 4′ disposition, but with a compass widened to C to $c^3$ from C/E to $c^3$.

### Petit ravalement of single-manual harpsichords

The petit ravalement of single-manual harpsichords, involving a change in both the compass and disposition, is relatively common. In its simplest form it meant increasing the dimension of the keyboards by the width of two naturals, removing the keyblocks at the sides of the case, and altering the disposition to 2 × 8′. The (*c.* 1605) AR, 1635 AR and the 1644a AR singles were altered in this way. But usually the transformation was slightly more complicated, involving widening the keyboard and giving the instrument the disposition 2 × 8′, 1 × 4′ by adding a third register in the gap. In carrying out these alterations several problems had to be overcome.

To increase the compass from C/E to $c^3$ to C to $c^3$ (or C, D to $c^3$) two extra naturals were required and four (or three) notes had to be added. If the original keyboard was used and the spacing of the keytails, jacks and strings maintained, then the keyblocks had to be narrowed or removed entirely, and the bridges and registers extended to carry the extra notes. Since the keyboard was widened only in the bass, but the space gained for the wider keyboard came from both the bass and treble sides, the keyboard had to be moved towards the treble. If two notes were added to either end of the bridges and registers, the movement of the keyboard resulted in a shortening of the effective scalings by two semitones. Adding an extra set of 8′ strings lengthened their scalings by a semitone, giving new 8′ scalings roughly one semitone shorter than before. But the 4′ scalings were left two semitones too short. These changes would have a somewhat detrimental effect on the overall tone quality, but at least string breakages would occur less frequently, and any deleterious effect on the tone was more than compensated for by the advantage of the increased compass and updated disposition.

Most petit-ravalement singles have neither their original keyboards with a bass enlargement nor their original string spacing. Instead, the keyblocks have been thinned to enlarge the space between them, new keyboards and registers with a smaller three-octave span have been made, and the bridges have been repinned to match. This means that at least one extra natural can be squeezed into the treble, increasing the compass to C to $d^3$. Reducing the string spacing destroys the geometry of the instrument's scalings, and gives treble string lengths which are no longer Pythagorean. However, adding the extra notes $c^{\sharp 3}$ and $d^3$ in the treble effectively moves the keyboard to the left and enforces longer scalings than when the top note was $c^3$, as before. This lengthening of the scalings is more than the semitone needed to return the ravalement scalings to their original value, even when the bridges are extended as far as possible towards the treble. Normally, the resulting scalings were so long that string breakages were unavoidable. The solution to this was then to move the nut towards the bridges. In fact normally it is necessary to move only the 8′ nut: the 4′ scalings are not affected by adding a second 8′ choir and, as mentioned above, are about a semitone shorter (at 4′ pitch) than the new long 8′ scalings.

The 1639 IR single was originally one of the large 'English' chromatic-bass-octave single-manual harpsichords with an original compass of C to $d^3$. This was enlarged by the method above to a fifty-five-note compass which was probably $G_1$, $A_1$ to $d^3$ (the keyboard is now lost). Here the keyblocks were thinned, new registers and a keyboard were made with a three-octave span of only 455mm, and the bridges were extended and repinned. Space for a third register in the gap to give a 2 × 8′, 1 × 4′ disposition was gained by cutting away both the wrestplank and upper belly rail. Although the altered instrument did not have the full resources of a five-octave eighteenth-century English harpsichord, it was capable of playing most of the literature of the early and middle part of the century. Installing the new action was a fairly easy task, and the case work needed no alteration at all. The new treble 8′ scalings were close to those normally used in native English harpsichords. But the extension of the bass compass downwards gives rise to a new problem not encountered in those instruments where the bass short-octave compass was replaced by a chromatic bass octave, with the lowest played note, C, the same in both cases. Here, extending the compass down to $G_1$ gives bass string lengths which were intended for C but now sound $G_1$, a fourth lower. (Ideally they should be twenty-five per cent longer.) At their new pitch the bottom strings would be very slack and the tone quality would be seriously compromised.

### *Grand ravalement of single-manual harpsichords*

The problem of crowding a large number of notes into the small case of the single-manual harpsichords was easily solved by widening the case. Normally this was done by adding material only on the treble side, leaving the spine side unaltered.

Again the ravalement procedure was carried out either by using the original keyboard and keys, or by remaking these and the registers with a narrower three-octave span. The 1627a IR harpsichord has had its compass widened from C/E to $c^3$ to C to $e^3$ simply by adding the required new keys and increasing the width of the case by about 90mm on the treble side. Adding the notes to the bass side of the keyboard has the effect of pushing the keyboard up towards the treble, so that the original keys play strings much shorter than before. Adding an extra set of strings to the 8′ choir effectively lengthens their scalings, but even allowing for this the new scalings would be shorter than typical Ruckers string lengths by a minor third for the 8′ strings and a major third for the 4′ strings. For some reason the soundboard was replaced in this instrument, and a new soundboard with only an 8′ bridge installed. But the opportunity of repositioning new bridges to give scalings closer to the originals was not taken, and the present scaling of the long 8′ $c^2$ is 305mm, about a minor third shorter than normal Ruckers scalings.

Most grand ravalements of single-manual harpsichords avoid the problem of shortening the scalings by remaking the keyboard with a smaller octave span. For the normal C/E to $c^3$ singles the new compass is usually C to $f^3$. Adding the extra notes in the bass pushes the keyboard towards the treble but, by using a shorter three-octave span and reducing the width of the bass keyblock, the treble keys are pushed towards the bass. Making these adjustments and moving the nuts away from the gap gave string lengths which, although they were no longer accurately Pythagorean, were at least closer to the original Ruckers scalings. More importantly, these new scalings gave strings close to their breaking point. Instruments ravalé in this way are the 1609 AR, 1618 AR and the 1645 IC.

The grand ravalement of the 1637a IR single, which had an original compass of C to $c^3$ chromatic, offered more scope than the narrow C/E to $c^3$ short-octave instruments discussed above. Here the bass compass could be extended below C and the treble extended above $c^3$. By narrowing both the three-octave span and the bass keyblock, and by making the lowest natural touchplate narrower than the rest, the compass was extended down to $A_1$ and, by widening the case, up to $f^3$ in the treble. But the bass strings now sounded $A_1$, a minor third below the original pitch of C. To help to compensate for the shortness of the strings the nut was moved as close to the tuning pins as possible in the bass. This then gave strings which were more centre-plucking. The resulting loss of clarity in the bass is noticeable. Both here and in the 1639 IR discussed above, increasing the bass compass without lengthening the case seriously compromises the sound of the lowest strings.

### *Conversion of single-manual harpsichords to double-manual harpsichords*

The conversion of a single-manual harpsichord into a double involves a considerable amount of work. New keyboards, jacks and registers have to be made and the case sides and baseboard have to be lengthened to accommodate the second keyboard. The nameboard has to be narrowed to allow the second keyboard to slide under it, and the lid front flap has to be widened and lengthened. In comparison to all this, only a relatively small amount of extra work was involved in moving the treble cheek piece outwards to extend the compass above the original $c^3$. Not surprisingly therefore, most of the single-to-double conversions are of the grand ravalement type, with a treble and sometimes a bass compass extension achieved by moving the case sides.

Exceptions to this are the few large Couchet singles which, because of their initial wide compass, were converted to doubles without widening the case, and are therefore of the petit ravalement type: the (*c.* 1650)b IC, where the compass was $F_1$, $G_1$, $A_1$ to $c^3$ altered to $F_1$, $G_1$ to $c^3$; the 1652 IC with a compass of $G_1/B_1$ to $c^3$, where the bottom E♭ key was split to give B♭/E♭; and the n.d. IC, where the $F_1$ to $d^3$, $e^3$ compass was increased by first narrowing the three-octave span of the keyboards and repinning the bridges first to $F_1$ to $e^3$ and then to $F_1$ to $f^3$. In the first two of these instruments even the original pinning and string spacings were used. In all three the new disposition was the expected 2 × 8′, 1 × 4′.

The single-to-double conversion of the smaller C/E to $c^3$ singles were all of the grand ravalement type. By decreasing the three-octave span of the keys and by moving the treble case side outwards the compass was extended in both the treble and bass. Since the bass scalings could not be increased, it is rather surprising that the bass compass was extended downwards as far as $G_1$, either chromatically, or by missing out $G^{\sharp}{}_1$ ($G_1$, $A_1$), or by using a $G_1/B_1$ short octave. Examples of converted C/E to $c^3$ singles are; 1639b AR ($G_1$ to $d^3$), 1651b AR ($G_1$, $A_1$ to $f^3$) and 1654 AR ($G_1/B_1$ to $f^3$). The spine of the 1651b AR has been moved outwards and new soundboard wood added on the bass side, but the bass scalings have not been much increased and are still almost twenty per cent shorter than those of the normal Ruckers doubles, which sound the same bottom note ($G_1$). The other two instruments have even shorter scalings in the bass, with even graver consequences to the sound of the lowest notes.

Two examples exist, both unique, of large singles converted into doubles. The 1636 AR originally had a compass of C to $c^3$. It was converted to a double by widening the case in the treble and replacing the original wrestplank with a new longer and wider one. The nameboard and wrestplank were repositioned closer to the player on the spine side, and the spine lengthened accordingly. Because the original bass scalings seem to have been somewhat longer than in the earlier singles (see also 1651a AR), the new wide wrestplank, relatively wide registers, and the positioning of the bass portion of the nut near the new nameboard gave relatively long bass scalings, even for the new bottom note of $F_1$ (which was still shorter than the $G_1$ of a normal Ruckers double, however).

The second large single-to-double conversion is the 1680 IC, which probably had an original compass of $F_1$ to $d^3$. This instrument was widened only on the bass side. The original spine was cut off at the belly rail and cut down to the level of the soundboard. A new full-height spine was glued to the side of the old spine, thus widening the instrument by an amount equal to the width of the original spine. The new compass was $F_1$ to $f^3$, which, with only two extra naturals, was easily fitted into the new space by using a smaller octave span. However, the new scalings are very non-Pythagorean: those of the extreme treble, intended for the note $d^3$ but now sounding $f^3$, are extremely long and must have required the use of a very hard-drawn wire.

The ravalement of those single-manual harpsichords discussed above left the soundboard, and usually the bridges intact. New soundboard wood (or non-original soundboard wood from old instruments) was added to the treble or bass side or both. However, it was also the practice to use the wood from an old Ruckers soundboard and to resplice it with additions to form a new one. Completely new bridges and soundboard barring were added to the composite soundboard in the builder's usual style. Although seemingly unconventional, this practice was in fact more common than it would otherwise appear from this survey, since there are a number of Flemish (but non-Ruckers) and early French instruments not mentioned above whose soundboards have been used in this way to make false 'Ruckers' instruments (e.g. '1590a HR', '1612 HR' and '1615 HR' (p. 278), 'n.d. IR' (p. 280), etc.).

The soundboard of the 1632 IR is basically a single-manual Ruckers soundboard with sections added on the spine, tail and treble side to make it into a double-manual one. The rose has been repositioned to locate it in a more normal position and the old rose hole has been carefully filled in with new wood. The wreath has been repainted very much in the style of the original. The added sections of soundboard wood have been painted with flowers and arabesques in the style of the original soundboard. The resulting instrument has long bass scalings and all of the design features necessary for good sound production.

The 1671/1673 IC soundboard was respliced in an even more complicated fashion. Here original wood located between the cutoff bar and the spine, and normally inactive, was replaced with new wood. As far as possible this old wood was reused in the acoustically active part of the new composite soundboard under the bass section of the new 4′ and 8′ bridges. Inevitably, small sections near the spine had to be filled in with new wood, and new wood was added in the treble. Here also, the original rose hole was carefully filled in and most of the original soundboard decoration (consisting only of bronze powder scallops and arabesques with no flower or bird painting) was obliterated. Thus, beginning with what appears to have been a small C to $c^3$ single, an excellent new $F_1$ to $f^3$ double was made. The new bridges, extended in the bass to give long scalings there, sit almost entirely on old original soundboard wood.

The soundboard of the 1621 AR has also been respliced to convert it from a single- to a double-manual harpsichord. The section of the soundboard which was originally on the bass side of the instrument and which contained the rose was joined to two new pieces of wood and lengthened with new wood. New wood was also added to the treble side of the soundboard. The original soundboard painting was retained and new flower groups added to the new wood in a style similar to the

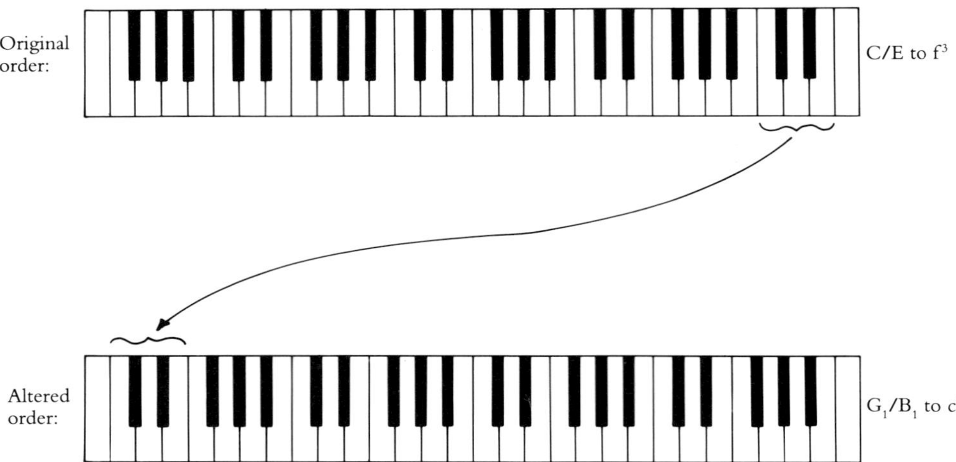


Fig. 11.1 Alignment of the Ruckers lower manual: method 1.

later Andreas instruments. Only about a half of the new composite soundboard is original, since a very large area of wood, especially in the bass, had to be added to accommodate the downward extension of the compass to $F_1$.

Instruments altered in the manner of the 1632 IR, the 1671/73 IC and the 1621 AR doubtless sounded very good when the ravalement was completed. The scalings, plucking points, and soundboard barring and layout were typical of the best instruments produced before, during and after the time of these alterations. However, it is clear that the altered soundboards, especially those consisting of pieces patched together from elsewhere on the original board, did not have contours similar to that of the original instruments or of a comparable Ruckers double-manual instrument; moreover, the bridges were located on it in new positions and with a new stiffness coefficient. The resulting sound, which must have been very different from that expected by the original makers, is characteristic not of seventeenth-century Flanders but of their eighteenth-century rebuilders.

### *Alignment of double-manual harpsichords*

As has been mentioned elsewhere, no Ruckers extant double-manual harpsichord was made with aligned keyboards (see Chapter 8, p. 181). Because the fashion or musical taste for unaligned double-manual instruments declined around 1650, the first and simplest alteration which could be made to a double was to align the keyboards without altering the number of string choirs, or the jacks or registers. The pitch which survived into the latter half of the seventeenth century and the eighteenth century was the so-called Corista pitch at R. For the

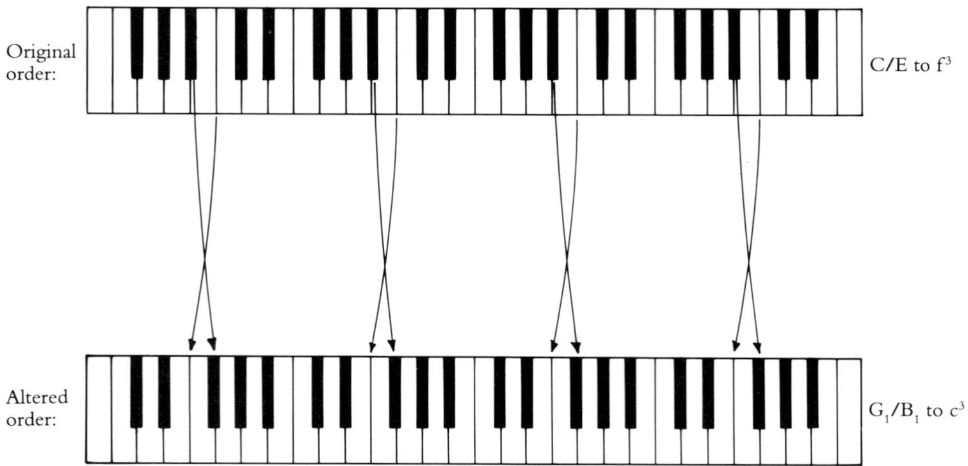


Fig. 11.2 Alignment of the Ruckers lower manual: method 2.

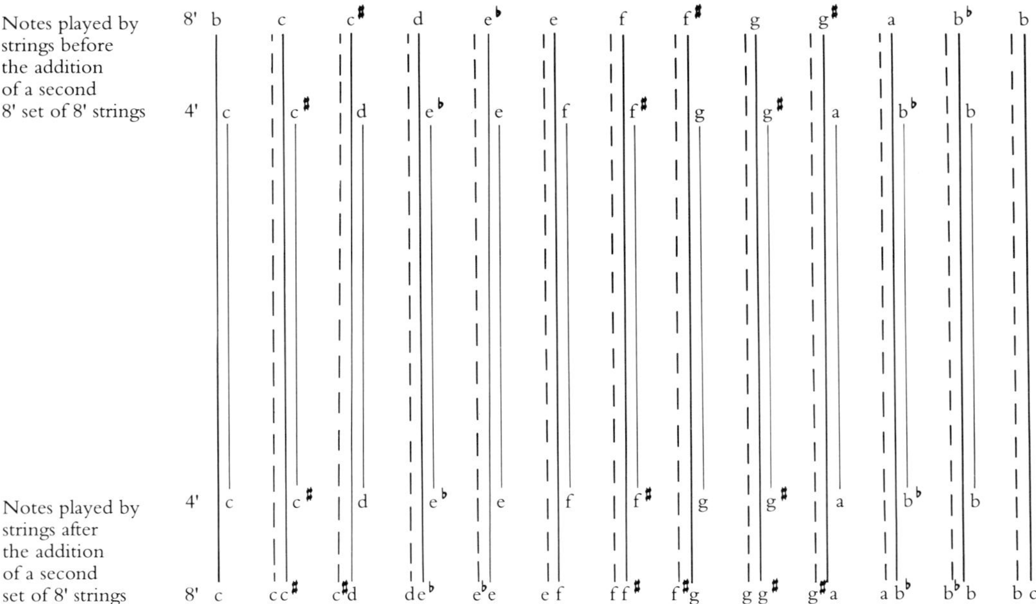


Fig. 11.3 The van Blankenburg problem. After the addition of the second 8′ string (dashed line), the original 8′ string must play a note at a pitch a semitone higher. The pitch of the 4′ strings remains unchanged.

normal transposing harpsichord, the upper manual at this pitch was left basically unaltered, except that the wooden block in the bass and the short-octave cranked keys were removed. New keys were made to fill the space left by these and extra keys extended the compass down to $G_1/B_1$. The alteration to the lower-manual keys was slightly more complicated. Within the original compass C/E to $f^3$ of the lower manual there is already a sufficient number of keys to yield the aligned compass $G_1/B_1$ to $c^3$ of the upper manual; it is necessary only to alter their order. The simplest method of doing this was to move the keys of the notes for $c^3$ to $e^3$ down to the bass to become the notes C to E, and to shift all the remaining keys up towards the treble. The bottom key became $G_1/B_1$ and the top $f^3$ key became $c^3$; these were left unaltered. But it was also possible to move each note *b*♭ up to become new *f*♯ so that the intervening naturals *b* and *c* became *e* and *f*.

Whichever method was used, because the lower-manual balance rail was slightly angled, being closer to the player in the bass than in the treble, the holes for the balance pins for the altered keys had to be redrilled either in the keys or the balance rail. Normal Ruckers double-manual harpsichords which were aligned without adding an extra set of 8′ strings are the 1615 AR and the 1640b AR (the 1633b AR was converted into a single-manual harpsichord using its original lower manual, with its C/E to $f^3$ compass at a pitch R − 4).

The problem of aligning the larger 'French' Ruckers doubles (see p. 180) is similar to that already described, except that the pitch rôle of the manuals is interchanged. The lower manual with its $G_1$ to $c^3$ compass at a pitch R can be left entirely unaltered. The upper manual with a block in the bass followed by the F to $f^3$ compass has to be aligned with the lower manual. Again, the simplest method of doing this is to move the notes $c^3$ to $e^3$ down to the bass to become C to E and then to shift the F to $b^2$ keys up to the treble. New keys for $G_1$ to $B_1$ have then to be made to fill out the space left by the removal of the wooden block. The 1616 HR was altered in this way (at some time the top $c^3$ key was moved to the bass to become an $F_1$, giving the exceptional $F_1$ to $a^2$, $b^2$ compass (see Russell 1959/1973, plate 36)).

As the next step after the alignment, a number of Ruckers doubles gained an extra set of 8′ strings, thus altering the disposition from the original 1 × 8′, 1 × 4′ to 2 × 8′, 1 × 4′. The addition of the second set of 8′ strings can be represented schematically – see Fig. 11.3.

Here the added strings are represented by a dashed line, the 4′ strings by a short solid line and the original 8′ strings by a solid line. It can be seen clearly that the original string is now plucked by the jack for the note one semitone higher. As a result, the effective scalings are increased by an amount equivalent to one full semitone, with all of the implications that this has for string breakages, strength of wire, and problems of pitch. It is the van Blankenburg problem.

Strangely, a number of aligned instruments with a $G_1$/

$B_1$ to $c^3$ compass and an added set of 8′ strings, but no other alterations, seem to have ignored the van Blankenburg problem. The scalings of the long 8′ strings are simply a semitone too long (e.g. 1637b IR and 1640b IR). Whether this means that stronger wire was used to string these instruments so that they could be tuned to the same pitch, or whether they were tuned a semitone flat to their previous pitch now seems impossible to determine.

But with some instruments it is clear that whoever altered them was aware of the van Blankenburg problem. Sometimes the measures taken to avoid it were very drastic. Fleischer, in aligning the 1618c IR double, replaced the soundboard and bridges with entirely new bridges and a soundboard which gave the instrument a long 8′ scaling of about 340mm (4′ scaling = 2 × 160m = 320mm). Although this is about a semitone shorter than Hass (1723), Fleischer's Hamburg contemporary, with a scaling of 366mm, it compares with Gräbner (1739) at 339mm and Horn (*c.* 1780) at 349mm. A less drastic and very ingenious method of overcoming the van Blankenburg problem was adopted by the builder who aligned the 1627b IR double. The compass was left at $G_1/B_1$ to $c^3$, although new keyboards were made. The bass notes were left with the jacks plucking strings whose scaling was longer than in the original design. But a space was left in both the keytails and the string-band between the notes d and e♭, so that all of the keys from e♭ to $c^3$ are cranked one semitone towards the treble. This shortens the tenor and treble scalings by one semitone, reducing the 8′ scalings to their original values. As mentioned earlier, van Blankenburg (see Appendix 10) suggests a similar solution whereby all the keys are moved one semitone towards the treble and an extra $A_1$ is added in the bass to fill up the space left. But the solution adopted by the rebuilder of the 1627b IR double is superior to van Blankenburg's, since the foreshortening of the bass strings is reduced and the treble 8′ scalings are left unaltered.

The alignment of the 1608 AR double was done in a rather unusual way. The compass was changed from $G_1/B_1$ to $c^3$ to C to $d^3$ for both manuals. Because the new compass has one more note, an extra key was made for c♯$^3$ and an extra set of strings was added in the treble. Here the 8′ scalings are increased by two semitones – one semitone from moving the keyboard towards the bass, and one semitone from adding an extra string. The 4′ scalings are lengthened by one semitone. The scalings were reduced somewhat by moving the treble ends of both the 8′ and 4′ nuts towards the gap. But the amount the nuts can be moved is limited: the 4′ nut is already very near the gap and the space between the 8′ and 4′ nuts is partly filled with the 4′ tuning pins. As a result, the treble scalings are still relatively long. The 8′ $c^2$ scaling is 379mm and the 4′ $c^2$ scaling is 2 × 178mm = 356mm (the original scalings were about 351mm and 2 × 175mm = 350mm respectively). The 1618c IR double mentioned above, although it was aligned and given a compass of $G_1/B_1$ to $c^3$ by Fleischer in 1724, was also later altered to a C to $d^3$ compass. Shifting the keyboard down towards the bass lengthened both the 8′ and 4′ scalings by an amount equivalent to a tone in pitch (8′: $c^2$ = 382mm; 4′:$c^2$ = 180mm × 2 = 360mm).

### *Petit ravalement of Ruckers double-manual harpsichords*

Although the lowest key of a normal Ruckers double-manual harpsichord in its original state sounded a string whose pitch was $G_1$, the key from the player's point of view was a C. Aligning the keyboards therefore gave the player the extra *notes* down to $G_1$, though the *pitch* of the bottom note remained the same. The top note $c^3$ was all that was required in Flanders until about 1650. In the second half of the seventeenth century, however, the need for aligned harpsichords coincided with the need for a larger treble compass. Initially at least, the most common requirement was the small but important extension to $d^3$.

Several of the doubles with a petit ravalement use the original spacing of the strings and keys. Adding the extra natural width to the keyboard requires more space; this was achieved by thinning the keyblocks on one or both sides of the keywell. Adding notes to the treble part of the keyboard exacerbates the van Blankenburg problem, because they force the keyboard to be moved towards the bass, lengthening the scalings instead of shortening them. The usual solution is to move the nuts towards the gap to reduce the scalings, and to gain as much space from the keywell on the treble side as possible, so that moving the keyboards as a whole towards the bass is avoided. Examples of petit ravalement instruments altered to give a $G_1/B_1$ to $d^3$ compass are the 1612b HR, 1618b IR and the 1642b IR doubles.

By respacing the strings and making a new keyboard with a smaller octave span, two effects can be achieved. First, by narrowing the treble keyblock, space for the extra $d^3$ can be made. The smaller octave span of the keys and string band moves the position of the strings towards the treble and shortens their effective scalings. Obviously shortening is greater for the bass than for the treble strings. The long treble scalings were probably less problematical than might be predicted, since fortunately the fine treble strings would be more work-hardened, and therefore stronger, and could withstand the increased tension without breaking. Secondly, reducing the octave span of the strings and keys means that more notes can be added in the bass, in addition to the extra $c^{\sharp 3}$ and $d^3$ added in the treble. The 1624 IR was altered in this way to give a compass of $G_1$, $A_1$ to $d^3$, and the 1628 AR to give $A_1$ to $d^3$.

Clearly the large 'French' doubles could also be given a petit ravalement to increase the treble compass to $d^3$. The 1628b IR large double was given a $G_1$ to $d^3$ compass by making new keyboards with a small octave span, but leaving the spacing of the strings unaltered. To achieve this the keys splay out in the treble to reach the new notes added only on the treble side. The scalings were thus increased by only one semitone as a result of adding an extra choir of 8′ strings. No attempt was made to shorten the scalings by moving the nuts, probably because the instrument – obviously altered in France judging from the style of the keyboards, registers and decoration – was then ideally suited to play at the low French chamber pitch without problems of string breakages.

Plate 11.1 The 1642b IR double-manual harpsichord. This is a good example of an aligned double with a petit-ravalement compass of $G_1/B_1$ to $d^3$, and a fine later outer decoration and stand. Copyright, Hugh Gough, New York.

### *Keyboard coupling in double-manual harpsichords*

In their original state the keyboards of a Ruckers double were intended to play at different pitches: they were uncoupled and operated completely independently of one another. In a few instruments (e.g. 1612b HR, 1616 HR, 1615 AR and 1640b AR) no coupling mechanism was added after alignment and ravalement and the disposition was left unaltered from the original 1 × 8′, 1 × 4′. With a single 8′ and 4′ on each manual and no possibility of coupling, the only effect of having two manuals was the contrast in tone colour resulting from the different plucking points of the two rows of jacks plucking the same string. Because of the problem of damper interference, the two manuals could not be played simultaneously to provide a contrast in tone colour. As with the instrument in its original state with unaligned keyboards, the jacks of one manual had to be pulled off before the other manual could be used. Since the dampers had to leave the strings completely when a row of jacks was disengaged, the dampers must have been cut with an obliquely angled (rather than horizontal) edge touching the string. The fact that at least four instruments survive without the possibility of coupling the manuals suggests that, to many musicians and harpsichord builders, rapid tonal and volume contrast between manuals was not very important.

In those aligned and petit-ravalement instruments where manual coupling is a feature, it is most easily achieved by using a dogleg row of jacks. If the ends of the upper-manual keys are shortened slightly, they can operate on the second row of jacks with doglegs cut in them in the usual way. Sometimes the register for the fourth row of jacks is blanked off (e.g. 1618b IR), but often this register is used as well as the other three rows to give typical dispositions such as:

| (a) | (b) | (c) |
|---|---|---|
| ← 4′ | → 8′ | ← 4′ |
| → 8′ | ← 4′ | → 8′ |
| ← 8′ dogleg | ← 8′ dogleg | ← 8′ dogleg |
| ← 8′ | ← 8′ | → 8′ |

Disposition (a) leaves the original two rear rows of jacks plucking in the same direction as in the original Ruckers state, but disposition (b) provides more contrast between the lower-manual 8′ and the upper-manual 8′. However, in both (a) and (b) the single 8′s on each manual can play in dialogue with one another (e.g. in *pièces croisées*), and any or all of the registers available on the lower manual can be contrasted with the single 8′ dogleg. This gives a very versatile disposition, although it requires one more row of jacks than the equally versatile French shove-coupler system discussed below. Not so versatile is disposition (c) – either with the two rear registers as indicated or in the position shown in (b). Many instruments ravalé in Flanders have this disposition, however, as do many Flemish instruments which were newly built in the eighteenth century. Here a dialogue between a single 8′ on each manual is impossible. On the other hand, one can play two 8′s on the upper manual, a registration not available on any other North European instruments.

In France the usual solution was to abandon the fourth register completely – either by making wide registers to fill up the space in the gap, or simply by inserting a strip of wood into the gap to fill the space left vacant. Such instruments use a typical French shove coupler. Dogs on the lower-manual keys reach up and activate the ends of the upper-manual keylevers when the upper keyboard is in its rear position. This is the method found also on French grand ravalement double harpsichords, and naturally in doubles newly made in the eighteenth century.

### *Grand ravalement of Ruckers double-manual harpsichords*

As the musical need for a larger compass and a greater flexibility of disposition grew during the eighteenth century, so the desire increased to enlarge the old Ruckers instruments to a state comparable with the latest contemporary harpsichords. Because a double-manual harpsichord *à grand ravalement* – that is to say with five octaves from $F_1$ to $f^3$, a manual coupler, and perhaps even a peau de buffle register and genouillère – best satisfied this desire, there is a relatively large number of Ruckers and Couchet instruments which have been subjected to this process.

The enlargement of the case of a Flemish instrument on both the spine and cheek side was a major undertaking, and this probably accounts for the fact that most instruments were widened only on the treble side. For the normal size of transposing harpsichord, two different compasses are found in those instruments whose original key spacing and string spacing were retained. In the first of these, only the treble part of the compass was increased. The widening of the case and soundboard in the treble and the extension of the compass are all carried out leaving the keyboard in its original position in the instrument. Such instruments (e.g. 1620c AR, 1646 IC) have a $G_1/B_1$ to $f^3$ compass and are therefore simply aligned instruments extended in the treble. Two instruments of the second type (1599 HR and 1624 AR – the latter now a single) have adopted a unique method of grand ravalement. Here the original keyboard was extended down to $F_1$ by adding new extra keys below the original $B_1$, and up to $f^3$. The case and soundboard were widened on the treble side by an amount sufficient to accommodate the new keyboard, now wider by six Ruckers naturals. The altered keyboard was inserted into the instrument with the bottom $F_1$ key in the position of the original $B_1$ key. The original keys, shifted towards the treble, would play strings sounding an augmented fourth – $F_1$ to $B_1$ – higher than originally. Adding the second 8′ string lengthens the scalings by a semitone, making them shorter overall by a perfect fourth. Since the average Ruckers harpsichord scalings are about 356mm, the new scalings would, in theory, be $356 \times 3/4 = 267$mm. The actual $c^2$ scalings of the 1599 HR harpsichord are now 270mm, and that of the 1624 AR double are 261mm. It seems unlikely, however, that these instruments were strung in iron and tuned a fourth higher than R. Instead they may have been strung in brass and tuned to a pitch R or slightly higher.

Rather than using the original Ruckers octave span as above, respacing the strings and making new keyboards with a narrower octave span gave the builder carrying out the ravalement more flexibility. If a narrower octave span was used and the keys shifted towards the treble, extra bass notes could be added and the van Blankenburg problem avoided simultaneously. Instruments altered in this way are the 1612a HR ($G_1$, $A_1$ to $f^3$), the 1617 IR ($G_1$ to $f^3$) and the 1614 AR ($A_1$ to $e^3$) doubles. Obviously the further the keyboard is shifted towards the treble, the shorter the scalings become, and the more notes can be added in the bass. Sometimes, as on the 1623 AR, a new wrestplank was made which was wider than the original but which still left enough room for three registers in the gap. This enabled the nuts to be positioned closer to the bridges. The resulting shorter scalings enabled the keyboard to be shifted far enough towards the treble to allow the bass compass to be extended down to $F_1$, giving $F_1$, $G_1$ to $f^3$.

Because of their larger original bass compass the big 'French' Ruckers doubles were relatively easy to alter to give the grand ravalement five-octave compass of $F_1$ to $f^3$. By repinning the bridges, making new keyboards with a smaller octave span to match the new string spacing, and extending the case by less than 50mm it was possible to alter the 1646b AR double to give a full $F_1$ to $f^3$ compass (initially the compass was increased to $e^3$, and then later without widening the case to $f^3$). Since the instrument originally went down to $G_1$, the extension down to $F_1$ was easily accomplished using a keyboard with a smaller octave span. The van Blankenburg problem was solved partly by inserting the extra bass notes so as to push the keyboard towards the treble, thus shortening the scalings, and partly by moving the new nuts towards the gap.

By way of contrast to this simple, efficient method, the grand ravalement of the 1627c IR 'French' double, although carefully carried out, is clumsy in conception. Here the original string spacing and bridge and nut pinning was maintained. The extension of the compass down to $F_1$ and up to $f^3$ was accomplished by widening the case on both sides. On the bass side the original spine was cut down to the level of the soundboard liner and a new spine positioned a few millimetres from the original. A new strip of soundboard wood was jointed to the original, running over the cut-down spine to the new spine liner. The extensions to the bass ends of the bridges, added to take the extra bass strings, run over the original spine and spine liner. In an attempt to free the bridges and enable them to vibrate, a saw cut was made through the original spine and liner a few millimetres below soundboard level for both bridges. This must have helped the bass soundboard area and bridges to vibrate, but the ends of the bridges are still much stiffer than if the soundboard had been left completely free. On the treble side the original cheek has also been left in position behind the keywell with the new cheek beside it. But unlike the spine, the original cheek has been cut down to a level below the soundboard. This enables the extension to the 4′ hitchpin rail to run unhindered to the new cheek liner, and the new treble extensions to the soundboard and bridges are also left completely free to vibrate.

The ravalement of the 1627c IR harpsichord, in which both the treble and bass sides were enlarged, was considerably more work than the ravalement of the 1646b AR harpsichord. The method used for the 1627c IR instrument has the advantage that, because the original pinning of the bridges and nuts was left, the spacing of the strings was not changed, and the scalings therefore remained Pythagorean in the treble. In the 1646b AR instrument, and of course all others in which the string spacing is altered, the string lengths in the treble do not accurately halve with each octave rise in pitch. To some extent this can be compensated for by repositioning the nuts, but in fact the slight inaccuracies in those instruments with reduced octave spans do not seem to have a noticeably detrimental effect on the sound. The advantage of maintaining Ruckers' spacing of the strings, especially when the bass sound is compromised by the bridges running over the original spine and spine liner as in the 1627a IR instrument, is therefore minimal. Unfortunately we will probably never know whether the eighteenth-century harpsichord builders who altered these instruments considered the advantages and disadvantages of one type of ravalement over another, and whether or not there was a general consensus about the importance of accurately Pythagorean scalings, new versus old soundboard wood, and the stiffness of the soundboard and bridges.

Just as some single-manual harpsichords were reworked by resplicing their soundboards and incorporating these within a new case, so this process occurred for double-manual instruments. Whereas three instruments survive which were converted from singles into doubles by resplicing the soundboard, there is only one extant example of this process for doubles. The reason for this is fairly obvious. The double-manual harpsichords were already fairly large instruments designed to sound $G_1$ as the bottom note. The bass strings were therefore already long and the extension to $F_1$ could be carried out with little compromise, although in the normal doubles finding the extra space to add the naturals from $G_1/B_1$ down to $F_1$ was a problem. In the large 'French' doubles going down to $G_1$ chromatically there was little compromise, either in string length or in space constraints, in extending the compass down to $F_1$. For both the normal and the 'French' doubles the treble had to be extended by moving the cheek out to achieve the *grand ravalement* treble compass to $f^3$. A builder not willing to make any compromises at all in the ravalement of a Ruckers double is faced with no alternative: the soundboard must be respliced and the case both widened and lengthened.

The ravalement of the (1612) IR double in the Instrument Museum of the Conservatoire NSM, Paris, is an example of such an uncompromising ravalement. Here the length of the spine was increased by almost 200mm and the width of the tail by about 40mm. The inside case width was increased from about 760mm to 878mm allowing ample room for the grand ravalement $F_1$ to $f^3$ compass, and giving enough space at both the bass and treble ends of the bridges to enable the soundboard to vibrate freely. About 75mm of new wood was added in the middle of the soundboard, and 45mm along the bass side. New bridges we made as well as new barring and a new 4′ hitchpin rail.

The new design is extremely good and a great credit to the (anonymous) builder. The string scalings are accurately Pythagorean in the treble and double in length down to $c^1$ in both the 8′ and 4′ (see catalogue entry for the (1612) IR). The lengths of the bass strings are very long and exceed those of other French builders such as Goermans, Taskin and Blanchet by 50 to 150mm. The ingenuity and subtlety of the new design is reflected in the exceptionally fine sound of the instrument.

## CHAPTER TWELVE

# Ruckers clavecimbels, music and performance practice

Relative to the number and importance of the keyboard instruments which survive from sixteenth- and seventeenth-century Flanders, the amount of surviving Flemish keyboard music from this period is rather small. The most important composers contemporary with the Ruckers who were actually born in the Low Countries are Sweelinck and Pieter Cornet, both of whom have left some notable keyboard music. Composers such as Philips and Bull, although born in England, lived and wrote music in Flanders for a large part of their mature careers. They must have known not only the instruments built by the Ruckers, but the makers themselves. It is entirely appropriate to play their music on Ruckers instruments, since their compositions seem to have been affected by the compass and disposition (and probably sound and action as well) of the instruments they encountered in Flanders. The justifiable addition of Philips and Bull to the list of keyboard composers active in the Low Countries in the period contemporary with the Ruckers greatly increases the body of important music composed for the Flemish clavecimbels.

### CLAVECIMBEL COMPOSERS IN THE LOW COUNTRIES CONTEMPORARY WITH THE RUCKERS

By far the largest body of surviving late sixteenth- and early seventeenth-century clavecimbel music composed by a native of the Low Countries is that of Jan Pieterszoon Sweelinck (1562–1621). Sweelinck lived a quiet but productive life as organist of the Oude Kerk in Amsterdam, where he worked for forty-four years. During his time there, Artus Gheerdinck, the organ and clavecimbel builder, was carillonneur at the Oude Kerk. Strictly speaking, Sweelinck was not a Flemish composer, as Amsterdam was a part of the Protestant Dutch Provinces, which were struggling for independence from the Spanish Netherlands during most of Sweelinck's lifetime. But Sweelinck was one of the most famous teachers and organists of his time; his influence spread throughout Northern Europe, and would certainly have been felt in Antwerp. In 1604 he made a journey to Antwerp to buy a harpsichord for the city of Amsterdam, and this almost certainly would have been a Ruckers instrument. The music he wrote is well suited to the clavecimbels of the Ruckers family: it can all be played on an instrument with a C/E short octave going up to $a^2$ in the treble. In particular, his echo fantasias can be played to good effect on coupled mother-and-child virginals.[1]

There survives a small but excellent group of clavecimbel pieces by Pieter Cornet (*c.* 1570/80–1633). Cornet lived and worked in Brussels as organist at the church of St Nicolas, and at the Chapel Royal for Albert and Isabella, both of whom were very well disposed to his music. Cornet's music often makes use of tenths in the bass[2], playable only on a short octave, and sometimes

[1] See John Koster, 'The mother and child virginal and its place in the keyboard instrument culture of the sixteenth and seventeenth centuries', *Colloquium: Ruckers Klavecimbels en Copieën*, (Antwerp, 1977), 90–1. Sweelinck would almost certainly have known the double mother-and-child virginals by Martin van der Biest, a one time colleague of Hans Ruckers in Antwerp (see Chapter 1, pp. 5–6). A typical van der Biest double virginal is the splendid instrument in the Germanisches Nationalmuseum, Nuremberg, Cat. No. MI 85.

[2] My thanks to Lucy Carolan, who carried out a survey for me of the compasses and notes used in the music of England and the Low Countries in the period contemporary with the Ruckers family. This included both the published and manuscript English and Flemish sources, including especially the Fitzwilliam Virginal Book.

goes as high as $b^{\flat 2}$ in the treble, implying that Cornet would have expected a full four-octave keyboard compass to $c^3$.

Peter Philips (*c.* 1560–1628) was born in England, although he spent his adult life after he was thirty in Antwerp and Brussels. He was a stubborn adherent to the Catholic Church, and had to leave England in 1582 'pour la foy Catholique'. He went to Rome, where he worked with Felice Anerio (and where his patron was Cardinal Alessandro Farnese, namesake of and cousin to the Duke of Parma – see p. 4). He travelled around Europe with Thomas, Lord Paget and went to Antwerp in 1588 before the sailing of the Armada. He settled first in Brussels in 1589 and then in Antwerp in 1590, where he was married. Philips went to Amsterdam in 1593 'to sie and heare an excellent man of his faculties'. This almost certainly must have been Sweelinck, who composed a set of variations on Philips' famous pavan of 1580 (*Fitzwilliam Virginal Book*, vol. I, p. 313).

Returning from Amsterdam, Philips was arrested and thrown into prison in Middleburg for an alleged plot against the life of Queen Elizabeth I. While in prison (Philips was soon exonerated of the charges of treason, and released) he composed the famous *Pavana Dolorosa* and *Galliarda Dolorosa*, which make extensive use both of tenths in the bass, and of a crucial bottom G♯. This could be played only on an instrument with a broken octave in the bass, i.e. with the bottom D/F♯ and E/G♯ split so that both notes could be played on the accidental keylevers. The composition of this piece with its unusual keyboard arrangement was almost certainly a result of Philips having seen an instrument by Lodewijck Grouwels while in Middleburg. Just such an instrument exists in the Metropolitan Museum of Art, New York (Catalogue No. 89.4.1196)[3], made by Grouwels in Middleburg in 1600. This instrument originally had the normal four-octave compass from C to $c^3$, with a bottom broken octave. That is, it had a short octave with the bottom F♯ and G♯ split so that they sounded the accidental notes as well as the D and E of the short octave tuning. Such an instrument would suit Philips' *Pavana Dolorosa* and *Galliarda Dolorosa* perfectly.

In 1597 Archduke Albert admitted Philips to his household as an organist of the Chapel Royal, where he would have worked alongside Cornet and later John Bull. Philips composed and worked in Brussels from then until his death in 1628. He never lost contact with Antwerp, however, and Phalèse, the famous Antwerp music publisher, printed most of his major collections. He almost certainly would have known Ioannes Ruckers, who was appointed court organ and harpsichord builder to Albert in 1614. When Albert died in 1621, Philips was held in such high regard that he led the procession of chaplains of the Chapel Royal in the funeral cortège. He had reached a position at court similar to that of Handel in England a century later, and was really as Flemish as Handel was English.

Another contemporary of Sweelinck, Cornet, Philips and of Ioannes and Andreas Ruckers was the English-born John Bull (1562/3–1628). Bull had the classic English choir-school training, was sent to join the Chapel Royal in his early teens, and later became a Gentleman of the Chapel Royal. After an initial period of penury, he gradually became well known and appreciated at court. But having already been forced to marry in 1607 because he had got his wife with child, he was forced to flee England in 1613 to avoid prosecution for adultery. He went to Flanders, never to return to England.

For a time Bull worked in the court chapel for Albert and Isabella, but the scandal in England caught up with him and he had to leave. From 1615 he was assistant organist at Antwerp cathedral; he became organist in 1617. Bull wrote a fantasia on a theme of Sweelinck when the latter died in 1621. Obviously Bull would also have known Ioannes Ruckers, who tuned the cathedral organ, and also Andreas Ruckers and the other instrument builders, musicians, and artists active in Antwerp's busy cultural life. Bull lived and worked there until his death in 1628.

These composers working in Flanders all moved in circles which intersected at many different points. Sweelinck came to Antwerp to buy a harpsichord which was almost certainly a Ruckers instrument. Sweelinck knew and appreciated the music of both Bull and Philips, who in turn were avid protagonists of Sweelinck. Cornet, Bull and Philips all worked at the royal chapel in Brussels, and would have known Ioannes Ruckers there. Bull and Philips both had strong professional and personal ties with Antwerp: Bull worked at the cathedral; Philips had his music published there and was married to an Antwerp woman.

Obviously the music of each of these composers was

[3] E. Winternitz, *Keyboard Instruments in the Metropolitan Museum of Art: A Picture Book* (New York, 1961), Plate 7. See also Koster, 'The mother and child virginal–', 84f, who describes this instrument, signed LODOVVICVS GROVVELVS ME FECIT 1600'. Koster failed to notice that the top two treble jackslots, and the bottom bass jackslot are not original, so that the original compass had only forty-seven notes, and not fifty as he claims. X-rays of the keyboard's original balance rail, taken for me by Stewart Pollens of the Metropolitan Museum, confirm that the original compass did not have any split enharmonic keys and that only the bottom D/F♯ and E/G♯ keylevers were split. There is therefore no escaping the fact that the original scalings were non-Pythagorean, as are the present scalings with the additional notes.

limited by the compass, disposition and keyboard action of the instruments which the Ruckers and the other contemporary Antwerp builders were making. And the tuning system and pitch of the instruments had to suit the music. It is necessary therefore to examine the relationship between the instruments built in the Ruckers tradition and contemporary music and performance practice.

## THE SHORT OCTAVE AND MEANTONE TUNING

The normal C/E short octave began to appear in the period around 1520.[4] Early keyboards began with G (the gamma ut) or F, and gradually extensions appeared going down to C, usually without any of the accidentals above C until the note B♭ was reached.[5]

The reason for the lack of the four bottom accidentals (C♯, E♭, F♯ and G♯) was both a musical one and a matter of economics. Pieces in this early period tended not to be written with more than one accidental (*b*♭) and did not modulate far from the home key. Accidentals, if they were required, occurred because of modal writing, or as a result of the transposition of a piece. Also, the temperaments in use during this period simply did not allow writing in or modulation into remote keys. In normal writing of the period the notes in the lowest octave were used as roots to the chords higher up. There was no musical necessity for accidentals in the bottom octave, since they were the roots of chords which were unplayable in the temperament used. An organ builder, knowing that these four notes would never be required, could reduce the cost of his instrument considerably by not building four of the largest pipes in the organ.

As Meeùs has pointed out (see footnote 4), it must have been a short step for someone to convert an old organ finishing at F in the bass to one that extended to C, using the short-octave arrangement. He simply added an E key below the F, and reused the F♯ and G♯ – or added them if they were missing – and made pipes for the E, F♯ and G♯ keys which were tuned to C, D and E respectively.

Therefore, probably as a result of its familiarity in organs, the short octave became the standard keyboard arrangement in stringed keyboard instruments as well. In parallel with this, meantone tuning had become the standard system of keyboard temperament.[6] In fact the two go together – any keyboard instrument, with a short octave was almost certainly tuned using meantone temperament. As has already been said, the accidentals below B♭ in the bass were never required as the roots of chords, since these could not be played in meantone tuning or any modified meantone temperament. That inversions of meantone chords might need the missing accidentals, or that they might be used as lower auxiliary notes, did not seem to bother contemporary musicians.

In the early part of the sixteenth century, either because the practice of equipping organs with a short octave had not yet become standard, or because meantone tuning was not the established temperament, stringed keyboard instruments were often made without a short octave. The 1550 virginal by Ioes Karest discussed in Chapter 2 (pp. 23ff) had a compass of C, D to $f^3$, even though the 1548 virginal by the same builder had a short octave. The 1537 Hans Müller harpsichord had a C, D to $g^2$, $a^2$ compass, and so had three 'unnecessary' accidentals (E♭, F♯ and G♯) in the bass octave. But from the middle of the sixteenth century onwards, the short octave became almost universal both in Italy and north of the Alps. Exceptions to this were the instruments made and used in England, as will be discussed in more detail below.

Although there is considerable documentary evidence that meantone tuning was the common keyboard temperament throughout most of the sixteenth and seventeenth centuries,[7] there is only one clue to be found on

4 Nicolas Meeùs, 'La naissance de l'octave courte e ses différentes formes au 16ᵉ siècle'. diss, Université Catholique de Louvain (1971).

5 Most of the evidence for this comes from old organ contracts, but two other interesting examples are pointed out by Edwin M. Ripin in 'The Norrlanda organ and the Ghent altarpiece', *Festschrift to Ernst Emsheimer*, Musikhistoriska museets skrifter 5 (Stockholm, 1974), 193–6. He has reconstructed the keyboard on the organ in the painting of the 'Mystic Lamb' by van Eyck in Ghent, before it was repainted. It began with a G; the accidentals G♯, B♭, c♯ and e♭ were all missing, and f♯ was the first accidental. The Norrlanda Organ (late fourteenth century) now in the Musikhistoriska Museet, Stockholm, had a manual keyboard beginning on c with c♯, e♭, f♯ and g♯ placed normally above it (but with b♭ and b both as lower notes), but the pedal board began at C with the naturals laid out side by side in the usual 'long-octave' way, and B♭ as the first accidental. Needless to say there are anomalies which presently defy explanation: the German clavicytherium (*c.* 1480) in the Royal College of Music, London (RCM No. 1), was found by Bill Debenham to have had an unusual compass with keys playing the apparent notes E, E♯, F, G, G♯, A and then chromatically to $g^2$ (see Elizabeth Wells, 'The London clavicytherium, *Early Music*, VI/4 (1978), 568–71).

6 See Mark Lindley, *Lutes, Viols and Temperaments* (Cambridge, 1984), 43–50.

7 This evidence includes treatises by: Nicola Vicentino, *L'antica musica ridotta alla moderna prattica* (Rome, 1555; facs., Kassel, 1967); Gioseffo Zarlino, *Le istitutioni harmoniche* (Venice, 1558; facs., New Haven, Conn., 1968); Thomas Morley, *A plaine and easie introduction to practical musicke* (London, 1597; facs., London, 1952); Michael Praetorius, *Syntagma Musicum II: De Organographia* (Wolfenbüttel, 1619; facs., Kassel, 1958); Marin Mersenne, *Harmonie universelle* (Paris, 1636; facs., Paris, 1965); Jean Denis, *Traité de l'accord de l'espinette* (Paris, 1650; New York, 1969; English translation, Cambridge, 1987); Klaas Douwes, *Grondig Ondersoek van de Toonen der Musijk* (Franeker, 1699; facs., Amsterdam, 1970).

Ruckers instruments that they were tuned in meantone. The two manuals in both the normal and the chromatic-bass 'French' double-manual harpsichords are separated in pitch by a musical interval of a fourth: one manual is at R, the other at R − 4. On these instruments each of the *e*♭s on the keyboard at R is required to play a *g*♯ on the keyboard at R − 4 (see Chapter 6, Fig. 6.13 and Chapter 8, Plate 8.1 and Fig. 8.4). In order to avoid the problem that the putative *g*♯ would sound an *a*♭ 41 cents too sharp,[8] doubled strings were provided for these notes, and the action was arranged so that the keys operated jacks sounding the correct pitches (see Chapter 6, p. 108). Any historical temperament other than meantone (just intonation or Pythagorean temperament, for example) would result in many more than one conflict per octave, and equal temperament would require none; so the Ruckers doubles *must* have used meantone temperament or one of its variants. There seems no reason to suggest that all of the other models of Ruckers clavecimbels were tuned using a temperament other than meantone.

## THE KEYBOARD AND ACTION AND THEIR EFFECT ON THE PLAYER

### *Keyboard touch and balance ratio*

The mechanics of the keyboard and action of any keyboard instrument will have a great effect on the way a musician will perform; in particular, the point along the keylever at which the balance point is placed strongly affects the feel or touch of the instrument under the fingers of the player. The closer the balance point is to the near end of the keylever, the harder will be the touch of the keyboard; the keys lifting the jacks will feel heavy, but the player will have a strong sense of the exact point at which the jack plucks the string. The further towards the rear of the keylever the balance point is, the lighter will be the touch, and the player will have to make very little effort to execute fast passages and difficult ornaments. But the sense of contact between the finger and the string will be lost, and both the sensation and the control of the point of pluck will not be as great.

In Chapter 6 (p. 118) the balance ratio was defined as the ratio of the distance along the keylever, from the near end of the natural's touchplate to the natural's balance point, divided by the length of the rear of the keylever from the natural's balance point to the tail of the keylever. This is equivalent to the mechanical advantage of the keylever: the larger the balance ratio, the lighter the touch experienced by the player, and the smaller the balance ratio, the heavier the touch. Table 12.1 compares the balance ratios of some Ruckers instruments with

Table 12.1 *Comparison of Ruckers balance ratios with those of eighteenth-century instruments*

| Type of instrument | Balance ratio | |
|---|---|---|
| Ruckers virginals | 0.53–0.56 | |
| Ruckers single-manual harpsichords | 0.59–0.61 | |
| | upper manual | lower manual |
| Ruckers double-manual harpsichords | 0.60 | 0.55 |
| Dulcken double-manual harpsichords | 0.70 | 0.70 |
| Taskin double-manual harpsichords | 0.79 | 0.80 |
| Kirkman double-manual harpsichords | 0.85 | 0.87 |

those of harpsichords made by some of the most important eighteenth-century makers.

A keylever with its balance point half-way along its length would have a balance ratio of 1.00, and would have a very light touch indeed. As can be seen, the balance ratio of the Kirkman lower-manual keys is not far from this; indeed, Kirkman keyboards are so centre-balanced that the tails of the keys require lead weighting to compensate for the heavy keyplate ends, otherwise the tails of the keys would not return under the weight of the jacks. At first it seems absurd to have to compensate for a design intended to lighten the touch by adding lead weights. The point is that, once the keys achieve a natural balance in this way, their large mechanical advantage makes it seem to the player that it is effortless to cause the jacks to pluck the strings. The Ruckers instruments, with a balance ratio of just over 0.50, have their balance points placed only about a third of the way along the keylever, and so have a comparatively heavy touch. Even if the keylevers were made to balance naturally about the balance point by adding lead weights at the keyplate end, the low value of the balance ratio of the keylever would still give the player the sensation of having to make a distinct effort to cause the jacks to pluck the strings. The natural balance of the keylever, whether it is achieved by adding lead weights as in the eighteenth-century English tradition, or by shaving away wood as in the French tradition, is not as important as the balance ratio when it

[8] This is assuming normal quarter-comma meantone, with perfectly pure major thirds in the 'home' keys. If a less extreme form of meantone tuning were used, say, sixth-comma meantone, the difference is still 20 cents, a discrepancy the ear finds musically intolerable, and which would still therefore require the use of the doubled strings for all *e*♭/*g*♯s.

comes to determining the sensation of lightness of touch to the player.

### *Keyboard layout and action cloths*

There are various ways of spacing out the sharps at the tail ends of the naturals. Five sharps have to be fitted into the space occupied by seven naturals, such that two sharps are placed at the back of the first three naturals, and three sharps are placed at the back of the next four naturals. It is clear that the space occupied by the seven natural keytails and the five sharps cannot be divided into twelve equal divisions. In Ruckers instruments the tails of the naturals *c*, *e*, *f* and *b* are much wider than those of *d*, *g* and *a*. The space for the fingers between the sharps on these narrow natural keytails makes it virtually impossible for the player to get his fingers between the sharps and must have affected contemporary fingering patterns. (However, since one would normally be playing in meantone in the 'home' keys, it was rarely necessary to move the hands into awkward positions towards the rear of the keys.) Ruckers keyboards were, however, inconvenient for later music, and this explains why many were replaced.

The cloths used in the Ruckers keyboards are tightly woven and matted. When a keylever is depressed the woollen fibres compress to their final thickness very quickly. There is enough 'give' in the cloth to bring the keys to rest quietly and quickly, and yet it is hard and resilient enough to give a crisp feel to the action unlike that produced with most modern materials. This, combined with the somewhat unfavourable (compared to the eighteenth century) balance ratio of the keylevers, gives the player a strong impression in his fingers of the jacks plucking the strings, and a greater feeling of contact with the instrument. It does, however, require the player to exert a greater force while playing. This is exacerbated by the fact that, unlike the eighteenth-century instruments mentioned above which have keylevers cut away underneath to balance naturally on the balance rail, Ruckers keys do not have a natural balance, but are quite strongly 'tail-heavy'. The extra effort required of the player, coupled with the impossibility of playing between the sharps, means that a considerable alteration is necessary to the technique and fingerings used by players accustomed to eighteenth-century or most modern reproduction instruments. I shall not discuss here how the technique of a performer playing a Ruckers-model keyboard with its low balance ratio and heavy touch might differ from that of a player performing on an eighteenth-century style keyboard. Nevertheless, the figures in Table 12.1 show that it is really impossible to use the same technique on both. There is no point in a musician complaining that he finds the seventeenth-century keyboard too heavy to play. The contemporary musicians had a technique adapted to the keyboards and instruments they were playing. It is up to the modern performer to discover what this technique was, and in so doing discover fingerings, phrasings and techniques suited to the correct interpretation of the contemporary keyboard music.

Most instruments with original keyboards and keys which have not received too much use show that the tails of the natural touchplates were lettered in red, possibly in sanguine, with their note name: *c*, *d*, *e*, *f*, *g*, *a*, *h*, repeating each octave, with the bottom (C/E) labelled *c*. The practice of lettering the natural names was also common on Italian instruments in the period contemporary with the Ruckers. In Italian instruments this was usually done in ink which was absorbed into the boxwood touchplates; it therefore survived better and is much more apparent. Lettering the keys in this way was a practice so widespread that it can hardly have been used only as a guide to help the learning child, and must reflect the transition from solmization to the modern 'one pitch to a note' system.

### *Implications of Ruckers-style dampers*

Virtually all seventeenth- and eighteenth-century harpsichords that I have seen with apparently original jacks have dampers with sloping sides. As explained in Chapter 5, this is a very efficient way of damping the strings, especially when the dampers are doubled, two to a jack, as they are in the larger sizes of virginal and in the unison registers of the harpsichords. The dampers in Ruckers instruments have the typical 'mouse ear' shape, which presents an angled edge to the string, and maintains its shape and position because of its conical form. The use of this type of damper is really the only effective way of damping the heavy bass strings vibrating with a large amplitude in the larger sizes of muselar virginals. In harpsichords, when a register is disengaged, the dampers come away from the strings and leave them undamped and free to vibrate, or to be engaged by another set of jacks. (As mentioned in Chapter 6, it is essential in Ruckers double-manual harpsichords that the dampers leave the strings entirely when the register is disengaged. With only one set of strings used in common by both keyboards, the dampers of the jacks belonging to one manual would otherwise cause interference when the jacks of the other manual were in use.)

In those instruments with two sets of unison strings, if the player disengages one of the 8′ sets of strings, it is left undamped while the other set of strings is sounding. But because the two sets of unison strings are physically very close to one another, and both are sharing the same bridge, the acoustical coupling between the two choirs is very strong. What this means is that if one of the sets of strings is disengaged and left undamped, then it will vibrate in sympathy with the set of sounding strings. This produces a halo of sound shimmering in the background, an effect startlingly different from the total silence following the normal crisp damping provided by the doubled sloping dampers. Duarte, writing to Huygens in 1648 (see Appendix 17), said of the harpsichord being built by Couchet that it was to have '3 different strings of which 2 strings are at unison and one at the octave and all three of which can be played together or each string separately with or without the octave . . . But they have a better tone because the unused string which is not played moves of its own accord, producing such a sweet quiet tone through the principal sound, which does not occur when all three strings are played together.'

Couchet, writing directly to Huygens (Appendix 18), implies that the instrument eventually made for Huygens had a 2 × 8′ disposition, without a 4′, and that he himself preferred an instrument with an octave, i.e. with the old-fashioned 1 × 8′, 1 × 4′ disposition. Musically, the problem with having an undamped choir of strings vibrating in sympathy is that the tonality of the previous harmonies are left sounding when the music modulates into a new key. But with only one set each of unison and octave strings, the fact that the dampers were not in contact with the strings when only a single row of jacks was engaged did not matter much as there was little acoustical coupling between the unison and octave bridges. The bridges are located far apart on the soundboard and are separated by the heavy 4′ hitchpin rail, so that the energy of the strings on one bridge cannot cause those of the other to vibrate. Perhaps Couchet was more sensitive than Duarte to the unpleasant effect caused by the undamped strings in the 2 × 8′ instruments.

Although the classical way of cutting the dampers is much more efficient, virtually all modern builders use flag dampers with a horizontal lower surface. Jacks with this type of damper tend to be thrown back up by the heavy bass strings, or the shape of the dampers becomes distorted and the dampers lose their effectiveness. But even if less efficient, these dampers always remain in contact with the strings when the register of jacks is disengaged. The use of this type of damper seems to arise because most modern musicians are also unable to accept the sound of the unplucked strings vibrating in sympathy, even though the problem really only arises in single-manual harpsichords with two 8′ registers. In double-manual harpsichords the unused 8′ strings can be left in contact with their dampers on the unused manual. In single-register instruments such as virginals and spinets, and in double-manual harpsichords and singles disposed 1 × 8′, 1 × 4′, it is a positive disadvantage *not* to cut the dampers with a sloping edge.

## THE PITCH SCHEME OF RUCKERS CLAVECIMBELS

In Chapters 4 and 8, the relative pitches of the various models of Ruckers virginals and harpsichords were determined. This was done by a mathematical comparison of the treble and bass scalings of each model with the treble and bass scalings of the normal 6-voet virginals and harpsichords. Also, for the 1612a HR double-manual harpsichord, whose original scalings cannot any longer be determined and compared because of alterations to it, the usual features of Ruckers normal construction practice in laying out the soundboard and bridges were used to determine its original compass and pitch. The different models of clavecimbels made by the Ruckers were found to correspond to eight different pitches, with basic intervals of a tone, a fourth, a fifth and an octave between them.

These eight pitches group very naturally into the scheme shown in Table 12.2.

It thus appears that these instruments belong to two families, each having members separated from one another by fourths and fifths, the two families being one tone apart. According to this arrangement, one family consists of instruments pitched at R − 5, R, R + 4 and R + 8, and the other family, a tone higher, at R − 4, R + 2, R + 5, and R + 9.

The analogy between the scheme suggested and a consort of say, recorders, viols or lutes is obvious. The difference is that recorders and viols normally only play monophonically, and only lutes are individually expected to play polyphony. But although lute music exists intended to be played by a consort of lutes, the pitch relationships of the members of the consort do not cover such a wide span as those in the Ruckers scheme. Furthermore, the idea of a consort of keyboard instruments poses certain theoretical problems involving tunings and the limited number of tonalities in which the music could be written. Also, there seems not to be a single piece of surviving music which indicates that four differently-pitched keyboard instruments were meant to play together. The famous duet by Giles Farnaby[9] is only

[9] Giles Farnaby, '[For Two Virginals]', *The Fitzwilliam Virginal Book*, ed. J. A. Fuller Maitland and W. Barclay Squire (Leipzig, 1899; facs., New York, 1963), Vol. 2, 202.

Table 12.2. *The pitch scheme of Ruckers clavecimbels*

| Pitch | Pitch level | Description |
|---|---|---|
| R + 9 | | 2½-voet virginals, Douwes 2-voet 4-duimen virginals |
| R + 8 | | child virginals, the 3-voet virginals of Britsen, Douwes 3-voet virginals |
| R + 5 | | 4-voet harpsichords, 4-voet virginals |
| R + 4 | | 4½-voet virginals |
| R + 2 | | 5-voet virginals |
| R | | 6-voet virginals, normal 6-voet harpsichords, upper manual of normal doubles |
| R − 4 | | lower manual of normal doubles |
| R − 5 | | one manual of 1612a HR double |

for two players, and these both play instruments at the same pitch.

The double virginals, although they could be coupled and played together from the one keyboard, could also be played separately by two players. The harpsichord/virginal combinations *must* have been played by two separate players, otherwise the combination of the two instruments in one case makes no sense. But how were they played? What music did they play? Were they played with a 4-voet quint clavecimbel playing a 'middle' part? The instruments mentioned in the Fugger inventory of about 1566 are intriguing.[10] Among them are two keyboard instruments with more than one manual. One is described as 'a harpsichord with two keyboards, made in Cologne, so that two can play together on each one' – presumably the perfect instrument for the Farnaby duet. But the second is remarkable: 'a harpsichord with four keyboards. Four persons can play together on it with four different voices [or parts]. Has no rose, and is very lovely in resonance. Made in the Netherlands'.

It seems highly unlikely that all four keyboards of this instrument were at the same pitch. The fact that the instrument came from the Netherlands suggests that the large number of pitches and models in the Ruckers tradition arose out of an earlier tradition where a multiplicity of pitches were also to be found. But what were the pitches of the Fugger inventory instrument? And how was it used for the performance of music? If the Ruckers instruments were played together by four players, then it must have been in a way similar to the Fugger instrument, whatever that might have been.[11]

## THE RUCKERS VIRGINALS

The compass of most Ruckers virginals is the standard C/E to $c^3$. The treble compass to $c^3$ is surprising in the light of the contemporary music. There is virtually no keyboard music composed in the period up to 1625 that goes above $a^2$, whether it is Flemish, English or French. And yet even the earliest 1581 HR double virginal has a $c^3$ compass. The 1583 HR quint virginal and the virginal part of the 1594 HR single-manual harpsichord/virginal combination both have treble compasses reaching only to $a^2$ (both without $g^{\sharp 2}$), and are therefore in keeping with the music. But all subsequent virginals, at least until the period around 1625–30, must be considered ahead of their time as far as the written music is concerned. The music as performed may, of course, have used the notes above $a^2$ either for ornamentation or for the performance of divisions. The upper notes may also have been needed for transposition. Pieces going up to $g^2$ could be transposed up a fourth, but the fact that most of the music does go to $a^2$ means that pieces could not be transposed up a fourth without exceeding the $c^3$ compass.

The 1629 IR 4½-voet spinett virginal has the unusual compass C/E to $d^3$, with an original top note not found on any other extant virginal, and found at a date when the

[10] See Richard Schaal, 'Die Musikinstrumenten-Sammlung von Raimund Fugger d.J.', *Archiv für Musikwissenschaft*, XXI (1964), 212–16, and Douglas Alton Smith, 'The musical instrument inventory of Raymund Fugger', *The Galpin Society Journal*, XXXIII (1980), 36–44.

[11] There is a distinct possibility that the Ruckers themselves may have made harpsichords with four keyboards. See Appendix 15, which lists the instruments on sale in Paris in the eighteenth century. The entry for 2 May [1768] (p. 303) gives: 'Excellent double-ended harpsichord by Ruckers, rectangular in shape with 4 keyboards, nicely painted. 1,000 livres.' What kind of an instrument was this? A double-manual harpsichord/virginal combination has three keyboards, although only two of them are usable at the same time. An instrument consisting of two double-manual harpsichords placed back to back would indeed have four keyboards, although only two would be usable together. I strongly suspect that this instrument is of this type, but there may of course also have been keyboards (belonging to virginals?) on the long sides, with single-manual harpsichords at the ends.

written music was only just starting to reach above $a^2$. Ignoring the second manual of the doubles, which reaches to $f^3$ because of its transposing function, the upward extension of the compass to $d^3$ is found on only two other Ruckers instruments, both harpsichords, built before 1650. One of these is the 1639 IR single-manual harpsichord which originally had the compass C to $d^3$, and which therefore marks the beginning of the upward extension of the compass to match the later written music. The other is the 1612a HR double-manual harpsichord, which originally had one manual at a pitch of R − 5 with the same C/E to $d^3$ compass. It seems highly unlikely that the 1629 IR and the 1612a HR instruments, standing exactly an octave apart in pitch, have the same compass through sheer coincidence. There are two obvious reasons for their having identical compasses. Possibly the compass may have been taken this high so that the *pitch* of the top note $d^3$ was the same as that of the top $c^3$ of the instrument's nearest neighbour in the pitch scheme above: the top keys of the instruments at R + 4 and at R + 5 would then sound the same pitch, and the top keys of the R − 5 and R − 4 instruments would also sound the same pitch. A player who owned an instrument like the 1612a HR or the 1629 IR could then transpose pieces written to $c^3$ up a tone to the pitch of the more common types of instruments at R − 4 and R + 5. The fact that the written music only goes to $a^2$ suggests, however, that the reason for the top $d^3$ note may have been to enable upward transpositions of a fourth.

### *Why different sizes of virginal?*

The array of sizes and pitches of Ruckers virginals is quite bewildering. In all there are six models of spinett virginal, with three models of muselar virginal duplicating the sizes and pitches of three of these. So a potential customer buying a Ruckers virginal had a choice of nine different models. One of the many questions growing out of this work which I have been unable to explain is why so many different models of virginal were made, and how these models of instrument fitted into the daily musical life and practice of the sixteenth and seventeenth centuries.[12] Gaspard Duarte,[13] writing in May 1648 (see Appendix 17, p. 305), says of the small clavecimbels: 'Now concerning the small harpsichords with unison or with an octave, each of which has its own beauty. They are usually one tone higher, and are of my invention of a few years ago. They are used in small chambers for playing courantes, allemandes and sarabandes . . .'

The smaller clavecimbels, with a smaller soundboard area producing less sound, would indeed be more suited to 'small chambers' than to large ones. But could they not also play fantasias, and other dance movements? Why, if the smaller instruments are designed for small rooms with small acoustics, are they not designed at pitches of, say, a major or minor third above reference pitch R, or a sixth or a seventh? Why are they found only at a tone, a fourth and a fifth above R? Was there some theoretical reason based on Greek classical writings, or was it just a practical reason based on convenience in calculating the scalings and the size of case? Or, was it merely a practical and mundane reason having to do with offering a choice to the customer commensurate with the size of his pocketbook?

There is a similar lack of evidence about how the combination of the mother with the child virginal was used. The child could be drawn out of its storage space beside the keyboard of the mother, and placed above the mother's jacks in order to couple the actions of the two. The musician could then play 1 × 8′, 1 × 4′ from the keyboard of the mother with a solo 4′ on the upper keyboard of the child. Koster[14] makes a good case for suggesting that they might be used for 'echo' effects, such as those in Sweelinck's echo fantasias. But even though the keyboards of the two could be coupled, they are clearly two independent instruments, just as much as the harpsichord and virginals are in the rectangular harpsichord/virginal combinations. Both types of double instruments must have been played separately by two players. No music survives for this combination, even though the use of both types of double clavecimbels in this way must have been a fairly common practice.

And what about the 2½-voet virginals? Because their keys were cranked inwards towards the centre of the instrument, the spacing of the jacks and the ends of the keylevers would not match those of a putative 'mother' 5-voet virginal an octave lower. The 2½-voet virginal could therefore be used only on its own as a solo instrument, or with a 5-voet virginal played by a separate

12 See my article, 'Ioannes and Andreas Ruckers: a quatercentenary celebration', *Early Music*, VII, 4 (1979), 460–2, with comments on the questions raised there by Ian Harwood, 'Flemish harpsichord pitches', *Early Music*, VIII, 2 (1980), 221–2.

13 Gaspard Duarte, a rather pompous, self-important man of commerce (he was an immensely wealthy Antwerp diamond merchant), was at the same time an accomplished musician and a man of letters. His claim to have invented the 5-voet harpsichord a few years before writing this letter in March 1648 is dubious. A 5-voet harpsichord would presumably be at the same pitch, R + 2, as a 5-voet virginal. The first extant 5-voet clavecimbel is the virginal by Ioannes and Andreas Ruckers of 1604, and it seems highly unlikely to me that no one else would have thought of building a harpsichord at this pitch in the intervening forty-four years. For a biography of Duarte see W. J. A. Jonckbloet and J. P. W. Land, *Musique et musiciens au ᵉXVIIᵉ siècle* (Leiden, 1882), clxxiv–clxxxiii.

14 See Koster, 'The mother and child virginal'.

player in a way similar to the uncoupled 6-voet mother and child. To the modern ear the aggressively high and piercing sound of one of these little instruments makes their very existence surprising. Why were such instruments made when the same amount of work and very little more material was required to make a larger, lower-pitched instrument? Were they used to accompany a g–d$^1$ consort of recorders (i.e. an f–c$^1$ consort a tone high), which, because they actually sound an octave above their written pitch, were actually playing at R + 9? It is indeed difficult to enter into the musical world of this period and to get a realistic idea of what normal musical practice might have been.

### *The harpichordium stop*

Only the muselar virginals had a harpichordium. As explained in Chapter 5, p. 77, probably because the amplitude of vibration of the end-plucked spinett virginal strings was very small, the regulation of the lead hooks of the harpichordium stop would have been very difficult on such an instrument. For the same reason the treble strings of the muselar virginals, which are very fine and also have a small amplitude of vibration, are not equipped with a harpichordium. The effect of the stop is to produce a snarling bass accompaniment to the open, rather flute-like treble sound. The C/E to f$^1$ compass of the harpichordium covers most of the bass accompaniments encountered in the literature of the period, but pieces whose melody line does not cross down into the region below f$^{\sharp 1}$ are difficult to find. Clearly the stop is not intended to be used everywhere; it is certainly not appropriate to slow dances or fantasias. A piece in which the use of the harpichordium stop would be fitting, with its repeated drone bass, and also possible because the bass never goes above f$^1$ and the right hand never descends below f$^{\sharp 1}$, is given below:[15]

## HARPSICHORD REGISTRATION

### *The solo 4′*

Although there was in any case little option open to a player faced with the limited possibilities of one 8′ and one 4′, the sheer difficulty of changing the registers on a Ruckers harpsichord implies that the music of this period was not conceived in terms of varied colouring. The registration could be altered at the beginning or end of a piece, or between movements, but never in the middle. The obvious choices of registration are the solo 8′, and the 8′ and 4′ combined together. The modern harpsichordist should remember that the 2 × 8′ disposition was not generally available on North European harpsichords until about 1650.

It is important to note, however, that even in single-manual harpsichords the 8′ register can be turned off, leaving just a solo 4′. From the builders' point of view, it would have been much easier to fix the 8′ register permanently in position so that it could never be disengaged. The stability of the regulation would be increased, since the 8′ upper jackslide would never move. (This fact was not overlooked by a number of Italian builders making 2 × 8′ instruments, where one register is fixed and permanently engaged.) There would also not be any disadvantage in doing so from the point of view of tuning – the 4′ would be disengaged while the 8′ was tuned, and then engaged and brought into pitch with the tuned 8′.

But the 8′ can be disengaged in Ruckers harpsichords, and the reason for this can only be that the solo 4′ was considered a desirable registration by the musicians of the sixteenth and seventeenth centuries. Most modern harpsichordists ignore this possibility, just as they ignore the

[15] Fuller Maitland and Barclay Squire, eds., *The Fitzwilliam Virginal Book*, Vol. 2, 268.

large number of octave keyboard instruments languishing in the reserve collections of most museums. Octave instruments, and octave registrations, were much more popular in the historical period than they are today, and there is a clear need to try to understand how they were used if the modern quest for authentic performance is going to be carried forward.

### *The buff stop*

Another way to vary harpsichord registration was to use the buff stop in the 8′ strings. Except in the late harpsichords by the Couchets the buff was always split; and so its use was like that of the harpichordium stop in the muselar virginals, to give a contrasting sound in the bass and treble registers. The soft moose-leather pads touching the strings near their ends quickly damp out the higher harmonics of the strings, and produce a muted sound like that of the gut strings of a lute or harp. This contrasts with the metallic bell-like sound of the normal un-buffed harpsichord strings. Like the virginal harpichordium which extends from C/E to $f^1$, the harpsichord buff stop splits between $f^1$ and $f\sharp^1$,[16] and both types of stop provide a strong contrast in the tonal colour of the treble and bass registers. The intention was to produce the effect of two different timbres from the one instrument, like the split-stop or half-stop registrations available on contemporary organs.

Such organ registrations were relatively common on Spanish organs[17], but do not seem to have been so common elsewhere in Europe. That the split harpichordium and buff stops exist on Flemish clavecimbels implies that split stops must have been available on contemporary Flemish organs as well. Abraham van den Kerckhoven[18] was organist at the Chapel Royal in Brussels (1648–after 1684) to the Archduke Leopold Wilhelm of Austria. Kerckhoven's surviving keyboard music is all for organ, and several of the pieces have the clear instruction '*half register*', indicating that he expected split-stop registrations to be used. The cornet stops on many organs surviving from this period are split-register stops operating on only the treble half of the keyboard. As with the harpichordium, the use of a markedly different type of sound in the treble and bass does not seem appropriate to pieces like fantasias or pavans, and was probably used more for fast, light, dance pieces.

## THE MUSICAL FUNCTION OF DOUBLE-MANUAL HARPSICHORDS

A Ruckers double-manual harpsichord in its original state seems quirkish to even the most inexperienced eye. The two keyboards separated by an interval of a fourth, and the distorted cranked keys with a wide block next to them in the upper-manual seem an eccentric aberration on the part of their builders. Why, one asks, did the Ruckers go to all of the expense and effort to make such instruments whose only purpose was to facilitate one of the easiest possible transpositions?

To us it may seem an easy transposition, but it is difficult for us today to understand the processes of composition, modal theory, and performance practice that were prevalent in the sixteenth and seventeenth centuries, and that made instruments like the Ruckers double-manual transposing harpsichord necessary. We are so used to dealing with only one standard pitch, with a very small number of clefs (usually only the treble G2 clef, and the bass F4 clef), and with a vast array of vocal and instrumental music written in all keys, and modulating to degrees that would have been unthinkable in Ruckers' time, that it is difficult for us to imagine now how the appearance of a single sharp in a key signature would cause singers and instrumentalists alike to experience difficulties.

The age in which the Ruckers lived and worked marks the end of the period in which music was primarily vocal. Instruments in the sixteenth century were used mostly to accompany the voice, and the composition of the small number of strictly instrumental pieces was still governed by the rules and practices which applied to vocal music. In the late Renaissance the importance given to the classical writers, and in particular the Greek theorists, is very difficult for us to appreciate. In fact, all of the implications of the theorists and of modal writing on the compositional principles and techniques are still not fully understood.

Andrew Parrott has made an important contribution to our understanding of sixteenth- and early seventeenth-century notation.[19] Numerous clefs were used in writing the music of this period, in a way which is very characteristic: the composer chose particular clefs in combination with one another, and not necessarily to suit the range or tessitura of the part. Two clef combinations, with slight

16 In double-manual harpsichords the buff cross-over is between $f^1$ and $f\sharp^1$ on the keyboard at a pitch of R − 4, and between $c^1$ and $c\sharp^1$ on the keyboard at reference pitch R.

17 See for example the music of Francisco Correa de Arauxo in *Libro de Tientos* . . . Vol. 1 (Alcala, 1626), Monumentos de la Música Española, VI, ed. Santiago Kastner (Barcelona, 1948), and Charles Jacobs, *Francisco Correa de Arauxo* (The Hague, 1973), 31.

18 Antoon van den Kerckhoven, *Werken voor Orgel*, Monumenta Musicae Belgicae, II, ed. J. Watelet (Berchem–Antwerp, 1933), p. xviii, and No. 16, p. 7.

19 Andrew Parrott, 'Transposition in Monteverdi's Vespers of 1610. An "aberration" defended', *Early Music*, XII, 4 (1984), 490–516.

variants, occur: the so-called high clefs or 'chiavette', and the normal clefs:

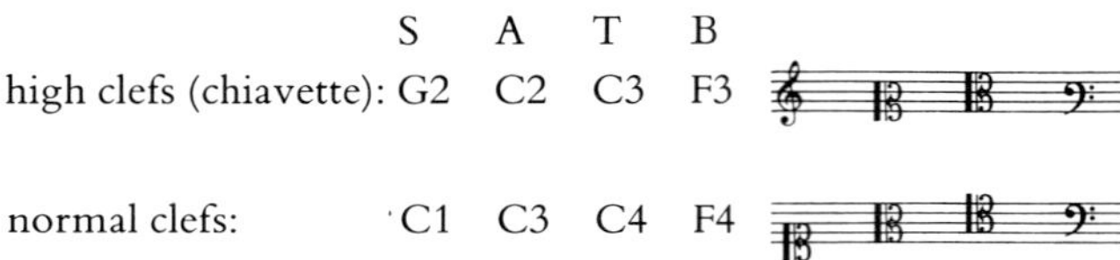


Whether a piece is written in high or in normal clefs is most easily ascertained by looking at the clef of the lowest part: normal clefs have the (in modern times now standard) bass clef (F4), whereas high clefs use the baritone (F3 or C5) clef (or rarely, the tenor (C4) or the alto (C3) clef).

If pieces which were composed in the high clefs are played or sung at the written pitch, then the tessitura is abnormally high in relation to that usually required. If, however, the high-clef pieces are transposed down a fourth or fifth, the range and tessitura are normal. That these chiavette movements were transposed is often confirmed by the continuo or organ parts, which are written a fourth or a fifth lower than the voice or instrumental parts above the continuo line.[20] Transposition down a fifth (e.g. from C to F) involved the addition of a flat to the signature and could be accomplished by imagining an equivalent clef change (e.g. from G2 to C2 for the soprano part or from C4 to F4 in the bass part). Transposition down a fourth (e.g. from C to G) required the addition of a sharp to the key signature and the appropriate clef changes, and was often considered less desirable.

To the singers the question of transposition never really arose. The notes for the singers were not viewed as fixed pitches (as they are today), but of intervallic relationships, and the position or type of clef in conjunction with the key signature (i.e. the presence or absence of a flat) determined where the tones and semitones occurred in the scale, and therefore the position of the solmization syllables.

Rubrics heading the organ parts of the manuscript pieces, or instructions at the beginnings of published pieces, have very clear instructions about transpositions. '*Alla quarta*', '*Alla 4*', or '*quartam vel quintam inferiorem*' (a fourth or a fifth lower) are typical instructions to organists. One particularly clear rubric to remind an English organist *not* to transpose is 'play it not fower notes Lower but as it standeth'.[21]

The required transpositions were easily carried out by singers, but required more skill and expertise from instrumentalists. Although the most common transpositions were of a fourth or a fifth, transpositions of a tone and of a minor third were also common, with more complicated transpositions necessitating more complicated changes to the key signature. Tracts written during the sixteenth and seventeenth centuries say that skilled instrumentalists, whether keyboard, wind or string players, were capable of carrying out the necessary transpositions with facility. But there were obviously players – students, assistant organists, etc. – who would not have had this facility. Many organs seem to have had a transposing keyboard, presumably for this eventuality.[22] For rehearsals and training, it was necessary to use a harpsichord to avoid the expense of engaging blowers to operate the bellows of the organ. A student or assistant taking these rehearsals would have found the Ruckers double-manual harpsichord, with its keyboards separated in pitch by a fourth (or by an upward transposition of a fifth), indispensable. But harpsichords were also frequently used in church services, and the many records of Ruckers harpsichords in Antwerp churches attest to their use there for rehearsal and for the services themselves.

However, although an experienced keyboard player could perform the necessary transposition down a fourth or a fifth, it would seem that in many cases organists at least preferred to have the part transposed for them to the sounded pitch. A number of Italian vocal pieces with organ accompaniment have the vocal parts written in high clefs, but the organ parts are written out for the organist a fourth lower. Praetorius actually expects the organist to sit down and write out (intabulate) his part from the vocal parts transposed to the appropriate pitch. All this would be unnecessary for a keyboard player with a Ruckers double-manual harpsichord. (And clearly lute, chitarrone and theorbo players would have to have their parts transposed for them in the tabulature that they were reading.)

By far the most common intervals of transposition were those of a fourth, a fifth, and a tone. A normal Ruckers double-manual harpsichord provided for a downward transposition of a fourth, or an upward transposition of a fifth. But the downward transposition of a fifth (or its octave) was not provided for in these instruments. Perhaps this then explains the existence of

[20] See Jeffrey Kurtzman, 'An aberration amplified', *Early Music*, XIII, 1 (1985), 75 and footnote 5. Also Caroline Anne Miller, '*Chiavette*: A new approach', diss., University of California, Berkeley (1960).

[21] J. Bunker Clark, *Transposition in Seventeenth Century English Organ Accompaniments and the Transposing Organ* (Detroit, 1974), 43. This book is an excellent guide to the common necessity of organ transpositions of a fourth and a fifth both on the Continent, and in England in the first half of the seventeenth century. See also Nicolas Meeùs, 'Renaissance transposing keyboards', *Fellowship of Makers and Restorers of Historical Instruments*, XLV and LVII (1977) for a more theoretical approach to the subject.

[22] See Bunker Clark, *Transposition*, 7ff and 23ff.

double-manual harpsichords such as the 1612a HR. This harpsichord had one manual at a pitch of R − 5, and the other at R − 4. Although the usual pitch R for playing the normal clefs was not provided for, this harpsichord would offer the harpsichordist or organist the instant alternative of a transposition downwards by *either* a fourth *or* a fifth (or the upward transposition to their octaves).

## THE CHROMATIC-BASS-OCTAVE SINGLES

The Ruckers workshops seem to have begun to produce single-manual harpsichords with a chromatic bass octave from about 1636 onwards (e.g. 1636 AR, 1637a IR, 1639 IR, 1679 IC). Although there is very little Flemish clavecimbel music on which to base a judgement, none that exists for this or the earlier period requires a chromatic bass octave; it can all be played on the short octave.[23] The production of chromatic-bass-octave singles in Flanders, where accidentals in the lowest octave were not required by the native music, is probably explained by the fact that such instruments were being made especially for the English market. Two of the instruments quoted (1637a IR and 1639 IR) have apparently been in England since earliest times, and were probably sent there directly from the Ruckers workshops.

In England, keyboard instruments had a 'long' bass octave as a matter of course. The Theeuwes claviorganum (see Chapter 2, p. 26) had a chromatic bass octave down to C, even though Theeuwes was a Flemish émigré and would have been used to making clavecimbels in Antwerp with a short octave. Obviously when he made instruments for the English market they had to suit the local music. Also, the extant English virginals (the oldest is dated 1638) all had a chromatic bass octave. Not surprisingly, English music contemporary with the active production of the Ruckers workshops does require F♯ and G♯ very often, used either in chordal inversions, or as lower auxiliary notes, but rarely as chordal roots.

Even in Antwerp, and in the clavecimbel workshops there, instruments with a chromatic bass octave were referred to as *op sijn engels*, or 'in the English style', and were said to have 'the basses straight on in the English way . . .'[24] The Ruckers and Couchets were obviously making these instruments for a specialist English market, with a compass to match the requirements of the English music. In the correspondence between Sir Francis Windebank and Balthazar Gerbier, (see Appendix 16, p. 304), Windebank writes from England about the Ruckers harpsichord that he has received: 'The Virginal which you sent me, is com safe, and I wish it were as usefull as I know you intended it. But the workman, that made it, was much mistaken in it, and it wantes 6 or 7 Keyes, so that it is utterly unserviceable. If either he could alter it, or wolde change it for another that may have more Keyes, it were well; but as it is, our musick is marr'd.' This has sometimes been taken to mean that Windebank received a double-manual harpsichord with transposing keyboards with which he was unfamiliar, and that he did not understand why the upper-manual keyboard had not been filled out instead of having a block of wood at the bass end.

But nowhere in this correspondence is a double-manual harpsichord mentioned. It seems to me much more likely that Windebank received a short-octave clavecimbel, and found that he could not play English music on it. In fact he seemed to have expected to be able to play music going down to $A_1$ since he found the instrument lacking '6 or 7 Keyes' – $A_1$ to E♭, to fill out the notes below the E of the short octave, would require seven additional keys. And in fact even in the Fitzwilliam Virginal Book (transcribed no later than 1619), numerous pieces require a low $A_1$. Obviously contemporary English instruments must have had compasses at least down to $A_1$ by 1615. Windebank, ordering a 'virginal' from the best Flemish maker in 1638, would have expected his instrument to reach at least as far as this note.

John Bull, when he was organist in Antwerp cathedral, sometimes advised on organs for other churches and other cities. In 1617 he advised the cathedral churchwardens of 's-Hertogenbosch (now in southern Holland) that their new organ should have keyboards with all the semitones, and with twenty-nine white keys and twenty black ones. This specification could only mean C to $c^3$, with a chromatic bass octave. Presumably Bull must have felt frustrated with the keyboards he encountered in the Low Countries. More than half of the large number of his compositions in the Fitzwilliam Virginal Book require either a bottom F♯ or a G♯ or both, and a number need a low $A_1$ and a C♯ as well. Either he simply could not play his music and that of his English contemporaries on the Flemish instruments, or he would have had to modify it to eliminate the low accidentals so it would suit the normal short octave. Did Philips tell Bull about the

23 See footnote 2.

24 See J. Lambrechts-Douillez and M. J. Bosschaerts-Eykens, 'Documenten betreffende de familie Couchet', *Mededeling van het Ruckers-Genootschap*, V (Antwerp, 1986), 28. Contract between Simon Hagaerts and Angela van den Brant (Ioannes Couchet's widow): 'den achtvoet steert med drij registers ende drij snaeren de bassen recht vuyt [sic] op sijn engels ongeschildert voor de somme van sevenentachtich guldens' ('the 8-voet harpsichord with three registers and three [sets of] strings the basses straight on in the English way, unpainted for the sum of 87 guilders' – here 'recht vuyt' is an old form of 'rechtuit', 'straight on').

broken-octave instruments of Grouwels in Middleburg, on which most of Bull's music would have been playable? Bull would surely have preferred a Grouwels clavecimbel with its bottom F#s and G#s to one of the Ruckers' instruments with the normal short octave. His recommendations to the authorities in the 's-Hertogenbosch cathedral would at least have ensured that his music could be played there.

## THE CHROMATIC-BASS-OCTAVE DOUBLES

In addition to the chromatic-bass-octave single-manual harpsichords which the Ruckers made for the English market, they also made chromatic-bass double-manual harpsichords (see Chapter 3, p. 45). These instruments originally had one manual at a pitch of R − 4 with a chromatic bass down to F, with the second manual at reference pitch R and a chromatic compass down to $G_1$. All of the instruments with this compass seem to have been special export models made for France, where, without exception, they all seem to have been since earliest times, and where the larger compass down to $G_1$ must have been needed. The period in which these instruments were built – they are the 1616 HR, 1627c IR, 1628b IR and 1646b AR – covers most of the first half of the century. This suggests that, as in other parts of Northern Europe, the use of harpsichords with keyboards at different pitches was known in France, where they must have been used in a way similar to that already discussed. Presumably, as in England, the use of a chromatic bass octave was a requirement of the music. What the musical necessity for a chromatic bass octave during this period was is not known, since I know of no original French music now extant that requires this. Also, importation of these instruments over such a long period suggests that they were continually appreciated in France and that, at least in the first half of the seventeenth century, the limited 1 × 8′, 1 × 4′ disposition that the Flemish instruments offered was sufficient for the music being played.

## THE COUCHETS AND THE CHANGE IN MUSICAL TASTE AND FASHION

By 1655 the last of the harpsichord-building Ruckers was dead. From that date on, the tradition was carried on by Ioannes Couchet and his sons. Except for the chromatic-bass singles, the Ruckers introduced very little innovation into the instruments they built in the seventy or so years in which they were active. But that changed with the Couchets, who extended the tradition in all of its aspects.

In 1646 Ioannes Couchet built a double which introduced a number of new features. It had an upper-manual compass of $G_1/B_1$ to $c^3$, so making it the first instrument with the $G_1/B_1$ short octave. It was designed to play a semitone above R at a pitch not found in any other Ruckers/Couchet instrument, and at a pitch which does not fit into the scheme discussed above (see pp. 224 and 271). Also, the buff stop was not split on this instrument (neither was it on the 1645 IC single-manual harpsichord), but was a continuous bar that operated on all strings from treble to bass. None of the later harpsichords seems to have had a split buff either. Hence the buff was no longer used to produce contrasts between treble and bass parts, but to produce an overall effect, as it is today.

The $G_1/B_1$ short octave again appears in 1652 in a remarkable single-manual Couchet harpsichord, this time as a conscious design feature, since it is not simply the compass at the transposed pitch of the lower manual. It originally had a 2 × 8′ disposition, but with three registers, two of them sharing the same choir of strings. Couchet and Duarte mention instruments of this type coming from the Couchet workshops (see Appendices 17 and 18), but this is the first extant Ruckers-tradition harpsichord with this disposition. Also most unusual is the original trapwork that seems to have enabled the registers to be changed, either using pedals or a genouillère.

Ioannes Couchet's extant instruments reveal two further innovations. He is probably the first to have extended the compass downwards to $F_1$, and the first to have left us with a Flemish harpsichord at a pitch of R + 2. Both of these features appear in the (*c.* 1650)b IC harpsichord, which, although it now has two, originally had only one manual.

The tendency to innovation was carried on by the next generation of Couchets. In 1679 Ioseph Ioannes made a single-manual harpsichord that was considerably longer than the usual singles, had a chromatic C to $c^3$ compass, and a conservative 1 × 8′, 1 × 4′ disposition, but with three registers, two of which plucked the same 8′ choir of strings. Last of all, the n.d. IC was originally extremely long, at a pitch of R + 2, and it had the large compass from $F_1$ to $d^3$, $e^3$, with a chromatic bass.

It is important to note here that every single Couchet harpsichord is individual in some way. I do not think this is just a quirk of fate; probably quite the contrary. In 1648, after the signing of the Treaty of Münster, which meant the closing of Antwerp's port, there was a strong economic decline in Antwerp's fortunes. If harpsichord production had gone on at the same rate after 1648, we would probably have many more instruments showing the effect of innovation and change, and the parallel change in musical taste and fashion.

What seems to emerge from all of this? Composers were certainly extending the range of their music, and the compasses of the instruments were increased to match this. There is no indication from Flemish music of what compasses were used in the Low Countries, although low bass compasses were required in the music of England and France. As has already been seen, English music went down to bottom $A_1$, even before 1615. By about 1650 English clavecimbel music began to demand a low $G_1$, and there must have been instruments in England which fulfilled this requirement.[25] Chambonnières (1601/2–72) owned a Couchet harpsichord (see Appendix 19), which almost certainly would have fulfilled the needs of his music. Chambonnières' music goes down to $G_1$, and uses tenths, $A_1$ to $c^\sharp$, but none of the chromatic notes between $G^\sharp{}_1$ and $E^\flat$, so needs a $G_1/B_1$ short octave.[26] In the treble $c^3$ is never exceeded, and so a harpsichord like the 1652 IC with a $G_1/B_1$ to $c^3$ compass, and a 2 × 8′ disposition would probably be the type of harpsichord Chambonnières would have owned.

Louis Couperin's (c.1626–61) music uses $A_1$ very frequently, and occasionally $G_1$ and $B^\flat{}_1$.[27] $B^\flat{}_1$ is never used with $E^\flat$, but $B_1$ also occurs, although never with $B^\flat{}_1$ in the same piece. If this means that Louis Couperin was using a $G_1/B_1$ short octave, then the apparent $E^\flat$ was tuned *either* to $B_1$ or to $B^\flat{}_1$. But of course this music could also be played on instruments like the Ruckers 'French' harpsichords with a chromatic bass octave from $G_1$.

Clearly implied by the Couchet innovation is a desire for variety in registration. The instruments with two sets of jacks both plucking the same set of strings would provide two colours that were quite different. The close-plucking register would be more nasal, the far-plucking one rounder and less brilliant. The addition of the machine to the 1652 IC suggests that there was also a desire to change the tone colour quickly and in the middle of a piece or movement, something which was impossible with the normal arrangement of registers projecting out of the cheek side of the instrument.

Noticeably lacking among the surviving instruments by Couchet is a contrasting double harpsichord (i.e. one capable of tonal variety between manuals at the same pitch). Mersenne (1636) and de la Barre (1648) suggest that contrasting doubles were known in France, and so the idea must have reached Antwerp at around this time. Either because of conservatism in the building tradition (which did not seem to apply to the Couchets), or because there was no musical requirement for them, contrasting doubles were probably not made in Antwerp before 1700. This is discussed further below.

## RAVALEMENT OF RUCKERS CLAVECIMBELS AND IMPLICATIONS FOR LATER MUSIC AND PERFORMANCE PRACTICE

### *Ravalement of Ruckers virginals*

Although seventy per cent of the surviving Ruckers virginals have been altered in pitch or compass, none of them has been subjected to a grand ravalement (the eighteenth-century practice of increasing the size of the case to accommodate more strings or longer strings for a downward extension of the compass). Altering the C/E short octave to a chromatic octave starting on C did not require longer strings, as the same note was sounded before and after the alteration. But instruments like the 1598 HR 6-voet spinett virginal, which was extended down to $G_1/B_1$, or the 1632 AR 4-voet virginal, with altered treble scalings suitable for tuning to reference pitch, have bass strings that are simply too short for the pitch that they are expected to play. Few ravalements of this type survive, either because the rebuilders knew that the result would be unacceptable if carried out, or because those that were carried out were found to be unsatisfactory, and so were disposed of or destroyed.

Clearly, unless the C/E short octave was retained and only an upward extension of the compass was made, the harpichordium would not survive the ravalement process. Even if the only alteration was the filling out of the short octave to make it into a chromatic bass octave, there would not be enough hooks on the harpichordium bar for the additional notes, and the bar itself would not be long enough for extra hooks to be added to it. If the ravalement was carried out by squeezing more notes onto the bridges by repinning them, then the spacing of the hooks would no longer match the string spacing. Needless to say, since so many virginals have been altered in some way, there are very few which survive with their harpichordium stops.

### *Ravalement of Ruckers harpsichords*

Many alterations of the petit and grand ravalement type were carried out very competently, giving Ruckers harp-

[25] Lancelot Edwin Whitehead, 'Stringed keyboard instruments in early modern England 1520–1720', diss., University of Edinburgh (1988), Appendix 6. The earliest appearance of $G_1$ he has found occurs in a piece by J. Tresure, 'Courant Variola', *c.* 1650 (Christ Church MS 1236).

[26] *Œuvres complètes de Chambonnières*, ed. P. Brunold (New York, 1967).

[27] *Pièces de Clavecin de Louis Couperin*, ed. Davitt Moroney (Monaco, 1985).

sichords a new lease of life in the eighteenth century. These instruments were made to resemble contemporary native instruments in disposition, sound quality and decoration. (Their relationship with the music of that period naturally belongs in a discussion of eighteenth-century performance practice, and not in a study such as this.) But not all of the instruments subjected to the ravalement process were carried out with a clear understanding of the principles underlying the design features which lead to the production of a good tone. There seemed to be a certain amount of blind faith in the ability of the Ruckers instrument to sound well no matter how the scalings or plucking points were altered, or what was done to the soundboard so long as its original wood was incorporated into the soundboard of the final instrument. Soundboards of small single-manual harpsichords and of virginals were hacked about and used as soundboards for double-manual instruments in such a way that the thickness contours of the resulting composite board were unrelated to those normally found in Ruckers double-manual harpsichords. Often the bass compass of single-manual instruments was extended downwards without any attempt at lengthening the case to give the necessary length to the strings.

In all these Ruckers instruments that have been altered during the eighteenth century a careful analysis of the plugged holes in the line of the hitchpins and in the bridges shows the existence of earlier alterations which are revealing about compasses and dispositions around the end of the seventeenth century, a period from which very few keyboard instruments survive.

### *The 2 × 8′ disposition*

Analysis of the string-band strips made for both altered single-manual and double-manual harpsichords shows that in most instruments the alteration was begun by replacing the 4′ stop by an 8′ stop, without altering the compass (see Chapter 11, p. 208). From the position of the plugged bridge-pin holes, it is clear that these instruments were changed to the disposition 2 × 8′ by adding another set of strings to the 8′ bridge in a position directly above that of the original 4′ strings. This meant that in theory the original registers and jacks could still be used, as the spacing and position of the jacks relative to the strings had not been changed. However, because the new 8′ string was added on the bass side of the jacks, there was a lengthening of the scale (the van Blankenburg Problem; see p. 209), which would have required a lowering of the pitch; and as there are no instruments surviving in this condition, it is not clear how the 4′ jacks were used in practice with this type of alteration. Perhaps the 4′ jacks were cut off at the top just above the level of the damper, and extended with new wood at the bottom to raise the quills up to the new level of the added 8′ string. This procedure would have carried out the conversion to a 2 × 8′ disposition with relatively little work. Alternatively, new jacks could have been made to fit the 4′ register.

Analysis of the string-band strips also shows that the 2 × 8′ disposition occurred as an intermediate state of many of the instruments that were given a petit ravalement. At this stage, either new strings and keys were added to those already present, or the jacks, registers and keyboards were remade and the strings were respaced closer together in order to squeeze more notes into the original case. Here the string-band strip shows that there was once a set of paired plugged holes in the 8′ bridge but no plugged holes in the 4′ bridge with the same spacing. Taking the alteration only this far meant that the width of the gap did not have to be changed, since there were still only two registers and two rows of jacks.

No matter how the alteration to give the 2 × 8′ disposition was carried out, it seems to have been enormously popular during the second half of the seventeenth century, and the early part of the eighteenth century. It occurred not only in ravalement harpsichords to bring them into line with the latest taste, but also in newly-built native instruments in Flanders (Hagaerts), France (Bellot, Blanchet) and England (Haward, Hancock).

### *The transition from transposing to contrasting double-manual harpsichords*

The last two extant transposing harpsichords made in the Ruckers/Couchet tradition were both made in 1646 (1646b AR, 1646 IC), and, as has already been pointed out, none of the earlier instruments they built was a contrasting double of the type so familiar to us today. But by 1650 some form of the contrasting double-manual harpsichord was known at least in France. Mersenne in 1636 describes a double that seems to have been of the contrasting type, as did de la Barre, court harpsichordist to Louis XIII, writing in October 1648: 'this master, who is still young, was the first to discover the invention of making harpsichords with two manuals, not in the style of Flanders which only play the same strings, but different in that they are capable of sounding different strings on each keyboard, and properly speaking, they are two harpsichords joined in one, and by consequence the work is doubled.'[28] I think it is most significant that there are no harpsichords later than 1646 built in the

[28] See Edwin M. Ripin, 'The French harpsichord before 1650', *The Galpin Society Journal*, XX (1967), 43–7, and Jonckbloet and Land, *Musique et musiciens au XVII^e^ siècle*, cxlix–cxlx.

Ruckers tradition which were originally doubles, whether transposing or contrasting. Ioseph Ioannes Couchet (and possibly Ioannes II Couchet) probably carried on building harpsichords into the 1690s, and yet there are no double-manual harpsichords built in this forty-year period. In fact there are only a very few double-manual harpsichords at all from the second half of the seventeenth century.

Clearly the potential of the old transposing doubles which must have existed in vast numbers in this period was there, as was the germ of the idea of how they could be used. The potential that these instruments offered was not taken up, obviously because there was not yet the musical need for the contrast in volume and tone colour that they could have provided.

Even more surprising is the fact that at least four double-manual harpsichords survive to this day without the possibility of coupling the manuals, and three of these were left with only the original $1 \times 8'$, $1 \times 4'$ disposition on each manual. The keyboards were aligned, and in some cases the compass extended slightly, but otherwise nothing was done to increase the possibilities for additional registration. The alterations to all of these instruments were very competently and professionally carried out, and the cases of three of them are beautifully decorated. It is clear that neither the rebuilder nor his customer felt a need for any additional registration. The lack of double-manual harpsichords originating during the second half of the seventeenth century and into the first years of the eighteenth century is thus probably a reflection of a lack of musical interest in and need for the possibilities they offered. With the exception of a few French composers such as Louis Couperin (whose *pièces croisées* require two manuals, but not for purposes of contrast), the use of a double-manual harpsichord for music of this period is inappropriate.

### *Multiple pitches in the eighteenth century*

What we can learn from the altered Ruckers/Couchet instruments regarding performance practice often emerges in unusual ways. One of these relates to the pitch of the altered instruments. Taskin was one of the eighteenth-century French builders, along with his master Blanchet, who spent much of his time rebuilding old instruments. Taskin's work is meticulous in all of its aspects, and in particular that of stringing and scaling his instruments.[29] There is a high degree of uniformity both in the treble scalings and in the transition scalings from one material to another in the tenor and bass both in his altered instruments and in his newly-made ones. But there are two notable exceptions.

The 1788 Taskin in the Castello Sforzesco, Milan,[30] which he faked to look like an Andreas Ruckers harpsichord ('n.d.c A R', p. 282), and the 1680 I C, reworked by Taskin in 1781, both have similar scalings. The string gauges were marked by Taskin on the wrestplanks of both instruments, and these indicate the note at which the transition from red brass to yellow and from yellow brass to iron should occur in both the 4′ and 8′ registers. Both the treble scalings and the transition scalings indicate that Taskin intended these two instruments to be tuned to a pitch a semitone higher than that of all of his other instruments. Since the majority of Taskin's harpsichords seem to have been tuned to a pitch of about $a^1 = 409$Hz (see Chapter 4, p. 62), there must have been another pitch in Paris, which was not as common, a semitone higher at about $a^1 = 433$Hz.

De Bricqueville mentions two relevant harpsichords, neither of which was a Ruckers, on sale in 1759[31]. One was 'a harpsichord of new invention which raises or lowers by a semitone', the other also 'raises or lowers by a semitone as one wishes'. From this it would appear that these were instruments in which the keyboards were capable of being shifted sideways up or down to achieve the required pitch. Harpsichords were obviously required for this higher pitch, either by having sliding keyboards, or by being specially designed to be tuned solely to the high pitch, as in the two Taskin harpsichords just discussed.

## RUCKERS INSTRUMENTS IN MODERN TIMES

The research carried out for this book has been based primarily on the surviving Ruckers instruments, and not on archival or literary sources. A fairly complete picture of the Ruckers tradition of instrument building has been made possible mostly because there are a large number of surviving instruments from which information has been gathered. One thing now stands out very clearly to me: it has been the unrestored instruments, the neglected instruments and the unaltered instruments that have been the most important sources of information and discovery. Paradoxically, these instruments, with their original features from Ruckers' time or from the time of

29 See my article, 'Some principles of eighteenth-century harpsichord stringing and their application', *The Organ Yearbook*, XII (1981), 160–76.

30 Natale and Franco Gallini, *Museo degli Strumenti Musicali: Catalogo* (Milan, 1963), No. 604, 247–8. The date of this instrument is clearly 1788, not 1780 as given in the catalogue.

31 Eugène de Bricqueville, *Les ventes d'instruments de musique au XVIII^e^ siècle* (Paris, 1908), 10, 11 (see p. 302).

their ravalement in the eighteenth century have survived more by chance than by the serious intent of the owners or restorers of the instruments. Restoring instruments to playing condition obviously means that they can then again fulfil the original purpose for which they were conceived, and I am the first to admit that the restoration of instruments is beneficial to our understanding of the contemporary music written for them. But the restoration of a musical instrument results in its having to carry out functions that are required of no other object normally subjected to conservation; namely it must function mechanically and acoustically. Imposing these two conditions on top of the conservation of the wood, paintwork, metal, leather, cloth, paper, and bone has very serious consequences.

For one thing it means that the ephemera are normally lost, or their original relationship to the instrument is destroyed even if they are conserved alongside the instrument. Original strings, quills, dampers, keyboard action cloths, leather registers and the like have a limited lifetime and cannot go on being used in a playing instrument forever. The discovery of an original (or even eighteenth-century) quill in an instrument is a rarity, but is of great importance to our understanding of the way clavecimbels were regulated. The quill is of interest when removed from its jack, but its real value organologically is in its original position in the jack and in the instrument. The properties of a piece of original wire on a tuning pin are changed by the very process of removing it from the pin. Yet that piece of wire is capable of telling us something about the original pitch of the instrument if it is handled in the right way and the correct measurements are made using it. Left on the tuning pin it at least retains all of its original properties; what are its chances of survival at the end of the next hundred years if removed? It should be obvious to the reader of this book that it has been the study of these very ephemera which has been one of the things that has yielded up a large amount of information about the action and regulation of the Ruckers instruments in their original states. But there is doubtless much more information still to be recovered from Ruckers instruments, and certainly a great deal from other instruments of all periods: providing, that is, that enough instruments remain unrestored, unaltered and undamaged.

Also, because of the scarcity of Ruckers instruments in their original state, there has often been the temptation to remove alterations made to instruments after they were originally built. These alterations were often carried out by competent eighteenth-century harpsichord builders such as Taskin, Goujon, Hemsch, Kirkman, Shudi, Bull, or Fleischer. These later builders were each working in their own tradition in an effort to improve or modernize the instruments according to contemporary standards. The alterations they carried out are therefore just as important to our knowledge of the history of music, instrument making and performance practice as are the surviving Ruckers instruments in their original state. Even if an alteration or ravalement is anonymous, who is to say that future research will not discover who carried it out?

To undo the work of these late seventeenth- or eighteenth-century builders has two important effects. First, in general it destroys evidence of an historical practice which tells us a great deal about musical style and needs during that period. The compass, disposition and scalings of the altered instruments are all as important to our knowledge of musical history as the contemporary eighteenth-century instruments built in the native style. In particular, evidence of the practice of individual builders, and the way they approached the problem of carrying out an alignment or ravalement, is destroyed when an instrument is returned to its original state. Secondly, returning the instrument to its original state usually involves a great deal of alteration to the fabric of the instrument, and this destroys evidence not only of the altered state but also of the original state as well. It also means usually that new material, in the form of wood, cloth or leather, must be added to the instrument which has no relevance to its past history.

There may also be the temptation to take an instrument only part way back to its original state. For example, a single converted to a ravalé double may be taken back to its 'original' state with one manual and its original compass. But leaving it with a $2 \times 8'$, $1 \times 4'$ disposition gives it a new non-historical state which represents no previous state nor historical practice. The course which causes the least damage and alteration to the instrument and which preserves the greatest possible amount of organological and musicological information is to restore the instrument to the form which it had during its last period of genuine musical use.[32] This means that a Ruckers harpsichord with any sort of a ravalement, alignment or alteration should not, in general, be restored to its original or any previous state.

Since about 1960 there has been an enormous resurgence of interest in early music and early keyboard instruments. The revival of traditional methods of construction of clavecimbels, inspired mostly by Russell and Hubbard, together with an increased awareness of auth-

[32] Alfred Berner, J. H. van der Meer and G. Thibault-de Chambure, *Preservation and Restoration of Musical Instruments* (London, 1967), 7; John Barnes, 'Does restoration destroy evidence?', *Early Music*, VIII, 2 (1980), 213–18).

entic performance practice, has resulted in a tremendous demand for restored early keyboard instruments. But unfortunately our understanding of the instruments and their technology has not kept pace with this demand. As new instruments are discovered and pulled out of dusty attics, they are often instantly whipped into playing order with little understanding of or respect for the features they exhibit in their unrestored state. Few restorers have the time – because of commercial pressures – or the inclination to do a thorough documentation of the instruments which come to them for restoration. And many museums and public collections are just as guilty.

As a result, a great deal of information about these instruments is being lost and, because new instruments are turning up more infrequently, the possibility of recovering this information from the few remaining unrestored instruments is becoming less and less likely. Fragments of strings or complete strings which are old and possibly original are removed and often destroyed without recording even the note on the instrument from which they came. Keyboard cloths are replaced without first measuring the depth of touch of the keyboards. The lengths of jacks are altered without noting the original lengths or plucking order. The original keyboard cloths in conjunction with the original jacks and quills can give the lost motion before the first jack has plucked and after the last. Bird quill is replaced by plastic plectra, and the original plectrum holes in the tongues, shaped to suit the natural quills, are distorted to accept the modern material. When the baseboard of an instrument is removed, a wealth of information is available. The framing, soundboard barring, case materials, etc. are all readily accessible. Also, when the baseboard of the instrument is removed, it is easiest to measure the soundboard thickness either mechanically or with an electromagnetic thickness gauge. Not to record details such as these is, in my opinion, an organological sin.

There is now a distinct need for a reduction in the rate at which instruments are being restored. Ruckers instruments, and other instruments of the sixteenth and seventeenth centuries, are especially in need of being considered in a category of their own. There are few authentic instruments by the Ruckers left, and even fewer which are sufficiently robust to be considered for restoration to a playing state. Of special importance, naturally, are those few instruments which are basically in their original condition. Because such instruments are extremely rare, they must be restored with the utmost caution.

In the past the prestige of a museum, and of private collectors of instruments, has been based upon the number of restored and playing instruments they have in their care. If careful organological studies such as the present one are to be made in the future, then there will have to be a total change in the attitude of museums, musicians, conservators, and restorers to the restoration to playing condition of musical instruments.[33] Museums and collectors will have to be seen to be prestigious because they are *not* restoring unique, unaltered, or delicate instruments. A great deal of information about the musical and technological background of an instrument can be obtained without restoring it. Instruments can be measured, X-rayed, drawn, and the individual components can be analysed in a non-interactive way (such as using X-ray fluorescence and photogrammetry).

Unless there is a drastic rethinking of the way we approach the restoration of musical instruments, the prospects for the future of Ruckers instruments, and for all musical instruments, is very bleak indeed.

[33] See my paper, 'The conservation of historical keyboard instruments: to play or to preserve?', *Per una carta europea del restauro: conservazione, restauro e riuso degli strumenti musicali antichi*, ed. Leo S. Olschki (Venice, 1987), 291–7.

# Catalogue of Ruckers instruments

election of the instruments for inclusion in the catalogue below has been based on the principles of authentication outlined in Chapter 9. No instrument has been included here unless I was sure that it was genuine. Counterfeit instruments dishonestly attributed to Ruckers by their makers, instruments altered after being made and given fake inscriptions, roses, etc., are in a separate catalogue (p. 277). Instruments referred to in the literature but otherwise lost sight of have not been included.

## CONVENTIONS USED IN THE CATALOGUE

The virginals and single-manual harpsichords may be assumed originally to have had the compass C/E to $c^3$, four octaves with a bass short octave, unless otherwise specified. If no alteration is noted this is also the present compass. The double-manual harpsichords originally had their keyboards playing at pitches a fourth apart. Unless otherwise specified these instruments had an upper-manual compass of C/E to $c^3$ with a block of wood filling up the space of three naturals in the bass, and a lower-manual compass of C/E to $f^3$. Compasses always refer to the apparent notes played, and not to the note sounded, which may be at some transposed pitch. Pitches of instruments are given relative to reference pitch R (see Conventions and Definitions, p. xix). The 6-voet virginal, the normal C/E to $c^3$ single-manual harpsichord, and the C/E to $c^3$ upper manual of the normal doubles were all originally at a pitch of R. The C/E to $f^3$ lower manual of the normal double-manual harpsichords were at a pitch of R−4. Instruments at pitches other than these are specified each time they occur in the catalogue.

Unless otherwise noted the disposition of the single-manual harpsichords was originally:

← 4′
→ 8′

and the original disposition of the double-manual harpsichords was originally:

← 4′
→ 8′
- - - -
← 4′
→ 8′

Measurements of altered instruments include those of the original state as well as the present altered state wherever possible. Because the case heights were chosen by the builders with dimensions that were integral or half-integral units of the small Flemish duim before the baseboard was applied, the case-height measurements are usually given both with and without the thickness of the baseboard included.

To avoid repetition the lists of original scalings have only been given once, and have not been repeated for each instrument. Original scalings and plucking points are given in millimetres and are listed under the following entries:

Virginals:

| | |
|---|---|
| 6-voet spinett double mother and child – (*c*. 1600) HR | 6-voet muselar double mother and child – (*c*. 1610) HR |
| 5-voet spinett – (see Appendix 2) | 5-voet muselar – 1604 HR |
| 4½-voet spinett – 1629 IR | 4½-voet muselar – 1610 AR |
| 4-voet spinett – 1613b AR | |
| 2½-voet spinett – (*c*. 1610)a AR | |

Harpsichords:
4-voet harpsichord – 1627 AR
Normal single-manual harpsichord – 1637 AR
Normal transposing double-manual harpsichord – 1638b IR
Chromatic-bass 'English' single-manual harpsichord – 1679 IC
Chromatic-bass 'French' double-manual harpsichord – 1616 HR
Extended-bass long Couchet single-manual harpsichord – n.d. IC.

The literature references to the instruments are not meant to be exhaustive, and are given here in shorthand: author's surname (date) page or reference. The full reference may be found in the bibliography under the author and date. The first reference uses the convention followed in the rest of the main text and gives the number in Boalch (1974). Not included in the literature references are those from my catalogues in *The New Grove Dictionary of Music and Musicians*, ed. Stanley Sadie (London, 1980) and *The New Grove Dictionary of Musical Instruments*, ed. Stanley Sadie (London, 1984), which occur under the entries for 'Ruckers' and 'Couchet'.

## CATALOGUE OF HANS RUCKERS INSTRUMENTS

1581 HR

Hans Ruckers, 1581, double muselar mother-and-child virginal, Metropolitan Museum of Art, New York, No. 29.90.

*Case dimensions:* mother – length 1786mm; width 492mm; height 236mm without, 250mm with the baseboard; keywell 650mm.

child – length 800mm; width 372mm; height 132mm with, 126mm without the baseboard; keywell 648mm.

*Motto:* keywell flap of the mother – MVSICA DVLCE LABORVM LEVAMEN.

*General description:* This is the earliest extant Ruckers instrument. It is thought to have been a gift of Philip II of Spain to the Marquis de Oropeza of Cuzco, Peru, who was a descendant of the ancient Incas. It retains most of its original parts and decoration. The lid of the main instrument has a fine sixteenth-century Flemish painting showing a rural scene with a castle and elegantly dressed courtiers engaged in boating, dancing, music making and feasting. The soundwell, keywell, front flap, etc., instead of being decorated with printed paper patterns as is usual in the later Ruckers instruments, are here delicately painted, and give the instrument a rich, lavish appearance. Above the keyboard of the mother instrument are two relief medallions of Philip II of Spain and his fourth wife Anne of Austria. The soundboard painting is in the usual Hans Ruckers style and is very well preserved in both instruments, but especially in the child, which has been protected inside the mother instrument.

Neither instrument bears the usual HR rose with an angel playing a harp; instead both instruments have original roses of pierced parchment cut in geometrical patterns. The child has only the usual single rose, but the mother has two roses, one in the usual position above the keyboard and the second in the middle of the soundboard area to the right of the bass jackrail support. The mother's jackrail is not original, but the child's jackrail is signed 'HANS RVEKERS ME FECIT', and the initials HR are painted on the top of the toolbox on the left-hand side of the mother.

Most of the keys retain their original arcades. The parchment backing of the arcades, which was originally dyed red, has now faded and Hebrew writing is visible on it on many of the keys. The bone naturals have the usual scribed lines and nicks decorating them; like many early Flemish and other Ruckers instruments, the sharps are also decorated with similar nicks and scribed lines. The outside of the mother instrument is painted black, but underneath this there are clear traces of the original green and off-white imitation porphyry marble decoration.

Like the later Ruckers double virginals, the mother and child can be coupled by placing the child above the jacks of the mother instrument. The main instrument has a harpichordium stop, not only on the straight bass-section of the right bridge, but also on the curved descant part. The two sections are split between $e^1$ and $f^1$, and can operate separately or together on the treble and bass strings.

*Literature:* B. 2, Hirt (1955), 204–5; Curtis (1960/61), 51; Buchner (1956), Plate 210; Besseler (1959), 43; Winternitz (1961), Plate 6; Winternitz (1966), No. 26, 93; *The Connoisseur* (1916), 169; van der Meer (1971c), 137, 138, 143, 145; Russell (1959), 149; Lambrechts-Douillez (1977), 269; Koster (1977) 78; Koster (1980), 52; Germann (1978), 65, McGeary (1981), 27; Rueger (1982/86), Plate 1, 53, 56; Koopman (1987).

*Former owners:* Marquis of Oropeza, Cuzco, Peru; B. H. Homan, who gave it in 1929 to the Metropolitan Museum.

1583 HR

Hans Ruckers, 1583, 4-voet spinett virginal at R + 5, Instrument Museum of the Conservatoire N.S.M., Paris, No. E.986.1.2

*Present original compass:* C/E to $a^2$.

*Case dimensions:* length 1143mm; width 431mm; height 178mm without the baseboard; keywell 598mm.

*General description:* This is the second-oldest surviving Ruckers instrument, and the only Hans Ruckers clavecimbel at quint pitch. It has many features of other early Flemish virginals: its compass goes only to a$^2$ in the treble, the jackrail, soundwell, keywell, lid and flap decorations are painted rather than being covered by block-printed papers, the natural touchplates are of wood (box?) rather than bone, the sharps as well as the naturals have decorative nicks and scribed lines, and the case mouldings are painted with alternate stripes of black and varnished wood like the two Karest virginals. The nameboard is decorated with medallions representing Catherine de Medici and Diane de Poitiers, and the lid painting represents a Flemish hunting scene. The keys have many of their original arcades, the parchment backing of which is inscribed with Hebrew writing.

*Literature:* B. 2a, Thibault-de Chambure (1961), Plate 32, 145; Bridgman and Lesure (1961), Plate 287, 117; van der Meer (1971c), Plate 10, 131, 143; O'Brien (1977a), 43; Koopman (1987), footnote 20.

*Former owners:* The Strauss Collection, Paris; André and then François and Denis Meyer, Paris.

1591a HR

Hans Ruckers, 1591, 6-voet polygonal spinett virginal, Gruuthuuse Museum, Bruges, No. 2296.

*Ruckers number:* [?]/30.

*Case dimensions:* Length 1711mm; width 467mm; height 236mm with, 224mm without the baseboard; keywell 647mm.

*Motto:* lid – SCIENTIA NON HABET INIMICVM NISI INGNORANTEM [*sic*].

*General description:* This is the only Ruckers virginal which is polygonal in shape. It is otherwise identical to the usual 6-voet spinett virginals except that the inactive areas of soundboard at the rear corners have been eliminated. The front flap and its decoration are not original. But the outer decoration of the rest of the case and of the lid is original and shows the usual green and off-white imitation porphyry marble. The lid in two hinged sections is original, and the papered interior is original and shows traces of the original ochre wood-graining, although most of this has now disappeared except near the letters 'IN' of INGNORANTEM. The rose has been regilded and the flowers painted around it are not original, although the 'pearls' in the rose wreath are similar to those found on other earlier Hans Ruckers instruments.

The right-hand bridge, and therefore the present scalings, are not original. Most of the keyboard action, including many of the jacks, is original.

Plate C.1 The polygonal 1591a HR 6-voet virginal. Photograph by Raymond Russell.

The instrument has been signed 'Restauré en 1959 par Henri Maillefer à Renens (Suisse)'.

*Literature:* B. 5; Russell (1959), Plate 24; van der Meer (1971c), 140, 145; Henkel (1979a), 77; O'Brien (1974a), 77, 87; O'Brien (1979), 456, 458; McGeary (1981), 31; van der Meer (1983), Plate 161 p. 97, 96; Koopman (1987), footnote 26.

*Former owner:* Theodore Joseph Cannel (a painter and former director of the Académie Royale, Ghent).

(1591)b HR

Hans Ruckers, 1591?, muselar mother-and-child virginal, Yale University, New Haven, Conn., No. 4870.60.

*Present compass:* C to c$^3$.

*Ruckers number:* M/24.

*Case dimensions:* mother – length 1707mm; width 495mm; height 266mm with, 254mm without the baseboard; keywell 648mm.

child – length 820mm; width 420mm including the keyboard; height 133mm with the baseboard; keywell 648mm.

*General description:* The dating of this instrument is based only on the inscription '1591' (or '1590'?) which appears on the trunk of a tree in the left-hand side of the lid painting. Although it appears to have been decorated by Hans' usual soundboard decorator, it has many affinities with the (*c.* 1600) HR spinett double virginal in Milan. Like the Milan instrument, it has HR roses of differing diameters in the two parts, and the top double mouldings on the nameboard and faceboard of both instruments have curved rather than flat lower surfaces.

The conversion of the bass short octave to a chromatic bass octave was achieved by making a keyboard with a narrower octave span, new slides with a correspondingly narrow spacing, and by repinning both bridges. The jacks and tuning pins have also been replaced. The present straight bass-section of the right-hand bridge, the mother's removable nameboard and the mother's front flap are all replacements.

The lid painting depicts the contest between Apollo and Marsyas, the faceboard of the mother is painted with figures dancing and making music, and the whole of the outside of the case of the child virginal is painted with figures of children at play.

The stand is old and may be original to the instrument.

*Literature:* B. 6; Steinert (1892–3), No. 12, 6; Skinner (1933), Plate 12, 32ff; Hipkins (1888), Plate XX (the stand is upside down!), 47–8; Marcuse (1960), No. 4; Russell (1959), 149; Rephann (1968), No. 242, 28; van der Meer (1971c), 137, 145; Koster (1977), 81.

*Former owners:* Messrs Chappell, London; George Donaldson, London; Morris Steinert, New Haven, Conn.; Belle Skinner.

1594 HR

Hans Ruckers, 1594, single-manual harpsichord and octave virginal combination, Schloss Köpenick, East Berlin.

*Original virginal compass:* C/E to $g^2$, $a^2$.

Plate C.2 The rose from the virginal part of the 1594 HR harpsichord/virginal combination. It is made of a thin veneer of beech and 3 layers of parchment. Scale 1:1.

*Present harpsichord compass:* C to $c^3$.

*Case dimensions:* length 1804mm; width 709mm; height 224mm without the baseboard; keywell 683mm in the harpsichord, 596mm in the virginal.

*General description:* All evidence of the original outer decoration is hidden under the present gesso and black lacquer. The inner lid painting by Hieronymus Janssens of a similar instrument with courtiers is not original. The original soundboard decoration has entirely disappeared, and the present decoration is of a later date. Many of the interior mouldings and surfaces have been repainted a number of times.

The keys, keyframe and slides of the harpsichord part are not original. The instrument is of particular interest, because the plan of much of the construction is scribed onto the baseboard. Three transverse lines at the gap in the harpsichord indicate that it had the usual two registers and a disposition of $1 \times 8'$, $1 \times 4'$. The length and position of each 8′ and 4′ string for each *c* and *f* are indicated, as well as many of the structural parts of the instrument.

The harpsichord part has the usual harpsichord Ruckers rose, but the virginal has a geometrical rose composed of several layers of pierced parchment and beech veneer.

This is the only surviving harpsichord by Hans Ruckers.

*Literature:* B. 7; Krebs (1892), 125–6; Russell (1959), 149; van der Meer (1971c), 128; Schmidt (1978), 60–7; van der Meer (1983), Plate 160, p. 96; Heyde (1986), 153, 161, 164.

*Former owners:* The Kings of Prussia.

## CATALOGUE OF IOANNES RUCKERS INSTRUMENTS WITH HR ROSES

1595 HR

Ioannes Ruckers, 1595, child virginal at R + 8, Cincinnati Art Museum, Cincinnati, Ohio, No. 1914.299.

*Present compass:* C to $d^3$

*Case dimensions:* length 813mm; width 318mm; height 140mm with the baseboard.

*General description:* This is an example of a much-altered child virginal. The sides of the case were cut down to a level flush with the soundboard and then a new case was added. The lid, keyblocks and jackrail are also all not original. The keys within the original compass from (C/)E to $c^3$ are original; the extra keys for C, C♯, D, E♭, $c^{\sharp 3}$ and $d^3$ have been added to the sides of the original keyboard.

The instrument has the signature 'IOHANNES RVQVERS ME FECIT A° 1595'; although not original, it seems to follow the paint of an earlier signature. If this is indeed an instrument by Ioannes, he was only seventeen years old when he built it (and presumably the lost mother as well). The rose is of the type used by Ioannes Ruckers in his early instruments, and not that used by Hans. Unfortunately the original soundboard painting has disappeared and been replaced by a new painting which gives no clue to the identity of the true builder.

*Literature:* B. 7a.

*Former owner:* William Howard Doane, Cincinnati.

1598 HR

Ioannes Ruckers, 1598, 6-voet spinett virginal, Instrument Museum of the Conservatoire N.S.M., Paris, No. E.979.2.6.

*Ruckers number:* 6/61.

*Present compass:* $G_1/B_1$ to $c^3$.

*Case dimensions:* length 1660mm; width 479mm; height 234mm without the baseboard; keywell originally 651mm.

*Motto:* lid – DVLCISONVM REFICIT TRISTIA CORDA MELOS 1598.

*General description:* Since this virginal was built in the year that Hans Ruckers died, it could be by either Hans or Ioannes Ruckers. However, it is signed 'IOHANNES RVCKERS FECIT ANTVERPIAE', and also has a papier mâché rose of the type used by Ioannes Ruckers in some of his later instruments (e.g. 1604 HR and 1614 HR). Both of these point to Ioannes as the maker of this virginal. Also, this is the first instrument with a soundboard painted by the painter who worked on the other early clavecimbels of Ioannes Ruckers.

In the keywell is written 'François Chapelle a refait cette spinette e luy a donné de l'armonie 1739'; this probably refers to the alteration of the compass and scalings. The keyboard was remade without widening the keyframe or the keywell and with a very narrow three-octave span of only 455mm to extend the compass downwards. New jackslots were cut in the soundboard, new lower guides made and the bridges repinned to match the new closer spacing of the keys. The resulting scalings are therefore not accurately Pythagorean and correspond to a pitch about a tone higher than the original one (i.e. to roughly R + 2).

The lid, flap and sides have a very old vine-work decoration. The spine is plain, but underneath the present decoration of this and the front flap one sees traces of the original green porphyry marble which must once have decorated the whole of the outside of the instrument.

*Literature:* B. 8; Jacquot (1904), No. 132, 109; Russell (1959), Plates 25, 27 and 69, p. 47; Juramie (1948), 36; Thibault-de Chambure (1961), Plate 43, 146; Catalogue 8 (1962), No. 587; Thibault-de Chambure (1971), 80–1; van der Meer (1971c), 130, 135, 142, 145; McGeary (1981), 21; Gétreau (1985), Plate p. 91, 90; Koopman (1987), footnote 26.

*Former owners:* Jeanne Lyon, Paris; Marcel Salomon, Paris; The Comtesse de Chambure, Paris.

1599 HR

Ioannes Ruckers, 1599, a ravalé double-manual harpsichord of a small-compass normal transposing harpsichord, Händel-Haus, Halle.

*Original compass:* upper-manual – C/E to $a^2$ at a pitch of R; lower-manual – C/E to $d^3$ at a pitch of R − 4.

*Present compass:* $F_1$ to $f^3$.

*Case dimensions:* length 2244mm; width now 927mm, originally about 742mm; height 262mm with, 251mm without the baseboard; keywell now 901mm, originally about 716mm.

*Motto:* lid flap (not original) – MVSICA MAGNORVM SOLAMEN DVLCE LABORVM.

*General description:* This is the earliest surviving Ruckers double-manual harpsichord. The plugged doubled pinholes for $e^\flat/g^\sharp$ in the bridges and 4′ hitchpin rail prove that this was originally a transposing harpsichord, and the number of plugged pins below the bottom set of $e^\flat/g^\sharp$ pins proves that the bottom note of the lower manual was the usual short-octave C/E. But the original width of the instrument (716mm) indicates that it must have reached only to $a^2$ on the upper manual or to $d^3$ on the lower. The non-original jackrail ascribes the instrument to Hans Ruckers. But Hans was already dead in 1599, and the rose type and soundboard-painting style are both characteristic of those found on the early instruments of Ioannes. Thus no extant double-manual harpsichord can be ascribed to Hans.

The ravalement was carried out by fitting in the extra bass notes without widening the bass side of the case or decreasing the octave span. Thus the treble keys were moved to the right, effectively shortening the scalings to the point where brass would be the appropriate stringing material, rather than iron.

Unfortunately the cheeks have been cut away in the style of the eighteenth-century German and Viennese fortepianos, and the case and stand encrusted with gilded neo-baroque stucco work, probably of the late nineteenth or early twentieth century.

*Literature:* B. 9; Führer (1938), No. 55; Hirt (1955), 248–9; Sasse (1958), 91; Sasse (1966), Plate, 36–7; van der Meer (1971c), 126, 127, 142; O'Brien (1977a), 42;

Henkel (1979a), 74; McGeary (1981), 28; Shann (1984), 65.

*Former history:* formerly part of the Neupert Collection, Bamberg.

(*c*. 1600) HR

Ioannes Ruckers, undated, double spinett mother-and-child virginals, Castello Sforzesco, Milan, No. 595.

*Ruckers numbers:* M/15 and k/15.

*Case dimensions:* mother – length 1708mm; width 493mm; height 266mm with, 255mm without the baseboard; keywell 647mm.

child – length 820mm; width 324mm; height 140mm with, 128mm without the baseboard; keywell 643mm.

*Scalings in millimetres:*

mother:

| | String length | Plucking point |
|---|---|---|
| $c^3$ | 183 | 63 |
| $f^2$ | 269 | 58 |
| $c^2$ | 367 | 71 |
| $f^1$ | 527 | 69 |
| $c^1$ | 708 | 86 |
| f | 936 | 95 |
| c | 1131 | 116 |
| F | 1366 | 129 |
| C/E | 1397 | 146 |

child at a pitch of R + 8:

| | String length | Plucking point |
|---|---|---|
| $c^3$ | 89 | 45 |
| $f^2$ | 136 | 44 |
| $c^2$ | 178 | 53 |
| $f^1$ | 261 | 47 |
| $c^1$ | 354 | 53 |
| f | 465 | 47 |
| c | 562 | 57 |
| F | 673 | 55 |
| C/E | 689 | 51 |

*General description:* This instrument is among those few in almost its original state (see Plate 3.9). Like other early Ioannes Ruckers instruments it is signed using the form 'IOANNES RVQVERS FECIT'. The back of the nameboard has 'Grimaldi Antonio Genova li [*sic*] 2/6/93' in a nineteenth-century hand. It has lost its exterior decoration everywhere except on the spine, which is the usual imitation green porphyry marble. The rest of the decoration is original and in very good condition. The lid painting is particularly fine. The soundboard painting, like the 1612a HR, is very sparse in comparison with later soundboard paintings on Ioannes Ruckers instruments.

This is the only spinett double virginal, and the only 6-voet spinett virginal with unaltered scalings.

*Literature:* B. 70a; Gallini (1963), No. 595, 241; van der Meer (1971c), 136, 143.

1604 HR

Ioannes Ruckers and Andreas Ruckers, 1604, 5-voet muselar virginal at a pitch of R + 2, Brussels Museum, No. 2927.

*Ruckers number:* 5/34.

*Case dimensions:* length 1424mm; width 479mm; height 215mm without the baseboard.

*Scalings in millimetres:*

| | String length | Plucking point |
|---|---|---|
| $c^3$ | 163 | 76 |
| $f^2$ | 243 | 102 |
| $c^2$ | 330 | 148 |
| $f^1$ | 464 | 187 |
| $c^1$ | 621 | 240 |
| f | 803 | 286 |
| c | 969 | 350 |
| F | 1156 | 397 |
| C/E | 1204 | 425 |

*General description:* Although much of the interior and exterior surface has been covered with a green eighteenth-century decoration, this is the only example of a 5-voet muselar virginal which has been unaltered musically. The jackrail, which undoubtedly belongs to the instrument, is signed IOANNES ET ANDREAS RVCKERS FECERVNT'. Also original is the HR rose, of the type used by Ioannes Ruckers before 1616, which is of papier mâché instead of lead. It is slightly smaller in diameter than the usual HR roses, probably because of the shrinkage of the papier mâché in drying.

The rack has its original cloths, three layers above and two layers below the tails of the keys. This is therefore one of the few instruments to retain its original depth of touch, which is found to be 9mm in the bass, and 8mm in the treble, measured at the front of the natural keys.

The original harpichordium (see Plate 5.2) is preserved separately in the museum. About ninety per cent of the jacks are original.

*Literature:* B. 11; Mahillon, Vol. IV (1893–1922), No. 2927; Russell (1959), Plate 26; Bragard and de Hen (1967), Plate IV–19, 142; Bragard and de Hen (1968), Plate IV–20, 157; de Maeyer (1969), No. 8, 26–8; de Maeyer (1972), No. 4, 14–17; van der Meer (1971c), 104, 134, 135, 145; O'Brien (1974a), 78, 81; O'Brien (1979), 455, 459; van der Meer (1983), 96.

*Former owners:* Abel Régibo, Ronse (Renaix); César Snoeck, Ronse (Renaix)

1610 HR

Ioannes Ruckers, 1610, double muselar mother-and-child virginal, Brussels Museum, No. 275.

*Ruckers numbers:* M/23 and k/23.

*Present compass:* C to $f^3$.

*Case dimensions:* mother – length 1709mm (not original); width 481mm (not original); height 269mm with, 255mm without the baseboard; keywell originally 647mm.

child – length 809mm; width 307mm without, 414mm with the keyboard; height 138mm with, 127mm without the baseboard; keywell originally 647mm.

*Original scalings:*

mother:

| | String length | Plucking point |
|---|---|---|
| $c^3$ | 180 | 88 |
| $f^2$ | 267 | 119 |
| $c^2$ | 366 | 167 |
| $f^1$ | 513 | 220 |
| $c^1$ | 693 | 302 |
| f | 943 | 422 |
| c | 1155 | 535 |
| F | 1395 | 643 |
| C/E | 1465 | 696 |

child at a pitch of R + 8:

| | String length | Plucking point |
|---|---|---|
| $c^3$ | 89 | 47 |
| $f^2$ | 133 | 42 |
| $c^2$ | 180 | 55 |
| $f^1$ | 261 | 51 |
| $c^1$ | 355 | 60 |
| f | 461 | 58 |
| c | 556 | 70 |
| F | 662 | 65 |
| C/E | 686 | 74 |

*General description:* This is a much-altered mother-and-child virginal, but it retains clear evidence of its original scalings. The ravalement has increased the compass by adding extra keys and strings beside the unaltered originals. The extra keys added to the treble forced the keywell brace of the mother into the space formerly occupied by the child, so that the latter cannot be stored in its original position. The outer case and keywell of both instruments have been painted in a reddish-brown wood-graining. But traces of the original *faux-marbre* green porphyry marble have been uncovered on the outer case of the mother virginal. Above the original paint there are no less than six layers (seven including a layer of gesso) of more recent paint on the outside of the mother. The child has a different sequence and number of layers of paint, making the history of the two difficult to tie together. The compass has been extended on both sides by adding new keys to the originals and by extending the registers and bridges to accommodate the extra notes.

The balance-rail cloth on both instruments is original. Original pieces of folded playing card (was Ioannes Ruckers a gambler?) were used to raise the sharps. The three layers of black cloth above the keys in the keyboard rack of the mother are original, as are the cloths glued to the tails of the keys.

*Literature:* B. 12; Mahillon, Vol. I (1893–1922), No. 275; van der Straeten (1875), 337; Hirt (1955), 204–5; Harich-Schneider (1958), 9; Russell (1959), Plates 29 and 30, 149; van der Meer (1971c), 137; de Maeyer (1972), No. 5, 18–21; O'Brien (1974a), 79, 81; McGeary (1981), 21.

*Former owner:* François-Joseph Fétis, Brussels.

1611 HR

Ioannes Ruckers, 1611, a 6-voet muselar virginal, Vleeshuis Museum, Antwerp, No. VH 2112.

*Ruckers number:* 6/16.

*Case dimensions:* length 1712mm; width 493mm; height 241mm with the baseboard; keywell 652mm.

*General description:* The jackrail of the instrument is signed 'IOANNES RVCKERS FECIT ANTVERPIAE'. The Andreas Ruckers rose in the soundboard is genuine, but does not fit the hole it is in, and the way it is glued in place is not original. Also, traces of the soundboard painting are in the usual style of Ioannes, and not of Andreas Ruckers instruments of this period. Thus the instrument must be ascribed to Ioannes Ruckers, not to Andreas.

Underneath the keyboard in the treble corner of the keywell is written 'nieuw Aecken gemaeckt von P.L.Cl. 1769 meert' ('new "hooks" made by P.L.Cl. in March 1769'); this probably refers to the jacks. These, although made in the style of Ruckers, are of plank-sawn and not quartered beech, they are not tapered in the Ruckers fashion, and their tongues have a circular quill hole and lack the usual leather pad at their base.

The instrument retains its original keyboard cloths. The non-original lower cloth above the original material can be pulled back at the ends to enable the original depth of touch to be measured. This is found to be 8mm in the bass and 7mm in the treble.

The front flap is not original, but is marbled like the rest of the instrument in reddish brown. Therefore the exterior decoration is not original; no traces of the original green imitation porphyry marbling remain.

The lid which is usually exhibited with the instrument is too small and does not belong to this virginal.

The stand, however, seems original and is an extremely fine example of typical turned and arcaded seventeenth-century Flemish furniture.

*Literature:* B. 15 and 75 (under Andreas Ruckers); van der Straeten, Vol. III (1875), 338; Génard (1876), Plate 2, 79; Lunsingh Scheurleer (1939), Plate 6, 47; Denucé (1941), Plate 16; Russell (1959), Plate 28; Catalogue 11 (n.d.), No. 32; Lambrechts-Douillez (1961), 128, 130; Lambrechts-Douillez (1968), Plate 10, 238; Lambrechts-Douillez (1970a), Plate, 14–16; van der Meer (1971c), 133, 141, 143; Germann (1978), 71; O'Brien (1979), 462; Lambrechts-Douillez (1981a), Plate 418, 148.

*Former owners:* A. Jacob-Wens, Antwerp; Steen Museum, Antwerp.

1612a HR

Ioannes Ruckers, 1612a, a ravalement of a double-manual harpsichord which originally had one manual at a pitch of R − 5, Fenton House, Hampstead, the property of H.M. Queen Elizabeth II.

*Original compass:* one manual – C/E to $d^3$ at a pitch of R − 5;

the other manual – C/E to $c^3$, probably at a pitch of R − 4.

*Present compass:* $G_1, A_1$ to $f^3$.

*Case dimensions:* length 2296mm; width now 881mm, originally about 735mm; height 270mm with, 251mm without the baseboard; keywell now 848mm, originally about 702mm.

*General description:* This is a unique example of a double-manual harpsichord which originally had one manual at a pitch of R − 5, with the second manual probably at a pitch a tone higher at R − 4 (see Chapter 8, pp. 178ff for an analysis of how the original state was determined). Originally there were three registers, and the most likely disposition would have been

← 4′
→ 8′ dogleg
← 4′

with the 8′ shared between the two manuals on a dogleg, and two rows of 4′ jacks, one for each manual.

The instrument is now brilliantly lacquered in the style of a typical English ravalement. The modern papers in the keywell and soundwell are most inappropriate, since the instrument could never have had this appearance after its extension and eighteenth-century modernization.

*Literature:* B. 16; exhibited at the Inventions Exhibition in London (1885) and Vienna (1892); Lees-Milne (1953), Plate 7; Russell (1957), 12; Harich-Schneider (1958), 11; van der Meer (1971c), 113, 115; O'Brien (1977a), 41, 43; O'Brien (1977b), 68; Clayson and Garrett (1981); Mactaggart (1983), 78–96.

1612b HR

Ioannes Ruckers, 1612, aligned and petit-ravalement of a normal double-manual harpsichord, Musée d'histoire locale, Amiens.

*Ruckers number:* St/34.

*Present compass:* $G_1/B_1$ to $d^3$, with a split $B_1/E^\flat$ key.

*Case dimensions:* length 2232mm; width 789mm; height 254mm without the baseboard; keywell 762mm.

*General description:* This instrument typifies a very conservative alignment of a normal Ruckers double-manual transposing harpsichord. The lower manual was aligned and the upper-manual compass extended down to $G_1/B_1$. Two notes were added to the treble and one to the bass to extend the compass to $d^3$ and to enable the $B_1/E^\flat$ key to be split. A third set of strings was not added and the keyboards are not coupled, so that no loud–soft contrast is possible, but the difference in the plucking points results in a tonal difference between the two manuals.

The soundboard is in good decorative order, although the arabesques have been repainted and a number of the flower groups heavily retouched or entirely repainted.

The alignment is dated 1730, and the builder who carried it out also labelled the bridges with the eighteenth-century gauges to be used in restringing the instrument. These seem to copy the original Ruckers stringing plan (see Chapter 4 and Table 4.6, p. 65).

*Literature:* B. 17a = 30c; Thibault-de Chambure (1971), 78; van der Meer (1971c), 118; Bédard (1977), 115; Dowd (1978), 108, 113.

(1614) HR

Ioannes Ruckers, 1614?, 6-voet muselar virginal, Brussels Museum, No. 2930.

*Ruckers number:* 6/20.

*Case dimensions:* length 1668mm; width 491mm; height 239mm without the baseboard; keywell 651mm.

*General description:* The outer decoration now consists of a geometrical pattern of brown and yellow ochre, but faults in this reveal the original green and white porphyry marbled decoration underneath. The lid interior, keywell and faceboard are all painted with figures of animals and humans engaged in various activities. The entire soundboard has been painted over with flowers, etc. in a very bad imitation 'Ruckers' style. The date 1614 does not appear anywhere on the instrument. The rose, like a number of other Ioannes

Ruckers HR roses from this period, is made of papier mâché.

Some soundbars are missing or replacements, and there are non-original wooden buttons with screws (piano style) and non-original bars under both bridges. This instrument is a good example of over-restoration.

*Literature:* B. 19 = 30a; Mahillon, Vol. IV (1893–1922), No. 2930; van der Meer (1971c), 132; de Maeyer (1969) No. 7, 25–6; O'Brien (1974a), 78.

*Former owner:* César Snoeck, Ronse (Renaix).

1616 HR

Ioannes Ruckers, 1616, aligned double-manual harpsichord, originally a chromatic-bass-octave 'French' double, M. Nirouet, Paris.

*Ruckers number:* St/17.

*Original compass:* upper manual – F to $f^3$ at a pitch of R – 4; lower manual – $G_1$ to $c^3$ at a pitch of R.

*Present compass:* $G_1$ to $c^3$.

*Case dimensions:* length 2251mm; width 830mm; height 267mm with the baseboard; keywell 805mm.

*Scalings in millimetres:*

| | 8′ | 4′ |
|---|---|---|
| $c^3$ | 175 | 82 |
| $f^2$ | 266 | 125 |
| $c^2$ | 356 | 172 |
| $f^1$ | 523 | 258 |
| $c^1$ | 672 | 340 |
| f | 912 | 479 |
| c | 1110 | 585 |
| F | 1386 | 739 |
| C | 1571 | 850 |
| $G_1$ | 1698 | 964 |

*General description:* The outer decoration painted in panels is not original, and is probably eighteenth-century French. The lid, which is in one piece without a flap, is not original. The interior of the lid, keywell and front flap are painted in mythological scenes. The keys, which have hollowed-out arcades with black naturals and white sharps, are in the style of many seventeenth-century French harpsichords and are not original. The upper-manual keyframe is original, however, and indicates that the original compass of the upper manual was F to $f^3$ (with a block three naturals wide in the bass). It still retains four transposer plates and four sets of doubled strings for the $e^{\flat}/g^{\sharp}$ notes in each choir. From the position of these plates and tuning pins, and from the width of the case, it can be inferred that the original compass of the lower manual was $G_1$ to $c^3$ chromatic. This is thus the earliest extant plucked keyboard instrument known to me which went chromatically down to $G_1$.

The soundboard decoration, although varnished over and slightly retouched, is in basically good order. The paper strip decorations above the soundboard have been replaced with a painted decoration in the style of the paper patterns. It retains its original oak turned and arcaded Flemish stand.

*Literature:* B. 22; Russell (1959), Plate 36, 45; van der Meer (1971b), 48; van der Meer (1971c), 118, 141, 145; Dowd (1978), 110, 112, 113; O'Brien (1985), footnote 13.

*Former owners:* Edgar Castil, Paris; Casadesus family.

## CATALOGUE OF IOANNES RUCKERS INSTRUMENTS WITH IR ROSES

n.d. IR

Ioannes Ruckers, undated, combined single-manual harpsichord and octave virginal, Berlin Musikinstrumentenmuseum, No. 2232.

*Case dimensions:* length 1818mm; width 707mm; height 229mm without, 243mm with the baseboard; keywell of harpsichord part 687mm.

*Mottoes:* longside virginal keywell flap (not original) – OMNIS SPIRITVS LAVDET DOMINVM;
shortside harpsichord keywell flap (not original) – GLORIA DEO.

*General description:* Although the instrument has its original compass, only the keyframe of the virginal is original, the new keyboards having a three-octave span of 483mm (harpsichord) and 475mm (virginal). The bridges and thus the scalings are also not all original. The soundboard is original, but it has been doubled in thickness by adding a new second soundboard with new barring below the old one. The virginal's lower guide and the belly rail behind the nameboard, and all of its tuning pins are not original. Most of the rest of the instrument is original, including the internal harpsichord bentside, which shows signs of being scorched by a strong heat source during bending. The harpsichord registers are original, and the wrestplank painting indicates that there was originally a buff stop. The harpsichord jackrail has its original two layers of damping cloth tacked with pairs of tacks at the ends and one-third and two-thirds of the way along the rail.

The lid painting, on canvas glued to the inside of the lid, shows the conversion of Saul/Paul. The lid itself and the outer decoration (in an unusual version of semi-precious stones on a steel-grey background) are not original. The style of the soundboard painting suggests that the instrument was built about 1628, or in the period just following.

*Literature:* B. 70; Sachs (1922), No. 2232, Plate; Sachs (1923), Plate 10; Russell (1959), 149; Otto (1965), Plate p. 134, 27; Ernst (1967), Plate X, 68; Berner (1971), Plate, 61–2; van der Meer (1971c), 128, 143; Lambrechts-Douillez (1977), 273; Schmidt (1978), 60; McGeary (1981), 22, 29; Krickeberg (1981), Plate 5, 28–31.

*Former owner:* César Snoeck, Ronse (Renaix).

(1612) IR

Ioannes Ruckers, 1612?, grand ravalement of a normal double-manual harpsichord, Instrument Museum of the Conservatoire N.S.M., Paris, No. E.1.

*Present compass:* $F_1$ to $f^3$.

*Case dimensions:* length now 2401mm, originally about 2201mm; width now 906mm; height 266mm with, 253mm without the baseboard; keywell now 878mm, originally about 755mm.

*General description:* This may be the earliest harpsichord to use the Ioannes Ruckers double-manual rose. The date is slightly uncertain, however, as it is written on a non-original part of the soundboard added in the eighteenth-century ravalement. The soundboard painting, with its use of birds and very intricate and delicate arabesques, is more in the style of the Ioannes soundboard paintings from 1616 to 1624. This, together with the use of the IR double-manual rose, which is otherwise not found until 1618, suggests to me that the date of this harpsichord is later than 1612. Perhaps 1617 was mis-read and copied as 161Z, and this has been interpreted as 1612?

The ravalement was carried out by widening the instrument on both the bass and treble sides. In the process dovetailed pieces were added to the wrestplank, belly rail, and toolbox liners. Most of the internal framing was either replaced or supplemented with additional wood. The original strapwork decoration (the only existing Ioannes strapwork case decoration) can be seen on the spine side, and the extension to the spine near the tail is also visible. The 4′ hitchpin rail was extended, new bridges and nuts were made and the entire action was replaced. The date was probably originally written on the wrestplank, and transferred to the soundboard in the process of the grand ravalement. The painting of the pieces added to the soundboard has been done very carefully in the style of the original. Technically, and from a design point of view, it is one of the most beautiful and ingenious harpsichord ravalements that I know.

The main lid shows the contest between Apollo and Marsyas and was painted by Jan Brueghel the Elder (The Velvet Brueghel) and Hendrik van Balen. The front flap shows Orpheus taming the wild animals and is by Paul Bril.

*Literature:* B. 31; Chouquet (1875), No. 222; Chouquet (1884), No. 327; Hirt (1955), 8–11; Thibault-de Chambure (1971), 78–80; van der Meer (1971c), 127, 144; Dowd (1978), 109, 113; Rueger (1982/86), Plate 71, 94; Gétreau (1985), Plate p. 91, 90–2; O'Brien (1985), 84–8; Papineau-Couture (1989).

*Former owners:* It is supposed to have been given by Maria de Medici to Elizabeth of France (wife of Philip IV of Spain), and to have been placed in the Escorial, where it later became the property of Maria Theresa. It is supposed then to have been given to Madame de Maintenon. In 1861 it belonged to L. Clapisson, Paris.

1617 IR

Ioannes Ruckers, 1617, English grand ravalement of a normal double-manual harpsichord, Dr Robert Johnson, Los Angeles.

*Present compass:* $G_1$, $A_1$ to $f^3$.

*Case dimensions:* length 2235mm; width now 917mm; height 270mm with the baseboard (not original); keywell now 842mm.

*General description:* This is an English ravalement of a normal transposing double-manual harpsichord. It is brilliantly lacquered on the outside of the case in black, and in red inside the lid. The stand is a typical English carved trestle stand.

Most unusually this harpsichord uses a virginal rose instead of a double-manual harpsichord rose. However, as it dates from the beginning of the period when Ioannes began to use the three different types of roses – according to the type of instrument – it seems likely that he had, in 1617, not yet firmly established the new rose tradition. Although the case has been widened, the entire inside of the soundwell is decorated with old Flemish block-printed papers. Close examination of these papers and careful comparison with similar papers from other instruments shows that these papers came from an instrument built after 1642. Thus they must have been taken from another Flemish instrument and glued into the soundwell at the time of the ravalement. A string-band strip made for this instrument shows the presence originally of the usual e♭/g♯ doubled strings and hitchpins in the usual positions. The soundboard painting and arabesques are typical of the other soundboard paintings of Ioannes Ruckers from the period around 1617.

*Literature:* B. 33; van der Meer (1971c), 109.

*Former owner:* Morris Steinert, Boston.

1618a IR

Ioannes Ruckers, 1618, child virginal at a pitch of R + 8,

Instrument Museum of the Conservatoire NSM, Paris, No. E.653. c.317.

*Ruckers number:* k/26.

*Case dimensions:* length 809mm; width 305mm (the keyboard projects a further 90mm); height 134mm without the baseboard.

*General description:* This is a fine example of an unaltered Ruckers child virginal. The soundboard painting is in reasonably good condition, and the papers are very well preserved. The 'name'-batten above the keys is papered, and is held in place with its original wooden beech pegs. The keys retain most of their Ioannes-style parchment and paper arcades. There is the usual slit in the baseboard to allow the keys to be operated by the jacks of the original mother, and even the cloth pads underneath the key levers appear to be original.

This is the first extant Ioannes Ruckers virginal to use the characteristic IR virginal rose used from this date onwards.

*Literature:* B.34; Chouquet (1884), No. 317; Thibault-de Chambure (1971), 81; van der Meer (1971c), 139; O'Brien (1974a), 81; Gétreau (1985), Plate p. 93, 92–3.

*Former owner:* A. Colin, Paris.

1618b IR

Ioannes Ruckers, 1618, aligned and extended normal double-manual harpsichord, Schloss Cappenberg, Westphalia, No. C.3370.

*Ruckers number:* St/12.

*Present compass:* $G_1/B_1$ to $d^3$.

*Case dimensions:* length 2210mm; width 784mm; height 268mm with, 254mm without the baseboard; keywell 757mm.

*General description:* This is a harpsichord with many interesting original and later features. Many of the jacks are original, and some of them retain their original dampers. Most of the keyboard cloths and both balance-rail cloths are original. The upper manual has two added treble keys marked St/57, probably from a late Andreas Ruckers single-manual harpsichord. The depth of touch of the upper manual can be measured and has been found to average 6.6mm.

The plan of the instrument is scribed on the baseboard in the usual way. The outside case paint has been removed, and the case is varnished so that one can see the wooden pegs holding the case joins and framing in place, and also the charring and blackening on the bentside caused by the heating used to effect the bending (see Plate 6.2, p. 91).

The second 8′ choir has been added to the left of the original, thus effectively lengthening the scaling. To compensate for this the 8′ nut has been moved toward the gap (about 10.5mm in the treble and 4.5mm in the bass). The strings, although not original, seem to copy the original sizes with those gauges available in the eighteenth or nineteenth century (see Chapter 4, pp. 63ff).

The soundboard painting is in reasonably good condition, although only the 'ghosts' of most of the arabesques remain.

*Literature:* B. 35; van der Meer (1971b), 49; van der Meer (1971c), 122, 123; O'Brien (1977a), 37; O'Brien (1977b), 62.

*Former owner:* Loeb Family, Haus Kaldenhoff, near Hamm in Westphalia.

1618c IR

Ioannes Ruckers, 1618, aligned normal double-manual harpsichord, Lund University, Kulturhistoriska Museet, Lund, Sweden.

*Present compass:* C to $d^3$.

*Case dimensions:* length 2235mm; width 790mm; height 260mm with the baseboared; keywell 760mm.

*General description:* This is a much-altered double-manual harpsichord. Most of the changes were made by the Hamburg harpsichord builder Johan Christoph Fleischer in 1724. The soundboard, bridges, nuts, soundboard mouldings, barring, 4′ hitchpin rail, wrestplank veneer, tuning pins, registers, keys, keyframes, lid, stand and cheekpiece are all not original. The Fleischer compass was $G_1/B_1$ to $c^3$; this was later changed by adding one note and making new keylevers to give C to $d^3$.

The inside of the case is painted in vermilion, the outside in imitation tortoise-shell. The soundboard painting is by Fleischer. The soundboard is signed near the gap: 'Iohannes [*sic*] Ruckers me fecit Antwerpiae [*sic*] Anno 1618' and 'Iohan Christoph Fleischer auxit et restituit Hamburgi [*sic*] Anno 1724'.

*Literature:* B. 35a.

*Former owner:* Queen Louisa Ulrica of Sweden (1720–82), daughter of King Friedrich Wilhelm of Prussia.

1619 IR

Ioannes Ruckers, 1619, aligned normal double-manual harpsichord/virginal combination, Brussels Museum, No. 2935.

*Ruckers number:* *ſt* on the harpsichord keys.

*Present compass:* harpsichord – $G_1/B_1$ to $c^3$;
virginal – C/E to $c^3$ at a pitch of R + 5.

*Case dimensions:* length 2188mm; width 817mm; height 254mm without the baseboard; keywell 750mm.

*General description:* This instrument is an example of disastrous over-restoration. Most of the instrument and its decoration are not original. The original parts are: the roses, the 'cheek' longside containing the virginal with its upper moulding, most of the keylevers, the keyframes, the sharps of the virginal and of the upper manual of the harpsichord, the harpsichord jackrail, the harpsichord registers and three of their bone plates, the lower guides of the harpsichord and virginal, the right-hand support of the virginal jackrail and the virginal nameboard. The soundboard (which is not tapered in thickness) and the bridges are all replacements. The soundboard barring is not original and is totally atypical of Ruckers normal practice. Most of the interior framing cannot be seen, but is probably also not original. The papers in the lid, soundwell, keywells and flaps are all modern, made during the time when Closson was curator of the Brussels Museum (1924–36). The painting inside the lid is modern. It represents Apollo and the nine Muses and is in the style of a similar painting by Marten de Vos (1532–1603, Antwerp) in the Musée des Beaux Arts, Brussels. The soundboard painting is roughly in the style of the early Ioannes painter, and may be copied from the original soundboard. Although the scalings are modern, they are fairly close to the Ruckers normal practice and make clear the fact that the virginal was at quint pitch an octave above the original lower manual of the harpsichord.

*Literature:* B. 36 = 37; Mahillon, Vol. IV (1893–1922), No. 2935; James (1930), Plate XXXVII, 117; Norlind (1939), Fig. 85, 134; Pols (1942), Plate 10; Lyr (1952), 16; Hirt (1955), 290–1; Russell (1959), 45, 149; Collaer and van der Linden (1961), Plate 261; Harrison and Rimmer (1964), Plate 115; van der Meer (1971b), 49; van der Meer (1971c), 103, 129; O'Brien (1974a), 79, 84; Schmidt (1978), 60.

*Former owners:* Abel Régibo, Ronse (Renaix); César Snoeck, Ronse (Renaix).

1620 IR

Ioannes Ruckers, 1620, 6-voet muselar virginal, on loan from the New England Conservatory of Music to the Boston Museum of Fine Arts (MFA No. 10.1974).

*Ruckers number:* 6/3[?].

*Present compass:* C to $f^3$.

*Case dimensions:* length 1707mm; width 495mm; height 243mm without the baseboard; keywell now 776mm, originally 652mm.

*Motto:* lid (not original) – OMNIS SPIRITVS LAVDET DOMINVM.

*General description:* This is a much-altered 6-voet virginal. The keywell was widened on both sides to extend the compass, but the keyboard was not moved up or down and thus the scalings were not changed. A section was added to the bass of the left-hand bridge to carry the new extra notes. The extensions to the keys caused the second figure of the Ruckers serial number to be cut away. The soundboard painting is in reasonably good condition (the arabesques have been repainted), although it and the non-original papers have been heavily varnished over.

The stand is probably eighteenth century; it resembles that under the Dulcken harpsichord in the Smithsonian Institution in Washington.

*Literature:* B. 39; van der Meer (1971c), 134; Koster (1977), 78ff; McGeary (1981), 29.

*Former owner:* Messrs Chickering, Boston, Mass.

1622 IR

Ioannes Ruckers, 1622, 6-voet muselar virginal, Metropolitan Museum of Art, New York, No. 11.176.1.

*Ruckers number:* 6/38.

*Present compass:* C to $f^3$.

*Case dimensions:* length 1706mm; width 488mm; height 228mm without the baseboard; keywell originally 647mm.

*Motto:* lid – OMNIS SPIRITVS LAVDET DOMINVM.

*General description:* The outside of the case is now painted black, but underneath one sees the heavily textured surface and traces of paint, from the original green and off-white imitation porphyry marble. The decoration is in basically very good order and is mostly original. The soundboard painting style is very similar to that of the 1624 IR double-manual harpsichord.

The compass was extended on both the treble and bass sides by moving the keywell braces and extending the nameboard, and the bass of the left-hand bridge was also extended with an additional section mitred to the end. The original tuning pins are labelled with their note names and confirm the original compass of C/E to $c^3$. The keys are labelled with the gauge numbers (probably eighteenth century) corresponding to the scalings and compass of the ravalement.

The stand, with turned columns and carved ends, may be original, although it is not in the style of the other Ruckers instrument stands. It is certainly very old, as is revealed by the wear to the bottom stretchers from the players' feet.

*Literature:* B. 40; Hipkins (1888 and 1921), Plate XVIII, 41–2; van der Meer (1971c), 132; McGeary (1981), 20.

*Former owner:* Victor Mahillon, Brussels.

1623 IR

Ioannes Ruckers, 1623, double muselar mother-and-child virginal, Würtembergisches Landesmuseum, Stuttgart.

Plate C.3 The 1623 IR muselar double virginal. Copyright, George F. Harding Museum, Chicago.

*Ruckers number:* M/33 and k/33.

*Case dimensions:* Mother – length 1708mm; width 501mm; height 264mm with, 253mm without the baseboard; keywell 648mm;

child – length 806mm; width 305mm; height 136mm with, 124mm without the baseboard; keywell 645mm.

*Mottoes:* lid – AVDI VIDE ET TACE SI VIS VIVERE IN PACE; keywell flap – OMNIS SPIRITVS LAVDET DOMINVM.

*General description:* This instrument gives a remarkably good idea of the original appearance of a Ruckers mother-and-child double virginal (see Plate C.3). Although the outer-case paint of the mother is not original, it copies the original imitation green porphyry marble decoration. The soundboard painting is rather heavily retouched, but the papers on both instruments are intact and in good condition.

A paper label pasted to the bottom of the toolbox reads: 'Restauré dans les Ateliers du Berceau Royal. Instruments de Musique Anciens M. & A. Salomon, 14 rue Boissy d'Anglais, à Paris, 25 juin 1925'. The replacement jacks and the heavy varnish on the soundboards of both instruments may date from this restoration.

*Literature:* B. 41; James (1930), Plate 26, 106; Norlind (1939), Fig. 76, 117; Russell (1959), Plates 31 and 32, 149; van der Meer (1971c), Plate 11, 138; O'Brien (1974a), 83; McGeary (1981), 20, 29.

*Former owners:* M. & A. Salomon, Paris; George Harding (brother of U.S. President Harding), Chicago; Harding Museum, Chicago.

1624 IR

Ioannes Ruckers, 1624, aligned petit ravalement of a normal double-manual harpsichord, Le musée des Unterlinden, Colmar, France.

*Present compass:* $G_1, A_1$ to $d^3$.

*Case dimensions:* length 2237mm; width 789mm; height 267mm with, 254mm without the baseboard; keywell 763mm.

*General description:* The instrument is not signed by Ruckers and the present rose was made by the author. But from the construction and decorative points of view, there can be no doubt that the harpsichord is by Ioannes Ruckers. The records of the de Sade family, who owned the harpsichord until recently, indicate that there has been a Ruckers harpsichord among the family's effects since the eighteenth century.

The instrument went through an initial alignment giving it a compass of $G_1/B_1$ to $c^3$ with the original Ruckers string spacing; later it was given a petit ravalement compass of $G_1$, $A_1$ to $d^3$ by decreasing the string and key spacing to give a three-octave span of 472mm, and by a slight increase in the width of the keyframes. The lower-manual keyblocks were removed and the upper-manual keyblocks were sawn in half to serve as the new keyblocks for both manuals. In the process of these alterations the nuts were replaced and new keyboards were made.

*Literature:* There are no references to this instrument in the literature.

*Former owners:* Comte Xavier de Sade, Condé en Brie; Alan Rubin, London.

1627a IR

Ioannes Ruckers, 1627, grand ravalement single-manual harpsichord, Berlin Musikinstrumentenmuseum, No. 2227.

*Ruckers number:* ʃt/54.

*Present compass:* C to $e^3$.

*Case dimensions:* length 1815mm; width 810mm, originally about 711mm; height 228mm without the baseboard; keywell now 779mm, originally about 680mm.

*General description:* The ravalement was carried out by widening the case and adding the extra notes in the treble and bass without changing the octave spacing. Thus the keyboard is effectively moved toward the treble relative to its original position in the case. The soundboard, although it is painted in a good imitation of the Ioannes style, is not original, nor are the bridges, nuts, or the wrestplank and its veneer. However, many of the jacks are original; there are roughly equal numbers of the 8′ (with two damper holes) and 4′ (with only one damper hole) sets. It is thus clear that

Plate C.4 Plan view of the 1624 IR double-manual harpsichord. Scale 1:10. Copyright, Chris Clarke, Veron, France.

the original disposition was the usual 1 × 8′, 1 × 4′, and from the original width of the instrument, the compass must have been C/E to $c^3$. This is confirmed by the keylevers from F to $c^3$, which are original and numbered.

The outer case decoration is a type of strapwork and is continuous around the case and across the ravalement join. This, together with the fact that it has a white gesso ground never used by the Ruckers, confirms that it is not original. Since the case sides are 9 duimen high (the other strapwork decoration singles were always 9½ duimen high), it is likely that the original outer-case decoration would have been the usual plain imitation marble.

*Literature:* B. 43; van der Straeten, Vol. III (1875), 329; Sachs (1922), No. 2227, Plate; Sachs (1923), Plate 6; Otto (1965), 27; Winternitz (1966), No. 34, Plate 113; Ernst (1967), 68; Otto (1968), Plate 14, 64; Berner (1971), 60; van der Meer (1971b), 51; van der Meer (1971c), 111, 115; O'Brien (1977a), 37, 41; Germann (1978), 74; McGeary (1981), 26; Heyde (1986), 221; Koopman (1987).

*Former owners:* Edmond van der Straeten; César Snoeck, Ronse (Renaix).

1627b IR

Ioannes Ruckers, 1627, aligned normal double-manual harpsichord, P. de la Raudière, Château de Villebon (Eure et Loire), France.

*Present compass:* $G_1/B_1$ to $c^3$.

*General description:* This is a conservative alignment of a normal Ruckers double-manual harpsichord. The nuts have not been moved, and the problem of avoiding the long scalings produced when the second set of strings is added (the van Blankenburg problem) has been solved in a unique way. The keytails and string-band have a space between d and $e^{\flat}$ and the keys crank upwards by one semitone for all of the notes above this point, so that the scalings of the long (added) string are effectively shortened by one semitone. The alignment is dated 1701.

The case is lacquered dark green with gold bands in the usual French style. The stand is old, although probably not original, and the lid is definitely not original. The instrument was restored in 1924 by G. Simer.

*Literature:* B. 44b.

*Former owners:* The instrument was bought by Sully, who was a minister to Henry IV, for the Château de Villebon. It was sold in 1904, and again in about 1920 to Salomon, Paris. It was bought again in 1927 by the present owner for the château.

1627c IR

Ioannes Ruckers, 1627, grand ravalement of an extended-bass-compass 'French' double-manual harpsichord, formerly the property of Claude Mercier-Ythier, Paris.

*Original compass:* upper manual – F to $f^3$ at a pitch of R – 4; lower manual – $G_1$ to $c^3$ at a pitch of R.

*Present compass:* $F_1$ to $f^3$.

*General description:* This instrument is an interesting example of the process of ravalement. Initially it was aligned and given the compass $G_1$ to $d^3$ without widening the case or altering the bridge pinning, but by using a small octave span, and by adding extra strings at the top and bottom. This alteration dates from 1753 and is signed, probably by Jean Goujon, who also carried out the ravalement of the 1632 instrument below. Later the original case sides were cut down to the level of the top of the soundboard and a new spine and cheek were added outside the original case sides. New liners and new strips of soundboard wood extend the compass down two semitones (i.e. from $G_1$ to $F_1$) and upwards by four semitones to $f^3$ (i.e. from $d^3$ to $f^3$).

The extra keys, signed 'FA', were added beside those of Goujon, and the nameboard was extended at both ends to reach out to the new cheek and spine pieces. The original marbled decoration on the spine was visible when the baseboard was removed because of a small space left between the original and the added spine. The little toolbox flap from the original spine was moved to the treble side and used as a support for the lower guides.

*Literature:* B. 44a; Dowd (1978), 109, 113; O'Brien (1985), footnote 13.

*Former owners:* Salomon, Paris; Mme Bailly, Paris; Claude Mercier-Ythier, Paris.

1628a IR

Ioannes Ruckers, 1628, double virginal converted to a normal 6-voet muselar single virginal, Brussels Museum, No. 2926.

*Ruckers number:* M/34.

*Present compass:* C, D to $f^3$.

*Case dimensions:* length 1708mm; width 472mm; height 266mm with the baseboard; keywell now 755mm, original 646mm.

*General description:* The Ruckers number, visible only under ultraviolet light on the tail of the keyframe, proves that this was originally a double virginal. The space for the child beside the keyboard of the mother has been filled up, and the whole of the case and lid have been veneered with simple naive inlay. The bridges (and therefore the scalings) and jacks are not original, although the soundboard, soundbars, wrestplank, rose, etc. are. There is presently a pedal arrangement at the treble end which seems to have once controlled a buff stop or the harpichordium.

*Literature:* B. 45; Mahillon, Vol. IV (1893–1922), No. 2926; van der Meer (1971c), 132; O'Brien (1974a), 80.

*Former owners:* Louis Jouret, Brussels; César Snoeck, Ronse (Renaix).

1628b IR

Ioannes Ruckers, 1628, aligned and petit ravalement of an extended-compass 'French' double-manual harpsichord, Versailles Palace, France.

*Original compass:* upper manual – F to $f^3$ at a pitch of R – 4; lower manual – $G_1$ to $c^3$ at a pitch of R.

*Present compass:* $G_1$ to $d^3$.

*Case dimensions:* length 2274mm; width 835mm; height 254mm without the baseboard; keywell 806mm.

*General description:* This is a fine example of a French petit ravalement of a Ruckers extended-compass double-manual harpsichord. The exterior decoration is in the style of Louis XIV and has been attributed to Claude III Audran (1658–1734). The interior of the lid is painted with a pastoral scene. Rather remarkably, considering the lavish nature of the rest of the instrument's decoration, the spine retains its original Ruckers marbling in excellent condition.

The bridges were not repinned when the compass was extended to $d^3$ and the second set of 8′ strings was added, but the extra natural width was achieved by decreasing the octave span of the naturals and fanning out the tails of the keys to reach the extra notes added.

The keys are dated 1706 and may be by Blanchet. The date of the ravalement makes this harpsichord eminently suitable for the interpretation of the music of François Couperin (le Grand), and his contemporaries.

*Literature:* B. 47; Dufourcq (1946), 535; Kinsky (1930 and 1951), No. 1, 125; Hirt (1955), 250, 251; van der Meer (1971c), 109; Dowd (1978), 111, 113; Dowd (1984), 21, 31ff, 70; O'Brien (1985), footnote 13.

*Former owner:* Musée de Cluny, Paris.

1629 IR

Ioannes Ruckers, 1629, 4½-voet spinett virginal at a pitch of R + 4, Brussels Museum, No. 2511.

*Ruckers number:* 4½/11.

*Present original compass:* C/E to $d^3$.

*Case dimensions:* length 1282mm; width 478mm; height 220mm with, 190mm without the baseboard; keywell 677mm.

*Scalings in millimetres:*

| | String length | Plucking point |
|---|---|---|
| $d^3$ | 121 | 54 |
| $c^3$ | 139 | 54 |
| $f^2$ | 199 | 51 |
| $c^2$ | 274 | 65 |
| $f^1$ | 402 | 62 |
| $c^1$ | 550 | 73 |
| f | 717 | 71 |
| c | 859 | 82 |
| F | 1018 | 83 |
| C/E | 1056 | 93 |

*Motto:* lid – OMNIS SPIRITVS LAVDET DOMINVM.

*General description:* This is one of two extant 4½-voet virginals and the only extant spinett virginal of this length. Most of the instrument is in original condition, except for some very heavy non-original bars under the soundboard. The right-hand bridge, unusually, is of cherry, not of beech. The date is written on the non-original jackrail, but is also visible under ultraviolet light on the soundboard. Most of the soundboard decoration has disappeared.

*Literature:* B. 49; Mahillon, Vol. IV (1893–1922), No. 2511; van der Meer (1971c), 131; O'Brien (1974a), 76; O'Brien (1977a), 43; O'Brien (1977b), 68; O'Brien (1979), 462; McGeary (1981), 29; Shann (1984), 65; Mactaggart (1985), 107.

1632 IR

Ioannes Ruckers, 1632, normal single-manual harpsichord converted into a ravalé double-manual harpsichord. Musée d'art et d'histoire, Neuchâtel.

*Present compass:* $G_1$ to $e^3$.

*Case dimensions:* length now 2254mm; width now 873mm; height now 279mm with, 265mm without the baseboard; keywell now 842mm, originally 645mm.

*General description:* The usual scribed lines on the baseboard indicate that this was originally a single-manual harpsichord with two registers, and the original width between the keyblocks (645mm) suggests that it originally had a compass of C/E to $c^3$.

The monogram on the keylevers indicates that the ravalement to a double was carried out by Jean Goujon in 1745. The original case sides appear to be enclosed inside the present case, with about 10cm having been added to either side of the case. The points at which the lengthened bridges pass over the original case sides have been cut away so that the soundboard and bridges can vibrate freely. The rose was repositioned and most of the soundboard carefully repainted in exactly the same style as the original Ruckers soundboard painter. The exterior case and stand have been lavishly decorated in the style of Louis XV.

The 8′ ravalement scalings are very precise, halving with each octave rise in pitch, and follow the usual eighteenth-century practice, but the 4′ scalings are almost a tone shorter than those of the 8′ strings (normally in France they were only about a semitone shorter).

*Literature:* B. 53; Hirt (1955), 252, 256; van der Meer (1971c), 110; O'Brien (1977a), 41; Rueger (1982/86), Plate 15, 58.

1636 IR

Ioannes Ruckers, 1636, 6-voet muselar virginal, Harvard University, Cambridge, Mass.

*Ruckers number:* 6/70.

*Present compass:* C to $f^3$.

*Case dimensions:* length 1708mm; width 497mm; height 240mm with, 227mm without the baseboard; keywell now 763mm, originally 645mm.

*Motto:* lid (not original) – DVLCISONVM REFICIT TRISTIA CORDA MEJOS [*sic*].

*General description:* This is a much-altered 6-voet virginal. The keyboard has been widened at both ends, and the bridges were extended and repinned to take the extra notes (one bridge is a modern replacement). The soundboard painting appears all to be non-original, but some of the flowers are vaguely in the style of the late Ioannes Ruckers/Couchet painter. The date is painted on non-original papers in the lid, and also between the left-hand bridge and spine, an unusual position. Was the date originally 1639, and not 1636? If so, it would explain the discrepancy in the Ruckers number (see Chapter 3, p. 50). The outside of the instrument has a heavy carved oak case glued to the original poplar case. The stand, also of oak, is in the style of seventeenth-century Flemish furniture and may be original.

The keyboard has four layers of original black cloth sewn to the top of the rack. The (eighteenth-century?) string gauges are marked on the keys by the builder responsible for the ravalement to the 1622 IR and 1632 AR virginals.

*Literature:* B. 55a (=56?); van der Meer (1971c), 132, 142, 145; McGeary (1981), 21.

1637a IR

Ioannes Ruckers, 1637, a grand ravalement of a chromatic-bass-octave 'English' single-manual harpsichord, Russell Collection, Edinburgh, No. 5.

*Original compass:* C to $c^3$.

*Present compass:* $A_1$ to $f^3$.

*Case dimensions:* length now 1830mm, originally about

1824mm; width now 840mm; height 243mm with, 230mm without the baseboard; keywell now 814mm, originally about 734mm.

*General description:* Originally this was one of the few 'English' Ruckers singles with a chromatic bass compass going from C to $c^3$. It went through a number of alterations. One of the first seems to have been the replacement of the 4′ by an 8′ register to give 2 × 8′, without altering the compass. It was later widened, the bridges were repinned, and new keyboards, registers and jacks were fitted. The workmanship suggests that this was done in England (but probably not in the workshops of either Kirkman or Shudi). There is an original pedal to operate the 4′ register, with two stop levers functioning in the usual way for the two 8′ registers.

The soundboard decoration is in good condition, although some of the groups and arabesques have been retouched. The outer case is in red lacquer with gilt and ink-wash vine and garland decoration.

*Literature:* B. 59; Newman and Williams (1968), No. 5, Plate, 11; Barnes (1971a), 36; van der Meer (1971b), 49–51; van der Meer (1971c), 113–15; O'Brien (1977a), 44; O'Brien (1979), 453.

*Former owners:* J. C. Horsley, R.A.; Hugh Gough, London; Raymond Russell, London.

1637b IR

Ioannes Ruckers, 1637, normal Ruckers double-manual harpsichord restored to its original state with unaligned keyboards, Museo degli Antichi Strumenti Musicali, Rome, No. 817.

*Ruckers number:* *ft*/14.

*Case dimensions:* length 2239mm; width 784mm; height 265mm with, 254mm without the baseboard; keywell 760mm.

*Motto:* keywell flap – ACTA VIRVM PROBANT.

*General description:* Although the lid is not original, most of the instrument's other original features are retained. It was restored in 1969–70 by John Barnes to its original state, with the manuals separated by a fourth in pitch and a disposition of 1 × 8′, 1 × 4′. It is thus the only restored transposing harpsichord. (Unfortunately through recent neglect it has already deteriorated to a point where it is no longer playable.) The soundboard painting and paper decorations are rather badly damaged, but the exterior marbling is in reasonably good condition: this is one of the few Ioannes Ruckers harpsichords with its original outer-case marbling not replaced by some later decoration. It is also one of the few doubles to retain its original keyblock decoration, and has many of its original key arcades.

*Literature:* B. 71 = 59a; van der Meer (1966), 114–21; van der Meer (1971b), 49; van der Meer (1971c), 119, 122; Cervelli (1976), 322; Dowd (1978), 107, 113; McGeary (1981), 18; Koopman (1987), footnote 3.

*Former owner:* Evan Gorga, Rome.

1638a IR

Ioannes Ruckers, 1638, 6-voet muselar virginal, Brussels Museum, No. 2933.

*Ruckers number:* 6/68.

*Present compass:* C to $d^3$.

*Case dimensions:* length 1709mm; width 494mm.

*Motto:* lid – MVSICA MAGNORVM EST SOLAMEN DVLCE LABORVM.

*General description:* The soundboard, bridges, scalings, and soundboard barring are all not original. The date is written on the (non-original) soundboard. The papers and the decoration of the interior of the lid are in reasonably good condition, and the outside of the lid and case show traces of the original olive green and off-white porphyry marbled decoration. The natural keyplates are very worn, showing that the instrument has been heavily used.

*Literature:* B. 60; Mahillon, Vol. IV (1893–1922), No. 2933; van der Meer (1971c), 133, 136; McGeary (1981), 28.

*Former owner:* César Snoeck, Ronse (Renaix).

1638b IR

Ioannes Ruckers, 1638, normal double-manual harpsichord with original unaltered keyboards, Russell Collection, Edinburgh, No. 6.

*Ruckers number:* *ft*/41.

*Case dimensions:* length 2243mm; width 786mm; height 269mm with, 255mm without the baseboard; keywell 759mm.

*Scalings in millimetres:*

unison scalings:

| Lower-manual note | Upper-manual note | String length | Plucking point* |
|---|---|---|---|
| $f^3$ | $c^3$ | 174 | 86 |
| $c^3$ | $g^2$ | 235 | 92 |
| $f^2$ | $c^2$ | 354 | 101 |
| $c^2$ | $g^1$ | 477 | 110 |
| $f^1$ | $c^1$ | 704 | 123 |
| $c^1$ | g | 891 | 132 |
| f | c | 1196 | 145 |
| c | G | 1413 | 156 |
| F | C | 1664 | 173 |
| C/E | ($G_1$/$B_1$) | 1693 | 175 |

* These are for the lower manual; subtract 33 for the upper-manual plucking points.

octave scalings:

| Lower-manual note | Upper-manual note | String length | Plucking point* |
|---|---|---|---|
| $f^3$ | $c^3$ | 84 | 61 |
| $c^3$ | $g^2$ | 113 | 65 |
| $f^2$ | $c^2$ | 175 | 71 |
| $c^2$ | $g^1$ | 235 | 74 |
| $f^1$ | $c^1$ | 348 | 77 |
| $c^1$ | g | 452 | 80 |
| f | c | 621 | 84 |
| c | G | 754 | 86 |
| F | C | 931 | 89 |
| C/E | ($G_1$/$B_1$) | 958 | 91 |

* These are for the lower manual; subtract 34 for the upper-manual plucking points.

*General description:* This is the only surviving double-manual harpsichord with its keyboards in their original condition. The rest of the instrument is also in a basically unaltered state. It was apparently used for some time with only one 8′ on the upper manual and one 4′ on the lower, with the two middle registers stored inside the instrument case. The transposing plates were removed and the recesses for them in the nuts filled, the register projections on the cheek side were removed and the Ioannes Ruckers rose was replaced with an Italian style gothic geometrical rose. The upper and lower guides, keyboard cloths, soundboard and case are all in very good condition. The outside of the case is decorated in black lacquer with vine-work and 'classical' heads in the style of the jack-rail paper (Type 24, p. 143). The buff stop has survived almost intact.

*Literature:* B. 61; Marcuse (1952), 417–18; Russell (1959), Plates 33–5, 45; Newman and Williams (1968), No. 6, Plates, 13; Ripin (1968), 34; Barnes (1971a), 37–8; van der Meer (1971b), 48; van der Meer (1971c), 117, 121; O'Brien (1977a), 45; Wittmayer (1977), 104; Dowd (1978), 107, 113; Henkel (1979a), 74, 108; O'Brien (1979), 456, 461; Koster (1982), 48; Mactaggart (1983), 79; van der Meer (1983), Plate 137, 95; Shann (1984), 65, 67; O'Brien (1985), footnote 21; O'Brien (1987), 294.

*Former owners:* E. Spence, Florence (before 1896); Sir B. Samuelson, sold 1915; Mrs Lotta van Buren Bizallion, who lent it to Yale University; Raymond Russell, London.

1639 IR

Ioannes Ruckers, 1639, petit ravalement of an extended-compass 'English' single-manual harpsichord, Victoria and Albert Museum, London, No. 1739–1869.

*Original compass:* C to $d^3$.

*Present compass:* probably $G_1$, $A_1$ to $d^3$.

*Case dimensions:* length 1733mm; width 785mm; height 212mm with, 201mm without the baseboard; keywell 758mm.

*General description:* Analysis of the original pinning of the bridges from the plugged bridge-pin holes shows that this harpsichord originally had a compass of C to $d^3$ chromatic. It was later altered in England by adding an extra 8′ choir of strings and an extra register (the additional space being gained on the soundboard/belly-rail side of the gap). The keyboards, registers and jacks were replaced and the compass extended by narrowing the keyblocks, using a smaller three-octave span, and by repinning the bridges accordingly. The ravalement keyboard was lost in a fire in Kirkman's factory in 1853, but the most likely compass was probably $G_1$, $A_1$ to $d^3$, giving a $c^2$ scaling of 339mm.

Although heavily varnished over, the soundboard painting is in good condition. The outer case is lacquered black with intertwined vines and flowers around the edges of the case sides. The non-original lid is painted with an elaborate rococo design.

*Literature:* B. 62; Russell (1959), Plate 13; Russell (1968), Fig. 13, 42; van der Meer (1971b), 51; van der Meer (1971c), 111, 115; O'Brien (1977a), 45; Schott (1985), No. 16, plates, 57–8.

*Former owners:* Queen Charlotte (wife of George III); Messrs Kirkman and Sons, London.

1640a IR

Ioannes Ruckers, 1640, 5-voet muselar virginal originally at a pitch of R + 2, Gemeentemuseum, The Hague, No. EC 34-x-1976.

*Ruckers number:* 5/46.

*Present compass:* C to $c^3$.

*Case dimensions:* length 1470mm; width 483mm; height 218mm with, 204mm without the baseboard; keywell now 700mm, originally 648mm.

*Motto:* lid – MVSICA LABORVM DVLCE LEVAMEN.

*General description:* The conversion of the short octave to a chromatic bass octave was achieved by adding the extra keys only on the bass side of the keyframe and by moving only the bass keywell brace to widen the keywell. The bridges were replaced, the new left-hand bridge having a curved portion in the bass to take the extra added strings. The new scalings are only slightly longer than the usual 5-voet virginal scalings, but the new position of the strings on the bridges meant that the tuning pins had to be moved to match the new bridge-pin positions.

Some of the jacks and tongues are original. The rose is of vellum or leather, pierced in a geometrical pattern, and is not original – the marks of the rounded tabs used to hold the original rose to the soundboard can be seen underneath the rose hole. The leather of the soundboard jackslides is in very good condition.

Although both the original jackrail (with the signature) and rose are missing, there is no doubt that this virginal is by Ioannes Ruckers. The style of the soundboard decoration, and the decoration of the lid are all in the usual style of the late instruments of Ioannes Ruckers, and in particular that of the 1642a IR 5-voet virginal.

*Literature:* B. 109b; McGeary (1981), 27.

*Former history:* Formerly in the Rijksmuseum, Amsterdam, on loan from the Koninklijk Oudheidkundig Genootschap.

1640b IR

Ioannes Ruckers, 1640b, aligned normal double-manual harpsichord, Graf Landsberg-Velen, Schloss Ahaus, Westphalia.

*Ruckers number:* ſt/14.

*Present compass:* $G_1/B_1$ to $c^3$.

*Case dimensions:* length 2254mm; width 784mm; height 268mm with, 255mm without the baseboard; keywell 759mm.

*General description:* This is another 'classic' example of an aligned Ruckers double. The alignment was done in the simplest way: the lower-manual keys were reordered, and keys from an (Andreas Ruckers?) harpsichord were used to fill out the bass octave of the upper manual. A second set of 8′ strings was added, lengthening the scale, since the 8′ nut was not moved (i.e. the van Blankenburg problem was ignored).

The soundboard painting is in good condition, and the outer case has a beautiful red chinoiserie decoration. The inside of the lid is painted with a scene depicting the contest between Apollo and Pan, the front flap depicts Apollo and the Muses and both are probably by Artus Wolfort (1581–1641), Antwerp, an almost exact contemporary of Ioannes Ruckers. The keys have many original arcades.

*Literature:* B. 63; Reuter (1968), 123–8; van der Meer (1971b), 49; van der Meer (1971c), Plates 4–5, 118, 143; O'Brien (1974a), 81; Lambrechts-Douillez (1977), 266; Wittmayer (1977), 97–108.

*Former owners:* Made for Alexander, Reichsgraf von Velen, Freiherr von Raesfeld, in 1640, and still in the same family.

1642a IR

Ioannes Ruckers, 1642, 5-voet muselar virginal at a pitch of R + 2, Musikmuseet, Stockholm.

*Ruckers number:* 5/78.

*Case dimensions:* length 1474mm; width 486mm; height (not original) 216mm with, 202mm without the baseboard; keywell 652mm.

*Motto:* lid – MVSICA LABORVM DVLCE LEVAMEN.

*General description:* Except for those in the lid, the papers on this instrument are in poor condition. The outer surface of the case is painted vermilion red, but underneath this the original imitation green porphyry marbled decoration can be seen.

Probably in the eighteenth century the original compass was increased to C to $c^3$ chromatic. This was reduced to C/E to $c^3$ in a recent restoration by moving the keywell braces back to their original positions, and by replacing the old cut-down left-hand piece of faceboard and moulding with a new piece. There was once a harpichordium, probably operating up to $f^1$. The strings are not now properly spaced on the straight section of the right-hand bridge for the (equally-spaced) harpichordium hooks. Thus the bass scalings are not quite those of the original state.

The rose is of a unique type among those of Ioannes Ruckers. Like the earlier roses, this one has a star-shaped pattern on the back surface, caused when a backing plate with channels in it to bleed off the excess lead was pressed against the back of the mould. It has a larger diameter than the earlier Ioannes virginal roses, and the angel's harp faces to his right instead of to his left. The reason for a new design is not clear; the earlier rose's cast may have become unusable. The present rose was cast just before Ioannes' death in 1642. Quite naturally it was this later casting which was copied by Couchet for his virginal rose, and not the somewhat smaller earlier Ioannes Ruckers rose.

*Literature:* B. 63a; van der Meer (1971c), 133, 135; McGeary (1981), 27; van der Meer (1983), Plate 159 p. 96, 96.

1642b IR

Ioannes Ruckers, 1642, aligned petit ravalement of a normal double-manual harpsichord, Hugh Gough, New York, N.Y.

*Ruckers number:* ſt/24.

*Present compass:* $G_1/B_1$ to $d^3$.

*General description:* This is a very fine example of a Ruckers aligned double-manual harpsichord. The enlarged compass of $G_1/B_1$ to $d^3$ was obtained by reducing the octave span of the keyboards and fitting the added $c^{\sharp 3}$ and $d^3$ into the original space between the keyblocks. Space for these extra notes was obtained by extending the bridges and nuts in the treble.

The interiors of the lid and lid flap are decorated with

very fine paintings showing scenes from classical mythology. The exterior of the case has Italianate vine-work decoration, and the instrument sits on a delicate gilt stand.

*Literature:* B. 64; *Musical Times,* XLV (1904), 431; Catalogue 3 (1909), 170; Marcuse (1952), 418–19; van der Meer (1971b), 49; van der Meer (1971c), Plate 6, 119, 143; Gough (1971), 4–6; Lambrechts-Douillez (1977), 272; Dowd (1978), 108, 113; Koster (1980), 59–9.

*Former owners:* Cornelius Winklaar, Zaandam (1832); F. R. Leyland of Speke Hall and South Kensington; Countess Dudley; Richard Newton, Henly-on-Avon.

## CATALOGUE OF ANDREAS RUCKERS INSTRUMENTS

(*c.* 1605) AR

Andreas Ruckers, undated, single-manual harpsichord, Vleeshuis Museum, Antwerp, No. VH 2136.

*Ruckers number:* ʃt/2.

*Case dimensions:* length 1826mm; width 723mm; height 240mm with the baseboard; keywell 692mm.

*General description:* The existence of forty-five original tuning pins, forty-five 4′ hitchpins, and the conformity to the 49cm rule all confirm the original C/E to $c^3$ compass of this harpsichord. After alteration it seems to have had forty-eight notes. This figure suggests C, D to $c^3$; however, the second set of 8′ tuning pins is staggered to indicate their note names in the French way, giving ?$e^{\flat 3}$ as the top note (the bottom note is indeterminate, since the staggering of the pins does not allow any intelligible reading).

The 8′ nut is a modern replacement in oak, but is in the same position as the original. The lid and lid flap are original, and have paintings on the inside. The lid flap seems to have been painted by the same (modern) artist who painted the inside of the 1646 IC double in Brussels. Most of the soundboard painting is not original, but what little remains of it, the type of rose, and the Ruckers number suggest that the date of this harpsichord is about 1605.

*Literature:* B. 130; Génard (1859), 26; Génard (1876), 26; van der Meer (1971b), 50, 52; van der Meer (1971c), 113; Catalogue 11 (n.d.), No. 35, 19–20; Lambrechts-Douillez (1970a), 18–19; Lambrechts-Douillez (1981a) 152; O'Brien (1974a), 83, 85.

*Former history:* formerly exhibited in the Steen Museum, Antwerp.

1608 AR

Andreas Ruckers, 1608, aligned normal double-manual harpsichord, Russell Collection, Edinburgh, No. 3.

*Ruckers number:* ʃt/19.

*Present compass:* C to $d^3$.

*Case dimensions:* length 2230mm; width 794mm; height 268mm with, 255mm without the baseboard; keywell 764mm.

*Motto:* ACTA VIRVM PROBANT is written on the baseboard inside the keywell, and is presumably copied from the original keywell flap.

*General description:* This is a very fine instrument which has suffered a number of alterations. The original lower-manual keys and keyframe survive; these indicate that the first alteration was to align the keyboards in such a way as to give a compass of C to $d^3$. Because the scale was lengthened when adding the second (long) 8′ (i.e. the van Blankenburg problem), and because the keyboard was shifted to the left, making the scale still longer, new 8′ and 4′ nuts were positioned closer to the gap to reduce the scalings. Unfortunately the exact disposition and number of registers at this stage of the instrument's history cannot now be determined.

At some time around the end of the eighteenth century, it was converted to a pianoforte, still with the compass C to $d^3$. Then, in 1928, it was converted back to a harpsichord with a new upper manual, and in the process the piano action was lost. The stand was also cut down, presumably to make it a more comfortable height. In 1953 new keyboards were again made with the spurious compass $G_1/B_1$ to $c^3$, $d^3$, and it was given an equally spurious disposition with a *peau de buffle* row of jacks, a shove coupler and a mixture of hard leather and quill registers.

The lid and lid flap both have very fine paintings and are signed 'P.C. IV' (probably Pieter Codde (1619–1666)). The outer case is painted in green lacquer with gold and black vine-work borders. The soundboard painting has virtually all disappeared.

*Literature:* B. 72; Catalogue 4 (1927), Lot 1904; Russell (1959), Plate 38, 43; Lambrechts-Douillez (1970b), Plate 5; Newman and Williams (1968), No. 3, 7; van der Meer (1971c), 104, 141; Barnes (1971a), 38–9; O'Brien (1987), 295.

*Former owners:* Charles van Raalte, Brownsea Island, Dorset; Sir Arthur Wheeler, Brownsea Island; Miss D. L. Smith, Wickhambrook, Suffolk; Raymond Russell, London.

1609 AR

Andreas Ruckers, 1609, ravalé single-manual harpsichord, Prof. Peter Williams, Chapel Hill, N.C.

*Present compass:* C to $d^3$ (modern).

*Case dimensions:* length 1834mm; width now 787mm;

height 243mm with the baseboard; keywell now 756mm.

*General description:* About 70mm has been added to the treble side of this single-manual harpsichord to widen its compass from the original C/E to $c^3$. From the style of the outer-case decoration, which is now veneered, and the hinges, the ravalement must have taken place in the eighteenth century in England. The soundboard painting is in good condition and most of the printed papers are old. Unfortunately the 8′ bridge is a replacement (eighteenth-century) and the keys, registers, jacks, nuts, scalings, etc. are all those of Dolmetsch, who carried out a major 'restoration' of the instrument which changed the eighteenth-century compass, scalings, and plucking points.

*Literature:* B. 73; van der Meer (1971b), 50; van der Meer (1971c), 106; Mactaggart (1979), 63; O'Brien (1987), 295.

*Former owners:* Arnold Dolmetsch, Haslemere; Herbert Lambert, and then Mrs Lambert, Bath.

(*c.* 1610)a AR

Andreas Ruckers, undated, 2½-voet virginal at a pitch of R + 9, Private, Australia.

*Ruckers number:* [?]/51.

*Case dimensions:* length 711mm; width 380mm; height 185mm at the back, 76mm at the front, both with the baseboard; keywell 651mm.

*Scalings:* see Appendix 3, p. 289.

*General description:* This is a unique example of a Ruckers instrument at R + 9, and is the only 2½-voet Ruckers clavecimbel. Apart from its unusual pitch, it has a number of features which are not normal in Ruckers instruments. Because of the extremely short strings demanded by such a high pitch, there is not enough space between the bridges for the normal width of register and jacks. The jacks and jackslots are therefore narrower than normal, and the bass and treble keytails are cranked in towards the middle of the instrument to line up with the jacks. Also, the case has an unusual shape, being high at the back and low at the front, with sloping case sides.

Unfortunately the instrument is undated and, without any other instruments of its type to compare it to, its number does not help in giving it an approximate date. However, details of the style of the rose and the soundboard decoration suggest a date of around 1610. The soundboard lacks the usual flower, bird and insect decoration, but is painted with the normal scallops and arabesques, and a red and white chain pattern around the rose. The case is painted with the mottled green *faux* porphyry marble, and the inside of the lid has a fine painting of courtiers in a rural setting near a castle and waterway. (For a full description with plates, see Appendix 3, p. 287.)

*Literature:* There is no reference to this instrument in the literature.

*Former owner:* Hans Adler, Johannesburg, South Africa.

1610b AR

Andreas Ruckers, 1610, 4½-voet muselar virginal at a pitch of R + 4, Museum of Fine Arts, Boston, No. 17.1792.

*Ruckers number:* 4x/35.

*Case dimensions:* length 1307mm; width 454mm; height 204mm with, 191mm without the baseboard; keywell 650mm.

*Scalings in millimetres:*

| | String length | Plucking point |
|---|---|---|
| $c^3$ | 137 | 81 |
| $f^2$ | 201 | 95 |
| $c^2$ | 276 | 121 |
| $f^1$ | 398 | 147 |
| $c^1$ | 546 | 190 |
| f | 722 | 230 |
| c | 876 | 281 |
| F | 1057 | 327 |
| C/E | 1108 | 354 |

*Motto* (not original): OMNIS SPIRITUS [*sic*] LAUDET [*sic*] DOMINUM [*sic*].

*General description:* Although the rose is not original, the style of the soundboard painting is correct for an Andreas Ruckers instrument of 1610. This is the only 4½-voet muselar Ruckers virginal that exists, and the only Ruckers muselar virginal in which the left-hand jackrail support, instead of being attached to the soundboard, is attached to the side of the left-hand keywell brace, and flies up over the soundboard. The jackrail, nameboard, toolbox flap, front flap and lid are all not original. But the harpichordium with its finger stop and the iron hold-down pins are original and in relatively good condition. Ten of the jacks are original and some of the keys have remnants of their original arcades.

*Literature:* B. 74; Bessaraboff (1941), No. 295, Plate; Catalogue 5 (1941); Galpin (1965), Plate 24; Russell (1959), 45, 46; van der Meer (1971c), 134, 135; McGeary (1981), 29; van der Meer (1983), 96, 97.

*Former owner:* Canon Francis W. Galpin.

1613a AR

Andreas Ruckers, 1613, 4-voet spinett virginal at a pitch of R + 5, Brussels Museum, No. 274.

*Ruckers number:* 4/11.
*Case dimensions:* length 1139mm; width 444mm; height 189mm with, 178mm without the baseboard.
*General description:* The scalings and compass of this virginal are original and confirm that it was originally at quint pitch. The case has been repainted and the interior repapered with modern papers. The soundboard has lost all traces of its original decoration.

Although the jacks and register guides are replacements, the original soundboard, soundboard barring, bridges, framing, etc. make this instrument a good example of its type.
*Literature:* B. 76; Mahillon, Vol. I (1893–1922), No. 274; Russell (1959), 47; van der Meer (1971c), 131; O'Brien (1974a), 84–5; McGeary (1981), 31; Shann (1984), 65.
*Former owners:* Matthias Van den Gheyn, 1740 (celebrated organist and composer of Louvain, born in 1721); Chevalier Xavier van Elewyck, Louvain (Van den Gheyn's biographer).

1613b A R
Andreas Ruckers, 1613, 4-voet spinett virginal at a pitch of R + 5, Brussels Museum, No. 2928.
*Ruckers number:* [4]/40.
*Case dimensions:* length 1138mm; width 440mm; height 190mm with the baseboard.
*Scalings in millimetres:*

| | String length | Plucking point |
|---|---|---|
| $c^3$ | 122 | 56 |
| $f^2$ | 175 | 72 |
| $c^2$ | 243 | 60 |
| $f^1$ | 348 | 56 |
| $c^1$ | 473 | 70 |
| f | 608 | 64 |
| c | 742 | 72 |
| F | 881 | 72 |
| C/E | 916 | 85 |

*Motto:* on lid (not original) – OMNIS SPIRITVS LAVDET DOMINVM.
*General description:* Like the 1613a A R, this virginal has its original scalings, but has lost its original papers and soundboard decoration. The case has been repainted, but the original imitation porphyry marble decoration is visible through faults in the later paint, although it is difficult to tell whether the base colour is dark red or dark green. The jacks are original, although the tongues have non-original leather plectra. The register leather on the soundboard and the lower guide (of walnut) is not original. The top two natural keylevers, $b^2$ and $c^3$, have traces of their original arcades.
*Literature:* B. 77; Mahillon, Vol. IV (1893–1922), No. 2928; Russell (1959), 47; van der Meer (1971c), 131; McGeary (1981), 29.
*Former owners:* M. Haveaux, Rebecq-Rognon; César Snoeck, Ronse (Renaix).

1613c A R
Andreas Ruckers, 1613, child virginal at R + 8, Cincinnati Art Museum, Cincinnati, Ohio, No. 1914.300.
*Present compass:* C/E to $d^3$.
*Case dimensions:* length 835mm; width 330mm plus 96mm keyboard projection; height 140mm with the baseboard.
*General description:* This instrument is a typical 'motherless child', and is in reasonably good condition. Some of the soundboard decoration has disappeared, but the arabesques and long sinewy leaves and stems of the flowers are typical of the soundboard-painting style of Andreas Ruckers instruments of about 1613.

The action is entirely a replacement, with new keylevers, key facings, jacks, etc. The additional two treble notes have been squeezed in by narrowing the octave span, and by repiercing the jackslots through the original leather jackslides.
*Literature:* B. 133; Catalogue 6 (1949), No. 52; van der Meer (1971c), 139.
*Former owner:* William Howard Doane, Cincinnati.

1614 A R
Andreas Ruckers, 1614, ravalement of a normal double-manual harpsichord, Leonard Elmhirst, Dartington Hall, Devon.
*Present compass:* $A_1$ to $e^3$.
*General description:* This is a typical English eighteenth-century ravalement of a Ruckers harpsichord. The case was widened and the octave span narrowed to accommodate the extra notes. New keyboards, jacks and slides were made and the bridges and nuts were repinned and extended. The harpsichord now has a lute register, which was also probably a feature of the eighteenth-century alteration (subsequent 'restorations' have made a positive dating of the lute impossible). The outer case and lid are veneered. Although the blue arabesques, scallops and 'snowflakes' are retouched, the basic paintwork of the soundboard is in good condition. The inside of the main lid depicts St Theresa's home town of Avila in Spain, with the cathedral which breaches the town battlements. The painting is seventeenth-century and is attributed to van der Meulen (1632–90).

The instrument is greatly over-restored. The spine and cheek side, the internal framing, jacks and slides, and baseboard are all modern, as is the soundboard barring, with many stifle bars under the 8′ bridge.

*Literature:* B. 78; Boddington Catalogue, No. 12; van der Meer (1971c), 110.

*Former owners:* Dr Blow, Bath; Rev. John Bower, Bath; General Hopkinson, J. Kendrich Pyne and Boddington College, Manchester; Howard Head, London; W. C. Priestly and Messrs Angell, Bath.

1615 A R

Andreas Ruckers, 1615, simple alignment of a normal double-manual harpsichord, Vleeshuis Museum, Antwerp, No. VH 2113.

*Ruckers number:* ʃt/4.

*Present compass:* $G_1/B_1$ to $c^3$.

*Case dimensions:* length 2244mm; width 789mm; height 265mm with the baseboard; keywell 760mm.

*Mottoes:* main lid – CONCORDIA RES PARVAE CRESCVNT DISCORDIA MAXIMAE DILABVNTVR; lid flap – OMNIS SPIRITVS LAVDET DOMINVM.

*General description:* Although only one of the original keys remains, it is clear from the repinning of the lower-manual balance rail that the compass was altered from C/E to $f^3$ to $G_1/B_1$ to $c^3$. This alignment was carried out without adding a third set of strings and, in fact, without removing the wooden block from the bass side of the upper-manual keyframe.

As the rose is missing, the authorship of the instrument has to be decided on the basis of the workmanship and decoration. Both Andreas and Ioannes were using roses 65mm in diameter up until about 1616, so this provides no clue. But the decoration of the soundboard and especially the lid is clearly that of the Andreas Ruckers decorator. The style of the wreath around the rose, the shape of the sinewy leaves and stems on the flowers, and the depiction of various types of animals are all characteristic of the early Andreas decorator. Furthermore, the date is painted on the soundboard, whereas the Ioannes decorator painted the date on the wrestplank during this period. Also characteristic of Andreas is the square cross-section of the treble part of the 4′ hitchpin rail instead of the narrow high hitchrail found on Ioannes harpsichords (see pp. 190–1).

Although it is in a poor state of preservation, this harpsichord retains a number of original features. The buff stop, registers, and register hold-down blocks are all original. It is one of only three original Ruckers doubles (the others are the 1616 H R and the 1640b A R) to retain its transposing plates for the $e^\flat/g^\sharp$ doubled strings. The keyboard rack cloths are original. The upper-manual rack has three layers of original cloth above the keys and two layers below; the lower manual has four layers above the keys and the lower cloths are missing. Using a virginal key of the correct length from the front of the key to the balance point, the depth of touch of the upper manual with original upper and lower cloths was found to be 6.5–7mm.

Except for the soundboard painting, the decoration is in good order. The exterior of the case is marbled with a unique 'fan' white scumble on the usual reddish-brown background.

*Literature:* B. 79 = 80; de Burbure (1863), 29; van der Straeten, Vol. III (1875), 334; Génard (1876), Plate 3, 79; Marcuse (1952), 417ff; Hubbard (1965), 65; Ripin (1968), 34; Lambrechts-Douillez (1970a), Plate 7, 16; van der Meer (1971b), 48; van der Meer (1971c), Plate 3, 117, 144; Libin (1975), 47; O'Brien (1977a), 37; Germann (1978), 71; Dowd (1978), 106, 113; Henkel (1979a), 133; Lambrechts-Douillez (1981a), Plate 425, 154; McGeary (1981), 29; Koopman (1987), footnote 3; Catalogue 11 (n.d.), No. 33.

*Former owners:* St Jacobskerk, Antwerp; formerly exhibited in the Steen Museum, Antwerp.

1617 A R

Andreas Ruckers, 1617, 6-voet spinett virginal, Deutsches Museum, Munich, No. 37588.

*Ruckers number:* 6/23.

*Present compass:* C to $f^3$.

*Case dimensions:* length 1658mm; width now 458mm, originally about 20–25mm more; height 241mm with, 229mm without the baseboard.

*General description:* The compass of this, one of the few Ruckers spinett 6-voet virginals, has been enlarged without altering the original scalings or plucking points. Both keywell braces were moved to widen the keywell for the extra notes, and the extra jackslots were pierced through the soundboard. The lower guide is entirely new. Additions were made to the original keyframe in both the treble and bass, and both the original and added keylevers received new touch-plates (ebony naturals and bone-topped sharps). The bridges were extended to carry the additional strings. For some reason the front of the instrument has been cut away to eliminate the front flap and its recess.

The lid has engraved papers printed (almost certainly in what is now Belgium) in both French and Flemish with the year 1720 in numerous different chronograms. This suggests that this may be the date of the alteration, or at least it indicates the earliest possible date for the alteration. The rose is not original, but is the same casting as the 1633a A R in Brussels, and suggests that both instruments at one time passed through the hands of the same restorer.

The original soundboard painting has entirely disappeared; the present naive soundboard painting is of a more recent date.

*Literature:* B. 82; Wallner (1925), 239–47; van der Meer (1971c), Plates 8 and 9, 105, 130.

*Former owners:* Bought from the stringed instrument restorer at the Brussels Museum, C. Houtshout, in 1913.

1618 AR

Andreas Ruckers, 1618, single-manual harpsichord, Berlin Musikinstrumentenmuseum, No. 2224.

*Ruckers number:* ƒt/1.

*Case dimensions:* length 1828mm; width (not original), 728mm; height 242mm with, 229mm without the baseboard; keywell now 697mm.

*Motto:* lid – 1618 / SOLI / DEO GLORIA.

*General description:* The harpsichord received a grand ravalement, probably in the eighteenth century, and from the renumbering of the keys it is clear that the compass was widened to C to $f^3$. It appears from the plugged tuning-pin holes in the wrestplank that the disposition was both 1 × 8′, 1 × 4′ and 2 × 8′ with this widened compass. At some time (pre-1922) it was brought back to its original width and compass, and amazingly retained its original scalings and plucking points, registers and lower guides and many of its original keys and jacks. The outer decoration and the tuning pins are not original.

The original jacks resemble those of the 1618b IR and seem to have been made by the same person. The baseboard is original and retains the scribed plan of the instrument on it. Originally there was a buff, split between $f^1$ and $f\#^1$; there are the usual holes for the wire hold-down pins in the 8′ bridge, and a plugged square hole in the cheek for the usual projection of the right-hand portion of the buff register.

*Literature:* B. 83; Sachs (1922), No. 2224, Plate IX; Ernst (1967), Plate IX, 63ff; Otto (1965), 27; Otto (1968), No. 13, Plate 64; van der Meer (1971b), 51; van der Meer (1971c), 111, 115, 144; Berner (1971), 53; McGeary (1981), 32; Krickeberg (1981), Plate 4, 26–8; Heyde (1986), 153.

*Former owner:* César Snoeck, Ronse (Renaix).

1620a AR

Andreas Ruckers, 1620, 4-voet spinett virginal at a pitch of R + 5, Smithsonian Institution, Washington, D.C., No. 303,543.

*Ruckers number:* 4/69.

*Case dimensions:* length 1143mm; width 450mm; height 190mm with the baseboard.

*Motto:* lid – SIC TRANSIT GLORIA MVNDI.

*General description:* This virginal retains many of its original features, including many different original papers inside, its original keys and touchplates, its original key arcades and twelve original jacks. The case exterior, especially the spine, shows the typical mottled surface texture of the original green and white imitation porphyry marble paint underneath a layer of more recent red-brown paint. The balance rail cloth is original, but the leather or card squares normally found on the sharps balance pins are missing. The cloth on the tails of the keys on which the jacks rest and the upper touch-rack cloths are all original. Much of the soundboard painting is of a later date, but follows the outlines of the original.

*Literature:* B. 85; Steinert (1892–3), No. 13, 28; Hirt (1955), 176–7; Checklist (1967/75), Fig. 6, 46; Hoover (1969), Plates 2–5, 6ff; van der Meer (1971c), 131; Germann (1978), 61; McGeary (1981), 31.

*Former owners:* Morris Steinert, New Haven, Conn.; Hugo Worch, Washington, D.C.

1620b AR

Andreas Ruckers, 1620, 6-voet muselar virginal, Brussels Museum, No. 1597.

*Ruckers number:* 6/27.

*Present compass:* C to $c^3$.

*Case dimensions:* length 1712mm; width 492mm; height 241mm with, 227mm without the baseboard; keywell now 696mm, originally 647mm.

*General description:* This is a normal 6-voet muselar virginal which has a keywell widened to convert the original short-octave base into a chromatic one. The bass keywell brace was moved to the left and four new keys were added to a bass extension of the keyframe. The treble notes were left unaltered; thus the scalings and plucking points of the notes from E to $c^3$ are original.

Although the instrument has an impressive appearance, little of the decoration is original. The outer paint of the case and lid is not original, and all of the printed paper decorations are modern (almost certainly the papers which Closson had printed for the museum instruments). Some of the soundboard painting is visible but its general condition is not very good.

*Literature:* B. 86; Mahillon Vol. III (1893–1922), No. 1597; James (1930), Plate XXV, 105; van der Meer (1971c), 133, 136; O'Brien (1974a), 84–5; O'Brien (1979), 462; McGeary (1981), 29, 31.

*Former owners:* Victor-Charles and Joseph Mahillon, Brussels.

1620c A R
Andreas Ruckers, 1620, ravalé aligned normal double-manual harpsichord, Berlin Musikinstrumenten-museum, No. 2230.
*Ruckers number:* ft/68.
*Present compass:* $G_1/B_1$ to $f^3$.
*Case dimensions:* length 2248mm; width 873mm; height 268mm with, 254mm without the baseboard; keywell now 842mm, originally about 763mm.
*General description:* The alignment and ravalement were carried out in a manner similar to that of the 1646 I C double. The original keyboards and string spacing were retained, but a second set of 8′ strings was added (perhaps when the alignment occurred and before the widening of the case). The case, soundboard, bridges, registers and keyboards were extended to increase the treble compass to $f^3$. The 8′ nut was not moved to counteract the longer scalings resulting from the addition of the second 8′ string. The wrestplank is not original, but the veneer from the old wrestplank was used to cover the new one.

The bridges and 4′ hitchpin rail show the doubled e♭/g♯ pins. Also, the wrestplank veneer shows the plugged double tuning-pin holes for these notes.

The decoration in the keywell is very similar to that found on the 1613b A R virginal and may date from the time when both instruments were in the Snoeck Collection. The outer case and lid are painted in a rather naive grisaille. The turned and carved oak stand, although painted grey to match the case, is original.
*Literature:* B. 84; Sachs (1922), No. 2230; Berner (1950), 239–43; Otto (1965), Plate p. 135, 27; Ernst (1967), Plate 12, 63–75; Berner (1971), 56–60; van der Meer (1971b), 49; van der Meer (1971c), 120, 141; Krickeberg (1981), Plate 6, 31–4.
*Former owner:* César Snoeck, Ronse (Renaix).

1620d A R
Andreas Ruckers, 1620, 6-voet muselar virginal, private, Gif-sur-Yvette, France.
*Present compass:* C to $g^3$.
*Case dimensions:* length 1706mm; width 492mm; height 244mm with, 228mm without the baseboard; keywell now 781mm, originally 652mm.
*Motto:* lid – ARS NON HABET INIMICVM NISI IGNORANTEM.
*General description:* This is a ravalé 6-voet muselar virginal. The original keys and touchplates were left with their original octave span and additions were made to the bass and treble sides of the keys and keyframe. Both of the keywell braces were moved to make space for the additional notes. It is not clear whether the present bridges date from the original alteration or from a more recent repair. They are at any rate longer than the original bridges would have been in order to carry the added strings of the ravalement.

The soundboard painting is somewhat retouched, but is in basically good condition and typical of the style of other Andreas instruments of this period. The date on the soundboard has the usual red arabesque flourishes on either side of it.
*Literature:* B. 88.
*Former owner:* Henri Prunières.

1621 A R
Andreas Ruckers, 1621, a normal single-manual harpsichord converted into a grand ravalement double-manual harpsichord, private, St Étienne, France.
*Present compass:* $F_1$ to $f^3$.
*General description:* This harpsichord represents a full-scale ravalement of a small single-manual Ruckers harpsichord into a large French double. The soundboard is a composite structure consisting of planks of Ruckers soundboard wood intermixed with new planks of wood. The Ruckers soundboard wood is painted in the style of the Andreas painter of 1621, whereas the new wood is painted more in the style of the Andreas painter working after about 1626.
*Literature:* not in Boalch; Dowd (1978), 109, 113.

1623 A R
Andreas Ruckers, 1623, ravalé normal double-manual harpsichord, private, England.
*Present compass:* $F_1,G_1$ to $f^3$.
*Case dimensions:* length 2348mm; width 926mm; height 297mm with, 282mm without the baseboard; keywell 875mm.
*General description:* This is another good example of an English grand ravalement of a normal Ruckers double-manual harpsichord. The case has been widened, the soundboard, bridges and nuts have been extended. The keyboards, registers and jacks are all in the style of typical English instruments of the eighteenth century. The keywell and outside of the case have been veneered and the ornate brass strap hinges complete the illusion of an English eighteenth-century harpsichord.

The soundboard and soundboard painting are very dark but in basically good condition. Remarkably, about a third of the eighteenth-century strings survive and are in regular use on this instrument, tuned to $a^1$ = 440Hz! Unfortunately the original bird quills have been replaced by hard leather plectra.
*Literature:* B. 91; van der Meer (1971c), 110.

*Former owners:* John Hullah, London; Capt. J. Lane, Wanstead; Messrs Morley, London; Mrs J. Cyriax, London; Mrs Grace Clark, Rickmansworth.

1624 AR

Andreas Ruckers, 1624, normal double-manual harpsichord converted into a ravalé single-manual harpsichord, Gruuthuuse Museum, Bruges, No. 2297.

*Present compass:* $F_1$ to $f^3$.

*Case dimensions:* length now 2136mm; width now 941mm; height 269mm with, 256mm without the baseboard; keywell now 910mm, originally about 767mm.

*Motto:* lid – 1624 / MVSICA LAETITIAE / COMES MEDICINA DOLORVM.

*General description:* From the join in the case sides it is clear that this instrument was enlarged in width from a smaller harpsichord. The existence of three double $e^{\flat}/g^{\sharp}$ 4′ hitchpins, the original inside case width of 767mm, and the case depth and original fifty-note compass are all characteristic of the usual Ruckers double-manual transposing harpsichord. The extension of the compass was carried out using the original string spacing and octave span. The extra notes in the bass were added without widening the bass side of the case. The notes from B to $c^3$ were moved upwards towards the treble, using shorter strings to give scalings which (except for the top few notes) are suitable for brass stringing. There is a buff stop in the style of J. P. Bull – a roll of cloth on a bar operated by a knee lever.

The jackrail retains its original cloths – two layers of black woollen material held in place with eight tacks. This is probably the only double-manual jackrail with its original cloth. Many of the jacks and tongues are original. The stand was originally from a virginal and is like that of the 1611 HR in Antwerp, but has unfortunately been cut down and lost its turned pillars in the process. The papers of the keywell and soundwell still exist, but are invisible under the present reddish-brown paint.

The decoration of the inside of the lid is in good condition, and even with much staining, the colours of the painting of the flowers, fruit and birds are extremely bright and transparent.

*Literature:* B. 92; van der Meer (1971b), 49; van der Meer (1971c), 121, 123, 125, 141, 145; Germann (1978), 72; Ripin (1968), footnote 5, 38; McGeary (1981), 27.

(1626) AR

Andreas Ruckers, undated, child virginal at R + 8, Sterckshof Museum, Deurne, Belgium, No. S2623.

*Ruckers number:* k/36.

*Present compass:* C,D to $c^3$.

*Case dimensions:* length 814mm; width 301mm; height 136mm without the baseboard; keywell now 680mm.

*General description:* This is a typical 'motherless' child. The compass was extended by widening the keywell on the bass side by roughly one natural's width, and by reducing the octave span of the keys. The tails of the keylevers are splayed out to use the original jackslots, but with one extra note in the treble and three in the bass.

The style of the soundboard painting, with a circle around the rose, and the arabesques indicates a date between about 1615 and 1628; the date 1626 has been estimated from the Ruckers number.

*Literature:* not in Boalch; O'Brien (1974a), 83.

1627 AR

Andreas Ruckers, 1627, single-manual harpsichord at a pitch of R + 5, Gemeentemuseum, The Hague, No. EC 545–1933.

*Ruckers number:* *4ft*.

*Case dimensions:* length 1232mm; width 694mm; height 190mm with the baseboard; keywell 669mm.

*Scalings in millimetres:*

unison scalings:

| | String length | Plucking point |
|---|---|---|
| $c^3$ | 121 | 45 |
| $f^2$ | 178 | 48 |
| $c^2$ | 238 | 50 |
| $f^1$ | 356 | 56 |
| $c^1$ | 461 | 60 |
| f | 628 | 65 |
| c | 749 | 73 |
| F | 876 | 82 |
| C/E | 886 | 83 |

octave scalings:

| | String length | Plucking point |
|---|---|---|
| $c^3$ | 60 | 28 |
| $f^2$ | 89 | 28 |
| $c^2$ | 117 | 29 |
| $f^1$ | 175 | 31 |
| $c^1$ | 237 | 32 |
| f | 339 | 33 |
| c | 419 | 35 |
| F | 529 | 40 |
| C/E | 543 | 40 |

*Motto:* lid – SIC TRANSIT GLORIA MVNDI.

*General description:* This is the only extant Ruckers harpsichord at a pitch of R + 5. Like the 4-voet virginals at this pitch, it was also referred to by its length as a 4-voet staartstuk, since it is labelled *4ft*. It is however almost 4 duimen longer than 4 voeten. Probably at some time in the eighteenth century the compass was changed to A to $f^3$ by rearranging the keys but still using the original registers and string spacing. The disposition was also changed to 2 × 8′, leaving the 4′ bridge unused. Adding the extra (long) 8′ string and rearranging the keys had the effect of lowering the pitch to the semitone between R and R + 2, probably so that it could play with other instruments. A restoration of 1964 returned the instrument to its original compass, disposition and pitch.

The soundboard decoration and the block-printed papers are in very good condition. The balance-rail cloth appears to be original. The belly rail was used as a backing piece during the cutting of the lower guide and provides many clues about the method of cutting the leather and wood of Ruckers lower registers.

Plate C.5 The 1627 A R 4-voet harpsichord at quint pitch with its original stand. Copyright, Haags Gemeentemuseum, The Hague.

The instrument has a very fine original turned and arcaded oak stand.

*Literature:* B. 94; Russell (1959), Plate 37, 45; Hubbard (1965), 61; van der Meer (1965), 117–21; Thomas and Rhodes (1967), 55; van der Meer (1968b), 209; van der Meer (1971c), 114, 115; Ripin (1970a), 37; O'Brien (1974a), 85, 87; O'Brien (1977a), 42; McGeary (1981), 31; van der Meer (1983), Plate 158 p. 95.

*Former owner:* D. F. Scheurleer, The Hague.

1628 A R

Andreas Ruckers, 1628, alignment and petit ravalement of a normal double-manual harpsichord, Dr Andreas Beurmann, Hamburg.

*Present compass:* $A_1$ to $d^3$ ($c^{\sharp 3}$ and $d^3$ are modern).

*Case dimensions:* length 2257mm; width 801mm; height 267mm with, 251mm without the baseboard; keywell 772mm.

*General description:* The rose in this harpsichord has the initials I R and was put in by Raymond Russell, who is probably also responsible for the atypical Ioannes Ruckers signature on the nameboard. But the instrument is undoubtedly by Andreas Ruckers. The soundboard painting style is similar to other instruments by Andreas Ruckers of this period (e.g. 1627 A R). Also, the rose hole is too small for the large double-manual rose that Ioannes was using in 1628 (i.e. from 1616 onwards). At some time the date has been altered to 1728, but the altered '6' is still faintly visible.

The lower bellyrail was used as a backing piece when the upper-manual lower guide was cut out, and shows the marks made by the chisel with gaps in the spacing of the jackslots for the notes of the short octave.

From the style of the black keyboards and the Louis XV stand it appears that the petit ravalement was carried out in France. New aligned keyboards were made with the compass $A_1$ to $c^3$ by using an octave span narrower than that used by Ruckers. The bridges and nuts were repinned and new registers and jacks were made. The keywell is decorated with baroque vine-work over the original Ruckers papers, which are still visible in places. The outside of the case is lacquered and ornamented with narrow gold bands surrounding garlands of flowers. The inside of the lid has a fine painting of a pastoral scene.

The extension of the treble compass was carried out by Vere Pilkington, by adding the notes $c^{\sharp 3}$ and $d^3$.

*Literature:* B. 46 = 47a (listed as Ioannes Ruckers); van der Meer (1971c), 109; Montague (1986), 258.

*Former owners:* Captain Lane, London; Raymond Russell, London; Vere Pilkington, Colares, Portugal.

1632 AR

Andreas Ruckers, 1632, 4-voet virginal with altered scalings, originally at a pitch of R + 5, Brussels Museum, No. 1593.

*Ruckers number:* 4/38.

*Present compass:* C to $f^3$.

*Case dimensions:* length 1136mm; width 448mm; height 203mm with, 184mm without the baseboard; keywell now 750mm, originally 648mm.

*Motto:* lid – SIC TRANSIT GLORIA MVNDI.

*General description:* This is an unusual example of a small 4-voet virginal originally at quint pitch whose compass has been extended and whose bridges have been moved apart to lower the pitch roughly to reference pitch. To enlarge the compass, the keys were squeezed together and both keywell cheeks and both keyframe sides were moved. Moving the bridges apart resulted in scalings which are no longer Pythagorean in the treble, and obviously the bass scalings are far too short in proportion to the treble scalings.

The soundboard decoration has disappeared entirely, but the instrument retains some of its original Ruckers papers. Also, traces of the original porphyry marbling are visible underneath a later case paint.

The keylevers, including the notes of the ravalement, have been marked with (eighteenth-century) gauge numbers.

*Literature:* B. 98; Mahillon Vol. III (1893–1922), No. 1593; van der Meer (1971c), 132; McGeary (1981), 28, 31.

1633a AR

Andreas Ruckers, 1633, 6-voet muselar virginal, Brussels Museum, No. 4600.

*Ruckers number:* 6/70.

*Present compass:* C,D to $f^3$.

*Case dimensions:* length 1706mm; width 495mm; height 245mm with the baseboard; keywell now 767mm, originally 652mm.

*Motto:* lid – MVSICA MAGNORVM SOLAMEN DVLCE LABORVM.

*General description:* The outer case is painted in imitation red wood-grain. But underneath this are traces of the original green porphyry marbling. The soundboard painting is in very bad condition with much retouching, but the date 1633 is clearly legible. Although the rose is a crude replacement of the original, the soundboard and lid decoration are clearly in the style of Andreas Ruckers. The compass was extended by adding keys from another Ruckers virginal which was numbered 6/36. Some of the jacks, also with this number, were used in this instrument, so that about eighty per cent of the jacks are by Ruckers. This is one of the few 6-voet virginals to retain its original harpichordium stop. It has lost its original lead hooks, and its original guide blocks and hand-stop. Originally the harpichordium worked on the notes C/E to $f^1$ inclusive. The decoration on the inside of the lid is original and in very good condition.

*Literature:* B. 97 (and 99?); McGeary (1981), 31 (given as 1632).

*Former owners:* Abel Régibo, Ronse (Renaix); Wanda Landowska, Paris.

1633b AR

Andreas Ruckers, 1633, conversion of a normal double-manual harpsichord into a single-manual harpsichord, Musikinstrumentenmuseum der Karl Marx Universität, Leipzig, No. 71.

*Ruckers number:* ſt/41.

*Present compass:* C/E to $f^3$ at a pitch of R − 4.

*Case dimensions:* length now 2112mm; width 788mm; height 268mm with, 254mm without the baseboard; keywell 762mm.

*General description:* This is one of the few Ruckers instruments which was made smaller instead of larger. Originally a normal double-manual harpsichord, it was cut down and its upper manual was discarded. The lower manual was given the compass C,D to $d^3$ (this was altered again in about 1912 to C/E to $f^3$) and a 2 × 8′ disposition. It seems likely that the first alterations took place in Italy.

The case and lid have been painted light blue with bands inside the panels formed by the cheek, tail, bentside, etc. The soundboard painting is in quite good condition, and has some amusing scenes of courting couples along with the usual flowers, birds, insects, etc.

*Literature:* B. 100; Kinsky (1910), Plate No. 71; Ruth-Sommer (1916), 69, 90; Rubart (1964); van der Meer (1971b), 49; van der Meer (1971c), 120; Henkel (1979a), 101ff; Henkel (1979b), 61; Heyde (1986), 165.

*Former owner:* Paul de Wit, Leipzig.

1634 AR

Andreas Ruckers, 1634, child virginal, originally at a pitch of R + 8, Instrument Museum of the Conservatoire NSM, Paris, No. E.980.2.502.

*Present compass:* C to $a^2$.

*Case dimensions:* length 812mm; width 327mm, plus keyboard projection 106mm; height 136mm with the baseboard; keywell 651mm.

*General description:* The compass and pitch of this virginal have been changed by replacing the keyboard with a new one filling out the original bass short octave. The original spacing of the tails of the keylevers and strings was maintained with one note added at the top (C/E to $c^3$ = forty-five notes with twenty-seven naturals; C to $a^2$ = forty-six notes also with twenty-seven naturals). In order to conform to normal French practice the three-octave span was decreased from 500mm to 473mm, and endblocks were added at the sides of the keys. Because the keys above C were moved towards the treble in the process of filling out the bass octave, the effective pitch was raised by a major third. The ravalement is dated 1763.

*Literature:* B. 102a; Gétreau (1985), 93.

*Former owner:* The Comtesse de Chambure, Paris.

1635 AR

Andreas Ruckers, 1635, a normal single-manual harpsichord, Dr Andreas Beurmann, Hamburg.

*Present compass:* C,D to $c^3$.

*Case dimensions:* length 1814mm; width 720mm; height 248mm with, 231mm without the baseboard; keywell 694mm.

*Motto:* lid – SIC TRANSIT GLORIA MVNDI.

*General description:* The namebatten with the signature and date is not original, and the rose is missing, but there is nothing to suggest that this instrument is not by Andreas Ruckers, nor that the date 1635 is not correct. Unfortunately nearly the whole of the 4′ area of soundboard (plus the part with the rose and the wreath behind the cutoff bar) from the 4′ hitchpin rail to the spine has been cut out, so that the only original parts of the soundboard are those under the 8′ bridge and that from $a^1$ to $e^2$ under the 4′ bridge. Much of the internal framing is not original, but is in the same position as the original. The lid papers are in a good state of preservation.

In addition to the usual flowers the soundboard painting shows a peacock, a group of monkeys smoking pipes, a dwarf holding a hoop through which a dog is jumping, another dwarf playing the bagpipes, etc. The 8′ bridge and nut, and parts of the lid and case are painted in gold paint.

*Literature:* not in Boalch; McGeary (1981), 31; Mactaggart (1985), 107.

*Former owners:* the front flap is inscribed: 'From Madame la Comtesse E de Pas, Chateau de Ramitz to Campbell M[ac]Kellar of Lerags'; Lady Kaye, London.

1636 AR

Andreas Ruckers, 1636, 'English' single-manual harpsichord ravalé into a double-manual harpsichord, Alec Cobbe, Hatchlands Park, East Clandon, Surrey.

*Original compass:* C to $c^3$.

*Present compass:* $F_1$ to $f^3$.

*Case dimensions:* length originally about 1965mm; width now 821mm, originally about 775mm; height 265mm without the baseboard; keywell now 793mm, originally about 734mm.

*General description:* This is a very interesting harpsichord, originally of a type quite different from the usual late single-manual harpsichords from the Andreas Ruckers workshop. It is the only known Andreas single which had the compass C to $c^3$ with a chromatic bass octave; it also had a very deep case – about 10.5 duimen instead of the usual 9 duimen. This suggests that it originally had a strapwork outer case decoration instead of the usual plain marbling. The plan of the instrument, including the 8′ *c* and *f*♯ strings, is scribed on the baseboard. This confirms the compass as C to $c^3$ and the disposition as 1 × 8′, 1 × 4′, since there are two registers marked out in the gap.

Most of the present framing is not original, although the soundboard bridges (extended in the treble and bass), the 4′ hitchpin rail, and the soundboard barring all appear to be by Ruckers (unusually, the 8′ bridge is of beech instead of cherry). The spine was moved towards the tail and the cheek was moved forward in the ravalement, so that the case additions in the keywell are not of the same length. On the basis of the wrestplank layout, the stop-levers and the soundboard mouldings, Phillippe Fritsch has identified the ravalement as the work of Hemsch.

The soundboard painting, which is seventeenth-century but not original, has in turn been extended by the Hemsch painter. The interior of the lid shows a pastoral scene; this has been extended at the time of the ravalement. The outside of the case has been painted with various mythological scenes which must also date from the time of the ravalement.

*Literature:* not in Boalch; O'Brien (1977a), 41; Germann (1981), 196.

*Former owner*: Michael Thomas, Norfolk.

1637 AR

Andreas Ruckers, 1637, a normal single-manual harpsichord, Germanisches Nationalmuseum, Nuremberg, No. MIR 1073.

*Ruckers numbers:* Both ſt/23 and ſt/24.

*Case dimensions:* length 1829mm; width 715mm; height 242mm without the baseboard; keywell 688mm.

*Scalings in millimetres:*

8′ scalings:

| | String length | Plucking point |
|---|---|---|
| $c^3$ | 171 | 61 |
| $f^2$ | 258 | 68 |
| $c^2$ | 348 | 76 |
| $f^1$ | 531 | 87 |
| $c^1$ | 698 | 96 |
| f | 963 | 112 |
| c | 1165 | 122 |
| F | 1351 | 139 |
| C/E | 1366 | 142 |

4′ scalings:

| | String length | Plucking point |
|---|---|---|
| $c^3$ | 83 | 36 |
| $f^2$ | 129 | 38 |
| $c^2$ | 173 | 41 |
| $f^1$ | 258 | 45 |
| $c^1$ | 338 | 48 |
| f | 474 | 51 |
| c | 580 | 54 |
| F | 717 | 58 |
| C/E | 736 | 62 |

*Mottoes:* main lid – SIC TRANSIT GLORIA MVNDI;
lid flap – SOLI DEO GLORIA ET SANCTVM NOMEN EIVS;
keywell flap – ACTA VIRVM PROBANT.

*General description:* This is one of the few Ruckers single-manual harpsichords in almost original condition. The only alteration it has suffered is that the top corners of the cheek have unfortunately been cut off in the style of the eighteenth-century fortepiano. Otherwise it retains most of its original musical and decorative features. Only the jacks are replacements. The outside of the case is painted in imitation strapwork holding large simulated jewels. The decoration of the exterior and interior is basically in very good condition. The keys retain their original arcades.

This instrument is unique in having two different Ruckers numbers. The keyframe and keys are marked St/23, but the registers and the case slot underneath the left-hand end of the jackrail are marked with the number 24. It seems that the parts for single-manual harpsichords numbers 23 and 24 somehow managed to get interchanged in the workshop.

*Literature:* B. 105; van der Meer (n.d.), 12; van der Meer (1971a), 63–4; van der Meer (1971b), 51; van der Meer (1971c), 111, 115, 142–6; O'Brien (1974a), 85; McGeary (1981), 18, 31, 32; van der Meer (1983), Plate 116 p. 73; Shann (1984), 65; Heyde (1986), 221; Hellwig (1985), Colour plate, 87–8.

*Former owner:* Dr Ulrick Rück, Nuremberg.

1639a AR

Andreas Ruckers, 1639, altered child virginal, originally at a pitch of R + 8, Gemeentemuseum, The Hague, No. EC 149-1950.

*Ruckers number:* k/59.

*Case dimensions:* length 796mm; width 325mm, plus keyboard projection 107mm; height 141mm with the baseboard.

*General description:* Although the present compass and scalings are the same as the original, the three-octave span of the keyboard is now 492mm instead of the usual 500mm; this appears to be a remnant of an intermediate compass. In the intermediate state three extra notes were added and the keyboard shifted one natural's width to the right, giving a compass of C,D to $c^3$ at a pitch of R + 9. The present keyblocks (of pine) and the sloping cheeks are not original. The leather upper registers and the red-brown imitation-wood case painting are also not original.

Many of the jacks and many of their tongues are original. The wire slides in the jackrail, and the lid and hinges are not original. Like all other child virginals, this one has a diagonal slot in the baseboard through which the jacks of the mother operated its keys when it was placed above the mother instrument.

*Literature:* B. 107; van der Meer (1971c), 139; O'Brien (1974c), 76, 84, 89.

*Former owner:* Abel Régibo, Ronse (Renaix).

1639b AR

Andreas Ruckers, 1639, a much-altered normal single-manual harpsichord, Gemeentemuseum, The Hague, No. EC 544-1933.

*Present compass:* now C/E to $c^3$; was $G_1$ to $d^3$ in the eighteenth century.

*Case dimensions:* length 1812mm; width now 718mm; height 227mm without the baseboard; keywell now 686mm.

*General description:* Although this harpsichord has its original compass, its conversion in eighteenth-century England to a double has left its mark indelibly on the instrument. As it stands, the instrument represents no historical state. The compass is that of the seventeenth century. The eighteenth-century disposition with two sets of 8′ strings and one 4′ set has been altered to 1 × 8′, 1 × 4′, but the scalings are representative of neither epoch. It retains its eighteenth-century keys, jackslides (cut down), jacks, keyframe, balance rail and key-guide system. The wrestplank, wrestplank veneer, nuts and 8′ bridge are all not original – only the 4′ bridge is original. The painting on the soundboard near the gap shows that part of the soundboard has been cut away to make room for the extra 8′ register. The pinning of the 4′ bridge and 4′ hitchpin rail show that the original string spacing of this harpsichord was the same as that of the 1644a AR single in Antwerp. The space for the discarded eighteenth-century upper manual has been rather crudely filled in with a wide 'namebatten'. None of the decoration, except for that of the soundboard, which is covered with a thick layer of brown varnish, is original.

*Literature:* B. 108; Boddington Catalogue, No. 12A; van der Meer (1964), 5–16; van der Meer (1971b), 48; van der Meer (1971c), 111, 115; Scheurwater and van Acht (1977), 36ff.

*Former owners:* J. K. Pyne; Boddington Collection, Manchester; Howard Head; E. Dodd Cramp, Byfield, Northants; J. Morley, London; D. F. Scheurleer, The Hague.

1640a AR

Andreas Ruckers, 1640, a normal single-manual harpsichord, Yale University, New Haven, Conn., No. 4878.60.

*Present compass:* C to $d^3$.

*Case dimensions:* length 1813mm; width 708mm; height 245mm with, 229mm without the baseboard; keywell 690mm.

*Mottoes:* main lid – 1640 / MVSICA LETITIAE / COMES MEDICINA DOLORVM;
lid flap – CONCORDIA MVSIS AMICA.

*General description:* Decoratively this instrument is a good example of a typical single-manual Ruckers harpsichord. It still retains its original marbled exterior and papered interior. The soundboard, although slightly retouched here and there, is in an excellent state.

This harpsichord is also a good example of a conservative *petit ravalement.* Its original compass of C/E to $c^3$ was increased to C to $d^3$ by making a new keyboard with a narrower octave span and by eliminating the keyblocks. This involved extending and repinning the bridges, respacing the tuning pins, and making new registers, lower guides, nuts and jacks. Somewhat unusually, it was not given two sets of 8′ strings.

The Flemish stand does not belong to this instrument, but was formerly under the 1648 AR in Copenhagen. With a lid cord instead of a stick, it would be a fine example of a Ruckers instrument in its original decorative order.

*Literature:* B. 109; Skinner (1933), Plate, 59ff; Hirt (1955), Plate, 12–13; Harich-Schneider (1958), 11; Rephann (1968), No. 250, 30; van der Meer (1971b), 51; van der Meer (1971c), 112, 115, 144; Germann (1978), 60; McGeary (1981), 20, 27.

*Former owners:* Charles Burney; The Rev. Thomas Twining, Colchester (died 1804); Miss Twining, Twickenham; Mrs A. B. Donaldson, Hampstead; Sir Algernon Oliphant; Miss Belle Skinner.

Plate C.6 The 1640b AR double-manual harpsichord with eighteenth-century gessoed decoration and stand.

1640b AR

Andreas Ruckers, 1640, normal double-manual harpsichord, Hôtel de Croix, Namur.

*Ruckers number:* ft/2.

*Present compass:* $G_1/B_1$ to $c^3$.

*Case dimensions:* length 2236mm; width 802mm; height 271mm with the baseboard; keywell 772mm.

*General description:* Although the outer decoration has been altered considerably, the instrument itself has been altered musically very little. It retains its original disposition with 1 × 8′, 1 × 4′, and has its original registers, jacks, buff, keyframes, etc. The nuts still have the original plates for separating the doubled e♭/g♯ strings, and there are doubled bridge pins and hitchpins for these notes. Except for fragments, the keys have all been lost, and the lower-manual keyframe has been repinned to align it with the upper manual, although the bass block in the upper manual has not been removed.

The soundboard painting is in very good condition, and even the note-names near the tuning pins are clearly visible. The outside of the case, the keywell, and the soundwell have been heavily gessoed over and then painted blue with a heavy gilt leaf- and vine-work decoration. The stand consists of four heavy caryatid figures connected together at the base by a lower stretcher. The lid is missing.

*Literature:* B. 109a; O'Brien (1974a), 83; Dowd (1978), 107, 113.

*Former owner:* The Comte Vizard de Bocarmé.

1643a AR

Andreas Ruckers, 1643, 5-voet muselar virginal at a pitch of R + 2, Gemeentemuseum, The Hague, No. EC 176-x-1952.

*Ruckers number:* 5/37.

*Present compass:* C to $c^3$.

*Case dimensions:* length 1500mm; width 477mm; height 217mm with, 204mm without the baseboard; keywell originally 650mm.

*Motto:* lid (not original) – OMNIS SPIRITVS LAVDET DOMINVM.

*General description:* Although the rose and jackrail are both missing this virginal is certainly by Andreas Ruckers. The soundboard-painting style is the same as the single- and double-manual harpsichords of 1640 and other instruments of this period by Andreas Ruckers. Also, all aspects of the construction are typical of the late work of Andreas Ruckers.

The bass octave was made chromatic by widening the keywell on the bass side and adding the extra, C, C♯, D and E♭ keys to an extension of the keyframe. The keyboard was not shifted, so that the scalings and plucking points of the notes from E upwards are the original ones. One of the strings of the four added notes is pinned on the left-hand bridge, but the three others are hitched directly to the elevated bass-section of the hitchpin rail and therefore sound only on the right-hand bridge.

The lid is of pine; it and its decoration probably date from the time of the ravalement in the eighteenth century. The instrument has its original harpichordium but is lacking the guide blocks and the hold-down pins going into the side of the bridge. This is one of the few Flemish virginals to retain its original lock on the front flap.

It has a simple arcaded oak stand, which, if it is not original, is at least very old, as is indicated by the very large amount of wear from the foot of the player on the lower stretcher.

*Literature:* B. 111; van der Meer (1971c), 134, 135, 144; O'Brien (1974a), 84–5; McGeary (1981), 29.

*Former history:* formerly in the Rijksmuseum, Amsterdam, on loan from the Koninklijk Oudheidkundig Genootschap.

1643b AR

Andreas Ruckers, 1643, grand ravalement of a normal double-manual harpsichord, Mrs Sheridan Germann, Boston, Mass.

*Present compass:* $G_1$ to $e^3$.

*Case dimensions:* length 2265mm; width now 845mm, originally about 795mm; height 265mm with the baseboard; keywell now 815mm, originally about 765mm.

*General description:* This is a conservative ravalement (probably from the first part of the eighteenth century) of a normal Ruckers double. The rose is missing, but the (non-original) namebatten is signed by Andreas Ruckers. The authorship of the instrument is confirmed by the style of the soundboard painting, which is identical to other instruments by Andreas Ruckers of this period. The construction marks on the original parts of the baseboard and on the soundboard corroborate the attribution to one of the members of the Ruckers family.

The style of the ravalement keyboards and the internal framing is clearly French, and details of the latter are very similar to those of Vater. The present jacks and registers are modern, so that the eighteenth-century disposition is uncertain. According to microscopic analysis done by John Koster, the wood of the 8′ bridge is of elm.

*Literature:* not in Boalch.

*Former owners:* sold in 1936 by the owners of the Château de Chenonceaux.

1644a AR

Andreas Ruckers, 1644, a normal single-manual harpsichord, Vleeshuis Museum, Antwerp, No. VH 2137.

*Ruckers number:* ƒt/16.

*Present compass:* C to $c^3$.

*Case dimensions:* length 1814mm; width 723mm; height 231mm with, 228mm without the baseboard; keywell 693mm.

*Motto:* lid – SIC TRANSIT GLORIA MVNDI.

*General description:* Since this harpsichord is signed 'ANDREAS RVCKERS DEN OVDEN ME FECIT ANTVERPIAE', it is one of the few late Andreas instruments which can definitely be ascribed to Andreas the Elder. The compass has been extended by adding two notes in the treble and two in the bass to the bridges and registers, and a long 8′ string has been substituted for the original 4′. The keyboard has been moved towards the treble (by the width of one natural), and the four extra keys to convert the short octave to a chromatic bass octave have been added on the left. Shifting the keyboard to the right has shortened the scalings by two semitones, and adding the extra set of 8′ strings has lengthened them by one semitone; the new scalings are therefore about one semitone shorter than originally.

The harpsichord still retains its original buff stop and many of the jacks are also original (some with original dampers!). One of the tuning pins (preserved separately from the instrument) may have the remnants of a bit of original string rusted to it (see Plate 4.1).

The papers and outer-case marbling are in good condition, although the soundboard painting has almost disappeared.

*Literature:* B. 112; Génard (1892), Plate 27, 195; Lunsingh Scheuleer (1939), 48; Russell (1959), 43; Hubbard (1965), 62; Lambrechts-Douillez (1968), 246; Lambrechts-Douillez (1970a), Plate 9, 18; van der Meer (1971b), 51; van der Meer (1971c), 104, 112, 115; O'Brien (1974a), 83; O'Brien (1977b), 61; Bédard (1977), 109–18; Lambrechts-Douillez (1981a), Plate 422, 153; McGeary (1981), 31; O'Brien (1984), 61–2; Catalogue 11 (n.d.), No. 34.

*Former history:* formerly exhibited in the Steen Museum, Antwerp.

1644b AR

Andreas Ruckers, 1644, 6-voet muselar mother-and-child virginal, Musikinstrumentenmuseum der Karl Marx Universität, Leipzig, No. 1093.

*Ruckers number:* M/28.

*Present compass:* C,D to $c^3$.

*Case dimensions:* (original mother instrument only) – length 1734mm; width 515mm; height 268mm with, 253mm without the baseboard; keywell now 701mm, originally 652mm.

*Motto:* lid (not original) – OMNIS SPIRITVS LAVDET DOMINVM.

*General description:* Originally this was the usual mother-and-child muselar double virginal. The compass was widened to fill out the bass octave, and in doing so the left keywell brace was moved to the left to allow space for the extra keys. As a result, the child could not fit in its normal space to the left of the keyboard, and probably for this reason it was discarded or lost. In about 1910 a new child was made to fit into the reduced space beside the keyboard. Also probably at this time, and in Heyer's workshops, the jacks were renewed, and the new papers were added. The bridges may have been renewed then also. There are numerous stifle bars (eight in all) across the whole of the area underneath the left-hand bridge.

Most of the soundboard painting has disappeared, but the outlines of it, and some colour, remain. The black outside-case paint is not original.

*Literature:* B. 113; Pols (1942), Plate 9; Rubart (1955), Plate 3, 19; Russell (1959), 149; van der Meer (1971c), 138; Henkel (1979a), 77, 101, 134; Henkel (1979b), 108; McGeary (1981), 29; Heyde (1986), 150, 167.

*Former owners:* Prince de Caraman Chimay; Heyer Collection, Cologne.

1646a AR

Andreas Ruckers, 1646, ravalé normal single-manual harpsichord, Vleeshuis Museum, Antwerp, No. VH 76.4.

*Present compass:* C to $f^3$.

*Case dimensions:* length 2007mm; width now 882mm; height 225mm without the baseboard; keywell now 852mm, originally about 680–90mm.

*General description:* This was originally a normal short-octave single-manual harpsichord. The case was widened in both the treble and the bass to extend the compass to C to $f^3$. The bridges were replaced and repinned, and an extra set of 8′ strings was added. New jacks, registers, keyboards and a new jackrail were made. During the course of the restoration of the instrument, when it was owned by William Post Ross, it was discovered that the internal framing had been altered (probably in the eighteenth century) to resemble that shown in Plate XXXV of Hubbard's book.

The interior of the lid is decorated with a painted engraving of a concert by C. van Loo, which has been glued in place. The block-printed papers and exterior paint are modern. Although heavily retouched and extended, much of the soundboard painting is original.

*Literature:* B. 115a; Hubbard (1965), Plate XXXV, footnote p. 52; Lambrechts-Douillez (1977), 273; Lambrechts-Douillez (1981a), Plate 424, 153.

*Former owners:* Alphonse van Neste, Brussels; William Post Ross, Boston, Mass.

1646b AR

Andreas Ruckers, 1646, a grand ravalement of an extended-compass 'French' double-manual harpsichord, Instrument Museum of the Conservatoire NSM, Paris, No. E.979.2.1.

*Original compass:* upper manual – F to $f^3$ at a pitch of R – 4; lower manual – $G_1$ to $c^3$ at a pitch of R.

*Present compass:* $F_1$ to $f^3$.

*Case dimensions:* length 2250mm; width now 904mm, originally about 835mm; height 255mm without the baseboard; keywell now 853mm, originally about 805mm.

*General description:* This is a particularly fine example of a large 'French' Ruckers double, altered in the eighteenth century to make it capable of playing the contemporary repertoire. The keyboards are dated 1756 and may be by Blanchet. It seems likely therefore that in 1756 the instrument was widened, the bridges were repinned and new jacks, registers and keyboards were made. Then in 1780, Taskin thickened the case sides and added the rear peau de buffle register and genouillère. Also at this time the instrument acquired its present stand and its splendid *vernis-martin* decoration.

The inside of the main lid and lid flap show mythological scenes, which seem to be by the same artist who painted the lid of the 1640b IR (Artus Wolfort (1581–1641). If so, the lid must have been painted some years before it was incorporated into this instrument, as Wolfort was already dead when this harpsichord was built.

*Literature:* B. 115; Thibault-de Chambure (1969), 113ff; Thibault-de Chambure (1971), 80; van der Meer (1971c), 120; Germann (1978), 74; Dowd (1978), 109, 111, 113; Bran-Ricci (1980), 138; Dowd (1984), 21, 70; Gétreau (1985), Plate 94, 94–8; O'Brien (1985), 79–84.

*Former owners:* Paul Eudel, Paris; Mme Adrien Allez; The Comtesse de Chambure.

1648 AR

Andreas Ruckers, 1648, normal single-manual harpsichord Musikhistorisk Museum, Copenhagen.

*Ruckers number:* *ft*/69.

*Present compass:* C/E to $c^3$ after several alterations.

*Case dimensions:* length 1826mm; width 711mm; height 241mm without the baseboard; keywell 684mm.

*Mottoes:* main lid – SIC TRANSIT GLORIA MVNDI;
lid flap – ACTA VIRVM PROBANT.

*General description:* This is one of the few extant Ruckers instruments decorated with strapwork holding large semi-precious stones against a marbled background. Most of the interior decoration is original and in reasonably good condition.

Like the 1627 AR quint harpsichord in The Hague, the upper belly rail shows chisel marks from the cutting of the Ruckers lower guides.

The instrument was altered in the eighteenth century by adding an extra set of 8′ strings and increasing the compass to C to $d^3$. This was done by decreasing the octave span of the keys and strings, by narrowing the keyblocks, and by extending the bridges and nuts. New registers and lower guides were required. The instrument was 'restored' in 1965 by Frank Hubbard and a number of major alterations were introduced. The compass was altered to C/E to $c^3$, using the eighteenth-century string spacing; the two sets of 8′ strings were left. The soundboard was removed (and planed to half its original thickness?), a new spruce soundboard was glued underneath the remains of the original soundboard, and the composite soundboard was reinstalled. The (?eighteenth-century) ivory keyplates were removed and replaced with bone. A new 4′ hitchpin rail was made which is far too wide and which comes very close to the 4′ and 8′ bridges in the treble. The soundboard is now very thick in the treble, a feature which is not characteristic of Ruckers harpsichords. The 8′ bridge is modern and is of beech, not cherry.

Like some other modern restorations, this has left the instrument in a state of musical and organological purgatory, in neither its eighteenth-century nor its original state. It has its seventeenth-century compass, but its eighteenth-century disposition and string spacing. The eighteenth-century keyboards have bone touchplates, ebony sharps (instead of bog oak) and modern arcades. And the acoustical function of the soundboard, 4′ hitchpin rail, and bridges has been drastically altered.

*Literature:* B. 117; van der Meer (1971b), 51; van der Meer (1971c), Plate 1, 112, 115, 142; Henkel (1979a), 133; McGeary (1981), 18, 31, 32; Heyde (1986), 221.

*Former owners:* Otto van Copenhagen, Providence, R.I.; Gustav Leonhardt, Amsterdam.

(1651)a AR

Andreas Ruckers, 1651?, a normal single-manual harpsichord, Peter Maxwell-Stuart, Innerleithen, Scotland.

*Ruckers number:* *ft*/2.

*Present compass:* C to $d^3$.

*Case dimensions:* length 1864mm; width 732mm; keywell 700mm.

*Mottoes:* main lid – SIC TRANSIT GLORIA MVNDI;
lid flap – SOLI DEO GLORIA;

keywell flap (not original) – LAVS DEO.

*General description:* The instrument, signed 'ANDREAS RVCKERS AND.[REAS] F.[ILIVS] FECIT ANTVERPIAE', is the only one which can definitely be ascribed to Andreas the Younger. The date is written on the soundboard and has been retouched in a recent restoration, so that it is now impossible to tell if the third numeral was originally a '5' or a '4'. There is a subtraction on the back of the namebatten, suggesting that the age of the instrument was calculated during the eighteenth century; the date of the instrument was then read as 1651. However, the '5' is made in a very uncharacteristic way: the bottom curved sweep of the figure is usually very bold on other instruments, whereas on this one it is tight and constrained. The whole numeral is much more like an altered '4'. Unfortunately there are not enough numbered instruments from this period to help decide the date. If this harpsichord was actually made in 1641, then it is reasonable that the son should sign himself 'AND.[REAS] F.[ILIVS]' to avoid confusion with his father. Andreas Ruckers the Elder died sometime between June 1651 and 24 March 1653. If it was made in 1651, then Andreas the Elder must still have been alive (and also making instruments) at the age of 72.

The instrument suffered at least two compass and disposition alterations. It was first changed to 2 × 8′, 1 × 4′ with a compass of C/E to $d^3$ using the old bridge pinning and string spacing. In the present, second alteration, the compass was altered to C to $d^3$ with the same disposition. In this state the three-octave span was reduced to enable the extra natural notes to be fitted in, and the bridges and nuts were repinned. New jacks, in a style similar to the old Ruckers jacks with oval damper holes, were made for this state.

Decoratively the instrument is in very good order. The papers are well preserved and the outside of the case has its original marbling, also in good condition. The soundboard painting has been extensively retouched, but in general the instrument gives a good idea of how a Ruckers harpsichord must have looked originally. The keywell flap and painted stand are modern.

*Literature:* B. 118a; van der Meer (1971b), 50; van der Meer (1971c), 113; O'Brien (1974a), 83; Mactaggart (1979), 63; McGeary (1981), 32; O'Brien (1984), 61–2; Mactaggart (1985), 106, 107.

*Former owners:* it seems likely that the instrument has always been at Traquair House, Innerleithen, and was brought directly from Antwerp to Scotland for the Stuart family.

1651b AR

Andreas Ruckers, 1651, ravalé double-manual harpsichord of a normal single-manual harpsichord, Victoria and Albert Museum, London, No. 1079–1868.

*Present compass:* $G_1$,$A_1$ to $f^3$.

*Mottoes:* (all not original) main lid – SIC TRANSIT GLORIA MVNDI;
lid flap – MVSICA DONVM DEI;
keywell flap (now lost) – ACTA VIRVM PROBANT.

*General description:* This is an English ravalement of a small single-manual Ruckers harpsichord. The case was widened in the treble and bass, and new keyboards, jacks, registers, bridges, nuts, jackrail and wrestplank were made for the instrument in the English style, probably around 1715–20. The case was also lengthened to give sufficient space for the addition of a second keyboard. In fact, the bass strings are far too short for the new bottom note ($G_1$).

The added sections of new soundboard wood in the bass and treble and the new wrestplank veneer have been painted over in the style of the original. The border scallop and arabesque designs have been removed and the position of the arabesques painted over with leaf designs. The spine still has its original red marble decoration, but the rest of the case has all been repainted.

This is one of the harpsichords which is claimed to have belonged to Handel.

*Literature:* B. 118; van der Straeten (1875), 334; James (1930), Plate XLII; Pols (1942), Plate II; Juramie (1948), 40; Kenyon (1949), Plate opp. p. 209; Hirt (1955), 14–15; Harich-Schneider (1958), 9; Russell (1959), Plate 14; Russell (1968), 43ff; Ripin (1968), 38; van der Meer (1971b), 48; van der Meer (1971c), 105, 112, 115; O'Brien (1977a), 41; McGeary (1981), 18, 26, 31; Schott (1985), No. 15, Plates, 53–6, 74 (listed as 1631!).

*Former owners:* Christopher Smith; Lady Rivers; Mr Wickham; Canon Hawtry; Dr Chard; Mr Hooper; Messrs Broadwood.

1654 AR

Andreas Ruckers, 1654, ravalé double-manual harpsichord of a normal single-manual harpsichord, Germanisches Nationalmuseum, Nuremberg, No. MINe 85.

*Present compass:* $G_1$/$B_1$ to $f^3$.

*Mottoes:* main lid – SIC TRANSIT GLORIA MVNDI;
keywell flap (not original) – ACTA VIRVM PROBANT.

*General description:* The grand ravalement carried out on this harpsichord to convert it from a normal single-manual harpsichord into a double was done by moving out the cheek to extend the treble compass, lengthening the spine and cheek sides at the front to accommodate the second manual, and by making new keyboards, jacks, registers, jackrail, bridges, nuts and wrestplank. The ravalement seems to have been carried out in Flanders, as is indicated by Flemish writing on the present jacks and keylevers. The case has been repainted in imitation marble in the style of the original decoration.

Although the rose is not original, the style of the workmanship and decoration confirm that the instrument is indeed by Andreas Ruckers.

*Literature:* B. 119; Führer (1938), No. 133; van der Meer (n.d.), 12; van der Meer (1971a), 65–7; van der Meer (1971b), 48, 52; van der Meer (1971c), 112, 115; O'Brien (1977a), 41; McGeary (1981), 18, 31; Hellwig (1985), Plate 9, 89–90.

*Former owner:* Dr Hans Neupert, Bamberg.

## CATALOGUE OF IOANNES COUCHET INSTRUMENTS

### 1645 IC

Ioannes Couchet, 1645, single-manual harpsichord, Russell Collection, Edinburgh, No. 7.

*Present compass:* C to $c^3$.

*Case dimensions:* length 1813mm; width originally about 710mm; height 243mm with, 231mm without the baseboard; keywell originally about 682mm.

*General description:* This harpsichord was originally a normal short-octave single-manual instrument. It was ravalé by extending the treble side of the case and repinning the bridges using a smaller three-octave spacing to give a compass of $A_1, B_1$ to $f^3$. A second set of 8′ strings was added and a new action made. From the style of the outer decoration and from the style of the new action, the ravalement must have been done in England in the early part of the eighteenth century.

A second change was made to the instrument, probably not very long before it was bought by Raymond Russell. The ravalement addition to the case was removed and the cheek was moved back to its original position (actually the case is now about 8mm narrower than originally). The keyboards were remade to give it a compass of C to $c^3$, and like many unenlightened modern restorations, this has left the instrument in a state of organological purgatory, awaiting a purification and return either to its original or to its eighteenth-century condition.

The existence of the hold-down pins in the 8′ nut for the buff batten, and of the plugged hole in the cheek for the buff batten extension, prove that this harpsichord originally had a buff register. However, there is no V-shaped nick in the back of the 8′ nut for the stop-block between the two sections of the split buff. This must indicate that the original buff was not split, a feature not found on any earlier Ruckers/Couchet harpsichord.

*Literature:* B. 1 (Couchet); Williams and Newman (1968), No. 7, 17; Barnes (1971a), 35–6; O'Brien (1977a), 46.

*Former owners:* Messrs Legg, Cirencester; Raymond Russell, London.

### 1646 IC

Ioannes Couchet, 1646, aligned and ravalé normal double-manual harpsichord, Brussels Museum, No. 276.

*Ruckers number:* ʃt/17.

*Original upper-manual compass:* $G_1/B_1$ to $c^3$.

*Present compass:* $G_1/B_1$ to $f^3$.

*Case dimensions:* length 2226mm; width now 856mm, originally about 785mm; height 264mm with the baseboard; keywell now 830mm, originally about 759mm.

*Ravalement disposition:*

→ 8′<br>
← 4′<br>
← 8′ dogleg<br>
→ 8′

*General description:* Like virtually all Couchet harpsichords, this one is unusual in a number of respects. First, it originally had an upper manual with the bass extending to $G_1/B_1$, instead of the usual type with C/E as the bottom note and the space to the left filled by a wooden block. It is thus the first known Ruckers/Couchet instrument with an original $G_1/B_1$ short octave, and probably also the first extant instrument of any kind designed with this compass. Secondly, it had an original scaling of 338mm, that is, between those instruments at R ($c^2$ = 358mm) and those at R + 2 ($c^2$ = 320mm). The implied pitch is about a semitone above R. Thirdly, the original buff stop was not split, but was continuous from treble to bass, like the 1645 IC above. In addition, the soundboard painting lacks the usual scalloped borders and arabesques.

This harpsichord is now a good example of an aligned transposing double with a conservative ravalement carried out very competently. The lower-manual keys were aligned to match those of the upper manual, and both keyboards were extended to $f^3$ in the treble by adding about 70mm to the cheek side. The bridges and soundboard were extended and filled out, and new upper and lower guides and a new set of jacks were made. An extra set of 8′ strings was added without changing the spacing of the existing strings. The ravalement disposition gives 2 × 8′ on the upper

Plate C.7 Plan view of the 1650a IC 6-voet muselar virginal. Scale 1:10. Copyright, Vleeshuis Museum, Antwerp.

manual, but does not allow a single lower-manual 8′ to contrast with a single 8′ on the upper. To make this registration possible, the plucking direction of the lower-manual jacks was altered, and a new set of dogleg jacks, plucking to the right and interchangeable with those of the ravalement, was made. Either disposition can thus be selected by choosing either the modern or the ravalement set of jacks. The ravalement disposition, with 2 × 8′ on the upper manual, is a feature of many eighteenth-century Flemish harpsichords; this, together with the workmanship of the jacks, points to Flanders as the country in which the ravalement was carried out.

The 4′ bridge is a replacement. The soundboard painting is in excellent condition and is almost un-retouched.

This instrument shares, with the 1646b A R in Paris, the distinction of being the latest transposing harpsichord.

*Literature:* B. 2 (Couchet); Mahillon, Vol. I (1893–1922), No. 276; Ernst (1955), 69; Russell (1959), 45; de Maeyer (1969), No. 12, 33; Meeùs (1970), 15–29; Ripin (1971a), 19; van der Meer (1971b), 49; van der Meer (1971c), 121; O'Brien (1974a), 81; O'Brien (1977a), 38, 46; Koster (1982), footnote 5; Shann (1984), 67.

*Former owner:* de Sorlus.

1650a IC

Ioannes Couchet, 1650, 6-voet muselar virginal, Vleeshuis Museum, Antwerp, No. VH 67.6.

*Case dimensions:* length 1708mm; width 498mm; height 242mm with, 230mm without the baseboard; keywell 650mm.

*General description:* This is the last surviving Ruckers/Couchet virginal. It is a little-altered 6-voet muselar virginal. The decoration of the outer case and the front flap is not original, and the papers are recent, but the rest of the decoration is in its original state. The soundboard painting is very well preserved and the instrument even has almost all of its key arcades. The soundboard painting and the holes for the wires in the side of the bass section of the bridge show that there was originally a harpichordium.

The case mouldings do not have the usual Ruckers/Couchet shape; they have had a red stripe painted down the middle instead of being left in plain varnished wood.

The lid painting shows a group of skittles players with a view of Antwerp in the background across the river Scheldt. The coats of arms of the Marquesses of Antwerp and the Rockox family indicate that this instrument was owned by the descendants of Nicolaas Rockox, Burgomaster of Antwerp, who died in 1640.

The turned and carved stand is probably original.

*Literature:* B. 9 (Couchet); Lambrechts-Douillez (1967), 100; Lambrechts-Douillez (1970a), Plate, 17; Lambrechts-Douillez (1970b), Plates 2, 6; van der Meer (1971c), 133; Bédard (1971), 41; Lambrechts-Douillez (1977), 271; Lambrechts-Douillez (1981a), Plate 419, 144, 149.

*Former owner:* Abel Régibo, Ronse (Renaix).

(*c.* 1650)b IC

Ioannes Couchet, undated, large single-manual harpsichord with an extended bass octave, originally at a pitch of R + 2, converted into a double-manual harpsichord, Metropolitan Museum of Art, New York, No. 89.4.2363.

*Ruckers number:* ft/34.

*Original compass:* $F_1$,$G_1$,$A_1$ to $c^3$.

*Present compass:* $F_1$,$G_1$ to $c^3$.

*Case dimensions:* length now 2290mm, originally about 2168mm; width 859mm; height 267mm with, 253mm without the baseboard; keywell 831mm, 795mm between the keyblocks.

*Present disposition:*

← 8′ (split)
← 4′
→ 8′ dogleg
← 8′ lute (split)

*General description:* The case, lid and stand are decorated lavishly in the style of Louis XIV. However, the instrument has been totally redecorated during the conversion from a single- to a double-manual instrument; the few traces of the original decoration (on the original keyblocks, etc.) are totally out of keeping with its present elegant appearance.

The scribed lines on the baseboard under the gap indicate that there were originally only two registers: the original disposition must have been 1 × 8′, 1 × 4′. The original tuning-pin positions are marked f, g, a, b, h, c . . . c, indicating that the original compass was $F_1, G_1, A_1$ to $c^3$. This is consistent with the width of thirty-three naturals between the keyblocks. Also, the pitch c string (whose 8′ bridge pin is 49cm from the nameboard) was originally played by the $b^{\flat 1}$ key, and the string played by $c^2$ was 314mm long. This confirms that $c^3$ was the original top note, that $F_1$ was the bottom note providing that $F^\sharp{}_1$ and $G^\sharp{}_1$ were originally missing, and that the pitch of the instrument was originally at R + 2.

Both keyboards date from the conversion from a single- to a double-manual instrument. The present disposition is very interesting: it is authentic to the alteration and can be confirmed on the basis of the construction and numbering of the registers. There are holes in the 8′ nut for the pins which originally helped to position the buff batten. Thus there was originally a buff stop. Like the 1645 IC and 1646 IC, however, it was not split, since there is no wedge nicked out of the middle of the rear surface of the 8′ bridge for the stop-block characteristic of the earlier split-buff stops.

The present jacks, which date from the conversion, are in the style of the usual Ruckers/Couchet jacks with blind damper holes instead of slots, but are thinner than was usual Ruckers practice. The soundboard is unpainted except for gold-painted scallops and arabesques along the bridges and case sides, and a gold 'wreath' of arabesques and vine-work.

*Literature:* B. 8 (Couchet); Catalogue 2 (1904), No. 2363; Winternitz (1966), No. 37, Plate, 118; Hubbard (1968), 69; Wolters (1969), 21; Ripin (1969), 169–78; Ripin (1970a), 37; van der Meer (1971b), 48; van der Meer (1971c), 114, 115; Thomas and Rhodes (1973), 121; Dowd (1978), 113; Rueger (1982/86), Plate 87, 100, 121.

1652 IC

Ioannes Couchet, 1652, double-manual harpsichord made from a single-manual harpsichord, private, France.

*Original compass:* $G_1/B_1$ to $c^3$.

*Present compass:* $G_1/B_1$ to $c^3$ (split $E^\flat$).

*Original disposition:* 2 × 8′.

*Case dimensions:* length now 2180mm, originally about 2087mm; width 790mm; height 260mm with, 248mm without the baseboard; keywell 760mm.

*General description:* This is the last extant instrument by Ioannes Couchet. Like all of the instruments bearing the name Couchet, it is interesting and unusual. It indicates both a change in musical tastes and the inventiveness of its maker.

It is now a double-manual harpsichord. But the cheek, spine and baseboard all show that it was converted to a double from a single-manual instrument. The present disposition with 2 × 8′, 1 × 4′ is usual for eighteenth-century French harpsichords. However, the 4′ hitchpins are driven into a thin strip of fruitwood glued to the top of the soundboard, and both this and the 4′ bridge lie on top of the original soundboard painting. This indicates that the instrument did not originally have a 4′ bridge or register. It is thus the earliest extant instrument built in the Ruckers/Couchet tradition with a 2 × 8′ disposition. Also, the gap has never been widened and the lines scribing the plan of the instrument on the baseboard show that the gap originally contained three registers! By analogy with the 1679 IC single, the most likely disposition is therefore

→ 8′
← 8′
→ 8′

with two rows of jacks both plucking the short 8′ set of strings.

Unlike the earlier Couchet and Ruckers instruments, the upper jackslides did not project through the cheek in the usual way to enable the registration to be changed. But there is a plugged hole on the spine side which apparently served for this purpose, probably in conjunction with some type of trapwork mechanism. The evidence for this is that the spine, except for a large rectangular area near the registers and wrestplank, has its original marbling. The rectangular area is clear unpainted poplar. From the appearance of the marbling at its edge, it was apparently covered by a box which would itself originally have been marbled. The box probably contained some type of trapwork which alternated the two registers controlling the jacks plucking the same set of strings. This may then be the earliest example of a machine stop; it certainly predates the mention of a pedal in Mace (Mace (1676), 235–6; see James (1930), 120, and Boalch (1974), 65) by more than twenty years.

The usual analysis of the case width and the position of the pitch c string in conjunction with the 49cm rule shows that the original compass was $G_1/B_1$ to $c^3$, playing at reference pitch R. The 1646 IC in Brussels also originally had a $G_1/B_1$ compass on the upper manual, where it was simply the result of transposing the lower-manual compass of C/E to $f^3$ down a fourth. For the present instrument the $G_1/B_1$ was obviously a result of design, which must nevertheless have been suggested by instruments like the 1646 IC. The extension of the compass from C/E to $G_1/B_1$ gives the range found in the large 'French' doubles, but without the lowest four accidentals ($G^\sharp{}_1$, $B^\flat{}_1$, $C^\sharp$ and $E^\flat$). Since meantone tuning was still the common temperament for keyboard instruments in 1652, however, the lack of these accidentals in the bass would not have been found a great limitation (though $B^\flat{}_1$ is in fact as likely a pitch as $B_1$ for the $E^\flat$). The 1652 IC instrument is thus the earliest instrument specifically designed with a $G_1/B_1$ compass.

Because the instrument originally lacked a 4′ bridge, the soundboard is barred differently from the usual Ruckers/Couchet system. There is one large single cutoff bar in roughly the position occupied by the 4′ hitchpin rail, with long soundbars running from this to the spine liner, and placed as usual perpendicular to the spine. The rose too is placed in a position further from the gap and spine than usual, in order to be nearer the isolated 8′ bridge.

*Literature:* not in Boalch; Dowd (1978), 113; Dowd (1984), 20ff.

## CATALOGUE OF INSTRUMENTS BY IOSEPH IOANNES OR IOANNES II COUCHET

### 1671/73 IC

Ioseph Ioannes Couchet, 1671/73, grand ravalement double-manual harpsichord of a small single-manual harpsichord, Kenneth Gilbert, Chartres, France.

*Present compass:* $F_1$ to $f^3$.

*General description:* This is a 'collage' instrument, with a soundboard from an old Couchet harpsichord placed in a French eighteenth-century case. The keyboards are dated 1757; William Dowd feels that they, and the essential part of the rebuilding of the harpsichord, can be attributed to Blanchet. In reusing the old soundboard, the idea seems to have been to place parts of the Couchet soundboard wood under the new extended bridges (see Chapter 11, p. 211).

The holes used to position the original 8′ bridge are visible in the original part of the soundboard. From the location of these near the original notes *c* and *f*♯, it is clear that the original top note was $c^3$, and that the compass probably went down either to C/E, or to C chromatically. There is no sign of any positioning holes for the 4′ bridge, nor of any plugged 4′ hitchpins; this and the lack of space between the original rose wreath and the 8′ bridge implies that there was no 4′ register and the original disposition was 2 × 8′.

A few traces of the usual bronze powder arabesques and scallops were not totally erased from the soundboard when it was reused and repainted. Among these is visible the date 1673 and not the 1671 which appears on an Andreas-style white ribbon in the repainted eighteenth-century part of the soundboard.

The instrument was reworked in 1778 by Taskin, who probably added the peau de buffle register and the genouillère.

*Literature:* not in Boalch; Germann (1979), 476; Dowd (1984), 21, 72, 97.

### 1679 IC

Ioseph Ioannes Couchet, 1679, chromatic-bass single-manual harpsichord with three registers, Smithsonian Institution, Washington, D.C.

*Ruckers number:* ꞙt/1.

*Present original compass:* C to $c^3$.

*Case dimensions:* length 1929mm; width 761mm; height 219mm without the baseboard; keywell 732mm.

*Scalings in millimetres:*

8′ scalings:

| | String length | Plucking point |
|---|---|---|
| $c^3$ | 175 | 60 |
| $f^2$ | 268 | 67 |
| $c^2$ | 356 | 73 |
| $f^1$ | 524 | 84 |
| $c^1$ | 687 | 89 |
| f | 863 | 106 |
| c | 1108 | 116 |
| F | 1355 | 134 |
| C | 1485 | 147 |

4′ scalings:

| | String length | Plucking point |
|---|---|---|
| $c^3$ | 86 | 38 |
| $f^2$ | 132 | 42 |

| | | |
|---|---|---|
| $c^2$ | 177 | 45 |
| $f^1$ | 263 | 48 |
| $c^1$ | 338 | 51 |
| f | 475 | 55 |
| c | 583 | 57 |
| F | 750 | 59 |
| C | 866 | 60 |

*Original disposition:*

→ 8′
← 4′
→ 8′

*General description:* Although it has a number of new and individual characteristics, this harpsichord is clearly built in the earlier Ruckers tradition.

It is the only extant Ruckers/Couchet single-manual harpsichord with its original chromatic-bass-octave keys, compass and disposition. It is about 100mm longer than the usual short-octave singles. It is also the only Ruckers/Couchet instrument with its original three registers. The three registers are so placed that the 4′ jack is situated between the two sets of 8′ jacks, which, because there is only one set of 8′ strings, both pluck the same string. Separating the two 8′ rows of jacks with the 4′ row produces the maximum tonal difference between the two 8′ registers.

The rose is the usual IC double-manual rose, even though the instrument only has one keyboard. The soundboard is unpainted except for bronze powder scallops around the bridges and case sides, and vine-work arabesques around the rose. Underneath the exterior green case paint the original red marbling is visible. Mottled slightly with a weak scumble, it is in panels on each case-side surface, not continuous around the outside of the case, as is usual. The interior of the lid is painted with a scene attributed to van Kessel.

*Literature:* B. 5 (Couchet); Steinert (1892), No. 24, 14; Koster (1977), 80; Dowd (1978), 113.

*Former owners:* Morris Steinert; Mrs Norman Learned, Washington; Ethelbert Nevin II.

1680 IC

Ioseph Ioannes Couchet, 1680, ravalé double-manual harpsichord of an extended-bass-compass single-manual harpsichord, Museum of Fine Arts, Boston, No. 1977.54.

*Original compass:* probably $F_1$,(,$G_1$,$A_1$) to $d^3$.

*Present compass:* $F_1$ to $f^3$.

*General description:* This is the last surviving dated instrument from the Ruckers/Couchet tradition. It has suffered numerous alterations to the extent that its original state can now only be guessed. Originally it was a single-manual harpsichord; the cheek has been extended by a lap joint in the process of converting it to a double. The original spine is contained inside the instrument. From its position the original inside width can be estimated to be about 863mm. This suggests that the original keyboard had thirty-four naturals (see Table 8.1). Using the 49cm rule to locate the position of the original pitch c string and locating the original plugged tuning pin gives $d^3$ as the original top note, and implies $F_1$ as the lowest note. (The somewhat unlikely $E_1$ ($C_1/E_1$?) to $c^3$ at a pitch R + 2 is not entirely to be excluded.) A harpsichord by the elder Ioannes Couchet with the $F_1$ to $d^3$ compass is mentioned in the correspondence of 19 July 1648 from Duarte to Huygens (see Appendix 17).

The initial conversion to a double-manual harpsichord may have been done by Blanchet, who signed the keys in 1758. It was then modified by Taskin in 1781, who added a fourth row of jacks (the peau de buffle), the stand and the genouillère. Taskin also stamped the wrestplank with the gauges of the strings that he intended to use; these and the scalings suggest that it was originally designed to sound a semitone above Taskin's usual pitch of $a^1$ = 409Hz.

*Literature:* B. 8 (Couchet); Hubbard (1965), Plate XIII; Ripin (1970b), 70; Dowd (1978), 109, 113; Dowd (1984), 21, 73ff.

*Former owners:* Karl Freund Collection; Mrs J. Henry, Lancashire; Sibyl Marcuse (purchased from Ginsburg and Levy, New York in 1942); Edwin M. Ripin, New York.

n.d. IC

Ioseph Ioannes Couchet, undated, grand ravalement double-manual harpsichord made from an extended-bass single-manual harpsichord at a pitch of R + 2, Nydahl Collection, Stockholm, No. KL 59.

*Original compass:* $F_1$ to $d^3$,$e^3$.

*Present compass:* $F_1$ to $f^3$.

*Case dimensions:* length now 2725mm, originally about 2630mm; width now 925mm, originally about 918mm; height 254mm without the baseboard; keywell 887mm (unaltered).

*Motto:* in keywell – NON NISI MOTA CANO.

*Scalings in millimetres:* Although both the bass and treble ends of the 8′ and 4′ bridges are not original, and the nuts have been replaced and repositioned, the original scalings can be estimated:

| | 8′ | 4′ |
|---|---|---|
| $e^3$ | 135 | 66 |
| $c^3$ | 161 | 78 |
| $f^2$ | 246 | 117 |

| | | |
|---|---|---|
| $c^2$ | 327 | 159 |
| $f^1$ | 499 | 244 |
| $c^1$ | 635 | 314 |
| f | 858 | 455 |
| c | 1077 | 573 |
| F | 1512 | 746 |
| C | 1879 | 913 |
| $F_1$ | 2170 | 1125 |

*General description:* This is probably the last of the instruments produced by the Ruckers/Couchet family, and is certainly one of the most interesting. It was originally a single-manual harpsichord with the usual 1 × 8′, 1 × 4′ disposition. It was both very long and very wide compared to the usual Ruckers/Couchet instrument; so long that red brass strings could not have been used in the extreme bass. The inside case width of 887mm gives room for thirty-five naturals (see Table 8.1), or five octaves less one natural.

The usual string-band-strip analysis shows that the bottom thirteen notes on the 8′ bridge were back-pinned, implying a fully chromatic bass octave. Assuming a bottom note of $F_1$ corroborates the position of $c^2$, located by the 49cm rule. This implies $e^3$ as the top note; the top $e^{\flat 3}$ must have been lacking, otherwise the treble ends of the bridges would have extended over the treble soundboard liner.

Although the 49cm rule locates the original 8′ note $c^2$, it is clear from the original position of the nut that the scalings for this note (and the other treble notes of both the 4′ and 8′ strings) correspond to a pitch a whole tone higher than R. This instrument is therefore exceptional in that the 49cm rule locates the *played* note $c^2$, even though the pitch of this note is at R + 2 (and pitch c is therefore played by the $b^{\flat 1}$ key). The plugged hole in the cheek for the projecting registers is wide enough for only two registers, so that the original disposition must have been 1 × 8′, 1 × 4′.

The first alteration added a second unison set of strings and added a top $e^{\flat 3}$ to give $F_1$ to $e^3$ with a 2 × 8′, 1 × 4′ disposition. The original rows of 4′ and 8′ tuning pins were used, adding one note in the treble, and staggering the second set of tuning pins in the usual French way. The space for the extra register was gained from both the belly-rail and wrestplank sides of the gap.

The next alteration seems to have been made by Taskin, whose typical label is found on the inside of the instrument, glued to the bentside. He extended the case length and made new keyboards to convert it to a double-manual harpsichord. Taskin also increased the thickness of the spine, and remade the internal framing in his usual way. The compass was left at $F_1$ to $e^3$. The sixtieth jack has Taskin's usual mark and the date 1768, making this Taskin's earliest dated work.

A later alteration added an extra set of keys, jacks and register holes for a top $f^3$ note, but this seems not to have been done by Taskin.

The exterior of the harpsichord is one of the most lavish and beautiful I have seen. It has a background of red lacquer with brilliant polychrome lacquer decorations. The stand is an elaborately-carved rococo creation. The lid is in one piece without a lid flap, with an interior painting in the style of David Teniers the Younger (1610–90) which is comparable in quality with the best of Teniers' work.

*Literature:* B. 12 (Couchet).

# Catalogue of unauthentic Ruckers instruments

## UNAUTHENTIC 'HANS RUCKERS' INSTRUMENTS

'n.d.a HR'
'Hans Ruckers', undated, double-manual harpsichord, Brussels Museum of Musical Instruments, No. 2510; B. 25.

This harpsichord is a genuine Flemish instrument, originally of a type not encountered anywhere else in the Flemish tradition. It is the subject of an article by John Koster, 'A remarkable early Flemish transposing harpsichord', *Galpin Society Journal* XXXV (1982), 45–53, who shows it originally to have had transposing keyboards with a 16′ register. It is discussed here in Chapter 2, p. 32. It has a rose which is the same casting as the roses in the '1636a IR' (B. 57), '1637 HR' (B.29), and '1658 HR' (B. 24), and so it seems likely that all four of these instruments were faked by the same person (see Plate F.2).

'n.d.b HR'
'Hans Ruckers', undated, double-manual harpsichord, Brussels Museum of Musical Instruments, No. 2934; B. 26.

A Flemish double-manual harpsichord, with many features similar to the instruments of Ruckers. There is no rose and no signature, and the attribution to Hans Ruckers is hypothetical. This harpsichord originally had transposing keyboards with compasses of C/E to $a^2$ (upper manual) and C/E to $d^3$ (lower manual), a 1 × 8′, 1 × 4′ disposition, and only three registers. It is described fully in Chapter 2, p. 29.

'n.d.c HR'
'Hans Ruckers', undated, small virginal, Instrument Museum, Leipzig, No. 36; B. 26a.

A small rectangular virginal possibly originally at a pitch of R + 9 (brass stringing). It is in the shape of a sewing box with drawers in the padded lid. It is an early instrument with a compass of C/E to $g^2$,$a^2$, probably from the period about 1570–90. It has a pierced parchment rose, and was attributed to Hans Ruckers by Kinsky.

'n.d.d HR'
'Hans Ruckers', undated, double-manual harpsichord, formerly the property of the Hearst family, New York, present location unknown; B. 28 = 32.

A large double-manual instrument. Photographs of this instrument in the Russell Collection, Edinburgh, show it to be a beautifully-decorated harpsichord, probably of French origin. It has a compass of $F_1$ to $f^3$, painted decorations in the style of Boucher, and a gilt stand in the style of Louis XV. The width of the tail is too great for it to have been a Ruckers instrument.

'n.d.e HR'
'Hans Ruckers', undated, a single-manual harpsichord, Smithsonian Institution, Washington; B. 30.

A modern pastiche instrument of no particular style. It appears to date from the late nineteenth or early twentieth century. It has a compass of C/E to $f^3$, and is disposed 1 × 8′, 1 × 4′.

'1573 HR'
'Hans Ruckers', 1573, single-manual harpsichord, Deutsches Museum, Munich; B. 1.

This is a small single which has been reworked and 'restored' a number of times. It has a pastiche case and lid decoration, and a 'baroque' cabriole-leg stand. The rose appears to be a genuine Andreas Ruckers rose in which the top of the letter A has been cut apart and the two sides of the letter then bent into a vertical position to make an H. It has a spurious compass, scaling and disposition.

'1590a HR'
'Hans Ruckers', 1590, double-manual harpsichord, property of M. A. Hanlet, Brussels; B. 3.

A much reworked instrument, possibly of Flemish origin. It is now a grand ravalement $G_1$ to $e^3$ double, although it started out as a much smaller instrument. The present three-octave span of the keys is 476mm, but it appears once to have had strings (and keys) with a three-octave spacing of about 500mm. However, the usual Ruckers markings are missing from the soundboard, so that, although it may have been Flemish, it is not by one of the Ruckers.

'1590b HR'
'Hans Ruckers', 1590, a large French double-manual harpsichord, Instrument Museum of the Conservatoire NSM, Paris, No. E.233; B. 4.

A very fine French double, which is mostly the work of Jean-Claude Goujon, dating from before 1749. It has a complicated history but was reworked by Joachim Swanen in 1784. The original compass was $G_1$ to $d^3$; this was enlarged in steps to $F_1$ to $e^3$ in 1749, and finally to $F_1$ to $f^3$ in 1784. It has fake Ruckers papers, a soundboard painting vaguely in the style of the late instruments of Andreas Ruckers, and a fake HR rose.

'1610 HR'
'Hans Ruckers', 1610, a medium-sized (4½-voet?) spinett virginal, Händel-Haus, Halle, German Democratic Republic; B. 14.

A reworked virginal of compass C/E to $f^3$. It may originally have been designed like the Ruckers 4½-voet instruments to sound at R + 4, but it now has modified scalings which, referred to $c^2$, vary from 150mm (*sic*) at $f^3$ to 366mm at $f^1$. It has many Flemish features; among these are the keywell/faceboard papers, which appear original. The lack of defects in these would date the instrument to the early part of the seventeenth century. It has an elaborate carved and turned baluster stand.

'1612 HR'
'Hans Ruckers', 1612/1774, a large double-manual harpsichord, Brussels Museum of Musical Instruments, No. 3848; B. 17.

A large French double-manual harpsichord of compass $F_1$ to $f^3$, with a composite soundboard some of which has been taken from a (Flemish?) virginal. The case and lid are painted with scenes from the career of Louis XIV by van der Meulen. Besides the fake Ruckers signature the instrument bears the inscription 'Mis a Ravalement par Pascal Taskin à Paris 1774'. Taskin may well be responsible for the whole of the instrument. This is probably the instrument referred to in Appendix 15, p. 303.

'1613 HR'
'Hans Ruckers', 1613, a French double-manual harpsichord, Yale University Collection of Musical Instruments, New Haven, Conn., No. 4886.72; B. 18.

This is a very important seventeenth-century French double-manual harpsichord. It is signed underneath the soundboard 'Faict par Michel Richard 1688'. It has a compass of $G_1/B_1$ to $c^3$ with a split low $E^\flat$. It has a casting of an Andreas Ruckers rose in the soundboard, with the top of the A split and spread out to form an H.

'1615 HR'
'Hans Ruckers', 1615, a French double-manual harpsichord, private ownership, Marseilles, France; B. 21.

A large French double made by putting a large case around a Flemish (but not Ruckers) soundboard taken from a double-manual harpsichord. The soundboard shows signs of the pinning for doubled $e^\flat/g^\sharp$ strings, but none of the other usual Ruckers construction marks. The rose is like those used by Hans Ruckers before 1598. The soundboard painting is a confection of neo-Ruckers styles, with the date painted in an Andreas Ruckers-style ribbon near the spine. The (modern) keyboards have a compass of $F_1,G_1$ to $f^3$. The lowest upper-manual jack is inscribed '1732', presumably the date in which the instrument was built, and has the initials IG: those of Jean Goujon, who must have carried out the work on the instrument.

'1620 HR'
'Hans Ruckers', 1620, the mother part of a 6-voet muselar virginal, Instrument Museum of the National Conservatory, Lisbon; B. 23.

Formerly a double mother-and-child virginal of the muselar type, with the child part now missing. This is

Plate F.1 The '1590 HR' double-manual harpsichord built by Jean-Claude Goujon in 1749, and altered in 1784 by Joachim Swanen. Musée Instrumental du CNSM de Paris, Cliché Publimages-Labo 4.

Plate F.2 The rose from the French '1636a IR' double-manual harpsichord.

Plate F.3 The elaborately decorated '1628 AR' double-manual harpsichord. Photograph by Raymond Russell.

one of the few non-Ruckers Flemish virginals. The keywell nameboard is not removable, but has instead a harpsichord-style namebatten above the keys which with their keyblocks must be removed before the keyboard can be withdrawn. It has the usual C/E to $c^3$ compass, and scalings comparable with those found on similar Ruckers virginals. The painted keywell and soundwell decorations and the lid painting suggest that this instrument dates from the period 1570–90.

'1637 HR'
'Hans Ruckers', 1637, a single-manual harpsichord, Brussels Museum of Musical Instruments, No. 4276, B. 29.

This is a large single-manual harpsichord, probably of late seventeenth-century Flemish origin. It has been much reworked, and much of it is not original. The outside of the case is covered with a very heavy carved oak decoration. It has a rose which is the same casting as the roses in the 'n.d.a HR' (B. 25), '1636a IR' (B. 57), and '1658 HR' (B. 24), and so it seems likely that all four of these instruments were faked by the same person.

'1644a HR'
'Hans Ruckers', 1644, a French double-manual harpsichord, property of M. and Mme Jacottet, Rivaz, Switzerland; B. 23b.

A late eighteenth-century French double with a compass of $F_1$ to $f^3$ and a genouillère machine to vary the registration. The casting of an Andreas Ruckers rose has had the top of the A cut and reshaped to form an H. The soundboard displays a mixture of styles, but is based mostly on the decoration of early Ioannes Ruckers instruments. There is a small piece of wood incorporated into the stand which has some original Flemish block-printed paper still glued to its surface! This is one of the finest-sounding instruments I have heard.

'1644b HR'
'Hans Ruckers', 1644, a double-manual harpsichord, Nydahl Collection, Stockholm; B. 30b.

Although it originally had two keyboards, this double-manual harpsichord now is left with only one. The compass is $G_1$ to $e^3$. The Italianate scrolls in the keywell are similar to those of some German harpsichords of the Saxon school, and suggests this as the place of origin. The stand is elaborately carved in the style of Louis XV.

'1658 HR'
'Hans Ruckers', 1658, a small double-manual harpsichord, Germanisches Nationalmuseum, Nuremberg, No. MINe 84; B. 24.

Originally a small double with a compass of only C/E to $c^3$, it now has a chromatic C to $c^3$ compass. Most of the instrument is of a softwood (pine?) and the style of construction suggests the Low Countries as the place of origin. It has many features in common with the Gheerdinck virginal, also in the Germanisches Nationalmuseum, and may be by him. Like the 'n.d.a HR' (B. 25), the '1636a IR' (B. 57), and the '1637 HR' (B. 29), it appears to have a recast Hans Moermans rose, and so it seems likely that all four of these instruments were faked by the same person.

## UNAUTHENTIC 'IOANNES RUCKERS' INSTRUMENTS

'n.d. IR'
'Ioannes Ruckers', undated, a French double-manual harpsichord, the property of Yannick le Gaillard, Paris; B. 136a = 138.

This is a large French double of the late eighteenth century with the inscription 'Refait par Pierre Dubois à Paris Anno 1780'. There is a normal Ioannes Ruckers double-manual rose in the soundboard, but with some damage to the letter I. The compass is $E_1$ to $f^3$, typical of French instruments of the period around 1780. The style of the soundboard painting suggests that the soundboard came from a seventeenth-century French harpsichord.

'1627 IR'
'Ioannes Ruckers', 162[7], a double-manual harpsichord, Yale University Collection of Musical Instruments, New Haven, Conn., No. 4876.60; B. 44.

A double, almost certainly a seventeenth-century French instrument, with a fifty-note ($G_1/B_1$ to $d^3$?) compass which has been widened to give $F_1$ to $e^3$. The keyboards were made by Dolmetsch in 1908, when he was working with Chickerings. The jackrail is inscribed 'IOHANNES RVCKERS ME FECIT ANTVERPIAE 162[7]', and the nameboard 'H RVKHER ANTWERPIAE'. The namebatten has 'Refait par Blanchet Facteur du Roi A Paris 175[6]', but the attribution to Blanchet is modern (see Boalch). The rose is like a Ioannes Ruckers virginal rose, but is not an original casting. There are printed papers hidden in the keywell on the spine side and evidence of the former position of the nameboard and jackrail, indicating that at least the spine may have come from a Ruckers instrument. There is a fake butt joint in the bentside. The soundboard painting is a mixture of styles, with Couchet-style arabesques, and painted motifs drawn from both early Ioannes Ruckers and late Andreas Ruckers instruments.

'1629 IR'
'Ioannes Ruckers', 1629, a single-manual harpsichord, Vleeshuis Museum, Antwerp, No. VH 2138; B. 50.

This is a large single-manual Flemish harpsichord probably dating from the late seventeenth century. The original compass had fifty-eight notes, probably $G_1$ to $e^3$ (giving a $c^2$ scaling of 345mm). This was later extended in the treble to $f^3$. It has only two registers and the disposition $1 \times 8'$, $1 \times 4'$, like a normal Ruckers harpsichord. The rose is a genuine Ioannes Ruckers single-manual model, but does not belong to this instrument. Because of its large compass this is a very interesting harpsichord of a type not otherwise found in the production of the Flemish workshops.

'1632a IR'
'Ioannes Ruckers', 1632, a French double-manual harpsichord, private ownership, France (formerly J. Martinod, Paris); B. 52a.

This is another of the large French doubles from the workshop of Jean Goujon. Goujon signed the underside of the soundboard with his full name, and put his initials (IG) and the date 1757 on the original lowest key ($G_1$) of the lower manual. The soundboard is composed of ten to twenty pieces, some of them parts of a virginal, all carefully joined together, and has a Ioannes Ruckers virginal rose of the type used after 1618 (was 1632 the date of the virginal from which the rose and pieces of soundboard were taken?). The original compass was $G_1$ to $e^3$; this was later extended to $F_1$ to $f^3$.

'1632b IR'
'Ioannes Ruckers', 1632, a Flemish single-manual harpsichord by Simon Hagaerts, which has been subjected to an eighteenth-century ravalement. Instrument Museum of the Conservatoire NSM, Paris, No. E.980.2c; B. 52x.

The rose in the soundboard of this instrument is an Andreas Ruckers type with the damaged initials S and H on either side of the angel instead of those of Andreas Ruckers. Probably at the time of the ravalement the top of the jackrail was signed 'IOANNES RUCKERS ME FECIT ANTVERPIAE . 1632'. There are now two manuals with a compass of $F_1$ to $f^3$, and a $2 \times 8'$, $1 \times 4'$ disposition.

'1634 IR'
'Ioannes Ruckers', 1634, an English double-manual harpsichord, Ham House, Richmond, the property of the Victoria and Albert Museum, No. HH 109; B. 54.

An English double made in the early part of the eighteenth century. It was counterfeited to give the appearance of a genuine Ruckers double-manual harpsichord with silk-screened papers in the soundwell and keywell, and panelled marbling on the outside of the case. The keyboards have a compass of $G_1$ to $e^3$, and there are three rows of jacks with a dogleg coupler. This instrument is probably by the same builder who made the '1646 AR' single-manual harpsichord below.

'1636a IR'
'Ioannes Ruckers', 1636, a French double-manual harpsichord, The Palace of Holyroodhouse, Edinburgh; B. 57.

This is a large French double, originally with a bass compass down to $E_1$, but now with the compass $F_1$ to $f^3$. It has a beautiful chinoiserie outer decoration. The rose is the same casting (except for the letter I) as the roses in the 'n.d.a HR' (B. 25), '1637 HR' (B. 29), and '1658 HR' (B. 24); all four of these instruments were probably faked by the same person (see Plate F.2).

'1636b IR'
'Ioannes Ruckers', 1636, a French double-manual harpsichord, property of Raymond Touyère, Geneva; B. 55.

This is a fine French double with the date 1766 on the keys. In a recent restoration it was discovered to be the work of Guillaume Hemsch, brother of the better-known Henri Hemsch. It has an IR rose, a French shove coupler and action, and keyboards with the compass $F_1$ to $f^3$.

'1642 IR'
'Ioannes Ruckers', 1642, a small single-manual harpsichord, formerly the property of Wanda Landowska, now reputed to be in Belgium; B. 65.

Like many other unauthentic harpsichords, this appears to be a product of a late nineteenth- or early twentieth-century faker's workshop. It has a stand with cabriole legs of an exaggerated curvature; they and the case have applied stucco decorations in a neo-rococo style. The lid has an applied painting, and is in one single piece with a lip moulding surrounding the whole. The instrument was restored by Claude Mercier-Ythier, who reports that it is now in Belgium.

## UNAUTHENTIC 'ANDREAS RUCKERS' INSTRUMENTS

'n.d.a AR'
'Andreas Ruckers', undated, a double-manual harpsichord, property of Knud Kaufmann, Brussels; B. 134.

A double-manual harpsichord which has been much reworked. It has a compass of $F_1$ to $d^3$.

'n.d.b AR'
'Andreas Ruckers', undated, a French double-manual harpsichord, School of Design, Providence, Rhode Island; B. 131.

This is a typical late eighteenth-century French harpsichord. It has gold bands decorating the outside of the case and a stand with cabriole legs in the style of Louis XV. The compass is $E_1$ to $f^3$, a typical range for French instruments of the last quarter of the eighteenth century.

'n.d.c AR'
'Andreas Ruckers', n.d., a French double-manual harpsichord, Museo del Castello Sforzesco, Milan; B. 130a.

A large French double which seems to have been made entirely by Pascal Taskin in 1788. Except for a vaguely 'Flemish' soundboard painting and an Andreas Ruckers rose in the soundboard, no other attempt was made to counterfeit the appearance of an Andreas Ruckers harpsichord.

'1617 AR'
'Andreas Ruckers', 1617, a double-manual harpsichord, Germanisches Nationalmuseum, Nuremberg; B. 81.

A large double, heavily decorated probably in modern times. It has an Andreas Ruckers signature on the jackrail, and an 'HR' rose in the soundboard. The compass is $G_1$ to $e^3$. According to Elfrid Gleim, it may be by Hieronymus Mahieu, Brussels (about 1730).

'1621 AR'
'Andreas Ruckers', 1621, a French double-manual harpsichord, Palace Museum, Sinaia, Romania; B. 88a.

This is a French eighteenth-century double. It is signed 'ANDERIAS [*sic*] RVCKERS', and has the usual French disposition, compass and decoration.

'1622 AR'
'Andreas Ruckers', 1622, a double-manual harpsichord, Hochschule für Musik, Frankfurt am Main; B. 89.

An eighteenth-century French double using a soundboard from an earlier instrument which may have been Flemish. The present compass is $G_1$ to $d^3$, with the usual French disposition, but the soundboard has fifty plugged holes in the wrestplank, bridges and 4′ hitchpin rail, indicating an original $1 \times 8'$, $1 \times 4'$ disposition and a probable compass of $G_1/B_1$ to $c^3$. But all the usual Ruckers construction marks are missing. It was reworked by Blanchet in 1725.

'1628 AR'
'Andreas Ruckers', 1628, a French double-manual harpsichord, property of Dr Rodger Mirrey, London; B. 95.

This is a large French double, with a very elaborate decoration. It was converted into a piano, and then converted back into a harpsichord in the twentieth century. The soundboard consists of several pieces taken from seventeenth-century virginals, and the soundboard painting cleverly conceals many of the joins in the wood. The rose is a very bad casting of an Andreas Ruckers rose. The present compass is $F_1$ to $f^3$ (see Plate F.3).

'1636 AR'
'Andreas Ruckers', 1636, a double-manual harpsichord, Conservatory of San Pietro a Majella, Naples; B. 101.

This is a much-'restored' instrument, much of which is not original. It is probably of Italian construction, and bears the date 1851 on the keys, which may be when the attribution to Ruckers was faked.

'1636 AR'
'Andreas Ruckers', 1636, a French double-manual harpsichord, Marchesa da Cadaval, Colares, Portugal; B. 104.

This is a French double, reported to have been 'rebuilt' by Pascal Taskin in 1782. It has a peau de buffle register and a genouillère. The soundboard consists of pieces taken from Flemish virginals.

'1639 AR'
'Andreas Ruckers', 1639, a Flemish single-manual harpsichord, Brussels Museum of Musical Instruments, No. 3908; B. 106.

This is a Flemish single with many features that are very similar to normal Ruckers practice. It was originally a $1 \times 8'$, $1 \times 4'$ instrument with a compass of C/E to $c^3$. The original position of the 8′ $c^2$ string is

49cm from the back of the nameboard, and the soundboard construction marks are similar to those used by Ruckers. But neither the internal construction, the dovetailed case joints, nor the soundboard painting are like those usually found on Andreas Ruckers instruments. The rose is a crude casting, and bears little resemblance to a genuine Andreas Ruckers rose.

'1646 AR'
'Andreas Ruckers', 1646, an English single-manual harpsichord, the property of The Lord Tollemache, Helmingham Hall, Stowbridge, Suffolk; B. 116.

An English single which is almost certainly by the same builder who made the '1634 IR' above. The rose appears to be a genuine Andreas Ruckers rose, and the original from which the casting for the '1634 IR' rose was made. The spine and spine liner appear to have come from a Flemish instrument which was probably by Ruckers. Otherwise the instrument bears only a superficial affinity to the Ruckers normal construction practices. It has an interesting pedal mechanism which engages the registers one after the other successively, to give a sort of 'swell' effect.

## UNAUTHENTIC COUCHET INSTRUMENTS

'n.d. IC'
'Ioannes Couchet', undated, a French double-manual harpsichord, Russell Collection, Edinburgh, No. 29; B. 7 (Couchet).

This instrument appears to have been made by Goermans in 1764, and then reworked in 1783/4 by Pascal Taskin. Taskin obliterated the original signature around the rose, changed the initials in the rose from IG to IC, and stained the soundboard to make it look old. He also redecorated the case and lid, added a peau de buffle register and a genouillère, and probably passed the instrument off as a genuine Couchet double-manual harpsichord which he had modernized (see Germann (1979)).

'1669 IC'
'Petrus Ioannes Couchet', 1669, Gemeentemuseum, The Hague, No. EC 134-x-1952; B. 4 (Couchet).

Originally a single, probably with a compass of $G_1/B_1$ to $d^3$, this instrument was widened and converted into a double-manual harpsichord with a compass of C to $f^3$. There is a Couchet virginal rose in the soundboard but, other than this, there is no resemblance to any of the other Ruckers/Couchet instruments or style of building. If the instrument is indeed by Petrus Ioannes Couchet, then he was working in a tradition quite different from the other members of the Ruckers/Couchet family, and I have therefore not included this instrument among the rest of the instruments which are so clearly a part of this tradition (see footnote 2, p. 197).

Besides the above instruments, there are others which have either disappeared, have been mis-attributed, or which I have not been able to find or trace:

*Small virginals falsely attributed:*
'1617 HR' (B. 22a)
'1620 HR' (B. 12a = 23a)
'n.d. HR' (B. 26a)
'n.d. HR' (B. 26b)

*Instruments lost or destroyed:*
1614 HR (B. 20)
1637 IR (B. 58)
n.d. IR (B. 69)

*Namebattens or roses separated from their instruments:*
n.d. IR (B. 71a) Ioannes Ruckers double-manual rose and soundboard fragment.
'1634 IR' (not in Boalch) An eighteenth-century soundboard dated 1634 with a genuine Ioannes Ruckers single-manual harpsichord rose in it (private ownership, Paris).
'1619 AR' (B. 83b) namebatten.

*Instruments untraced and unseen:*

| | |
|---|---|
| n.d. HR (B. 27) | 1626 AR (B. 93) |
| 1610 IR (B. 13) | 1630 AR (B. 96) |
| 1619 IR (B. 38) | 1634 AR (B. 102) |
| 1626 IR (B. 42) | 1644 AR (B. 114 = 113?) |
| 1629 IR (B. 42) | 1655 AR (B. 120) |
| 1630 IR (B. 51) | 1656 AR (B. 121) |
| 1632 IR (B. 52) | 1659 AR (B. 122) |
| 1636 IR (B. 56 = 55a?) | 1667 AR (B. 123) |
| n.d. IR (B. 65a) | n.d. AR (B. 124) |
| n.d. IR (B. 66) | n.d. AR (B. 125) |
| n.d. IR (B. 67) | n.d. AR (B. 126) |
| n.d. IR (B. 68) | n.d. AR (B. 127) |
| 1651 IC (B. 3) (Couchet) | n.d. AR (B. 128) |
| n.d. IC (B. 10) (Couchet) | n.d. AR (B. 129) |
| n.d. IC (B. 11) (Couchet) | n.d. AR (B. 131) |
| 1619 AR (B. 83a) | n.d. AR (B. 132) |
| 1623 AR (B. 90) | |

B. 10 = B. 137 is a double-manual harpsichord by Pascal Taskin dated 1770, and is entirely the work of Taskin.

# Appendices

## 1 THE DUIM

At the time the Ruckers lived and worked in Antwerp there was no standardization of the unit of length from country to country or even from city to city. In most European centres the unit of measure was the foot (*pied, Fuss, piede* or *voet*), which was usually divided into 12 units.[1] However, in many parts of Northern Europe, the foot was divided into 11 units instead of 12. Antwerp was one such place, and there each unit dividing the *voet* or foot was called a *duim* or thumb. Edwin Ripin[2] was the first to record that the voet used by the Ruckers would have been divided into 11 duimen. He suggested that the duim would equal either 25.7mm or 26.6mm. Thomas and Rhodes[3] confirm that the Antwerp voet had 11 duimen, but suggest that one duim was equal to 25.8mm. More recently Dr Lambrechts-Douillez has given the value of one duim as 26.07mm.[4]

However, although it seems clear that the Antwerp voet did contain 11 duimen, none of the above values of the duim agrees with the actual lengths of the instruments built by the Ruckers family. For example, the average length of the single 6-voet muselar virginals is about 1708mm. This should be equal to 66 duimen, and straightforward division gives 1708/66 = 25.879mm.

Because there are a number of virginals whose length has never been altered, I have decided to use the lengths of these instruments in order to discover the length of the voet and duim being used in the Ruckers workshops. Table A1.1 shows the unaltered lengths of Ruckers virginals classified according to the type and length of each instrument.

From Table A1.1 it can be seen that, for example, for the 4-voet virginals, and for the 6-voet muselar virginals, the lengths were simply divided by the number of duimen in the nominal length of the instrument. However, for some types of instrument such as the mother-and-child virginals, the 6-voet spinett virginals, etc., the actual lengths of the instruments differed from their nominal lengths by an integral number of duimen units, and each of these has been corrected accordingly.

The average value of the duim calculated from Table A1.1 is 25.881mm. This has been rounded off to 25.88mm and used throughout this work. The corresponding value of the Antwerp voet is thus 284.7mm.

As has been shown in Chapters 5 and 6, this value of the duim gives virginal widths and other large dimensions (such as the length and width of virginal lids) which are integral or half-integral multiples of this 25.88mm unit. However, it is equally clear that many of the other distances in Ruckers virginals and harpsichords are integral multiples not of this unit, but of one slightly smaller. A careful analysis of the case heights, the width of the interior braces and framing, and the distances separating scribed lines on the baseboards of both virginals and harpsichords shows that measurements smaller than 1 voet seem to have been measured with a rule divided into duimen which were, on average, 25.477mm long. Therefore the value of the duim used for short measurements throughout this work has been taken to have a value of 25.48mm and the voet a value of 280.3mm. The 25.88mm duim I have called the long duim; the 25.48mm duim I have called the short duim.[5]

1 The English word 'inch' derives from the Old French word of Latin origin *uncia*, meaning a twelfth part. Thus we get also '*ounce*', where one Troy ounce is one twelfth of a Troy pound.

2 Edwin M. Ripin, 'The "three foot" Flemish harpsichord', *Galpin Society Journal*, XXIII (1970), 35–9.

3 W. R. Thomas and J. J. K. Rhodes, 'Harpsichord strings, organ pipes and the Dutch foot', *The Organ Yearbook*, IV (1973), 112–21.

4 Jeannine Lambrechts-Douillez, 'Aperçu historique sur la facture de clavecin à Anvers aux XVI^e^ et XVIII^e^ siècles', *La facture de clavecin du XV^e^ au XVIII^e^ siècle* (Louvain-la-Neuve, 1980), 62.

5 Many cities used a large and small unit of the same measure simultaneously. Usually this variation manifested itself in the ell used to measure cloth. For example, in Trieste the ell used to measure woollen material measured 676.75mm, whereas that used to measure silk was 642.14mm. But many other cities such as Augsburg, Cologne, Cracow, and Brussels had a large and a small foot. See *Aide-Mémoire à l'usage des officiers d'artillerie de France*, II (Paris, 1819), 896ff.

Table A1.1 *The large duim calculated from the length of unaltered Ruckers virginals*

|  |  |
|---|---|
| *6-voet muselar virginal* | |
| 1591a HR | $\frac{1711}{66} = 25.924$mm |
| 1611 HR | $\frac{1712}{66} = 25.939$mm |
| 1620 IR | $\frac{1704}{66} = 25.818$mm |
| 1622 IR | $\frac{1708}{66} = 25.879$mm |
| 1628a IR | $\frac{1708}{66} = 25.879$mm |
| 1638a IR | $\frac{1709}{66} = 25.894$mm |
| 1650a IC | $\frac{1708}{66} = 25.879$mm |
| 1620d AR | $\frac{1705}{66} = 25.833$mm |
| 1633a AR | $\frac{1706}{66} = 25.848$mm |
| *6-voet spinett virginal* | |
| 1598 HR | $\frac{1660}{64} = 25.938$mm |
| 1617 AR | $\frac{1658}{64} = 25.906$mm |
| *6-voet mother-and-child virginals* | |
| 1581 HR | $\frac{1786}{69} = 25.884$mm |
| (1591)b HR | $\frac{1711}{66} = 25.924$mm |
| (*c.* 1600) HR | $\frac{1708}{66} = 25.879$mm |
| 1623 IR | $\frac{1708}{66} = 25.879$mm |
| *5-voet muselar virginal* | |
| 1604 HR | $\frac{1424}{55} = 25.891$mm |
| 1640a IR | $\frac{1470}{57} = 25.789$mm |
| 1642a IR | $\frac{1474}{57} = 25.860$mm |
| 1643a AR | $\frac{1500}{58} = 25.862$mm |
| *4½-voet spinett virginal* | |
| 1629 IR | $\frac{1282}{49.5} = 25.899$mm |
| *4½-voet muselar virginal* | |
| 1610b AR | $\frac{1304}{50.5} = 25.822$mm |
| *4-voet spinett virginal* | |
| 1583 HR | $\frac{1143}{44} = 25.977$mm |
| 1613a AR | $\frac{1139}{44} = 25.886$mm |
| 1613b AR | $\frac{1138}{44} = 25.864$mm |
| 1620a AR | $\frac{1143}{44} = 25.977$mm |
| 1632 AR | $\frac{1136}{44} = 25.818$mm |
| *2½-voet spinett virginal* | |
| (*c.* 1610)a AR | $\frac{711}{27.5} = 25.855$mm |

Thomas and Rhodes (see footnote 3) have suggested that Douwes, when writing about the scalings and case-lengths of Flemish and Dutch clavecimbels, was using the Frieshoutvoet which was divided into 12 units instead of 11. In fact Douwes (see Appendix 8) says, 'But I should also say that such clavecimbels as are called 6-voet are not fully 6 voeten long, but are about a third of a voet shorter.' Thus for Douwes an Antwerp 6-voet virginal was about 5⅔ Frieshoutvoeten long. If he was speaking of the 6-voet virginals, which were the most common, their length would be about 1708mm. One Frieshoutvoet would then be about 1708/5⅔ = 301.4mm and the duim used by Douwes would be $^{1}/_{12}$ of this or 25.12mm. Douwes also speaks of 'a little clavecimbel of 2 voet and 4 duimen'. Using a Frieshoutvoet of 12 duimen each with a length of 25.12mm gives a length of 703mm. By way of comparison, the (*c.* 1610)a AR virginal has a length of 711mm.

These calculations seem to confirm Thomas' and Rhodes' contention that Douwes was using the 12-duimen Frieshoutvoet, and explain why an instrument which is 2½ (i.e. 2 voet 5½ duimen) Antwerp voeten long should be described by Douwes as 2 voet 4 duimen in length.

## 2 THE HAGAERTS 5-VOET SPINETT VIRGINAL

There are no existing 5-voet spinett virginals by a member of the Ruckers family. In fact very few Ruckers 5-voet muselar virginals exist: there are three instruments by Ioannes (1604 HR, 1640a IR, 1642a IR) and only one by Andreas (1643a A R). It seems fairly certain that the Ruckers would have made 5-voet spinett virginals but, considering that 6-voet spinett virginals were much less popular than the same size of muselar virginals (only one in five of the surviving 6-voet virginals is of the spinett type), it is not surprising that no Ruckers 5-voet spinett virginal has survived. However, a 5-voet spinett virginal made by Cornelius Hagaerts in 1636 is now in the Rockox House in Antwerp.[1] (See Plate A2.1.)

Like the Ruckers, Hagaerts was an Antwerp clavecimbel builder, and he lived and worked in a period contemporary with Ioannes and Andreas I and II. He entered the Guild of St Luke in 1626/27 and died on 17 June 1642.[2] Although few instruments by Cornelius Hagaerts or his son Simon exist, it seems likely that they would have made a range of instrument models similar to those made by the Ruckers.

In fact the 5-voet virginal is very similar in style to the Ruckers instruments, with papered decorations, a painted soundboard and a gilded lead rose. Like the Ruckers instruments, the Hagaerts virginal is numbered and bears the cipher 5/14. The upper part of this number indicates that we are dealing here with a 5-voet instrument (see Chapter 3). The lower part of the number indicates that this was the fourteenth 5-voet virginal made by Hagaerts. If we assume that Hagaerts began numbering his 5-voet instruments in 1626 when he joined the Guild, this amounts to a production rate of about 1.4 5-voet virginals a year. Because of the scarcity of Ruckers 5-voet instruments, it is almost impossible to compare this with the production rate of either Ioannes or Andreas.

Using the average value of the large duim obtained from the lengths of Ruckers instruments (1d = 25.88mm – see Appendix 1), 5 voeten would have a length of 5 × 11 × 25.88mm = 1423.4mm. By way of comparison the Hagaerts 5-voet spinett

[1] C. A. Bom, 'Restauratie en beschrijving van het Hagaerts virginaal, Antwerpen, 1636', *Mededelingen van het Ruckers-Genootschap*, II (Antwerp, 1982), 29–49.

[2] J. Lambrechts-Douillez and M.-J. Bosschaerts-Eykens, 'Dokumenten betreffende de familie Hagaerts', *Mededelingen van het Ruckers-Genootschap*, II (Antwerp, 1982), 11–24.

Plate A2.1 Plan view and internal view of the 1636 spinett virginal by Cornelius Hagaerts. Scale 1:10. The Rockoxhuis Museum, Antwerp, Kredietbank.

virginal is 1428mm long and the 1604 HR muselar virginal is 1424mm, showing clearly that both Hagaerts and Ruckers were using the same standard of length. The Hagaerts virginal is 477mm wide, the Ruckers virginal is 479mm wide, and both of these are very close to 18.5 duimen (18.5d = 478.8mm).

The string lengths and plucking points of the Hagaerts and 1604 HR 5-voet virginals are compared in the table A2.1 below.

The treble scalings of the Hagaerts virginal are slightly shorter than those of the Ruckers, the bass scalings slightly longer. It seems clear however that the two instruments were intended to be tuned to the same pitch, namely R + 2. The plucking points of the Ruckers muselar virginal vary from about 45% of the string length in the treble to about 35% in the bass. The plucking points of the Hagaerts spinett virginal vary from about 45% in the treble to only 10% in the bass; these figures are very similar to the Ruckers 6-voet spinett virginals (see Catalogue entry for (*c.* 1600) HR). Had a Ruckers 5-voet spinett virginal survived, it therefore seems likely that it would have had scalings, plucking points, and case dimensions which were similar to those of the Hagaerts virginal.

Table A2.1 *Hagaerts and Ruckers 5-voet virginal scalings and plucking points in millimetres*

| Note | 1636 Hagaerts spinett virginal String length | 1636 Hagaerts spinett virginal Plucking point | 1604 HR muselar virginal String length | 1604 HR muselar virginal Plucking point |
|---|---|---|---|---|
| $c^3$ | 154 | 69 | 163 | 76 |
| $f^2$ | 234 | 70 | 243 | 102 |
| $c^2$ | 318 | 83 | 330 | 148 |
| $f^1$ | 443 | 83 | 464 | 187 |
| $c^1$ | 605 | 96 | 621 | 240 |
| f | 812 | 99 | 803 | 286 |
| c | 990 | 114 | 969 | 350 |
| F | 1169 | 110 | 1156 | 397 |
| C | 1212 | 120 | 1204 | 425 |

# 3 THE 2½-VOET VIRGINAL

Douwes (see Appendix 8) refers in his stringing lists to clavecimbels 2 voet 4 duimen in length. I have recently discovered two instruments of this type, and measurement of their scalings has enabled a determination of their pitch (see below). Both of these instruments are virginals; one is by Andreas Ruckers (see catalogue entry for (*c.* 1610)a AR),[1] the other is by Georgius Britsen and is dated 1686 (Brussels Museum of Musical Instruments, No. 631).[2]

Douwes says that these instruments should have a length of 2 voet 4 duimen. The Ruckers virginal has a length of 711mm, almost exactly 27.5 duimen (27.5 duimen = 711.7mm). The instrument is therefore 2 voet 5½ duimen or 2½ Antwerp voeten in length, and not 2 voet 4 duimen. It is exactly one-half the length of the 5-voet virginals and, as will be shown below, has string lengths which were designed to be half as long as the 5-voet instruments. The reason for the length given by Douwes almost certainly arises from the unit of measure he was using. As Thomas and Rhodes have shown,[3] Douwes appears to have been using the Frieshoutvoet, with 12 duimen to the voet. If each duim was 25.1mm long (see Appendix 1, p. 285), 2 voet 4 duimen in the Friesland measure then equal 703mm, which is very close to the length of the Ruckers instrument. The length of the Britsen virginal is 753mm or very close to 29 Flemish duimen (= 2 voeten 7 duimen). Because the Ruckers virginal is almost exactly 27.5 duimen long I will always refer to these instruments as 2½-voet virginals.

The Ruckers and Britsen instruments have a great deal in common. Unlike the Ruckers '3-voet' instruments, which are always child virginals belonging to a large mother virginal, both of these virginals are completely independent instruments. They were never a part of another larger instrument – neither has a slot in the baseboard to allow the jacks of a putative mother to operate its keys. Both show traces of the original green *faux* porphyry marble exterior decoration under a layer of more recent paint, whereas the child instruments always had a papered exterior decoration which was protected inside the mother instrument. Both virginals have sloping case sides with the spine about twice as high as the front of the instrument. They both have an original lid (which the child virginals did not); the closed instrument resembles a small writing desk with the lid, supported by the sloping sides, providing the writing surface.

The scalings of the two virginals are compared in Table A3.1 below.

The right-hand bridge of the Britsen virginal consists of a curved treble section mitred to a straight bass section. The left-hand bridge is straight. The scalings produced by the resulting combination are quite accurately Pythagorean and give an

[1] I would like to express my thanks to the owners of this instrument, and to William Bright for their generous help in supplying me with information and photographs of this instrument.

[2] V. C. Mahillon, *Catalogue déscriptif et analytique du Musée Instrumental du Conservatoire Royal de Bruxelles*, No. 631, Vol. II (Ghent–Brussels, 1893–1922; facs., Brussels, 1978), 44. P. Collaer and A. van der Linden, *Historische Atlas van de Muziek* (Amsterdam, 1961); J. H. van der Meer, 'Beiträge zum Cembalobau der Familie Ruckers', *Jahrbuch des Instituts für Musikforschung Preussischer Kulturbesitz* (1971), 135.

[3] W. R. Thomas and J. J. K. Rhodes, 'Harpsichord strings, organ pipes and the Dutch foot', *The Organ Yearbook*, IV (1973), 114.

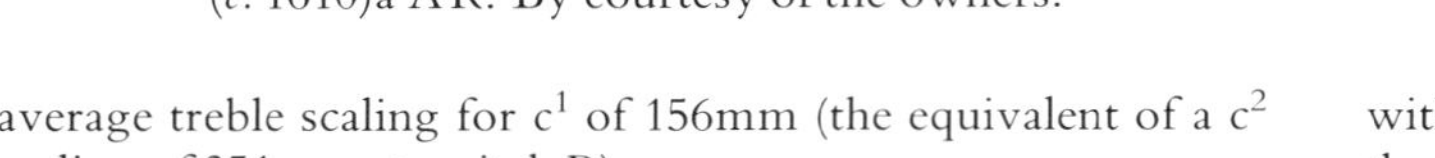

Plate A3.1 The 2½-voet virginal by Andreas Ruckers, (*c.* 1610)a AR. By courtesy of the owners.

Plate A3.2 The 2½-voet virginal by Georgius Britsen, 1686.

average treble scaling for $c^1$ of 156mm (the equivalent of a $c^2$ scaling of 351mm at a pitch R).

Because the right-hand bridge of the Ruckers virginal (like the 3-voet child virginals) consists only of two straight segments, its scalings are not accurately Pythagorean. Plotted logarithmically, the scalings of this virginal produce a graph with two curved sections each of which corresponds to one of the *straight* sections of the bridge. Because the bridge mitre occurs between $b^{\flat 1}$ and $b^1$, very near to $c^2$, and because the scalings here deviate most markedly from their theoretical Pythagorean values, the string length of $c^2$ does not give a good representation of the scalings as a whole.

Plate A3.3 The keyboard of the 1686 Georgius Britsen 2½-voet virginal. The bass and treble keytails are cranked in towards the centre of the keyboard to match the narrow spacing of the jack slots. Scale 1:5.

The scalings near $d^1$ and around $f^{\sharp 2}$ to $g^{\sharp 2}$ are longest, and therefore the strings near these notes are closest to their breaking point. Using the scalings of these notes and converting them to the equivalent length for $c^2$ gives 157.5mm.

In Chapter 4 (p. 57) it was assumed that the pitch of this type of instrument was R + 9. If this is true, then converting the above scalings to a pitch R should give values which compare with the average Ruckers scalings found in Chapter 4. Correcting for their pitch a ninth higher than R is accomplished by multiplying these scalings by 9/4. This gives an equivalent scaling for $c^2$ of 354mm for the Ruckers 2½-voet virginal. These compare with an average treble scaling of 354.8mm found for all other Ruckers virginals in Chapter 4, and confirm the pitch of R + 9.

Because of the high pitch of these instruments the scalings are necessarily very short. In particular the C/E scaling of the Ruckers instrument is shorter than the width of the keyboard from C/E to $c^3$ (650mm). Therefore there is not enough space between the bridges for the normal width of registers and jacks. The jacks and jackslots have therefore been narrowed to fit between the bridges, and the bass and treble keys are cranked in towards the middle of the instrument to line up with the jacks – see Plate A3.3. The resulting narrow spacing of the jacks corresponds to a three-octave width of only 456mm for the Ruckers virginal compared with the usual three-octave keyboard span of 500mm. Clearly it is because of the narrow spacing of the jacks that these 2½-voet instruments are not used as the 'children' of the 5-voet instruments an octave lower. Because jacks of the putative 5-voet mother instruments have the same spacing as the keys, they cannot be used to operate the tails of the 2½-voet virginals in the same way as the usual 6-voet/3-voet mother-and-child virginals.

Table A3.1 *Scalings of the two 2½-voet virginals in mm.*

| Note | Andreas Ruckers (*c.* 1610)a | Georgius Britsen (1686) |
|---|---|---|
| $c^3$ | 75 | 73 |
| $f^2$ | 114 | 112 |
| $c^2$ | 147 | 154 |
| $f^1$ | 226 | 232 |
| $c^1$ | 320 | 332 |
| f | 418 | 442 |
| c | 507 | 548 |
| F | 599 | 662 |
| C/E | 606 | 681 |

## 4 THE STRINGING OF INSTRUMENT TYPES NOT IN DOUWES

Klaas Douwes lists the gauges and stringing materials for five different types of Flemish clavecimbel (see Appendix 8). The instruments listed are all short-octave instruments, and, from the close correspondence between the case lengths of the instruments listed and the actual lengths of Ruckers virginals, it appears that Douwes had virginals specifically in mind here. However, from the similarity in string length between say, the normal short-octave single-manual harpsichord and the 6-voet virginals, it would seem that Douwes' lists could be applied to harpsichords as well. Therefore to string a short-octave single harpsichord, Douwes' list for the 6-voet clavecimbels could be used for the 8′ choir and the list for the 3-voet clavecimbels used for the 4′ choir. Similarly Douwes' list for the 4-voet clavecimbels could be used to string the unison choir of the small 4-voet harpsichords (e.g. the 1627 AR) and the octave choir of the normal short-octave double-manual harpsichords.

Notably absent in Douwes is the stringing list for the 4½-voet clavecimbels, the unison choir of the normal double harpsichord, the octave choir of the 4-voet harpsichord, and both the large double and large single chromatic-bass harpsichords. However, as was noted in Chapter 4 (see footnote 7, p. 57), the gauges used for the treble notes of the different sizes of instrument are essentially the same after correcting for the pitches of the various different types of instrument. This fact can be used to predict the treble note gauges of the instrument types not listed by Douwes, and comparison with the other instruments as close in size as possible allows the gauges of the bass notes to be estimated.

### STRINGING OF THE SHORT-OCTAVE INSTRUMENTS

From Douwes' lists it is clear that the three lowest notes, C, D and E, of the short-octave instruments are always strung with red strings (red brass), the subsequent notes from F to $c^{\sharp}$ with yellow strings (yellow brass) and the remainder from d to $c^3$ with white strings (iron). Using this and making the comparisons mentioned above, it is possible to estimate the following stringing lists:

To string the unison of a short-octave double-manual harpsichord:

|  | No. | |
|---|---|---|
| C | 0 | red |
| D E | 1 | red |
| F G | 2 | yellow |
| A $B^{\flat}$ | 3 | yellow |
| B c $c^{\sharp}$ | 4 | yellow |
| d $e^{\flat}$ e f | 5 | white |
| $f^{\sharp}$ g $g^{\sharp}$ a $b^{\flat}$ | 6 | white |
| b $c^1$ $c^{\sharp 1}$ $d^1$ $e^{\flat 1}$ $e^1$ $f^1$ | 7 | white |
| $f^{\sharp 1}$ $g^1$ $g^{\sharp 1}$ $a^1$ $b^{\flat 1}$ $b^1$ $c^2$ $c^{\sharp 2}$ | 8 | white |
| $d^2$ $e^{\flat 2}$ $e^2$ $f^2$ $f^{\sharp 2}$ $g^2$ $g^{\sharp 2}$ $a^2$ | 9 | white |
| $b^{\flat 2}$ $b^2$ $c^3$ $c^{\sharp 3}$ $d^3$ $e^{\flat 3}$ $e^3$ $f^3$ | 10 | white |

To string a 4½-voet clavecimbel:

|  | No. |  |
|---|---|---|
| C | 2 | red |
| D | 3 | red |
| E | 4 | red |
| F G | 5 | yellow |
| A B$^{\flat}$ B | 6 | yellow |
| c c$^{\sharp}$ | 7 | yellow |
| d e$^{\flat}$ e | 7 | white |
| f f$^{\sharp}$ g g$^{\sharp}$ a b$^{\flat}$ | 8 | white |
| b $c^1$ $c^{\sharp 1}$ $d^1$ $e^{\flat 1}$ $e^1$ $f^1$ | 9 | white |
| $f^{\sharp 1}$ $g^1$ $g^{\sharp 1}$ $a^1$ $b^{\flat 1}$ $b^1$ $c^2$ $c^{\sharp 2}$ | 10 | white |
| $d^2$ $e^{\sharp 2}$ $e^2$ $f^2$ $f^{\sharp 2}$ $g^2$ $g^{\sharp 2}$ $a^2$ | 11 | white |
| $b^{\flat 2}$ $b^2$ $c^3$ $c^{\sharp 3}$ $d^3$ | 12 | white |

To string the octave of a 4-voet harpsichord:

|  | No. |  |
|---|---|---|
| C | 5 | red |
| D | 6 | red |
| E | 7 | red |
| F G A | 8 | yellow |
| B$^{\flat}$ B c c$^{\sharp}$ | 9 | yellow |
| d e$^{\flat}$ e f f$^{\sharp}$ g g$^{\sharp}$ a b$^{\flat}$ b | 10 | yellow |
| $c^1$ $c^{\sharp 1}$ $d^1$ $e^{\flat 1}$ $e^1$ $f^1$ $f^{\sharp 1}$ $g^1$ $g^{\sharp 1}$ $a^1$ $b^{\flat 1}$ | 11 | white |
| $b^1$ $c^2$ $c^{\sharp 2}$ $d^2$ $e^{\flat 2}$ $e^2$ $f^2$ $f^{\sharp 2}$ $g^2$ | 12 | white |
| $g^{\sharp 2}$ $a^2$ $b^{\flat 2}$ $b^2$ $c^3$ | 13 | white |

## STRINGING THE CHROMATIC-BASS HARPSICHORDS

The stringing of the large 'French' doubles and the large 'English' singles with a chromatic bass octave poses a special problem, since Douwes lists only short-octave instruments. The string gauges must have been similar for the short-octave and the chromatic-bass instruments, since the lengths of the

Table A4.1. *Transition notes calculated for two Ruckers harpsichords (1616 HR and 1639 IR)*

| | | Transition note: Red brass to yellow brass | Transition note: Yellow brass to iron |
|---|---|---|---|
| Ruckers chromatic-bass-octave single-manual harpsichord | 4′ | E/F | d/e$^{\flat}$ |
| | 8′ | F$^{\sharp}$/G | c$^{\sharp}$/d |
| Ruckers chromatic-bass-octave double-manual harpsichord | 4′ | $B_1$/C | B/c |
| | 8′ | D/E$^{\flat}$ | d/e$^{\flat}$ |

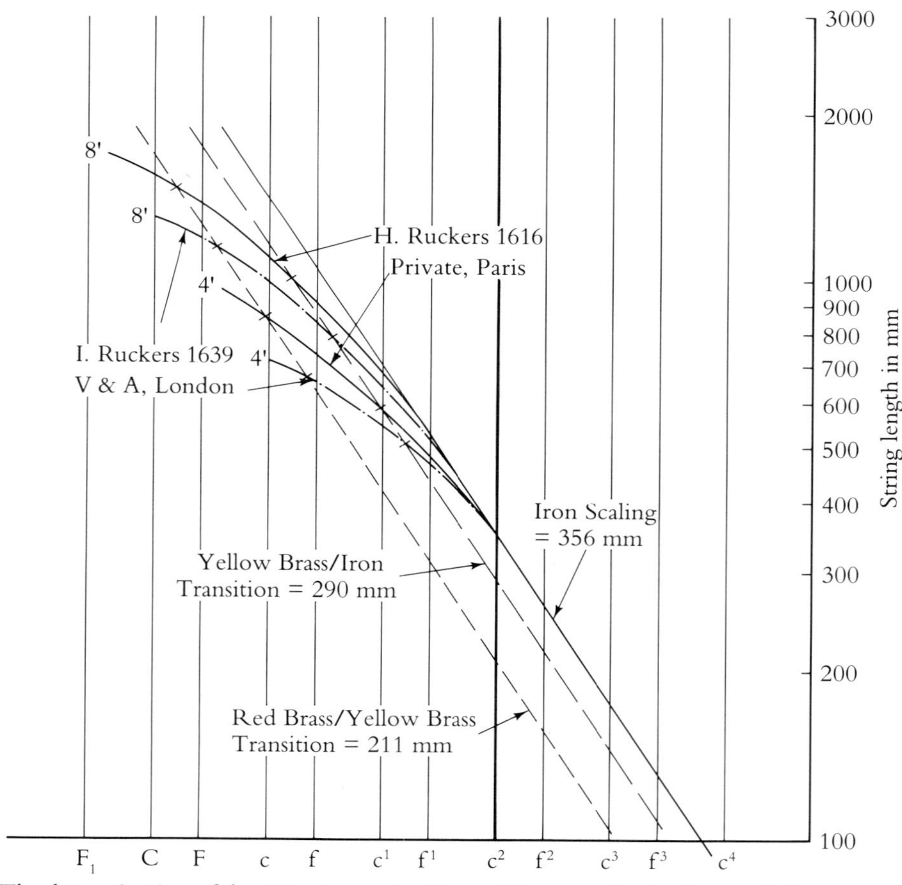


Graph A4.1 The determination of the stringing-material transition notes in the chromatic-bass-octave harpsichords.

instruments and the scalings of the two were almost identical. The problem is to decide where the transition from red to yellow brass, and from yellow brass to iron, should occur.

In Chapter 4 (p. 61) the transition scalings for the changes from red to yellow brass, and from yellow brass to iron were calculated and found to be 211mm and 290mm respectively. Graph A4.1 plots the original scalings of the 1616 HR double-manual and the 1639 IR single-manual harpsichords, each of which also originally had a chromatic bass octave. The intersection of the 211mm red/yellow brass transition line, and the 290mm yellow brass/iron transition line with the scaling curves gives the transition notes for these two instruments. These are listed in Table A4.1.

## 5 DOUWES SCALINGS AND RUCKERS INSTRUMENTS

Douwes' string-gauge lists (see Appendix 8) seem to apply to Ruckers instruments. In these lists the bottom three short-octave notes of all sizes of instrument are strung in red brass. The next notes up to $c^\sharp$ are strung in yellow brass and the notes from d to $c^3$ are strung in iron. This type of stringing plan is valid only if the scalings of a high-pitched model of instrument are derived from those of a low-pitched model by multiplying the lengths of the strings for each note by a constant factor less than unity. For example, an instrument at a pitch R + 5 would have scalings which are ⅔ of those of another at R. This would be true in the treble; if the transitions from red to yellow brass and from yellow brass to iron occur at the same played notes, then the scalings in the bass must also be different by a factor of ⅔. As was shown in Chapter 4, Ruckers instrument scalings *are* derived from one another by multiplying by a constant factor for each note throughout the entire compass.

In addition, the pitches of the instruments being spoken of by Douwes seem to be the same as those of Ruckers. Table 4.8 shows that if the stringing lists of Douwes are arranged according to the pitch differences found for Ruckers instruments, the treble notes are, in most cases, strung with strings of the same gauge, as would be expected.

Douwes' scaling lists, on the other hand, are less easy to apply to Ruckers instruments (see Table A5.1). First, the lengths Douwes gives are never listed to an accuracy greater than half a duim. Thus it is unlikely that any of the measurements are very accurate. Secondly, many of the scalings are inconsistent. Only those of the 6-voet clavecimbel are Pythagorean between $c^1$ and $c^3$; for all the other sizes, the length of $c^1$ is less than twice the length of $c^2$ (the $c^1$ scaling of the 4-voet clavecimbel is particularly short). Thirdly, the scaling ratios of the higher-pitched instruments to the 6-voet clavecimbel are not usually the expected ones (see column headed 'ratio'). For example, the scaling ratio of the 6-voet to the 3-voet clavecimbel would be expected to be 2:1, since the two are an octave apart. In Table A5.1 we see that the scaling ratio is 2.00 for $c^2$ and $c^3$ (14:7 and 7:3½ respectively). But the scaling ratio is 2.15 for $c^1$, 2.05 for c, and only 1.90 for C. If Douwes' 5-voet and 4-

Table A5.1 *Comparison of Douwes scalings with those of Ruckers instruments*

| | 6-voet clavecimbel | | | | 5-voet clavecimbel | | | |
|---|---|---|---|---|---|---|---|---|
| | Douwes | | | | Douwes | | | |
| Note | duimen | mm | (*c.* 1600) HR in mm | ratio | duimen | mm | 1604 HR in mm | ratio |
| $c^3$ | 7 | 176 | 183 | 1.00 | 6½ | 163 | 163 | 1.08 |
| $c^2$ | 14 | 352 | 367 | 1.00 | 13 | 327 | 330 | 1.08 |
| $c^1$ | 28 | 703 | 708 | 1.00 | 25 | 628 | 621 | 1.12 |
| c | 45 | 1130 | 1131 | 1.00 | 39 | 980 | 969 | 1.15 |
| C | 59 | 1482 | 1397 | 1.00 | 50 | 1256 | 1204 | 1.18 |

| | 4-voet clavecimbel | | | | 3-voet clavecimbel | | | |
|---|---|---|---|---|---|---|---|---|
| | Douwes | | | | Douwes | | | |
| Note | duimen | mm | 1613a AR in mm | ratio | duimen | mm | (*c.* 1600) HR in mm | ratio |
| $c^3$ | 5 | 126 | 117 | 1.40 | 3½ | 88 | 89 | 2.00 |
| $c^2$ | 10 | 251 | 244 | 1.40 | 7 | 176 | 178 | 2.00 |
| $c^1$ | 18 | 452 | 472 | 1.56 | 13 | 327 | 354 | 2.15 |
| c | 31 | 779 | 748 | 1.45 | 22 | 553 | 562 | 2.05 |
| C | 41 | 1030 | 921 | 1.44 | 31 | 779 | 689 | 1.90 |

The column headed 'ratio' gives the ratio of Douwes 6-voet clavecimbel scalings to Douwes scalings for the instrument in question.

voet clavecimbels have the same pitch as those of Ruckers, then the scaling ratios should be 9:8 = 1.125 for the 5-voet virginals at R + 1, and 3:2 = 1.50 for the 4-voet virginals at R + 5. The ratios of the Douwes scalings shown in Table A5.1 are near these, but vary erratically on either side of the expected values.

In order to compare the scalings listed by Douwes with those of actual Ruckers instruments we must first of all know what the length of Douwes' duim unit was. In Appendix 1 an approximate value of 25.12mm was found. Using this the lengths of Douwes' strings can be calculated; these are listed in Table A5.1. Also listed for comparison are the *c* scalings of a 6-voet, 5-voet, 4-voet and child (3-voet) virginal made by one of the members of the Ruckers family. Only here and there do the Ruckers string measurements and Douwes' scalings converted into millimetres approximate to one another. Nor can this be ascribed to the impossibility of calculating Douwes' values accurately. Douwes' C scalings are consistently much longer than those of Ruckers: the Ruckers C scalings are longer than their tenor c scalings by a factor of 1.23–1.24, whereas Douwes' C scalings are 1.28–1.41 longer than his tenor c scalings. To me this suggests that Douwes was dealing with chromatic-bass-octave instruments, rather than the Ruckers short-octave instruments.

Considering how systematic and orderly the Douwes string-gauge lists are, the scaling lists show a surprising lack of internal consistency. Douwes' lists for the 4-voet and 3-voet clavecimbels were copied by Reynvaan (see Appendix 9). But Reynvaan's lists are also very confused; he introduces some new models of clavecimbel which, from their treble scalings at least, clearly correspond to Douwes' models of a different length. What is clear is that, because of the lack of internal consistency of Douwes' scaling lists, they do not help in understanding the string plan of Ruckers instruments or of Flemish instruments in general, and should not be applied to them. It is tempting, for example, to use the short duim (= 25.48mm) to calculate the length of the 6-voet $c^2$ string length (14 duimen). This gives 356.7mm, which is very close to the average Ruckers scalings (355.0mm) found in Chapter 4. Unfortunately this apparent agreement does not then extend to the other sizes of Ruckers instruments, or even to the bass notes of the 6-voet clavecimbel: the Douwes scaling lists simply cannot be applied to the Ruckers instruments.

# 6 CLASSIFICATION OF RUCKERS INSTRUMENTS ACCORDING TO THEIR ORIGINAL STATE

## *virginals*

*6-voet spinett mother and child*
(*c.* 1600) HR

*6-voet spinett virginal*
1591a HR, 1598 HR, 1617 AR

*5-voet spinett virginal*
(no extant example known – see Appendix 2)

*4½-voet spinett virginal*
1629 IR

*4-voet spinett virginal*
1583 HR, 1613a AR, 1613b AR, 1620a AR, 1632 AR

*child (3-voet) spinett virginal*
1595 HR, 1618a IR, 1613c AR, (1626) AR, 1634 AR, 1639a AR

*2½-voet spinett virginal*
(*c.* 1610)a AR

*6-voet muselar mother and child*
1581 HR, (1591)b HR, 1610 HR, 1623 IR, 1628a IR, 1638a IR, 1644b AR

*6-voet muselar virginal*
1611 HR, (1614) HR, 1620 IR, 1622 IR, 1636 IR, 1620b AR, 1620d AR, 1633a AR, 1650a IC

*5-voet muselar virginal*
1604 HR, 1640a IR, 1642a IR, 1643a AR

*4½-voet muselar virginal*
1610b AR

## *harpsichords*

*standard single-manual harpsichords*
1627a IR, 1632 IR, (1605) AR, 1609 AR, 1618 AR, 1621 AR, 1635 AR, 1637 AR, 1639b AR, 1640a AR, 1644a AR, 1646a AR, 1648 AR, (1651)a AR, 1651b AR, 1654 AR, 1645 IC, 1671 IC

*chromatic-bass-octave singles*
1637a IR, 1639 IR, 1636 AR

*standard double-manual harpsichords*
1599 HR, 1612b HR, (1612) IR, 1617 IR, 1618b IR, 1618c IR, 1624 IR, 1627b IR, 1637b IR, 1638b IR, 1640b IR, 1642b IR, 1608 AR, 1614 AR, 1615 AR, 1620c AR, 1623 AR, 1624 AR, 1628 AR, 1633b AR, 1640b AR, 1643b AR, 1646 IC

*chromatic-bass-octave doubles*
1616 HR, 1627c IR, 1628b IR, 1646b AR

*quint single-manual harpsichord*
1627 AR

*standard single-manual harpsichord/virginal combination*
1594 HR, n.d. IR

*special single-manual harpsichords*
(*c.* 1650)b IC, 1652 IC, 1679 IC, 1680 IC, n.d. IC

*sub-quint double-manual harpsichord*
1612a HR

*standard double-manual harpsichord/virginal combination*
1619 IR

## 7 TRANSPOSITION BY A TONE IN MEANTONE TUNING

The tuning system in most common use during the Ruckers period was ordinary quarter-comma meantone. This system uses pure major thirds in the 'home' keys, and the comma is divided among four fifths – usually those between *c* and *e*, *f* and *a* or *g* and *b*. In this system the common intervals have the sizes listed below in cents: these are compared with the corresponding equally-tempered and pure intervals.

Interval sizes in cents

| | Fifth | Fourth | Major third |
|---|---|---|---|
| Equal temperament | 700.00 | 500.00 | 400.00 |
| Pure interval | 701.96 | 498.04 | 386.31 |
| Meantone interval | 696.58 | 503.42 | 386.31 |

Using the sizes of the meantone intervals above, the size of all of the other intervals can be calculated; these are listed in Table A7.1. From this it can be seen that in meantone a whole tone has a value of 193.16 cents. Adding this value to every note produces new notes a tone higher, most of which have the same value as the untransposed notes, except for e♭/c♯ and b♭/g♯: see Table A7.1.

For a double-manual harpsichord of the type discussed in Chapter 8, pp. 178–80, with two keyboards a tone apart, there would be a conflict in the tuning of the notes e♭/c♯ and b♭/g♯ in each octave. In moving from one manual to the other to effect a transposition of a tone, either one would have to retune the strings for these notes, or the instrument would have to be provided with *two* sets of doubled strings, transposing plates, etc. in each octave.

Table A7.1 *Meantone tuning and tone transposition*

| Untransposed | | Addition of one tone to pitch of | Transposed | |
|---|---|---|---|---|
| Note | Pitch | untransposed note | Pitch | Note |
| c | 0.0 | | | |
| c♯ | 76.05 | | | |
| d | 193.16 | 193.16 + 0.0 = | 193.16 | c |
| ★e♭ | 310.26 | ,, + 76.05 = | 269.21 | c♯★ |
| e | 386.31 | ,, + 193.16 = | 386.31 | d |
| f | 503.42 | ,, + 310.26 = | 503.42 | e♭ |
| f♯ | 579.47 | ,, + 386.31 = | 579.47 | e |
| g | 696.58 | ,, + 503.42 = | 696.58 | f |
| g♯ | 772.63 | ,, + 579.47 = | 772.63 | f♯ |
| a | 889.74 | ,, + 696.58 = | 889.74 | g |
| ★b♭ | 1006.84 | ,, + 772.63 = | 965.79 | g♯★ |
| b | 1082.89 | ,, + 889.74 = | 1082.89 | a |
| c | 1200.00 | ,, + 1006.84 = | 1200.00 | b♭ |
| c♯ | 1276.05 | ,, + 1082.89 = | 1276.05 | b |
| d | 1393.16 | ,, + 1200.00 = | 1393.16 | c |
| . | . | . | . | . |
| . | . | . | . | . |
| . | . | . | . | . |

## 8 KLAAS DOUWES ON CLAVECIMBELS

Source: Klaas Douwes, *Grondig Ondersoek van de Toonen der Musijk* (Franeker, 1699; facs., Amsterdam, 1970), Part 2

### CHAPTER 5, 104: ON CLAVECIMBELS

Clavecimbels[1] are musical instruments which have a very agreeable tone and are therefore usually used for pleasure and entertainment. They are best suited to play all sorts of melodies and musical pieces. There are different kinds. In some the jacks stand roughly midway between the bridges. These are the most common and are called *muselars*. In some, the jacks stand near the bridge on the left-hand side and these are called *spinetten*.

[1] *Klavecimbels* – Hubbard translates this as harpsichord. It is because the Flemish word clavecimbel or klavecimbel has a generic meaning – plucked keyboard instrument – that I have used it throughout this work. It is usually clear when Douwes means virginal and when he means harpsichord. Probably because Hubbard used 'harpsichord' here, some researchers, notably Edwin Ripin, were led to search for harpsichords specifically of the lengths listed by Douwes.

The little ones are called *scherpen* because they have a high and sharp sound. There are still other kinds which have the keyboards at one end and run to a point at the other end, and these are called *steertstukken*.[2] They come in many sizes; some *steertstukken* are 8 voeten long, some clavecimbels are 6 voeten long, some 5 voeten, some 4 voeten, some 3 voeten and some yet smaller. The pleasantness of the sound depends upon the soundboard being of the correct thinness and upon the bars under the soundboard being in the right places. The readiness of speech depends upon the strings being the correct distance from the jacks, and upon the jacks and tongues being well made. In order to have a good tone, both bridges must be positioned so that the upper octaves differ in length by half. But the lower octaves must not differ in length by half because the long strings, which are much thicker than the shorter, cannot by nature by made to stand so high in tone. And the lowest octave, where copper strings are used, could in any case not stand so high in tone. Also, the clavecimbels would have to be too long, in which all octaves doubled in length.

Therefore I shall now say the following about the length of the strings:

A six-voet clavecimbel then requires the upper string

| | | |
|---|---|---|
| that is the highest C [$c^3$], should have a length of | 7 | duimen |
| the second C from the top [$c^2$] | 14 | |
| the third C [$c^1$] | 28 | |
| the fourth C [c] | 45 | |
| the fifth C [C] | 59 | |

These lengths must be taken between the bridges, since what is beyond the bridge does not affect the sound.

A five-voet clavecimbel requires

| | | |
|---|---|---|
| that the upper C [$c^3$] should have a length of | 6½ | duimen |
| the second C [$c^2$] | 13 | |
| the third C [$c^1$] | 25 | |
| the fourth C [c] | 39 | |
| the fifth C [C] | 50 | |

A four-voet clavecimbel:

| | | |
|---|---|---|
| the first or top C [$c^3$] | 5 | duimen |
| the second C [$c^2$] | 10 | |
| the third C [$c^1$] | 18 | |
| the fourth C [c] | 31 | |
| the fifth C [C] | 41 | |

A three-voet clavecimbel:

| | | |
|---|---|---|
| the first or top C [$c^3$] | 3½ | duimen |
| the second C [$c^2$] | 7 | |
| the third C [$c^1$] | 13 | |
| the fourth C [c] | 22 | |
| the fifth C [C] | 31 | |

When all these octaves have been given the above lengths, then the other strings or notes located in between will also have the correct lengths. For a small difference [in the string lengths] is not important, since one string can be pulled a little tighter than another. This can be done easily in the tuning.

But I should also say that such clavecimbels as are called six-voet are not fully six voeten long, but are about a third of a voet shorter.

Then similarly, the 5-, 4-, and 3-voet also have not the full length, but are normally a bit shorter, which is why I have also given the length of the strings.

The notes or keyboards of clavecimbels compare with those of most organs, namely from C to C four octaves [i.e. from C to $c^3$]. But a few large harpsichords go lower to G or F [i.e. $G_1$ or $F_1$] similar to some large organs, and encompass 4 octaves and a fifth.

## CHAPTER 15, 119: WAYS AND MEANS TO STRING CLAVECIMBELS AND CLAVICHORDS[3]

For this three kinds of strings are made: red, yellow and white. The red are made from red copper, which is the weakest and softest, and are used for the lowest or deepest basses. The yellow are made of yellow copper and these are a bit harder than the red ones, and are used on clavecimbels for the bass strings which follow. The white are made of iron and are the hardest and also have a clearer sound. They are all wound upon little wooden spools, each with its number, consecutively from number 1 to number 12 – of which the first is the thickest, carrying on to the twelfth which is the finest.

The clavecimbels, which because of their pleasant sound are used mostly for enjoyment and entertainment, are strung not just with red and yellow, but mostly with white strings, since the white are clearer in tone. But the clavichords, which are mostly used for instruction in the art, have only red and yellow strings, since these do not rust as easily as the white and will therefore last much longer. The thickest are placed at the bottom in the bass where the strings are the longest, and continuing on, so that the finest come at the top in the descant as will be shown here:

To string a six-voet clavecimbel:

| | | | |
|---|---|---|---|
| C | No. | 1 | red |
| D E | | 2 | |
| F G | | 3 | yellow |
| A $B^{\flat}$ | | 4 | |
| B c $c^{\sharp}$ | | 5 | |
| d $e^{\flat}$ e f $f^{\sharp}$ g | | 6 | white |
| $g^{\sharp}$ a $b^{\flat}$ b $c^1$ $c^{\sharp 1}$ $d^1$ | | 7 | |
| $e^{\flat 1}$ $e^1$ $f^1$ $f^{\sharp 1}$ $g^1$ $g^{\sharp 1}$ $a^1$ | | 8 | |
| $b^{\flat 1}$ $b^1$ $c^2$ $c^{\sharp 2}$ $d^2$ $e^{\flat 2}$ $e^2$ | | 9 | |
| $f^2$ $f^{\sharp 2}$ $g^2$ $g^{\sharp 2}$ $a^2$ $b^{\flat 2}$ $b^2$ $c^3$ | | 10 | |

2 *Steertstukken* – tail pieces. Here it is clear that Douwes is speaking of harpsichords and not virginals.

3 The stringing lists of the clavichords have not been given, since they are not relevant here.

To string a five-voet clavecimbel:

|  | No. |  |
|---|---|---|
| C | 1 | red |
| D | 2 | |
| E | 3 | |
| F G | 4 | yellow |
| A $B^{\flat}$ | 5 | |
| B c $c^{\sharp}$ | 6 | |
| d $e^{\flat}$ e f $f^{\sharp}$ g | 7 | white |
| $g^{\sharp}$ a $b^{\flat}$ b $c^1$ $c^{\sharp 1}$ $d^1$ | 8 | |
| $e^{\flat 1}$ $e^1$ $f^1$ $f^{\sharp 1}$ $g^1$ $g^{\sharp 1}$ $a^1$ | 9 | |
| $b^{\flat 1}$ $b^1$ $c^2$ $c^{\sharp 2}$ $d^2$ $e^{\flat 2}$ $e^2$ | 10 | |
| $f^2$ $f^{\sharp 2}$ $g^2$ $g^{\sharp 2}$ $a^2$ $b^{\flat 2}$ $b^2$ $c^3$ | 11 | |

To string a four-voet clavecimbel:

|  | No. |  |
|---|---|---|
| C | 2 | red |
| D | 3 | |
| E | 4 | |
| F G | 5 | yellow |
| A $B^{\flat}$ | 6 | |
| B c $c^{\sharp}$ | 7 | |
| d $e^{\flat}$ e f $f^{\sharp}$ g | 8 | white |
| $g^{\sharp}$ a $b^{\flat}$ b $c^1$ $c^{\sharp 1}$ $d^1$ $e^{\flat 1}$ | 9 | |
| $e^1$ $f^1$ $f^{\sharp 1}$ $g^1$ $g^{\sharp 1}$ $a^1$ $b^{\flat 1}$ $b^1$ | 10 | |
| $c^2$ $c^{\sharp 2}$ $d^2$ $e^{\flat 2}$ $e^2$ $f^2$ $f^{\sharp 2}$ $g^2$ | 11 | |
| $g^{\sharp 2}$ $a^2$ $b^{\flat 2}$ $b^2$ $c^3$ | 12 | |

To string a three-voet clavecimbel:

|  | No. |  |
|---|---|---|
| C | 3 | red |
| D | 4 | |
| E | 5 | |
| F G | 6 | yellow |
| A $B^{\flat}$ | 7 | |
| B c $c^{\sharp}$ | 8 | |
| d $e^{\flat}$ e f $f^{\sharp}$ g $g^{\sharp}$ a | 9 | white |
| $b^{\flat}$ b $c^1$ $c^{\sharp 1}$ $d^1$ $e^{\flat 1}$ $e^1$ $f^1$ $f^{\sharp 1}$ | 10 | |
| $g^1$ $g^{\sharp 1}$ $a^1$ $b^{\flat 1}$ $b^1$ $c^2$ $c^{\sharp 2}$ $d^2$ $e^{\flat 2}$ | 11 | |
| $e^2$ $f^2$ $f^{\sharp 2}$ $g^2$ $g^{\sharp 2}$ $a^2$ $b^{\flat 2}$ $b^2$ $c^3$ | 12 | |

To string a little clavecimbel of two voeten and four duimen:

|  | No. |  |
|---|---|---|
| C | 4 | red |
| D | 5 | |
| E | 6 | |
| F G A | 7 | yellow |
| $B^{\flat}$ B c $c^{\sharp}$ | 8 | |
| d $e^{\flat}$ e f $f^{\sharp}$ g | 9 | white |
| $g^{\sharp}$ a $b^{\flat}$ b $c^1$ $c^{\sharp 1}$ $d^1$ $e^{\flat 1}$ | 10 | |
| $e^1$ $f^1$ $f^{\sharp 1}$ $g^1$ $g^{\sharp 1}$ $a^1$ $b^{\flat 1}$ $c^2$ $c^{\sharp 2}$ | 11 | |
| $d^2$ $e^{\flat 2}$ $e^2$ $f^2$ $f^{\sharp 2}$ $g^2$ $g^{\sharp 2}$ $a^2$ $b^{\flat 2}$ $b^2$ $c^3$ | 12 | |

Here it should be noted that it is not important within a note or two whether a string is a number too coarse or too fine. Likewise the instruments of some [makers] are strung a bit more heavily, and of others more finely. If, nonetheless, the strings are short and coarse and pulled tight, they will give a dull or dark sound. And if they are long and fine, they will give a cranky and rattling sound. Therefore the middle way is the best. Similarly, it makes very little difference if red or yellow strings are used. But the red ones can stand lower in pitch than the yellow ones. Should one require thicker strings than No. 1, one can buy annealed potter's wire as thick as one needs, ensuring that the dirt has been removed. These are very well fitted to string the lowest notes in the *Pedal*, and they have a very good sound.

## 9 'HARPSICHORD' ENTRY IN REYNVAAN'S *DICTIONARY*

Source: Joos Verschuere Reynvaan, 'Harpsichord', *Muzijkaal Kunst-Woordenboek* (Amsterdam, 1795), 111–15

### HARPSICHORD

CEMBALO or CIMBALO. (*Italian*) A clavecimbel; cymbals; also a bell or handbell, from which in Italian the clavecimbel would seem to have derived its name. It is not a *cymbal* with a keyboard, as it would seem from the way the name is written, or as it could mistakenly be taken to mean. But it is a kind of reclining *harp*, whose strings are set in motion by *jacks*, touchers or springers, which is why the English refer to this instrument by the term *Harpsichord*. Probably Guido Aretino, who is assumed to be the inventor of the clavecimbel, gave rise to the change in the position of the *harp* from vertical to horizontal, and instead of moving the strings with the fingers, they were made to speak with jacks. There are several kinds of clavecimbels, such as *staartstukken*,[1] which are the best; *vierkanten*,[2] which have the keyboard on the right-hand side and which produce a rumbling in the bass which is unpleasant and which cannot easily be prevented, since the jacks in descending divide the strings into two parts which are of such a length as to sound against one another. *Spinett* virginals, in which the keyboard is on the left-hand side, do not have this problem. The last two kinds are falling out of use. The first is called *staartstuk* because

[1] *Staartstukken* – tail pieces. It is clear that Reynvaan, like Douwes and van Blankenburg, always uses *staartstuk* to mean harpsichord and never virginal. I have therefore always translated it as harpsichord.

[2] *Vierkanten* – rectangles. Likewise, here Reynvaan always intends virginals.

at the back it ends in a point, like a tail. The second is called *vierkant* because of its oblong rectangular shape. The *virginal* has only one string to each *key*, whereas the *harpsichord* has three, which are controlled by registers in which the *jacks* stand in a grating. Two of three strings are tuned in *unison* and the third, or *octave*, is one *octave* higher than the *unison*. There are some of this type which have three *unisons* with an *octave*, and therefore four *registers*. There are also those with two *unisons* and in fact most have three *registers*. There are *clavecimbels* which encompass four *octaves*, from great C to $c^3$; five *octaves* from *contra* $F_1$ to $f^3$, which are even sometimes extended to $a^3$. Also some in between these two, with special high and low notes. Some of the *harpsichords* are eight voeten long or more, some 6 voeten, some 5 voeten, some 4 voeten, some 3 voeten, and some even smaller. At the beginning of the last century, the best clavecimbels had only 45 *keys*, in which the lowest octave consisted of the eight notes C, E, F, G, A, B♭, B and c;[3] which were shortened by weaving into one another to C, F, D, G, E, A, B♭. This is now called a short octave, but at the time it had the name 'a clavecimbel with the new enlargement', because, in the last century, they were made only down to F and up to $a^2$, in the same way that organs were once made, which were sometimes arranged as above both with and without B♭. At this time people had so little experience in *transposition* that, in order to enable them to play a piece *transposed* a *fourth* lower, a special second keyboard was made for the clavecimbel. The two keyboards had only two choirs of strings, and yet four registers. There were namely one *unison* and the *octave*, the double row of strings making the true *unison* not having yet been introduced. One of the keyboards had to remain mute when the other was being used. The lower *keyboard* stood a fourth lower than the *chamber* or *opera pitch*, and had five *keys* too many at the top. Similarly, the upper *keyboard* might have had the same superfluity of notes at the bottom, but in place of the lower *keyboard bass* notes, which might have been used, not only was [the upper] left without *keys*, but in their place a wooden block was made, and beside this a *short octave*. This was achieved with great difficulty, since the *keys*, because of the previously-mentioned entangled order, had to reach over one another crosswise. This is evidence of how unnecessary the filling out of the *bass* notes was felt to be at that time. About fifty years later, however, improvements began to be made, which happened with very little difficulty. All that had to be done was to rearrange the *keys* of the lower *keyboard*, either to $c^3$ or $d^3$. And at the lower end of the upper keyboard, in place of the wooden block, as many *keys* were added as there was space for. As a result the *keyboard*, depending on how large or small it was, was as complete as practicable. This having been done, the third row of *jacks* was lengthened slightly and cut according to the position of the topmost *keyboard*. This row of jacks could then be moved both by the top and by the bottom *keyboard*, being therefore of much better use.[4] For then one could play *piano* on the upper keyboard and *forte* on the lower one. After this, an attempt was made to add a third string, which at first turned out to be a drawback instead of an advantage. For the bridges on the soundboard were placed as far from one another as the strings could bear in order to produce the required note. Say that the top $c^3$ was 6½ duimen, then the additional $c^3$, if it were placed on the left side, would have to be 7 duimen long, because of the slope of the bridge. This is the measure of the next string, which is a semitone lower than $c^3$. This is a serious disadvantage for such harpsichords, since they could then not reach the required pitch, and the strings would be much more likely to break. In order to prevent this, the new added string must not be lengthened, but placed at the other side of the old $c^3$, or near its own *unison*. Thereby it can be improved and brought up to pitch. The beauty of the sound depends upon the soundboard being properly thin, and the bars under the soundboard being in the right place. The readiness of speech depends upon the strings being properly placed relative to the *jacks*, not too close and not too far. For if too near, the crow-quill of the jack must be too short and will remain hanging upon the strings; if too long, the quill loses its strength because of its length. And particularly, the jacks and tongues must be well made. In order to produce a good tone, both bridges must be so positioned that the upper *octaves* differ in length by one half. But the lower *octaves* must not be longer by one half, since the long strings, which are much thicker than the short ones, can *inherently* not be tuned so high. And the very lowest *octave*, which has copper strings, can in any case not stand so high. Anyway *clavecimbels* would have to be too long, if all *octaves* were to be longer by half. Therefore we should now say something about the length of the strings.

The top or highest $c^4$ [*sic*] of *an 8-voet clavecimbel* should be 7 duimen long; the second $c^2$ from the top 14 duimen; the third $c^1$ from the top 28 duimen; the fourth c from the top 45 duimen; the fifth C from the top, or the lowest, 62 duimen. These lengths must be reckoned between the bridges, since what is beyond the bridge has no effect on the pitch.

In *a 6-voet clavecimbel*, the upper or highest $c^3$ should be 6½ duimen; the second $c^2$ 13 duimen, the third $c^1$ 25 duimen, the fourth c 43 duimen, and the fifth C 60 duimen.

In *a 5-voet clavecimbel*, the upper or highest $c^3$ should be 6 duimen; the second $c^2$ 12 duimen; the third $c^1$ 24 duimen; the fourth c 40 duimen, and the fifth C 58 duimen.

In *a 4-voet clavecimbel*, the upper or highest $c^3$ should be 5 duimen; the second $c^2$ 10 duimen; the third $c^1$ 18 duimen; the fourth c 31 duimen, and the fifth C 41 duimen.

In *a 3-voet clavecimbel*, the upper or highest $c^3$ should be 3½ duimen; the second $c^2$ 7 duimen; the third $c^1$ 13 duimen; the fourth c 22 duimen, and the fifth C 31 duimen.

*The strings of the octave* are calculated in proportion to these measurements. For example, taking a 5-voet clavecimbel, since it is of medium size, the upper or highest $c^3$ is 3½ duimen, the second $c^2$ 6½ duimen; the third $c^1$ 12 duimen; the fourth c 23 duimen, and the fifth C 33 duimen.

If all these *octaves* are given these lengths, the other strings or notes which lie in between will also have their proper length,

[3] Reynvaan omits the note D. But this seems to have been a simple omission, since he includes it in the short-octave list which follows immediately in the same sentence.

[4] Reynvaan is clearly describing a dogleg register in which, by being 'cut', the jacks could be operated by either keyboard.

for a slight difference does not matter, since one string can be pulled up a bit tighter than another, which can be made good in the tuning.

But one must also take into account that those clavecimbels called 6-voet are not wholly 6 voeten in length, but about a third of a voet shorter. The same applies to the 5-, 4- and 3-voet, which also do not all have the full length, but are ordinarily somewhat shorter. The *clavecimbels* that are longer than the 6-voet run higher than $c^3$ and lower than C, and can be calculated in proportion to the data given above.

The sound of the *basses* depends mainly on the space which they have on the bridges. Therefore it is preferable that they be placed with more space than with less. Similarly, everyone will understand why the space should be in direct *proportion*, since large strings need more room than smaller ones.

The *clavecimbel* is played in essentially the same way as the *organ*. There are *harpsichords* equipped with one, and some with two *keyboards*. There are however also *virginals* which have two *keyboards*, but this second *keyboard* is in fact a special, small *clavecimbel*, a small *spinett*, which has been placed on the [large] *virginal* which has been constructed to accept it. Such types are called *de moeder met het kind* [the mother with the child].

The *keys* of the *keyboard* are played and move the *jacks*, which pluck the strings by means of crow-quills, the best [material] for this purpose. The lower strings are made of copper [alloy] and the upper ones of iron. These strings lie upon the bridges, and are stretched across the soundboard and held in place by means of small copper [alloy] pins and at the bottom by tuning pegs which can be moved for tuning.

# 10 VAN BLANKENBURG ON THE CLAVECIMBEL

Source: Quirinus van Blankenburg, *Elementa Musica* (The Hague, 1739; facs., Amsterdam, 1972), Part 1, Chapter 28, 142–6; Part 2, Chapter 7, 174

## ON THE CLAVECIMBEL

1. This instrument is not a cymbal with keyboard (as the name seems more to imply), but a reclining harp, whose strings are set in motion by means of *jacks*, that is to say touchers, which are called springers[1] in France. The instrument which tapers and becomes narrow at the end is called by us *staartstuck*,[2] but in France Clavessin.

2. It is only with this that we shall deal here. Of the virginals we will say in passing only that the type whose keyboard stands toward the left is regular and playable. These are called Spinetten. But those which have the keyboard on the right-hand side are good in the right hand, but grunt in the bass like young pigs. One cannot prevent this because the jack in falling divides the string in two parts which are of such a length that they can sound against each other.

3. At the beginning of the previous century the best clavecimbels had only 45 keys of which the lowest octave consisted of the eight notes of Guido, C D E F G A B♭ B c, which were shortened by weaving through one another thus: C F D G E A B♭. This is now called a short octave, although formerly it had the name of a clavecimbel with the new enlargement, because in the preceding century they were made only down to F and up to $a^2$, such as I have seen also on organs in my youth.

4. At that time they were so inexperienced in transposing that, in order to be able to transpose a piece a fourth lower, they made expressly a special second keyboard in the clavecimbel. This seems unbelievable, but the proof, which is very remarkable, will be confirmed, since the renowned Ruckers from the beginning of the previous century until more than thirty years after made only instruments in which, first, there were, for the two keyboards, only two strings, but nevertheless four registers (for the unison was then unknown), whereby one keyboard had to be dumb when the other was played. Secondly, the lower keyboard stood a fourth lower than organ pitch and had at the top five keys too many, so that the upper keyboard could have had the same overflow at the bottom. But instead of making the beautiful basses of the lower keyboard play, not only did they leave it without keys, but they made in their place a wooden block and next to it a short octave – and this with great difficulty since the keys, because of the recently-mentioned entangled notes, had to cross over one another. This proves how unnecessary it was to fill in the notes of the bass at that time.

5. About fifty years later these two faults began to be corrected, which took place with very little difficulty, since they only had to displace five keys in order to change *f* into *c* and to add a new octave at the bottom of the upper keyboard. Thereby the clavecimbel was given both above and below a long keyboard of 50 keys, that is, four octaves and a *b*♭ [*sic*] below the lowest c above this total. We can see the proof of this alteration by removing a wooden batten from the front of the keyboard, for we can see the new wood on the upper [keyboard], and the confusion of the numbers where Ruckers had numbered the keys on the lower keyboard.

6. Later on they undertook to add a third string. N.B.: here it must be reported that one can make a mistake instead of enjoying an advantage. For it is known that Ruckers placed the bridges on the soundboard as far from one another as ever the strings could bear if they were to attain the required pitch. Supposing that Ruckers top *c* is 6½ duimen long, then the new *c* which one has placed on its left side next to it will, because of the slant of the bridge, be seven duimen long, which is the measure of the nearby string a half tone lower than *c*. I have

[1] A jack is called a *Springer* in German, not in French.

[2] *Staartstuck* – tail piece. As in Appendices 8 and 9.

found various harpsichords which have been harmed by this lengthening, on the one hand through the breaking of strings because the instrument cannot easily stand so high, and on the other hand through the heavy weight of the strings which press too hard on the soundboard, which is harmful to the tone, as one can prove with *mutes* or by laying some lead on the bridge. Added to the above, it can sometimes happen that the bridge sinks in so low in the bass that the strings touch the octave. My advice is that one should not lengthen the Ruckers measure to seven duimen, but that one should add the new string on the other side of the above-mentioned *c*, near its own unison. This can be done without the least pressure on the soundboard. Then one should add a jack to each register, displace the whole keyboard a half-tone higher, and make a key for the string left open down in the bass, which will then be $A_1$. Thus the harpsichord will be improved in tone and can stay in tune and is enriched by the above-mentioned $A_1$, which is very useful as a fifty-first key in the place where otherwise the fiftieth is as good as useless.[3] This being done, one arranges that, by a little lengthening, the third jack is moved both by the lower and by the upper keyboard, and then the latter is no longer mute, since one can play on the upper *piano* with one string, and on the lower *forte* with three strings. But the fourth register, which stands in front, is not only useless but even a hindrance.

7. All harpsichords with two keyboards at present have three strings, so that the instrument seems now to be complete. At this point one might have asked what moved us to describe it in such detail. There are three reasons, of which the smallest is important enough to oblige us to do it. The first is that the clavecimbels (they were sold during the maker's lifetime for twenty, the small harpsichords for twelve and the virginals for six pounds Flemish) at present have reached so high a price that certain entrepreneurs have set out to abuse people by fitting to a small harpsichord – which had only one keyboard, two registers, and forty-five keys – two keyboards with the full number [of keys], and four registers of which the fourth, as was mentioned above, is useless. This one then calls a clavecimbel by Ruckers with two keyboards. But the opposite is true, for it is then a forced instrument which perhaps sounds lovely but is certainly soft in tone. One can recognize them by their breadth, which must be of fifty complete keys and a block at each end between the side-boards. The second reason concerns the large clavecimbels which some have undertaken to enlarge still further. This I have always seen to succeed very poorly. For if one, in order to place a greater number of strings on the bridge, reduces each space slightly with compasses, the clavecimbel will lose the power it had from the Ruckers because of the weight of the added strings. The tone of the basses depends particularly on the space which they have on the bridge. Therefore the clavecimbel makers should be careful to allow them too much space rather than too little. Those who will open the eyes of their understanding can see forthwith that there is no proportion in giving the large strings no more room than small ones.

8. Now we come to the third reason, which is a description of the great advantage one can enjoy from the good use of the above-mentioned superfluous jack. It will come as a surprise when we say that we can bring about by this exceptional method such wonderful and pleasant results as will give the ignorant as well as the learned the very greatest pleasure.

9. All that is necessary for this is that we give the fourth jack, which up to now has been an outcast, a more important function than the other three. This may be done by positioning it with its register one-and-a-half or two duimen from the bridge in the bass and as close to it as possible at the top. If someone wants to know what the result of this will be, let him take a writing quill and touch a string close to the bridge and then far off, and then he will hear the difference between a spinett and a round tone. This is a thing which was well known to us for years. But that one, by making such a spinett in a two-manual Ruckers clavecimbel, could generate more than a dozen fine variations of tone (such as happens with many registers in an organ) has been unknown until our time.

10. In 1708 I made a two-manual harpsichord of Ioannes Ruckers of the year 1625 function according to this discovery, and named the four registers *Spinetta*, *Unisonus*, *Cymbalum*, *Octava*, or, to use the language of organs, *Trompet*, *Bourdon*, *Prestant*, *Octaaf*. And in order to be able to take the listener by surprise more quickly through unexpected changes, we brought the stops to the front in order to be able to move them with a stroke of the hand while playing, whereby we were able to use the keyboards alternately and also together.

11. This instrument made such an impression at that time that many nobles, ministers, and even princes did me the honour of coming to hear me play on it, and being unable to understand how it was that a clavecimbel could produce such a variety of effects, asked me whether or not there was another instrument secretly hidden inside it. Whereupon I removed the bar (which covers the jacks) and showed them that it simply consisted of the four registers, and that one could as desired add a lute and a harp of new discovery which does not press the strings, without mentioning an improvement in tone which we could incorporate into the best harpsichords without affecting the soundboard.

12. In order to enjoy the fruit of a refined clavecimbel such as this, a good master would be needed to bring out the beautiful effects of all the changes and combinations of different tones. But a student who can play only what has been required of him can have some pieces specially made for him, considering that this clavecimbel is not only convenient for ordinary use, but even better for such pieces. But should someone say, where is the instrument and where are the pieces? The first we can show him at any time, and the second we can make while playing. So that here all difficulty is removed, for the student is helped at once, and meanwhile, if he is well taught, he can learn to produce similar effects from his own ideas which he can then afterwards do also on a much more beautiful instrument and even on an organ on which all imaginable changes can be found.

[3] Seemingly van Blankenburg was unaware of the $G_1/B_1$ short octave!

### CHAPTER 7, 174, PART 2

11. Further, we will also warn the student that he, in order to acquire a good judgement of the sound, should always keep his harpsichord well tuned, and also should learn to tune it himself, which is the best means of training his ear. One should be warned that this instrument is a kind of thermometer which rises and falls with the cold and warmth, so that someone who has a keen ear will be able to use it to tell if one room is warmer than another. Moreover, copper [alloy] strings drop much more through warmth than iron ones, so that when there is a change in the weather the copper [alloy] and iron strings differ with one another. One would wish that they would rise and fall uniformly. Therefore it would greatly help if they were all of copper [alloy], but since they do not sound as clear as iron in the treble, clavecimbels are seldom made in this way. There is a difference in the string lengths; a top *c* of iron is seven duimen long, but of copper [alloy] five-and-a-half duimen; an octave lower, the length of the iron string is fourteen, of the copper [alloy] eleven duimen. But the third *c* is not two times fourteen, but about twenty-five or twenty-six duimen. For here the length of the iron strings must be reduced in order to be able to place [strings of] copper [alloy] and iron next to one another at the beginning of the lowest octave. The little rectangular virginals, which are called 5-voet, are capable of being strung in copper [alloy] [strings], the lengths of which may be investigated. Furthermore, according to the greater or lesser distance between the bridges one can choose finer or coarser strings.

## 11 CONTRACT BETWEEN IOES AND GOOSEN KAREST[1]

Source: Antwerp City Archives. Notaris S. Hertogen s. (Zeger Hertoghen, senior), Prot. 1534–39, No. N2070, fos. 10r–11r

Friday 8 February 1538[2]

Master Joos[3] Karest builder of clavecimbels on the one [side] and Goosen Karest, painter, his brother on the other side, both residents of the city of Antwerp, have admitted and declared out of their own free will and knowledge, also, as they said, being unrestrained and untempted by anyone, to have concluded with one another a contract of employment or wages in the way and manner that follows. Namely that the forenamed Goosen has undertaken and arranged herewith with the forenamed master Joos his brother and admits and accepts to work with him within the same master Joos' house and nowhere else, either at painting or finishing[4] instruments, or else at whatever is within his ability, for and to the requirements of the same master Joos his brother, and not for himself nor for anyone else whoever it may be, in any way. And in order to do and fulfil the work as described above, the said master Joos shall be bound and covenanted, at his outlay and burden, to give and to pay to Goosen his brother all materials of paint and gold that for the same work he will require and utilize. But the tools and other instruments that he will use in his work, these Goosen himself must pay for, as well as his livelihood and food and this all without outlay or burden of master Joos his brother. And this for a period and a term of three years following each other consecutively having started at last Candlemas[5] and so ending at Candlemas as one shall write anno fifteen hundred and forty in the style of Brabant. And such work by the said Goosen shall be done and fulfilled during these three years: namely from Shrove Tuesday to Easter, always coming to work in the morning as soon as there is daylight, and in the evening remaining to work with candles until eight o'clock, and from Easter until mid-August always in the morning at six o'clock and in the evening as long as there is daylight, and from mid-August until Shrove Tuesday he shall come to work in the morning at seven o'clock or earlier if there is daylight, and remain working in the evening until eight o'clock with candles. In the winter he shall work in the morning until after half past eleven and in the summer until after eleven, and always, winter and summer, being back within one hour's time to work as described above. For if he does not fulfil and achieve it thus and if during these three years he loses any hours, days, weeks, months, or more time, whether it occurs from sickness, laziness, negligence or inattention, this master Joos his brother would not dare pay him for, and nevertheless he Goosen would always have to repay to the same Master Joos the lost or absented hours, weeks, months, or more time that he would have lost or have been absent, at the end of the said three years without any objection or entreaty. And for all the service of work as described above to be done by Goosen either during the said three years or possibly in the additional time that he will serve and work, master Joos his brother shall give him and such with this he promises and binds himself to do. First all workdays that he will work in the way described above, for each day six stuyvers from his own wealth and to be paid to him weekly 'work done, payment given'. And besides this remuneration of this covenanted and continuous service of work that Goosen shall do for his brother master Joos, also the latter, willing to promote his brother and to help him, so shall the same master Joos during these three years teach his brother Goosen his art of building clavecimbels of voicing and of playing them, as much as he can,

[1] I would like to thank Dr van Roey, Dr N. Meeùs and Mrs M. van Vaerenbergh for their generous help with the transcription and translation of this document.

[2] During this period the New Year began at Easter and not on 1 January, so this would now be reckoned as Friday, 8 February 1539.

[3] Joos – an alternative spelling of Ioes (see Chapter 1, p. 14).

[4] *Stofferen* – literally, to upholster. It seems likely that finishing is what is intended here.

[5] Candlemas – 2 February. By modern reckoning the contract would be binding from 2 February 1539 to 2 February 1542.

and as the same Goosen, according to his intelligence, will be able to understand and accept, and no more, and this all without the same Goosen's outlay or burden, or without for this at any time being entitled to retain or diminish anything from his earned wages or anything else. All of which the said parties have promised and promise herewith mutually and each to the other well and truly to fulfil, to pursue and to complete; and against this to say or do nothing, either by themselves or anyone else in their name in any way. And that a penalty of £12 Flemish will be charged at once to the one who will not entirely fulfil and satisfy this contract of employment; and the same penalty to be employed and distributed one-third of it in favour of the Royal Purse, and the other two-thirds to the benefit of the one who will abide by this contract in everything. And which charged penalty being paid or discharged or not, the said parties will remain indebted to each other to fulfil all that which is described above under engagement of their own selves and of their goods present and future, and notwithstanding all exceptions and legal or factual means of which each of them could make good or bad usage in any way contradicting this [contract]. And particularly the word of the law saying, etc.[6] The whole without treachery. In knowledge of the truth, the parties have demanded and admitted to each other that two public instruments with the same contents should be made of this [contract], of which both have signed with their own hand the one of the other. So done at Antwerp at the house of my notary called the Red Cross, etc. Present Niclaes de Voocht, draper, and Niclaes van Gheldere, merchant, both residents of the said city called and bidden as witnesses thereto, etc.

S. Hertoghen

[6] The consequences and meaning of this incomplete statement would presumably have been understood by the signatories to the document, and also by other notaries.

## 12 REGULATIONS OF THE GUILD OF ST LUKE PERTAINING TO THE CLAVECIMBEL BUILDERS

Source: Léon de Burbure, 'Recherches sur les facteurs de clavecins et les luthiers d'Anvers', *Bulletins de l'Académie Royale de Belgique*, 2$^{me}$ série, XV/2 (1863), 10–16

We, Jan van Immerseele, knight, Lord of Boudries, etc, sheriff of the City of Antwerp, and margrave of the land of Ryen, and we, burgomasters, aldermen and councillors of the abovementioned City of Antwerp, make known and certify as the strict truth, that Masters Joos Carest, Marten Blommesteyn, Jacop Theeuwes, Aelbrecht Van Neeren, Hans the organ maker, Christoffel Blommesteyn, Ghoosen Carest, Jacop Aelbrechts, Marten Van der Biest and Lodewyck Theeuwes, all clavecimbel makers, resident within this City, have unanimously made known to us by petition that they recently met and communicated with the deans, jurors and elders of the Guild of St Luke of this place, and having discussed and agreed with the same, that they, the petitioners were all willing and prepared to enter the said Guild, if they were to be granted and permitted the following points and articles which they had jointly drawn up and which are set out below, so that, among them and their successors in the making of clavecimbels and similar musical instruments, there should be order and policy, such as exist among the other trades and guilds of this City. This being so, the forementioned deans, jurors and elders of the said Guild, realizing that the said points and articles had a bearing upon the ordinances and franchises of us forementioned, dare not co-opt the forementioned petitioners freely into their guild without the previous consent and ordinances on our part; as a result of which the same petitioners and along with them the forementioned deans, jurors and elders of the said Guild of St Luke, unanimously and in all humility and reverence, prayed and desired of us that we, taking everything into account should, to the advancement and gain of the said Guild, consent to the abovementioned course, and in so doing agree to the wishes of the petitioners and those to come after them, and grant them and their successors the following points and articles, and to embody these in the proper form.

Having considered the above petition and the points it puts forward, and being inclined to grant the petitioners' desire, and considering also that the same points seem reasonable, we have granted, agreed and conferred the following:

1. In the first place, that the abovementioned petitioners shall be bound to appear together immediately before the said Guild of St Luke, and each to swear a suitable oath and also to pay the usual fees.

2. Furthermore, that the same petitioners, as free masters and guild brothers of the said Guild, within this City and its Liberties, shall remain free and unhindered to carry out their abovementioned trade of making and selling clavecimbels and similar musical instruments, as was their wont before, without having to make a test piece.

3. Furthermore, that these same petitioners and also their successors as clavecimbel makers shall be freely received into the said Guild, shall enjoy and use all such privileges and liberties as the said Guild now enjoys and later may obtain, in all ways and manners as the other masters and brothers of the Guild are wont to, and shall enjoy, in conformity with the ordinances and privileges now existing and at a later date to be promulgated.

4. It is to be understood that in future, after the said petitioners have been freely admitted as clavecimbel makers into the said Guild of St Luke, only such may be admitted as have made by hand and completed the following test piece, and that at the house of one of the aftermentioned assessors, who will have to provide him with all the necessary materials and tools, viz. a virginal or a harpsichord, five feet long or thereabouts, or

longer should he so desire, well and truly wrought, in the correct shape and proportions, and in accordance with its nature being sound in tone and properly quilled and strung.

5. Furthermore, the above-prescribed test piece having been completed, it will have to be brought to the chamber of the said Guild, where the prescribed assessors, in the presence of the deans and jurors of the said Guild and of two or three free clavecimbel makers, shall inspect and test the same, and declare upon oath whether or not the test piece has been made in accordance with the prescribed articles, and declare truthfully and without deceit whether he who made it should be accepted as a free clavecimbel maker in the said Guild.

6. Furthermore, should the abovementioned test piece be passed, then the assessor, in whose house it has been made and who has provided the required materials and tools, shall have and retain the same [clavecimbel] for his materials and trouble, without having to give or to pay anything to the workman who made it for his labour.

7. And should [the test piece] not [be passed], the workman who made it shall have to remove it and pay for and make good the materials and tools the assessor has provided.

8. Furthermore, that every year the deans and jurors of the said Guild of St Luke shall, from among the clavecimbel makers, choose and ordain two suitable and able assessors, who shall be bound to examine test pieces and testify upon them in a way conforming to the manner above laid down and upon the oath which they shall have sworn to that end.

9. Furthermore, that in future no one within this City and its Liberties shall be entitled to carry on the trade of making clavecimbels or similar musical instruments and afterwards sell them, unless he be first freely admitted into the said Guild of St Luke, having paid the usual fees and performed the prescribed test, upon pain of fine and forfeit, and any who will be found to have contravened this ordinance, for each occasion shall be fined the sum of six Guilders Carolus, to be divided in three parts, one third to the sovereign, one third to the City, and one third to the abovementioned Guild.

10. Furthermore, that each free clavecimbel maker of this City shall be bound and liable to place in each musical instrument made by him his own mark, signature or [coat of] arms, and that in the most obvious place, before he sells it or distributes it, upon pain of a fine of two Guilders Carolus, to be levied for each instrument he should have sold contrary to this ordinance, and [the fine] to be paid in three parts as aforesaid.

We reserve the right to ourselves and our successors, in office at any time, to add to, delete from, interpret, increase, diminish or change any point in this ordinance as may be deemed fit and suitable without fraud or ulterior motive. In good faith have we, sheriff and we, burgomasters, jurors and councillors forementioned, appended the seal of business of the forenamed City of Antwerp to this writ, on the 28th day of March, in the year of Our Lord 1557, in the style of Brabant.

[signed] Van Assiliers

## 13 'HARPSICHORD' FROM THE *ENCYCLOPÉDIE*

Source: D. Diderot and J. le R. d'Alembert, 'Clavecin', *Encyclopédie ou dictionaire raisonnée des arts, sciences et métiers*, VIII (Lausanne and Berne, 1780–2), 231–4

The best harpsichords that have been made up to now for the beauty of their tone are those of the three Ruckers (Hans, Ioannes and Andreas) as well as those of Ioannes Couchet, who, all working in Antwerp in the previous century, made an immense quantity of harpsichords, of which a very large number of originals are found in Paris, and recognized as such by true connoisseurs. One finds makers in our time who have copied and counterfeited the harpsichords of the Ruckers. The exterior can be misleading, but the tone quality always exposes the fraud. Nevertheless the incomparable harpsichords of the three Ruckers and of Couchet, as they have come from the hands of these masters, are absolutely useless today, since these great artists, who understood the tonal part superbly well, have succeeded very badly from the point of view of the keyboard. Besides this all these Flemish harpsichords are so small that the pieces or sonatas which are written today cannot be played on them. This is why they undergo a *grand ravalement*, giving them sixty-one keys in place of the fifty which they used to have. Moreover, in place of the 100 strings (because most of the harpsichords of the Ruckers were made with only two strings per key) they have been given 183 strings by adding a *grand unisson*, by which means the tone becomes even more manly and majestic.

It is in the art of enlarging the harpsichords of Ruckers that the late Blanchet has succeeded incomparably well. In order to achieve this he had to cut them on the treble side and on the bass side, to enlarge and even lengthen the whole case of the harpsichord, and finally to add some old sonorous fir,[1] the most even-grained that it is possible to find, to the soundboard to give it its new width and length. The wrestplank is completely remade in these sorts of harpsichords, which, all things considered, retain from their original state only the soundboard and about two-and-a-half feet of the right case-side. The accessory parts, such as the keyboards, jacks, registers, now are much more accurate and precise than they were made by the Flemish masters of the

[1] *Sapin* = fir. It is unclear whether Diderot is using *sapin* to mean literally fir, or whether he is using the word in a more generic sense to mean softwood, i.e. fir, spruce or pine. The Ruckers and Couchets used spruce for their soundboards, but many French makers used fir (*Abies alba*). The woods are notoriously difficult to distinguish except microscopically. Perhaps some French makers did add fir to the already existing spruce soundboard wood in the ravalement process.

previous century. A harpsichord by the Ruckers or by Couchet, artistically cut and enlarged, with jacks, registers and keyboards by Blanchet, has become today a very precious instrument.

The usual price of harpsichords simply and appropriately painted, coming from the hands of the maker, and made by an artist of Paris, would today be five to six hundred *livres*. For the best one pays seven hundred *livres*, but this only if the tone is so velvety that it approaches the beauty of the Flemish harpsichords about which we have just spoken.

## 14 THE PREPARATION OF BONE FOR KEYBOARDS

Source: Dom Bedos de Celles, *L'art due facteur d'orgues*, II (Paris, 1766–78) Chapter 3, 249–50

700. All these operations having been done, one puts the plates on the upper surface of the front of the [key]board. These plates are made from bone, or of black ebony. Plates of bone are preferable for the keyboards of organs, because this material is harder and lasts much longer. The bone used is from the legs of beef. The bone is sawn up, and one makes the strips the size of the keys. They are sold in Paris ready made at three sols each; but in the provinces if one is not able to get them from Paris, one is obliged to make them oneself. They are roughed out with the saw and with a file. Before they are finished, one whitens them in the following way.

701. One puts into a large pot a piece of quicklime the size of a fist, which one dissolves with a little water. The lime having become inactive, and reduced to a paste, one adds little by little almost two pints or three or four pounds of water. One adds to this a little ground alum. All this having been well mixed, one adds the bones. The pot is set on the fire and when it has boiled at the most two or three minutes, one removes the pot from the fire. The water having lost a little of its great heat, one gently removes all of the scum. It is allowed to cool entirely, and one removes the bones which one washes with fresh water. One lets them dry very slowly in air that is not too warm. If they are allowed to dry too quickly or in the sun, they will crack. It must be said that if one lets the bones boil for longer than the time I have given above, they will burn or calcify, and one has then spoiled the lot.

## 15 RUCKERS INSTRUMENTS SOLD IN PARIS SALES DURING THE EIGHTEENTH CENTURY

Source: Eugène de Bricqueville, *Les ventes d'instruments de musique au XVIII^e^ siècle* (Paris, 1908), 7–16[1]

A virginal by Ruckers, in the form of a long table.

Large virginal by Andreas Ruckers, and another smaller one which can be placed on the first to give two keyboards, 300 livres, 24 July 1771.

A harpsichord by Ruckers with paintings by Rubens, 3 July 1752.

A harpsichord by Ruckers, decorated with paintings by the Gobelins, on a gilt ground and with hinges also of gilt ormolu, 10 August 1752.

Very beautiful harpsichord in true lacquer *à ravalement*,[2] in a very good state, 24 August 1752.

Harpsichords by Ruckers, 13, 17, 20 July 1752.

Harpsichord by Ruckers *à ravalement* in old lacquer, 21 May 1753.

A harpsichord by Ioannes Ruckers. The stand and the case are completely gilt, and the inside is decorated with paintings in the style of Watteau, 13 August 1753.

An excellent harpsichord by A[ndreas] Ruckers. It is very old and in a good state, 12 November 1753.

Harpsichord by Ruckers with a marquetry stand. It has been made by Boule the father, with gilt ormolu ornaments and with beautiful paintings, 1753.

A harpsichord by Antoine[3] Ruckers with two keyboards and *à grand ravalement*. It is well painted and in a good condition. The price is 50 louis.[4] 3 October 1754.

A harpsichord by Ruckers newly painted, 7 October 1754.

A beautiful harpsichord by Ruckers with keyboards by Blanchet. It is *à grand ravalement*. The soundboard is from 1588. Parnassus is painted on the inside by a good master. The stand is carved and gilt. 17 April 1755.

A harpsichord by Ruckers painted by Oudry, 26 March 1755.

A harpsichord by Ruckers decorated by Martin;[5] two others also decorated by him and made by Ruckers are also on sale, 5 November, 20 November, 15 April 1755.

Harpsichord by Couchet, 25 louis, 24 February 1755.

1 Only the instruments by or attributed to Ruckers are listed here.
2 *À ravalement* – that is, with a compass greater than 4 octaves, C to $c^3$. A five-octave compass, $F_1$ to $f^3$, is called *à grand ravalement*.
3 Presumably Andreas is meant here, since no Antoine (Antoon in Flemish) is known among the members of the Ruckers clavecimbel builders.
4 One louis = 20 livres.
5 *Vernis martin* – a type of rich furniture decoration in which the object is gilt over its whole surface and then painted with flowers, animals, grotesques, strapwork, etc.

Very beautiful harpsichord by Ruckers, painted by Watteau, 11 March 1756.

Harpsichord by Ioannes Ruckers, painted by Rubens, 3 May 1756.

An excellent small harpsichord 3½ feet long with two keyboards, made by H. Ruckers in 1620.[6] It is ideal for carrying into the country, or for storing in a closet. The price is 150 livres. 27 August 1759.

Very beautiful harpsichord by Andreas Ruckers on an extremely rich stand of Boule marquetry. The paintings are by Patel. 18 October 1759.

A harpsichord by Ruckers decorated by Martin. Price: 300 livres. 31 December 1759.

An excellent harpsichord 7 feet 3 inches long made by Andreas Ruckers in 1601,[7] painted black and gold with decorations in the Chinese taste. A Bacchanalia is painted on the interior by Coypel. Those knowledgeable have valued it at 3,000 livres. It is being offered for 2,000. 29 December 1760.

Harpsichord by Ruckers, 400 livres, 4 March 1761.

Harpsichord by Andreas Ruckers, painted black with gold bands, and a gilt stand. 350 livres. 15 July 1762.

Harpsichord by Ioannes Ruckers, decorated by Martin. Exactly 1,800 livres. 5 September 1763.

Excellent harpsichord by Andreas Ruckers of 1608; *à grand ravalement* and keyboards by Blanchet. Decorated with very fine paintings inside and out, with a carved and gilt stand. 2,400 livres. 23 May 1765.

Harpsichord by Ruckers, 25 louis, 1780.

Very good harpsichord by Ruckers, 600 livres. 19 October 1780.

Harpsichord by Andreas Ruckers, rectangular, with two [choirs of] strings (Duchess of Lorges), 28 May 1767.

An excellent harpsichord, a masterpiece of Ruckers, containing a virginal richly ornamented, and decorated with a scene by Watteau representing a concert of animals. 30 December 1767.

One harpsichord by Ruckers, 30 louis, 27 April [1775].

Harpsichord by Ruckers with a stand of gilt ebony. 1 March 1766.

Excellent double-ended harpsichord by Ruckers, rectangular in shape with 4 keyboards, nicely painted. 1,000 livres. 2 May [1768].

Harpsichord by Ruckers, 400 livres. 10 March [1768].

Harpsichord by Ruckers at 600 livres.

Harpsichord by Ioannes Couchet of Antwerp, having 5 notes more than the keyboards *à grand ravalement*[8] and with all of its bass strings in gilt silver, 1,000 livres. It has been valued at 3,000. 10 September 1772.

Harpsichord by Ruckers with keyboards by Blanchet, and painted in *aventurine.*[9] 15 February 1773.

Very fine harpsichord by Ruckers, completely gilt and painted in miniatures with a scene inside, 24 June [1773].

Harpsichord by Ruckers, 30 louis, 24 June [1773].

Harpsichord *à grand ravalement* made in 1612 by Ruckers, superbly painted by van der Meulen, decorated with bronzes. It has been put in order by the celebrated artist Pascal Taskin. It contains 4 registers, of which one is a peau de buffle invented by this maker. It comprises 6 movements which one changes with the knees without the need to lift the hands from the keys, to give a piano, a forte and a crescendo in the cleanest, most sensitive manner.[10] Price: 260 louis in cash, from M. de la Chevardiere, music master, rue du Roule. 23 January 1777.

Excellent harpsichord by Ruckers with a virginal in the same soundboard, 12 May [1777].

Harpsichord by Ruckers of a new type producing [the effect of] the flute, the oboe and the vox humana. All by a Fleming newly arrived in Paris. From M. Goermans, harpsichord and harp merchant, rue de Limoges. 5 February 1778.

Harpsichord by Andreas Ruckers made in 1606 with a fine virginal by the same maker which it contains; paintings by Watteau and superb gilding. The stand is completely gilt, price, 100 louis. It has been valued at 4,000 [livres?] two years ago. There are no repairs necessary. Enquiries at the Hotel de Novioa, rue de la Planche, 20 December 1778.

Harpsichord by Andreas Ruckers [1630], 4,000 livres. 1 January 1778.

Harpsichord by Andreas Ruckers at 25 louis. 1 January 1778.

Harpsichord by Andreas Ruckers at 1,000 louis,[11] valued at 2,000. 12 November [1778].

Harpsichord by Ruckers decorated by Martin. 24 October [1779].

Harpsichord by Ruckers, decorated in gold with figures by Audran. 24 November [1779].

Harpsichord by Couchet, newly remade and given *à grand ravalement* compass by P. Taskin, with precious paintings and a foot mechanism to change the registration in from 10 to 12 ways (death of M. Demarville, receiver general of finances, rue du Sentier).

6 No double-manual harpsichord by the Ruckers exists which is 3½ pieds (= 1137mm) in length and it seems likely that this was a fake. This seems to be confirmed by the date, 1620. Hans Ruckers could not have made this instrument, since he died in 1598. And since Ioannes Ruckers never used the HR rose after 1616, it seems likely that this harpsichord was given an HR rose and dated 1620 by some disreputable person who did not realize this fact.

7 This instrument was also probably a fake. Its length (7 pieds 3 pouces = 2355mm) is about 10cm longer than the average Ruckers double. Also, we know that Andreas Ruckers was working with his brother Ioannes as late as 1604 (see catalogue entry for 1604 HR) when they used an HR rose. Therefore an instrument dated 1601 and bearing an Andreas signature and Andreas rose is immediately liable to suspicion.

8 Literally, with five notes more than an $F_1$ to $f^3$ compass – perhaps $C_1$ to $f^3$? Or was this perhaps one of the large extended-compass harpsichords of Ioseph Ioannes Couchet?

9 *Aventurine* – a kind of lacquer decoration where the paint is strewn with flakes of gold.

10 This seems to be a contemporary description of the '1612 HR' five-octave double-manual harpsichord, rebuilt by Taskin in 1774 (Brussels Museum of Musical Instruments, No. 3848, Boalch No. 17). It has paintings by van der Meulen on its case, and seems once to have been equipped with a genouillère.

11 1,000 louis = 20,000 livres! This is the highest price asked for a harpsichord, or for any other type of instrument, in these lists.

Harpsichord by Ruckers *à grand ravalement* with 4 registers, a peau de buffle, and a mechanism which produces a crescendo and diminuendo. From M. Schneller, harpsichord maker, Marché des Enfants Rouges. 10 January.

Excellent harpsichord by Ruckers *à grand ravalement* with keyboards by Blanchet, newly painted in green with gold bands, 1,500 livres from M. le Normant d'Étoiles, rue du Sentier. 14 June.

Old harpsichord by Ruckers, 50 louis, 19 November.

# 16 GERBIER–WINDEBANK CORRESPONDENCE CONCERNING A RUCKERS HARPSICHORD

Source: W. Noël Sainsbury, *Original Unpublished Papers Illustrative of the Life of Sir Peter Paul Rubens* (London, 1859), 208–10

### BALTHAZAR GERBIER TO SIR FRANCIS WINDEBANK

Right honnorable:

Brussels, Jan. 20/30, 1637–8.

The Virginall I do pitch upon is an excellent peece, made by Johannes Rickarts att Antwerp. Its a dobbel staert stick as called, hath foure registers, the place to play on att the inde. The Virginal was made for the latte Infante, hath a faire picture on the inne side of the Covering, representing the Infantas parke, and on the opening, att the part were played, a picture of Rubens, representing Cupid and Psiche, the partie asks £30 starling. Those Virginals w$^{ch}$ have noe pictures cost £15: – Y$^{r}$ hon$^{r}$ will have time enuf to consider on the sum, cause I can keepe the Virginal long enuf att my house.

I take my leave & rest

Yo$^{r}$ hon$^{rs}$, &c.,
B. Gerbier.

### SIR FRANCIS WINDEBANK TO BALTHAZAR GERBIER

Sir: Westminster, February 2, 1637–8.

In a lr̃e a part yo$^{u}$ are pleased to give me a testimony of yo$^{r}$ care of my privat little businesse concerning the Virginall, for w$^{ch}$ I retourne y$^{u}$ my most affectionat thankes.

If the Instrument, for sounde & goodnesse, be right, I do not much respect the accessories of ornament or paintings, & therfore if y$^{u}$ can meete w$^{th}$ a very good one plaine & w$^{th}$out these curiosities, I shold rather make choice of such a one. But I will advise w$^{th}$ y$^{r}$ good frende & myne Mr. Norgat, whose skill in these businesses is excellent, & then I will take the liberty to acquaint y$^{u}$ w$^{th}$ my further desires. Presenting my true love to yo$^{u}$ & making it my suite to y$^{u}$ to use me as freely, as by yo$^{r}$ many civilities you have obliged me to be (S$^{r}$)

Y$^{r}$ most faithful true servant
Fran. Windebank.

On the 2nd of March Windebank writes to Gerbier to send the Virginall mentioned in his former letter, if as good for use and music as he represented it to be for show, and he will give satisfaction for it whensoever he shall appoint.

### SIR FRANCIS WINDEBANK TO BALTHAZAR GERBIER (Extract)

S$^{r}$: Westminster, July 20, 1638.

The Virginall, w$^{ch}$ yo$^{u}$ sent me, is com safe, and I wish it were as usefull as I know yo$^{u}$ intended it. But the workman, that made it, was much mistaken in it, and it wantes 6 or 7 Keyes, so that it is utterly unserviceable. If either he could alter it, or wolde change it for another that may have more Keyes, it were well: but as it is, our musick is marr'd. Neverthelesse, I am exceedinglye behoulding to y$^{u}$ for it and do acknowledge as many thankes to be due to y$^{u}$, as if it had bene the most exquisit peece in the worlde. In that quality I beseeche yo$^{u}$ (S$^{r}$) com̃aunde

Yo$^{r}$ most faithfull and obliged
true frende to serve yo$^{u}$,
Fran. Windebank.

### BALTHAZAR GERBIER TO SIR FRANCIS WINDEBANK (Extract)

Brussels, July 23/Aug. 7, 1638.

Right Honnorable:

I have y$^{r}$ honors letter to me of 20/30 July, to which I have no more to say but that I must take patience, the Virginall proves not according expectation; Iff y$^{r}$ honor causeth the same sent to me agayne well conditioned and a just measure of the keyes desired annother Virginall to be; I will cause this to be sould as itt can, and annother made forthw$^{th}$ by Mr. Rickaerts, the same and the best master here, who saith this Virginall cannot be altered, and none elce made here on saille.

Humbly take my leave and rest yo$^{r}$ hon$^{rs}$, &c.,
B. Gerbier.

On 3 August, 1638, Windebank writes to Gerbier from Haines Hill. 'For the Virginall I desire yo$^{u}$ not to trouble y$^{r}$self, seeing the fault was myne that did not give better instruction.'

# 17 CORRESPONDENCE BETWEEN G. F. DUARTE AND CONSTANTIJN HUYGENS[1]

Source: J. A. Worp, *De Briefwisseling van Constantijn Huygens (1608–1687)*, IV (The Hague, 1915), 465, 477, 486, 488

Sir, I have received your honour's pleasant [communication] of the 27th of February, to which I should like to reply concerning the discourse of the large clavecimbels[2] with *one* full keyboard from G sol re ut [$G_1$]. Your honour will be pleased to know that the nephew of the late Joannis Rukarts, one Couchet by name, who worked with his uncle for sixteen years and whom I have found to be of a much more studious spirit, which my instruction has greatly helped, with investigations unheeded by the abovementioned uncle, such as rapid playing of the keys. One should investigate even the large instruments to make them obey promptly so that the subtleties and delicacies are discovered, and as well as these the length of the quills, keyboards and jacks as well as the sweetness of the tone, the thickness and length of the strings, all of which would take too long to explain. The extreme length of the large clavecimbels is 8 voeten more or less, the pitch Chorista, with 3 registers – that is, three different strings of which 2 strings are at unison and one at the octave and all three of which can be played together or each string separately, with or without the octave, like the ordinary clavecimbels that your honour mentions. But they have a better tone because the unused string which is not played moves of its own accord, producing such a sweet quiet tone through the principal sound, which does not occur when all three strings are played together. The second unison string is then somewhat sharper in sound than the other, which also causes a pleasant sweetness because of its being a large straw-breadth longer than the other. The virtue of the instruments arises also from the strings being slacker, thinner and longer rather than being thick, so that with these 3 strings one may play in five or six different ways, and yet these may be so soft in touch as a small clavecimbel, wherein lies the greatest art which very few masters know. So much concerning the large instruments, of which so far four have been made, the last being the best. They were sold for about 300 gulden and afterwards 20 or 30 less, so that one should have them made expressly. Now concerning the small harpsichords with unison or with an octave, each of which has its own beauty. They are usually one tone higher, and are of my invention of a few years ago. They are used in small chambers for playing courantes, allemandes and sarabandes. If your honour should desire to command of me in this or in any other things, I will prove that I am, Sir, your honour's humble servant,

In Antwerp, the 5th of March
1648 G. F. Duarte.

Sir, I have received your honour's very pleasant [communication] of the 27th of the previous month of April, and I have understood well your honour's desire for a harpsichord with a unison and a full keyboard, like that of Mrs Swan,[3] but of a length of that which Mr Couchet has sent to a certain Pater[4] by name, and about which I have often spoken with the same Couchet by often calling at his house, as he likewise often comes to mine. Now as regards the same sounding two tones lower than that of Mrs Swan, this can hardly be and it is neither the fashion, nor is it fit for any concert of voices. But there is the natural pitch of this land which one calls *Chorista*, and this is just one tone lower than that of Mrs Swan, serving for normal voices, while that of the same lady serving for extraordinarily good voices singing very high, and to play allemandes and courantes. At this same pitch I have tried four or five as well as my own clavecimbel like an organ at *Chorista*, which is of the correct pitch. And that is how your honour's must be, and it must also be somewhat longer than that of Pater. I have also recently discovered that each of the first strings of the two [unisons], which sounds sharp, should be played by the second jack, and the other string, which is somewhat more inclined by the front jack, which gives a quite different quality, which we have only recently tried out with a harpsichord. Lift the jackrail of Pater's harpsichord, and consider for yourself when a note is plucked and your honour shall clearly understand my meaning, such things and others more subtle taking too long to write out,

[1] Gaspard Duarte was an immensely wealthy diamond merchant and banker in Antwerp (he sold most of the stones used at the wedding of the Prince of Orange to Princess Mary of England). Although he seems to have been rather pompous and self-important, he was nevertheless a good musician and a man of letters. He owned a sumptuous mansion on the Meir in Antwerp, just a short distance from the workshops of Rubens and Couchet. Both the Prince of Orange and Huygens were among the many dignitaries who were guests at his home.

Constantijn Huygens was a man of state, a poet, a scholar, a scientist, a polyglot – he wrote excellent Latin, Greek, German, English, Italian, Spanish, French (the normal court language of the Stadhouder), as well as his native Dutch/Flemish – and an accomplished musician. In 1647 he published a collection of his own music in Paris. He was a tireless writer and correspondent. He exchanged letters with Mersenne, Descartes, Chambonnières, J. L. Guez de Balzac, and with ambassadors and the aristocracy at the courts of England, France, Flanders, Spain and Holland. He wrote letters to Henri du Mont, and to de la Barre, court musician to Louis XIII. Huygens was a champion of Chambonnières, and it was he who sent some of Chambonnières' music to Froberger in 1649. Huygens' favourite instrument was the lute, but he was also very proud of the fact that his new harpsichord was by Couchet, the builder of Chambonnières' instrument.

[2] *Clavesinglen* – from the rest of the correspondence it is clear that Duarte is referring to a harpsichord here.

[3] Lady Utricia Swann, née Ogle. Her father was Major Sir Thomas Ogle, who saw service in the Low Countries under the Stuarts. She was married to Sir William Swann, a man of letters and lover of music, who was a Royalist at the time of the Commonwealth. Lady Swann was a good singer and a pupil of Huygens.

[4] I have not been able to discover who Pater was.

and having not been studied by other masters. This must be by reason of very rapid playing to which the ordinary instruments will hardly respond. Your honour may always freely command me, without ceremony, and you will always find me ready to be, Sir,

In Antwerp, the 3rd of May 1648 — Your honour's humble servant G. F. Duarte.

Sir, I have received your honour's very pleasant [communication] of the 13th in which you express your thanks for the favours your honour's son is supposed to have heard here from us, which anyway does not conform to your honour's great merits and the obligation that I have to serve your honour. The clavecimbel will be ready this week with a unison and of the lowest ordinary *Chorista* pitch which one makes, a full keyboard extending down to ef fa ut [$F_1$] and up to the cadence of la sol re [$d^3$]. I don't doubt that your honour will be pleased with the lid which is left white inside, as is the part under the strings, and the front above the keys, which all can be painted according to your honour's wishes. The yellow border piece all around and the jackrail will be gilt this week. I hope that I shall be able to get to your honour's before your departure for Cleves, where I would ask your honour to deliver my humble greetings to My Lady the Princess of Orange,[5] for the honour which I received from Her Majesty. And I will always remain, Sir,

In Antwerp the 19th of July 1648 — Your honour's humble servant G. F. Duarte.

P.S. It is a great pleasure to me to understand that I will have the distinction to see your honour here this summer, which I should greatly esteem.

Sir, This shall serve only to let your honour know that the clavecimbel is now made, has a very sweet and lovely harmony, and has been much praised by all the music lovers. Mr Couchet has put his utmost ability into it, principally in the keyboards which are very delicate for two large strings. It should be sent to your honour tomorrow or the day after. It cannot be given for less than 30 pounds Flemish. Its length is 8 voeten. I would have said 28 pounds Flemish, but one must keep him satisfied. Your honour's acknowledgement of receipt, as well as your opinions about it will be eagerly received. I remain as always, Sir,

In Antwerp the 30th of July 1648 — Your honour's humble servant G. F. Duarte.

[5] Mary, Princess of Orange, later joint Monarch of Great Britain with William III.

## 18 LETTER FROM IOANNES COUCHET TO CONSTANTIJN HUYGENS

Source: J. A. Worp, *De Briefwisseling van Constantijn Huygens (1608–1687)*, IV (The Hague, 1915), 489

Considerate Sir, whom I have not met, this is to let your honour know that I have made your honour this clavecimbel according to your honour's order, that is with a unison at the proper pitch and a keyboard of ef fa ut [$F_1$]. The lower octave has also been made according to Mr Duarte's wish. This is the first that I have made in this way. Your honour should be aware that if your honour had paid 100 Pattekons, your honour would not have paid a stijver too much as regards the skill placed in it and the resonance it has. Your honour should take care over the person who will tune it, whom I understand to be Mr Pater your honour's friend and who is just now in Brussels and has not yet heard it. I expect him back to my house any day now. [Tell him] that he should always tune it to the correct pitch, wherefore your honour has a little flute, to which the gi sol re ut [probably $g^1$] should be tuned. In this way your honour will always hear the resonance perfectly, because if it stands too low or too high, then the resonance is impaired and is not correct, as it was intended. If this is done honour will result from my work. I don't have any doubt that your honour will be completely satisfied with it, of which I await a letter giving your reply, and your honour's pleasure and also [to know] if everything is according to your honour's wish. Moreover, if the occasion should ever arise again, that I should have to make another for a music lover, I would advise him to have the same type made with an octave; that would be my wish. This goes quicker and sharper than the unison, it is sweet and lovely in sound, then your honour would hear the difference. I have made one with the octave, and the same keyboard [compass] but a tone higher, and with an octave instead of a unison. It is still in Antwerp; Mr Duarte goes almost every week to visit the music lover and to hear his clavecimbel. And if he could get it out of his hands, he would not linger about long. I now have to make one for him.

Herewith, (I send) hearty greetings and commend you to God.

Your servant
Jan Couchet, clavecimbel maker.

# 19 OBITUARY POEM BY CONSTANTIJN HUYGENS ON THE DEATH OF IOANNES COUCHET

Source: J. A. Worp, *De gedichten van Constantijn Huygens naar zijn handschrift uitgegeven*, Vol. V (Groningen, 1895), 189 (for the year 1655).

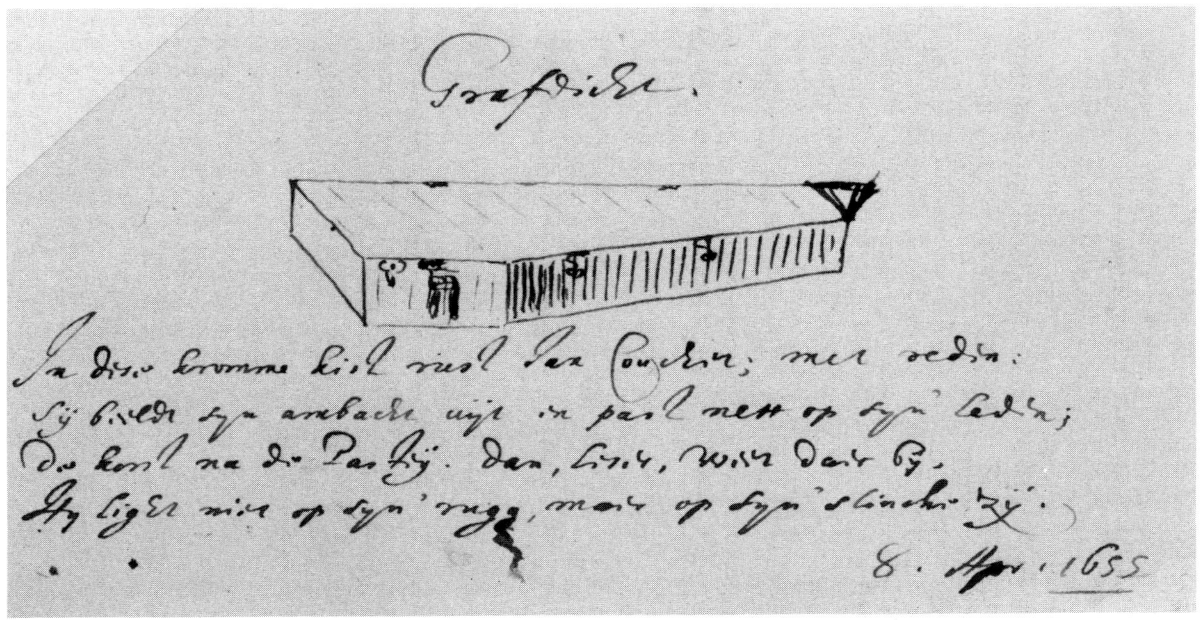



Grafdicht

In dese kromme kist rust Ian Couchet; met reden:
Sij beeldt syn ambacht uijt en past nett op syn' leden;
De korst na de Pasteij. Dan, leser, weet daer bij,
Hy light niet op syn' rugg, maer op syn' slincke zij.

8 Apr.

Obituary

In this crooked box rests Jan Couchet; for a good reason:
It shows his craft, and fits his shape exactly –
The crust fits the filling. Then, reader, know from this,
He lies not on his back, but on his left side.

8 April [1655]

Huygens noted the death of Ioannes Couchet in his *Dagboek* or diary on 2 April 1655.[1] A letter to Henri du Mont, composer and organist of the church of St Paul, in Paris, which he wrote on 6 April 1655, reads in part:[2]

As I finish off this letter, I have learned by post from Antwerp that the celebrated Couchet has passed away there. This is a signal waste to the dedicated [who are] interested in good clavecimbels. It is a comfort to me that I own one of the last of his invention with two keyboards[3] and made by him, like that of M[onsieur] de Chamboniere [*sic*]. It is quite excellent, and I don't believe that anyone will make another like it following [the death of] poor Couchet, which I greatly regret . . .

Two days later, on 8 April, Huygens wrote this curious epitaph to Couchet. Both the drawing and the poem are interesting. The instrument which Huygens draws as Couchet's coffin is clearly, from the position and number of the register projections on the cheek side, a single-manual two-register

[1] From the Antwerp archives, it appears that Couchet actually died on 4 April 1655. See J. Lambrechts-Douillez and M.-J. Bosschaerts-Eykens, 'De familie Couchet', *Mededelingen van het Ruckers-Genootschap*, V (Antwerp, 1986), 4.

[2] W. J. A. Jonckbloet and J. P. W. Land, *Musique et musiciens au XVIIe siècle* (Leiden, 1882), 24–5.

[3] Huygens surely means two *registers* here! Couchet himself says that the harpsichord he was sending to Huygens was disposed 2 × 8′, and I cannot imagine how only two registers would be disposed in a double. Huygens' sketch is clearly of a single, and nowhere else in the correspondence is a double-manual harpsichord mentioned.

harpsichord. It would seem almost certain that this is a sketch of Huygens' own Couchet harpsichord, which had a 2 × 8′ disposition, as we have seen from Couchet's letter to Huygens in the previous appendix. The poem then tells us that although a normal coffin would not have suited Couchet's shape, a harpsichord case would have fitted round his body like a pie-crust round its filling. My interpretation of this is that Couchet was a hunchback, or at least very stooped. With his feet down in the tail of the harpsichord case, his bent shape would have fitted into the keyboard end with his body lying on its left side.

If this is indeed the correct interpretation of Huygens' epitaph, it provides the only evidence we have of the physical appearance of any of the members of the Ruckers/Couchet family.

# Select bibliography


Abondance, Pierre, *see* Robin, Michel.

van Acht, Rob, and Scheurwater, Wouter. 1977. *Oude Klavecimbels: Hun Bouw en Restauratie. Old Harpsichords: their Construction and Restoration*, The Hague, 1977.

Adam, Alastair T. 1925. *Wire-Drawing and the Cold Working of Steel*, London, 1925.

Aide-Mémoire. 1819. *Aide-Mémoire a l'usage des officiers d'artillerie de France*, II Paris, 1819.

d'Alembert, J. le R., *see* Diderot, D.

Apel, Willi. 1969. *Pieter Cornet: Collected Keyboard Works*, ed. Willi Apel, Corpus of Early Keyboard Music, 26, 1969.

1972. *The History of Keyboard Music to 1700*, Bloomington, Ind.–London, 1972. Translation of *Geschichte der Orgel- und Klaviermusik bis 1700*, Kassel, 1967.

Appuhn, Horst. 1966. *Kloster Isenhagen: Kunst und Kultur im Mittelalter*, Lüneburg, 1966.

1976. *Riesenholzshnitte und Papiertapeten der Renaissance*, Unterschneidheim, 1976.

Bakeman, Kenneth. 1974. 'Stringing techniques of harpsichord builders', *The Galpin Society Journal*, XXVII (1974), 95.

Barnes, John. 1965. 'Pitch variations in Italian keyboard instruments', *The Galpin Society Journal*, XVIII (1965), 110–16.

1966. 'Two rival harpsichord specifications', *The Galpin Society Journal*, XIX (1966), 49–56.

1968. 'Italian string scales', *The Galpin Society Journal*, XXI (1968), 170–81.

1969. 'Some restoration problems in the Russell Collection', *Studia Musico-Museologica: Bericht über das Symposium: Die Bedeutung, die optische und akustische Darbietung und die Aufgabe einer Musikinstrumentensammlung*, Nuremberg–Stockholm, 1969, 117–25.

1971a. 'The Flemish instruments in the Russell Collection, Edinburgh', *Colloquium: Restauratieproblemen van Antwerpse Klavecimbels*, Antwerp, 1971, 35–9.

1971b. 'The specious uniformity of Italian harpsichords', *Keyboard Instruments: Studies in Keyboard Organology*, ed. Edwin M. Ripin, Edinburgh, 1971, 1–10.

1973. 'The stringing of Italian harpsichords', *Der klangliche Aspekt beim Restaurierung von Saitenklavieren*, ed. Vera Schwarz, Graz, 1973, 35–9.

1979. 'Bach's keyboard temperament', *Early Music*, VII, 2 (1979), 236–49.

1980a. 'Does restoration destroy evidence?', *Early Music*, VIII, 2 (1980), 213–18.

1980b. 'Instruments, restoration of', *The New Grove Dictionary of Music and Musicians*, ed. Stanley Sadie, 9, London, 1980, 254–5.

Barnes, John; O'Brien, G. Grant; Ripin, Edwin M.; and Schott, Howard. 1980. 'Harpsichord', *The New Grove Dictionary of Music and Musicians*, ed. Stanley Sadie, 8, London, 1980, 216–46.

Baudouin, Frans. 1977. *P. P. Rubens*, Antwerp, 1977.

Bédard, Hubert. 1971. 'Report on the restoration of the virginal by J. Couchet, 1650', *Colloquium: Restauratieproblemen van Antwerpse Klavecimbels*, Antwerp, 1971, 41–3.

1977. 'Harpsichord of 1644 by Andreas Ruckers: on putting it in playing condition', *Colloquium: Ruckers Klavecimbels en Copieën*, Antwerp, 1977, 109–18.

Bedos de Celles, Dom François. 1766–78. *L'art du facteur d'orgues*, Paris, 1766–88.

Bemetzrieder, Anton. 1771. *Leçons de clavecin, et principes d'harmonie*, Paris, 1771.

Benade, A. H. 1976. *Fundamentals of Musical Acoustics*, Oxford, 1976.

Benton, Rita. 1962. 'Hüllmandel's article on the clavecin in the *Encyclopédie Méthodique*', *The Galpin Society Journal*, XV (1962), 34.

Berger, K. 1976. *Theories of Chromatic and Enharmonic Music in Late 16th Century Italy*, Ann Arbor, Mich., 1976.

Berner, Alfred. 1950. 'Zum Klavierbau im 17. und 18. Jahrhundert: Kongressbericht', *Gesellschaft für Musikforschung* (1950).

1971. 'Der Ruckers-Bestand des Berliner-Musikinstrumenten-Museums: Bemerkungen zu den Konstruktionen',

*Colloquium: Restauratieproblemen van Antwerpse Klavecimbels*, Antwerp, 1971, 53–62.

Berner, Alfred, van der Meer, J. H., and Thibault-de Chambure, G. 1967. *Preservation and Restoration of Musical Instruments*, London, 1967.

Bessaraboff, Nicholas. 1941. *Ancient European Musical Instruments: An Organological Study of the Musical Instruments in the Leslie Lindsey Mason Collection at the Museum of Fine Arts, Boston*, Cambridge, Mass., 1941.

Besseler, Heinrich. 1959. 'Umgangsmusik und Darbietungsmusik im 16. Jahrhundert', *Archiv für Musikwissenschaft*, XVI, 1/2 (1959), 21–43.

van Blankenburg, Quirinus. 1739. *Elementa Musica*, The Hague, 1739; facs., Amsterdam, 1972.

Bliss, D. P. 1964. *A History of Wood-Engraving*, London, 1964.

Blunt, Wilfrid. 1950a. *Flower Books and their Illustrators*, Exhibition Catalogue, Cambridge, 1950.

1950b. *The Art of Botanical Illustration*, London, 1950.

Boalch, Donald H. 1956/74. *Makers of the Harpsichord and Clavichord, 1440–1840*, London, 1956; 2nd edn, Oxford, 1974. (All references in this book are to the 1974 edition.)

Boddington, Henry, *see* Pyne, James Kendrick.

Boerlin, Paul-Henry. 1962. 'Das Virginal des Andreas Ryff von 1572', *Zeitschrift für Schweizerische Archäologie und Kulturgeschichte*, XXII, 1/3 (1962).

Bosschaerts-Eykens, M.-J., *see also* Lambrechts-Douillez, Jeannine. 1983a. C. Verkoop van Ruckers-instrumenten in de 18[de] eeuw', *Mededelingen van het Ruckers-Genootschap*, III, Antwerp, 1983, 31–2.

1983b. 'Situering van de belangrijkste ateliers in de 16[de], 17[de] en 18[de] eeuw', *Mededelingen van het Ruckers-Genootschap*, III, Antwerp, 1983, 33–6.

Boston, J. L. 1954. 'An early virginal-maker in Chester, and his tools', *The Galpin Society Journal*, VII (1954), 3–6.

Bragard, Roger, and de Hen, Ferdinand. 1968. *Musical Instruments in Art and History*, London, 1968.

Bran-Ricci, Josianne. 1980. 'Clavecin à deux claviers, 1646', *Cinq années d'enrichissement du patrimoine national, 1975–1980*, Paris, 1980, 138.

de Bricqueville, Eugène. 1908. *Les ventes d'instruments de musique au XVIIIe siècle*, Paris, 1908.

Bridgman, Nanie, and Lesure, François. 1961. *Collection musicale André Meyer*, Abbeville, 1961.

Broadwood, James Shudi. 1862. *Some Notes Made by J. S. Broadwood, in 1838, with Observations by H. P. Broadwood*, London, 1862.

Bruni, A. 1890. *Un inventaire sous la terreur. État des instruments de musique, relevé chez les émigrés et condamnés*, Paris, 1890.

Buchner, Alexander. 1956. *Musikinstrumente im Wandel der Zeiten*, Prague, 1956.

de Burbure, Léon. 1863. 'Recherches sur les facteurs de clavecins et les luthiers d'Anvers, depuis le seizième siècle jusqu'au dix-neuvième siècle', *Bulletins de l'Académie Royal de Belgique*, 2me série, XV, 2, Brussels, 1863, 1–32.

Burney, Charles. 1771. *The present State of Music in France and Italy*, London, 1771.

1773. *The Present State of Music in Germany, the Netherlands and United Provinces*, Vol. 2, London, 1773.

1775. *The Present State of Music in Germany*, London, 1775.

Butsch, Albert Fidelis. 1969. *Handbook of Renaissance Ornament: 1290 Designs from Decorated Books*, New York, 1969.

Byrne, Maurice. 1966. 'A pitch for 1774', *The Galpin Society Journal*, XIX (1966), 136.

Catalogue 1. 1903. *Catalogue of Keyboard Musical Instruments in the Crosby Brown Collection*, New York, 1904.

Catalogue 2. 1904. *Catalogue of the Crosby Brown Collection of Musical Instruments of all Nations: I: Europe*, New York, 1904.

Catalogue 3. 1909. *Illustrated Catalogue of the Music Loan Exhibition held by the Worshipful Company of Musicians at Fishmongers Hall, June and July 1904*, London, 1909.

Catalogue 4. 1927. *Sale Catalogue of the Brownsea Castle, Brownsea Island, Dorset*, Seventh day of sale, Tuesday 21 June 1927, Musical Instruments and Armour and Arms.

Catalogue 5. 1941. *Catalogue of the Boston Museum of Fine Arts*, Cambridge, Mass., 1941.

Catalogue 6. 1949. *Collection of the Cincinnati Art Museum: Musical Instruments*, Cincinnati, 1949.

Catalogue 7. 1961. *V. Festival Gulbenkian de música: Exposição internacional de instrumentos antigos: Catalogo*, Lisbon, 1961.

Catalogue 8. 1962. *Catalogue of the exhibition 'Île de France–Brabant'*, Sceaux, 1962.

Catalogue 9. 1967. *A Checklist of Keyboard Instruments at the Smithsonian Institution*, Washington, D.C., 1967; rev. 1973, 1975.

Catalogue 10. 1967. *Treasures from Scottish Houses: 21st Edinburgh International Festival*, Edinburgh, 1967.

Catalogue 11. n.d.. *Catalogus Oudheidkundige Musea Vleeshuis Stad Antwerpen: V: Muziekinstrumenten*, Deurne–Antwerp, n.d.

Cervelli, M. Luisa. 1959. 'Italienische Musikinstrumente in der Praxis des Generalbass-Spiels: Das Arpichord', *Bericht über den siebenten internationalen Kongress, Köln, 1958*, Kassel, 1959, 76–8.

1976. 'Per un catalogo degli strumenti a tastiera del Museo degli Antichi Strumenti Musicali', *Accademie e Biblioteche d'Italia*, XLIV 4–5 (1976), 305–43.

Cervelli, M. Luisa, and van de Meer, J. H. 1966. 'Conservato a Roma il più antico clavicembalo tedesco', *Palatino: Rivista Romana di Cultura*, X, 3–4, Rome, 1966, 265–8.

de Chambure, *see* Thibault, G.

Chouquet, Gustave. 1875/1884. *Le Musée du Conservatoire National de Musique: Catalogue raisonné*, Paris, 1875; 2nd edn, 1884. (Pillaut, L., *1[er] supplément au catalogue de 1884*, Paris, 1894.)

Clapham, Michael. 1957. 'Printing', *A History of Technology, Volume III: From the Renaissance to the Industrial Revolution, c. 1500–1750*, Oxford, 1957, 377–410.

Clark, J. Bunker. 1974. *Transpositions in Seventeenth Century English Organ Accompaniments and the Transposing Organ*, Detroit, 1974.

Clayson, Richard, and Garrett, Andrew. 1981. 'Harpsichord by Hans Ruckers the Younger dated 1612: Workshop report on the restoration completed in October 1981', unpublished restoration report, Lyminge, Kent, ?1981.

Clerici, Fabrizio. 1946. *Allegorie dei sensi di Jan Brueghel*, Florence, 1946.

Closson, Ernest. 1905. 'La facture des instruments de musique en Belgique: Clavecins et pianos', *Le guide musical*, LI, 45 (1905), 703–7.

1908. 'Les Ruckers', *Biographie national*, col. 381–6, 1908.

1911. 'Quelle est l'année de la mort de Hans Ruckers, le vieux?' *Le guide musical*, LVII, 38–9 (1911), 571–2.

1932. 'L'ornementation en papier imprimé des clavecins anversois', *Revue Belge d'archéologie et d'histoire de l'art*, II (1932), 105–12.

1935, *La facture des instruments de musique en Belgique*, Brussels, 1935.

Clutton, Cecil. 1952. 'Arnault's MS', *The Galpin Society Journal*, V (1952), 3.

Clutton, Cecil, and Hodson, Alec. 1947. 'Defining the virginal', *The Musical Times*, LXXXVII (1947).

Collaer, Paul, and van der Linden, Albert. 1961. *Historische Atlas van de Muziek*, Amsterdam–Brussels, 1961.

Conand, Robert. 1963. 'The Yale collection of instruments', *The Consort: Journal of the Dolmetsch Foundation*, XX (1963).

Connoisseur. 1916. *The Connoisseur*, XLV (1916), 169.

Cooper, Francis M. C. 1972. 'The Leckingfield proverbs', *Musical Times*, CXIII (1972), 547–9.

Correa de Arauxo, Francisco. 1626/1948. *Libro de Tientos . . .* Vol. 1, Alcala, 1626; Monumentos de la Música Española, VI, ed. Santiago Kastner, Barcelona, 1948.

Curtis, Alan. 1960/61. 'Dutch harpsichord makers', *Tijdschrift van de Vereniging voor Nederlands Muziekgeschiedenis*, XIX, 1/2 (1960/61), 44–6.

1969. *Sweelinck's Keyboard Music*, Leiden–London, 1969.

Dale, William. 1913. *Tschudi: The Harpsichord Maker*, London, 1913; reprint, Boston, Mass., 1978.

Denis, Jean. 1643. *Traité de l'accord de l'espinette*, Paris, 1643; facs., New York, 1969; English translation, J. Panetta, Jr., Cambridge, 1987.

Denucé, J. 1941. *Het Vleeschhuis*, Antwerp, 1941.

Diderot, D., and d'Alembert, J. le R. 1751–65. *Encyclopédie ou dictionnaire raisonnée des arts, sciences et métiers*, Paris, 1751–65; and later editions: Geneva, 1778; Amsterdam, 1780; *Supplément*, Amsterdam, 1776–77; Lausanne–Berne, 1781.

van Dijck, Lucas, *see* Koopman, Ton.

Doerner, Max. 1949. *The Materials of the Artist and their Use in Painting*, London, 1949.

Douillez, *see* Lambrechts-Douillez, J.

Doursther, Horace. 1965. *Dictionnaire universel de poids et mesures anciennes et modernes*, Amsterdam, 1965.

Douwes, Klaas. 1699. *Grondig Ondersoek van de Toonen der Musijk*, Franeker, 1699; facs., Amsterdam, 1970.

Dowd, William R. 1978. 'A classification system for Ruckers and Couchet double harpsichords', *Journal of the American Musical Instrument Society*, IV (1978), 106–13.

1984. 'The surviving instruments of the Blanchet workshop', *The Historical Harpsichord*, I, ed. Howard Schott, New York, 1984, 17–108.

Dufourcq, Norbert. 1946. *La musique des origines à nos jours*, Paris, 1946.

Eckstein, D., Wazny, T., Bauch, J., and Klein, P. 1986. 'New evidence for the dendrochronological dating of Netherlandish paintings', *Nature*, CCCXX (3 April 1986), 465–6.

Eisenberg, Jacob. 1962. 'Virdung's keyboard illustrations', *The Galpin Society Journal*, XV (1962), 82.

Ellis, A. J., *see* Mendel, Arthur.

*Encyclopédie méthodique*, *see* Framéry, Nicolas-Étienne.

*Encyclopédie ou dictionnaire raisonnée des arts, sciences et métiers*, *see* Diderot, D.

Ernst, Friedrich. 1955. 'Der Flügel Johann Sebastian Bachs', *Ein Beitrag zur Geschichte des Instrumentenbaus im 18. Jahrhundert*, Frankfurt am Main, 1955.

1962. 'On harpsichord building in former times,' *Glareana*, XII, 1/2 (1962).

1964. 'Historische Tasteninstrumente im Frankfurter Besitz', *Das Musikinstrument*, XIII (1964), 126–8.

1967. 'Four Ruckers harpsichords in Berlin', *The Galpin Society Journal*, XX (1967), 63–75.

1969. 'Master Arnold Rucker', *The Galpin Society Journal*, XXII (1969), 35–9.

Fétis, François-Joseph. 1860–65. *Biographie universelle des musiciens et bibliographie général de la musique*, 8 Vols., Paris, 1860–65.

Finlay, Ian F. 1953. 'Musical instruments in 17th-century Dutch paintings', *The Galpin Society Journal*, VI (1953), 52–69.

Floetner, Peter. 1549. *Das Kunstbuch des Peter Floetner*, Zurich, 1549; facs., Berlin and Leipzig, 1882.

Ford, Charles. 1979. *Making Musical Instruments, Strings and Keyboards*, London, 1979.

Framéry, Nicolas-Étienne, and de Ginguené, Pierre-Louis. 1791/1818. *Encyclopédie méthodique*, 2 Vols., Paris, 1791/1818; see 'Musique', and 'Clavecin', and Vol. II, pp. 285–9.

Franciolini, Leopoldo, *see* Ripin, Edwin M., 1974a.

Fuchs, Leonhart. 1543. *New Kreüterbuch*, 1543; facs., Leipzig, 1939.

Führer. 1938. *Fürhrer durch das Musikhistorische Museum Neupert in Nürnberg*, Nuremberg, 1938.

Fuller Maitland, J. A., and Squire, W. Barclay, eds. 1899/1963. *The Fitzwilliam Virginal Book*, 2 Vols., Leipzig, 1899; New York, 1963.

Gallay, J. 1890. *Un inventaire sous la terreur. État des instruments de musique relevé chez les émigrés et condamnés*, Paris, 1890.

Gallini, Natale and Franco. 1963. *Museo degli Strumenti Musicali: Catalogo*, 2 Vols., Milan, 1963.

Galpin, Francis W. 1927. 'Ruckers', *Grove's Dictionary of Music and Musicians*, 4, 3rd edn, 1927; also 4th edn, 1940, and Supplementary Volume, 1940.

1937. *A Textbook of European Music and Instruments*, London, 1937.

1965. *Old English Instruments of Music: Their History and Character*, 4 Vols., London, 1965.

Gargiulo, Terenzio. ?1972. *Conservatorio de Musica S. Pietro a Majella*, ?Naples, ?1972.

Garrett, Andrew, *see* Clayson, Richard.

Génard, P. 1859. 'Les grandes familles artistiques d'Anvers: Ruckers', *Revue d'histoire et d'archéologie*, I, Brussels, 1859, 458–63.

1876. *Catalogue de musée d'antiquités d'Anvers*, Antwerp, 1876.

Germann, Sheridan. 1978. 'Regional schools of harpsichord decoration', *Journal of the American Musical Instrument Society*, IV (1978), 54–105.

1979. '"Mrs Crawley's Couchet" reconsidered', *Early Music*, VII, 4 (1979), 473–81.

1980–81. 'Monsieur Doublet and his confrères: The harpsichord decorators of Paris', *Early Music*, VIII, 4 (1980), 435–53; IX, 2 (1981), 192–207.

Gétreau, Florence, ed. 1985. *La facteur instrumentale europeénne: Suprématies nationales et enrichissement mutuel*, Paris, 1985.

*See also* Robin, Michel.

Gettens, R. J., and Stout, G. L. 1942/66. *Painting Materials: A Short Encyclopaedia*, New York, 1942; reprint, New York, 1966.

Gilchrist, Robert. 1977. 'An unusual harpsichord', *The Galpin Society Journal*, XXVII (1974), 74.

de Ginguené, Pierre-Louis, *see* Framéry, Nicolas-Étienne.

Gough, Hugh. 1971. 'Harpsichord of note', *Harpsichord*, IV, 1 (1971), 4–6.

van de Graaf, Johannes Alexander. 1958. 'Het de Mayerne manuscript als bron voor de schilder-techniek van de barok', diss., University of Utrecht, 1958.

*Grove's Dictionary of Music and Musicians*, *see* Sadie, Stanley.

Gug, Rémy. 1977. 'Über Analysen alter Cembalosaiten', *Collo-quium: Ruckers Klavecimbels en Copieën*, Antwerp, 1977, 125–8.

Haase, Gesine, *see* Krickeberg, Dieter.

Hacke, Walter. 1968. *Am Klavier: Werke europäischer Maler aus sechs Jahrhunderten*. Königstein im Taunus, 1968.

Hands, R. A. 1967. 'A scientific approach to the clavichord', *The Galpin Society Journal*, XX (1967), 89.

Harding, Rosamund. 1933. *The Pianoforte*, Cambridge, 1933; reprint, Cambridge, 1978.

Hardouin, Pierre-J. 1957/59/60. 'Harpsichord making in Paris: eighteenth century', *The Galpin Society Journal*, X (1957), 10; XII (1959), 73; XIII (1960), 52.

Harich-Schneider, Eta. 1958. *Die Kunst des Cembalo-Spiels*, Kassel, 1958.

Harley, Rosamond. 1982. *Artists' Pigments c. 1600–1835*, London, 1982.

Harrison, Frank and Rimmer, Joan. 1964. *European Musical Instruments*, London, 1964.

Hatton, Richard G. n.d. *Handbook of Plant and Floral Ornament*, New York, n.d.

1909. *The Craftsman's Plant Book*, London, 1909.

Haynes, Bruce. 1985. 'Johann Sebastian Bach's pitch standards: the woodwind perspective', *Journal of the American Musical Instrument Society*, XI (1985), 55–114.

Helenius-Öberg, Eva. 1986. *Svenskt Klavikordbygge 1720–1820*, Stockholm, 1986.

Hellwig, Friedemann. 1969. 'Aufgabenstellung und Methode bei der Restaurierung von Musikinstrumenten', *Studia Musico-Museologica: Bericht über das Symposium: Die Bedeutung, die optische und akustische Darbeitung und die Aufgaben einer Musikinstrumentensammlung*, Nuremberg–Stockholm, 1969, 103–12.

1976. 'Strings and stringing: Contemporary documents', *The Galpin Society Journal*, XXIX (1976), 91–104.

1978. 'Die röntgenographische Untersuchungen von Musikinstrumenten', *Maltechnik*, II, 2 (Munich, 1978), 103–15.

1979. 'Restoration and conservation of historical musical instruments', *Making Musical Instruments*, ed. Charles Ford, London, 1979, 155–75.

1985. *Atlas der Profile*, Frankfurt, 1985.

de Hen, F., *see* Bragard, Roger.

Henkel, Hubert. 1979a. *Beiträge zum historischen Cembalobau*, Leipzig, 1979.

1979b. *Kielinstrumente: Katalog: Musikinstrumentenmuseum der Karl-Marx Universität, Leipzig*, Vol. II, Leipzig, 1979.

Hess, Albert G. 1953. 'The transition from harpsichord to piano', *The Galpin Society Journal*, VI (1953), 75–94.

Heyde, Hubert. 1976. *Historische Musikinstrumente im Bachhaus Eisenach*, Eisenach, 1976.

1986. *Musikinstrumentenbau*, Leipzig, 1986.

Hind, A. M. n.d. *An Introduction to a History of the Woodcut*, New York, n.d.

1934. *A History of Woodcut: The XV$^{th}$ Century*, London, 1935.

Hipkins, Alfred James. 1883. 'Ruckers', *Dictionary of Music and Musicians (1450–1889)*, ed. Sir George Grove, London, 1883; reprint, 1890 and 1900.

1888. *Musical Instruments, Historic, Rare and Unique*, Edinburgh, 1888.

1896. *A Description and History of the Pianoforte and of the Older Keyboard Stringed Instruments*, London–New York, 1896.

1908. 'Ruckers', *Grove's Dictionary of Music and Musicians*, 2nd edn, London, 1908 (with additions by F. W. Galpin and Miss E. J. Hipkins).

Hirt, Franz-Joseph. 1955. *Meisterwerke des Klavierbaus*, Olten, 1955.

1968. *Stringed Keyboard Instruments*, Boston, 1968.

Hodson, Alec, *see* Clutton, Cecil.

Hollstein, F. W. H. n.d. *Dutch and Flemish Etchings, Engravings and Woodcuts 1450–1700*, Amsterdam, n.d.

Hoover, Cynthia A. 1969. *Harpsichords and Clavichords*, Washington, D.C., 1969.

Hubbard, Frank. 1950. 'Two early English harpsichords', *The Galpin Society Journal*, III (1950), 12–18; IV (1951), 19.

1951. 'Johannes Ruckers me fecit Antwerpiae 1613', *Museum Notes: Museum of Arts, Rhode Island School of Design*, Providence, R.I., 1951.

1956. 'The *Encyclopédie* and the French harpsichord', *The Galpin Society Journal*, IX (1956), 37–50.

1965. *Three Centuries of Harpsichord Making*, Cambridge, Mass., 1965.

Hüllmandel, Nicolas Joseph. 1791/1818. 'Clavecin', *Encyclopédie Méthodique*, Paris, 1791/1818.

Jacobs, Charles. 1973. *Francisco Correa de Arauxo*, The Hague, 1973.

Jacquot, Albert. 1904. *Musée retrospectif de la classe 17: Instruments de musique à l'exposition universelle internationale de 1900*, Paris, 1904.

James, Philip. 1930. *Early Keyboard Instruments from their Beginnings to the Year 1820*, London, 1930; reprint, London, 1960.

Jeans, Sir James. 1937. *Science and Music*, Cambridge, 1937; reprint, London, 1968.

Jonckbloet, W. J. A., and Land, J. P. W. 1882. *Musique et Musiciens au XVII$^{e}$ siècle*, Leiden, 1882.

Junghanns, Herbert. 1932. *Der Piano- und Flügelbau*, Leipzig, 1932.

Juramie, Ghislaine. 1948. *Histoire du Piano*, Paris, 1948.

Kastner, Santiago, *see also* Correa de Arauxo, Francisco.

1936. *Música Hispânica, o estile musical do Padre Manuel R. Coelho*, Lisbon, 1936.

Kenyon, Max. 1949. *Harpsichord Music*, London, 1949.

van den Kerckhoven, Antoon. (1933). *Werken voor orgel*, Monumenta Musicae Belgicae, II, ed. J. Watelet, Berchem–Antwerp, 1933.

Kinsky, George. 1910. *Musikhistorisches Museum von Wilhelm Heyer in Cöln, Katalog 1*, Cologne, 1910.

1930. *A History of Music in Pictures*, London, 1930; reprint, New York, 1951.

Koopman, Ton and van Dijck, Lucas. 1987. *Het Klavecimbel in de Nederlandse Kunst tot 1800*, Zutphen, 1987.

Koster, John. 1977. 'The mother and child virginal', *Colloquium: Ruckers Klavicimbels en Copieën*, Antwerp, 1977, 78–96.

1980. 'The importance of the early English harpsichord', *Galpin Society Journal*, XXXIII (1980), 45–73.

1982. 'A remarkable early Flemish transposing harpsichord', *Galpin Society Journal*, XXXV (1982), 45–53.

Kottick, Edward L. 1985. 'The acoustics of the harpsichord: response curves and modes of vibration', *The Galpin Society Journal*, XXXVIII (1985), 55–77.

Krebs, Carl. 1892. 'Die besaiteten Klavierinstrumente bis zum Anfang des 17. Jahrhunderts', *Vierteljahrschrift für Musikwissenschaft*, VIII (1892), 91–126.

Krickeberg, Dieter, and Haase, Gesine. 1981. *Tasteninstrumente des Museums*, Berlin, 1981.

Kurtzman, Jeffrey. 1985. 'An aberration amplified', *Early Music*, XIII, 1 (1985), 73–6.

de Lafontaine, Henry Cart. 1909. *The King's Music*, London, 1909.

Lambrechts-Douillez, Jeannine. 1961. 'Collections of musical instruments in Antwerp', *Music Libraries and Instruments: Hinrichsens Eleventh Music Book*, London, 1961.

1967. 'Muziekinstrumenten te Antwerpen', *Tijdschrift van de Stad Antwerpen*, XIII (1967), 100–1.

1968. 'De klavecimbelbouw te Antwerpen: een kunstambacht van wereldformaat (einde zestiende–begin zeventiende eeuw)', *Antiek: Tijdschrift voor Liefhebbers en Kenners van Oude Kunstnijverheid*, III (December, 1968), 237–52.

1969a. 'How to look at a collection of musical instruments with historical ears [sic]', *Studia Musico-Museologica: Bericht über das Symposium: Die Bedeutung, die optische und akustische Darbietung und die Aufgaben einer Musikinstrumentensammlung*, Nuremberg–Stockholm, 1969, 48–54.

1969b, 'Biographical notes on the Ruckers–Couchet family', *Galpin Society Journal*, XXII (1969), 98–9.

1970a. *Antwerpse Klavecimbels in het Museum Vleeshuis*, Antwerp, 1970.

1970b. 'Antwerpse klavicembels, oude muziek herleeft', *Actuele Onderwerpen*, AO 1310, Goes, 1970.

1971a. 'The Ruckers–Couchet instruments in the Museum Vleeshuis: restoration or copy?', *Colloquium: Restauratieproblemen van Antwerpse Klavecimbels*, Antwerp, 1971, 44–8.

1971b. 'Documents dealing with the Ruckers family and Antwerp harpsichord-building', *Keyboard Instruments: Studies in Keyboard Organology*, ed. Edwin M. Ripin, Edinburgh, 1971, 37–42.

1973. 'Hans Ruckers and his workshop', *Der klangliche Aspekt beim Restaurieren von Saitenklavieren*, ed. Vera Schwarz, Graz, 1973, 41–6.

1974. 'Archief documenten betreffende de Ruckers familie', and 'Catalogus Ruckers: documenten en instrumenten', *Bulletin of the Brussels Museum of Musical Instruments*, IV (1974), 33–54 and 65–70.

1977. 'The Ruckers family and other harpsichord makers', *The Connoisseur*, CXCIV, 782 (1977), 266–73.

1979. 'Couchet', *Algemene Muziekencyclopedie*, II (1979), 262.

1980a. 'Ruckers: 1. The family', *The New Grove Dictionary of Music and Musicians*, ed. Stanley Sadie, 16, London, 1980, 303–5.

1980b. 'Aperçu historique sur la facture de clavecin à Anvers aux XVI$^{e}$ et XVII$^{e}$ siècles', *La facture de clavecin du XV$^{e}$ au XVIII$^{e}$ siècle*, Louvain-la-Neuve, 1980, 59–66.

1981a. *Catalogus Muziekinstrumenten: Museum Vleeshuis Antwerpen*, Antwerp, 1981.

1981b. 'Hagaerts', *Algemene Muziekencyclopedie*, IV (1981), 135.

Lambrechts-Douillez, Jeannine, and Bosschaerts-Eykens, M.-J. 1982a. 'Stamboom der klavecimbelbouwersfamilie Ruckers–Couchet', *Mededelingen van het Ruckers-Genootschap*, I, Antwerp, 1982.

1982b. 'Dokumenten betreffende de familie Hagaerts', *Mededelingen van het Ruckers-Genootschap*, II, Antwerp, 1982, 11–24.

1983a. 'A. Hans Ruckers en Adriana Cnaeps', *Mededelingen van het Ruckers-Genootschap*, III, Antwerp, 1983, 9–13.

1983b. 'B. Joannes Ruckers(II) en Maria Waelrant', *Mededel-*

*ingen van het Ruckers-Genootschap*, III, Antwerp, 1983, 15–30.
1984a. 'A. Andreas Ruckers de Oude en Catharina de Vriese', *Mededelingen van het Ruckers-Genootschap*, IV, Antwerp, 1984, 17–36.
1984b. 'B. Andreas Ruckers de Jonge en Johanna Hechts', *Mededelingen van het Ruckers-Genootschap*, IV, Antwerp, 1984, 37–52.
1984c. 'C. 'Ruckers instruments sold during the 18th century', *Mededelingen van het Ruckers-Genootschap*, IV, Antwerp, 1984, 53–7.
1986a. 'A. Carel Couchet', *Mededelingen van het Ruckers-Genootschap*, V, Antwerp, 1986, 7–19.
1986b. 'C. Ioannes Couchet en Angela van den Brant', *Mededelingen van het Ruckers-Genootschap*, V, Antwerp, 1986, 20–38.
Land, J. P. W., *see* Jonckbloet, W. J. A.
Lees-Milne, James. 1953. *Fenton House Catalogue*, London, 1953.
Lehrs, Max. 1908. 'Die dekorative Verwendung von Holzschnitten im XV. und XVI. Jahrhunderts', *Jahrbuch der Königlich-Preussischen Kunstsammlungen*, XXIX (1908), 183 and Plate 7.
Leiss, Joseph. n.d. 'Die Geschichte der Papiertapete vom 16.–20. Jahrhundert', *Tapeten: Ihre Geschichte bis zur Gegenwart*, I, Braunschweig, n.d., 203–7.
Leonhardt, Gustav. 1971. 'In praise of Flemish virginals of the seventeenth century', *Keyboard Instruments: Studies in Keyboard Organology*, ed. Edwin M. Ripin, Edinburgh, 1971, 43–6.
van Lerius, T., *see* Rombouts, P.
Leschiutta, Sigfrido. 1983a. *Appunti per una bibliografia sul clavicembalo, clavicordo e fortepiano*, Padua, 1983.
1983b. *Cembalo, spinetta e virginale*, Ancona, 1983.
Lesure, François, *see also* Bridgman, Nanie.
1954. 'La facture instrumentale au Paris au seizième siècle', *Galpin Society Journal*, VII (1954), 11.
Libin, Laurence. 1975. 'A Dutch harpsichord in the United States', *Galpin Society Journal*, XXXVIII (1975), 43–52.
van der Linden, Albert, *see* Collaer, Paul.
Lindley, Mark. 1984. *Lutes, Viols and Temperaments*, Cambridge, 1984.
Lonicer, Adam or Lonericus, Adamus. 1569. *Kreuterbuch*, 1569; facs., Bamberg, 1975.
Lunsingh Scheurleer, Daniel F. 1939. 'Over het ornament en de autenticiteit van bedrukte papierstrooken in twee clavierinstrumenten', *Mededelingen van de Dienst voor Kunsten en Wetenschappen der Gemeente 's-Gravenhage*, The Hague, 1939, 45–9.
McGeary, Thomas. 1981. 'Harpsichord mottoes', *Journal of the American Musical Instrument Society*, VII (1981), 5–35.
Mactaggart, Ann and Peter. 1978. 'The Knole harpsichord: a re-attribution', *Galpin Society Journal*, XXXI (1978), 2–8.
1979. 'Tempera and decorated keyboard instruments', *The Galpin Society Journal*, XXXII (1979), 59–65.
1983. 'A royal Ruckers: decorative and documentary history', *Organ Yearbook*, XIV (1983), 78–96.
1985. 'The colour of Ruckers lid papers', *The Galpin Society Journal*, XXXVIII (1985), 106–11.
Mace, Thomas. 1676. *Musick's Monument*, London, 1676.
de Maeyer, René. 1969. *Exposition des instruments de musique des XVI$^{ème}$ et XVII$^{ème}$ siècles*, Brussels, 1969.
1972. *Catalogus van de Tentoonstelling Gewijd an Muziekinstrumenten uit de XVI$^{e}$ en XVII$^{e}$ Eeuw Behorend tot het Instrumentenmuseum van Brussel in Kasteel Laarne*, Brussels, 1972.
Mahillon, Victor Charles. 1893–1922. *Catalogue déscriptif et analytique du Musée Instrumental du Conservatoire Royal de Bruxelles*, 5 Vols., Ghent–Brussels, 1893–1922; facs., Amsterdam, 1978.
Marcuse, Sybil. 1952. 'Transposing keyboards in extant Flemish harpsichords', *Musical Quarterly*, XXXVIII (1952), 414–25.
1958. *Check-list of Western Instruments in the Collection of Musical Instruments I: Keyboard Instruments*, New Haven, Conn., 1958.
1960. *Musical Instruments at Yale: A Selection of Western Instruments from the 15th to 20th centuries: Catalogue*, New Haven, Conn., 1960.
1961. 'The instruments of the king's library at Versailles', *Galpin Society Journal*, XIV (1961), 34–6.
van der Meer, John Henry, *see also* Berner (1967), Cervelli (1967), Tagliavini (1986) and Weber, Rainer.
n.d.a. *Wegweiser durch die Sammlung Historischer Musikinstrumente, Germanisches Nationalmuseum, Nürnberg*, Nuremberg, n.d.
n.d.b. 'Ruckers', *Die Musik in Geschichte und Gegenwart*, XI, cols. 1049–56, n.d.
1960/61. 'Per ogni sorte di stromenti da tasti', *Tijdschrift van de Vereniging voor Nederlandse Muziekgeschiedenis*, XIX, 1/2 (1960/61), 67–9.
1964. 'An example of harpsichord restoration', *Galpin Society Journal*, XVII (1964), 5–16.
1965. 'A Flemish "quint" harpsichord', *Galpin Society Journal*, XVIII (1965), 117–21.
1966a. 'Flämische Cembali in italienischem Besitz', *Analecta Musicologica*, III (1966), 114–21.
1966b. 'Beiträge zum Cembalobau im deutschen Sprachgebiet bis 1700', *Anzeiger des Germanischen Nationalmuseums, Nürnberg* (1966), 103–33.
1968a. 'Harpsichord making and metallurgy: a rejoinder', *Galpin Society Journal*, XXI (1968), 175–8.
1968b. 'Notes', *Galpin Society Journal*, XXI (1968), 209.
1971a. 'Flämische Kielklaviere im Germanischen Nationalmuseum, Nürnberg', *Colloquium: Restauratieproblemen van Antwerpse Klavicimbels*, Antwerp, 1971, 63–76.
1971b. 'More about Flemish two-manual harpsichords', *Keyboard Instruments: Studies in Keyboard Organology*, ed. Edwin M. Ripin, Edinburgh, 1971, 47–56.
1971c. 'Beiträge zum Cembalobau der Familie Ruckers', *Jahrbuch des Instituts für Musikforschung Preussischer Kulturbesitz*, Berlin, 1971, 100–53.

1973. 'Zielsetzung bei der Restaurierung historischer Saitenklaviere', *Der klangliche Aspekt beim Restaurieren von Saitenklavieren*, ed. Vera Schwarz, Graz, 1973, 15–24.

1977. 'Flämische Kielklaviere: Forschung und Instrumentenpraxis', *Colloquium: Ruckers Klavecimbels en Copieën*, Antwerp, 1977, 13–26.

1979/80. 'Germanisches Nationalmuseum Nürnberg: Geschichte seiner Musikinstrumentensammlung', *Jahrbuch des Staatlichen Instituts für Musikforschung Preussischer Kulturbesitz* (1979/80), 9–78.

1983. *Musikinstrumente*, Munich 1983.

Meeùs, Nicolas. 1970. 'Le clavecin de Johannes Couchet, Anvers 1646: Un moment important de l'histoire du double clavecin en Flandre', *Bulletin of the Brussels Museum of Musical Instruments*, I (1970), 15–29.

1971. 'La naissance de l'octave courte et ses différentes formes au 16e siècle', diss., Université Catholique de Louvain, 1971.

1974. 'La facture de virginals à Anvers au 16e siècle', *Bulletin of The Brussels Museum of Musical Instruments*, IV (1974), 55–64.

1980a. 'Épinettes et "Muselars": une analyse théoretique', *La facture de clavecin du XVe au XVIIIe siècle*, Louvain-la-Neuve, 1980, 67–78.

1980b. 'Le diapason authentique: Quelques réflexions à propos du clavecin transpositeur des Ruckers', *La facture de clavecin du XVe au XVIIIe siècle*, Louvain-la-Neuve, 1980, 78–88.

Mendel, Arthur. 1948. 'Pitch in the 16th and early 17th centuries', *Musical Quarterly*, XXXIV (1948), 28–45, 199–221, 336–57, 575–93.

1949. 'Devices for transposition in the organ before 1600', *Acta Musicologica*, XXI (1949), 24–40.

1978. 'Pitch in western music since 1500: a re-examination', *Acta Musicologica*, I, 1/2 (1978), 1–93.

Mendel, Arthur, and Ellis, A. J. 1968. *Studies in the History of Musical Pitch*, Amsterdam, 1968.

Mersenne, Marin. 1636. *Harmonie universelle*, Paris, 1636; facs., Paris, 1965; English translation (instruments section only), The Hague, 1957.

Meyer, Franz Sales. 1922. *Handbuch der Ornamentik*, Leipzig, 1922; English translation: *Handbook of Ornament*, New York, 1957.

Meynell, Francis and Morrison, Stanley. 1923. 'Printers' flowers and arabesques', *The Fleuron*, I (1923), 1–43.

Miller, Caroline Anne. 1960. '*Chiavette*: a new approach', diss., University of California, Berkeley, 1960. Reviewed by Roland Jackson in *Current Musicology*, XIX (1975), 113–16.

de Mirimonde, Albert P. 1967. 'Les sujets de musique chez Gonzales Coques et ses émules', *Bulletin Musées Royaux/ Beaux-Arts de Belgique*, XVI (1967), 179.

1968. 'La musique et la fantastique chez David Rijckaert III', *Jaarboek van het Koninklijk Museum voor Schone Kunsten*, Antwerp, 1968, 177.

1974. *Sainte-Cécile: Metamorphoses d'un thème musical*, Geneva, 1974.

Montague, Jeremy. 1986. 'Salerooms: Instruments', *Early Music*, XIV, 2 (1986), 258.

Morley, Thomas. 1597. *A Plaine and Easie Introduction to Practicall Musicke*, London, 1597; facs., London, 1952.

Morrison, Stanley, *see* Meynell, F.

Morse, Philip M. 1948. *Vibration and Sound*, New York, 1948.

Mould, Charles M. 1968. 'James Talbot's manuscript', *Galpin Society Journal*, XXI (1968), 40.

1971. 'The Tabel harpsichord', *Keyboard Instruments: Studies in Keyboard Organology*, ed. Edwin M. Ripin, Edinburgh, 1971, 57.

1976. 'The development of the English harpsichord with particular reference to the work of Kirkman', diss., University of Oxford, 1976.

Moxon, Joseph. 1683. *Mechanick Exercises on the Whole Art of Printing*, London, 1683; reprint, London, 1958.

Murray, John J. 1972. *Antwerp in the Age of Plantin and Brueghel*, Newton Abbot, Devon, 1972.

Music Libraries and Instruments. 1961. *International Association of Music Libraries and the Galpin Society Conference of 1959: Music Libraries and Instruments: Hinrichsen's Eleventh Music Book*, London, 1961.

Neupert, Hanns. 1925. *Vom Musikstab zum modernen Klavier*, Bamberg, 1925; reprint, 1926 and Berlin, 1952.

1933. *Das Cembalo*, Kassel, 1933.

Neven, Armand. 1970. 'L'arpicordo', *Acta Musicologica*, XLII (1970), 230–5.

Newman, Sidney, and Williams, Peter. 1968. *The Russell Collection and other Early Keyboard Instruments in Saint Cecilia's Hall, Edinburgh*, Edinburgh, 1968.

Nissen, Klaus. 1951. *Die botanische Buchillustrationen*, Stuttgart, 1951.

Norlind, Tobias. 1939. *Systematik der Saiteninstrumente: Heft 2: Geschichte des Klaviers*, Stockholm–Hanover, 1939.

Öberg, *see* Helenius-Öberg, Eva.

O'Brien, G. Grant. 1974a. 'The numbering system of Ruckers instruments', *Bulletin of the Brussels Museum of Musical Instruments*, IV (1974), 75–89.

1974b. 'The 1764/83 Taskin harpsichord in the Russell Collection, Edinburgh', *The Organ Yearbook*, V (1974), 91–107.

1976. 'Attitudes to musical instrument conservation and restoration', *Bulletin of the Fellowship of Makers and Restorers of Historical Instruments*, III (1976), 15–21.

1977a. 'The determination of the original compass and disposition of Ruckers harpsichords', *Colloquium: Ruckers Klavecimbels en Copieën*, Antwerp, 1977, 38–47.

1977b. 'The stringing and pitches of Ruckers instruments', *Colloquium: Ruckers Klavecimbels en Copieën*, Antwerp, 1977, 48–71.

1979. 'Ioannes and Andreas Ruckers: a quatercentenary celebration', *Early Music*, VII 4 (1979), 453–66.

1980a. 'Ruckers 2: The instruments', *The New Grove Diction-*

*ary of Music and Musicians*, ed. Stanley Sadie, 16, London, 1980, 305–10.

1980b. 'Couchet', *The New Grove Dictionary of Music and Musicians*, ed. Stanley Sadie, 4, London, 1980, 831–2.

1980c. 'Il 400° anniversario della nascita di Ioannes e Andreas Ruckers', *Gli Strumenti Musicali*, IV (1980), 36–46.

1981a. 'Some principles of eighteenth-century harpsichord stringing and their application', *The Organ Yearbook*, XII (1981), 160–76.

1981b. 'Eight Ruckers pitches', *Early Music*, IX, 1 (1981), 80.

1983. 'The authentic instruments from the workshops of Hans and Ioannes Ruckers', *Mededelingen van het Ruckers-Genootschap*, III, Antwerp, 1983, 37–44.

1984. 'The authentic instruments from the workshops of Andreas Ruckers I and Andreas Ruckers II', *Mededelingen van het Ruckers-Genootschap*, IV, Antwerp, 1984, 61–8.

1985. 'Les Ruckers d'Anvers: La vogue de leurs clavecins en Europe des XVII^e^ et XVIII^e^ siècles', *La facture instrumentale europeénne: Suprématies nationales et enrichissement mutuel*, ed. F. Gétreau, Paris, 1985.

1986. 'The authentic instrument from the workshops of Ioannes Couchet and his sons', *Mededelingen van het Ruckers-Genootschap*, V, Antwerp, 1986, 45–49.

1987. 'The conservation of historical keyboard instruments: to play or to preserve?', *Per una carta europea del restauro: Conservazione, restauro e riuso degli strumenti musicali antichi*, ed. Leo S. Olschki, Florence, 1987.

O'Brien, G. Grant; Barnes, John; Ripin, Edwin M.; and Schott, Howard. 1980. 'Harpsichord', *The New Grove Dictionary of Music and Musicians*, ed. Stanley Sadie, 8, London, 1980, 216–46.

Olschki, Leo S., ed. 1987. *Per una carta europea del restauro: Conservazione, restauro e riuso degli strumenti musicali antichi*, Florence, 1987.

Ott, Alfons. 1968. *Tausend Jahre Musikleben: 800–1800*, Munich, 1968.

Otto, Irmgard. 1965. *Musikinstrumentenmuseum Berlin*, Berlin, 1965.

1968. *Das Musikinstrumenten-Museum Berlin*, Berlin, 1968.

Overton, John. 1957. 'A note on technical advances in the manufacture of paper before the nineteenth century', *A History of Technology, Vol. 3: From the Renaissance to the Industrial Revolution c. 1500–c. 1750*, Oxford, 1957, 411–16.

Panetta, J., Jr., *see* Denis, Jean.

Papineau-Couture, François. 1989. *Clavecin de Ioannes Ruckers, 1612: dessin, technique et notice organologique*, Société des amis du Musée Instrumental, Paris, 1989.

Parrott, Andrew. 1984. 'Transposition in Monteverdi's Vespers of 1610. An "aberration" defended', *Early Music*, XII, 4 (1984), 490–516.

Paul, John. 1981. *Modern Harpsichord Makers*, London, 1981.

Peeters, Flor. 1971. 'Organ music: Abraham van den Kerckhoven', *The Organ and its Music in the Netherlands 1500–1800*, ed. F. Peeters and M. A. Vente, Antwerp, 1971.

Pellegrino, Francesco. 1530. *La fleur de la science de pourtraicture: patrons de broderie, façon arabicque et ytalique*, Paris, 1530; facs., Paris, 1908.

Pillaut, L., *see* Chouquet, Gustave.

Pols, André M. 1942. *De Ruckers en de Klavierbouw in Vlaandern*, Antwerp, 1942.

Praetorius, Michael. 1619. *Syntagma Musicum II: De Organographia*, Wolfenbüttel, 1619; facs., Kassel, 1958.

Pyne, James Kendrick. 1888. *Catalogue of Musical Instruments Principally Illustrative of the History of the Piano. The Property of Henry Boddington*, Manchester, 1888.

Randall, Robert H. 1951. *An Introduction to Acoustics*, Cambridge, Mass., 1951.

Rephann, Richard. 1968. *Checklist: Yale Collection of Musical Instruments*, New Haven, Conn., 1968.

Reuther, Rudolf. 1968. 'Das Ruckers-Cembalo der Grafen von Landsberg-Velen', *Westfalen*, 46 (1968), 123–8.

Reynvaan, Joos Verschuere. 1795. *Muzijkaal Kunst-Woordenboek*, Amsterdam, 1795.

Rimbault, Edward F. 1860. *The Pianoforte . . . with Some Account of the Clavichord, the Spinet, the Virginal and the Harpsichord*, London, 1860.

Ripin, Edwin M. 1967. 'The French harpsichord before 1650', *The Galpin Society Journal*, XX (1967), 43–7.

1968. 'The two-manual harpsichord in Flanders before 1650', *The Galpin Society Journal*, XXI (1968), 33–9.

1969. 'The Couchet harpsichord in the Crosby Brown collection', *Metropolitan Museum Journal*, II (1969), 169–78.

1970a. 'A "three foot" Flemish harpsichord', *The Galpin Society Journal*, XXIII (1970), 35–9.

1970b. 'Expressive devices applied to the eighteenth-century harpsichord', *The Organ Yearbook*, I (1970), 64–80.

1970c. 'A reassessment of the fretted clavichord', *The Galpin Society Journal*, XXIII (1970), 40.

1971a. 'Antwerp harpsichord building: The current state of research', *Colloquium: Restauratieproblemen van Antwerpse Klavecimbels*, Antwerp, 1971, 12–23.

1971b. 'On Joes Karest's virginal and the origins of the Flemish tradition', *Keyboard Instruments: Studies in Keyboard Organology*, ed. Edwin M. Ripin, Edinburgh, 1971, 65–74.

1974a. 'The instrument catalogues of Leopoldo Franciolini', *Music Indexes and Bibliographies*, Vol. 9, Hackensack, N.J., 1974.

1974b. 'The Norrlanda organ and the Ghent altarpiece', *Festschrift to Ernst Emsheimer*, Musikhistoriska museets skrifter 5, Stockholm, 1974, 193–6.

1975. 'Towards an identification of the chekker', *The Galpin Society Journal*, XXVIII (1975), 11.

Ripin, Edwin, M., Barnes, John, O'Brien, G. Grant, and Schott, Howard. 1980. 'Harpsichord', *The New Grove Dictionary of Music and Musicians*, ed. Stanley Sadie, 8, London, 1980, 216–46.

Robert, N. 1660. *Diverses fleurs dessinées et gravées d'après le naturel*, Paris, 1660; facs., London, 1975.

Robin Michel. 1988. *Instrumentistes et luthiers parisiens XVIIe–*

*XIXe siècles: Délégation a l'action artistique de la ville de Paris*, Paris, 1988.

Robin, Michel, Abondance, Pierre, and Gétreau, Florence. 1982. *Clavecin Goujon-Swanen: documentation organologique No. 1*, Société des amis du Musée Instrumental du C.N.S.M., Paris, 1982.

Rombouts, P., and van Lerius, T. 1872–76. *De Liggeren en Andere Historische Archieven der Antwerpsche Sint Lucasgilde*, 2 Vols., Antwerp–The Hague, 1872–76; facs., Amsterdam, 1961.

Rubart, Paul. 1955. *Führer durch das Musikinstrumenten-Museum der Karl-Marx Universität*, Leipzig, 1955.

Rueger, Christoph. 1982/86. *Musical Instruments and Their Decoration*, London, 1982/86.

Russell, Raymond. 1954. 'Ruckers', *Grove's Dictionary of Music and Musicians*, 5th edn, ed. E. Blom, London, 1954; also Supplementary volume, London, 1961.

1957. *Catalogue of the Benton Fletcher Collection of Early Keyboard Instruments at Fenton House, Hampstead*, London, 1957; revised, London, 1969.

1959. *The Harpsichord and Clavichord*, London, 1959; reprint, London, 1973.

1968. *Victoria and Albert Museum: Catalogue of Musical Instruments: I: Keyboard Instruments*, London, 1968.

Ruth-Sommer, Hermann. 1916. *Alte Musikinstrumenten*, Berlin, 1916.

Sachs, Curt. 1913. *Reallexikon der Musikinstrumente*, Berlin, 1913.

1922. *Sammlung alter Musikinstrumente bei der Staatlichen Hochschule für Musik in Berlin: Beschreibender Katalog*, Berlin, 1922.

1923. *Das Klavier: Handbuch des Instrumentenmuseums der Staatlichen Hochschule für Musik*, Berlin, 1923.

1942. *The History of Musical Instruments*, New York and London, 1942.

Sadie, Stanley, ed. 1980. *The New Grove Dictionary of Music and Musicians*, 20 Vols. London, 1980.

ed. 1984. *The New Grove Dictionary of Musical Instruments*, 3 Vols. London, 1984.

Sainsbury, W. Noël. 1859. *Original Unpublished Papers Illustrative of the Life of Sir Peter Paul Rubens*, London, 1859.

Samoyault-Verlet, Colombe. 1966. *Les facteurs de clavecins parisiens: Notices biographiques et documents (1550–1793)*, Paris, 1966.

Santagata, E. 1930. *Il museo storico musicale di S. Pietro a Majella*, Naples, 1930.

Sasse, Konrad. 1958. *Das Händel-Haus in Halle*, Halle–Saale, 1958.

1966. *Katalog zu den Sammlungen des Händel-Hauses in Halle: 5: Musikinstrumentensammlung: Besaitete Tasteninstrumente*, Halle–Saale, 1966.

Scheurwater, W., *see* van Acht, R.

Schmidt, Martin-Christian. 1978. 'Ein Beitrag zum Cembalobau von Hans Ruckers aus instrumentenkundlicher und handwerklicher Sicht', *Neue Museumskunde*, XXI 1 (1978), 60–7.

Schott, Howard. 1971. *Playing the Harpsichord*, London, 1971.

1974. 'The harpsichord revival', *Early Music*, II, 4 (1974), 85.

1977. 'The sixteenth century in England, the Netherlands, France, Germany, Poland, Iberia and Italy (Early music for harpsichord: Part 3)', *Early Music*, V, 1 (1977), 67–73.

1985. *Victoria and Albert Museum: Catalogue of Musical Instruments, Volume I: Keyboard Instruments*, London, 1985.

Schott, Howard; Barnes, John; O'Brien, G. Grant; and Ripin, Edwin M. 1980. 'Harpsichord', *The New Grove Dictionary of Music and Musicians*, ed. Stanley Sadie, 8, London, 1980, 216–46.

Schwarz, Vera, ed. 1973. *Der klangliche Aspekt beim Restaurieren von Saitenklavieren*, Graz, 1973.

Shann, R. T. 1984. 'Flemish transposing harpsichords: an explanation', *Galpin Society Journal*, XXXVII (1984), 62–71.

Shortridge, John D. 1960. 'Italian harpsichord building in the 16th and 17th centuries', *Contributions from the Museum of History and Technology: United States National Museum*, Bulletin 225, Paper 15, Washington, D.C., 1960, 93–107.

Skinner, William. 1933. *The Belle Skinner Collection of Old Musical Instruments*, Holyoke, Mass., 1933.

Skowroneck, Martin. 1974. 'Das Cembalo von Christian Zell, Hamburg, 1728, und seine Restaurierung', *The Organ Yearbook*, V (1974), 79–87.

1977. 'Cembalobauer des 20. Jahrhunderts als Kopisten', *Colloquium: Ruckers Klavecimbels en Copieën*, Antwerp, 1977, 27–35.

Smith, Douglas Alton. 1980. 'The musical instrument inventory of Raymund Fugger', *The Galpin Society Journal*, XXXIII (1980), 36–44.

Snoeck, César. 1894. *Catalogue de la collection d'instruments de musique anciens au curieux de C. C. Snoeck*, Ghent, 1894.

1903. *Catalogue de la collection d'instruments de musique flamands et néerlandais de C. C. Snoeck*, Ghent, 1903.

Soly, Hugo, *see* Voet, Leon.

Squire, W. Barclay, *see* Fuller Maitland, J. A.

Steinert, Morris. 1892. *Catalogue of the M. Steinert Collection of Keyed and Stringed Instruments*, Vienna, 1892.

Stellfeld, J. A. 1942. 'Bronnen tot de geschiedenis der Antwerpse clavecimbel- en orgelbouwers in de XVIe en XVIIe eeuwen', *Vlaamsch Jaarboek voor Muziekgeschiedenis*, Antwerp, 1942, 3–110.

1945. 'Johannes Ruckers de jongere en de koninklijke kapel te Brussel', *Hommage à Charles van den Borren*, Antwerp, 1945, 289.

Stout, G. L., *see* Gettens, R. J.

Strack, Wolfgang. 1979. 'Christian Gottlob Hubert and his instruments', *The Galpin Society Journal*, XXXII (1979), 38.

van der Straeten, Edmond. 1867–88. *La musique aux Pays-Bas avant le XIXe siècle*, 8 Vols., Brussels, 1867–88.

Sylvius, Balthasar. 1554. *Variarum protractionum quas vulgo Maurusias vocant Libellus*, Paris, 1554; reprint, The Hague, 1893.

Tagliavini, Luigi Ferdinando and van de Meer, John Henry. 1986. *Clavicembali e spinette dal XVI al XIX secolo*, Bologna, 1986.

Thibault, Geneviève, Comtesse de Chambure, *see also* Berner.

1961. 'Les collections privées de livres et d'instruments de musique d'autrefois et d'aujourd'hui', *Music, Libraries and Instruments: Hinrichsen's Eleventh Music Book*, London, 1961, 131–47.

1969. 'The restoration of harpsichords at the Paris "Musée Instrumental du Conservatoire National Supérieur de Musique" ', *Studia Musico-Museologica: Bericht über das Symposium: Die Bedeutung, die optische und akustische Darbietung und die Aufgaben einer Musikinstrumentensammlung*, Nuremberg–Stockholm, 1969, 113–16.

1971. 'Les clavecins et épinette de Ruckers au Musée Instrumental du Conservatoire National Supérieur de Musique', *Colloquium: Restauratieproblemen van Antwerpse Klavecimbels*, Antwerp, 1971, 77–82.

Thomas, Michael. 1971. 'String gauges of old Italian harpsichords', *The Galpin Society Journal*, XXIV (1971), 69–78.

Thomas, William R., and Rhodes, J. J. K. 1967. 'The string scales of Italian keyboard instruments', *The Galpin Society Journal*, XX (1967), 49–62.

1971. 'Schlick, Praetorius and the history of organ-pitch', *The Organ Yearbook*, II (1971), 58–76.

1973. 'Harpsichord strings, organ pipes and the Dutch foot', *The Organ Yearbook*, III (1973), 112–21.

1974. 'The octave clavichord (*c.* 1750) in the Russell Collection, Edinburgh', *The Organ Yearbook*, V (1974), 88–91.

1979. 'Harpsichords and the art of wire-drawing', *The Organ Yearbook*, X (1979), 126–39.

1980. 'Pitch', *The New Grove Dictionary of Music and Musicians*, ed. Stanley Sadie, 14, London, 1980, 779–86.

Thompson, Daniel V. 1936. *The Materials of Medieval Painting*, London, 1936.

Tournay, Jean. 1980. 'A propos d'Albertus Delin (1712–1771): Petite contribution à l'histoire du clavecin', *La facture de clavecin du XV^e au XVIII^e siècle*, Louvain-la-Neuve, 1980, 139–232.

Tretbar, Charles F. 1893. *The M. Steinert Collection of Keyed and Stringed Instruments*, New York, 1893.

Turnbull, Rupert Davidson, *see* Vytlacil, Vaclav.

Véliz, Zahira. 1982. 'Francisco Pacheco's comments on painting in oil', *Studies in Conservation*, XXVII 2 (1982), 49–57.

Villanis, Luigi Alberto. 1901. *L'arte del clavicembalo*, Turin, 1901.

Vicentino, Nicola. 1555. *L'antica musica ridotta alla moderna prattica*, Rome, 1555; facs., Kassel, 1967.

Voet, Leon. 1973. *Antwerp: The Golden Age*, Antwerp, 1973.

Voet, Leon, and Soly, Hugo. n.d. 'De kaart van Virgilus Bononiensis: 1: Het plan en zijn auteur', *De Stad Antwerpen van de Romeinse Tijd de 17^de Eeuw: Topographische Studie Rond het Plan van Virgilius Bononiensis*, Antwerp, n.d.

Vytlacil, Vaclav, and Turnbull, Rupert Davidson. 1935. *Egg Tempera Painting*, New York, 1935.

Wallner, Bertha Antonia. 1925/26. 'Die Musikinstrumentensammlung des Deutschen Museums in München', *Zeitschrift für Musikwissenschaft*, VIII (1925–26), 239–47.

Ward-Jackson, Peter. 1967/69. *Some Main Streams and Tributaries in European Ornament from 1500 to 1750*, London, 1969; reprint from the *Bulletin of the Victoria and Albert Museum*, III, 2–4 (1967), 58–71, 90–103, 121–134.

Watelet, J., *see* van den Kerckhoven, A.

Weber, Rainer. 1975. 'Some researches into pitch in the 16th century with particular reference to the Accademia Filarmonica of Verona', *The Galpin Society Journal*, XXVIII (1975), 7–10.

Weber, Rainer, and van der Meer, J. H. 1972. 'Some facts and guesses concerning doppioni', *The Galpin Society Journal*, XXV (1972), 22.

Wells, Elizabeth. 1978. 'The London clavicytherium', *Early Music*, VI, 4 (1978), 568–71.

Williams, Peter, *see* Newman, S.

Winternitz, Emanuel. 1961. *Keyboard Instruments in the Metropolitan Museum of Art: A Picture Book*, New York, 1961.

1966. *Musical Instruments of the Western World*, London, 1966.

Wittmayer, Kurt. 1977. 'Der Bau von Kopien . . .', *Colloquium: Ruckers Klavecimbels en Copieën*, Antwerp, 1977, 97–108.

Wolfenden, Samuel. 1916. *The Art of Pianoforte Construction*, London, 1916; reprint, Woking, 1975 and 1977.

Wolters, Klaus. 1969. *Das Klavier*, Berne–Stuttgart, 1969.

Wood, Alexander. 1944. *The Physics of Music*, London, 1944; reprint, London, 1965.

Worp, J. A. 1895. *De Gedichten van Constantijn Huygens*, 9 Vols., Groningen, 1892–99; *see* Vol. V (1895), 189.

1915. *De Briefwisseling van Constantijn Huygens (1608–1687)*, IV (The Hague, 1915), 465, 477, 486, 488–9; V (The Hague, 1916), 200, 233.

Wraight, Denzil. 1987. 'The conservation of keyboard instruments', *Per una carta europea del restauro: Conservazione, restauro e riuso degli strumenti musicali antichi*, ed. Leo S. Olschki, Florence, 1987, 299–304.

Zarlino, Gioseffo. 1558. *Institutione harmoniche*, Venice, 1558; New Haven, Conn., 1968.

Zuckermann, Wolfgang. 1969/70. *The Modern Harpsichord: Twentieth-Century Instruments and Their Makers*, New York, 1969; London, 1970.

# Index